全国普通高等学校优秀教材一等奖 第一版

"十二五"普通高等教育本科国家级规划教材 第三版

Book One

# 英语国家社会与文化入门

上册
第四版
Fourth Edition

## AN INTRODUCTION TO MAJOR ENGLISH-SPEAKING SOCIETIES AND THEIR CULTURES

主编　朱永涛　王立礼

编者　石同云　宋云峰　Ann Aungles
　　　John Hill　Jerusha McCormack

高等教育出版社·北京

### 图书在版编目（CIP）数据

英语国家社会与文化入门．上册／朱永涛，王立礼主编．
—— 4 版．—— 北京：高等教育出版社，2020.5（2021.12 重印）
ISBN 978-7-04-053458-0

Ⅰ．①英… Ⅱ．①朱… ②王… Ⅲ．①英语－阅读教学－高等学校－教材 ②文化－概况－国外 Ⅳ．①H319.37

中国版本图书馆 CIP 数据核字(2020)第 017194 号

| 策划编辑 | 张 凯 | 责任编辑 | 王代军 | 封面设计 | 张 楠 |
| 版式设计 | 孙 伟 | 责任校对 | 张 凯 | 责任印制 | 韩 刚 |

| 出版发行 | 高等教育出版社 | 网 址 | http://www.hep.edu.cn |
| 社 址 | 北京市西城区德外大街4号 | | http://www.hep.com.cn |
| 邮政编码 | 100120 | 网上订购 | http://www.hepmall.com.cn |
| 印 刷 | 辽宁虎驰科技传媒有限公司 | | http://www.hepmall.com |
| 开 本 | 850mm×1168mm 1/16 | | http://www.hepmall.cn |
| 印 张 | 26.25 | 版 次 | 2000年12月第1版 |
| 字 数 | 630千字 | | 2020年 5 月第4版 |
| 购书热线 | 010-58581118 | 印 次 | 2021年12月第6次印刷 |
| 咨询电话 | 400-810-0598 | 定 价 | 65.00元 |

本书如有缺页、倒页、脱页等质量问题，请到所购图书销售部门联系调换
版权所有 侵权必究
物 料 号 53458-00

# 第四版前言

《英语国家社会与文化入门》由高等教育出版社于2000年出版，分别在2005年和2011年出版第二版及第三版。长期以来，《英语国家社会与文化入门》在全国各高校英语专业使用，有众多的学习者，并受到读者的普遍欢迎和好评。同时，读者也期待我们不断更新内容，跟上形势变化的节奏和时代前进的步伐。这也正是我们的心愿和努力的方向。我们的理念是，英语学习者在学习语言的同时必须了解和学习主要使用英语的国家的历史、地理、政治、经济、社会、文化等各个方面。只有这样才有能力运用英语进行深入的跨文化国际性交流。了解英语国家的社会与文化能够拓展读者的视野，使他们接触多元文化，获得观察世界的新角度，使思维更加敏捷活跃。编者基于对《英语国家社会与文化入门》重要性的认识以及对广大读者负责的态度，在过去二十年的时间内，对此书进行了包括此次在内的三次修订，每一次都认真总结教材使用情况并听取读者反馈的意见，做了细致严肃的修改，使《英语国家社会与文化入门》的质量不断提高。本书曾获得"全国普通高等学校优秀教材一等奖（第一版）"，被列入"普通高等教育'十一五'国家级规划教材"和"普通高等教育'十二五'国家级规划教材"。

这次修订的重点是更新信息内容，补充了自上次修订以来相关国家所发生的重大事件及其发展；调整了部分课文；重新设计了练习，去掉选择题，增加问答题和讨论/研究题目，目的是突出重点，以便学习者掌握课文的主要内容，并且协助学习者分析课文内容，进行独立思考。

《英语国家社会与文化入门》的英语名称改为 An Introduction to Major English-Speaking Societies and Their Cultures。

上册保留原有的20个单元，但内容有很大的补充和增加。

下册从22个单元改为20个单元。主要变化在有关美国这一部分：对原有的单元做了调整，去掉了 Religion in the United States、Technology in America、Sports and Scenic Spots in America 和 American Popular Culture: Movies and Music，补充了两个新单元：The Land and the People of the USA 和 Environmental Issues and Environmental Movements in the USA。第三版下册第11单元 American Way of Life: A Search for Credible Generalization 由本文作者重新改写，新的题目是：What Is "American" About the USA?

不可否认，调整单元结构不但给修订工作带来很大的工作量，而且从情感上编者对有些被删的课文还是有些不舍的。这些课文都是作者精心撰写的，并受到读者喜爱的，但权衡话题的轻重性和为控制全书的篇幅，我们还是做了调整。新增加的 The Land and the People of the USA 对美国做了比较全面的介绍：涵盖地理特征和人口的主要方面，如种族、移民、宗教等等。Environmental Issues and Environmental Movements in the USA 讨论了当今世界不可避免的重要话题，不管我们学习什么专业，我们都需要知道我们赖以生存的地球在发生什么变化，我们都应该加强对保护环境的认识。我们通过美国环境问题和环保运动这一单元对这些全人类面临的普遍问题给予关注和思考。读者反馈原来的 American Way of Life: A Search for Credible Generalization 过于理论化，读起来有些困难，这次原作者重写了课文，从标题就可以看到，新课文对美国的"特色"从社会、文化与价值观等层面进行介绍和分析，也就是，美国和其他国家的主要区别、最具本国特征的方面是什么。文字也比较通俗易懂了。

　　为了加深读者对课文内容的印象，同时加强理解和掌握，我们为读者提供了丰富的配套学习资源。该资源同课后练习答案可登录 http://abook.hep.com.cn 获取，具体使用方法请参考郑重声明页。

　　本书的课文作者与第三版基本一致，这里要补充的是，在第四版新增加的课文中，The Land and the People of the USA 的课文由美国教授 Bob Eckhart 撰写；Environmental Issues and Environmental Movements in the USA 的课文由加拿大教授 Ruth Gamberg 撰写。英国教授 Richard Sanders 审校了英国部分里 6 个单元，全书其他 34 个单元均由新西兰专家 Helen Wylie 审校。在此，向上面所有为《英语国家社会与文化入门》做出贡献的外国专家教授致以真诚的感谢。

　　本书的编者是王立礼、宋云峰、龚雁、滕继萌、石同云、翟峥。衷心感谢大家的努力和合作。

主　编<br>
2019 年 4 月

# 第三版前言

《英语国家社会与文化入门》于2000年出版第一版，2005年出版第二版，一直以来有广大的读者群，并受到使用者的好评。现在出版的第三版根据使用者的反馈，对单元的安排做了以下调整：上册的澳大利亚部分删除了 Unit 16 Religion in Australia Today 和 Unit 19 Bureaucratic Power and Whistle-Blowers，原因是许多读者认为这两章较难，且专业性较强，不适合本科，特别是低年级本科学生。我们认为他们的意见很好。本部分的作者重新编写了两篇课文：Unit 16 Australian Cultural Life 和 Unit 19 Australia in the World Today。这两篇新课文的语言相对容易，包含的内容重要，涉及面广泛，对读者了解现代澳大利亚很有帮助。同时，原 Unit 17 From Penal Colony to "Free Migration" 的题目改为 Work and Family Life，并增添了许多新内容。下册的变化是美国部分增加了两个单元，即 Unit 11 American Way of Life: A Search for Credible Generalizations 和 Unit 12 The Women's Liberation Movement in America。原来的 Unit 14 Early American Jazz 被 Unit 16 American Popular Culture: Movies and Music 替换，原因是 Early American Jazz 的题目比较狭窄，而新章的内容更能反映美国的大众文化。下册从原有的20个单元增加到22个单元。

第三版基本保持原书的课文、注释和练习的风格，但每个单元增加了相关网站，以便师生对某些感兴趣的话题增进了解和展开进一步的研究。这些网站是经过编者精心挑选的，大多数是稳定的官方或机构的网站。第三版保留的课文大多有改变，主要是信息更新或增添必要的新内容。注释和练习也作了相应的变化。相信第三版较之前两版有明显的改进，希望能继续受到读者的欢迎。

上册的英国部分由英国专家 John Hill 撰写，爱尔兰部分由爱尔兰专家 Jerusha McCormack 撰写，澳大利亚部分由澳大利亚专家 Ann Aungles 撰写。下册的加拿大部分由加拿大专家 Ann Rogers 撰写，美国部分由美国专家 Morton Schagrin 和 Helen Young 撰写，新增加的 Unit 11 American Way of Life: A Search for Credible Generalizations 由美国专家 John Blair 撰写，Unit 12 The Women's Liberation Movement in America 由 Jerusha McCormack 撰写。外交政策一章由美国问题专家梅仁毅教授撰写。新添的 Unit 16 American Popular Culture: Movies and Music 由滕继萌教授撰写。新西兰部分由新西兰专家 Helen Wylie Bartle 修改并审稿。美国专家 Elizabeth Schultz 参与了 Unit 7 American Literature 的修改。全书的修订由 Helen Wylie Bartle 审稿。在此，主编向他们深表衷心的感谢，没有他们的共同努力，本书是不可能完成的。

主　编
2011年3月

# 第二版前言

《英语国家社会与文化入门》自出版以来得到广大使用者的好评。第二版在第一版的基础上进行了修改和增删,力求有所改进和完善。从所包括的国家方面,第二版上册增加了"爱尔兰",共 4 个单元。"英国"由原来的 12 章改为 10 个单元。"澳大利亚"由原来的 4 章改为 6 个单元,特请澳大利亚专家重新编写,内容更加充实,也更好地体现了澳大利亚这个国家的特点。"新西兰"的原 2 章进行了修改,并移到下册。原 12 章"美国"做了适当的调整,增加了有关二战结束后的美国外交政策的内容。"加拿大"也做了部分修改。

每单元有如下调整:第一,将重点内容提示(Focal Points)放到课文的前面,便于使用者阅读课文时抓住重点内容。第二,保留生词部分,但去掉音标,因为读者只要能识别生词即可,不要求准确地读出来。第三,有些课文有一定的改变,主要是更新信息。个别课文增加了较多的内容。第四,注释(Explanations)仍为本书的特色之一,内容更加充实详尽,以帮助使用者自学。第五,练习部分遵循由浅入深的原则,设计了正误判断题、多项选择题、填空题和解释题。练习均有答案,解释题有参考答题,供使用者参考。

英国部分由英国专家 John Hill 撰写,爱尔兰部分由爱尔兰专家 Jerusha McCormack 撰写,澳大利亚部分由澳大利亚专家 Ann Aungles 撰写,美国部分课文由美国专家 Morton Schagrin 和 Helen Young 分别撰写,外交政策第一章由美国问题专家、北京外国语大学梅仁毅教授提供,加拿大部分由加拿大专家 Ann Rogers 撰写,新西兰部分由新西兰专家 Helen Wylie Bartle 修改和审校。在此,主编向他们深表谢意。

主 编
2005 年 5 月

# 第一版前言

《英语国家社会与文化入门》是一套关于主要英语国家(英国、美国、加拿大、澳大利亚和新西兰)的社会与文化背景的教科书,旨在帮助英语专业学生和英语自学者了解这些国家的社会与文化概貌,如地理、历史、政治、经济、社会生活和文化传统等方面的基本知识。同时,通过课文的学习和各种练习的实践,达到提高英语水平的目的。本书分上、下两册,上册介绍英国、澳大利亚和新西兰,下册介绍美国和加拿大。本书适用于各类大专院校(包括电大、成人教育学院)英语专业一、二年级学生及具有同等英语水平的自学者。

本书主编在北京外国语大学英语系一年级教授过数年美国历史课,参与了英语系二年级欧洲文化入门的授课和教科书的编写工作。这两门课均受到学生的欢迎。学生通过听课,阅读简易的英语课本,在扩大知识面和英语掌握上都有很大的收获。这一成功的教学经验说明,英语教学必须实行语言教学与文化知识课紧密结合的原则,而且应从低年级开始有计划地逐步实施。只有这样,英语教学才能进一步深化。随着社会的进步和科技的高速发展,中外各种交流越来越密切,这种结合必将更加重要。本书的编撰正是基于这样的认识。

根据以上编撰宗旨和认识,本书在课文的编写及练习的设计上作了一些新的尝试。首先,本书力图符合中国学生的具体情况,适应他们的实际需要。英语学习刚刚起步的中国读者急需一本大众化的英语国家文化背景教科书。为此,我们邀请了数位在中国有过教学经验的外国专家撰写了本书的大部分课文。这些专家分别来自英国、美国、加拿大和新西兰等国家。他们都有各自的特长,并从自己的国家带来了新鲜的思想。他们对中国学生的特点和需要有一定了解,因此,他们编写的课文通俗易懂,基本词汇量不超过 2 500 个,英语地道、内容新颖。本书的中国编者是北京外国语大学英语系有着丰富教学经验的老师。他们根据中国学生的需要对难点作了精心注释,并设计了方便学生学习的练习。

其次,本书在编写中试图体现教学应以学生为中心、学生自己是学习的主人的教学思想。为了帮助学生理解课文、掌握英语、吸取知识,注释部分尽量做到详细、实用,希望能起到教师课堂引导的作用。注释的内容包括重大事件和人物的历史背景、典故、语言难点或学生不容易理解的地方等。每课编有重点内容提示(Focal Points),以帮助学生掌握课文的组织结构和中心思想。每课课文后都设计了多项选择题、填空题及解释题,这些练习不仅可以帮助学生记忆各种信息,巩固和提高文化和语言知识,还可以帮助学生复习、归纳所学内容。书后附有练习题的答案,供学生参考。此外,每章都编有思考题，供学生进行口语练习或用英语开展跨文化比较讨论时使用。

　　本册的英国部分由英国专家 John Hill 博士及加拿大专家 Ann Rogers 博士撰写。澳大利亚和新西兰驻华大使馆为本书的编写提供了有关他们国家的书面材料。中央广播电视大学的鄂鹤年先生为本书的编写和出版做了大量的工作。北京外国语大学的熊德辊教授、外交学院张益庭教授及国务院发展中心世界发展研究所吴晋研究员审阅了本书。主编谨向他们表示谢意。

主编　朱永涛
1997 年 6 月

# Contents

## The United Kingdom of Great Britain and Northern Ireland

- **UNIT 1**   A Brief Introduction to the United Kingdom   *003*
- **UNIT 2**   Northern Ireland   *023*
- **UNIT 3**   The Government of the United Kingdom   *043*
- **UNIT 4**   Politics, Class and Race   *061*
- **UNIT 5**   The UK Economy   *087*
- **UNIT 6**   British Literature   *107*
- **UNIT 7**   British Education System   *131*
- **UNIT 8**   British Foreign Relations   *149*
- **UNIT 9**   The British Media   *171*
- **UNIT 10**   Sports, Holidays and Festivals in Britain   *189*

## The Republic of Ireland

- **UNIT 11**   Land, People, and History   *211*
- **UNIT 12**   Politics and Economy   *233*
- **UNIT 13**   Irish Culture: How the Irish Live Now   *255*
- **UNIT 14**   Irish Culture: Language, Literature and Arts   *277*

## Australia

| UNIT 15 | The Land and the Peoples of the Dreaming | 297 |
| UNIT 16 | Australian Cultural Life | 313 |
| UNIT 17 | Work and Family Life | 333 |
| UNIT 18 | Australia as a Liberal Democratic Society | 349 |
| UNIT 19 | Australia in the World Today | 365 |
| UNIT 20 | From Racism to Multiculturalism | 385 |

# The United Kingdom of Great Britain and Northern Ireland

| UNIT | | |
|---|---|---|
| ❶ | A Brief Introduction to the United Kingdom | 003 |
| ❷ | Northern Ireland | 023 |
| ❸ | The Government of the United Kingdom | 043 |
| ❹ | Politics, Class and Race | 061 |
| ❺ | The UK Economy | 087 |
| ❻ | British Literature | 107 |
| ❼ | British Education System | 131 |
| ❽ | British Foreign Relations | 149 |
| ❾ | The British Media | 171 |
| ❿ | Sports, Holidays and Festivals in Britain | 189 |

# UNIT 1

# A Brief Introduction to the United Kingdom

## Go over the following focal points before reading the text:

- Effects of UK's imperial past
- A member of the European Union
- A multiracial society
- Class, regional and economic differences
- The significant role of London
- The cultural and economic dominance of England
- The invasion of the Roman Empire
- King Arthur
- Vikings from Scandinavia
- William the Conqueror
- Parliament's dominance over the throne
- Physical features of Scotland
- The cultural division between highland and lowland
- Independence of Scotland for 300 years
- Strong Scottish identity
- A brief introduction to Wales
- Wales' unification with the UK

# The United Kingdom of Great Britain and Northern Ireland

 Text

**Area:** total: 244 100 km²
land: 241 590 km²
water: 3 230 km²
(Note: Including Rockall and Shetland Islands)
**Population:** 66.05 million (2017 est.)

## A Brief Introduction to the United Kingdom

The full name of the country we are studying is the United Kingdom of Great Britain and Northern Ireland. It is a complicated name for what is in many ways a complicated country. Most people know something about it because its huge overseas **empire** gave it an important international role which only came to an end in the years following the Second World War. However, the things that people know about the UK (which they will probably call simply Britain or, wrongly, England) may have little to do with how most real British people live their lives today.

For one thing, the days of empire are now long enough ago that only old people remember it as anything of any importance in their lives[1]. Britain is no longer an **imperial** country, though the effects of its imperial past may be often **encountered** in all sorts of ways; not least in the close relationships which exist with the fifty or more countries which used to be a part of that empire, and which maintain links through a loose (and voluntary) organisation called the Commonwealth of Nations[2]. But more important today in Britain's international relations is the European Union[3], of which the UK has been a member since 1973, and it is more useful when considering modern Britain to emphasise its role as a European nation, rather than its membership of the Commonwealth. However, Britain's decision to withdraw from the EU in the 2016 **referendum** incurs uncertainty in its future relationship with Europe. The UK remains a relatively wealthy country, a member of **the Group of Seven (G7)** large developed economies.

One other obvious effect of that old imperial role lies in the make-up of the British population itself. **Immigration** from some of those Commonwealth countries, which

empire *n.*
帝国
imperial *adj.*
帝国的
encounter *v.*
遇到，遭遇
referendum *n.*
全民公决，公投
the Group of Seven (G7)
西方七国集团
（美、日、德、英、法、意、加）
immigration *n.*
移民

was encouraged in the 1950s and 1960s, has produced a population of which 1 in 10 are of non-European **ethnicity** (2011 **census**). They themselves, or their parents or grandparents, were born in India, Pakistan, South Africa, the countries of the **Caribbean**, to name only the most common[4].

This introduces what is the key theme of the chapters about the United Kingdom: as is the case for most, or all, countries, it is not possible to sum up the British people with a few simple phrases. Many people who think of Britain think of the English gentleman. But this is just a **stereotype** which never applied to the majority of the British people, and really has little validity today. The UK is one nation, with a single passport, and a single government having **sovereignty** over it all, but as the full name of the nation suggests, it is made up of different elements. It includes four parts: England, Scotland and Wales comprising Great Britain, the largest of the British Isles, and Northern Ireland, a province on the neighbouring Island of Ireland[5]. So in discussing Britain and the British some consideration has to be made of these differences: for example a woman from Scotland would not be pleased if we were to call her an "English gentleman"! She is Scottish and female, and sees her identity as different from that of men and separate from the English.

But this distinction between the four **constituent** countries is only one, and perhaps the simplest, of the differences which divide the United Kingdom. It has been already pointed out that the UK is now a **multiracial** society, and these quite recent groups of immigrants have brought aspects of their own cultures with them which sit side by side with more traditionally British ways of life. For example, many are Muslims, while most British people (in name at least) are Christians. And clearly involved in the above example of the Scottish woman is the fact that men and women do not have the same experience of life in Britain. Also Britain is divided economically: it is a society with a class-structure.[6] It is possible to **exaggerate** the importance of this class-structure, because of course most countries have some kind of class-system, but it is true to say that the class-structure of UK society is relatively obvious. The culture of a factory worker whose father was a factory worker may be quite different from that of a **stockbroker** whose father was a stockbroker: they will **tend** to read different newspapers, watch different television programmes, speak with a different accent, do different things in their free-time, and have different expectations for their children.

Another difference which marks British society is that of region. Even within each

---

ethnicity *n.*
种族地位，种族特点，种族渊源
census *n.*
人口普查
Caribbean *n., adj.*
加勒比海（的）
stereotype *n.*
模式化观念，刻板印象
sovereignty *n.*
主权
constituent *adj.*
组成的，构成的
multiracial *adj.*
多种族的
exaggerate *v.*
夸张
stockbroker *n.*
股票（证券）经纪人
tend *v.*
倾向（于），趋向（于）

# The United Kingdom of Great Britain and Northern Ireland

of the four countries there are different regions: the difference between the "highland" and "lowland" Scots has a long historical significance. For example: north and south England are also considered to be culturally distinct, though the boundary between them is not marked on any map, and exists only as a rather unclear mental attitude[7]. Nevertheless, there is some basis to the distinction in economic terms as the south is on average wealthier than the north.

Part of the reason for that economic difference between north and south is found in another distinction which marks British society, a distinction which can be seen in many societies but is perhaps particularly obvious in the UK, that is, the difference between the capital and the provinces. London is in the south of the country, and is dominant in the United Kingdom in all sorts of ways. It is by far the largest city in the country, with about one seventh of the nation's population; it is the seat of government;[8] it is the cultural centre, home to all the major newspapers, TV stations, and by far and away the widest selection of **galleries**, theatres and museums. Also it is the business centre, headquarters of the vast majority of Britain's big companies; it is the financial centre of the nation, and one of the three major international financial centres in the world. London is a huge weight in Britain's economic and cultural life, and to some extent the rest of the country lives in its shadow.

## England

**Population:** 54.786 million (2015 est.)
**Area:** 130 423 km$^2$

England is a highly **urbanised** country, with 80% of its population living in cities, and only 2% of the population working in agriculture. Its largest city is the capital, London. England is physically the largest of the four nations, and it has by far the largest population. This dominance in size is reflected in a cultural and economic dominance too, which has the result that people in foreign countries sometimes make the mistake of talking about England when they mean the UK.[9] Significantly, people in England sometimes make that mistake too, but people in the other three nations would not: they might call themselves British, or they might call themselves **Scottish** or **Welsh** or **Irish**, but they certainly wouldn't call themselves (or like to be called) English. So

gallery *n.*
画廊，美术馆
urbanised *adj.*
城市化的
Scottish *n., adj.*
苏格兰人，苏格兰的
Welsh *n., adj.*
威尔士人，威尔士的
Irish *n., adj.*
爱尔兰人，爱尔兰的

oddly, of the four nations, the English feel most British, and therefore have the weakest sense of themselves as a separate "English" culture within Britain.¹⁰

The British history has been a history of invasions. Before the first century AD Britain was made up of many tribal kingdoms of **Celtic** people: a powerful culture **originating** in central Europe.¹¹ Then in 43 AD Britain was invaded by the Roman Empire¹², and England and Wales (though not Scotland or Ireland) became a part of the Roman Empire for nearly 400 years. As the Roman Empire came under threat from the east, the Roman armies and Roman protection were withdrawn from Britain, and Britain was again divided into small kingdoms, and again it came under threat from outside, this time from **Germanic** peoples: the **Angles**, and the **Saxons**.

One of the best-known English legends **derives** from this time. In the fifth century AD it is said that a great leader appeared, united the British, and with his magical sword, **Excalibur**, drove the Saxons back. This is the story of King Arthur¹³, and has been **embellished** by singers, poets, novelists and even filmmakers ever since.

Although King Arthur's real existence is in doubt, you can visit places associated with his legend, such as the cliff-edge **castle** at **Tintagel** in **Cornwall**. According to legend Arthur gathered a company of **knights** to him, who sat together at Arthur's castle at **Camelot** (possibly the real hilltop **fort** at Cadbury Hill in **Somerset**). Conflict between his knights led to Arthur creating the famous "round table" at which all would have equal **precedence**.¹⁴ Perhaps this could be seen as an indicator of the way in which the English have wished to see their **monarch** as something other than a remote dictator, and have in fact managed to gradually bind the monarchy into a more democratic system, rather than completely rejecting it.¹⁵

Whatever Arthur's success, legend or not, it did not last, for the Anglo-Saxons did succeed in invading Britain, and either absorbed the Celtic people, or pushed them to the western and northern edges of Britain.¹⁶ Despite the fact that contemporary English people think of King Arthur as their hero, really he was fighting against them, for these Anglo-Saxon invaders were the forefathers of the English, the founders of "Angle-land" or "England" as it has become known.

Two more groups of invaders were to come after the English: from the late 8th

---

Celtic *adj.*
凯尔特人的，凯尔特语的
originate *v.*
开始；起始于
Germanic *adj.*
日耳曼人的
Angles *n.*
盎格鲁人（5世纪由德国北部移居英国）
Saxons *n.*
撒克逊人（原住德国，一部分于5世纪中叶至6世纪上半叶移居英国）
derive *v.*
由⋯而来
Excalibur *n.*
亚瑟王之魔剑
embellish *v.*
传颂，歌颂
castle *n.*
城堡
Tintagel
廷塔哲岬（在英格兰西南部，传说中的亚瑟王诞生地）
Cornwall
康瓦尔（英国西南部一郡，首府为Bodmin）
knight *n.*
（中古时的）骑士；武士
Camelot *n.*
卡米洛，传说中亚瑟王之宫殿所在地
fort *n.*
要塞；堡垒，城堡
Somerset
索美塞得郡（英格兰南部一郡）
precedence *n.*
上席；较高位置
monarch *n.*
君主；帝王

# The United Kingdom of Great Britain and Northern Ireland

century on, raiders from **Scandinavia**, the **ferocious** Vikings[17], threatened Britain's shores. Their settlements in England grew until large areas of northern and eastern England were under their control. By then the English heroes were truly English (Anglo-Saxon), such as King Alfred the Great[18], who turned the tide in the south against the Vikings. There remains to this day a certain cultural divide between northerners and southerners in England, which while not consciously "Saxon" **versus** "Dane", may have its origins in this time.[19] The richer southerners tend to think of northerners as less **sophisticated** than themselves, while northerners think southerners **arrogant** and unfriendly. They are also marked by having distinctly different accents.

The next invaders were the **Normans**, from northern France, who were **descendants** of Vikings. Under William of Normandy (known as "William the Conqueror"[20]) they crossed the English Channel in 1066, and in the Battle of Hastings, defeated an English army under King Harold[21]. This marks the last time that an army from outside the British Isles succeeded in invading. William took the English **throne**, and became William the First of England. The Tower of London[22], a castle in the centre of London which he built, still stands today.

The Normans did not settle England to any great extent: rather they imported a ruling class. The next three hundred years may be thought of as a Norman (and French-speaking) **aristocracy** ruling a largely Saxon and English-speaking population. It is this situation which produced another of England's heroic legends. This is the legend of Robin Hood[23], the Saxon nobleman oppressed by the Normans, who became an **outlaw**, and with his band of "merry men" hid in the forest of Sherwood in the north midlands of England. From this secret place, armed with their **longbows**, they then went out to rob from the rich to give to the poor. He has featured in many television series and films, both British and American. Some writers have seen in the popularity of this legend of a rebellion hidden in the green wood a clue to the English character: a richly unconventional **interior** life hidden by an **external** conformity.[24] But, like all stereotypes, this one has its weaknesses, as many English people, especially young people, like to display their unconventionality externally — for example English **punk rockers** with their vividly **dyed spiky** hair[25]. But it is certainly true that the lifeless fronts of many English houses **conceal** beautiful back gardens. Gardening is one of the most popular pastimes in England, and the back garden provides a place where people's outdoor life at home can go on out of the public gaze. This may contrast with people from other countries whose

---

Scandinavia
斯堪的纳维亚（北欧国家的原称，指：瑞典、挪威、丹麦、芬兰、冰岛）
ferocious *adj.*
凶残的；野蛮的
versus *prep.*
对（多用于诉讼或竞技等之中，缩写作 v. 或 vs.）
sophisticated *adj.*
世故的；城府深的
arrogant *adj.*
骄傲自大的
Normans *n.*
诺曼人
descendant *n.*
后代，后裔
throne *n.*
王位
aristocracy *n.*
贵族；贵族阶层
outlaw *n.*
不法之徒，草莽英雄
longbow *n.*
大弓
interior *adj.*
内部的
external *adj.*
外表上的
punk *n.*
朋克摇滚乐；小混混，小流氓
rocker *n.*
摇滚乐手，摇滚乐迷
dyed *adj.*
染色的
spiky *adj.*
竖起的；直立的
conceal *v.*
隐藏，掩盖

outdoor life might be more social — sitting on the front **porch** watching passers-by.

The next few hundred years following the Norman invasion can be seen as a process of joining together the various parts of the British Isles under English rule, so that any English identity eventually became swamped by the necessity of adopting a wider British identity, both to unite the kingdom internally, and to present a single identity externally as Britain became an imperial power.[26] At the same time power was gradually transferred from the monarch to the parliament. Charles the First's attempt to **overrule** parliament in the 1640s led to a civil war in which parliamentary forces were victorious, and the king was **executed**. After a gap of 11 years in which England was ruled by parliament's leader, Oliver Cromwell[27], the monarchy was restored. Further conflict between parliament and the king led to the removal of the Scottish house of Stuart[28] from the throne, and William and Mary[29] were imported from Holland to take the throne, thus finally establishing parliament's dominance over the throne.

## Scotland

**Population:** 5.405 million (2016 est.)
**Area:** 77 080 km$^2$

Scotland is the second largest of the four nations, both in population and in geographical area. It is also the most confident of its own identity because alone amongst the non-English **components** of the UK it has previously spent a **substantial** period of history as a unified state independent of the UK. Thus it is not a big leap for the Scottish to imagine themselves independent again.[30]

Physically, Scotland is the most **rugged** part of the UK, with areas of **sparsely** populated mountains and lakes in the north (the Highlands), and in the south (the Southern Uplands). Three quarters of the population lives in the lowland zone which **spans** the country between these two highland areas. The largest city is **Glasgow**, in the west of this zone. Scotland's capital city is **Edinburgh**, on the east coast forty miles away from Glasgow. It is renowned for its beauty, and dominated by its great castle on a high rock in the centre of the city. Both cities have ancient and internationally respected universities dating from the 15th century.

Scotland was not conquered by the Romans, though they did try to, and for a

---

porch *n.*
门廊
overrule *v.*
推翻；否定
execute *v.*
处决
component *n.*
组成部分
substantial *adj.*
大量的，可观的；实质的
rugged *adj.*
崎岖的；不平坦的
sparsely *adv.*
稀少地
span *v., n.*
跨越
Glasgow
格拉斯哥，苏格兰最大城市
Edinburgh
爱丁堡，苏格兰首府

# The United Kingdom of Great Britain and Northern Ireland

while occupied as far as the edge of the northern highland zone. But the difficulty of maintaining their rule there caused them to **retreat** to a line roughly equivalent to the contemporary boundary between England and Scotland. Along this line, from sea to sea[31], they, like the Chinese, built a wall to mark the northern edge of their **domain**, and to help defend it. It is called "Hadrian's Wall"[32] after the Emperor of Rome at the time of its building and, although ruined, lengths of it can still be seen and walked along.

Nor was most of Scotland conquered by the Anglo-Saxons, although an Angle Kingdom was established in the southeast — hence Edinburgh's Germanic name[33]. British Celts displaced from the south by Saxon invasion occupied the area around what is now Glasgow, and in this same period (around the 6th century AD) people from northern Ireland invaded the southwest. They were called the Scots, and it is they that gave the modern country of Scotland its name. The original Scottish Celts, called the Picts, were left with the extensive but unproductive highland zone. The division between highland and lowland Scotland remains a cultural divide today, in much the same way as north and south England see themselves as different from each other. There are even areas in the highlands where (in addition to English) people speak the old Celtic language, called "**Gaelic**".

Like England, Scotland began to experience Viking raids in the 9th century, and it was the pressure from this outside threat that led Scottish kings to unify, forming an independent singular Scottish state at just about the same time that Anglo-Saxon England was also unifying. The presence of this larger powerful kingdom on its southern doorstep was the key factor in Scottish politics from that time on, with frequent wars between the two. William Shakespeare's play *Macbeth*[34] is set in the Scotland of this period. The town of Berwick upon Tweed near the Scottish border in present day England is said to have **changed hands** thirteen times as a result of Anglo-Scottish conflict. Despite the conflict, there were close ties between the two countries with extensive **intermarriage** between the two aristocracies, and even between the royal families. A Hollywood movie, *Braveheart*, told the story of William Wallace's[35] uprising in 1298, which was **quelled** by the English. But only a few years later the Scots, under the leadership of Robert the Bruce[36], were victorious at the Battle of Bannockburn[37], leading to 300 years of full independence.

In 1603, however, Queen Elizabeth the First[38] of England died childless, and the next in line to the throne was James the Sixth of Scotland[39], so he also became James

**retreat** *v.*
撤退
**domain** *n.*
领土；领地
**Gaelic** *n.*
盖尔语
**change hands**
（财产等）转换所有者；易手
**intermarriage** *n.* 异族通婚；近亲通婚
**quell** *v.*
镇压

the First of England, uniting the two thrones. But for another hundred years Scotland maintained its separate political identity. However, in 1707 by agreement of the English and Scottish parliaments, Scotland joined the Union. There followed two rebellions in 1715 and 1745 in which the **heir** to the Stuart claim (**deposed** in 1688 by the English parliament) to the British throne attempted to **reassert** his right to rule Britain, gathering support in Scotland then marching with an army into England. In 1745 this led to a brutal military response from the British army. The rebel army was destroyed at the Battle of Culloden (the last battle on British soil) in northern Scotland. Scottish highland clan (extended family group) culture was effectively destroyed at this time, and today exists largely as a way of parting tourists from their money by selling them "**tartan**" **souvenirs** or histories of "their" clan[40]. For following Culloden, and even more importantly, the agricultural changes of the 18th century which led to **depopulation** of the highlands, many Scots sought their fortune outside Scotland — in England, America, Canada, or Australia. So that there are more people of Scottish descent outside Scotland than in it, and many of those come back to find their "roots", forming a good target for the sellers of such souvenirs.

The dream of an independent Scotland has not **vanished**. Although Scotland elects its members of parliament to the London parliament in just the same way as the English do and sends 59 representatives to London, the Scotland Act 1998 provided for the establishment of the Scottish Parliament and Executive, following endorsement of the UK Government's proposals on devolution in a referendum in 1997 when the proposal to establish a Scottish Parliament was supported by 74.3% of the votes. The newly-elected Scottish Parliament had powers to make primary legislation in certain "**devolved**" areas of policy, in addition to some limited tax-varying powers. Other policy areas remain "reserved" areas for the UK government and parliament. In the first election to the Parliament, in May 1999, 129 Members of the Scottish Parliament (MSPs) were elected for a fixed four-year term. The Labour Party, which had traditionally done well in elections in Scotland, became the largest single party. The Scottish National Party, which wants an independent Scotland, is the second largest party and the Conservative Party the third largest in the Parliament. The Scottish National Party (SNP) was first elected to form the Scottish Government in 2007. The new government established a "National Conversation" on constitutional issues, proposing a number of options such as increasing the powers of the Scottish Parliament, federalism, or a referendum on Scottish independence from the United Kingdom. In rejecting the last option, the three

heir *n.*
继承人
depose *v.*
废黜（国王等）
reassert *v.*
再次申明
tartan *adj.*
用格子呢制的
souvenir *n.*
纪念品
depopulation *n.*
人口减少
vanish *v.*
消失
devolve *v.*
权力下放

# The United Kingdom of Great Britain and Northern Ireland

main opposition parties in the Scottish Parliament created a commission to investigate the distribution of powers between devolved Scottish and UK-wide bodies.[41] The Scotland Act 2012, based on proposals by the commission, was subsequently enacted devolving additional powers to the Scottish Parliament. After the 2011 elections gave the SNP an overall majority in the Scottish Parliament, a referendum on independence for Scotland was held on September 18, 2014. The referendum rejected independence by a majority of 55.3% to 44.7%. Following the referendum on the UK's membership of the European Union on June 23, 2016 (**Brexit**), where a UK-wide majority voted to withdraw from the EU whilst a majority within Scotland voted to remain, Scotland's First Minister, Nicola Sturgeon, announced that as a result a new independence referendum was "highly likely".

Scotland has a great tradition of innovation in the arts, philosophy and science. The inventor of the telephone was a Scot, and the first man to **transmit** a television picture was another. Its writers have given the world such well-known work as Walter Scott's[42] romances of highland Scotland, and "Auld Lang Syne"[43] (by Robert Burns, who wrote in the Scots dialect). But the work which many consider to best sum up Scotland's position is the famous novel *Dr. Jekyll and Mr. Hyde*, by Robert Louis Stevenson[44], which describes how the civilised scientist Dr. Jekyll transforms periodically into the crude and violent Mr. Hyde. This description of the **dual** nature of man is perhaps a good way to think of Scotland: superficially fully integrated into the UK, but concealed beneath this is a still-strong Scottish identity[45].

## Wales

Population: 3.089 million (2012 census)
Area: 20 776 km$^2$

The capital of Wales is Cardiff, a small city of about 346 100 people (2011 census) on the south coast. This southern area was an important element in Britain's industrial revolution, as it had rich coal **deposits**. Coal-mining became a key industry for the Welsh, employing tens of thousands at its height. So its disappearance has been a major economic and cultural blow. But South Wales has been very successful in attracting investment from abroad — particularly Japan and the United States, which has helped to create new industries to replace coal and steel.

---

Brexit
英国退出欧盟。由 Britain 和 exit 两词组合而成。
transmit *v.*
传送
dual *adj.*
双重的
deposit *n.*
矿藏，矿床

Wales is the smallest among the three nations on the British mainland, though larger than Northern Ireland. It is very close to the most densely populated parts of central England. Though it is hillier and more rugged than **adjacent** parts of England there is no natural boundary. So Wales has been dominated by England for longer than the other nations of the union. Nevertheless, what is remarkable is that despite this nearness and long-standing political integration Wales retains a powerful sense of its difference from England. It also retains its own language, Welsh. This is a Celtic **tongue** completely different from English, spoken by 19% of the population (2011 census), a much higher proportion of the population than that who can speak Gaelic in Scotland. Again, all those Welsh-speakers are also fluent in English.

Like the rest of Britain, before the arrival of the Roman Empire, Wales was a land of Celtic peoples, living in a number of small tribal kingdoms. Wales was conquered by the Romans eventually, though with difficulty. The Welsh **chieftain** Caradoc fought a long **guerrilla** campaign from the Welsh hills against the invader. When the Romans left Britain Wales was again a Celtic land, though again divided into separate kingdoms, but unlike England it did not fall to the Anglo-Saxon invaders of the fifth century.

But Wales was always under pressure from its English neighbours, particularly after the Norman Conquest, when Norman **barons** set up castles and estates in Wales under the authority of the English Crown. Thus there was a need to unify Wales to successfully resist the English. This did not happen until Llywelyn ap Gruffudd brought a large portion of Wales under his rule, and by a military campaign forced the English to acknowledge him as Prince of Wales in 1267. But when he died, the English king, Edward the First, set about conquering Wales, building a series of great stone castles there from which to control the population. These castles stand today as one of Wales' greatest tourist attractions (along with its beaches, cliffs and mountains), and tourism is now an important industry.

Edward the First named his son the Prince of Wales, and the first son of the monarch has held that title ever since (including the present day Prince Charles) to try to bring Wales into the British nation. The last real attempt to resist that process was in the early 15th century when Owain Glyndwr[46] led an unsuccessful rising against the English. Today Glyndwr and Llywelyn are more than simple historical figures for the Welsh: they are the almost legendary heroes of Welsh nationalism. Their brief campaigns are the only times in history when Wales existed as a unified independent

adjacent *adj.*
邻近的
tongue *n.*
（特定的）语言
chieftain *n.*
族长，酋长
guerrilla *n.*
游击战
baron *n.*
男爵（英国贵族中最低的一级爵位）

# The United Kingdom of Great Britain and Northern Ireland

nation[47].

   A hundred years after Glyndwr, in 1536, Wales was brought legally, administratively, and politically into the UK by an act of the British parliament.[48] This close long-standing relationship means that modern Wales lacks some of the outward signs of difference which Scotland possesses — its legal system and its education system are exactly the same as in England. Often official statistics are given for "England and Wales". However, Wales is different, and one of the key markers of that difference is the Welsh language — the old British Celtic tongue which is still in daily use. But as a source of the Welsh identity this is sometimes divisive[49], because 80% of the Welsh don't speak the language, and yet feel Welsh. Since most of the Welsh speakers are in the north, this deepens a cultural division between the more populated, industrial south, and the rural north of Wales.

   As in Scotland the Welsh people elect their MPs to the London parliament. The Welsh too have a nationalist party, "Plaid Cymru"[50] (the Party of Wales), which campaigns for an independent Wales. In May 1997, the Labour government of Tony Blair was elected with a promise of creating a devolved assembly in Wales; the Wales resulted in a "yes" vote. The National Assembly for Wales, as a consequence of the Government of Wales Act 1998, possesses the power to determine how the government budget for Wales is spent and administered, although the UK parliament reserves the right to set limits on the powers of the Welsh Assembly.

# Explanations

1. **the days of empire are ... as anything of any importance in their lives:**
   现在，帝国的时代已过去很久了，只有老人们把英帝国作为他们生活中有一些意义的一件事留在记忆中。anything of any importance: 重要的事。

2. **the Commonwealth of Nations:**
   英联邦国家组织，有 53 个成员国。由英国和其前殖民地在第二次世界大战结束和非殖民化后组成的松散国际组织，以取代第二次世界大战前的大英帝国。女王是这些国家的最高权力象征，每年举行定期会议，但英国并无实际控制权力。英国目前与这些国家仍保持经常性的来往和交流。

UNIT **1** A Brief Introduction to the United Kingdom

3. **The European Union:**
   欧洲联盟，简称欧盟。前身为欧洲共同体。到 2017 年为止，欧洲联盟有 28 个成员国（包括英国）。

4. **to name only the most common:**
   仅举出几个最具有代表性的国家和地区。指前面所提到的印度、巴基斯坦、南非以及加勒比海国家。

5. **and Northern Ireland, a province on the neighbouring island of Ireland:**
   再加上北爱尔兰——大不列颠岛临近的爱尔兰岛上的一个省，组成了一个完整的国家。

6. **Also Britain is divided economically: it is a society with a class-structure:**
   而且英国社会是根据经济状况来划分的，即它是有阶级结构的社会。

7. **north and south England are also considered ... a rather unclear mental attitude:**
   尽管英格兰北部和南部的分界线在任何地图上都没有标出，而且这种分野是一种相当模糊的心理态度，但这两个地区的文化迥然不同。

8. **it is the seat of government:**
   伦敦是（英国）政府所在地。seat: 场所；所在地。

9. **This dominance in size ... when they mean the UK:**
   面积上的主导地位也反映在文化和经济的主导地位上，其结果是别的国家的人有时在言谈话语中错误地用英格兰来代替英国。

10. **So oddly, of the four nations ... as a separate "English" culture within Britain:**
    所以，奇怪的是在这四个地区，英格兰人最觉得自己是英国人，并不特意把自己的"英格兰文化"区别于英国国内的其他文化。

11. **Before the first century AD ... in central Europe:**
    公元 1 世纪之前，英国是由许多凯尔特人的部落王国构成的，其强大的文化源于中欧地区。

12. **the Roman Empire:**
    罗马帝国。始于公元前 31 年，公元 192 年进入全盛时期，政治、经济和文化都得到充分发展。进入 3 世纪之后，罗马奴隶制社会陷于全面危机，经济衰退，政治混乱，基督教逐渐流行和传播。至帝国后期，戴克里先建立君主统治，各地爆发了广泛的人民起义，给帝国的统治以严重打击。393 年帝国分裂为西罗马和东罗马帝国。

13. **King Arthur:**
    亚瑟王，6 世纪时英格兰统治者，圆桌骑士的领袖。有关他的传说很多。

14. **Conflict between his knights ... have equal precedence:**
    亚瑟王的骑士们在开会时经常为排座次问题而争吵，致使亚瑟王采用著名的圆桌会议形式，这样，骑士们就无法分出地位的主次了。

15. **Perhaps this could be seen ... completely rejecting it:**
    或许这可以被用来象征英国人如何看待其君主的一种愿望，他们不希望把君主看作一位可望而不可即的

# The United Kingdom of Great Britain and Northern Ireland

统治者。事实上，英国人已逐渐将君主制融入一个更为民主的体制之中，而不是完全拒绝君主制。

16. **Whatever Arthur's success ... the western and northern edges of Britain:**
    无论亚瑟王的伟业如何，也无论是传说还是事实，他的伟业没有持续多久，因为盎格鲁－撒克逊人入侵了英国，或吸纳了凯尔特人，或将他们赶到英国西部或北部边缘地带。

17. **Vikings:**
    维京人，泛指8世纪到11世纪掠夺欧洲西海岸的北欧海盗。

18. **King Alfred the Great:**
    阿尔弗雷德大帝（849–899），英国历史上著名的国王，领导英国抗击北欧海盗的入侵。

19. **There remains ... origins in this time:**
    直到今天英格兰的北方人和南方人之间还存在着一定的文化差异，这种差异虽不像"撒克逊"与"丹麦人"之间的差异那样明显，但其根源可能产生于这段时间。

20. **William the Conqueror:**
    征服者威廉（约1028–1087），法国诺曼底公爵，英格兰第一位诺曼人国王（1066–1087在位）。1066年9月27日领兵渡海对英格兰开战，获全胜。同年圣诞节，威廉在威斯敏斯特教堂加冕为英格兰国王，史称威廉一世。

21. **King Harold:**
    哈罗德国王，英格兰最后一位撒克逊民族的国王，1066年诺曼人入侵英格兰时，在关键的黑斯廷斯战役中被杀。从此英格兰被征服，诺曼底统治者当了英国国王，即威廉一世。

22. **The Tower of London:**
    伦敦塔，位于泰晤士河北岸，伦敦塔桥附近，是伦敦著名古迹之一。威廉一世于11世纪为保卫和控制整个伦敦城而建造了该塔，占地18英亩。经历代君主扩建和修整，整个建筑反映了英国不同朝代的建筑风格。9个世纪以来，这里曾作过堡垒、王宫、监狱、皇家铸币厂和伦敦档案馆。现在是王冠、王袍、兵器和盔甲陈列馆。

23. **Robin Hood:**
    罗宾汉，英国传说中的一位著名撒克逊族绿林好汉，他和他的追随者们在森林里盘踞，以劫富济贫、杀贪官污吏为宗旨。

24. **Some writers ... by an external conformity:**
    在这个广为流传的绿林反叛的传奇故事中，一些作家看到了体现英国个性的迹象：表面上循规蹈矩，但内心世界却不同寻常。

25. **for example English punk rockers ... dyed spiky hair:**
    例如英国的一些朋克摇滚乐迷把头发理成鸡冠状，并染成鲜艳的颜色，以外在形式来表达他们的反叛心理。

26. **The next few hundred years ... as Britain became an imperial power:**
    诺曼人入侵后的几百年可以视作不列颠不同地区在英格兰统治下融合的时期，其结果是英格兰的身份最

# UNIT 1  A Brief Introduction to the United Kingdom

终让位于有必要采用的更宽泛的英国身份，一是因为王国内部统一的需要，二是当英国成为帝国时需要一个代表英国的单一身份。

27. **Oliver Cromwell:**

    奥利弗·克伦威尔（1599–1658）。英格兰军人和政治家。生于英格兰东部的亨廷顿，曾两次当选国会议员，由于反对国王、捍卫公民自由和宗教自由，很快成为英国资产阶级革命的领袖。1649年国王查理一世被处死后，议会宣布成立共和国，克伦威尔成为共和国首领，称为"护国公"。1649年，他又征服了爱尔兰人。

28. **the Scottish house of Stuart:**

    苏格兰斯图亚特王室。1371年，罗伯特二世成为该家族在苏格兰的第一代国王。1603年，该家族的苏格兰国王詹姆士六世继承英格兰王位（英格兰的詹姆士一世），斯图亚特家族从此成为英格兰王室。

29. **William and Mary:**

    威廉和玛丽。英国资产阶级革命王朝复辟时期的第二个国王是詹姆士二世。他和他的妻子都是天主教徒，他的统治遭到议会中资产阶级势力和新教徒的强烈反对。因此，英国议会于1687年邀请詹姆士二世的女儿新教徒玛丽和她的丈夫荷兰国王威廉（新教徒）到英国联合执政。威廉的军队在英国登陆时未遇任何反抗，詹姆士二世逃跑，这就是英国历史上1688年的"光荣革命"，又称"不流血革命"。1689年，议会通过"权利法案"，限制国王权力，从而开始了延续至今的君主立宪制。

30. **Thus it is ... to imagine themselves independent again:**

    所以对苏格兰来说，想象一下再次独立并不是遥不可及的事情。big leap: 一大步，跃进。

31. **from sea to sea:**

    从东岸到西岸。英国是个南北狭长、处于大西洋中的岛国。

32. **Hadrian's Wall:**

    哈德良长城，罗马人保卫不列颠北疆的屏障，长118公里，不列颠总督尼波斯监造，公元136年竣工。

33. **hence Edinburgh's Germanic name:**

    所以爱丁堡的名字源于日耳曼语。盎格鲁和撒克逊均为日耳曼部落。

34. *Macbeth*:

    《麦克白》，莎士比亚创作的四大悲剧之一。现实生活中的麦克白在1040年杀死堂兄，自立为苏格兰国王。1057年在一场战役中被英格兰支持的一方杀死。他大起大落的生平构成了莎翁戏剧创作的基本情节。

35. **William Wallace:**

    威廉·华莱士（约1270–1305），苏格兰最伟大的民族英雄之一。1298年7月3日，爱德华一世的军队入侵苏格兰。他率领苏格兰人民奋起反抗，在斯特灵的福尔柯克战役中被爱德华的军队打败。之后，继续带领其队伍在苏格兰各地与英军对抗，1305年被捕，后在伦敦被处决。

36. **Robert the Bruce:**

    罗伯特·布鲁斯（1274–1329）。14世纪苏格兰争取国家独立的斗士，1306年成为苏格兰国王。1314年，他率领苏格兰军队在班诺克本大败英格兰军队，迫使英格兰承认他的地位。根据北安普敦条约（1328年）

# The United Kingdom of Great Britain and Northern Ireland

的规定，英王承认他为苏格兰国王并完全放弃英格兰对苏格兰主权的要求。

37. **the Battle of Bannockburn:**

    班诺克本战役。苏格兰历史上的一次大决战。在这次决战中，由罗伯特·布鲁斯统率的苏格兰军队打败了爱德华二世带领的英格兰军队。苏格兰军队在敌强我弱的情况下，巧妙利用地形，粉碎了敌人的进攻。通过这次战役，苏格兰重获独立。

38. **Queen Elizabeth the First:**

    伊丽莎白一世（1533–1603）。英格兰历代最伟大的君主之一。在位 45 年中，她不愿发动战争，因而保证国家稳步走向繁荣。伊丽莎白时代是英国最辉煌的年代，以莎士比亚戏剧为标志的英国文学达到鼎盛。此外，英国航海业在这一时期开始发展，繁荣了对外通商。伊丽莎白实行了一系列强国政策，使英国成为海上霸主，走上了殖民主义道路。

39. **James the Sixth of Scotland:**

    苏格兰詹姆士六世（1566–1625）。1567 年起统治苏格兰，史称詹姆士六世。生于爱丁堡，一岁继承苏格兰王位。成年后竭力与英格兰女王保持良好关系，因为伊丽莎白无嗣，按次序来讲他可继承英格兰王位。1603 年，伊丽莎白逝世后，詹姆士六世继承英格兰王位，史称詹姆士一世。

40. **today exists largely ... histories of "their" clan:**

    （部族文化）现今的存在主要是为了向游客兜售"花格呢"纪念品和各部族所谓的历史资料。"their" 指来苏格兰寻根的游客。

41. **In rejecting the last option ... between devolved Scottish and UK-wide bodies:**

    苏格兰议会三个主要反对党否决了最后一个选项（即举行苏格兰独立公投），成立了一个委员会调查已得到权力下放的苏格兰与联合王国（中央政府）机构之间权力分配的问题。

42. **Walter Scott:**

    沃尔特·司各特（1771–1832）。苏格兰小说家，历史小说的首创者。他著名的作品都是写苏格兰和英格兰的历史，许多材料取自民间传说。其中有《苏格兰歌谣》《爱丁堡评论》《威弗利》等。

43. **Auld Lang Syne:**

    著名苏格兰民歌《友谊地久天长》，歌词作者为苏格兰诗人彭斯。歌曲的苏格兰语 auld lang syne 在规范的英语中是 old long since，或 long long ago。

44. **Robert Louis Stevenson:**

    罗伯特·路易斯·斯蒂文森（1850–1894）。苏格兰著名冒险故事和散文作家。他的作品种类繁多，构思精巧。主要著作有《新天方夜谭》故事集、《金银岛》《诱拐》《化身博士》《一个孩子的诗园》等。

45. **superficially fully integrated ... a still-strong Scottish identity:**

    表面上（苏格兰）已与英国融为一体，但实际上仍然保持了强烈的苏格兰身份特征。

46. **Owain Glyndwr:**

    欧文·格林道瓦尔（1354–1416），自称威尔士王子，率威尔士人反抗英格兰的统治但未成功。人们称他为威尔士的民族英雄。1400 年 9 月，他在威尔士北部发动起义，起义很快就发展成为威尔士的民族斗争。

1404 年，格林道瓦尔控制了威尔士大部分地区，建立了独立的威尔士议会，开始实施自己的外交和基督教会政策。1405 年，他遭到亨利王子的围剿，不久起义即告失败。

47. **Their brief campaigns ... as a unified independent nation:**
    他们短暂的反抗运动是历史上威尔士作为独立统一国家而存在的唯一时期。

48. **A hundred years after Glyndwr ... by an act of the British parliament:**
    格林道瓦尔死后的一百年，即在 1536 年，英国国会的一项法案使威尔士在法律、行政和政治上并入英国。

49. **But as a source of the Welsh identity this is sometimes divisive:**
    然而作为威尔士特征的一个来源，这（威尔士语）有时却具有分裂作用。

50. **Plaid Cymru:**
    The Party of Wales, 威尔士党，1925 年成立。该党派要求威尔士获取更大的自治权，同时希望与英格兰保持紧密的关系。

# Exercises

**I. Give the Chinese equivalents for the following:**

1. Robin Hood
2. Anglo-Saxons
3. King Arthur
4. the Vikings
5. referendum

**II. Decide whether the following statements are true (T) or false (F):**

1. Britain is no longer an imperial country. _____
2. The Commonwealth of Nations, which replaced the British Empire, is dominated by the United Kingdom. _____
3. 1 in 20 of the British population is of non-European ethnicity. _____
4. The stereotype of the English gentleman never applied to the majority of the British people. _____
5. When people outside the UK talk about England, they mistake it as Britain sometimes. _____
6. The Scots and Welsh have a strong sense of being British. _____

# The United Kingdom of Great Britain and Northern Ireland

7. Scotland was unified with England through peaceful means. _____
8. Wales is rich in coal deposits. _____

## III. Fill in the blanks:

1. The full name of the UK is the United Kingdom of _____ and _____.
2. The Island of Great Britain is made up of England, _____ and _____.
3. The United Kingdom has been a member of the _____ since 1973.
4. London is not only the political and business centre of the nation, but also the _____ and _____ centre.
5. Britain is a country with a history of invasions. In 43 AD Britain was invaded by _____; in the late 8th century they experienced the Viking raids from Scandinavia; and in the 11th century they suffered invasions from _____.
6. The Anglo-Saxons began to settle in Britain in the _____ century.
7. Charles the First, king of Britain, was executed, because he attempted to overthrow _____ in the English Revolution.
8. The battle of Bannockburn led by _____ succeeded in winning the full independence of Scotland for 300 years.
9. The capital of Scotland is _____, which is well-known for its natural _____.
10. Although Wales is the smallest of the three nations on the mainland, it's good at getting investment from abroad, particularly from _____ and _____.

## IV. Questions:

1. What are the differences between the following terms: England, Britain, and the United Kingdom?
2. In terms of international relations, which is more important to Britain — The European Union or the Commonwealth of Nations? Why?
3. What is the percentage of Britain's non-European ethnicity? Which countries or regions did these non-European immigrants mainly come from?
4. How dominant is England in the four countries that constitute the UK in terms of area, population, economy, and culture?
5. Who was King Arthur? Why are there so many legends about him?
6. Who was Robin Hood? What is he famous for?
7. What are the major characteristics of Scotland in geography and population?

8. What is the largest city in Scotland? What have you learned about this city from the text and other sources?
9. Has Scotland ever been conquered in history?
10. How did Scotland come to unite with England?
11. What was the result of the referendum on the independence for Scotland held in 2014?
12. Which city is the capital of Wales? What do you know about that city?
13. What percentage of the population in Wales can speak Welsh, a Celtic tongue completely different from English?
14. Why did Edward the First name his son the Prince of Wales?
15. What does the Welsh nationalist party "Plaid Cymru" campaign for?

V. **Topics for discussion or research:**
1. Do research on the sphere of the British Empire. Discuss in what ways the influence of the British Empire is still felt domestically in Britain and internationally.
2. Why does the author say that it is not possible to sum up the British people with a few simple phrases? Illustrate your point with facts or examples.
3. Why does the author say "the dream of an independent Scotland has not vanished"? How would you prove this point with past and present events taking place in Scottish history?
4. The author says, "The British history has been a history of invasion." Do research on the major invasions mentioned in the text. Discuss how each of the invasions influenced the British culture.

# UNIT 2

# Northern Ireland

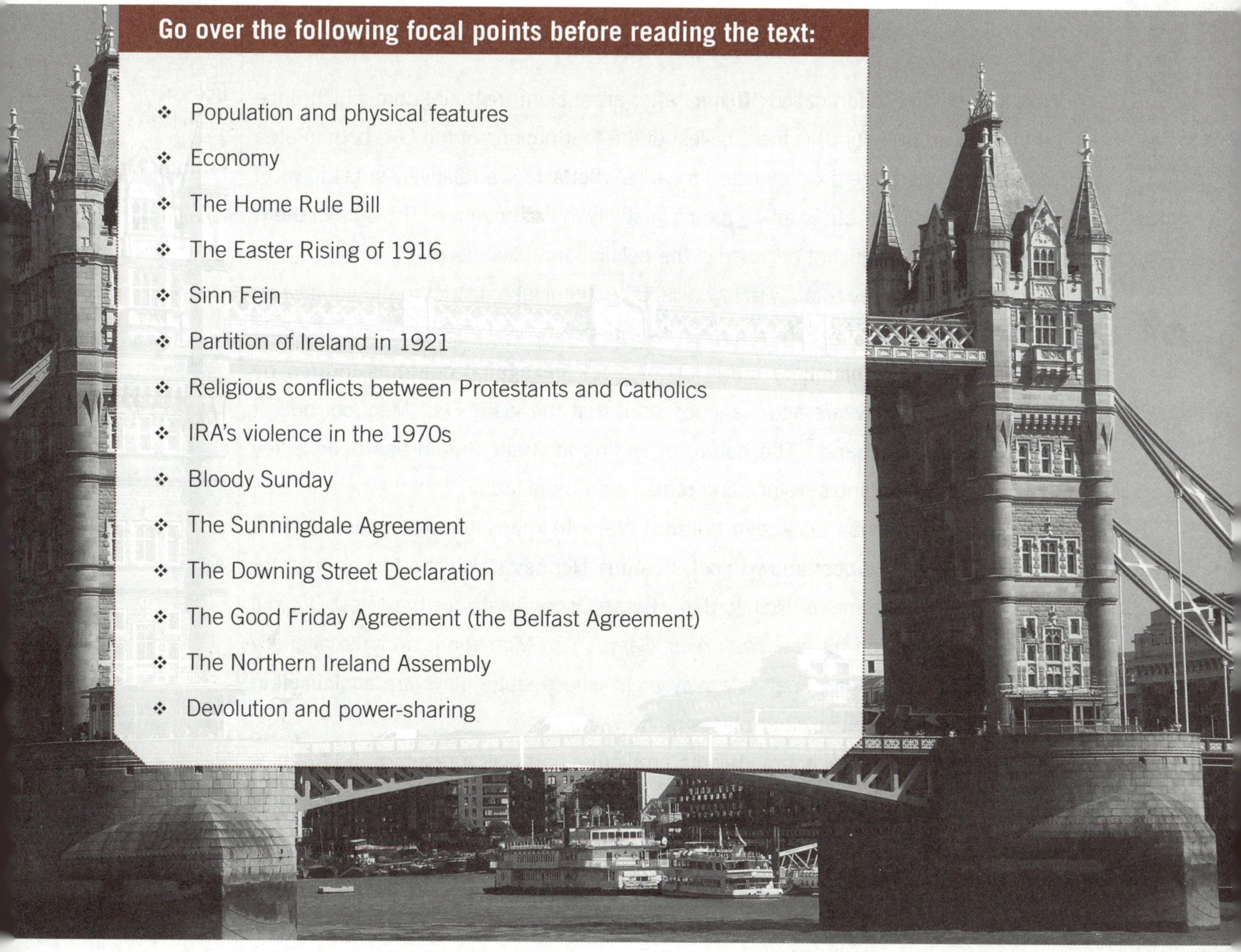

**Go over the following focal points before reading the text:**

- Population and physical features
- Economy
- The Home Rule Bill
- The Easter Rising of 1916
- Sinn Fein
- Partition of Ireland in 1921
- Religious conflicts between Protestants and Catholics
- IRA's violence in the 1970s
- Bloody Sunday
- The Sunningdale Agreement
- The Downing Street Declaration
- The Good Friday Agreement (the Belfast Agreement)
- The Northern Ireland Assembly
- Devolution and power-sharing

# The United Kingdom of Great Britain and Northern Ireland

## Text

**Population:** 1.811 million (2011 UK Census; 2.9% of UK population)
1.87 million (2017 estimate)
**Area:** 14 130 km²

### General Introduction

Northern Ireland (often called "**Ulster**" after an ancient Irish kingdom which once existed in that part of Ireland) is the smallest of the four nations of the UK, both in area and population. There are six counties. Its capital, **Belfast**, is a relatively small town of 532 928 people in 2014, but is much the biggest city in the province. Though Northern Ireland is small, it is significant because of the political troubles there.

Physically, it is mostly rural, with low hills, a beautiful lake district in the southwest, and a rugged coastline, which includes its most famous landmark, the "Giant's Causeway"[1], a rocky **promontory** made up of black **hexagonal** columns formed by cooling **lava** millions of years ago. Legend has it that the giant Finn MacCool built it to cross the sea to Scotland.[2] The nature of its link to Great Britain has been a key element in Northern Ireland's history, and remains an issue today.

Northern Ireland has an active cultural life with many theatres, restaurants, pubs and museums. Its best known poet, Seamus Heaney[3], won the Nobel Prize for Literature in 1995. Film-maker Neil Jordan won an Oscar award for the "Best Original Screenplay" in 1992 with his film *The Crying Game*[4]. Van Morrison is an internationally famous pop musician. Brian Friel[5] is a playwright whose stage plays are **acclaimed** in London and Dublin as well as other places of the world.

The Northern Ireland economy has its problems, partly as a result of the troubles discouraging investment, partly as a result of its **peripherality** in relation to the UK. Its wealth per head is the lowest of any UK region. Nevertheless living costs are also comparatively low. Industrial companies there include the aircraft manufacturer, Short Brothers (usually referred to as "Shorts"), which builds small commuter aircraft, as well as parts for other manufacturers such as Boeing, and the UK's largest shipbuilder,

Ulster *n.*
北爱尔兰
Belfast *n.*
贝尔法斯特（北爱首府）
promontory *n.*
海角
hexagonal *adj.*
六角形的，六边形的
lava *n.*
熔岩；火山岩
acclaim *v.*
受到称赞，赞扬
peripherality *n.*
周边

Harland and Wolff[6], which built the famous RMS *Titanic* and whose focus in recent years has been on **offshore** renewable energy (wind and marine-generated electricity).

This unit will concentrate on the political problems of Northern Ireland, because unfortunately that is what is best known about it, though often not well understood. However, you should remember that it is a place where ordinary life continues, to which the troubles are an addition, rather than the main preoccupation of everyday life.

## History

The Northern Ireland problem has resulted from conflict between **Protestants** and **Catholics** over the status of Northern Ireland. It is a historical problem left over by British colonial rule in the past.

Northern Ireland used to be part of Ireland. In 1169, Britain began to invade Ireland, and the conquest was completed in 1603. In 1801 Ireland was unified with Great Britain under the 1801 Act of Union — with the name "The United Kingdom of Great Britain and Ireland". To strengthen British control of Ireland, a "**plantation policy**" was practised, especially in the 17th century. The British government encouraged people from Scotland and Northern England to **emigrate** to Ireland. Many settled in the north. From the time of Queen Elizabeth I (i.e. from the late 1590s) the new settlers, loyal to the British crown and Protestants in religious **persuasion**, were granted land, position, and privileges which had been systematically taken away from the **indigenous**, Roman Catholic population.

These abuses constitute a vivid history of **massacre**, exile, systematic repression, and deprivation. In the 19th century, the island was scarcely able to support the population, and at times many people died as a result of **famine** (e.g. the 1845 Irish potato famine); great numbers of others crossed the Atlantic to America[7]. Between 1840 and 1900 there was a dramatic increase of population in most parts of Europe and the population of England rose from 16 million to 32 million. But during the same time the population of Ireland fell from 8.5 million to 4.5 million. Naturally the result has been a systematic and ingrained resentment against the British which is almost **endemic** in the native Irish culture and is evident even today.[8]

After 1801, Irish demands for an independent Irish state were never lost, and one of the key issues in late 19th century British politics was a campaign in parliament for what was called "home-rule" — Irish political control of Irish affairs. The Home Rule

---

offshore *adj.*
近海的，离开海岸的
Protestant *n.*
新教徒
Catholic *n.*
天主教徒
plantation policy
殖民政策
emigrate *v.*
移居（外国）
persuasion *n.*
信念，信仰
indigenous *adj.*
本土的
massacre *n.*
屠杀，残杀
famine *n.*
饥荒，饥饿
endemic *adj.*
某地流行的，某地特有的

# The United Kingdom of Great Britain and Northern Ireland

Bill[9] was finally passed in 1914, but the process was **overtaken** by the First World War and was **suspended** for the duration of the war.[10]

Along with the political campaign for home-rule there were groups who followed a more direct method of pursuing Irish independence, engaging in **guerrilla** activities against British institutions and the British military forces. During the First World War and immediately after, this activity increased, sometimes brutally **suppressed** by British forces. The Easter Rising of 1916[11] was the most spectacular event, in which the rebels took over Dublin's Post Office, forcing the British to retake it by military means. The leaders of the rebellion were executed. In 1905 the extreme nationalist party *Sinn Fein*[12] ("Ourselves") was founded by Arthur Griffith. In 1919 a nationalist guerrilla force called the Irish Republican Army[13] (IRA), which *Sinn Fein* supported, expanded the fighting. In the end the conflict became too great to ignore, and as *Sinn Fein* gained most of the Irish seats in the British parliament in 1918, Irish independence became inevitable.

However, there was a problem. The majority of Irish people were **descendants** of the original Celtic people who inhabited the British Isles before the Romans arrived 2000 years ago. Ireland was not invaded by the Romans, nor settled by the Anglo-Saxons who followed them into Britain, thus they were **ethnically** distinct from the majority of British people. Adding to this difference was religion: most Irish people remained Catholics, while most British people had become Protestants. But in the northeastern part of Ireland this was not, and still is not, the case. Due to the large number of British settlers there, many people were Protestants, thought of themselves as British, and wished the area to remain a part of the British state. In 1921 the idea of being a part of an independent Irish State, where most people were Catholic, did not appeal. On the other hand they could not "go home" — Ireland was their home: they had been there 250 years or more. They had shown in 1913 that they would not accept union with Ireland by organising a show of force, and put 100 000 armed men in the streets of Northern Ireland.

Faced with these conflicting demands the British government chose a **compromise** and organised a **partition** of Ireland. The southern 26 counties would form an independent Irish Free State, while the 6 northeastern counties would remain a part of the UK. This is what happened in 1921 with the Anglo-Irish Treaty, bringing an end to 700 years of British rule in southern Ireland. The Irish Free State was a **dominion** within the British Empire, but left the Commonwealth at the end of 1948 and became the

---

be overtaken by
（由于事件的变化而）遭受阻碍，无法进行
suspend *v.*
暂停，中止
guerrilla *n.*
游击队
suppress *v.*
镇压
descendant *n.*
后裔，后代
ethnically *adv.*
种族地
compromise *n.*
折中；妥协
partition *n.*
分离，分割
dominion *n.*
自治领；（常作D-）英联邦自治领

Republic of Ireland in 1949.[14] It did not recognise the status of Northern Ireland.

Unlike the other nations of the UK, Northern Ireland between 1921 and 1972 was given its own devolved Parliament to deal with Northern Irish internal affairs, based at Stormont[15] just outside Belfast. The problem was that in the 6 northern counties the population was not purely "Loyalist" or "Unionist"[16] (in favour of union with Great Britain, loyal to the British Crown, Protestant in religion). About a third of the population was Republican or Nationalist[17] (in favour of union with the Republic of Ireland, Roman Catholic in religion), many of whom resented the North's separation from the south and identified with the nationalist cause. To worsen the situation, the Protestants, being the majority, controlled the local democratically-elected parliament, and used that power to support their own economic and social dominance in the province. Catholics found it harder to get jobs, or to benefit from social programmes such as public housing. Communal tension and **segregation** were obvious. Unionists and nationalists tended to live and work in different areas, attend different schools, socialise with people from their own community and read different newspapers. Catholics were regularly harassed by a Protestant police-force and any indication of nationalist sentiment was ruthlessly repressed. Understandably resentment grew, and armed conflict between the two communities, known as the "Troubles", eventually **erupted**.

## The Troubles

The years following the end of the Second World War were relatively peaceful ones. The events triggering a popular revolt by Catholics in Northern Ireland were those surrounding the **Civil Rights Movement** in the United States. Traditionally, Ireland as a whole has strong links with America; and now, with the **advent** of television in the early 1970s, people in the North were able to witness how the American blacks campaigned for their equal rights. The American Civil Rights Movement thus provided a model for Catholics, who felt they had been treated in much the same way as American blacks. The result was a vigorous, but originally **pacifist**, campaign in Northern Ireland to regain civil rights for those Roman Catholics, conducted by means of marches, speeches, and sit-ins.

Groups of Protestants began to organise counter-demonstrations, and **rioting** broke out. Protestant mobs attacked Catholic areas. The police (the Royal Ulster **Constabulary**, RUC) were **overwhelmed** by the fighting, and the Northern Irish Prime

segregation *n.*
种族隔离；分离，隔离
erupt *v.*
爆发，突然发生
Civil Rights Movement
民权运动
advent *n.*
出现，到来
pacifist *adj.*
和平主义（者）的，反战主义（者）的
rioting *n.*
暴乱，骚乱
constabulary *n.*
警察
overwhelm *v.*
使不知所措

# The United Kingdom of Great Britain and Northern Ireland

Minister at the time asked London to send soldiers to help restore order. In 1969, the first British soldiers were seen on Northern Irish streets and were not withdrawn until 2007, 38 years later.

They came first to protect the Catholic people, and a news film of the time shows them being offered cups of tea by grateful Catholics. However, the longer they stayed, the more they were seen as the symbol of British rule in Northern Ireland. The IRA at this time split. The Official IRA thought as enough progress had been made they could concentrate on a political process, and **run candidates** for elections, but a strong **faction** felt that armed struggle was the only way to get the British out, and they separated from the officials, calling themselves the "Provisional IRA".[18] It is this group which continued the conflict in the following decades, and it is they that are usually referred to in discussion about the IRA.

In the early 1970s the IRA carried out a campaign of bombing and shooting, usually targeting the security forces, but often bombing city-centres. Usually they gave warnings, but not always. The British security forces were strengthened, with up to 20 000 soldiers, and 10 000 armed police in the province. They were forced to patrol in bullet-proof **armoured** cars, and to fortify police-stations and **barracks**, always being under threat of the IRA's activities. The Protestants formed their own illegal "**paramilitary**" groups and took revenge on Catholics, often murdering individuals **at random**. Catholics in mainly Protestant areas, and Protestants in mainly Catholic areas were threatened, and sometimes their houses burned down, causing each to flee.[19] The result was that Northern Irish cities became "**ghettoised**" into **exclusively** Protestant and exclusively Catholic areas.[20] As their children also attended separate schools the two communities hardly mixed at all. In 1971 the Northern Irish government took the desperate step of imprisoning terrorist suspects from both sides without trial, a policy known as "**internment**"[21], which targeted primarily Catholic men in the North. This suspension of civil rights caused anger on both sides, and, if anything, intensified the conflict.[22] The policy was ended in 1975 and is now seen as a major mistake in the handling of the crisis.

In the following year 1972, 468 people were killed in Northern Ireland, the worst year of the troubles. These included 13 Catholics who had been taking part in a peaceful (though banned) civil rights march. They were shot dead by British soldiers. This was a key event in strengthening Catholic opposition to the British presence.

---

run candidates
参加竞选
faction n.
宗派，派别
armoured adj.
武装的
barrack n.
兵营，军营
paramilitary adj. 半军事化的
at random
任意地，胡乱的
ghettoise v.
使集中居住，使成聚居区
exclusively adv.
全部地
internment n.
拘留，收容

This day has now been termed as "Bloody Sunday"[23], an important symbol of British oppression in Northern Ireland.

Fueled by centuries of **sectarian** distrust and downright hatred, the armed conflict was bloody, chaotic, and, ultimately, disastrous for all concerned. The pattern established was that of "**tit-for-tat**" or revenge killings, which took on a terrible dynamic of their own and seemed to become endemic within the North's culture. Because of increased inter-communal violence and terrorism, the Conservative government under Prime Minister Edward Heath decided that the Northern Irish parliament could not govern the province effectively, and suspended it, replacing it with "direct-rule" from London, a situation which lasted until 1998.

The IRA's bombing campaign extended to the mainland of Great Britain. There were many random attacks on people in public transportation or in public places, causing serious **casualties**. In 1984 Prime Minister Mrs Thatcher herself and most of her cabinet narrowly escaped when an IRA bomb exploded at the Conservative Party Conference in Brighton, killing five and seriously injuring two senior ministers. After the 1994 IRA ceasefire, **dissident** groups carried out **sporadic** attacks, the most brutal being the Real IRA's (split from the Provisional IRA in 1997 and opposed to the Republican ceasefire) Omagh bombing that killed 29 civilians in 1998.

Despite the bloodshed, the troubles settled down to a peculiar level of semi-acceptability.[24] People had got used to it. Both sides continued the conflict, but the British forces kept the scale down to a lower level than in the early 1970s, and through the late 1970s and the 1980s the death rate averaged around 90 per year. It didn't get worse, but neither could anyone see an end to it.

sectarian *adj.*
宗派的
tit-for-tat *n.*
以牙还牙，针锋相对
casualty *n.*
（事故、灾难等的）死伤者
dissident *adj.*
持不同意见的
sporadic *adj.*
不定时发生的；零星的

### Figure 1
### The Troubles in Numbers: 1969 – May 1994

| | | |
|---|---|---|
| Total Deaths | | 3 147 |
| of which: | Civilians (including paramilitaries) | 2 202 |
| | British forces (police and army) | 945 |
| Killed by | Republican paramilitary | 58% |
| | Loyalist paramilitary | 27.7% |
| | British forces | 10.9% |

# The United Kingdom of Great Britain and Northern Ireland

### Figure 2
### Main Political Groupings

|  | NATIONALISTS<br>(Want union with Ireland) | UNIONISTS<br>(Want union with UK) |
|---|---|---|
| Constitutional:<br>(legal) | SDLP – Social Democratic and Labour Party<br>Sinn Fein | UUP – Ulster Unionist Party<br>DUP – Democratic Unionist Party |
| Paramilitary:<br>(illegal) | IRA – Irish Republican Army<br>INLA – Irish National Liberation Army | UVF – Ulster Volunteer Force<br>UDA – Ulster Defence Association |
| NON-SECTARIAN: | Alliance Party | |

devolution *n.*
权力下放，分权
revitalise *v.*
使新生，给予…新的活力

## Towards a Solution

While attempting to maintain normality through a massive and increasingly effective security presence, successive British governments since direct rule have been committed to power-sharing **devolution** as a political solution to the troubles. Power would be shared by both unionist and nationalist communities. The 1973 Sunningdale Agreement[25] was reached between the main political parties in Northern Ireland, and importantly, the British and Irish governments. The agreement proposed the setting up of a new form of parliament — an assembly elected by proportional representation, and a power-sharing executive to allow the minority Catholic population political influence. Also a Council of Ireland would be established for north-south cross-border cooperation. This, especially the Irish involvement, outraged the Protestant loyalist majority. The massive and prolonged strike by the Protestant workforce eventually led to the collapse of the power-sharing mechanism[26].

In the 1980s, convicted IRA prisoners started a hunger strike, starving themselves to fight against the removal of "political prisoner" status.[27] One of them, Bobby Sands, ran for parliament and was duly elected before he died. Margaret Thatcher's government did not give in to this demand for political status and 11 prisoners starved to death. This event made it more difficult to dismiss the IRA as mere terrorists. It **revitalised** the political campaign of Sinn Fein, the legal political party which supports the IRA's right to fight. Its leaders spoke of a twin campaign for union with Ireland, both political and military, which they called the policy of "The Bullet and the Ballot Box"[28]. The **escalation** of violence on both sides, together with this mass hunger strike, made further action urgent.

The British government still felt that involving the Southern Irish in Northern Irish affairs was the right way to proceed despite the disaster of power-sharing in the 1970s. It should not be thought that the Irish government supported the IRA: they did not (in the civil war following independence in 1921, the Irish government's forces executed three times as many IRA men as the British ever had). The IRA was thus an illegal organisation there too. Nevertheless, the Irish do seek to protect the rights of Catholics in Northern Ireland. In 1985 the Anglo-Irish Agreement[29] was signed between the two governments, giving the Irish a right to consultation on Northern Irish matters through an intergovernmental body, recognising that the Republic of Ireland had a **legitimate** interest in the concerns of the Catholic minority in Northern Ireland. Greater cross-border cooperation to defeat terrorism was also an aim. This agreement, like the one before it, guaranteed the loyalist Protestant community their right to decide their future — either to join with the South, as part of an all-Ireland nation, or to remain as they were, in the separate political entity of Northern Ireland. Despite this provision, the loyalist politicians once again rejected this agreement. Huge Protestant protest followed with the "Ulster Says No" campaign. This time the government did not give in and the Anglo-Irish Agreement is still in effect. A series of big bombs in London in the late 1980s and early 1990s increased pressure on the British government to come up with a solution.

This pressure, and the more clearly political campaign of Sinn Fein, combined with the closer cooperation between the two governments, is what in 1993 enabled John Major and the Irish Prime Minister jointly to produce the Downing Street Declaration[30], which made it clear that the consent of a majority of people in Northern Ireland would be required before any constitutional change would come about. On this basis the British Government **reiterated** that Britain had "no selfish **strategic** or economic interest in Northern Ireland" (first declared by Secretary of State for Northern Ireland in 1990) and that "it is for the people of Ireland alone, by agreement between the two parts" to decide its future, "to bring about a united Ireland if that is their wish". All parties which established "a commitment to exclusively peaceful methods" were invited to join talks

escalation *n.*
逐步升级；逐步扩大
legitimate *adj.*
合法的，合理的
reiterate *v.*
重申
strategic *adj.*
战略上的

# The United Kingdom of Great Britain and Northern Ireland

about the future.[31]

Through the actions of a constitutional Nationalist politician, John Hume, leader of the SDLP[32], and the leader of Sinn Fein, Gerry Adams[33], in August 1994, to most people's surprise, the IRA declared a ceasefire.[34] Protestant paramilitary groups did the same. Everyone breathed a sigh of relief, but the problem was not solved, though for the moment no one was being killed.

In February 1995 the British and Irish governments published the Joint Framework Documents[35], reaffirming the need for self-determination in the North. It signaled that an agreement would have three strands: power-sharing devolution in Northern Ireland, the relationship between the north and south of Ireland, and the relationship between the British and Irish governments. These foreshadowed most of the details of the later Good Friday Agreement of 1998.

## The Good Friday Agreement[36]

As a result of multi-party negotiations beginning in June 1996, aided this time by the intervention of the US Senator George Mitchell[37], the Good Friday Agreement known also as the Belfast Agreement, emerged on April 10th 1998. The agreement was signed by the British government, the Irish government and eight parties of Northern Ireland. David Trimble, leader of Northern Ireland's main Protestant party the Ulster Unionists, and John Hume, leader of the moderate Catholic party Nationalist Social Democratic and Labour Party, were jointly awarded the Nobel Prize for Peace in 1998, "for their efforts to find a peaceful solution to the conflict in Northern Ireland".

The agreement assures the loyalist community that Northern Ireland "remains part of the United Kingdom and shall not cease to be so without the consent of the majority of the people of Northern Ireland."[38] The Irish government, for its part, undertook to revise articles of its Constitution that claimed **jurisdiction** over the North and expressed the hope that Ireland would once more be united as an Ireland to a new article that recognises "that a united Ireland shall be brought about only by peaceful means with the consent of the majority of the people, democratically expressed in both jurisdictions (i.e., both in the Republic and in the North) in the island …".[39] Britain would **repeal** its 1920 Ireland Act and acknowledge the possibility of the unification of Southern and Northern Ireland on the precondition that it should be approved by most people in Northern Ireland.

jurisdiction *n.*
司法权，管辖权
repeal *v.*
撤销；废除

The agreement also provided a basic framework for the political solution of Northern Ireland in three parts. Firstly, based on the principle of power-sharing, it established a devolved Northern Ireland Assembly of 108 members with legislative functions, elected by proportional representation and an Executive consisting of 10 ministers headed jointly by a First Minister and Deputy First Minister elected from the unionist and nationalist blocs in the Assembly. Ministerial posts in the Executive Committee are allocated on a proportional basis according to party strength in the Assembly.[40] Secondly, a "North-South Ministerial Council" with certain executive powers was set up for the Northern Ireland administration and the Irish government to cooperate on cross-border issues. Thirdly, an inter-governmental "British-Irish Council" was established to ensure internal cooperation within the British Isles as a whole.

The Agreement won overwhelming approval in referendums in May in both Northern Ireland (71% in favour) and the Republic of Ireland (94% in favour). The new Northern Ireland Assembly was elected in June 1998. In December 1999, power was formally devolved to Northern Ireland Assembly and its Executive Committee of Ministers under the Northern Ireland Act 1998 of the UK parliament.[41]

Devolution was **dogged** by problems such as **decommissioning**. The IRA did not fully decommission its arms until September 2005. The British government suspended the Northern Ireland Assembly and Executive and re-imposed direct rule on four occasions as disputes over decommissioning continued.[42] The longest period of suspension lasted from October 2002 to May 2007.

The 2006 St Andrews Agreement resulted in the restoration of the Northern Ireland Assembly, the formation in May 2007 of a new Northern Ireland Executive and a decision by Sinn Fein to support the Police Service, courts and rule of law. The prospects of long term peace and stable power-sharing government appeared.

Thus Northern Ireland today must be the only area in the world which is recognised as an independent entity but which is governed, in effect, by three separate jurisdictions: that of the Republic of Ireland, that of Great Britain, and that of its own elected executive government of ten ministers.[43]

The North of Ireland is now a quieter and more civilised place than it has been for the last 50 years. The laws that discriminated against Catholics have been systematically repealed to bring about a more equal society. The police force, once wholly Protestant, has now been integrated as a result of a policy of active recruitment

dog *v.*
困扰；折磨
decommission
*v.* 正式停止使用
（武器等）

# The United Kingdom of Great Britain and Northern Ireland

of Catholics and has been transformed into a new body, the Police Service of Northern Ireland, its **protocols** revised to ensure that police actions are fair as well as seen to be fair.

## Conclusion

The "Troubles" in Northern Ireland was a political headache for decades. People concerned became very tired of a low-grade conflict that seemed to go on and on and to be, for historical reasons, insoluble — or at least, without any will to solve it. Outsiders would fear to visit the area. The 1998 Belfast Agreement finally brought peace and hope to the land.

Yet the North still has far to go. The economy remains stagnant and unemployment high. Many young people leave for England and never return; their parents do not see a future for them in the North. A Northerner would be more warm and comfortable with someone of his own traditions and persuasion. Things might change, but probably only with the next generation.

Northern Ireland's current constitutional status is like this: it is part of the UK but with strong links to Ireland. In the past it had a clear Protestant majority. Yet the Catholic population is growing faster than the Protestants. So, ultimately, **demographic** trends seem likely to result in a Nationalist Northern Ireland and the Irish unification that neither the ballot nor the bullet could **procure**.[44]

protocol *n.*
协议
demographic *adj.*
人口的；人口统计的；人口学的
procure *v.*
取得，实现

# Explanations

1. **the Giant's Causeway:**
   巨人之堤，位于北爱尔兰贝尔法斯特西北约80公里处大西洋海岸。此堤道绵延数千米，是由几百万年前火山爆发而形成的数万根大小不均匀的玄武岩石柱组成，绝大部分石块为六边形棱柱。其奇妙之处在于这些规则的石头都平整光滑，却又高高低低，参差不齐，像是人工做出来的模型。1986年被列为世界自然遗产。

2. **Legend has it that the giant Finn MacCool built it to cross the sea to Scotland:**
   传说远古时代爱尔兰巨人要与苏格兰巨人决斗，于是开凿石柱，填平海底，铺成通向苏格兰的堤道，后堤道被毁，只剩下现在的一段残留。Finn MacCool 为爱尔兰半神话英雄。

3. **Seamus Heaney:**

    谢默斯·希尼（1939–2013），北爱尔兰诗人。主要作品有诗集《十一首诗歌》(*Eleven Poems*, 1965)、《博物学家之死》(*Death of a Naturalist*, 1966)、《通向黑暗的门》(*Door into the Dark*, 1969)、《北方》(*North*, 1975)等。1995 年获诺贝尔文学奖。

4. ***The Crying Game*:**

    《哭泣的游戏》，获 1992 年奥斯卡最佳原创剧本奖和多项奥斯卡提名。电影以北爱的政治形势为背景，描写了一位爱尔兰共和军成员与一名被劫持的英军士兵以及后者的女友（实际上是扮成女人的男人）三人之间复杂微妙的关系。故事充满悬念和刺激。

5. **Brian Friel:**

    布赖恩·弗里尔（1929–2015），爱尔兰当代著名剧作家和小说家。

6. **Harland and Wolff:**

    哈兰德和沃尔夫造船厂。位于北爱尔兰贝尔法斯特。20 世纪初建造了著名的皇家邮轮泰坦尼克号。19 世纪 90 年代，英国造船业在全球造船市场所占份额高达八成；贝尔法斯特的造船业相当有名；后来逐渐衰落。哈兰德和沃尔夫现在的工作重心已转向近海可持续能源（风能和海洋发电）。

7. **great numbers of others crossed the Atlantic to America:**

    大量爱尔兰人为躲避饥荒和压迫而逃往美国，使得如今美国人中有很高的爱尔兰后裔比例。这也是美国政客积极关注和支持北爱和平进程的重要原因。1998 年《北爱和平协议》的签订就有克林顿政府积极推动并派出前参议院多数党领袖乔治·米切尔牵头调解的功劳。

8. **the result has been ... and is evident even today:**

    结果造成爱尔兰人对英国人根深蒂固的怨恨。这种怨恨在爱尔兰民族文化中几乎是盛行的，甚至今天也显著存在。

9. **the Home Rule Bill:**

    自治法案。自由党政府于 1886 年和 1892 年提出过两个爱尔兰自治法案，但因党内激进派以及保守党的反对而失败。1912 年自由党政府在下院提出了第三个自治法案并得到通过，但遭到上院的否决。根据 1911 年的议会法，该法案搁置两年后至 1914 年正式生效。但第一次世界大战的爆发中止了爱尔兰自治的实现。随后发生了 1916 年复活节起义，改变了南爱公众的看法，南爱不接受这一自治法案。对自治法案的不同看法也导致了自由党内部的分裂和其后的衰落。

10. **but the process was overtaken ... the duration of the war:**

    但是自治法案的实施进程由于第一次世界大战而受阻，战争期间一切进展均暂时中止。

11. **The Easter Rising of 1916:**

    1916 年复活节起义。1916 年复活节清晨（4 月 26 日，星期一）"爱尔兰共和兄弟"和共和军的战士们在帕尔斯和康纳利领导下，发动了一次反英的武装起义，占领了都柏林总邮局，宣布成立爱尔兰共和国。但是，由于时机不成熟和筹划不周，五天后就被镇压了。16 名领导人被处死，160 人受到军事审判，122

# The United Kingdom of Great Britain and Northern Ireland

人被判处有期徒刑。

12. **Sinn Fein**:
    新芬党，北爱政党之一，成立于 1905 年。该党主张英国政府从北爱撤走，使南北统一，建立一个全爱尔兰共和国。新芬党也是爱尔兰共和军的官方政治组织。

13. **the Irish Republican Army**:
    爱尔兰共和军，一个非官方半军事组织，于 1919 年正式成立。其前身是 1913 年成立的民族主义组织——爱尔兰志愿军，其目的是武装推翻英国在爱尔兰及北爱尔兰的统治，为争取成立独立的爱尔兰共和国而斗争。该组织长期通过暴力活动以实现政治诉求。

14. **The Irish Free State was a dominion ... became Republic of Ireland in 1949**:
    爱尔兰自由邦是大英帝国的一个自治领，但于 1948 年底脱离英联邦，于 1949 成为爱尔兰共和国。二战中爱尔兰自由邦保持中立，拒绝对英国施以援手。

15. **Stormont**:
    斯多蒙特，北爱议会所在地，位于贝尔法斯特城外的斯多蒙特城堡。1922 至 1972 年间，北爱是通过自己的议会自治，占人口多数的新教徒垄断统治权。

16. **The problem was that ... "Loyalist" or "Unionist"**:
    问题是，在北爱的 6 个郡的人们不是纯亲英派或统一派。Loyalist or Unionist 亲英派或统一派。在北爱尔兰人口中亲英派或统一派约占 60%。这些人都是新教徒，并且控制着北爱议会。他们效忠英国女王，主张北爱尔兰与英国统一。

17. **Republican or Nationalist**:
    共和派或民族派。他们是天主教徒，主张北爱尔兰与爱尔兰共和国合并。

18. **The Official IRA ... the "Provisional IRA"**:
    1970 年爱尔兰共和军内部矛盾激化，公开分裂为"正统派"（the Official IRA）和"临时派"（the Provisional IRA）。正统派强调政治、经济领域里的斗争，反对极端的军事冒险行动，认为武装斗争只可作为自卫手段。临时派则坚持"不承认、不参加现政府机构"，主张使用暴力和恐怖袭击手段，但也未完全放弃政治斗争。2005 年 7 月 28 日，临时派宣布放弃武装斗争。

19. **Catholics in mainly ... causing each to flee**:
    新教徒居住区内的天主教徒以及天主教徒居住区内的新教徒均受到暴力袭击的威胁，他们的房屋有时被对方烧毁，致使他们双方各自逃离家园。

20. **The result ... exclusively Catholic areas**:
    结果是北爱城市被分割成新教徒和天主教徒两大聚居区。ghettoise: 使集中居住。

21. **a policy known as "internment"**:
    所谓的"拘留"政策。由于当时北爱局势紧张，流血事件频发，北爱政府为了控制局面采取了不进行审判就把恐怖主义嫌疑人投入监狱的做法。这不但没有解决危机，反而激起北爱天主教徒和新教徒的不满，1975 年北爱当局不得不放弃这项政策。

UNIT **2** Northern Ireland

22. **This suspension of civil rights ... intensified the conflict:**

    这种剥夺民权的做法引起了双方的愤怒，并且激化了冲突。If anything: 如果说它产生任何作用的话，只是激化了冲突。

23. **Bloody Sunday:**

    血腥星期日。事件发生在 1972 年 1 月 30 日，英国空降部队打死了 13 名为争取民权举行和平示威游行的天主教徒。这一事件激起了人们的强烈不满，大规模的反英示威在各地举行。在爱尔兰首都都柏林，英国使馆被烧毁。

24. **Despite the bloodshed ... level of semi-acceptability:**

    尽管有流血事件，冲突的缓解达到了双方都能部分接受的特殊程度。

25. **The 1973 Sunningdale Agreement:**

    1973 年《桑宁代尔协议》。该协议旨在北爱尔兰内部产生政治解决方案，但是爱尔兰共和国政府牵涉进来。协议提供了民族派和统一派之间的"权力共享"方案，以及一个促进南北爱双边合作的"爱尔兰理事会"。

26. **power-sharing mechanism:**

    权力分享机制。

27. **convicted IRA prisoners started hunger strike ... removal of "political prisoner" status:**

    被判有罪的爱尔兰共和军囚犯开始绝食斗争，以绝食来抗议政府取消其"政治囚犯"地位。撒切尔政府对爱尔兰共和军非常强势，不再把他们认定为政治犯，而是视其为纯粹的恐怖主义刑事犯，这引起愤怒。

28. **The Bullet and the Ballot Box:**

    暴力和民主手段，由新芬党领袖们提出。他们主张用政治和军事手段双管齐下实现爱尔兰的统一。Bullet 指暴力活动；Ballot Box 指民主选举活动。

29. **the Anglo-Irish Agreement:**

    1985 年英国和爱尔兰签署的《英爱协议》。根据协议，建立了一个常设联合秘书处，定期主持召开政府间会议，使爱尔兰政府能够对北爱事务提出看法和建议，讨论跨边界合作和安全问题。这个协议首次允许爱尔兰政府参与北爱事务，标志着英爱两国密切合作及推进北爱和平进程的开始。

30. **the Downing Street Declaration:**

    《唐宁街宣言》。1993 年 12 月，英国与爱尔兰共同发表了《唐宁街宣言》，双方都做出一定让步，同意北爱尔兰宪法地位的改变必须取得北爱尔兰大多数人的同意。宣言指出，英国"在北爱尔兰没有自私的战略和经济利益"，"只有爱尔兰人民自己通过双方协商"才能决定自己的未来，"如果爱尔兰人民愿意的话，可以组成统一的爱尔兰"。宣言还就爱尔兰共和军永久停止使用暴力和吸纳新芬党参加和平谈判达成共识。

31. **All parties which established ... were invited to join talks about the future:**

    凡承诺只采用和平方式的各方都被邀请参加会谈，讨论北爱的前景。

32. **John Hume, leader of the SDLP:**

    约翰·休姆（1937–），北爱社会民主工党领袖，社会民主工党创始人之一，北爱民权协会成员。1998

# The United Kingdom of Great Britain and Northern Ireland

年与北爱尔兰统一党领袖大卫·特林布尔共同被授予诺贝尔和平奖。

33. **Gerry Adams:**
格里·亚当斯（1949–），十几岁时即活跃在政治舞台上，参加街头抗议活动并与新芬党组织有联系。1978 年当选新芬党副主席，1983 年当选主席。1983–1992 和 1997–2011 年间当选为英国议会贝尔法斯特西区议员。

34. **the IRA declared a ceasefire:**
爱尔兰共和军"临时派"于 1994 年 8 月 31 日宣布停火，之后不久，北爱新教的准军事组织也宣布放弃暴力行动。作为回应，英国宣布解除对新芬党的长期禁令。两大敌对的武装组织相继宣布停火，为北爱和谈创造了必要条件。共和军的停火在 1996 年 2 月至 1997 年 7 月之间间断过，2005 年才宣布彻底放弃武装斗争。

35. **the Joint Framework Documents:**
《联合框架文件》。框架文件兼顾了各方的利益，基本上得到了北爱两大教派各政治势力的支持，为多党谈判奠定了基础。文件主要内容多在 1998 年的《北爱和平协议》中得到了体现。

36. **The Good Friday Agreement:**
《受难日和平协议》，又称为《贝尔法斯特协议》或《北爱和平协议》。1998 年 4 月 10 日在美国参议员乔治·米切尔的斡旋下，英爱两国政府与参加北爱多党谈判的各党派之间达成和平协议。该协议于 1998 年 5 月 22 日在北爱和爱尔兰全民公决中获得通过。协议规定只有在北爱大多数人同意的情况下才能改变北爱目前的政治地位。爱尔兰政府将修改其宪法的第二、第三条款，放弃对北爱尔兰的领土主权要求；英国方面则将废除 1920 年的爱尔兰法案，承认南北爱尔兰统一的可能性。协议决定建立一个按比例代表制选举产生的北爱尔兰地方议会和行政委员会，实现权力共享的政治原则。此外，将有"北南部长理事会"和"英爱理事会"（英爱政府间会议）两个协调机构来分别处理南北爱尔兰和英爱两国间的事宜。该协议是互相妥协与让步的结果，是一个值得载入史册的事件。Good Friday 是指每年复活节礼拜天前一周的周五，即耶稣受难日。

37. **the US Senator George Mitchell:**
乔治·米切尔在 1988 年至 1995 年间任美国国会参议院民主党议员，曾任参议院多数党领袖。1994 年出任美国北爱尔兰问题特使，主持和斡旋了北爱尔兰和平谈判。2009 年 1 月被奥巴马总统任命为中东问题特使。

38. **The agreement assures ... the people of Northern Ireland:**
这一协议向亲英派保证，北爱"仍将属于英国，并且只有征得北爱大多数人同意才能改变现状"。

39. **The Irish government, for its part ... in the island ...:**
爱尔兰政府方面负责修改宪法中关于爱尔兰拥有北爱管辖权的条款，并通过新的条款表达对爱尔兰再次获得统一的期盼："只有通过和平的方式征得爱尔兰岛双方（爱尔兰共和国和北爱）大多数人民主表达的同意才能统一爱尔兰……"。

40. **based on the principle of power-sharing ... according to party strength in the Assembly:**
根据权力共享原则，它建立了一个按照比例代表制选出的由 108 名成员组成的权力下放的立法机构——

北爱尔兰地方议会，以及一个由10位部长组成的行政委员会；行政委员会由首席大臣（First Minister，也译为首席部长）和副首席大臣（Deputy First Minister，也译为副首席部长）共同领导，地方议会中统一派和民族派各选出一人担任。行政委员会的部长职位根据地方议会中的统一派和民族派的席位力量比例相应分配。

41. **In December 1999 ... the Northern Ireland Act 1998 of the UK parliament:**
根据英国议会1998年《北爱尔兰法案》，英国于1999年12月正式将权力下放给北爱尔兰地方议会和由部长组成的行政委员会。英国是中央集权制，它对苏格兰、威尔士和北爱尔兰实施的权力下放与联邦制不同，理论上中央政府可以将下放的权力随时视需要而收回。中央政府的北爱尔兰事务大臣（Secretary of State for Northern Ireland）是内阁部长。2017年，北爱尔兰执政联盟分裂导致了提前选举。北爱尔兰事务大臣即表示如果当地政党无法按期组建政府，就有可能恢复对该地区的直接管辖。

42. **The British government suspended ... as dispute over decommissioning continued:**
（自1999年至2007年）由于在交出武器问题上的持续争议，英国政府曾四次暂停北爱尔兰地方议会和行政委员会的运作，恢复直接管辖。统一派拒绝在爱尔兰共和军手中握有武器的情况下与新芬党分享权力。而爱尔兰共和军总是一点点地交出武器（直到2005年才完全解除武装），这造成分权的北爱地方政府数次摇摇欲坠。

43. **Thus Northern Ireland today must be ... executive government of ten ministers:**
这样一来，今天的北爱肯定是世界上唯一的被认为是独立实体但又实质上是由爱尔兰政府、英国政府以及由北爱自行选出的十名部长组成的执行委员会政府三方共同实施司法管辖的区域。

44. **So, ultimately, demographic trends seem ... neither the ballot nor the bullet could procure:**
所以最终人口的趋势（天主教反对堕胎，教徒生育率高，人口增长速度比新教徒快）很可能导致出现一个民族派占多数的北爱尔兰，并由此带来靠投票或子弹都无法实现的爱尔兰的统一。ballot 与 bullet 是押头韵的比喻，指选举和武力暴力。

## Exercises

### I. Give the Chinese equivalents for the following:

1. Protestant and Catholic
2. the Irish Republican Army
3. Sinn Fein
4. the Easter Rising
5. The Good Friday Agreement
6. Northern Ireland Assembly

# The United Kingdom of Great Britain and Northern Ireland

## II. Decide whether the following statements are true (T) or false (F):

1. In 1801, Northern Ireland was united with Great Britain under the name the United Kingdom of Great Britain and Northern Ireland. _____
2. Faced with conflicting demands the British government chose a compromise and organised a partition of Ireland in 1921, leading to the founding of the Irish Free State. _____
3. Those who want to unite Northern Ireland with the Irish Republic are called unionists. _____
4. Sinn Fein is an illegal nationalist military organisation in Northern Ireland. _____
5. In Northern Ireland, Protestant majority used to be the ruling force before the 1999 devolution. _____
6. Influenced by the American Civil Rights Movement, the Catholics immediately took up arms and fought for their civil rights. _____
7. Threatened by the IRA in the early 1970s, the Protestants formed their own illegal paramilitary groups and took revenge on the Catholics. _____
8. The Anglo-Irish Agreement of 1985 gave the Republic of Ireland a right to consultation on Northern Irish matters through an intergovernmental body. _____

## III. Fill in the blanks:

1. Northern Ireland is well-known in the world for its most famous landmark, _____.
2. To pursue Irish independence, the most spectacular event in the Irish history was _____ of 1916, in which the rebels occupied Dublin's _____ and forced the British to take it back by military means.
3. The political troubles in Northern Ireland are conflicts between _____ and _____.
4. In 1971 the Northern Irish government took the action to imprison terrorist suspects from both sides without _____, a policy known as _____.
5. The British government sent troops to Northern Ireland in 1969 to help _____ and soon _____ was practised between 1972 and 1998.
6. In the early 1970s, the IRA split into the Official IRA and the Provisional IRA. The _____ carried out quite a number of terrorist attacks.
7. In the early 1980s, some convicted IRA prisoners went on a _____ and demanded for the status of _____. Eleven prisoners starved to death.

# UNIT 2  Northern Ireland

8. The 1998 Good Friday Agreement assures _____ that Northern Ireland "remains part of the United Kingdom and shall not cease to be so without _____ _____ of Northern Ireland".
9. The Belfast Agreement of 1998 on Northern Ireland set up a Northern Ireland Assembly and an Executive based on the principles of _____ and _____.
10. David Trimble, leader of the Ulster Unionists, and John Hume, leader of Social Democratic and Labour Party, won 1998 _____ Prize for _____.

## IV. Questions:

1. What are the geographical and economic features of Northern Ireland?
2. What did Britain do during its colonial rule of Ireland?
3. How serious was the famine in Ireland in the 19th century?
4. What happened to the 1912 Home Rule Bill?
5. When and how was the Irish Free State set up?
6. How did the Protestant majority treat the Catholic minority in Northern Ireland?
7. Who are nationalists, and who are unionists?
8. What is the nature of Sinn Fein and of the Irish Republican Army? Why did the IRA split in the early 1970s?
9. What happened on Bloody Sunday in 1972?
10. Why did direct rule from London replace Northern Irish parliament in 1972?
11. What are the main contents of the 1998 Good Friday Agreement/the Belfast Agreement? In what way is this Agreement similar to the Sunningdale Agreement?
12. What are the major political parties or groups in Northern Ireland and their different attitudes towards solutions to the political troubles?
13. How is power-sharing practised in the Northern Ireland Assembly and the Executive?
14. Is the development of Northern Ireland devolution smooth? What have been its problems in the 21st century?

## V. Topics for discussion or research:

1. What are the areas of conflicts between Protestants and Catholics in Northern Ireland?
2. Why was the Northern Ireland Assembly suspended several times?
3. What do you think should be the right solution to the political problem in Northern Ireland?

# UNIT 3

# The Government of the United Kingdom

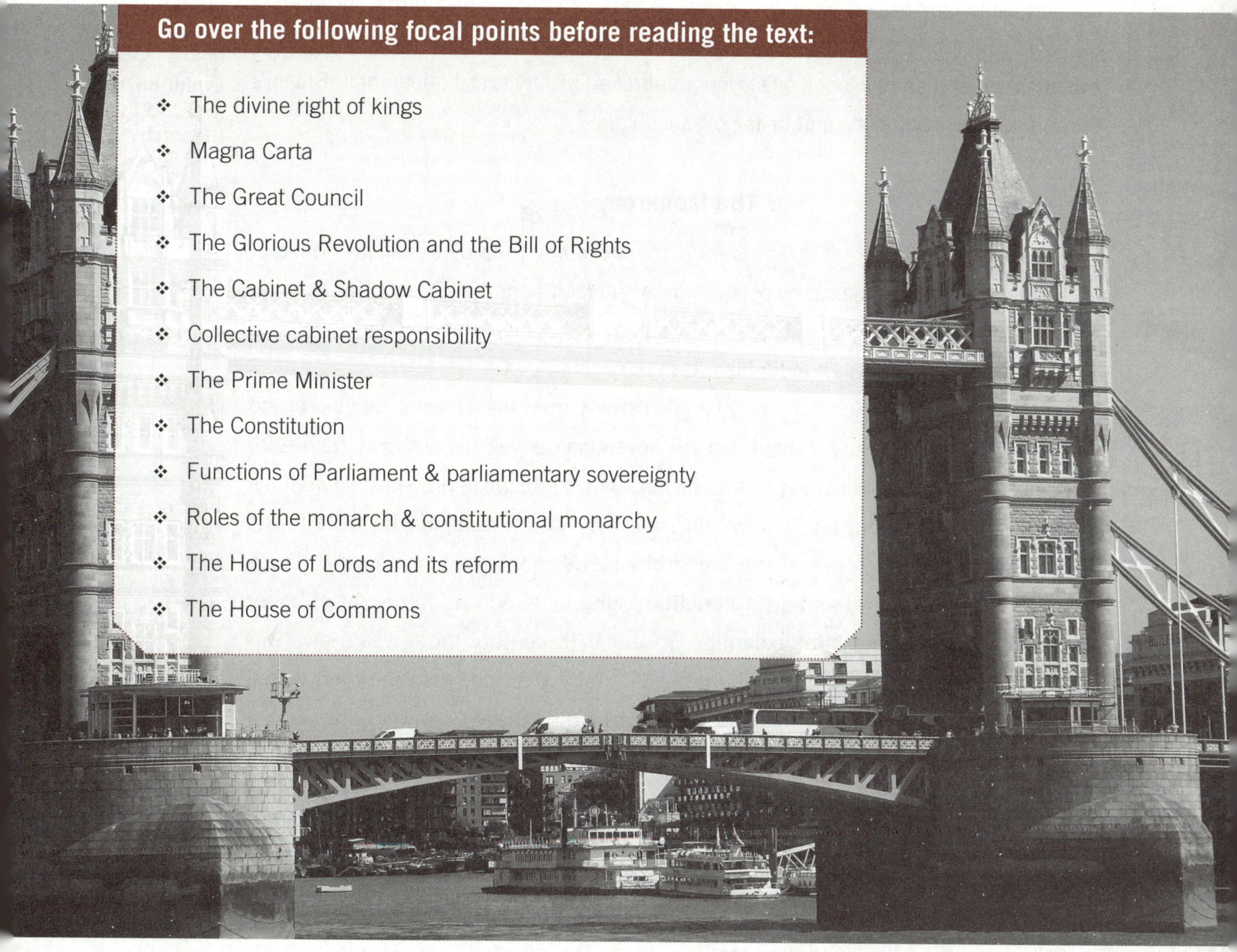

**Go over the following focal points before reading the text:**

- The divine right of kings
- Magna Carta
- The Great Council
- The Glorious Revolution and the Bill of Rights
- The Cabinet & Shadow Cabinet
- Collective cabinet responsibility
- The Prime Minister
- The Constitution
- Functions of Parliament & parliamentary sovereignty
- Roles of the monarch & constitutional monarchy
- The House of Lords and its reform
- The House of Commons

# The United Kingdom of Great Britain and Northern Ireland

 Text

Britain is **arguably** the oldest representative democracy in the world, with roots that can be **traced** back over a thousand years.[1] Other countries also have long political histories, but these histories are marked by periods of sudden, and often violent, change. Although Britain too has had its periods of political **instability**, in contrast to, say, France or the United States, the process of state-building has been one of **evolution** rather than revolution.[2] This long, unbroken history is still apparent in Britain's current political institutions and in its political culture.[3]

## The Monarchy

The oldest institution of government is the **Monarchy** (rule by the king or queen). This dates back to the Saxons who ruled from the 5th century AD until the Norman Conquest in 1066. The present Queen, Elizabeth II, is directly descended from King Egbert[4], who united England under his rule in 829.

The power of the monarchy was largely **derived** from the ancient doctrine of the "**divine** right of kings".[5] It was held that the **sovereign** derived his authority from God, not from his **subjects**. Because of this divine right, although there were sometimes battles between different families who insisted they were the **legitimate heirs** to the throne, the actual existence of the monarchy has seldom been questioned. For a thousand years Britain has had a **hereditary** king or queen as the head of state, although there was one brief exception. In the 17th century there was a civil war in England between republican "Roundheads"[6] (so-called because the men **defied** popular fashion and wore their hair cut very short) led by Oliver Cromwell, who wanted to abolish the monarchy, and royalists who wanted it to continue. The Roundheads succeeded in **ousting** the monarch, Charles I[7], in 1642 and ruled for just 18 years before the monarchy was restored.

While the king in theory had God on his side, in practice even in **medieval** times it was thought that he should not exercise absolute power.[8] Instead, the sovereign should be willing to receive advice from **prominent** men. The monarch's unwillingness to do

---

arguably *adv.*
可论证地，可能，大概
trace *v.*
追溯，查考
instability *n.*
不稳定性，不稳固
evolution *n.*
演变，演化
monarchy *n.*
君主政体，君主制
derive *v.*
取得，得到，形成
divine *adj.*
神授的，天赐的
sovereign *n.*
君主
subject *n.*
臣民
legitimate *adj.*
合法的，法律认可的
heir *n.*
继承人，继任者
hereditary *adj.*
世袭的，承袭的
defy *v.*
（公然）违抗，藐视
oust *v.*
驱逐，罢黜
medieval *adj.*
中世纪的
prominent *adj.*
著名的，杰出的

this led to many battles between the king and other powerful groups like the Church and powerful, land-owning feudal **barons**.

It was a gang of feudal barons and the Church which opposed some of King John's (1199–1216) policies. This opposition was so powerful that the king finally granted them a **charter** of liberty and political rights, still known by its medieval Latin name of Magna Carta[9]. Magna Carta placed some limits on the king's ability to **abuse** his royal power. This is still regarded as Britain's key expression of the rights of citizens against the Crown.

## Parliament

The word "parliament" comes from the verb "to **parley**", that is, to discuss or talk. The term was first used officially in 1236 to describe the gathering of feudal barons and representatives from **counties** and towns which the king occasionally **summoned** if he wanted to raise money. Traditionally, medieval kings were supposed to meet their own royal expenses out of their own wealth. If extra resources were needed — for example, if a king wanted to **wage** a war, which he frequently did — he would try to persuade the Great Council[10], a gathering of leading, wealthy barons which met several times a year, to give him some extra money. By the 13th century, kings found they could not **make ends meet** by asking for money from this quite small group, and so they widened the Great Council to include representatives of counties, cities and towns, to get them to contribute to their projects. It was in this way that the Great Council came to include both those who were summoned "by name"[11] (the House of Lords) and representatives of communities (the House of Commons). These two houses exist today and are collectively known as Parliament. The Commons quickly gained in political strength. They were willing to help the king by raising taxes and passing laws, but in return they wanted an increasing **say** in what the king was doing. In recognition of this, Henry IV **decreed** in 1407 that all money **grants** should be considered and approved by the Commons before being considered by the Lords, a **formula** which is almost the same today. The Commons also acquired law-making powers by the 15th century, a **prerogative** which had once belonged only to the king and his **Councillors**.

The civil war which brought the Roundheads to power in the 17th century was rooted in a dispute over the power of the king **vis-a-vis** Parliament.[12] James I[13] and his successor Charles I both insisted on their divine right as kings. They felt Parliament,

baron *n.*
（由国王直接分领地的）贵族；男爵
charter *n.*
宪章，共同纲领
abuse *v.*
滥用（职权等）
parley *v.*
（法语）讲话，会谈，谈判
county *n.*
（英国、爱尔兰及某些英联邦国家的）郡
summon *v.*
召唤，召集
wage *v.*
进行，展开
make ends meet
使收支相抵，勉强维持生计
say *n.*
发言权，话语权
decree *v.*
命令，颁布
grant *n.*
授予物（如补助金等）
formula *n.*
惯例，常规
prerogative *n.*
特权，独有的权利
councillor *n.*
议员；（市、镇等的）政务会委员顾问
vis-a-vis *prep.*
同…相对，同…相比

# The United Kingdom of Great Britain and Northern Ireland

representing the community, had no real political right to exist, but only existed because the king allowed it to do so. It was the effort to **reassert** the rights of Parliament that led to the Civil War[14]. The royalist armies were defeated and King Charles I was **executed** in 1649. But by 1660, Charles I's son was restored to the throne as Charles II[15].

The next King, James II[16], having apparently learned little from the experience of the previous decades, also tried to govern without the **consent** of Parliament. In 1688, leading politicians and church authorities invited James' son-in-law, William of Orange[17], to England to replace him. In return, William promised these representatives that he would declare governing without parliamentary consent to be illegal. This might have led to another civil war, but James ran away, and his Protestant daughter Mary and her husband William were made the joint monarchs in April 1689. This Glorious Revolution was bloodless and therefore was also called the Bloodless Revolution. In 1689 Parliament passed the Bill of Rights[18] which greatly limited royal power and granted Parliament control of finances and the army. The events of 1688–1689 established the **supremacy** of Parliament over the Crown and set Britain on the path towards constitutional monarchy.

## The Birth of the Prime Minister and Cabinet

To ensure good relations between Crown and Parliament, the king or queen met regularly with a group of important **Parliamentarians**, a group which became known as the **Cabinet**.[19] While Cabinet ministers were appointed by the sovereign, they had to have enough support in the House of Commons to enable them to persuade Parliament to pass laws and vote for taxes.

In 1714, the ruling Queen Anne died without producing an heir to the throne, and so Britain had to "import" a member of the royal family from Germany to rule Britain. The new King George I[20] spoke English very badly and was not very interested in politics anyway, so he left the job of chairing cabinet meetings to one of his ministers, and in time he came to be called the **prime minister**.

While a king or queen who was interested in politics remained very influential, the Parliament was slowly becoming more powerful, especially as it became more organised. In 1832, when a system for choosing the House of Commons by popular election replaced the monarch's job of appointing representatives, the modern political system was born.[21] Members of Parliament (MPs) **assembled** themselves into groups

---

reassert *v.*
重申，再断言
execute *v.*
将…处死
consent *n.*
同意，准许
supremacy *n.*
至高无上，最高地位
parliamentarian *n.* 国会议员
cabinet *n.*
内阁
prime minister
首相
assemble *v.*
召集，聚集

which eventually would become political parties, organised groups which presented their policies and ideas to the **electorate** for approval. The party with the most supporters in the Commons forms the government, and by tradition, the leader of that party becomes Prime Minister.

## The British Government Today

From this brief history we can see that British government today is deeply influenced by its long past. Britain is both a parliamentary democracy and a constitutional monarchy.[22] Parliamentary democracy or representative democracy[23] (rather than direct democracy) means that the people do not rule themselves directly but elect representatives to rule for them. Constitutional monarchy means that, while the Sovereign is the official Head of State, his/her powers are largely traditional and symbolic. The government at national and local levels is elected by the people and governs according to British constitutional principles.

Because of Britain's imperial past, when many other corners of the globe were ruled from London, we find similar systems of government in many former colonies.[24] Other countries which are governed according to the principles of British parliamentary democracy are Australia, Canada, New Zealand and India. All but India recognise the Queen as their head of state, and a representative of the Crown, called the **Governor-General**, is present in such constitutional monarchies in order to fulfil the role of the monarch.[25]

### The Constitution

British **governance** today is based upon the terms and conditions of the constitution. Israel and Britain are the only two countries without written constitutions of the sort which most countries have. Instead of having a single document which lists out the basic principles of how a country should be governed, the foundations of the British state are laid out in **statute** laws[26], that is, laws passed by Parliament; common laws[27], which are laws which have been established through common practices in the courts, not because Parliament has written them; and conventions[28], which are rules and practices which do not exist legally, but are nevertheless regarded as vital to the **workings** of government.

# The United Kingdom of Great Britain and Northern Ireland

### The Prime Minister and the Cabinet

The Prime Minister (PM) is the national leader, responsible for selecting politicians to form a government and directing and coordinating its work. He focuses more on decisions concerning the economy, foreign affairs, and defence. He chooses Cabinet ministers mainly from the leading and experienced figures of his own party in the House of Commons. The Cabinet — the country's top executive committee — usually consists of between 20 and 23 members, including the Prime Minister and the most senior of the government ministers — heads of government departments. The Cabinet carries out the functions of policy-making, the coordination of government departments and the supreme control of government.

A key discipline of the Cabinet is **collective cabinet responsibility**, also known as collective ministerial responsibility, which is a constitutional convention. It means ministers accept responsibility collectively for the decisions made in the Cabinet. They may disagree in Cabinet discussion, but once a decision is made, they are expected to support it publicly, even if they do not privately agree with it. If they feel they must dissent publicly, they are expected to resign, as Robin Cook, the then Foreign Secretary, did in March 2003 over the decision to invade Iraq without a second UN Security Council resolution.[29] The purpose is to show Cabinet solidarity. Cabinet discussion is secret, and no one is allowed to leak information to the media or public.

Another key term is the **Shadow Cabinet**, which is a senior group of the opposition party — the next largest party in the Commons — chosen by the Leader of the Opposition. In the House of Commons, the relevant Shadow Cabinet minister challenges and criticises policies and actions of the counterpart government minister and offers alternative policies.[30] Members of the Shadow Cabinet are often but not always appointed to a Cabinet post if and when their party gets into government.

### Parliament

Parliament has a number of different functions. First and foremost, it passes laws. Another important function is that it provides the means of carrying on the work of government by voting for taxation.[31] Its other roles are to **scrutinise** government policy, administration and expenditure and to debate the major issues of the day. Parliament meets in the **Palace of Westminster**, whose clock tower, **Big Ben**, is one of the most famous symbols of London.

---

collective cabinet responsibility
内阁集体负责制
Shadow Cabinet
影子内阁
scrutinise *v.*
检查，仔细观察
Palace of Westminster
威斯敏斯特宫，又称议会大厦
Big Ben
大本钟，即威斯敏斯特宫钟塔的大报时钟

**Parliamentary sovereignty** is a unique feature of UK government, which means that parliament has unlimited authority. Parliament is supreme in the British state because it alone has the power to change the terms of the Constitution.[32] For example, the decision for Britain to join the European Union (EU) required a constitutional change because it meant recognising that EU law would in particular cases be more important than British law. There are no legal **restraints** upon Parliament. It can make or change laws, change or **overturn** established conventions or even prolong its own life without consulting the electorate.[33] However, it does not assert its supremacy, but **bears** the common law **in mind** and acts according to **precedent**.

Strictly speaking, the Parliament today consists of the Queen, the House of Lords and the House of Commons[34]. These three institutions must all agree to pass any given legislation.

However, most everyday references to Parliament refer to the workings of the Lords and/or the Commons, with the Monarchy regarded as a separate institution. This is because even though the Queen must consent to pass a law, this consent is given as **a matter of course**.[35] The last royal refusal was in 1707.

### The Role of the Monarchy Today

The present sovereign, Queen Elizabeth II, was born on April 21, 1926; was married to Prince Philip, the Duke of Edinburgh, on November 20, 1947 and came to throne on February 6, 1952 (crowned on June 2, 1953). As we shall see below, she is the longest reigning monarch in British history, overtaking Queen Victoria's previous record reign in 2015.

The role of the monarch today is primarily to symbolise the tradition and unity of the British state. Obviously the Prime Minister and governing party at any given time will only represent those parts of the population that support its policies in elections. The Queen, however, because she is non-political, belongs to everybody. Under the terms of the constitution her other roles are as follows: she is legally head of the **executive**, an **integral** part of the **legislature**, head of the **judiciary**, **commander-in-chief** of the armed forces and "supreme governor" of the Church of England.[36] Every year, she presides over **the State Opening of Parliament** as Head of State.

Always a popular figure in the UK, not to mention other countries, the Queen has almost always had an excellent approval rating in opinion polls (between 70% and

---

parliamentary sovereignty 议会至尊
restraint *n.* 限制，约束
overturn *v.* 推翻，废除，使无效
bear sth. in mind 记住（某事）
precedent *n.* 先例，前例
a matter of course 理所当然的事
executive *n.* （政府的）行政部门，行政当局
integral *adj.* 基本的，不可缺少的
legislature *n.* 立法机关，议会
judiciary *n.* 司法部，司法系统
commander-in-chief *n.* 总司令
the State Opening of Parliament 议会开幕大典

# The United Kingdom of Great Britain and Northern Ireland

80% in the 21st century), which was often significantly higher than that of her elected Prime Ministers. In 2002, the Queen was ranked 24th in the 100 Greatest Britons poll. Most Britons felt the Queen's most important job was to represent Britain at home and abroad; her second most important job was to set standards of good citizenship and family life. While the Queen has indeed led an exemplary life, her children have been criticised for their poor behaviour. For example, her successor and son, Prince Charles, divorced his wife, Princess Diana in 1996 and married Camilla Parker Bowles in 2005. Stories came out in the press **alleging** that Charles and Diana had both had **extramarital** affairs.

While the Queen is independently wealthy, much of the financial support for the Royal Family comes from taxpayers, supposedly in **recognition** of the fact that the royal family fulfils its role on behalf of the British people.[37] The huge financial cost for maintaining the monarchy has been a source of debate and criticism.

Criticism of the Queen's children led to a more general criticism about the monarchy and the debate **came to a head** in November 1992 when a fire did a great deal of damage to Windsor Castle.[38] The government immediately offered 50 million pounds' worth of taxpayers' money to pay for repairs. The electorate was very angry: Britain was in a **recession** and basic things like hospitals and schools had been forced to cut their services because public money was so scarce. They thought it was very unfair that the Queen, who is very wealthy (The ***Forbes* magazine** estimated her property to be around £270 million in 2009) and does not have to pay taxes herself, should not have to pay for at least part of the repairs. The taxpayers were already paying for the running costs of Buckingham Palace, Windsor Castle, three other palaces, a royal **yacht**, a royal train and a royal plane. As a result of the controversy, the Queen offered to start paying taxes and to accept less public money to support her family. She also began to open Buckingham Palace to tourists in the summer months in order to raise money to pay for repairs. The death of Princess Diana in a car crash in 1997 and the reluctance of the Queen to hold a public **funeral** for her led to another royal crisis, with many people talking of abolishing the monarchy. However, the Queen's willingness to give in to popular demands once again **endeared** her to her subjects.[39]

A less well known role of the Queen, which is nevertheless very important to British politics, is that of a **confidante** to the Prime Minister. Every Tuesday the Prime Minister attends the Queen privately at Buckingham Palace. In her nearly 70 years on

---

allege *v.*
声称，断言
extramarital *adj.* 婚外的
recognition *n.*
承认
come to a head
（事情）达到决定性阶段
recession *n.*
（经济的）衰退，衰退期
Forbes magazine
《福布斯》杂志
yacht *n.*
快艇，游艇
funeral *n.*
葬礼
endear *v.*
使受喜欢，使受钟爱
confidante *n.*
知己的女友

the throne, the Queen has had weekly chats with 13 different Prime Ministers and they have said that her long experience and her political **neutrality** make her a good source of informed observation on the day to day problems of governance.[40] Interestingly, it is said that the Queen gets on much better with Labour Prime Ministers than with Conservative Prime Ministers.

Prince Charles has won his popularity by taking part in charity work and has sponsored the Prince's Trust, the Prince's **Regeneration** Trust, and the Prince's Foundation for the Built Environment. Since founding the Prince's Trust, he has established fifteen more charitable organisations.

In the 21st century, a series of celebratory events have boosted public support for the monarchy. The royal **Diamond Jubilee** was celebrated in 2012. The Queen became Britain's **Longest Reigning Monarch** on September 9, 2015 and was also the first British Monarch to see a **Sapphire Jubilee** (65 years) in 2017. The Queen's 90th birthday was celebrated in 2016. The wedding of Prince William[41] and Catherine Middleton in April 2011 and the birth to their son George, daughter Charlotte and second son Louis brought the country with new hope and joy.

### The House of Lords and the House of Commons

Below the Queen is the House of Lords. It consists of the **Lords Spiritual**, who are the **archbishops** and senior **bishops** of the Church of England; and the **Lords Temporal**, which refers to everyone else.[42] In the 19th century specialist **law lords**, appointed for life, were added to assist the House of Lords in its judicial capacity as the highest court of the UK.[43] In the 1960s, the idea of inherited titles became unpopular and after 1965 no new hereditary peerage was made. The Life Peerages Act 1958 empowered the Crown to create life peers and peeresses, who cannot pass on the titles to their children.[44] So, lords, usually called **peers**, are not elected and are not considered to represent anyone besides themselves. They sit in the Lords either because they have inherited the seat from their forefathers (**hereditary peers**) or because they have been appointed by the sovereign, at the suggestion of the Prime Minister, due to their outstanding career achievements (**life peers**).

Because peers are appointed or given the right by their birth into a particular family, in Parliament they speak and vote as individuals, not as representatives of the greater interests of the country — although of course **civic-minded** peers do try to serve

neutrality *n.*
中立，中立地位
regeneration *n.*
恢复，新生
Diamond Jubilee
钻石禧（登基60周年纪念）
Longest Reigning Monarch
在位时间最长的君主
Sapphire Jubilee
蓝宝石禧（登基65周年纪念）
Lord Spiritual
上议院的神职议员
archbishop *n.*
大主教，主教长
bishop *n.* 主教
Lord Temporal
上议院的世俗议员
law lord
上议院执掌最高司法职务的议员，上诉法院法官
peer *n.* 贵族
hereditary peer
世袭贵族
life peer 终身贵族
civic-minded *adj.*
关心公益的，热心公民事务的

# The United Kingdom of Great Britain and Northern Ireland

their country rather than their own interests. Unlike those who serve in the House of Commons, they do not receive salaries and many (especially hereditary peers) do not attend Parliament at all. Peers who do attend parliament are paid generous expenses, however.

The composition of the House of Lords has, over the years, been seen as sexist and **elitist** because of the way the majority of peerages are passed down through aristocratic **patrilineal** lines.[45] This has led to reforms in order to make the chamber more democratic and effective.

During the first term of the New Labour government, the House of Lords Act 1999 received Royal Assent,[46] reducing the number of hereditary peers to only 92 with the prospect of further reform when their natural right to sit in the Lords will be completely abolished (this further reform has not yet occurred). Before the 1999 reform, the House of Lords had 26 spiritual peers, 777 hereditary peers, 525 life peers and 27 law lords, totaling 1 355 members. After the reform, the 26 spiritual peers, 525 life peers and 27 law lords continued to sit in the House, but the 777 hereditary peers were only allowed to elect 92 of them to remain so as to provide continuity and experience during the transitional period.

How will the new members of the House of Lords be chosen is still an issue unsolved today. In June 2012, the government published a House of Lords Reform Bill[47], which would make the chamber mostly elected for the first time in its history. The bill would cut the number of members by nearly half and make 80% of peers elected. The remaining 20% would be appointed. However, the bill was withdrawn due to insufficient support in the House of Commons.

In July 2017, there were 806 members in the House of Lords: 91 hereditary peers, 690 life peers and 25 bishops. Of the 149 sitting days in the 2015–2016 session, 497 lords on average regularly attended the **sittings**.

The judicial function of the House of Lords has recently been removed. The **Appellate** Committee in the House of Lords, which involved the special group of law lords sitting from 1876 until 2009, used to serve as the Supreme Court (the highest appeal court) of the country. In 2005, the Constitutional Reform Act[48] was passed which provided the separation of the judicial from the legislative (Parliament) and executive (Government). The independent and separate UK Supreme Court, comprising of 12 senior judges, was established and opened on October 1st, 2009. The law lords in the

---

**elitist** *adj.*
杰出人物统治（论）的
**patrilineal** *adj.*
父系的，父传的
**sitting** *n.*
（议会的）开会
**appellate** *adj.*
（尤指法庭）上诉的，受理上诉的

Upper Chamber moved out to become the first judges in the new court.

Finally, there is the House of Commons (presided over by the **Speaker**) which currently consists of about 650 Members of Parliament (MPs) elected by the people to represent them. MPs represent voters in a particular area, known as a **constituency** or seat. The number of seats varies a little bit because of changes in the population. MPs are only allowed to sit for the lifetime of the parliament, that is, the length of time between General Elections when a new set of MPs is elected. However, MPs can be reelected a limitless number of times and so popular MPs have **veritable** careers as parliamentarians.[49] Unlike the Lords, MPs receive a basic salary of about £74 962 a year (from April 2016). This is about the same pay as an average middle class professional such as a doctor or an accountant would earn and it is thought that MPs will thus be able to identify with the "typical" voter they represent. They also receive **allowances** for secretaries and researchers, travel and so on.

Most MPs belong to political parties — Labour, the Conservatives and the Liberal Democrats are the major ones. The Prime Minister is of course the leader of the political party which wins the most seats in a general election.

The House of Commons is the real centre of British political life — it is the place where elected representatives make and debate policies as well as approve laws — and so its role is discussed in greater detail in the unit on British Politics. In the House of Commons, the Government ministers (PM and Cabinet) sit on the front bench (the front row) to the right of the Speaker and Opposition shadow ministers (leader of opposition party and Shadow Cabinet) sit on the front bench to the left of the Speaker. They are known as **frontbenchers**. Other MPs sit in the rows of benches behind their respective party leaders and are called **backbenchers**.

Speaker *n.*
下议院议长
constituency *n.*
选区，选举区
veritable *adj.*
名副其实的，十足的
allowance *n.*
津贴，补贴
frontbencher *n.*
前座议员
backbencher *n.*
后座议员

# Explanations

1. **Britain is arguably the oldest representative democracy ... a thousand years:**
   英国可以说是世界上最古老的代议民主制国家，其代议民主制度起源于一千多年以前。

# The United Kingdom of Great Britain and Northern Ireland

2. **Although Britain too has ... one of evolution rather than revolution:**
   尽管英国历史上也曾有过政治不稳定时期，但相对于法国、美国而言，英国的建国历程是一个逐渐演变而不是革命性剧变的过程。法国历史上曾有法国大革命，以及拿破仑一世发动的雾月政变；美国历史上有 1775 年至 1783 年的独立战争。其实，英国也有过革命性的剧变，如 17 世纪的英国革命。

3. **This long, unbroken history ... in its political culture:**
   这样长久持续的历史在英国现今的政治体系和政治文化中仍然有所体现。政治文化是指一个国家有关政权、政府制度及政策制定的理论和意识形态等。

4. **King Egbert:**
   埃格伯特国王，为西撒克逊之国王（802–839）。继位后为巩固其独立统治，使韦塞克斯脱离麦西亚联盟，825 年打败麦西亚国王，使韦塞克斯成为英格兰最强大的王国。

5. **The power of the monarchy ... the "divine right of kings":**
   君主政体的权力主要是依据古老的"君权神授"理论而来。"君权神授论"认为国王的统治权是上帝赋予的，所以人民对其统治的怀疑和反抗是罪恶的。这种理论引起了英国新兴资产阶级及代表其利益的议会的强烈反对。

6. **Roundheads:**
   以奥立佛·克伦威尔为首的圆颅党人，1642 年至 1652 年英国内战期间的议会派成员，因剪短发而得名。支持国王的一派称为"骑士派"（the Cavaliers）。

7. **Charles I:**
   查理一世，英国斯图亚特王朝国王（1625–1649），因对抗国会、压迫清教徒而引起内战，被以克伦威尔为首的圆颅党人打败，被国会处以死刑。克伦威尔领导的共和体持续了 18 年，1660 年克伦威尔去世后不久，流亡在法国的查理一世之子回国登位，重新恢复了君主制。

8. **While the King in theory ... should not exercise absolute power:**
   尽管在理论上国王有上帝站在他一边，但在实践中，甚至早在中世纪时，人们就已认为国王不能行使绝对权力。

9. **Magna Carta:**
   英国大宪章。1215 年，英国大封建领主和教会反对英王约翰的一些政策，迫使他签署了保证部分公民权和政治权利的文件，限制国王的权力。大宪章被认为是维护公民权不受王权侵犯的重要文件。

10. **the Great Council:**
    大议会。中世纪时，国王们需用钱时，常召集一些上层富裕的大封建领主筹钱，这些人组成了大议会。后来发现这些人人数太少，无法筹到更多的钱。13 世纪前后，国王们开始把各郡、市、镇的代表纳入大议会。

11. **those who were summoned "by name":**
    这里是指那些享有世袭贵族头衔的家族和大封建领主。

## UNIT 3  The Government of the United Kingdom

12. **The civil war which brought ... the power of the king vis-a-vis Parliament:**
    17 世纪的内战使圆颅党得以掌权，内战的根源是国王与议会的权力之争。

13. **James I:**
    詹姆斯一世。英国斯图亚特王朝第一代国王（1603–1625），他和他的儿子查理一世都极力宣扬"君权神授"理论，招致新兴资产阶级的反对，从而引发资产阶级革命（1640–1688）。

14. **the Civil War:**
    内战。为了保障议会的权力，1642 年至 1646 年和 1648 年至 1652 年间，议会派圆颅党人在克伦威尔的领导下，与支持查理一世的保皇党人之间爆发了内战，议会派获胜。查理一世于 1649 年被处决。

15. **Charles II:**
    查理二世。英国斯图亚特王朝国王（1660–1685），查理一世之子，于 1660 年封建王朝复辟后，回国继承王位，恢复了君主制。

16. **James II:**
    詹姆斯二世。英国国王（1685–1688），查理二世的弟弟，继位后置议会的权力于不顾，被 1688 年的"光荣革命"推翻。詹姆斯二世从小在欧洲流亡长大，是天主教徒，希望不放弃个人宗教信仰，这也不能被英国政坛所容忍。

17. **William of Orange:**
    亦称 Prince of Orange，即威廉三世。原为尼德兰联省（即当今荷兰、比利时、卢森堡及法国东北部）的执政者，后应英国资产阶级和新教派的邀请，在 1688 年的"光荣革命"后，与其妻玛丽（詹姆斯二世之女）共同执政，接受国会通过的《权利法案》，确立了资产阶级统治和君主立宪制度。

18. **the Bill of Rights:**
    《权利法案》，1689 年英国议会通过的宪法性文件。法案对国王权力加以限制，确立了议会所拥有的权力高于王权的原则，标志着英国君主立宪制的建立。

19. **To ensure good relations between Crown and Parliament ... as the Cabinet:**
    为使王室和议会保持良好关系，国王或女王常定期与议会一些主要议员碰面，这批人后来逐渐被称为内阁。

20. **George I:**
    乔治一世。英国汉诺威王朝第一代国王（1714–1727）。即位后组成以辉格党占统治地位的内阁，沃波尔（Sir Robert Walpole）成为英国第一任首相。

21. **In 1832, when a system for choosing ... the modern political system was born:**
    这里指的是英国 1832 年的"议会法"使下议院议员由民选产生，而不再是国王任命。

22. **Britain is both a parliamentary democracy and a constitutional monarchy:**
    英国既是一个代议民主制国家，又是一个君主立宪制国家。

23. **representative democracy:**
    代议制民主。值得一提的是，在代议制构架下，英国政治的新趋势是政府更多依靠全民公决来处理涉及

# The United Kingdom of Great Britain and Northern Ireland

宪政变革的重大议题，例如 2011 年 5 月关于全国大选制度是否需要变革的全民公决，2016 年 6 月关于英国是否应该退出欧盟的全民公决，以及 2014 年 9 月苏格兰是否应从联合王国独立出来的地区全民公决等。

24. **Because of Britain's imperial past ... in many former colonies:**
由于过去大英帝国的历史，世界上其他许多地方曾被英国统治过，人们发现在这些前殖民地国家存在着类似的政体。

25. **All but India recognise the Queen ... to fulfill the role of the monarch:**
除了印度之外（印度是共和国），其他三国都承认女王为其国家元首。在这些君主立宪制中有一名女王的代表，即总督，以便履行王室的职责。总督由女王根据英联邦有关国家政府的建议任命当地人担任。

26. **statute laws:**
成文法。指由议会通过的一些法案，如 1689 年的《权利法案》（the Bill of Rights）、英国和苏格兰合组为大不列颠王国的《1707 年联合法案》（Acts of Union 1707）以及《1972 年欧洲共同体法案》（European Communities Act 1972）等。

27. **common laws:**
普通法，判例法。指英国法庭历来通过的判决而形成的法令，而非议会通过的法案。

28. **conventions:**
习惯法。指法律上没有明文规定，但却对政体的运行起着非常重要作用的一些传统宪法规则和惯例。例如，首相由下议院获得多数席位的政党的领袖担任，国王/女王对议会通过的法案给予御准，内阁集体负责制等。英国宪法之所以被认为属不成文（unwritten）宪法是因为它没有被合编成一本法典。事实上，只有习惯法才是真正意义上的不成文。定义英国宪法更准确的词汇应该是"没有编成法典"（uncodified）。

29. **If they feel they must dissent publicly ... UN Security Council resolution:**
如果他们觉得必须公开反对，他们就会被期待辞职，正如前外交大臣罗宾·库克 2003 年 3 月因反对英国在没有联合国安理会第二次决议情况下就决定入侵伊拉克而愤然辞职。

30. **the relevant Shadow Cabinet minister ... offers alternative policies:**
影子内阁相关的部长会挑战并批评他所对应的政府部长的政策和行动，并提供（反对党的）替代政策。counterpart 对应物，如影子财政大臣对应政府内阁财政大臣。

31. **Another important function is that ... by voting for taxation:**
（议会的）另一个重要作用是通过投票决定税收制度，为政府工作的开展提供手段。

32. **Parliamentary sovereignty ... to change the terms of the Constitution:**
议会至尊是英国政府一个独有的特征，它意味着议会拥有无限的权力。议会在英国是至高无上的，因为它自己就有权修改宪法条款。议会的决定是最终结果，最高法院无权以"违宪"理由来废除议会法案。

33. **It can make or change laws ... without consulting the electorate:**
议会可以制定或修改法律，修改或推翻已成定规的习惯法，甚至可以不用征得选民同意而推迟大选日期。

# UNIT 3　The Government of the United Kingdom

34. **the House of Lords and the House of Commons:**
    英国的议会上院/上议院（the Upper House, the Upper Chamber）又称"贵族院"（the House of Lords），下院/下议院（the Lower House, the Lower Chamber）又称"平民院"（the House of Commons）。

35. **This is because even though ... as a matter of course:**
    这是因为尽管必须经女王同意方能通过一项法律，但是女王总是理所当然地同意。

36. **Under the terms of the constitution ... the Church of England:**
    按宪法规定，女王的其他职责是：她是法律意义上的行政首脑，立法机构中的不可缺少的一部分，司法机构首脑，军队最高统率，以及英国国教的"最高领袖"。

37. **While the Queen is independently wealthy ... the British people:**
    尽管女王自己很富有，但王室的许多资金开支源于纳税人，这自然是对王室代表英国人民履行职责的一种承认。

38. **Criticism of the Queen's children ... to Windsor Castle:**
    对女王子女行为的指责引起人们对君主制更为广泛的批评，1992年11月温莎堡遭火灾破坏，更使这场争论达到了高潮。Windsor Castle: 温莎堡，英国王室住所，位于离伦敦不远的温莎城。

39. **However, the Queen's willingness to give in ... endeared her to her subjects:**
    但女王顺应民意的作风使她再次赢得了人民的爱戴。例如，温莎堡火灾事件后，女王同意王室收入纳税；戴安娜王妃车祸去世后，女王最终同意为其举行公共葬礼。

40. **In her nearly 70 years on the throne ... on the day to day problems of governance:**
    近七十年在位期间，女王曾先后与十三位首相坚持每周交谈。这些首相称，女王长期积累的经验和其在政治上的中立态度，使她能为日常国家管理事务提出有见识的意见。

41. **Prince William:**
    威廉王子，深受国民爱戴，在2012年5月女王登基60周年（钻禧）庆祝活动前夕，一项民意调查显示，主张女王退位或去世后应将王位直接传给长孙威廉王子的人数（48%）高于主张女王将王位传予长子查尔斯王子的人数（39%）九个百分点。

42. **It consists of the Lords Spiritual ... which refers to everyone else:**
    上议院由神职议员和世俗议员组成，前者是指英国国教的大主教和最主要的几位主教，后者是指非神职的贵族议员。长期以来，世袭贵族、上诉法院法官、教会大主教和主教均为上院当然的议员。另一部分上院议员则是"终身贵族"或"新封贵族"。

43. **In the 19th century specialist law lords ... as the highest court of the UK:**
    19世纪，上院成员增添了终身任命的上诉法院法官，以协助上院行使其作为英国最高法院的司法职能。

44. **The Life Peerages Act 1958 ... who cannot pass on the titles to their children:**
    1958年英国议会通过了《终身贵族法案》，开始对那些为英国社会做出杰出贡献的人，由首相提名，王室授封他们终身贵族，但爵位不能传给后代。

# The United Kingdom of Great Britain and Northern Ireland

45. **The composition of ... through aristocratic patrilineal lines:**
    人们认为上议院的组成成分既表现出性别歧视，又体现出高人一等的优越感，因为大多数贵族爵位是父传于子的。

46. **the House of Lords Act 1999 received Royal Assent:**
    1999年《上议院法》获得御准。该法案取消了大多数世袭议员的席位，剩余的92名世袭议员今后也终将失去资格。"光荣革命"之后，国王逐渐成为没有实权的"虚君"，上院的权力逐步向下院转移。1832年"议会法"以民选取代了上院提名下院议员的权力，结束了上院凌驾于下院的历史。20世纪，上院否决和搁置下院议案的权力逐步被削弱。1911年"议会法"规定，上院不予通过的议案最多被搁置两年即自动生效；且上院不得否决下院提出的预算法案，搁置期最长不得超过一个月。1949年"议会法"规定，上院不得修改预算法案，财政预算案之外的议案仅可搁置一年。至此，管理国家最重要的立法权和财政权被完全转移到下院。

47. **House of Lords Reform Bill:**
    2011年5月，联合政府提出的上院改革方案的核心内容是，2015年后上院将由300名议员组成，其中80%由选民选举产生，20%沿用任命制，同时保留英国国教会主教的上院议员席位。2012年7月，该议案提交议会下院。但因草案过于粗糙，在议会辩论阶段获得的支持率不够，最终被撤回。

48. **the Constitutional Reform Act:**
    2005年《宪法改革法》实现了以司法权和立法权分离为目标的机构改革，2009年成立的独立的最高法院取代了原先上院里由上诉法院法官组成的最高上诉法院，使最高司法权与上院彻底脱钩。

49. **However, MPs can be reelected ... veritable careers as parliamentarians:**
    然而，议员可连任无限次，所以受欢迎的议员可以以国会议员为真正的职业。

## Exercises

**I. Give the Chinese equivalents for the following:**

1. constitutional monarchy
2. Prime Minister
3. the Bill of Rights of 1689
4. parliamentary sovereignty
5. the House of Lords & the House of Commons
6. hereditary peers & life peers

UNIT ❸ The Government of the United Kingdom

## II. Decide whether the following statements are true (T) or false (F):

1. In Britain, the process of state-building has been one of evolution rather than revolution, in contrast to France and the US. _____
2. Common laws are laws which have been passed in the House of Commons. _____
3. Britain is both a parliamentary democracy and a constitutional monarchy. _____
4. Life peers earned their titles through their outstanding career achievements. The titles cannot be inherited by their children. _____
5. Members in both the House of Commons and the House of Lords receive salaries for their service. _____
6. Only government ministers can sit on the front bench in the House of Commons and are called frontbenchers. _____
7. For a policy to become law, it should be finally approved by the Queen. _____
8. Britain for centuries has had an independent and separate Supreme Court of law lords. _____

## III. Fill in the blanks:

1. The doctrine of the "divine right of kings" held that the sovereign derived his authority from _____, not from _____.
2. In 1215, some feudal barons and the Church forced King John to sign the _____, which placed some limits on the power of _____.
3. In medieval times, kings would summon a group of wealthy barons and representatives of counties, cities and towns — a gathering called _____ to raise money.
4. During the civil war in the 17th century, those who represented the interests of Parliament were called _____, and those who supported the King were called _____.
5. In 1689, Parliament passed _____ to ensure that the King would never be able to ignore Parliament and _____ monarchy gradually came into being.
6. In the 18th century, King George I left the job of chairing cabinet meetings to one of his ministers who later came to be called _____.
7. The British Constitution consists of statute laws, _____ and _____.
8. The most important function of the Parliament is to _____.
9. Important MPs of the opposition party form _____ in the House of Commons.
10. With Labour's reform of the House of Lords, the number of _____ has been greatly reduced.

# The United Kingdom of Great Britain and Northern Ireland

IV. **Questions:**

1. What are the characteristics of the British constitutional monarchy? Which institution is the real centre of political life in the UK?
2. How has the English monarchy evolved gradually to the present constitutional monarchy?
3. How did the doctrine of the "divine right of kings", according to the author, lead to the English Civil War?
4. What were the causes of the Glorious Revolution in the 17th century? How do you understand the significance of the Glorious Revolution and the Bill of Rights?
5. What are the major characteristics of the British constitution? Why do we say that Britain does not have a written constitution?
6. What is the history of English Parliament? What are the two Houses of Parliament called?
7. Why does the author say that Parliament is supreme in the British state? What functions does Parliament have?
8. What role do the Prime Minister and Cabinet play in British government? How are Cabinet members chosen?
9. What are the principles of collective cabinet responsibility?
10. What is the Shadow Cabinet?
11. What role does the House of Commons play in British government?
12. Who are members of the House of Lords today? How did the Labour Government reform the House of Lords?

V. **Topics for discussion or research:**

1. What roles is the British monarchy playing today? In your opinion, should the monarchy be kept or abolished in the near future? Why?
2. What are the major changes which have led to the weakening of the House of Lords and the growing importance of the House of Commons in British politics?
3. Why does Britain want to reform the House of Lords?

# UNIT 4

# Politics, Class and Race

**Go over the focal points before reading the text:**

- Importance of general elections
- The formation of the government
- A "vote of no confidence"
- Procedures of general elections
- Members of Parliament (MP)
- First-past-the-post
- Proportional representation
- The Conservative Party
- The Labour Party
- The Liberal Democrats
- Margaret Thatcher
- Tony Blair
- Recent political trends in the UK
- The class system in British society
- The upper middle-class and lower middle-class
- The hereditary aristocracy
- Ethnic relations in Britain

# The United Kingdom of Great Britain and Northern Ireland

## Politics

### General Elections — Why Are They Important?

Periodic national elections are very important in the Western model of democracy.[1] In the UK the citizen's right to vote for the candidate of their choice to represent them in parliament is a right that has been struggled for over the past two hundred years.[2] Although Members of Parliament have been elected to parliament for hundreds of years, in 1832 only 5% of the adult population were allowed to vote; by 1884 persistent political campaigning had increased this to 25%; by 1919 it was 75%; and in 1928 it reached the current level of about 99%[3] (those excluded are Lords,[4] certain categories of **convicted** criminals, the legally insane, and resident foreign citizens — except UK resident citizens of the Irish Republic,[5] who may vote). The Representation of the People Act 1969 reduced the minimum voting age of all people from 21 to 18. The election is seen as an opportunity to influence future government policy — or, less positively, that whatever else the failings of the political system, at least the election provides the opportunity to "kick the **rascals** out".[6]

### When Do Elections Occur?

As you will remember from the previous unit the British people are represented in parliament by one of 650 Members of Parliament (MP) representing the 650 geographical areas or "constituencies" into which the United Kingdom is divided. The party which holds a majority of those "seats" in parliament forms the government, with its party leader as the Prime Minister (PM). After a government has been in power for five years it has to resign and hold a general election, in which all British adults are given the chance to vote again for their constituency's MP. A government cannot continue for longer than five years without a new election except in exceptional circumstances (it has happened twice last century, when elections were delayed until the end of the First and Second World Wars). However, the Prime Minister can call an election sooner than five years. This can happen (as in 1979) when the government loses a "vote of no confidence" in the House of Commons. That is, an MP (usually

---

convict *v.*
证明…有罪，宣判…有罪
rascal *n.*
流氓，无赖

a member of an opposition party) puts forward a statement for the MPs to vote on saying that "This house no longer has confidence in the Government". If a majority of MPs agree, then the government has effectively lost its ability to govern and is forced to resign and call a new general election. An early election might also happen if the Prime Minister decided that the government was currently very popular (perhaps the economy was booming) and called a new election in the hope of winning another five years rather than wait the full period and risk becoming unpopular in the meantime and losing the election.

Under the Fixed-term Parliaments Act 2011[7], all future general elections were to take place on the first Thursday in May every five years, except in exceptional circumstances. The Prime Minister could call a General Election within the five-year period, but only with the consent of Parliament.

**Who Can Stand for Election as an MP?**

Anyone who is **eligible** to vote can stand as an MP. It is necessary only to make a deposit of £500 (a quite easily obtainable amount in the UK) which is lost if the candidate does not receive at least 5% of the vote.[8] This is supposed to stop people running just for a joke. In most cases, if you are not the candidate put forward by one of the main political parties you are unlikely to persuade many people to vote for you. They will see it as a wasted vote even if they respect you and your ideas, because it will be hard for you to win most votes in any one constituency or even if you were to win the seat you would be powerless in parliament against the big parties' representatives.[9] A vote for an independent candidate effectively prevents the voter from contributing to the competition between the big parties as to which of them will form a government.[10] There are some small parties which have electoral success — usually these are associated with the politics of a particular region, such as the Scottish National Party. But people who want to make an impact in national politics must usually join one of the big parties, and apply to be chosen as their candidate in one of the constituencies.

**What Happens in an Election?**

Once the date has been set, everyone on the "electoral register" (the list of citizens eligible to vote) receives a voting card in the mail with details of when and where to vote. The electoral register is compiled from a variety of sources, but it is the citizen's

eligible *adj.*
在法律上合格
的，有资格的

# The United Kingdom of Great Britain and Northern Ireland

own responsibility to check they are on the list — people sometimes forget to re-register when they move house for example.

Meanwhile the political parties get their electoral campaigns under way normally around four weeks before voting day. This involves advertisements in newspapers, door-to-door campaigning (candidates or their local supporters come and knock at people's doors trying to persuade voters to vote for them), postal deliveries of **leaflets**, and, for the main parties, strictly limited "party electoral broadcasts" on the television: each main party is given a few 10-minute periods of time on national TV to "sell" their policies to the public.[11] The time is given free, and the amount of time is broadly **proportional** to the percentage of the vote which the party received at the previous election.[12] They are not allowed to buy more time as this would favour richer parties over poorer ones. Likewise the amount each candidate is allowed to spend in his or her constituency campaign is strictly limited to around £30 000, depending upon the size and nature of the constituency for the same reason of fairness. Nevertheless, the national campaign, other than that on TV, is not limited,[13] with the big three parties spending significantly larger amounts nationally. For example, in the 2015 General Election, the Conservative Party spent £15.6 million while the Labour Party spent £12.2 million, with total spending by all political parties nationally reaching over £37.56 million. In addition to the parties' own publicity, newspapers and TV programmes devote a great deal of time to studying the party **election manifestos**, discussing the campaign, interviewing politicians, and predicting the results: a lot of money is spent by the media on "**opinion polls**", in which samples of the British population are asked how they will vote, and the results are then applied to the whole country to try and guess the election result.[14] They are often wrong!

The campaigns are not simply about telling people how good your policies are, but also about telling them how bad your opponents are. So they can be quite aggressive and critical.[15] Many British people complain that the campaigns are too negative, that the politicians do not properly explain their own policies, but instead explain why people shouldn't vote for their opponents.

On the Election Day, people go to their local voting station (often in a public building taken over for the day, such as a school or a community centre). They give their electoral cards to the official who checks them off on his or her list and hands over to each voter another card with all the candidates' names on it. The voters take this

---

**leaflet** *n.*
传单，小册子
**proportional** *adj.* 比例的，成比例的
**election manifesto**
竞选宣言
**opinion poll**
民意测验

into a private booth and put an "X" beside the name of the candidate of their choice. Secrecy is an important part of the process because it means each voter is under no pressure from anyone to vote one way or another since no one knows for whom he or she has voted.[16] They then fold the card and take it to the sealed box beside the official and push it through a **slit** in the top. Voting is not compulsory in the UK. The **turnout rate** in the 2017 general election was 68.7%, the highest level in 25 years.

When the voting closes at the end of the day (voting takes place from 7: 00 to 22: 00), the counting begins. Under close supervision, teams of volunteers check the voting cards in each constituency. The results come out over a period of a few hours. Television stations devote long night-programmes to monitoring the process as the results are gathered in from around the country, and keep a running count of the seats won by each party.[17] It can be quite tense and exciting in a **close** election. Usually by the early morning it is clear which party is going to form the next government — as soon as they have won 326 constituencies, which will give them a majority of MPs in the House of Commons. This is a time for great celebration for them and their supporters, and great disappointment for the losers.

If no single party wins an absolute majority (326 seats), a rare situation in the 20th century but one which has happened twice already in the 21st century (2010 and 2017), a hung parliament[18] is the result. Then the party winning the most number of seats may seek to form a **coalition government** with a smaller party (with over 326 seats altogether) or form a minority government. For example, in 2010, the Conservative Party ruled jointly with the Liberal Democrats in a formal coalition government, and in 2017, the Conservative Party (318 seats) was able to form a minority government with agreement from the Democratic Unionist Party of Northern Ireland (10 seats) that it would provide parliamentary support to the Conservative Party on key votes in the House of Commons. After the June 2017 election, there were 650 members in the House of Commons: Conservative 317, Labour 262, Scottish National Party 35, Liberal Democrats 12, and the rest being shared by smaller parties.

### What Is the First-past-the-post (FPTP)[19] Election System?

In British general election, voting takes place in 650 constituencies. In each constituency, there are several candidates, each representing a political party or standing as an independent. Voters vote for one of them and the candidate who

slit *n.*
狭长的口子
turnout rate
投票率
close *adj.*
比分接近的，结果不定的
coalition government
联合政府

# The United Kingdom of Great Britain and Northern Ireland

receives the most votes wins and becomes the MP for the constituency in Parliament. All other votes are **disregarded**. The party that wins the majority of constituencies wins the election. The leader of the winning party naturally becomes Prime Minister and he or she is invited to Buckingham Palace to the monarch and asked to form a government.

One **recurring** result of the FPTP electoral system is that it tends to lead to the larger political parties (normally the Conservative and Labour Parties) being overrepresented in Parliament in relation to the proportion of votes cast for them. The system thus leads to unproportional representation — the percentage of seats gained in Parliament by the different parties does not match the percentage of votes won overall by each party. The FPTP normally benefits the two major parties, and is extremely unfair to many others.[20] In particular, it harms those small parties whose votes are spread widely across the country instead of concentrating in particular areas (smaller parties with highly concentrated support, such as the Scottish National Party, can do very well, however).

A system of proportional representation (PR) would distribute seats according to percentage of votes gained nationally.[21] That means, if a party gains 40% of the total votes, then it should get 40% of the seats.

Whilst there is no doubt that PR would be "fairer", the FPTP is defended on the ground that it usually provides a government with a working parliamentary majority and thus leads to a strong and stable executive.[22] Besides, the system is easy to understand and the votes can be counted and winners declared quickly. In contrast, PR might produce unstable, inefficient coalition governments in which no party would have a majority of MPs in Parliament. It could also lead to a rapid increase in the number of smaller parties.

The Liberal Democrats, which has consistently lost out as a result of the FPTP electoral system, has for a long time called for reform of election system, but in a national referendum in May 2011, the British people rejected any change. However, at present, the elections for the European Parliament, the Scottish Parliament and the Welsh and Northern Irish National Assemblies all use some form of PR.

**Political Parties**

There are three major national parties: the Conservative Party and the Labour

disregard *v.*
不理会，忽视
recur *v.*
复发，重现

Party are the two biggest, and any general election is really about which of these two is going to govern. The Liberal Democrats, for a long time Britain's "third" party, usually receives up to about 20% of the votes: not enough to form a government, but enough to have a big impact on which of the other two parties does so.[23] Any citizen can join any of these parties and so take part in their internal politics: it is just a question of paying a small annual fee. All encourage people to join since it means more money for their campaigns, and greater **legitimacy** for their policies.

In terms of their origins, the Labour Party[24] is the newest of these three, formed in 1900 by a union between the trade unions and socialist groups with the aim of providing independent working class representation in Parliament. Helped by the extension of the **franchise** to working class men in 1885, it quickly replaced the Liberal Party as one of the two biggest parties (19th century politics had essentially been a competition between the Liberals and the Conservatives). Labour is formally a socialist party.[25] That is to say its members believe a society should be relatively equal in economic terms, and that part of the role of government is to act as a "**redistributive**" agent: transferring wealth from the richer to the poorer by means of taxing the richer part of society and providing support to the poorer part of society[26]. As well as this redistributive role, they see the government as the right body to provide a range of public services available to all, such as health, education and public transport. The Labour government that came to power with an absolute majority in 1945 had a major effect on British society. It started the world's first comprehensive Welfare State, setting up the National Health Service to provide high quality health care for all, free "from cradle to grave",[27] and providing a range of **social security** payments such as unemployment benefit and old age pension (to replace or **supplement** wages in case of unemployment, sickness, poverty, and old age). And, most controversially, it "nationalised" (changed from private to state ownership) a wide range of key industries, making the UK into a mixed economy with both private enterprises and a large state-owned sector.[28] All this government activity required money, so the Labour Party became identified as a party of high public spending and high taxation levels.

The Conservative Party[29], founded in 1834, is the party that has spent most time in power. In the post-1945 period the party of government has changed fairly frequently, as Labour government have been replaced by Conservative and **vice versa**. From 1979 to 1997, the Conservative Party won 4 elections **in a row** and was in power for

---

legitimacy *n.*
合法性，合理性
franchise *n.*
选举权
redistributive *adj.* 再分发的，重新分配的
social security
社会保障
supplement *v.*
增补，补充
vice versa
反之亦然，反过来也一样
in a row
接连地，连续地

# The United Kingdom of Great Britain and Northern Ireland

18 years, but thereafter the Labour Party formed governments until 2010. Basically the Conservatives are seen as the party of the individual, protecting the individual's right to acquire wealth and to spend it in ways they choose, and so favouring economic policies which businessmen prefer, such as low taxes. They receive a lot of their party funding from big companies. But in the past this economic policy was coupled with a **paternal** sense of obligation to the less fortunate in society,[30] which meant that even though the "big" government which Labour set up in the post-1945 era was against their principles, they did not **dismantle** it when they came to power. Thus the difference between the Labour Party and the Conservative Party is one of degree, not an absolute.[31] However, as we shall see in the section below, neither party has stood still, and there have been **substantial** changes in both parties in recent years.

The Liberal Democrats[32] was the third biggest party until 2015 when it was surpassed by the Scottish National Party in terms of seats (though not in votes cast). The party originates from the Liberal Party, which dominated in the 19th century and early 20th century.[33] In March 1988, a majority of the Liberals agreed to a **merger** with the Social Democratic Party under the new title the Social and Liberal Democrats, but the party was renamed the Liberal Democrats in 1989. To some extent it may be seen as a party of the "middle", occupying the ideological ground between the two main parties. As such, at election time they may receive votes both from those who usually vote Labour and from those who usually vote Conservative. Many people see them as comparatively flexible and **pragmatic** in their balance for support of the individual (individual liberty) and the social (government interference).[34] The party supports free trade, free market and Britain's membership of the European Union (EU). It calls for reform of electoral system to make government more representative and democratic.

There are small parties supporting the independence of Scotland and Wales (i.e. the Scottish National Party (SNP) and Plaid Cymru — the Party of Wales). They receive a small share of the national vote but because their vote is regionally concentrated they win significant parliamentary representation. Indeed in 2015, the SNP won 56 of the 59 parliamentary seats in Scotland with only 4.6% of the UK-wide national vote, and indeed, only 50% of the vote in Scotland. There are also political parties which only organise in Northern Ireland (see the politics of Northern Ireland). The main UK political parties do not organise in Northern Ireland at all.

Other small parties which have clear special aims are the UK Independence Party

---

**paternal** *adj.* 父系的，父亲（般）的
**dismantle** *v.* 废除，取消
**substantial** *adj.* 重大的，实质性的
**merger** *n.* 合并
**pragmatic** *adj.* 讲究实际的，实用主义的

(UKIP), the Green Party, and the British National Party,[35] etc. The UKIP was founded in 1993 and has campaigned strongly for Britain's exit from the EU. In the 2015 general election, it came the third in terms of votes — 12.7%, though only won one seat — a victim of having support spread widely across the country. The Green Party is a left-wing political party believing in social justice, **environmentalism** and nonviolence (it won one seat in the 2010, 2015 and 2017 general elections) and the British National Party is a far-right party associated with strong nationalism and hostility to immigration.

### Recent Political Trends

The 1970s was a decade of problems in the UK. The economy did badly, with high inflation and low growth. Many large private companies went bankrupt, and the nationalised industries were seen as inefficient. To maintain living standards trade unions campaigned for higher pay. There were many strikes (esp. nationwide miners' strikes) when these demands were not met, which added to the problems. Relations between workers and managers were frequently very bad. **Trade union** leaders became national figures, negotiating directly with the government and apparently having a lot of power. Many people saw this influence as undemocratic. The decade **culminated** in the winter of 1978-79 when there was a series of public sector strikes. The Labour government faced a vote of no confidence in the House of Commons, which it lost, causing a general election in 1979. This was won by the Conservatives under their leader Margaret Thatcher who thus became the UK's first woman Prime Minister.

Mrs Thatcher was strongly committed to the idea of small government and free-market economics, and less concerned with being "fatherly" (paternalistic concern for the less privileged). State intervention was deemed by her to encourage laziness and discourage **entrepreneurship**.[36] As a result the 1980s saw the most substantial changes to British society since the late 1940s. Much of the change was to undo the work of the 1945 Labour government, in that one of the Conservative Party's major policies was the privatisation of nationalised industries: British Aerospace, British Airways, British Telecom, British Petroleum, the electricity, gas and water companies, and many others, including much public housing (council houses), were gradually sold off, until today when little remains to be sold.[37] The policy is generally seen as a success because many of the privatised companies have done very well, becoming very efficient and profitable. There were negative consequences, however, as the process of becoming

environmentalism *n.*
环境保护论
trade union 工会
culminate *v.*
达到顶点
entrepreneurship *n.*
企业家精神

# The United Kingdom of Great Britain and Northern Ireland

efficient enough for private investors to buy them involved the huge businesses in getting rid of many of their workers. So unemployment went up quickly in the early 1980s, from 1 million jobless to 3.5 million, and the level of poverty rose for the first time from 1945. Government welfare payments became less generous too. So through the 1980s many people got richer, but many got poorer: Britain became a less equal society, and many thought public services, such as health, education and transport, got worse. The leader of the Liberal Party described the 1980s as a time of "private affluence and public **squalor**"[38]. Nevertheless many businesses boomed, and simplified government regulations attracted many foreign businesses.

Part of the mechanism of change was a less redistributive taxation system:[39] tax rates were cut, allowing people to keep more of what they earned. It was an attempt to change local government taxes which led to Mrs Thatcher's downfall, because many citizens refused to pay the new "**Poll Tax**" which was seen as unfair. To maintain their popularity the Conservatives abandoned the new tax and elected a new leader: John Major.[40] He continued Thatcher's policies, but perhaps a little less forcefully and won the 1992 general election against all expectations.

Thus the 1980s saw British politics move to the "right", away from the "public" and toward the "private"; away from the "social" and toward the "individual", and all political parties made appropriate adjustments as they saw fit.

Faced with this national (and international) trend away from big government socialism towards free market individualism (and four successive election defeats), the Labour Party in the 1990s was forced to think of change too. For one thing, owing to **deindustrialisation**, the traditional working class was **shrinking**. So the Labour Party became less overly "socialist", giving up its commitment to "public ownership of the means of production", and was careful about suggesting policies which would need tax increases. The desire to win elections forced it to make broad appeals to different social groups. Tony Blair reformed the party into a catch-all party termed as New Labour. New Labour's "Third Way" philosophy appeared a compromise between unrestricted free market capitalism (associated with Margaret Thatcher) and centralised state socialism (associated with "old" Labour).[41] So New Labour stressed fairness and equal opportunities while promoting efficiency in economic development.

The mid-1990s saw steady economic growth and steadily reducing unemployment figures. These are usually good signs for a government, but John Major's Conservatives

squalor *n.*
悲惨，贫困
Poll Tax
人头税
deindustrial-
isation *n.*
使非工业化，减少…的工业比重
shrink *v.*
收缩，减少

were unpopular: well behind Labour in the opinion polls. Part of the reason for this was that the Conservatives had been in power for so long and people were ready for a change. Also there had been a lot of stories in the news about government corruption. Additionally the Conservatives were seen as divided internally on their policy towards Europe: some pro-**integration**, some against.[42] In particular, there was division on the topic of **monetary** union — whether the UK should give up its own currency (the pound) and join with the rest of the EU in creating a new European currency (the **Euro**). At the same time, popular government services such as health and education were not seen to be "safe" with the Conservatives. All these factors mean that the reformed new-look Labour Party under its new leader Tony Blair became more popular, and it won the election in 1997.

New Labour led Britain into a period of smooth economic development and won two more elections (2001, 2005). But the party was split over Blair's Iraq policy (the war in Iraq). Blair had to resign in 2007 and was replaced by Gordon Brown.[43] Unfortunately, the Brown government was troubled by the financial crisis of 2008 and lost the election in 2010. So Gordon Brown resigned the party leadership and was replaced as Labour Party leader by Ed Miliband. Miliband was unable to revive the Labour Party's fortunes in the 2015 general election, however, and resigned immediately after Labour's defeat.

Conservative leader David Cameron formed a coalition government with the Liberal Democrats after the election in 2010 because he did not win enough seats in the House of Commons for the Conservative Party to form a government on its own. This was the first formal coalition government in the UK after the Second World War. However, Cameron managed to lead the Conservative Party to victory with a majority of seats in the House of Commons in the 2015 election. After the June 2016 referendum over Britain's membership of the European Union, which resulted in a narrow 52%: 48% victory for those supporting Britain's withdrawal from the EU, David Cameron resigned as Prime Minister and Conservative Party leader as he campaigned for the UK to remain inside the EU.[44] Theresa May was elected as party leader and thus automatically became Prime Minister, the second female PM in Britain.

In the summer of 2015, Jeremy Corbyn was elected the Labour Party leader. He was the most left wing candidate who had no previous leadership experience and who, for 30 odd years, had consistently opposed the centrist policies of New Labour.

integration *n.*
结合，综合，融成一体
monetary *adj.*
货币的，金融的
Euro *n.* 欧元

# The United Kingdom of Great Britain and Northern Ireland

Indeed, Corbyn's election as leader represented the Labour Party turning its back on New Labour generally, rejecting the moderate policies of Blair and Brown, and **reverting** back to policies more associated with its past socialist traditions, involving high public spending and nationalisation.[45] This led to major **strife** in the Labour Party and a revolt amongst many Labour MPs against Corbyn's leadership throughout 2016. However, Corbyn triumphed in another leadership contest only 12 months after his first leadership victory with an even bigger majority of votes amongst members of the party.

In 2016, Theresa May appeared to be in a very dominant position within British politics, particularly with the Labour Party in apparent **turmoil** over Corbyn's leadership. In May 2017, therefore, May called a new general election three years earlier than required to give the Conservative Party a bigger parliamentary majority and more authority in conducting the forthcoming Brexit negotiations between the UK and the EU.[46] The election result turned out to be very embarrassing for Theresa May with the Conservative Party losing 13 seats instead of gaining an increased majority and ended in another hung parliament. May was able to form a government only when the Democratic Unionist Party of Northern Ireland agreed to provide the Conservative Party with parliamentary support in key votes.[47] The poor performance of the Conservative Party in the June 2017 election was largely the result of a major swing amongst younger voters towards the Labour Party, energised by its new "socialist" policies and the sudden and dramatic popularity of its new leader Jeremy Corbyn. Although much older than May, Corbyn gained large numbers of votes from younger voters, tired of the **austerity** policies pursued by governments since the financial crisis of 2008, and attracted by his radical ideas associated with higher public spending, abolition of university student fees and renationalisation of basic public services to include the railways and the water industry. Corbyn's impressive performance in the 2017 general election (the Labour Party did not win the election, but came far closer to doing so than anyone expected) **cemented** his leadership of the Labour Party for some years to come. In contrast, Theresa May's poor performance weakened her and put her leadership of the Conservative Party and her position as Prime Minister for the long term in doubt.

## Class

Social class is a complex topic, but one which is difficult to avoid when discussing British society, which is often seen as a society in which "class" is more important

---

revert *v.*
恢复，回到…上
strife *n.*
冲突，斗争，争吵
turmoil *n.*
混乱
austerity *n.*
财政紧缩
cement *v.*
巩固；粘牢

than in other countries. This is true to a certain extent, but should probably not be exaggerated. Most countries have some kind of class structure, in that there exist broad groups within society which share types of employment, income levels, and certain cultural characteristics. But important in the idea of "class" is that it makes a difference to an individual's "life-chances" as to which group or class he or she is born into.[48] So if a middle-class couple (perhaps a doctor and a teacher) have a child, it is more likely that that child will also acquire middle-class education, employment and income levels, than will the child of working-class factory workers. This is certainly the case in the UK, though it should be stressed that it is far from impossible for the working-class child to acquire middle-class status: it is simply statistically much more unlikely than for his middle-class school-friend.[49]

If asked, about half the British population would describe themselves as middle-class, and half as working-class. Employment would be the main guide they would use: manual (or "blue-collar") workers would usually call themselves working-class, and office (or "white collar") workers would usually call themselves middle-class. However there is a **hazy** area around unskilled office-work and skilled well-paid manual work which leads to sub-divisions such as "lower middle-class" being used; and the term "upper middle-class" might be used to describe doctors and lawyers and so on who have relatively high incomes and high-status professions — especially in families with long traditions of such employment.[50] This would differentiate them from the majority of middle-class people today, most of whom have working class parents or grandparents. This reflects the huge expansion of the middle-class over the 20th century, and especially since 1945, when more equal social policies were adopted by the government.

Such class-divisions are not simply economic: a working-class car-worker may earn more money than a middle-class university teacher, but there are additional cultural differences. An obvious one in the UK is which newspaper people read. The car-worker probably (though not certainly) reads a paper like *The Sun*[51]: a newspaper with little hard news[52] but with plenty of articles on TV **soap operas**, television and film stars, the Royal family, and sport. The university teacher might read *The Telegraph*, *The Times* or *The Guardian*:[53] larger newspapers with longer stories, covering national and international news, "high" culture such as theatre and literature, and so on. Strangers would probably be able to place each of them in the right class simply by listening to

---

hazy *adj*.
模糊的，不明确的，灰蒙蒙的
soap opera
肥皂剧

# The United Kingdom of Great Britain and Northern Ireland

the way they speak: regional accents tend to be stronger amongst the working-class.

Another factor marking off what might be termed an "upper middle-class" is education.[54] Most Britons (working or middle-class) go to the same kind of free state schools, but about 7% of the UK population attends independent schools, which are expensive private schools, but which tend to give children a better chance to go to the best universities (for example about half the students at Oxford and Cambridge, the top two universities, come from independent schools). This is important not simply because this offers a good education, but because it offers a network of connections: the top levels of many aspects of British society — arts, media, industry and politics contain a very high proportion of "**Oxbridge**" (the two university names are often run together in this way) graduates.[55] When hiring they tend to hire fellow Oxbridge graduates. For example: although former Prime Minister John Major was a lower middle-class boy who did not go to university at all, reflecting the possibility for social advancement in British society, about 90% of his 22 senior government ministers were Oxbridge graduates, reflecting the advantage that such an education gives.

What is distinctive about the British class system, and which marks it as different from the American or Chinese social structure, is that it has also retained a hereditary aristocracy. Among the students at the independent schools attended by the upper-middle-class above would be a thin scattering of aristocratic children, who will inherit titles: **baronets, barons, dukes** etc., and usually fortune. Many are from families which have held wealth and position for centuries, and own historic "great" houses in the country. That the hereditary aristocracy also can sit and vote in the House of Lords, the upper house of the British parliament, is a political inheritance which distinguishes the British aristocracy from its neighbours in Europe.[56]

But their significance should not be over-stated. Their number is very small. Their position has also changed with the century. Though still influential they do not dominate UK society, nor even that "**power-elite**" which holds a disproportionate share of wealth and influence at the top of UK society (though without forming what most people would think of as a separate "class").[57] Many of the very rich in the UK are not aristocrats, but businessmen and entrepreneurs. The majority of working "Lords"[58] in the House of Lords are not from aristocratic families either, but have been made "life peers" (who are lords for their lifetime, but whose children cannot inherit the title) out of recognition for achievement in UK society (for example Margaret Thatcher, a grocer's daughter,

**Oxbridge** n.
牛津大学和剑桥大学
**baronet** n.
准男爵（级别在男爵之下）
**baron** n. 男爵
**duke** n. 公爵
**power-elite**
（总称）权力中坚

was made a life peer when she retired as an MP). Real power in parliament rests in the elected House of Commons rather than the House of Lords. The Labour Party reform of the Upper House includes a commitment to end the right of hereditary peers to sit in the House of Lords (presently only 92 of them can sit in the House of Lords). The aristocratic family's great house in the country is probably open to the public in order to raise money for its **upkeep**.

## Race

People abroad often think of the UK as an exclusively "white" country. It is not. According to the 2011 census, Asian/Asian British and Black/Black British comprise about 9.9% of British population. Although small ethnic minority populations have lived in the UK for a long time, particularly in port cities such as Liverpool and Bristol, the majority of such immigrants have arrived since the 1950s. Mostly they originated in countries of the now almost **vanished** British Empire. Due to the post-war shortage of labour, the British Nationality Act 1948 allowed free entry of citizens from the **Commonwealth** countries. It was only when racial conflicts and riots started to occur in the late 1950s that later Immigration Acts or Nationality Acts began to restrict coloured immigrants step by step. Two areas of the world in particular have supplied the majority of Britain's recent immigrants: South Asia, that is, India, Pakistan, Bangladesh and Sri Lanka; and Caribbean countries such as **Jamaica** and **Trinidad**; though there are smaller groups from all over the world — Africa, China, etc. The number of Chinese has grown rapidly in recent decades. The 433 150 Chinese makes 0.7% of the UK population (2011 census). The biggest concentration of ethnic minorities is in London and some other large cities like Birmingham, Manchester, Bradford, etc. Since the Second World War, Britain has gradually become a **multiracial** and **multicultural** society.

This has a number of consequences for British society, mainly positive, though with some indirect negative effects. On the positive side such immigrant groups bring their culture with them, which increases the variety and interest within British culture: for example, the UK, which used to have a bad reputation for food, now has a **cuisine** as varied as any country, with Indian and Chinese restaurants in every community, especially in bigger cities. This variety in restaurant food has resulted in more experimentation at home, so that shops now carry a much wider variety of goods to supply the demand, and there are many TV programmes and books devoted to all

# The United Kingdom of Great Britain and Northern Ireland

kinds of different cooking.

Likewise British music has been invigorated by the newcomers, with many black British performers having **chart**-topping record success.[59] **Crossover** music between Asian and Afro-Caribbean sounds has resulted in new forms of popular music.[60]

Of course most immigrants do not open restaurants or become musicians. Most simply get jobs, start small businesses and live private lives not unlike their neighbours, although perhaps with different religious beliefs, and different family structures (For example Islam, practised by many South Asian immigrants, is now thought to be the UK's biggest active faith, as the number of practising Christians has fallen). Their children go to school alongside their white neighbours, and have no national identity other than British. They become citizens of the UK, and take part in and contribute to that society like the rest.

The negative side of things lies largely in the attitude of some of their white neighbours. In many countries where there has been substantial immigration, there has also been trouble in the process of **assimilating** those immigrants, and unfortunately the UK is no exception. Immigration is not evenly spread across the country, so some areas, especially the larger cities, and particular areas within those cities have quite high proportions of ethnic minorities. Some parts of London have more than 30% of the population from non-white groups. Often people used to an ethnically uniform society feel their way of life to be threatened by the newcomers, and perhaps see themselves as being in economic competition with them, especially if they do feel economically insecure, and fear losing their jobs.[61] For some people too, cultural difference is seen not as positive and interesting but as distasteful. Fortunately, various Race Relations Acts have been passed in the past decades, making **racial discrimination** illegal in all aspects of social life, such as education, employment, housing, advertising and so on. But despite much progress, and much official action to minimise racism, both subtle and overt oppression remains.[62]

While there is a growing ethnic minority middle-class, and many individual success stories, by most measures the immigrant population is worse off economically speaking than the white population as a whole. Individuals from ethnic minorities are more likely to be unemployed; and they are under-represented in politics too, though there are now a number of black and Asian MPs (the 2017 general election produced the most diverse parliament[63] yet with 52 ethnic minority MPs out of 650, a rise from 41 in the

chart *n.*
每周流行唱片排行榜
crossover *adj.*
混合的；转型的
assimilate *v.*
使同化
racial discrimination
种族歧视

2015 election) and in May 2016 Labour's Sadiq Khan (of Pakistani family background and a practising Muslim) was elected London mayor. But there are also a number of small political parties in the UK with overtly racist policies. Their followers sometimes carry out violent attacks on members of the minority communities. Their electoral support remains low, however, though their impact is high. The National Front, the best known of such racist groups in the late 20th century, never succeeded in getting an MP elected. More recently the National Front has been overshadowed by the British National Party as the most significant extreme nationalist and anti-immigrant, bordering on racist, party.[64] It too has not achieved any significant electoral success.

Anti-racist organisations (with black and white members) campaign against them, which sometimes leads to violent clashes between the two. Many immigrants believe the police and justice system to be unfair in their dealings with them, and statistics suggest they are right (for example, on average, African-Caribbean men convicted of the same kind of crime as white men are given longer prison sentences by the judge). This kind of unfairness has led in the past to quite large-scale street violence. Following such riots (particularly in the early 1980s) efforts have been made to **address** the problem. It is probably true to say that things are improving, but that much progress still needs to be made.

address *v.*
处理，对付

# Explanations

1. **Periodic national elections are very important in the Western model of democracy:**
   周期性的大选在西方民主制度中非常重要。西方民主制主要指西方国家中定期举行的议会及总统选举制。英国通常每 5 年进行一次大选，在 650 个选区内选出 650 名议员。

2. **In the UK the citizen's right to vote ... over the past two hundred years:**
   英国人民为了争取选举权——选举代表公民自己利益的议员——而进行了 200 多年不断的奋斗。of their choice to represent them in parliament 修饰名词 candidate。

3. **Although Members of Parliament ... the current level of about 99%:**
   英国人民争取选举权的斗争是漫长的。1836 至 1848 年间工人阶级为得到普选权而掀起了宪章运动 (The Chartist Movement)。1832、1867、1884 年的三个法案逐步拓展了选民的范畴。1919 年的法案取消了对男性选民的财产要求，使得 21 岁以上男子普遍获得了选举权，同时也给予了 30 岁及以上的女性选举权（有财产条件要求）。1928 年法案把女性选民的年龄降至 21 岁并取消了财产限制，使女性的选举权

# The United Kingdom of Great Britain and Northern Ireland

与男性完全平等。

4. **those excluded are Lords:**
   按英国的选举制度，Lords（上议院议员，大多是世袭贵族）因在上议院中已有被封的席位，所以不能参加选举。

5. **UK resident citizens of the Irish Republic:**
   侨居英国的爱尔兰共和国公民（有投票权）。英国在历史上与爱尔兰共和国有着千丝万缕的联系，爱尔兰长期是英国的殖民地。经过几个世纪的抗争，爱尔兰南部的 26 个郡于 1922 年获得独立，成为后来的爱尔兰共和国。北部的 6 个郡仍归属英国。

6. **The election is seen as ... to "kick the rascals out":**
   大选被视为是影响未来政府政策的一次良机，或者退一步说，不管政治体制存在着什么样的缺陷，大选至少可以给人们一次"把无赖踢出去"的机会。"无赖"在这里是指选民们讨厌的政客。

7. **the Fixed-term Parliaments Act 2011:**
   2011 年 9 月 15 日英国议会通过了《议会固定任期法》。根据该法案，英国放弃了此前首相在 5 年任期内征得女王同意即可解散议会提前举行大选的宪法惯例，明确规定大选时间为任期第 5 年 5 月的第一个星期四。同时该法案规定，在以下情况下可以提前大选：下院议员三分之二以上多数批准，议会通过对政府的不信任案，或 14 天内本届议会无法组成新政府。

8. **Anyone who is eligible to vote ... receive at least 5% of the vote:**
   任何一个有资格选举的人都可以成为议员候选人。当然，必须先付 500 英镑保证金（押金），并且获得至少 5% 的选票才能收回押金。

9. **They will see it as a wasted vote ... against the big parties' representatives:**
   即使选民们尊重你及你的主张，他们也会把投给你的这张票视作废票。因为你很难在任何一个选区赢得最多选票，或者即使你获胜赢得议员席位，在议会中面对大党的多数议员们，你还是无能为力。意思是在英国，小党或独立候选人没有获胜执政的机会。

10. **A vote for an independent candidate ... will form a government:**
    投票选举独立候选人实际上使选民无法参与大党之间争夺执政权的竞争。意思是说，投给他的这张票完全是浪费。

11. **This involves advertisements in newspapers, ... to the public:**
    竞选运动的方式主要有在报纸上登竞选广告、上门游说（候选人或其支持者挨门挨户敲门，试图劝说选民投他们一票）、邮寄竞选传单，主要政党还可以在电视上进行有严格时间限制的"政党竞选电视演讲"：各大党可有数次公开演讲的机会，但每次只有 10 分钟，在国家电视台向公众"推销"他们的政策。

12. **The time is given free, ... at the previous election:**
    （电视台）提供的时间是免费的，但时间的长短按该党上一次大选中获得的投票率分配。

13. **the national campaign, other than that on TV, is not limited:**
    除了电视演讲以外，各党用于全国竞选运动的资金不受限制。

## UNIT 4  Politics, Class and Race

14. **A lot of money is spent ... to try and guess the election result:**
    媒体花巨资做"民意测验",抽样调查选民会投谁的票,然后根据调查结果试图猜测大选结果。

15. **So they can be quite aggressive and critical:**
    所以他们往往相互指责,火药味很浓。候选人在竞选活动中,不仅要鼓吹自己的政策多么好,还得向公众显示对手的政策有多么糟糕。

16. **Secrecy is an important part ... for whom he or she has voted:**
    保密在投票过程中至关重要,它意味着每个选民都不受任何外界压力而能进行自主投票,因为没有人知道他或她投了谁的票。

17. **Television stations devote long night-programmes ... won by each party:**
    电视台用很长的夜间节目监测整个选举过程,随着选举结果由全国各地汇总而来,随时报道各党所获席位的最新数据。

18. **hung parliament:**
    悬浮议会。当没有一个单一党派在英国下议院占据多数席位时,就属于"悬浮议会",也称为"无多数议会"。出现悬浮议会时,有三种办法组成新政府:首先是由议席最多的政党与一个较小的党派(议席合计超过半数)联合执政,如2010年保守党与自由民主党组成的联合政府。二是由议席最多的政党单独执政,成为少数党政府(最好得到一个或几个其他小政党的支持并确保这些政党在重要法案表决中不反对政府),执政会比较艰辛。例如在2017年6月的大选中,保守党议席未过半,只能依靠北爱尔兰民主统一党允诺在议会投票中对它的支持来维持少数党政府。三是在两大党席位差距不大的情况下也有可能由议席第二多的政党与一个较小的党派联合(议席合计超过半数);2010年工党也曾尝试与自由民主党联合,但自由民主党认为这会有违民意,选择了与保守党合作,尽管其政策思想更接近工党。

19. **First-past-the-post:**
    "简单多数票当选",即每一个选民只能投一票给一个候选人,在这个选区内获得选票最多的候选人当选为本选区的下议院议员(赢得议会一个席位)。又被称为简单多数制、单选区出线制(Simple Majority Voting)。英国大选是选议会议员,投票结束后,计算每个党派的候选人赢下多少选区,席位过半的党获得执政权,其党魁自然出任首相。

20. **The system thus leads to unproportional representation ... unfair to many others:**
    以2015年大选为例可以看出政党获得的选票和得到的议席的百分比是多么不成比例。保守党选票占36.8%,议席却占50.8%(330个);自由民主党以7.9%的选票仅得到1.2%的议席(8个);英国独立党选票多达12.6%(排第三位),仅拿下1个议席(0.2%)。自由民主党和英国独立党选民分散在全英各选区,在选区中又不够强大到夺冠,所以很吃亏。而苏格兰民族党只在59个选区参选,关注的是地区议题,又受益于此前苏格兰独立公投的影响,所以以4.7%的选票获得了8.6%(56个)的议席,创造了历史记录(2010年大选该党仅获得6席)。在这种制度下,投票给自由民主党常常被视为是浪费选票。

21. **A system of proportional representation (PR) ... votes gained nationally:**
    比例代表制是根据全国获得的选票的百分比来分配相应比例的席位。

# The United Kingdom of Great Britain and Northern Ireland

22. **EPTP is defended ... stable executive:**
    为简单多数制辩护的理由是它通常会形成一个有议会过半席位的好运转的政府，从而使得政府（行政）高效、稳定。

23. **The Liberal Democrats ... which of the other two parties does so:**
    自由民主党长期是英国的第三大党，它通常能获得多达约20%的选票，这个数目不够组建政府，但却足以对其他两党谁能执政产生重大影响。自由民主党在2015和2017年两次选举中都失去了第三大党的地位。

24. **the Labour Party:**
    工党，英国议会第二大党。1900年成立，原名劳工代表委员会，1906年改用现名。1997年至2010年连续执政13年。2010年5月大选失利，成为反对党。近年来，工党更多倾向关注中产阶级利益，与工会关系一定程度上有所疏远。主张保持宏观经济稳定增长，建立现代福利制度。外交上主张积极参与国际合作，视与美国和欧盟关系为两大外交支柱，支持欧盟一体化建设，反对英国脱离欧盟。2015年5月大选失败，埃德·米利班德辞去工党领袖职务。9月工党领袖选举结果出炉，激进左翼候选人杰里米·科尔宾以59.5%得票率当选工党新领袖。

25. **Labour is formally a socialist party:**
    工党形式上是个社会主义党。实际上，欧洲的社会主义党很复杂，一般都不是根据马克思、恩格斯关于社会主义理论建立的政党。

26. **part of the role of government ... to the poorer part of society:**
    政府的一部分职责即是充当"再分配"代理人：向富裕阶层收税转而资助贫穷阶层，以达到将富人的一部分财产再分配给穷人的目的。

27. **It started ... "from cradle to grave":**
    工党政府在世界上最早实行全民福利国家，建立了全民医疗制度，为所有国民提供高质量、免费的终生医疗保健。**National Health Service:** 全民医疗制度，指1948年开始实施，主要靠赋税维持的免费医疗制度。**from cradle to grave:** 从摇篮到坟墓；意指从生到死，一生。

28. **it "nationalised" ... and a large state-owned sector:**
    工党将大批工矿企业国有化，使得英国经济成为一个既有私有企业，又有国有企业的混合经济体系。

29. **The Conservative Party:**
    保守党，英国议会第一大党。保守党前身为1679年成立的托利党，1834年改称现名。1979至1997年间曾4次连续执政18年。2010年大选后与自由民主党组成联合政府，领袖戴维·卡梅伦出任首相。2015年5月英国大选后，保守党获议会席位过半，组成保守党政府单独执政。支持者一般来自企业界和富裕阶层。主张自由市场经济，严格控制货币供应量，减少公共开支，压低通货膨胀，限制工会权力，加强"法律"和"秩序"等。近年来，提出"富有同情心的保守主义"，关注教育、医疗、贫困等社会问题。强调维护英国主权，反对"联邦欧洲"，不加入欧元区。2016年6月英国民众在全民公决中以微弱多数选择了英国退出欧盟，卡梅伦因此辞去首相和党的领袖职务，特蕾莎·梅被选为党的领袖并接任首相。

UNIT **4** Politics, Class and Race

30. **But in the past this policy ... to the less fortunate in society:**
    但是在过去几年中,（保守党的）这一经济政策已附加上一种对社会贫困阶层"慈父"般的义务。指保守党也开始关注社会贫困阶层的问题。

31. **Thus the difference between ... not an absolute:**
    所以工党与保守党之间的差别只是程度不同，而不是截然相反。意即两党在政策的实施方面开始越来越相互靠拢。

32. **the Liberal Democrats:**
    自由民主党。20 世纪 70 年代，工党变得更加左倾，工会势力更趋强大。1979 的选举失利导致工党内部于 1980 年分裂，若干温和派的领导人于 1981 成立了社会民主党。后来该党与自由党合并，成为现今的自由民主党。自由民主党 2010 年与保守党组成联合政府，但因其政策主张被保守党压制，被选民认为没有遵守竞选承诺而失信，在 2015 年选举中惨败。

33. **The party originates from ... early 20th century:**
    18、19 世纪，英国政治是托利党（the Tory Party）和辉格党（the Whig Party）两党分别在某时间段长期执政（托利党 1770–1830 年，辉格党 1714–1770 年）。1828 年，辉格党更名为自由党。1834 年，托利党更名为保守党。自由党在 19 世纪后半叶以及 20 世纪前期的多年中长期掌权执政，但无奈因党派内部分裂而被新兴的工党超越（1922 年）。20 世纪保守党和工党两党轮流交替执政，保守党在位时间更长。

34. **Many people see them as ... the individual and the social:**
    许多人认为自由民主党在均衡个人（个体自由）和社会（政府干预）关系方面较为灵活，讲求实际。

35. **the UK Independence Party, the Green Party, and the British National Party:**
    the UK Independence Party: 英国独立党；the Green Party: 绿党；the British National Party: 英国国家党

36. **Mrs. Thatcher was strongly committed ... discouraging entrepreneurship:**
    撒切尔夫人强烈信奉小政府和自由市场经济，对政府的"慈父般"的形象不屑一顾。她认为政府的干预是鼓励懒惰而不是鼓励企业家精神。

37. **Much of the change was ... until today when little remains to be sold:**
    很大一部分变化是取消了 1945 年工党政府所做的工作。因为他们的重大政策之一是使国有化了的工业重新私有化，如英国的航天工业、航空公司、电信局、石油公司、电力、煤气和水公司以及很多其他行业，包括公共住房，都被逐步卖掉了，至今已无财产可卖了。

38. **private affluence and public squalor:**
    少数人富裕起来了，而大部分百姓的生活却贫困化了。

39. **Part of the mechanism of change was a less redistributive taxation system:**
    变化机制中的一部分是削弱再分配性质的税收制度。减税是一种表现形式。导致撒切尔首相下台的地方税种人头税（Poll Tax）也因为不论贫富、人人都缴同样数额而受到民众的抗议。

# The United Kingdom of Great Britain and Northern Ireland

40. **John Major:**
    约翰·梅杰。1990 年 12 月至 1997 年 5 月任英国首相，继续推行撒切尔夫人保守的经济政策，但采取较为温和的方式。

41. **New Labour's "Third Way" philosophy ... associated with "old" Labour:**
    新工党的"第三条道路"哲学显得是介于毫无限制的自由市场资本主义（与撒切尔相关）和集权的国家社会主义（与旧工党相关）之间。

42. **Additionally the Conservatives were seen as ... some against:**
    此外，人们认为保守党内部在对欧洲的政策上意见分歧很大。一些人支持（欧盟进一步的）一体化，一些人则持反对意见。

43. **Blair had to resign ... Gordon Brown:**
    托尼·布莱尔于 2007 年 6 月 27 日正式向英国女王递交辞呈辞去英国首相职务，由工党新领袖财政大臣戈登·布朗接任，入主唐宁街 10 号。英国大选是选出哪个党派执政，党魁自然成为首相。所以布莱尔辞职，工党任期未满，新党魁可以自然接任首相职务。

44. **After the June 2016 referendum ... UK to remain inside the EU:**
    卡梅伦认为英国继续作为欧盟成员国符合英国利益，但鉴于党内疑欧派的压力，保守党推出了 2016 年 6 月的旨在决定英国是否留在欧盟的全国公投。公投结果是民众以微弱多数支持英国退出欧盟，卡梅伦由此辞职，特蕾莎·梅被选为党的领袖并接任首相。

45. **Corbyn's election as leader ... high public spending and nationalisation:**
    科尔宾当选为工党领袖代表着工党基本背弃了之前新工党的理念，不再推崇布莱尔和布朗的温和主义政策，而是重新回归更接近过去的社会主义传统的政策，如高公共开支和国有化。工党在 2017 年 6 月的大选中收获了更多的议席，主要是因为它以激进的思想得到了青年人的支持，如主张更高的公共开支、取消大学学费和把包括铁路和水工业在内的基础公共服务国有化。

46. **In May 2017 ... Brexit negotiations between the UK and the EU:**
    2017 年 5 月，梅在保守党任期还差三年未满的情况下决定提前举行大选，希望借此扩大保守党在议会的议席过半优势，从而使得保守党政府在即将到来的英国与欧盟展开的英国脱欧谈判中能有更高决策效力（减少脱欧谈判进程中来自议会其他党派的阻力）。

47. **The election result ... parliamentary support in key votes:**
    选举结果对特蕾莎·梅来说是非常尴尬的，保守党（出乎意料地）非但没能增加席位，扩大已有的议席过半优势，反而失去了 13 个席位（议席未过半，丢掉了多数党单独执政的机会），导致又一个悬浮议会。梅只能依靠北爱尔兰（右翼的）民主统一党允诺在议会关键投票中对它的支持来组建少数党政府。

48. **But important in the idea of "class" ... is born into:**
    但是"等级"观念的一个重点即在于一个人出生于何种阶层会影响到他一生的机遇。

49. **though it should be stressed that ... his middle-class school-friend:**
    尽管这里应强调指出，工人阶级的孩子不是不可能取得中产阶级地位，但从数据上来看，这种可能性要比他那些出生于中产阶级家庭的同学小得多。

50. **However there is a hazy area ... of such employment:**
    然而，存在一个界定不清的阶层，即非技术性办公室职员和技术性强、收入高的体力劳动者。因而中产阶级又细分为"中下阶级"和"中上阶级"，而"中上阶级"则指医生、律师等拥有相对高收入、高地位职业的那些人，尤其是指家族中有从事此种职业的传统的那些人。

51. ***The Sun*:**
    《太阳报》。属英国通俗报纸或流行小报（"popular paper" or "tabloid"）。此类报纸主要是为娱乐群众，较少严肃的新闻报道。

52. **hard news:**
    时事性强、必须及时报道的新闻。与"soft news"相对，后者指趣味性强但不一定及时报道的新闻。

53. ***The Telegraph, The Times* or *The Guardian*:**
    《每日电讯报》《泰晤士报》或《卫报》。这些都是英国重质量的严肃大报（quality paper）。《卫报》被认为政治观点左倾。

54. **Another factor marking off what might be termed an "upper middle-class" is education:**
    使所谓的"中上阶级"有别于其他人的另一因素是教育。中上阶级有钱送他们的子女进学费昂贵的私立学校，如伊顿公学等，使孩子受到更好的教育，进入一流的大学。

55. **This is important not simply because ... graduates:**
    这一点很重要，不仅是因为这可以提供良好的教育，更因为这可以提供一个关系网——英国社会的许多方面：艺术、媒体、工业和政治领域的上层人物中有很大比例是牛津剑桥毕业生。

56. **That the hereditary aristocracy ... from its neighbours in Europe:**
    世袭贵族还能继承在英国议会上议院的席位及投票权，这种政治权力的承袭是欧洲其他国家贵族所没有的。

57. **Though still influential ... as a separate "class":**
    尽管他们仍有影响力，但却不可能主宰英国社会。甚至那些在英国社会最高层，拥有极大财富和影响力的"权力中坚"（尽管他们并没有像大多数人认为的那样形成一个独立的阶层）也不能主宰英国社会。这里的 power-elite 是指英国中上统治阶级及有权势的社会力量，如企业界巨头等。

58. **working "Lords":**
    这里的 working Lords 是指上院中的积极分子。终身贵族通常积极参与上院政事，而许多世袭贵族一般都不参加例会，只有少数人比较积极。上院在改革后也只允许不到 100 名世袭贵族保留上院议员身份。

59. **Likewise British music has been invigorated by ... record success:**
    同样，英国的音乐界也因新移民的加入而活跃起来。许多英国黑人表演家荣登流行唱片排行榜。

60. **Crossover music between ... in new forms of popular music:**
    亚洲与非洲、加勒比海音乐之间的融合，形成了新的流行音乐形式。

# The United Kingdom of Great Britain and Northern Ireland

61. **Often people used to an ethnically uniform society ... losing their jobs:**
    通常，习惯于单一种族社会的人们会觉得他们的生活方式受到新来者的威胁。尤其当他们确实觉得经济上不稳定，担心失去工作时，会害怕新来者在经济上与自己竞争。

62. **But despite much progress ... oppression remains:**
    但是尽管已有了很大进步，官方也做了极大努力减少种族歧视，公开和隐藏的种族压迫仍然存在。

63. **the 2017 general election produced the most diverse parliament:**
    2017大选选出的下议院议员最具多样性，女性（208名）、男女同性恋者、双性恋者与跨性别者（45名）、少数族裔（52名）以及残疾者人数都比过去有所增加。

64. **More recently the National Front ... bordering on racist, party:**
    最近，国民阵线党的风头已经被英国国家党盖过，后者成为最重要的极端民族主义和反移民（近乎种族主义）的政党。英国国家党是英国极右派政党，1982年从国民阵线党分裂出来。

## Exercises

**I. Give the Chinese equivalents for the following:**

1. Members of Parliament
2. first-past-the-post
3. proportional representation
4. hereditary aristocracy
5. the Conservative Party
6. racial discrimination

**II. Decide whether the following statements are true (T) or false (F):**

1. In British general elections, citizens directly vote for the Prime Minister. _____
2. The election campaign lasts for 3 months. _____
3. The House of Commons decides a "vote of no confidence". _____
4. The 1945–1950 Labour government practised the world's earliest Welfare State, providing social security benefits and free health care to people. _____
5. The key party belief of the UK Independence Party was for Scotland to gain independence from the UK. _____

6. From 1979 to 1997, the New Labour Party won 4 consecutive elections and was in power for quite a long time. _____
7. One of the distinctive features about the British class system is that it has also retained a hereditary aristocracy. _____
8. The majority of Britain's postwar immigrants have mainly come from South Asia and Caribbean countries. _____

### III. Fill in the blanks:

1. In the UK, a general election usually occurs once every _____ years. Britain is divided into about _____ constituencies with each of them represented by a Member _____.
2. The party which wins majority seats in the House of Commons forms _____ and its leader becomes _____.
3. Unproportional representation means the percentage of _____ gained in Parliament does not match the percentage of _____ won by each party.
4. There are two major political parties in the UK: _____ and _____.
5. Mrs Thatcher was committed to the idea of _____ and a key practice of her Conservative government in the 1980s was _____.
6. Jeremy Corbyn as party leader is very _____-wing, believing in such policies as _____ and _____.
7. _____ was elected as party leader and became UK Prime Minister in 2016.
8. People who do unskilled office work and skilled well-paid manual work are likely to be described as _____ class.
9. A university teacher would probably read newspapers like _____ while a manual worker would probably read _____.
10. Great contributions have been made by immigrants in _____ and _____.

### IV. Questions:

1. Who can vote and who cannot vote in British general election? When were women allowed to vote?
2. How are British Members of Parliament elected?
3. What is the first-past-the-post election system?
4. Why are small parties and independent candidates powerless in general elections for the formation of a government? What is a wasted vote?

# The United Kingdom of Great Britain and Northern Ireland

5. Can a big/rich party buy TV time to broadcast their policies in an election campaign?
6. What are the major political parties in the UK today? Which is currently in power, and which is in opposition?
7. What are the major beliefs of the Conservative Party and the Labour Party?
8. What were Mrs Thatcher's policies to deal with the economic problems of the 1980s and what were their effects?
9. Why did the Labour Party win the 1997 election?
10. Why did Theresa May call a general election in 2017 three years earlier than required? What was the election result?
11. How are people in the UK divided into different classes? In what way is the British class system similar to or different from that of the United States and Europe?
12. What are the characteristics of the hereditary aristocracy in the UK?
13. What are some of the positive and negative effects of non-white immigrants in British society according to the author?
14. What is the general situation of racial relations in the UK today?

## V. Topics for discussion or research:

1. What are the advantages and disadvantages of first-past-the-post and proportional representation?
2. What are the postwar political trends in the UK? Are these trends more democratic or less democratic?
3. In what way is the British general election different from the American system?
4. What are some of the characteristics of Britain as a multi-racial and multi-cultural society?

# UNIT 5

# The UK Economy

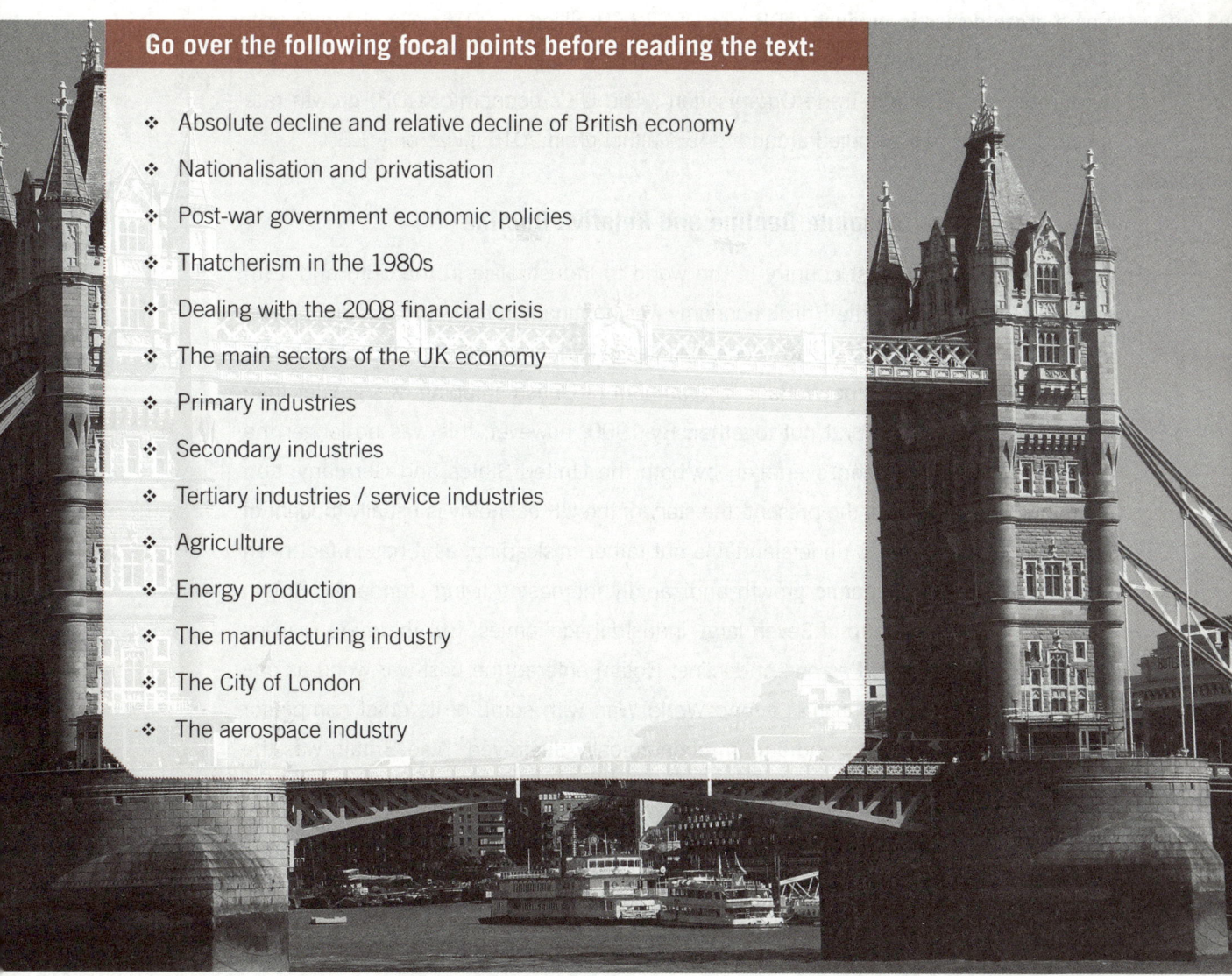

**Go over the following focal points before reading the text:**

- Absolute decline and relative decline of British economy
- Nationalisation and privatisation
- Post-war government economic policies
- Thatcherism in the 1980s
- Dealing with the 2008 financial crisis
- The main sectors of the UK economy
- Primary industries
- Secondary industries
- Tertiary industries / service industries
- Agriculture
- Energy production
- The manufacturing industry
- The City of London
- The aerospace industry

# The United Kingdom of Great Britain and Northern Ireland

 Text

The United Kingdom of Great Britain and Northern Ireland is a major developed capitalist country. It is now the world's 5th largest national economy (both in 2015 and 2016, measured by GDP, behind the United States, China, Japan and Germany) and has a **gross domestic product** (GDP) of US$2 629 billion in 2016 (4% of the world). The UK is not only a member of the G7, G8 and G20 major economic blocks[1], but also a member of the World Trade Organisation[2]. The UK's economic (GDP) growth rate since the 1950s has averaged around 2.45% although in 2016 it was only 1.8%.

## Absolute Decline and Relative Decline[3]

The UK was the first country in the world to industrialise in the 18th and 19th centuries. By the 1880s the British economy was dominant in the world, producing one third of the world's manufactured goods, half its coal and iron, half its cotton (it became known as "Workshop of the World"). The amount of British shipping was greater than that in the rest of the world put together. By 1900, however, this was no longer the case, the UK having been overtaken by both the United States and Germany; and certainly from 1945 until the present, the story of the UK economy is usually thought of as one of decline. This is understandable but rather misleading, as it has in fact been a period of steady economic growth and rapidly increasing living standards. Britain remains one of the Group of Seven large industrial economies. But there are reasons for describing this period as one of decline. Britain entered the post-war world as one of the successful **allies** of the Second World War, with some of its chief competitor nations such as Germany and Japan, economically destroyed. Also Britain was the centre of a still vast empire. **Statistically**, the UK was second only to the United States in the international economy. Thus Britain was then in an apparently strong economic position, a position it clearly no longer occupies, which indicates some sort of decline.[4]

But the basic positive-seeming facts describing the size of the economy, the high proportion of world trade that was British, and so on, in 1945, did not reveal important negative facts about the UK's position even then.[5] Firstly, the country had gone heavily

---

gross domestic product
国内生产总值
ally *n.*
同盟国，同盟者
statistically *adv.*
统计上地，统计学地

into debt in order to finance the war, selling many of its **accumulated** overseas **assets**[6], and borrowing large amounts from the United States and Canada. These debts meant that the UK entered the post-war era with a major economic problem.

Secondly, the era of empire was over. India, popularly known as "the Jewel in the Crown" of the British Empire, gained its independence in 1947, only two years after the end of the war. This was the largest element in the empire, providing raw materials and a big market for British goods. This relationship with India was no longer available, and the rest of the empire quickly followed India in gaining independence, leaving Britain as just a medium-sized European country, with a population only one fifth the size of the US.

Thirdly, despite the relatively rapid and trouble-free process of **decolonisation**, Britain was still forced to maintain a substantial and expensive military presence in many overseas locations until the process was completed (mostly by the end of the 1960s).[7] Also its position as one of the **shapers** of the post-war world required substantial military contributions — both as one of NATO's[8] six major partners, and as a member of **the UN Security Council**. All this had the result that Britain spent a higher proportion of its national wealth (and especially of its research and development **budget**) on the military than most of its competitors. Military expenditure tends not to **generate** an economic **return** in quite the same way as other industrial investment.[9]

Fourthly, although Britain was quite badly damaged by German bombing during the war, its industry survived comparatively unaffected. This contrasted greatly with some of its competitors — especially the main losers in the conflict, Germany and Japan, which had, more or less, to start again from nothing. This apparent disadvantage for them may **ultimately** have worked in their favour in that as they had to invest, they could invest in the most modern equipment and new products.[10] British industry, however, could continue with its older factories and pre-war products, and given its other economic problems, did so — a problem in the long-term.[11] So while Britain looked securely wealthier than them in 1945, a catching-up with the UK was inevitable as they recovered.

This failure to invest sufficiently in industry also reflects a long-standing and continuing problem in the UK economy. Even without the particular circumstances of the post-war world, relatively low rates of investment (the amount of money businesses put aside from profits to reinvest in the business in new products and production methods) were characteristic of the British economy **in relation to** other developed

---

accumulate *v.*
积累，累计
asset *n.*
（常用复数）资产
decolonisation *n.* 非殖民（地）化，去殖民（地）化
shaper *n.*
塑造者
the UN Security Council
联合国安理会
budget *n.*
预算，预算拨款
generate *v.*
产生；导致，造成
return *n.*
（常作复数）收益，赢利
ultimately *adv.*
最后，最终；终于
in relation to
与…相比

# The United Kingdom of Great Britain and Northern Ireland

economies.¹² Economists have pointed to the lack of a close relationship between industry and banks in the UK — again a contrast, particularly with the two most successful post-war economies, Japan and Germany, where banks and industrial firms have very close links. Economic historians have suggested that this may be due to the fact that the UK was the first economy to industrialise, and industrial firms, without foreign competition, grew used to financing their own development, without the need to borrow from banks.¹³ Banks therefore, not able to find good investment opportunities in the UK, looked overseas for investment opportunities. A low rate of domestic industrial investment coupled with a very high rate of overseas investment is still a characteristic of the UK economy. So, amongst European nations, Britain is the largest investor in China, but sells fewer of its own manufactured goods here than do Germany or France.

The point to note is that the comparatively strong economic position Britain found itself in 1945 was in many ways deceptive. So the decline from Britain's apparently good fortunes at that point until now is thus not as extraordinary as it might seem, being the result of already existing basic problems.¹⁴ And it should also be remembered that this was not an absolute decline: Britain is not poorer, or producing less than it was in 1945 and that in fact (like most countries) it is a lot wealthier and more productive than it was then. The problem is that though it has improved, other countries have improved more rapidly, hence the **slide** from being the 2nd largest economy (after the United States) to being the 6th or 5th, as it is at present. And even many smaller economies have overtaken the UK in terms of output per head of population.¹⁵ Britain's GDP per capita decreased from the 7th highest in the world in 1950 to the 21st in 1981 and 19th in 2016. So the UK has experienced economic decline, but this decline is relative to some other economies rather than absolute. Nevertheless, this relative failure is a serious cause of concern to the UK governments.

## Recent History

In 1945, the first majority Labour government brought a range of basic industries into public ownership through a process of nationalisation in order to promote full employment and better services in the public interest. The Bank of England was nationalised in 1946, alongside **civil aviation**, the coal industry and the railways in 1947, electricity in 1948, gas in 1949, iron and steel in 1951 and the post office in 1969. The Conservative governments in the 1950s and 1960s broadly accepted the

slide *n.*
滑落，下落
civil aviation
民用航空业

new **status quo** and made only minor changes.[16] The British economy in these two decades enjoyed smooth and rapid development although the growth rates were lower than the rates of other European countries such as France and West Germany.

The British economy went through a particularly bad period in the 1970s. The oil price rises (caused primarily by the world oil crisis of 1973/4) at that time led to very high rates of **inflation** (up to 25%) in the mid-1970s. This caused many workers to strike for more pay. The fall in the value of the UK currency (the pound) even forced the Labour (socialist) government to borrow from the International Monetary Fund.[17] British industry, notably the car industry, appeared to be doing badly, with increasing imports relative to exports. All these negative economic facts led to a change of government at the general election in 1979, when the British people voted in the Conservative Party under Margaret Thatcher,[18] with the promise of a **radical** programme of reform.

Mrs Thatcher's economic policies of neo-liberalism (termed as Thatcherism) were marked by **monetarism** (to beat inflation) and **privatisation** (to promote efficiency).[19] **Bureaucracy** was reduced (e.g. foreign exchange controls were lifted[20] and rules governing banks loosened). Tight **fiscal** and monetary policies were practised to control the money supply. Taxes were reduced and public spending (e.g. on welfare) was cut. And throughout the 1980s an extensive programme of privatisation (or denationalisation) was carried out, with many state-owned businesses being sold back to the private sector with the aim of improving their competitiveness, for example, British **Petroleum** (1979), British **Aerospace** (1981), British **Telecom** (1984), British Steel (1988), British Gas (1986), British Airways (1987), as well as the water (1989) and electricity (1990) companies. Many council houses were sold to their **tenants**. The reform seemed in some ways to be successful in that inflation came under control, and many businesses, especially the newly privatised ones, made profits. With the decline of the coal and manufacturing industries, the new industries and the service sector enjoyed significant growth. The national economy as a whole grew at relatively high rates (better than many EU countries). The negative aspect was a rapid increase in unemployment, rising to almost 12% at its highest — the highest since the 1930s. So while companies were more efficient, producing the same amount with fewer workers, and therefore being able to pay higher wages and make higher profits, the cost was paid by the unemployed who had to live on low incomes from state support.[21] The gap between the rich and the poor was widened. Trade unions were greatly weakened and

---

status quo
现状
inflation *n.*
通货膨胀，物价飞涨
radical *adj.*
激进的；彻底的，根本的
monetarism *n.*
货币主义
privatisation *n.*
私有化，私人化
bureaucracy *n.*
官僚政治；（总称）政府官员，官僚；官僚主义
fiscal *adj.*
财政上的
petroleum *n.*
石油
aerospace *n.*
航空航天工业（或技术）
telecom =
telecommunication
电信
tenant *n.*
租户；承租人

# The United Kingdom of Great Britain and Northern Ireland

the role of market was strengthened.

Under Prime Minister John Major (1990–1997), Britain experienced **recession** between 1990 and 1992 and the economy **shrank** by 2.3%. But after that, the picture was brighter, with four years of steady growth, at rates higher than those in the rest of the European Union (EU). Unemployment fell to 7.7%, which was among the lowest in the EU. Inflation remained under control at very low levels. Privatisation continued with British Coal (1994) and British Rail (1994). Investment increased, encouraged by low **interest rates**. Britain's membership of the EU also made it an attractive location for inward investment by companies from outside the EU (especially from the US and Japan), from which it received a larger share than any other EU country.[22] Overall it was second only to the US as a **destination** for international direct investment.[23] It was also itself a major source of international investment — in fact it was the 2nd biggest international investor in the world in 1995.

When New Labour was in office, led by Prime Ministers Tony Blair (1997–2007) and Gordon Brown (2007–2010), it basically accepted the central reform measures of the Thatcher government. Helped by New Labour's pro-market policies instead of the more socialist ones of the past, the UK enjoyed an annual growth rate of 2.4% during Blair's term, compared with 2.1% on average during the previous half century. In 1998, the Bank of England was granted independence in setting monetary policy.[24] The government also kept taxes relatively low and abandoned traditional Labour policies, such as high public spending financed by large budget deficits and public ownership. It also introduced the National Minimum Wage and tax credits[25] for the low paid, which reduced poverty. New Labour also deserved credit for greater investment in UK **infrastructure**. Crossrail[26] and the successful Olympic bid owed much to Blair.

The UK went into a recession in the second quarter of 2008, brought about by the world financial crisis. The country was hit harder by the crisis because of the large size of its financial sector in proportion to its national income. For the first time the UK GDP **contracted** for six **consecutive** quarters. This was the longest and deepest recession since WWII. Some banks which were on the verge of collapse were taken into public ownership or partly nationalised. In March 2009, the Bank of England cut interest rates to a historical low of 0.5% (from 5% in October 2008) and began quantitative easing to boost lending as well as **reflate** the economy.[27] Yet, faced with the large budget deficit caused by the recession, the coalition government (comprising the Conservative

---

recession *n.* （经济的）衰退，衰退期
shrink *v.* 收缩；缩水
interest rates 利率
destination *n.* 目标；目的地，终点
infrastructure *n.* 基础设施；基础建设
contract *v.* 缩小
consecutive *adj.* 连续的
reflate *v.* 使通货再膨胀

Party alongside the Liberal Democrats) under the leadership of Prime Minister David Cameron (2010–2015) delivered an **austerity** package involving budget control and sharp cuts in public expenditure. Government cuts led to public sector job losses although the private sector enjoyed rising employment and efficiency. Recovery started in 2013 and by the end of 2014, UK growth had become the fastest in the G7 and in Europe.

In June 2016, Britain held a referendum on whether it should withdraw from the EU. Following the Brexit decision, the pound fell to a 31-year low against the US dollar, remaining around 15% lower against the dollar and 10% down against the euro. The Bank of England cut its interest rate from 0.5% to a new historic low of 0.25%, concerned about the potential negative effects of Brexit on the economy. Prices went up as a result of increases in import prices resulting from the fall in the pound exchange rate. In the long term there is a fear that Britain's withdrawal from the EU might force some banks and big businesses to relocate out of the UK.

## The Current UK Economy

National economies can be broken down into three main areas: "primary" industries, such as agriculture, fishing, and mining; "secondary" industries, to include manufacturing and construction; and **tertiary** industries, often described as services, such as banking, insurance, tourism, and retailing.[28]

Britain's agricultural sector is small (producing less than 2% of GDP) but efficient, producing about 60% of the UK's food needs with less than 1.6% of its workforce. Three quarters of Britain's land is used for agriculture, with about a quarter of that under crops — wheat and **barley** are the two commonest. The rest is grazing land for animals, including **cattle** (both **dairy** and **beef**), though sheep are the most numerous livestock. The beef industry was hit badly by the BSE disease[29] in cattle leading to a 1996 ban on beef exports, although it has recovered since. The best agricultural land is in the southeast of England.

The fishing industry provides less than two thirds of the UK demand for fish. Scottish ports land the majority of the fish caught.[30]

Energy production is an important part of the UK economy, accounting for 2.3% of GDP in 2016. Britain has large deposits of coal, mined for more than 300 years. However, today, coal can be produced more cheaply in other countries, and so almost

austerity *n.*
（财政）紧缩
tertiary *adj.*
第三的，第三产业的
barley *n.* 大麦
dairy (beef)
cattle 乳（菜）牛

# The United Kingdom of Great Britain and Northern Ireland

all coal mines in Britain have closed. During the 1960s, oil and gas were discovered under the North Sea. With the extraction of North Sea oil and gas that started in the 1970s until the 2000s the UK was self-sufficient in energy, and the UK became a net-exporter of oil and gas. Yet due to the decline in North Sea production, and the costs of mining and using coal cleanly, the UK returned to being an energy importer in 2004. It has become a net importer of oil (though still an exporter of oil products) and gas since 2005. In 2016, 36% of energy used in the UK was imported. The technology required to **extract** oil from the difficult **offshore** conditions has given UK companies a strong position in the offshore oil industry around the world. The energy companies — Shell (half Dutch), British Petroleum (BP), and British Gas[31] — remain three of the biggest companies in Britain[32]. The famous UK mining company RTZ[33] operates mines all over the world.

Nuclear energy and other **renewables**, such as wind power, have risen in importance. In 2016, nuclear energy supplied 19% of the UK's electricity[34] and the percentage is planned to grow sharply in future years. From the mid-1990s new renewable energy sources began to play an increasingly important part in the electricity generated. Wind power is its fastest growing supply and the UK became the world's 6th largest producer of wind power in 2017.

In the secondary sector of the economy, manufacturing industry remains important, though not as before. British companies are active in all major fields of manufacturing industry, but are particularly strong in **pharmaceuticals**[35] (the 10th largest in the world; GlaxoSmithKline and AstraZeneca being respectively the world's 6th and 8th largest drug companies in 2015), chemicals (ICI[36] was once the 2nd largest paint manufacturer in the world), aerospace (2nd largest in the world) and food and drink (Scotch whisky being a major export). The chemical and pharmaceutical industry is Britain's largest export earner. Britain also has a big electronics industry (the world's 5th largest in terms of production), but like the car industry (which includes Ford, GM, Peugeot, Nissan and Toyota[37]) this is in most cases foreign-owned. Britain's last major independent car company, Rover, was bought by the German company BMW in 1998, but was subsequently sold to the Chinese multinational Nanjing Automobile Group in 2005. A high-technology engineering industry has developed around the motor-racing business, with many of the world's racing cars, both for Formula One, and the American IndyCar Series being designed and built in Britain.[38] McLaren and Williams

extract *v.* 开采
offshore *adj.*
近海的，近岸的
renewables *n.*
再生性能源
pharmaceutical
*n.* 药物

are two of the most successful of these companies. The British Steel Plc (privatised in 1988) is the world's 3rd largest steel producer and one of the top ten exporters in the UK, but was bought up by the Indian multinational Tata Group in 2007. The UK is also the world's 2nd biggest defence exporter behind the US, with BAE Systems being the country's largest defence company.

    The UK manufacturing industry as a whole has experienced declining employment and productivity. Total employment fell from 7.1 million in 1979 to 2.7 million in 2016. In the 1970s, manufacturing accounted for 25% of the economy. In 2016, it accounted for only 10%. The steel industry, which employed about 350 000 people when it was nationalised in 1967, now has only about 30 000 in 2016. A major challenge comes from emerging economies which are able to produce goods more cheaply than the UK. The global economic slowdown and rising energy and materials costs have also affected manufacturers. However, it is believed that modern British manufacturing can thrive by playing to its strengths of design, technology, creativity, innovation and service. Since the 21st century, British manufacturing has become increasingly hi-tech. Globalisation also offers new opportunities with the discovery of new markets.

    In contrast to the decline of the manufacturing industry, the service sector's share of the economy has risen from 46% in 1948 to around 80% of GDP in the mid-2010s. The biggest segments within services are: government, education and health (19% of GDP); property (12%); professional, scientific and technical activities and administrative and support services (12%); wholesale and **retail** trade (11%); finance and insurance (8%); tourism; etc. The Internet is now the UK's 2nd biggest economic contributor behind the property sector, having overtaken manufacturing and retail, accounting for about 12% of the GDP in 2016, which is a bigger share than in any other G20 country. The World Wide Web, an Internet-based hypermedia initiative for global information sharing, was invented by a Londoner/scientist Tim Berners-Lee (Father of the Internet)[39] in 1989. In 2014, the UK ranked the 8th major tourist destination in the world and London is the 2nd most visited city in the world just behind Hong Kong. Britain is also home to the world's largest advertising company, Wire & Plastic Products Group[40]. The country is a major international provider of services.

    The financial sector is an important part of the service industry, as London is now the world's largest financial centre (followed by New York, Singapore, Hong Kong and Tokyo). By 2009, it accounted for 10% of the UK GDP, the highest of all G7 economies.

retail *n.*
零售，零卖

# The United Kingdom of Great Britain and Northern Ireland

London has the greatest concentration of foreign banks in the world and is the world's largest foreign exchange market. As well as banking, dealing in commodities and insurance are important processes in "The City"[41] — the name given to the historic area at the centre of London where all this business is concentrated, at the heart of which is the London Stock Exchange, one of the busiest **share-dealing** centres in the world.[42] Besides, the City is the home of the Bank of England — the central bank of the UK, Lloyds of London — a famous insurance company and the London Metal Exchange which deals with industrial metals. The UK currency pound sterling is the world's 3rd largest reserve currency after US dollar and the euro and is also one of the ten most-valued currencies in the world.[43]

Britain is famous for its free trade tradition and ideology. It is a leading global trading nation, as the 2nd largest exporter and 5th largest importer of commercial services, and the 10th largest exporter and 5th largest importer of merchandise (2016). In the mid-2010s, trade accounted for 29% of the country's GDP. Its trade in goods is in deficit while the trade in services is in surplus.[44] The EU is the biggest supplier and market for the UK (hence there is considerable concern over the potential negative consequences of the Brexit decision). In 2016 it bought 44% of British exports and provided 53% of the country's imports. At the country level, the US and Germany are the largest destination for UK exports and Germany, China and the US are the top import origins for the UK. The UK has the biggest share of financial services exports in the world. In 2016, it had the 2nd largest inward foreign direct investment and the 3rd largest outward foreign direct investment.

### Case Study: The Aerospace Industry[45]

Aerospace is one of the UK's highest value adding manufacturing sectors. After the US, the UK's aerospace industry is the 2nd in the world, with a global market share of 17% in 2015. It is capable of producing the full range of aerospace products from civil and military aircraft (including helicopters) to missiles, satellites, and jet engines.[46]

The first powered flight in the world was made by the Wright Brothers[47] in the US in 1903. It was in 1908 when the first such flight was made in the UK. But only a few years later came the First World War which forced the rapid development of the aviation industry, and by 1918 the British industry was the biggest and most **sophisticated** in the world, producing 1 250 aircraft each month.

---

share-dealing
股票交易
case study
案例研究
sophisticated
*adj.* 先进的

# UNIT 5 The UK Economy

After the war the new aircraft types provided the base for the development of the civil aviation industry. A **converted** First World War **bomber** crossed the Atlantic Ocean in 1919,[48] and a civil **airline**, Imperial Airways, was started in 1924. International air races provided an **incentive** for technological development, and a British plane, the Supermarine S6B, powered by a Rolls Royce engine, broke many speed records.[49] Rolls Royce became the most successful aero-engine manufacturer at this time. The aircraft-building industry was reduced to a few major companies by a series of **mergers**.

One of the most significant developments of the inter-war period was the development of **radar** by the UK's Marconi Company in 1922. And when Englishman Frank Whittle[50] developed the world's first practical jet engine in 1937, the foundations had been laid for the three major branches of the aviation industry: aircraft, engines and aviation electronics, with British companies prominent in each field.[51]

Sadly, in 1939 war came again to provide another **spurt** of technological change, with many successful British aircraft designs in action, such as the Spitfire **fighter** and Lancaster bomber, and culminating in the jet-powered Meteor.[52] The Rolls Royce Merlin engine became the best-selling aero-engine of all time with 166 000 produced. The wartime government, seeing the importance that the aircraft industry had gained (it employed 1.8 million workers by the end of the war), planned a range of civil aviation types to take over from wartime production. These included the world's first jet-powered civil airliner, the **Comet**.

However, the years following the Second World War were problematic for the UK industry. It continued to produce the full-range of products, even selling some of its aircraft to the United States. But in most markets British companies were in **head on** competition with American companies such as Boeing and McDonnel-Douglas, which were larger, having the advantage of being **preferential** suppliers to the enormous US market, both civil and military.[53] The British industry merged into two main aircraft groups: the British Aircraft Corporation, and Hawker-Siddeley Aviation, with Rolls-Royce as the main engine builder, and Westland in helicopters. Nevertheless British civil airliners of the 1960s such as the **Trident** and the VC10 sold much less well than their American equivalents. Nor did British military aircraft sell very well overseas, with the exception of the unique Vertical Take-off and Landing Harrier, bought by the US Marines alongside many other customers.[54]

The answer to the problem lay in **collaborative** projects with other European

---

convert *v.*
改建，改装
bomber *n.*
轰炸机
airline *n.*
航空公司
（airliner 则指客机，班机）
incentive *n.*
刺激，鼓励
merger *n.*
（公司、企业等的）兼并
radar *n.* 雷达
spurt *n.*
（活动等的）突发性开展；急剧上升
fighter *n.*
战斗机，歼击机
Comet *n.* 彗星
head on
迎面的，正面的
preferential *adj.*
优先的，优惠的
Trident *n.*
三叉戟（飞机或导弹等）
collaborative *adj.* 合作的，协力完成的

# The United Kingdom of Great Britain and Northern Ireland

aircraft manufacturers which faced the same problems. The first of these was between Britain and France to produce the world's first **supersonic** civil airliner, Concorde.[55] The aircraft was a technical success but a commercial failure, only 16 being built for British Airways and Air France. However the successful collaboration led to more such programmes between Britain and France, including the Jaguar combat aircraft, and three types of helicopter, including the Lynx, which holds the world speed record for helicopters.[56]

Many other collaborative programmes between Britain and other European countries developed, including the **Tornado** combat aircraft — a project between Britain, Germany, and Italy. The European Fighter Aircraft was another such **venture**. Westland developed helicopter in association with an Italian company.

But the most successful programme has been in civil airliners where the **Airbus** series of aircraft has effectively competed with American companies. This is an ongoing programme between France, Germany, Britain and Spain. British companies build the wings. British Aerospace also build their own range of regional jets, including the successful 146 (popular with Chinese airlines) famous for being the quietest jet airliner.

The industry has been through some major changes of ownership in the last 40 years. Rolls-Royce, in attempting to build a revolutionary new engine for the American company, Lockheed[57], went bankrupt, and had to be **rescued** by the government in 1971. BAC and Hawker Siddeley were also nationalised — as one company, British Aerospace, in 1977 by the Labour government. But both Rolls-Royce and British Aerospace were privatised in the 1980s by the Conservatives and have since been very successful both in individual projects and in international joint-ventures. The third main arm of the industry is GEC **Avionics** (renamed BAE Systems Avionics in 1999 and Selex ES in 2013), producing a wide range of electronic systems including the technologically advanced **cockpit** of the Boeing 777 airliner[58]. Smaller companies produce a wide range of equipment from **ejection seats** to **landing gears**.

The Aerospace Industry is now profitable, with a turnover of over £31 billion in 2016 (of which 90% came from exports), ranking Britain the 2nd in the world. The aerospace enjoyed 39% growth in the 5 years (2011–2015), outpacing the wider manufacturing industry. With 634 companies in 2013 (250 more than in 2008), it accounted for 0.9% of UK economic output. It employed 120 000 people in direct aerospace sector jobs and 118 000 in indirect jobs in 2016. It has been through difficult times, particularly in

---

supersonic *adj.*
超音速的，超声速的
tornado *n.*
龙卷风
venture *n.*
风险事业
Airbus
空中客车
rescue *v.*
营救，救援
avionics *n.*
航空电子技术
cockpit *n.*
（飞行员）座舱
ejection seat
（飞机的）弹射座椅
landing gear
（飞机）起落架

the 1970s, moving in and out of public ownership. But it has found success in links with Europe — a pattern it shares with the rest of the UK economy.

## Explanations

1. **G7, G8 and G20 major economic blocks:**
   七国集团（七国集团首脑会议，Group 7 Summit）、八国集团和 20 国集团主要经济体。

2. **the World Trade Organisation:**
   世界贸易组织，简称 WTO，成立于 1995 年 1 月 1 日，总部设在日内瓦。

3. **absolute decline and relative decline:**
   绝对衰退和相对衰退。作者认为英国经济一直在持续发展中，但因其他国家发展速度较之英国更快，所以英国在世界经济中的地位相对衰退。

4. **Thus Britain was then ... which indicates some sort of decline:**
   因此，当时英国明显占据的经济强国地位在今天看来已成为过去，这在某种意义上意味着英国在走下坡路。

5. **But the basic positive-seeming facts ... the UK's position even then:**
   那些描述 1945 年英国经济规模以及英国在世界贸易中占有高份额的看似正面的数据，掩盖了当时英国已处于极为不利地位的负面事实。

6. **accumulated overseas assets:**
   长期积累的海外资产。英国在历史上有很多海外殖民地，故有此说。

7. **Thirdly, ... the process was completed (mostly by the end of the 1960s):**
   第三，尽管非殖民化的过程相对而言迅速、平静，英国还是被迫在此过程结束之前（大多是到了 20 世纪 60 年代末）在许多海外殖民地区驻扎大量军队，军费开支巨大。

8. **NATO:**
   其全称是 "North Atlantic Treaty Organisation"，北大西洋公约组织（简称北约），建立于 1949 年。

9. **Military expenditure ... other industrial investment:**
   军费开支往往不会像其他工业投资那样产生经济收益。

10. **This apparent disadvantage ... the most modern equipment and new products:**
    这看似不利的条件却可能反而最终对他们有利。正因为他们不得不投资，所以他们可以投资于最现代化的设备和新产品。

11. **British industry, however ... a problem in the long-term:**
    而英国工业能够靠旧工厂和战前的产品生存下去，再加上其他经济问题，也确实这样做了，所以造成了一个长期的问题。did so 即等于 did continue with its older factories and pre-war products。

12. **Even without the particular circumstances ... other developed economies:**
即使没有战后这些特殊情况，英国经济与其他发达国家相比，投资率（即企业从利润中抽取再投资于新产品和新生产方式的那部分钱）还是相对较低。

13. **Economic historians have suggested that ... to borrow from banks:**
经济历史学家认为，这也许是因为英国是首先实现工业化的国家，企业在没有外来竞争的情况下已习惯于自己为自身的发展融资，而不需要从银行贷款。

14. **So the decline from Britain's apparently good fortunes ... basic problems:**
所以，英国从当时的表面繁荣到现在的衰退，就显得比较正常了，因为这是那些早已存在的基本问题造成的。

15. **And even many smaller economies ... output per head of population:**
甚至许多小国经济在人均国民生产总值上也超过了英国。per head of population = per capita。

16. **The Conservative governments ... made only minor changes:**
保守党在20世纪五六十年代基本接受了工党的国有化事实，仅做了微小的调整。钢铁工业是受到公有化和私有化两种经济政策交替影响的典型代表。它1949年被工党政府收归国有，1953年被保守党政府私有化，1967年又被工党政府国有化，撒切尔政府期间再次被私有化。

17. **The fall in the value of the UK currency ... the International Monetary Fund:**
英国货币（英镑）的贬值甚至迫使工党政府向国际货币基金组织借贷。The International Monetary Fund: 国际货币基金组织。1945年成立，是联合国管理和协调国际金融业务的专门机构，总部设在华盛顿。

18. **Margaret Thatcher:**
玛格丽特·撒切尔，英国历史上第一任女首相（1979–1990），保守党领袖（1975–1990）。

19. **Mrs. Thatcher's economic policies ... privatisation (to promote efficiency):**
撒切尔夫人的新自由主义经济政策（被冠名为撒切尔主义）的特色是货币主义（旨在击退通货膨胀）和私有化（为提高效率）。货币主义政策重视有效地控制货币供给量。

20. **foreign exchange controls were lifted:**
外汇管制被取消。

21. **So while companies were more efficient ... to live on low incomes from state support:**
公司的效益增加是因为减少了工人而不减产量，所以能提高工资并获得更高利润。这是以那些只能靠国家救济的低收入的失业工人为代价的。

22. **Britain's membership of the EU ... a larger share than any other EU country:**
英国的欧盟成员国身份也使其能吸引欧盟之外的外国公司的投资（尤其是美国和日本），它所获得的外资份额大过其他欧盟国家。

23. **Overall it was ... international direct investment:**
总体而言，英国是接受国际直接投资的第二大国，仅次于美国。direct investment: 直接投资，是国际投资的一种方式，其特点是投资者通过输出生产资本直接在外国开办企业，或收购当地企业，或与当地合办企业，取得各种直接经营企业的权利。

24. **In 1998, the Bank of England was granted independence in setting monetary policy:**
英格兰银行，1694 年成立。1946 年被国有化，成为英国的中央银行，是世界上第一家中央银行。1998 年英格兰银行不再是国有制，获得独立地位，可以不受政府操纵独立制定英国的货币政策，如决定利率。

25. **the National Minimum Wage and tax credits:**
国家最低工资标准和税收抵免。

26. **Crossrail:**
是目前英国以及欧洲最大的铁路建设工程，预算 150 多亿英镑，2009 年开工建设，预计 2020 年 12 月竣工，有的线段 2021 年初竣工。全程长 118 公里，连接伦敦东部和中西部以及希思罗机场，将并入伦敦现有铁路网（包括伦敦地铁，被命名为伊丽莎白线），使首都的公共交通系统得到很大改善。工程主要特色是穿过伦敦市中心地底长达 21 公里的新建双连拱隧道。

27. **The Bank of England cut interest rates ... to boost lending as well as reflate the economy:**
英格兰银行将利率降至历史低点 0.5%（从 2008 年 10 月的 5%），并开始量化宽松以促进借贷和经济复苏。

28. **National economies can be broken down ... and retailing:**
国民经济可以分为三大领域：第一产业，即农业、渔业和矿业；第二产业，如制造业和建筑业；第三产业，即人们常说的服务行业，如银行业、保险业、旅游业和零售业。tertiary industry: 第三产业，也称"服务业"。

29. **BSE disease:**
"疯牛病"，始发于牛的一种传染性大脑疾病。BSE 全称为 Bovine Spongiform Encephalopathy, 俗称"mad cow" disease。1993 年发病高峰期间，英国每周约有 1 000 个疯牛病例发生。

30. **Scottish ports land the majority of the fish caught:**
捕获的鱼大多在苏格兰港口卸货。

31. **Shell (half Dutch), British Petroleum (BP), and British Gas:**
壳牌公司（英国和荷兰合资）、英国石油公司、英国天然气公司是英国三大能源公司。

32. **the biggest companies in Britain:**
英国最大的公司排名年年有变，成绩突出。2016 年英国排名前 10 位的公司是：1. 汇丰银行（HSBC）——全球第四大银行（论资产）；2. 英国石油公司（British Petroleum）——全球第七大石油和天然气公司；3. 英国保诚集团（Prudential Plc）——跨国人寿保险公司；4. 渣打银行（Standard Chartered Plc）；5. 沃达丰（Vodafone）——世界第二大移动电话公司，仅次于中国移动；6. 乐购（Tesco）——食品杂货零售商，全球三大零售企业之一；7. 葛兰素史克（GlaxoSmithKline Plc）——世界第六大制药公司；8. 国家电网公司（National Grid Plc）；9. 阿斯利康（AstraZeneca Plc）——生物制剂和制药公司；10. 英美烟草公司（British American Tobacco）——总部设在伦敦，行业排名全球第五。

33. **RTZ:**
力拓锌业公司是 1962 年由力拓公司（the Rio Tinto Company）和联合锌业公司（the Consolidated Zinc Corporation）合并而来。英国在国际采矿工业中，以其三家采矿公司的活动而具有重要的位置——

# The United Kingdom of Great Britain and Northern Ireland

力拓锌业公司（RTZ）、联合金矿公司（CGF）和英国石油公司（BP）的国际矿物公司。

**34. In 2016, nuclear energy supplied 19% of the UK's electricity:**

2016 年，英国总发电量中，核电占 19%。煤炭发电所占比例急剧下跌至 9%；天然气发电飞涨至 42%；风能和太阳能发电占 14%，其中风能比例是 11.5%，首次超过了煤炭。

**35. pharmaceuticals:**

制药业，医药品。葛兰素史克（GlaxoSmithKline）由葛兰素威康和史克必成于 2000 年合并而成。阿斯利康制药公司（AstraZeneca）由前英国捷利康公司和前瑞典阿斯特拉公司于 1999 年合并而成，2013 年总部迁至英国剑桥。

**36. ICI:**

Imperial Chemical Industries（帝国化学工业集团），创建于 1926 年，主要经营油漆、药品、塑料和石油化工产品。是全球最大的建筑装饰漆供应商之一，拥有多乐士（Dulux）等油漆品牌。2007 年被荷兰阿克苏诺贝尔公司收购。

**37. Ford, GM, Peugeot, Nissan, Toyota:**

福特（美国）、通用（General Motors，美国）、标致（法国）、日产（日本）、丰田（日本），这些都是世界有名的汽车公司，在英国投资建厂生产汽车。英国的汽车工业曾提供给世界一大批优秀的车型和品牌，比如劳斯莱斯、宾利、阿斯顿马丁、捷豹、摩根以及罗孚。

**38. A high-technology engineering industry ... being designed and built in Britain:**

赛车带动了一种高技术机械工业的发展。不论在一级方程式赛车上还是在美国印第安纳波利斯汽车大赛上都出现了很多由英国设计和制造的世界级赛车。

**39. Tim Berners-Lee (Father of the Internet):**

蒂姆·伯纳斯·李 1989 年正式提出万维网的设想。1990 年，他在日内瓦的欧洲粒子物理实验室里开发出了世界上第一个网页浏览器。他最杰出的贡献是免费把万维网的构想推广到全世界，让万维网科技获得迅速的发展，深深改变了人类的生活面貌。英国计算机产业的另一大贡献是设计了世界上第一个用于手提电脑的调制解调器。

**40. Wire & Plastic Products Group:**

WPP 集团，世界顶级的品牌沟通服务集团，全球三大广告传播集团之一。

**41. "The City":**

"伦敦城"是英国首都市中心区的一部分，也是英国金融和商业中心。在一平方英里的地区集中了许多家大银行和金融公司，例如英格兰银行、伦敦证券交易所（股票与债券）、伦敦劳埃德（保险）等。这里也是世界最大外汇交易市场、最大黄金现货交易市场、重要保险市场、重要船贷市场和非贵重金属交易中心。

**42. As well as banking, dealing in commodities ... the busiest share-dealing centres in the world:**

同银行业一样，商品交易和保险业也是"伦敦城"的重要业务——"伦敦城"指的是伦敦中心区一块历史悠久的区域，所有以上交易都集中在这里，其中最重要的是世界最繁忙的股票交易中心之一——伦敦证券交易所（1802 年开业）。

UNIT ❺ The UK Economy

43. **The UK currency pound sterling ... ten most-valued currencies in the world:**
    英国货币英镑是继美元和欧元之后的世界第三大储备货币，也是世界上十大最有价值的货币之一。

44. **Its trade in goods is in deficit while the trade in services is in surplus:**
    英国是商品贸易逆差，服务贸易顺差。

45. **The Aerospace Industry:**
    英国航空航天产业占全球市场份额17%，世界排名第二，仅次于美国。著名公司包括罗尔斯·罗伊斯公司（Rolls-Royce, 世界第二大飞机发动机制造商）、英国宇航公司（BAE Systems, 世界第二大国防承包商）、空客英国公司（Airbus UK）、庞巴迪英国公司（Bombardier Aerospace）等。

46. **It is capable of producing ... missiles, satellites, and jet engines:**
    它能够生产从民用和军用飞机（包括直升机）到导弹、卫星和喷气发动机的全系列航天产品。

47. **the Wright Brothers:**
    莱特兄弟（Orville 1871–1948 和 Wilbur 1867–1912），美国飞机发明家，航空先驱者。

48. **A converted First World War bomber crossed the Atlantic Ocean in 1919:**
    一架改装过的第一次世界大战时的轰炸机于1919年飞越了大西洋。英国战后利用军用飞机的优势发展民用航空工业。

49. **International air races ... broke many speed records:**
    国际航空竞赛刺激了技术的发展，一架装备有罗尔斯·罗伊斯发动机的英国飞机 Supermarine S6B 打破了许多飞行速度的纪录。Rolls Royce: 既是著名的高档小轿车制造商（Rolls-Royce Motor Cars Limited），也是顶级发动机公司（Rolls-Royce Plc.），其发动机为世界航空工业广泛采用。Rolls Royce 通常在汽车领域被翻译成劳斯莱斯，而在航空发动机领域被翻译成罗尔斯·罗伊斯。

50. **Frank Whittle:**
    弗兰克·惠特尔（1907–1996）。英国工程师，1930年取得喷气式引擎基本设计的专利。1941年一架装有他设计的喷气式引擎的飞机首次飞行成功。1948年被封为勋爵。

51. **And when Englishman Frank Whittle ... British companies prominent in each field:**
    当英国人弗兰克·惠特尔于1937年发展完善了世界上第一个实用的喷气发动机，航空工业中三大领域——机身、引擎和航空电子技术都已奠定了基础。英国公司在这三大领域中均占领先地位。

52. **Spitfire fighter ... the jet-powered Meteor:**
    Spitfire fighter: 喷火战斗机；Lancaster bomber: 兰卡斯特轰炸机；the jet-powered Meteor: meteor 原意为流星，此处指一种喷气式飞机。

53. **But in most markets ... both civil and military:**
    但在大多数市场，英国公司遭到了来自美国波音、麦道（这两家公司已于1996年合并）等公司的激烈竞争。波音和麦道公司规模更大，在美国巨大的民用和军用市场中享有特惠供应商的优势。

54. **Nor did British military aircraft ... alongside many other customers:**
    英国军用飞机在海外销路也不太好，除了独具垂直起降性能的鹞式飞机卖给了美国海军陆战队和其他国

# The United Kingdom of Great Britain and Northern Ireland

家用户以外。

55. **The first of these ... first supersonic civil airliner, Concorde:**
 第一个此类合作项目是英法合作生产的世界第一架超音速客机——协和式飞机。

56. **However the successful collaboration led to more ... the world speed record for helicopters:**
 然而，这一成功的合作使英法两国进行了更多的类似合作项目，包括生产美洲豹战斗机和三种直升机，其中山猫直升机是世界上速度最快的直升机。

57. **Lockheed:**
 洛克希德公司创建于1912年，总部设在美国马里兰州，1995年与另一公司合并更名为洛克希德·马丁公司，目前为全球第一大国际承包商，生产各种军用飞机。

58. **the technologically advanced cockpit of the Boeing 777 airliner:**
 波音777大型客机技术先进的驾驶舱。

# Exercises

**I. Give the Chinese equivalents for the following:**

1. absolute decline and relative decline
2. nationalisation and privatisation
3. tertiary industries
4. National Minimum Wage
5. London Stock Exchange
6. Rolls Royce

**II. Decide whether the following statements are true (T) or false (F):**

1. For a long time after the Second World War, Britain was burdened with high expenditure on military defence. _____
2. In the 1970s, with the soaring price of oil and high rates of inflation, Britain went through a bad period. The Labour Party had to step down from the government in 1979. _____
3. As a result of Mrs. Thatcher's monetary and privatisation policies, unemployment fell

slowly. _____

4. Faced with the 2008 financial crisis, the Brown Labour government practised austerity and cut public spending. _____
5. The chemical, pharmaceutical and aerospace industries are Britain's chief export earners. _____
6. With the decline of the manufacturing industry, British tertiary/service industry now produces half of the national wealth. _____
7. Radar and engine developments were UK's significant contributions to the world's aerospace industry. _____
8. As a major trading nation in the world, Britain exports more goods than it imports. _____

### III. Fill in the blanks:

1. Since 1945, the UK economy has experienced _____ decline rather than _____ decline.
2. A low rate of _____ industrial investment coupled with a very high rate of _____ investment is a characteristic of the UK economy.
3. In the 1970s, the devaluation of the UK currency forced the Labour government to borrow money from _____.
4. Mrs. Thatcher's economic policies were marked by _____ and _____.
5. The UK economy can be divided into three main sectors: _____ industries, secondary industries and _____ industries.
6. The discovery of the _____ oil and gas in the 1970s greatly helped to solve the energy problems in the UK.
7. GlaxoSmithKline is a big _____ company in the world while BAE Systems is Britain's largest _____ company.
8. _____ is the central bank of Britain.
9. _____ is one of the busiest share-dealing centres in the world.
10. Englishman Frank Whittle developed the world's first _____ in 1937.

### IV. Questions:

1. How should we understand "absolute decline" and "relative decline"?
2. What are the reasons for the relative decline of the post-war British economy?

# The United Kingdom of Great Britain and Northern Ireland

3. What is nationalisation? Why did the first Labour majority government introduce nationalisation?
4. What was wrong with the British economy in the 1970s?
5. What were Mrs. Thatcher's radical economic policies in the 1980s? Was her reform programme successful or not?
6. What were New Labour's economic achievements?
7. How did the Brown government deal with the 2008 financial crisis?
8. Which key words can best describe David Cameron's economic policies?
9. What does the tertiary sector industry mainly include in the UK economy?
10. What are the main components of Britain's energy sources? Which are of rising importance?
11. Of the manufacturing sector, in which fields is Britain particularly strong?
12. In what ways is the City of London so important?
13. How much do you know about Concorde?
14. Is Airbus a successful European collaborative project? What is Britain's role in it?

V. **Topics for discussion or research:**

1. Britain, like most developed economies, has seen a significant decline of secondary industry and a sharp growth in tertiary or service industries. Why is it so? Do you see a similar growth in tertiary industries in China in the past 20 years or so? Explain your points with examples.
2. Why and how did Mrs Thatcher practise privatisation in the 1980s? What was its legacy?
3. Research on one aspect of the UK industry that you are interested in and share with classmates your findings of its historical development, merits and lessons.

# UNIT 6

# British Literature

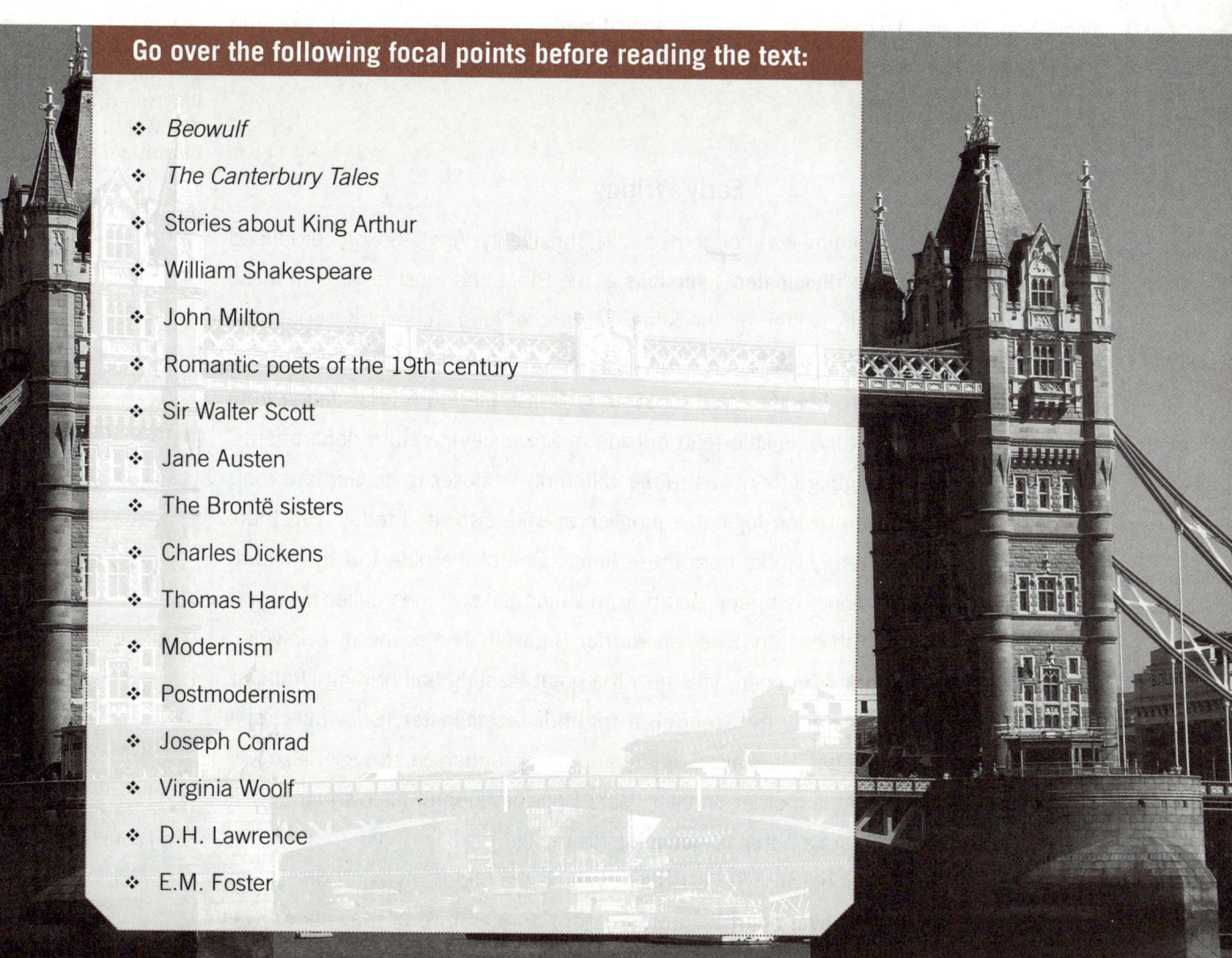

**Go over the following focal points before reading the text:**

- *Beowulf*
- *The Canterbury Tales*
- Stories about King Arthur
- William Shakespeare
- John Milton
- Romantic poets of the 19th century
- Sir Walter Scott
- Jane Austen
- The Brontë sisters
- Charles Dickens
- Thomas Hardy
- Modernism
- Postmodernism
- Joseph Conrad
- Virginia Woolf
- D.H. Lawrence
- E.M. Foster

# The United Kingdom of Great Britain and Northern Ireland

 **Text**

In this unit we will consider one aspect of Britain's artistic **output**, that for which it is perhaps best known: literature.[1] The major literature competition, the annual Man Booker Prize[2], is televised as an important national event, causing a great deal of discussion: the novel which wins, or is even **short-listed** for the prize, is likely to become a **best-seller**. The rich variety of theatre performance available in London is one of its main attractions to visitors.[3]

## Early Writing

Much early British writing was concerned with Christianity: Anglo-Saxons produced beautifully **illustrated** (or "**illuminated**") **versions** of the Bible: the most famous of these is the Book of Kells[4], partly written on the Scottish island of Iona. Today it is kept in the library of **Trinity** College in Dublin, the capital of Ireland. Outside of the church, few people in this period were **literate**. Even today early British literature (that dating from before the sixteenth century), is little read outside of university literature departments, because the English language then was rather different — closer to its German roots — making it quite difficult even for native English speakers to read today. But there are a few well-known literary works from those times. One of the oldest of these early "Old English"[5] literary works is a long poem from Anglo-Saxon times called *Beowulf*. It tells the story of the 6th century Swedish **warrior** Beowulf. The scene of *Beowulf* is not England but **Denmark**. The poem tells how the great feasting hall of King Hrothgar, the **Dane**, is **raided** repeatedly by Grendel, a frightful sea **monster**. Beowulf comes from **Sweden** to aid Hrothgar. He **slays** Grendel and, in an undersea struggle, also kills Grendel's equally dangerous mother. In later years Beowulf, king of his own land, dies in the act of killing a fire dragon that is **menacing** his people.

With the Norman Conquest in 1066 Britain entered the Middle Ages (1066–1485), and the language of the **royal court** became French. So literature of that period was written in French or Latin. But one work from these times often studied today by middle school and college students is *The Canterbury Tales* by Geoffrey Chaucer (1343–1400).

---

output *n.* 产品，产物，输出
short-listed *adj.* 进入最后一轮候选名单的
best-seller *n.* 畅销书
illustrated *adj.* 有插图的
illuminated *adj.* 装饰华美的
version *n.* 版本
Trinity *n.* （基督教）三位一体（即圣父、圣子、圣灵合成一个神体）
literate *adj.* 有读写能力的
warrior *n.* 勇士
Denmark *n.* 丹麦
Dane *n.* 丹麦人
raid *v.* 袭击
monster *n.* 魔鬼
Sweden *n.* 瑞典
slay *v.* 屠杀
menace *v.* 威胁
royal court 宫廷

He was the first court poet to write in English. Written in a more recognizable version of English (known as "Middle English") than *Beowulf*, it is made up of a series of stories told by **pilgrims** to entertain each other on their way to the important Christian Church at Canterbury in southeast England.[6] It is notable for its diversity, both in the range of social types amongst the 31 pilgrims, and the range in style of the stories they tell.[7] "The Wife of Bath's Tale," for example, is a **romance** concerning King Arthur's times.

The **legend** of King Arthur[8] became established in literary form with the publication in 1138 of Geoffrey of Monmouth's *History of the Kings of Britain*, a Latin work which, though calling itself a work of history, invented material to fill the broad gaps in the historical records.[9] The stories of King Arthur's court, his **knights** and their famous round table, and the **quest** for **the Holy Grail** in the 5th century, are mostly inventions around a very few vague "facts". The best-known version of this story comes from around 1470 when Thomas Malory completed his *Le Morte D'Arthur* (*Death of Arthur*), making the story of Arthur's Queen Guinevere, and her love affair with his best friend and greatest knight Sir Lancelot, the stuff of the British imagination for centuries to come. Locations mentioned in the legends such as the ruined castle at Tintagel in Cornwall are popular tourist destinations.

## Elizabethan Drama

There was a general **flowering** of cultural and intellectual life in Europe during the 15th and 16th centuries which is known as "The **Renaissance**" ("rebirth"). In British culture one of the most successful and long-lasting expressions of this development lay in drama.[10] The first professional theatre opened in London in 1576, and others followed, producing the work of many notable **playwrights**, including Christopher Marlowe[11], Ben Jonson[12], and, of course, William Shakespeare[13].

Marlowe (1564–1593) was the earliest of this great **trio**, and his style is thought to have been a great influence on Shakespeare. His most famous play is *The Tragical History of Doctor Faustus*, the story of a man who sold his soul to the devil in return for power. It is thought that Marlowe had another career as a government agent, and that his death by murder in a Deptford (part of London) pub may have had something to do with that political activity.

William Shakespeare (1564–1616) is probably the best-known literary figure in the world, but little is known of his life. He came from a middle-class family in Stratford-

pilgrim *n.*
朝圣者
romance *n.*
浪漫故事，中世纪传奇故事
legend *n.*
传奇，传说
knight *n.*
骑士
quest *n.*
探索
the Holy Grail
（传说耶稣在最后晚餐中用的）圣杯、圣盘
flowering *n.*
繁荣
Renaissance *n.*
文艺复兴
playwright *n.*
剧作家
trio *n.*
三个（或三人）一组

# The United Kingdom of Great Britain and Northern Ireland

upon-Avon, but somehow he became a successful playwright and director of a theatre company in London. Records show him as a **shareholder** in the famous Globe Theatre (which has recently been faithfully reconstructed and puts on Shakespearean plays in the style which Shakespeare knew) and wealthy enough to buy his father the largest house in Stratford. Shakespeare's plays fall into categories, or classes. He **excels** in each kind. The **tragedies** include *Romeo and Juliet*, *Hamlet*, *Othello*, *King Lear*, and *Macbeth*. Among the **comedies** are *The Taming of the Shrew*, *A Midsummer Night's Dream*, *Twelfth Night*, and *The Tempest*. His history plays, based on English history, include *Richard III*, *Richard II*, *Henry IV*, and *Henry V*.[14] *Julius Caesar* and *Antony and Cleopatra* are tragedies on classical themes.[15] Among the best known are *Hamlet*[16], the most-performed play in the world: the story of a Danish **prince** seeking revenge upon his uncle for the murder of his father; and *Romeo and Juliet*[17], the story of two young lovers from **feuding** families which ends in a tragic double **suicide**.

Elizabethan drama, and Shakespeare in particular, is considered to be among the earliest work to display a "modern" **perception** of the world: full of moral doubts and political **insecurities**, where the right of those who **wield** power to do so is put in question.[18]

## The 17th Century

Literature cannot really be divided into exact periods. Any such divisions actually overlap and blend into one another. Thus the late Elizabethans are also Jacobeans. This term comes from the Latin form of the name of King James I, Jacobus.

A permanent **monument** of English literature style **commemorates** James's name. He ordered the translation of the **Holy Scriptures** known as the King James Bible (1611). This was not the first English translation. It owed a debt to the earlier versions done by William Tyndale (1492?–1535) and Miles Coverdale (1488–1568). There was also the Bible of the English College at Douai, France, which is still the chief English text used by Roman Catholics. There have been many translations since, especially mid-20th-century ones that clarify many passages in the light of modern **scholarship** and recently found ancient manuscripts.[19] Yet the King James Version will probably never be matched for **majesty** of language. For many generations it exerted a greater influence on style and standards of taste than any other single work in English.[20]

The *Essays* of Francis Bacon (1561–1626) made popular in English a literary form

---

shareholder *n.*
股东
excel *v.*
胜过，优于
tragedy *n.*
悲剧
comedy *n.*
喜剧
prince *n.*
王子
feuding *adj.*
有世仇的
suicide *n.*
自杀
perception *n.*
感觉，认识
insecurity *n.*
不安全
wield *v.*
行使，挥，操
monument *n.*
纪念碑，不朽的作品，典范
commemorate *v.* 纪念
the Holy Scriptures
（宗教）圣经
scholarship *n.*
学问，学术成就
majesty *n.*
庄重，权威

widely practiced afterwards. Bacon was a public figure and statesman of importance under both Elizabeth and James, rising to the high post of **Lord Chancellor**. A **scandal** ended his public service in 1621. He devoted the rest of his life wholly to literature and scholarship. *The Novum Organum* (1620) (the title means new instrument), written in Latin, sets forth a new method of approaching knowledge. *The New Atlantis* (1627) (a **Utopian fable**) is a study in political philosophy. These are representative of a large body of Bacon's work. Yet it is the most informal and casual of his works, the *Essays* (first published in 1597, and issued in final form in 1625), that is read most often.

The literary giant of the 17th century, John Milton (1608–1674) was much bound up in the **Puritan** Revolution. His literary talents showed themselves in early works. The twin poems "L'Allegro" (meaning the cheerful, or merry one) and "Il Penseroso" (meaning thoughtfulness) present two different views of life — that of the lively man and that of the thoughtful man. Religious and political disputes also interested Milton, and he wrote many **pamphlets** on these subjects. The most famous of them is *Areopagitica*. The title comes from the Areopagus, a Greek place of debate. *Areopagitica* gives one of the most **eloquent** of all **pleas** for freedom of the press. Milton took the side of Parliament in the Civil War and wrote pamphlets supporting the king's **execution**. During the **protectorate** he served as Latin secretary to Cromwell, composing many state documents in that language. When Charles II **came to the throne** in 1660, Milton's position was endangered. He was heavily fined. During his retirement from public life he produced his masterpieces: the **epic** *Paradise Lost*, its **sequel**, *Paradise Regained*, and the poetic tragedy *Samson Agonistes*.[21]

## The 18th Century

Eighteenth-century English literature is marked by a rather large shift from the **mood** and **tone** of 17th-century literature. For one thing, a second great political disturbance took place in the late 17th century. This was the revolution of 1688. King James II tried to make Catholicism the official religion of England. After a struggle, he was forced to give up the throne and withdraw to the Continent. Both of the English political parties, the Whigs and the Tories, offered the throne to Prince William of Orange and his wife Mary as **co-monarchs**. Together they ruled England from 1689 until Mary's death in 1694. William died in 1702.

Intellectual activity sets the 18th century apart. It was an age of wit, when great

---

Lord Chancellor （英国）大法官
scandal *n.* 丑闻
Utopian *adj.* 乌托邦的
fable *n.* 寓言
Puritan *adj.* 清教的
pamphlet *n.* 小册子，（讨论时事问题的）小册子刊物
eloquent *adj.* 雄辩的
plea *n.* 恳求，请求
execution *n.* 处决
protectorate *n.* 护国公政体，护国时期
come to the throne 登上王位，登基
epic *n.* 史诗
sequel *n.* 续篇，续集
mood *n.* 情绪
tone *n.* 语调
co-monarch *n.* 共同作为君主

# The United Kingdom of Great Britain and Northern Ireland

thinkers and writers argued. It was an age of **skepticism**, when thinking men questioned all facts and beliefs. **Conversationalists** and letter writers flourished in literary circles and gathered in London clubs. The first important dictionary of the language was produced. The theatre was lively, with a great number of **satirical** comedies. **Satire**, making fun of people and things, expressed the spirit of the time. Prominent on the stage, satire also found a powerful **medium** in a form that came to full growth in this century — the novel.[22]

Jonathan Swift (1667–1745), Irish-born, became a priest of the Church of Ireland and later dean of St. Patrick's Cathedral in Dublin. He spent a number of his early years in England, and he was interested in English politics all his life. His name is linked with the fanciful account of four voyages known to us as *Gulliver's Travels*. The first voyage is to Lilliput, the land of tiny people, and the second to Brobdingnag, the land of giants. The simplified versions of the stories of these two voyages appeal to children. Yet the whole of Gulliver's adventures form the most bitter and **hard-thrusting** satire in the English language. It touches every **vice**, **folly**, and mere weakness of mankind. *Gulliver's Travels* reaches a powerful **climax** in its fourth part. The human race, represented by filthy creatures called Yahoos, is shown as inferior to a noble **breed** of thinking, talking, **high-minded** horses known as Houyhnhnms.

Scotland produced a much-loved poet, Robert Burns[23], who wrote in Scottish **dialect**. Among the most cherished of his poems are "Holy Willie's Prayer", "To a Mouse," and "To a Louse". Among his songs are "Comin' thro' the Rye" and "Auld Lang Syne". He remains the beloved folk poet of Scotland.

Daniel Defoe (1660–1731) led an active life as a journalist and political **pamphleteer**. More than once his opinions carried him into prison. He wrote many books, including the novel *Moll Flanders*. Defoe's first and greatest novel appeared in 1719. This was *Robinson Crusoe*[24], the most famous tale of **shipwreck** and solitary survival in all literature.

## The Romantic Period

Roughly the first third of the 19th century makes up English literature's romantic period. Writers of romantic literature are more concerned with imagination and feeling than with the power of reason, which marked the 18th century. Perhaps the rather

---

skepticism *n.* 怀疑主义
conversationalist *n.* 健谈者，善于辞令者
satirical *adj.* 具有讽刺性的
satire *n.* 讽刺，讥讽
medium *n.* 媒介
hard-thrusting *adj.* 有强烈推动力的
vice *n.* 邪恶
folly *n.* 愚行
climax *n.* 高潮
breed *n.* 种类，类型
high-minded *adj.* 具有崇高理想和原则的
dialect *n.* 方言
pamphleteer *n.* 写小册子的人
shipwreck *n.* 船舶失事，海难
romantic *adj.* 具有浪漫色彩的

violent and ugly world about them drove 19th-century writers to a literary **refuge**.²⁵ Napoleon's wars had **racked** Europe. The Industrial Revolution had changed England into a nation of factories.

Two poets offered what had been called romantic poetry's "Declaration of Independence." This was a volume of poems called *Lyrical Ballads*, written by William Wordsworth²⁶ and Samuel Taylor Coleridge²⁷. Wordsworth's **verses** are about country scenes and country people. Representative of his other work is the long **autobiographical** poem *The Prelude* and such shorter poems as "My Heart Leaps Up When I Behold" and "I Wandered Lonely as a Cloud," also called "**Daffodils**". Wordsworth's poetry varies widely. Some is written in plain language, and in other poems the style is complex. Both Wordsworth and his good friend Coleridge were distinguished for writings on criticism and principles of poetry. Coleridge's major work of this sort is the autobiographical *Biographia Literaria*. The most famous of his poems is "The **Rime** of Ancient **Mariner**".

Three men brought the Romantic Movement²⁸ to its height. *George Gordon, Lord Byron*²⁹ (1788–1824), travelled widely in Europe, part of the time an **exile** because of scandals related to his marriage. At the age of 36 he died of a fever in Greece, where he had gone as a volunteer to fight for Greek independence. His large body of work includes the partly autobiographical *Childe Harold's Pilgrimage*. *Don Juan* owed its title and parts of its story to the old legend of the great lover. Byron retells the story in the form of satire.

John Keats³⁰ came from origins as plain as Byron's were aristocratic. His father kept a **livery stable**. It is fortunate that Keats's **genius** showed itself early, since he died of **tuberculosis** in Rome at the age of 25. Keats was superb at pictorial poetry — painting a picture with words. His art is nowhere greater than in the two poems "**Ode** on a **Grecian Urn**" and "Ode to a **Nightingale**".³¹

Percy Bysshe Shelley's³² writing has a wide range. The lovely musical quality of his work appears in the fine verses of "Ode to the West Wind" and "To a **Skylark**". "The Revolt of Islam", renamed as "The Rise of Islam", preaches revolution, and *Defense of Poetry* upholds the place of imagination and love in the arts. The long poem *Adonais* is a beautiful **lament** written on the death of Keats. A month before his 30th birthday Shelley drowned while sailing in **the Mediterranean**. His ashes lie in the same Roman **cemetery** where Keats is buried.

---

refuge *n.* 逃避
rack *v.* 破坏
verse *n.* 诗句
autobiographical *adj.* 自传体的
daffodil *n.* 黄水仙
rime *n.* (rhyme) 押韵诗
mariner *n.* 水手
exile *n.* 放逐
livery stable (出租马与马车的)代养马房
genius *n.* 天才
tuberculosis *n.* 肺结核
ode *n.* 颂歌
Grecian *n. adj.* 希腊人(的)
urn *n.* 瓮
nightingale *n.* 夜莺
skylark *n.* 云雀
lament *n.* 挽歌
the Mediterranean 地中海
cemetery *n.* 公墓

# The United Kingdom of Great Britain and Northern Ireland

## The 19th Century Novel

This spirit of **Romanticism** also occurred in the novel, notably in Mary Shelley's (the poet Shelley's wife) *Frankenstein*[33] (1818), the story of science gone wrong through the disastrous consequences of an arrogant scientist's (Dr. Frankenstein) attempts to create life.[34] In the process he only creates a monster. But the novel's sympathies are with the monster's struggle to make sense of his existence in a world that rejects him.[35]

In Scotland there developed a type of romanticism different from that of Byron, Keats and Shelley. Its spokesman was Sir Walter Scott[36], whose voice has a worldwide influence and popularity. Most of Scott's **themes** came from medieval and Scottish history. He wrote a number of romantic novels. *Waverley, Rob Roy, The Heart of Midlothian*, and *Ivanhoe* are but a few of his widely read novels. Scott had a great influence on such American writers as James Fenimore Cooper, Washington Irving, and Nathaniel Hawthorne. His novels remain popular today, and several have been the subjects of Hollywood films.

Jane Austen[37] wrote six novels published between 1811 and 1818. These stories (often set in the pretty southwest town of Bath) of middle-class women in search of husbands are known for their fine writing, **subtle characterization** and controlled studies of **manners**. The novel of manners pictures in detail the manners and customs of a certain social class. Jane Austen, who excelled at this form of writing, is indeed one of the greatest of all English novelists. A delightful, almost **flawless stylist**, she has devoted admirers of her *Sense and Sensibility, Pride and Prejudice*, and *Emma*, among other works. In the spirit of the 18th century, **rationality** is praised, but in the contemporary spirit of Romanticism, this is balanced with the imaginative and the personal.[38] This balance is seen in the title of *Sense and Sensibility*, which was made into a highly successful film by a Chinese director, Ang Lee. *Pride and Prejudice* has been made into films and TV dramas.

Perhaps the most famous literary family in British history are the Brontë sisters[39], and they too were influenced by the Romantic Movement. They were three daughters (Charlotte, Emily and Ann) of the **vicar** of a village church in Haworth in Yorkshire, and as such, poor, but educated and respectable. They had a brother who was a failed painter and **alcoholic**, and two other sisters who died in childhood. All were tragically to die before their father. Given their short lives they did not produce much, but among their works are some of the best-loved novels in English, Charlotte Brontë's *Jane Eyre*

Romanticism *n.*
浪漫主义
theme *n.* 主题
subtle *adj.*
微妙的
character-
ization *n.*
人物刻画
manners *n.*
风度，礼仪
flawless *adj.*
无瑕的
stylist *n.*
具有独特风格
者，自成流派者
rationality *n.*
理性
vicar *n.*
教区牧师
alcoholic *n.*
嗜酒者

and Emily's *Wuthering Heights* (both published in 1847) being the most successful. Both have been filmed several times. Their novels reflect both their local geography: the wild high **moors** of the Yorkshire hills, which their home backed onto, and their uncertain economic position, because of which they could not hope for a respectable marriage of equals, being too poor.[40] Thus *Jane Eyre* tells the story of an **orphan**, who has a loveless childhood at a terrible **boarding school**, and who goes to work for a rich man as a **governess** to his child. He becomes attracted to her because of her independence and free spirit. However, he has a secret in his past: a mad former wife locked up in the **attic** of his house. The secret discovered, Jane runs away. Later she becomes the object of attention of a vicar, who wishes to marry her as he feels she will make a suitable wife for a **missionary**. But in true romantic fashion, this worthy but **passionless** lover is rejected, and Jane returns to the darker, but **passionately** romantic, figure of her previous employer, Mr. Rochester.

The Brontës had trouble getting published, and in fact had to use male **pseudonyms** in order to gain acceptance. But one of Charlotte's friends was another female novelist, Elizabeth Gaskell. She represents a more realistic aspect of the 19th century novel, concerned with social comment, not just personal freedom. A vicar's daughter from Manchester, she was concerned with the situation of the workers in the new industrial cities. Her novel *North and South* describes the division that this economic change was emphasizing in British society at that time, both in terms of class, and geography — the north was the industrial part of England, and those in the south, where power lay, remained ignorant of it. She was supported in her work by the greatest British storyteller of the 19th century, Charles Dickens[41].

Dickens too was concerned with the state of the nation, and having suffered as a child worker himself when his father was imprisoned for debt, he had personal reasons for bringing the suffering of the poor to light.[42] He wrote many well-known novels, including *Pickwick Papers*, which showed a rare comic gift, *Oliver Twist*, the story of an orphan child drawn into crime in the London **underworld**, *David Copperfield*, his own favourite book, and *Great Expectations*, which traces the growth of Philip (Pip) from a boy of shallow dreams to a man of depth and character.

Later in the 19th century Robert Louis Stevenson[43] also wrote Scottish historical romances. The adventures in *Treasure Island* and *Kidnapped* **thrill** readers young and old. Steveson was also a master of the short novel. His most famous one was *The*

moors *n.* 沼泽地
orphan *n.* 孤儿
boarding school 寄宿学校
governess *n.* 家庭女教师
attic *n.* 阁楼
missionary *n.* 传教士
passionless *adj.* 毫无热情的
passionately *adv.* 热烈地
pseudonym *n.* 假名，笔名
underworld *n.* 罪犯社会
thrill *v.* 激动，使兴奋

# The United Kingdom of Great Britain and Northern Ireland

*Strange Case of Doctor Jekyll and Mr. Hyde*, a story again concerned with the conflict between the rational and the emotional, sensual side of man's nature, represented in the single person of the scientist Dr Jekyll, who transforms himself into the wild Mr. Hyde.[44]

Thomas Hardy[45] lived well into the 20th century but did his major work as a novelist in the 19th century. Among his better-known novels are *The Return of the Native* (1878), *Tess of the D'Urbervilles* (1891), and *Jude the Obscure* (1896). These books fall into the **prose** group that Hardy called novels of character and environment. They offer powerful, realistic studies of life. Although Hardy ranks high as a novelist, we should not overlook the fact that he was a first-class poet. As a prose writer he is the last of the 19th century. As a poet he belongs to the 20th century.

## Literature in the 20th Century and Onwards

Any summary of the complex 20th century is difficult. It has seen wars and revolutions. Breakthroughs in science have affected millions of lives. Never have so many words and ideas been printed or passed on, through radio and television.[46]

The 20th century marked the end of the British Empire, which was replaced by the Commonwealth of Nations. Yet English civilisation and culture continue to have a strong influence on the rest of the world. The **heritage** of English literature forms an outstanding part of that culture.

20th century literature can be broadly divided into two **stylistic** periods: **Modernism**[47], and **Postmodernism**[48]. These periods roughly correspond to literature written before the Second World War (1939–1945) and literature written after it. Both are characterised by a high degree of **experimentation**.

Modernism in literature can be seen as a reaction against the nineteenth century forms discussed above, which can be thought of as **assuming** understanding between writer and reader, resulting in the simple communication of an agreed version of the "world".[49] This **approach** to writing is known as "**Realism**". Instead, Modernist writers express the difficulty they see in understanding and communicating how the world works. Often, therefore, Modernist writing seems disorganised, hard to understand. It often portrays the action from the viewpoint of a single confused individual, rather than from the viewpoint of an all-knowing impersonal narrator outside the action.[50]

One of the most famous of English Modernist writers is Joseph Conrad[51]. He was

---

prose *n.*
散文体
heritage *n.*
遗产
stylistic *adj.*
文体上的
Modernism *n.*
现代主义
Postmodernism *n.*
后现代主义
experimentation *n.*
实验
assume *v.*
假设
approach *n.*
途径，方法
Realism *n.*
现实主义

raised in Poland, but became a sailor, and ended up as the captain of a British ship. He got British citizenship and settled in England, where he wrote his books in English. They are Modernist in their concerns with moral uncertainty: what is right? And in their concerns with factual uncertainty: what is true?[52] Conrad's most famous novel is *The Heart of Darkness* (1902), a story of a riverboat journey in central Africa to investigate an **exploitative** European **ivory** trader called Mr Kurtz. The journey is a symbolic one representing the darkness at the heart of man.[53] Mr Kurtz's last words, "The horror! The horror!" are among the best known in English literature. A film based on the novel has been made by the well-known American director, Francis Ford Coppola, but set in Vietnam in the 1960s, and called **Apocalypse** *Now*.

Virginia Woolf[54] is another writer associated with Modernism, and one of the most famous writers of the century. She was part of the intellectual "Bloomsbury group" named after the **fashionable** area of London in which they lived, which included other writers, philosophers, and painters. Her work was concerned with the individual **consciousness**, especially the female consciousness. Her novels have become important to **feminists** for the way they show women's personalities to be limited by society.[55] *Mrs. Dalloway* (1925), *To the Lighthouse* (1927), and *Orlando* (1928) are among her best-known books. She sometimes used what has been called the "**stream of consciousness**" technique: the apparently unorganised flow of thought onto page.[56] Woolf also wrote a great deal of literary criticism and numerous essays including *A Room of One's Own*.

Less experimental, D. H. Lawrence[57] and E. M. Forster[58] both wrote novels in this period which are critical of the modern world. Lawrence felt that society forced too many rules on people and kept them from living a full, natural life. His forceful writing on daring themes shocked many. *Sons and Lovers*, based partly on his own life, is one of his finest novels. The novels of E. M. Forster concerned themselves with personal relations. In his most notable book, *A Passage to India*, Forster examined the relationships between Englishmen and Indians. In *Howard's End* he contrasts the artistic, romantic Schlegel sisters with the forceful, **unethical** business-people, the Wilcoxes. But in what we might see as a typical move for a British writer, the two families are brought together to create a new "**hybrid**"[59].

Moving into the post-war period, one of the most famous novels in English appeared: George Orwell's *1984* (written in 1948) is a powerful satire on the **totalitarian**

---

**exploitative** *adj.* 剥削性的
**ivory** *n.* 象牙
**Apocalypse** *n.* (《圣经》)启示录
**fashionable** *adj.* 上流社会的，时髦豪华的
**consciousness** *n.* 意识
**feminist** *n.* 女性主义者
**stream of consciousness** 意识流
**unethical** *adj.* 不道德的
**hybrid** *adj.* 混合成的
**totalitarian** *adj.* 极权主义的

# The United Kingdom of Great Britain and Northern Ireland

tendency in modern states. It is set in an extremely unpleasant England ruled absolutely by "Big Brother." This depressing story is characteristic of the post-war years, and begins "Postmodernism". The horrors of the Second World War **undermined** ideas of human progress, and of meaning in life, however well hidden. So while Modernists were scientists of human existence, looking for buried meaning below confusing surfaces, Postmodernists can be thought of as abandoning that search.[60] Meaning does not exist outside of the human head, likewise it does not exist inside a book, waiting to be discovered,[61] instead it is made in the process of reading a book, or of making sense of the world.

So writers like John Fowles play a game with the reader, constantly demonstrating the **fictionality** of their writing, and inviting the reader to put together different pieces freely. Fowles' most successful novel, *The French Lieutenant's Woman* (1968), set in the small holiday resort of Lyme Regis, describes a **Victorian** gentleman's education into his own freedom by the mysterious girl, Sarah. The story's main postmodern "trick" is that the reader is offered a choice of endings.[62]

Not all writers can be squeezed into the definitions Modern or Postmodern.[63] Many post-war writers continue traditional themes: Graham Greene[64] wrote novels of morally and religiously troubled **expatriates**, sometimes concerned with spies. Spy fiction in general is one of the strong points of contemporary British fiction: the best known writer is John Le Carre. His novels (such as *Smiley's People*) have been made into internationally distributed TV serials. In popular fiction, Ian Fleming's fantastic James Bond[65] stories are even better known, especially for their numerous film versions

Among the newer novelists are William Golding (1911–1993), Doris Lessing (1919–2013), Kingsley Amis (1922–1995), John Braine (1922–1986) and Margaret Drabble (1939–). Golding was also a poet and playwright. His *Lord of the Flies* (1954) was an immediate success in Britain and soon found a wide audience in the United States. Golding was awarded the Nobel Prize in Literature in 1983. Doris Lessing's most famous novels are *The Grass Is Singing* (1950) and *The Golden Notebook* (1962), and her most recent novel is *Alfred and Emily* (2008). In 2007, Lessing won the Nobel Prize in Literature for her **rigorous** depiction of women's experience. She is the eleventh woman to win the Nobel Literature Prize, and also the oldest person ever to win the prize. Kingsley Amis' first novel, *Lucky Jim* (1954), is perhaps his most famous. The novel satirizes the **high-brow** academic set of a **redbrick university**, seen through the

**undermine** *v.*
破坏
**fictionality** *n.*
虚构性
**Victorian** *adj.*
维多利亚时期的
**expatriate** *n.*
移居国外者，侨民
**rigorous** *adj.*
精确的，缜密的
**high-brow** *adj.*
（自以为）文化修养或趣味很高级的
**redbrick university**
19世纪末或20世纪初创建的英国大学

eyes of its protagonist, Jim Dixon, as he tries to make his way as a young lecturer of history. The novel was perceived by many as part of the Angry Young Men movement of the 1950s which reacted against the **stultifications** of conventional British life. John Braine, also associated with the Angry Young Men movement, is chiefly remembered today for his first novel, *Room at the Top* (1957), although he wrote twelve works of fiction. Margaret Drabble is a novelist, biographer and critic. Her first novel is *The Summer Bird-Cage* and most recent novel is *The Sea Lady* (2006). It is said that "Each of Margaret Drabble's novels has been an accurate, honest record of its time in the idiom of its time." As of 2016, Drabble has published 19 novels.

Perhaps the most **controversial** of contemporary British writers is Salman Rushdie (1947–). He is a British Indian novelist and essayist. His first success came with his second novel, *Midnight's Children* (1981), which won the Booker Prize in 1981 and "The Best of Booker" in 2008. Much of his fiction is set on the Indian subcontinent. His style is often classified as **magical realism** mixed with historical fiction, and a dominant theme of his work is the story of the many connections, **disruptions** and migrations between the Eastern and Western world. His novel, **The Satanic Verses** (1988), aroused a big **controversy** with many protests from Muslims in several countries. Some of the protests were so violent and threatening that Rushdie was forced to go into hiding for a period of time until the danger was over. He published *The Enchantress of Florence* in 2008. His latest novel *The Golden House*, published in 2017, marks his change from magic realism to realism. Since 2000, Rushdie has lived in the United States, and was elected to the American Academy of Arts and Letters. In 2012, he published *Joseph Anton: A Memoir*, an account of his life following the controversy over *The Satanic Verses*.

Another writer worthy of our attention is Kazuo Ishiguro[66]. Ishiguro is one of the most **celebrated** contemporary fiction authors in the English speaking world, with four Booker Prize nominations. His novel *The Remains of the Day* won the 1989 prize, and was made into a successful movie staring Oscar award winning big names Anthony Hopkins and Emma Thomson. A number of his novels are set in the past. His novels often end without any sense of resolution. The issues his characters confront are buried in the past and remain unresolved. His recent works include *When We Were Orphans* (2000), *Never Let Me Go* (2005), and *Nocturnes* (2009). His seventh novel, *The Buried Giant*, was published in 2015 in both the United States and the United Kingdom. In

---

stultification *n.* 愚蠢，荒谬，可笑
controversial *adj.* 有争议的
magical realism 魔幻现实主义
disruption *n.* 破裂
*The Satanic Verse* 《撒旦诗篇》
controversy *n.* 争议
celebrated *adj.* 著名的

# The United Kingdom of Great Britain and Northern Ireland

2017, the Nobel Prize in Literature was awarded to Ishiguro "who, in novels of great emotional force, has uncovered the abyss beneath our illusory sense of connection with the world."

Ian McEwan (1948– ) is a successful novelist and screenwriter. In 2008, *The Times* featured him on their list of "The 50 greatest British writers since 1945". McEwan began his career writing Gothic short stories. These were followed by three novels of some success in the 1980s and early 1990s. His 1997 novel, *Enduring Love*, about the relationship between a science writer and a stalker, was popular with critics, and adopted into a film. His next novel *Amsterdam* (1998) won the Man Booker Prize. His following novel **Atonement** (2001) won **acclaim**, and was adapted into an Oscar-winning film. The novel, set in three time periods, 1935 England, Second World War England and France, and present-day England, concerns the understanding and responding to the need for personal atonement. His other works include *Saturday* (2005), *On Chesil Beach* (2007), *Solar* (2010), *Sweet Tooth* (2012), *The Children Act* (2014), and *Nutshell* (2016).

To look at a list of the most respected contemporary British writers is to be struck by the variety of many of their origins[67]: Salman Rushdie (India), Grace Nichols (**Guyana**), Kazuo Ishiguro (Japan), V. S. Naipaul (**Trinidad**) amongst many others. This too is an aspect of the postmodern world: a mixing of cultures on a grand scale. But this mixture, this "**hybridity**", has always been a part of British writing, with its multinational and class-divided internal **status**, its imperial past, and its current highly international economy.[68] British literature continues to reflect that complexity.

atonement *n.*
赎罪
acclaim *n.*
称誉，高度评价
Guyana *n.*
圭亚那
Trinidad *n.*
特立尼达
hybridity *n.*
混杂物，杂合性
status *n.*
地位，身份

# Explanations

1. **In this unit we will consider one aspect ... it is perhaps best known:**
   本章将探讨英国文艺产品的一个方面：文学。这可能是英国最为闻名的方面。

2. **Man Booker Prize:**
   布克文学奖，为世界最受关注的文学奖项之一，1969 年开始颁发，每年授予一部最优秀的英语小说。

3. **The rich variety of theatre performance ... is one of its main attractions to visitors:**
   伦敦舞台丰富多彩的演出是该城市吸引游客的重要原因之一。

UNIT 6 British Literature

4. **the Book of Kells:**
   凯尔斯书，四部福音书，内有华美的手抄饰画，约 7 世纪后期开始绘制，8 世纪完成。

5. **Old English:**
   英格兰的盎格鲁－撒克逊人的语言，使用时期约在 5–12 世纪期间。

6. **Written in a more recognizable version of English ... in southeast England:**
   （乔叟著的）《坎特伯雷故事集》是用中古英语写成的，它比《贝奥武夫》(*Beowulf*) 更易读懂。该书由朝圣者讲述的一系列故事组成。这些朝圣者在赴坎特伯雷大教堂的途中彼此讲着故事作为娱乐。

7. **It is notable for its diversity, both in the range of social types ... the stories they tell:**
   该作品以丰富多彩而著名，这不仅表现在 31 个朝圣者的各种社会类型，还体现在他们所讲述故事的不同风格上。

8. **The legend of King Arthur:**
   亚瑟王的传说包括一系列有关亚瑟王的故事，部分是神话，部分为历史。最早的传说可追溯到 6 世纪。12 世纪时，亚瑟王的故事传遍英国，此后一再被传诵，至今仍不断出现以亚瑟王为主题的各种艺术形式的作品。

9. **a Latin work which, though calling itself a work of history ... in the historical records:**
   这部拉丁文作品虽自称是部史书，但它却编造了许多材料来填充历史记录中的空白。

10. **In British culture one of the most successful ... this development lay in drama:**
    在英国文化中，体现这一发展的最成功、最长久的方面就是戏剧了。

11. **Christopher Marlowe:**
    马洛（1564–1693），英国重要诗人和戏剧家，主要作品包括《帖木儿》《浮士德博士》《马耳他岛的犹太人》等。他对伊丽莎白时期戏剧的发展起了巨大作用，为莎士比亚和詹姆斯王朝剧作家开辟了道路。

12. **Ben Johnson:**
    本·琼森（1572–1637），英国戏剧家、诗人、评论家，被公认为伊丽莎白一世和詹姆斯一世时期仅次于莎士比亚的剧作家，他是运用语言和刻画人物性格的大师，主要作品有《人人高兴》《人人扫兴》《黑假面具》《炼金术士》等。

13. **William Shakespeare:**
    威廉·莎士比亚（1564–1616）是文艺复兴时期英国著名的戏剧家和诗人。他创作了大量的传世之作，其中包括喜剧、悲剧和历史剧。他的剧本至今仍在世界各地上演，并为人们所普遍阅读。莎士比亚文采横溢，作品的题材广泛，内容深邃，所创造的各类人物以及喜怒哀乐场面给人以深刻难忘的印象，富有跨越地域和时空的永久艺术魅力。

14. **The tragedies include *Romeo and Juliet*, ... *Richard II*, *Henry IV*, and *Henry V*:**
    莎士比亚创作的悲剧包括《罗密欧与朱丽叶》《哈姆雷特》《奥赛罗》《李尔王》和《麦克白》等；喜剧中有《无事生非》《仲夏夜之梦》《第十二夜》《暴风雨》等；根据英国历史创作的历史剧有《理查

# The United Kingdom of Great Britain and Northern Ireland

三世》《理查二世》《亨利四世》《亨利五世》等。

15. ***Julius Caesar* and *Antony and Cleopatra* are tragedies on classical themes:**
《裘力斯·恺撒》和《安东尼与克娄巴特拉》是根据古典题材创作的悲剧。

16. ***Hamlet*:**
《哈姆雷特》是莎士比亚最著名的悲剧，也是世界文学中最具魅力的戏剧。哈姆雷特是丹麦王子，因父王被谋杀而郁郁寡欢。他的叔父杀死了他的父亲，篡夺了王位并娶了哈姆雷特的母亲为妻。哈姆雷特欲为父亲报仇，但他的内向和谨慎使他犹豫不决。同时，国王也在策划杀死哈姆雷特。最后戏中的主要人物同归于尽。

17. ***Romeo and Juliet*:**
《罗密欧与朱丽叶》。在一个舞会上，罗密欧与美丽的姑娘朱丽叶相遇并深深地爱上了她。因为两家是世仇，他们不能结婚。在一场街战中罗密欧的好友被朱丽叶的表兄杀死，罗密欧则刺死了后者。罗密欧不得不逃走。朱丽叶被迫将要嫁人，她服药假死。但由于事故，罗密欧没有及时得到消息，他误认为朱丽叶真死了，他自己也服毒自杀。朱丽叶醒来后发现爱人已死，她便随心爱的人而去。该剧歌颂了青年男女的纯洁爱情，反映了作者人文主义思想。

18. **full of moral doubts and political insecurities ... is put in question:**
这个世界充满道德的疑问以及政治上的不安全，那些运用权力造成这一现象的人们是否有权这样做受到了质疑。

19. **that clarify many passages in the light of modern scholarship ... ancient manuscripts:**
（这些新的翻译）根据现代学术研究成果和最新发现的古老手稿澄清了许多段落篇章。

20. **For many generations it exerted a greater influence ... any other single work in English:**
世代以来，这部圣经对英语的写作风格和品位标准产生了巨大影响，这是任何其他英语作品不能比拟的。

21. ***Paradise Lost*, *Paradise Regained* and *Samson Agonistes*:**
弥尔顿的三篇具有史诗气魄的巨作：《失乐园》《复乐园》和《力士参孙》。《失乐园》以基督教圣经中亚当和夏娃受魔鬼撒旦引诱堕落，失掉上帝的恩宠为主题。《复乐园》是《失乐园》的自然继续，描写耶稣在荒原上战胜撒旦的诱惑，恢复亚当丧失的谦虚与自制。在《力士参孙》中，参孙通过忏悔，从自我谴责而达到精神重振与胜利。

22. **Prominent on the stage, satire also found a powerful medium ... the novel:**
讽刺在戏剧中是很突出的。后来，讽刺又找到了一个强有力的媒介，这一文艺形式在18世纪得到充分发展，这一形式就是小说。

23. ***Robert Burns*:**
罗伯特·彭斯（1759–1796），杰出的苏格兰诗人，深受中国读者的喜爱。课文中提到的诗和歌有《圣威利的祈祷》《致小鼠》《致虱子》《穿过麦田》和《友谊地久天长》。

24. ***Robinson Crusoe*:**
《鲁滨逊漂流记》是笛福的著名小说，该作取得了即时和永久的成功，译成多种语言，在全世界流行。

在小说中鲁滨逊乘坐的船遭遇海难，他被冲到一个孤岛上，并在那里生存了 24 年。在岛上他遇到一位当地人，鲁滨逊称他为"礼拜五"，后者成为鲁滨逊的仆人与同伴。他们两人共同经历了许多危险，最后回到英国。

25. **Perhaps the rather violent and ugly world about them ... to a literary refuge:**
他们周围那个充满暴力和丑恶的世界可能使 19 世纪的作家到文学中寻求庇护。

26. **William Wordsworth:**
威廉·华兹华斯（1770–1850），英国诗人，以其对大自然的崇拜、人道主义思想以及对民主自由主义的同情而闻名。他是英国早期浪漫主义的领导人之一。他的诗作很多，其中有课文中提到的《抒情歌谣集》《序曲》等。

27. **Samuel Taylor Coleridge:**
柯尔律治（1772–1834），英国诗人、散文家、评论家。柯尔律治与华兹华斯相遇并结为好友，他们同是英国浪漫主义运动的伟大诗人。作为评论家柯尔律治被认为是英国浪漫主义运动的代言人。课文提到的《古舟子咏》是他的代表诗作。

28. **the Romantic Movement:**
浪漫主义作为一种思潮产生于 18 世纪末、19 世纪初的欧洲资产阶级革命时代。在文学艺术史上，浪漫主义和现实主义是两大主要思潮。浪漫主义在反映现实上，善于抒发对理想世界的热烈追求，常用热情奔放的语言、瑰丽的想象、夸张的手法等。

29. **George Gordon Byron:**
拜伦（1788–1824），英国诗人。在他的作品和生活中他创造了"拜伦式英雄"，即富有挑战性的、忧郁的年轻人，总是沉思于神秘的、不可饶恕的罪行之中。拜伦被看作浪漫主义的化身。拜伦出身贵族，私人生活浪漫，因此他的生平比他的诗作更引人注意，受到更详尽的分析。拜伦的主要作品有课文中提到的《恰尔德·哈罗尔德游记》和《唐璜》。

30. **John Keats:**
济慈（1795–1821），英国浪漫主义诗人。他出身贫苦，当过医生的学徒，后来才以写诗为业。他对当时英国社会现实不满，希望在一个"永恒美丽的世界"中寻找安身立命之处。济慈的诗以文辞声调之美而著称，在艺术上对后代英国诗人有很大影响。

31. **His art is nowhere greater than his two poems ... "To a Nightingale":**
他的艺术在他的两首诗《希腊古瓮》和《夜莺颂》里达到最高峰。这两首诗咏叹了青春、美和生命的瞬息即逝。

32. **Percy Bysshe Shelley:**
雪莱（1792–1822），英国浪漫主义诗人。他生于贵族家庭，早年深受卢梭、潘恩和葛德文等人的思想影响。雪莱创作的诗题材广泛，气势壮阔。他既写了具有政治思想的诗作，也写了优美的抒情诗、爱情诗，显示出诗人丰富的想象力，瑰丽的色彩和动人的音韵。他的主要作品包括课文提到的《西风颂》《云雀颂》和《伊斯兰的叛变》（后改名为《伊斯兰的崛起》）。

# The United Kingdom of Great Britain and Northern Ireland

33. *Frankenstein*:
    《弗兰肯斯坦》（1818）是玛利·雪莱运用哥特式故事和科幻小说相结合的手法写成的一部恐怖小说。书中的弗兰肯斯坦是个专攻秘术的瑞士学者，他制造了一个由不同尸体的各部分组成的怪物，而最终却被自己制造的怪物杀死。根据此书改编拍摄的电影也很出名。

34. the story of science gone wrong ... attempts to create life:
    这个故事说明，当傲慢的科学家（弗兰肯斯坦博士）试图创造生命时，他带来了灾难性的后果。这时，科学就出毛病了。

35. But the novel's sympathies are with the monster's struggle ... that rejects him:
    在一个拒绝接受他的世界里魔鬼努力搞清自身存在的意义，对此小说寄予了同情。

36. Sir Walter Scott:
    司各特（1771–1832），英国小说家、诗人。生于苏格兰古老家族。1814 年写了《威弗利》，开创了历史小说的先河。随后发表一系列历史小说，如课文还提到的《罗布·罗伊》《米德洛西恩的监狱》和《艾凡赫》。其中《艾凡赫》最为著名，小说生动描写了 12 世纪英国"狮心王"理查在位时复杂的阶级矛盾和民族矛盾。司各特的历史小说丰富和发展了 19 世纪的欧洲文学，对法国的巴尔扎克，俄国的托尔斯泰，美国的库珀、欧文、霍桑等都产生过影响。

37. Jane Austen:
    奥斯汀（1775–1817），英国小说家。她出生在乡村牧师家庭，一生居住在乡间，对乡村绅士地主的生活了解深入，她的小说都以此为背景，以婚姻问题为中心题材。她的小说情节曲折，故事性强，人物描写生动，语言幽默巧妙。主要作品有课文提到的《理智和感情》《傲慢与偏见》《爱玛》等。她的作品多次被搬上银幕和电视。

38. but in the contemporary spirit of Romanticism ... with imaginative and the personal:
    在当时的浪漫主义精神之中，理性被想象力和个人因素所平衡。

39. the Brontë sisters:
    勃朗特姐妹。夏洛蒂、爱米丽、安妮三姐妹出身贫寒，幼年丧母，不得不在慈善学校度过童年。三个姐妹都喜欢写作。夏洛蒂的代表作《简·爱》是自传体小说，小说坦率而热情地塑造了一个个人天性欲望和社会世俗发生矛盾的妇女形象，该作问世后产生了巨大影响。爱米丽的《呼啸山庄》描写了强烈的爱憎情感，被一些文学评论家誉为第一部社会革命小说。以上两部小说均为英国文学中的重要作品。安妮的小说具有平静的力量和现实性，也得到一些评论者的称赞。

40. because of which they could not hope for a respectable marriage of equals, being too poor:
    因为他们过于贫困，他们无法希望得到体面的婚姻，嫁给同等的男人。

41. Charles Dickens:
    狄更斯（1812–1870），英国最伟大的现实主义小说家。幼年家贫，曾当过学徒，成名后仍接近贫苦人们。他一生辛勤创作，留下 20 余部小说，包括课文提到的《匹克威克外传》《雾都孤儿》《大卫·科波菲尔》和《远大前程》。狄更斯的小说情节曲折感人，人物形象鲜明生动，无论写景还是叙事，既真切又富想象力，

UNIT 6  British Literature

既含有尖刻的讽刺，又不乏幽默的夸张。狄更斯的作品无情地揭露和抨击了压迫穷人的不公正社会。

42. **Dickens too was concerned with the state of the nation ... the suffering of the poor to light:**
狄更斯也十分关注国家的状况。他儿时父亲因欠债入狱，他饱受童工之苦，因此，他有个人理由将穷苦人的遭遇写出来，让世人知道。

43. **Robert Louis Stevenson:**
罗伯特·路易斯·斯蒂文森（1850–1894），英国小说家和散文家，尤以冒险故事著称。他的作品种类繁多，构思巧妙，富有创造力量。他对苏格兰风土人情深感兴趣，研究过18世纪苏格兰历史，写了一些以苏格兰为背景的历史小说，其主要著作包括课文提到的《金银岛》《绑架》和《吉基尔医生和海德先生》。

44. **a story again concerned with the conflict ... transforms himself into the wild Mr. Hyde:**
这个故事也讲述了理性与感情之间的冲突，描述人本性中感性的一面，这一矛盾由同一个人体现出来，这人是吉基尔医生，他将自己变成了凶悍的海德先生。

45. **Thomas Hardy:**
哈代（1840–1928），英国小说家，诗人。他的作品揭露了19世纪后半叶的英国社会，描写了资本主义制度下小农的破产和他们无望的挣扎。他著有11部小说，代表作包括课文提到的《还乡记》《苔丝》和《无名的裘德》，此外《远离尘嚣》和《卡斯特桥市长》也很有名。他的作品反映了自然主义人生观，认为人受着自我无法控制的力量的左右。后来哈代转向诗歌创作，出版了《韦塞克斯诗集》。

46. **Never have so many words and ideas been printed or passed on, through radio and television:**
通过广播和电视，大量的文字与信息得到前所未有的传播。

47. **Modernism:**
现代派是20世纪初以来出现的各种文学新流派的总称。它包括象征主义、未来主义、超现实主义、意识流小说、存在主义文学、黑色幽默等等。现代派小说的大多数作品不重故事情节，而着重对人物内心世界的挖掘。文字语言往往不规范，意思含糊晦涩。爱尔兰作家乔伊斯，英国女作家伍尔芙，美国作家福克纳被公认为现代派的杰出代表。

48. **Postmodernism:**
后现代主义，这是二战以后，20世纪60年代至70年代出现的一种文学新流派，其主要特点是试图摆脱一切传统模式的束缚，否定权威，否定中心，提倡多元化。

49. **which can be thought of as assuming understanding ... an agreed version of the "world":**
那可以被认为是假设作家与读者之间的理解，其结果是对世界形成一种简单化的统一认识。

50. **It often portrays the action from the viewpoint ... narrator outside the action:**
现代派作品经常从一个困惑的个人角度描写故事，而不是以故事之外一个无所不知的、非个人化的角度。

51. **Joseph Conrad:**
约瑟夫·康拉德（1857–1924），英国航海家和小说家。他自幼向往海上生活，先后在不同的商船上工作，担任过水手、大副和船长等职务。海上的传奇经历为他的写作提供了丰富素材。他的作品有课文提到的《黑暗的中心》以及《群岛上的被遗弃者》《机会》和《胜利》等。以《黑暗的中心》为基础拍摄的影片《现

# The United Kingdom of Great Britain and Northern Ireland

代启示录》描绘了20世纪60年代的越南战争。

52. **They are Modernist in their concerns with moral uncertainty ... what is true:**
    他们是现代派，对道德的不确定表示关注：什么是对？他们也对事实的不确定表示关注：什么是真？

53. **The journey is a symbolic one representing the darkness at the heart of man.**
    这个旅程是象征性的，代表人类内心的黑暗。

54. **Virginia Woolf:**
    弗吉尼亚·伍尔芙（1882–1941），英国女作家。她对小说的写作形式做出了独特贡献，是现代派重要作家之一。除了小说，她还写文学评论。她的主要作品包括课文提到的小说《黛洛维夫人》《到灯塔去》《奥兰多》以及评论专著《一个自己的房间》等。其中《黛洛维夫人》是作家早期的佳作，描写黛洛维夫人一天24小时之内的生活，情节虽简单，但人物内心的刻画很细致，通过"意识流"手法将人物的思想、感情、个性和弱点都充分表现出来了。1941年伍尔芙投河自尽。

55. **Her novels have become important to feminists ... to be limited by society:**
    她的小说对女性主义者来说变得很重要，因为它们表现了妇女的个性是如何受到社会的局限的。

56. **She sometimes used what has been called "stream of consciousness ... thought onto page:**
    她有时运用被称为"意识流"的技巧，即用文字呈现出表面上毫无组织的意识流动。"意识流"是20世纪描写心理小说采用的一种叙述技巧。该叙述方式有意忽视故事情节的连贯和完整，运用人物内心独白、梦幻想象、自由联想、象征暗示、时空交错等手法来展现人物的意识流动轨迹，以达到挖掘人物内心世界的效果。

57. **D. H. Lawrence:**
    劳伦斯（1889–1930），英国著名小说家、诗人、散文家，现代派代表作家之一。作为矿工的儿子，劳伦斯对英国清教传统敢于反叛，他的作品辛辣地批评现代工业社会，他认为性是原始的潜意识，它对当代人由于工业社会造成的不适宜症能起到治疗作用。劳伦斯在写作上摒弃了英国传统的艺术表现形式，大量使用质朴的生活语言。他的主要小说包括《虹》《恋爱中的女人》《查泰莱夫人的情人》以及文中提到的《儿子们与情人们》等。

58. **E. M. Forster:**
    福斯特（1879–1970），英国小说家、散文家。生于伦敦，毕业于剑桥大学。初期的作品反映了摆脱维多利亚时代文学影响的特点。他摒弃了19世纪人们喜爱的繁缛辞藻和复杂的细节描写，采用更为流畅自如、更为口语化的写作风格。他的作品温和地讽刺了英国中上层阶级在道德和感情上的匮乏。课文提到的《霍华德庄园》是作家的成名之作，故事的女主人公玛格丽特·施莱格热爱艺术，富有浪漫主义色彩和自由想象力，她与商业成功而精神濒于崩溃的亨利·威尔考克斯结婚。作者以此暗示商业化的英国社会需要与浪漫的文化艺术相结合。《印度之行》是作家另一部佳作，描写了英国对印度的殖民统治的偏见与不公正。

## UNIT 6  British Literature

**59. But in what we might see as a typical move ... to create a new "hybrid":**
不过，最后这两家合到了一起，产生了一个新的"混合物"，我们可以看到这一处理对一位英国作家来说是颇具典型性的。

**60. So while Modernists were scientists of human existence ... as abandoning that search:**
因此，如果说现代主义作家是研究人类存在的科学家，力图寻找存在于令人迷惑的表象下面的隐藏意义，那么，可以认为后现代派作家放弃了这种寻求。

**61. Meaning does not exist outside of the human head ... waiting to be discovered:**
（对后现代派来说）人的大脑之外不存在任何意义，同样，书中也不存在等待人们去发现的意义。

**62. The story's main postmodern "trick" is ... offered a choice of endings:**
故事体现后现代主义的主要"伎俩"是给读者提供几种不同的结局，让他们选择。

**63. Not all writers can be squeezed into the definitions Modern or Postmodern:**
并不是所有的作家都可以归类到现代派或后现代派的定义中去。

**64. Graham Greene:**
格林（1904–1991），英国小说家，毕业于牛津大学。主要作品包括《事情的中心》《权利与荣耀》，描写冷战时期住在越南的美国人的《沉默的美国人》，古巴间谍故事《我们在哈瓦那的人》等。

**65. James Bond:**
詹姆斯·邦德，伊恩·弗莱明笔下侦探小说系列的主人公。邦德是英国情报机构的侦探，代号007。他常授命执行异常艰巨危险的任务，每次执行任务中，他都历经危险，出生入死，但最后总能化险为夷，并伴有浪漫故事发生。以小说为基础的007电影系列更是家喻户晓。

**66. Kazuo Ishiguro:**
石黑一雄，英国小说家，剧作家和短篇小说家。1954年生于日本，1960年全家移民英国。他在英国接受教育并成为英国公民。他的小说 *The Remains of the Day*（译为《去日留痕》或《长日将尽》）曾成功地改编为电影，获八项奥斯卡提名。2017年石黑一雄获诺贝尔文学奖，"他的小说富有激情的力量，在我们与世界联系的虚幻感下面，他展现了一个深渊"。

**67. To look at a list of the most respected contemporary British writers ... their origins:**
如果我们浏览一下当今英国最受尊敬的作家名单，这些作家背景的多样性必会给我们留下深刻印象。

**68. But this mixture, this "hybridity" ... highly international economy:**
但是，这种混合，即"杂糅"，一直是英国文学写作的一部分，它的背景包含了英国多民族的、阶级划分的内部地位，英国帝国历史，以及英国当前高度发展的国际经济。

# The United Kingdom of Great Britain and Northern Ireland

# Exercises

**I. Give the Chinese equivalents for the following:**
1. *The Canterbury Tales*
2. John Milton
3. The Renaissance
4. *Robinson Crusoe*
5. *Romeo and Juliet*
6. Virginia Woolf

**II. Decide whether the following statements are true (T) or false (F):**
1. Much early British literature was concerned with Christianity, and Anglo-Saxons produced many versions of the Bible. _____
2. Beowulf was a sea monster killed by a Swedish warrior. _____
3. "The Wife of Bath" is one of the tales contained in *The Canterbury Tales*. _____
4. There was a general flowering of culture and intellectual life in Europe during the 17th and 18th centuries which is known as "The Renaissance". _____
5. William Shakespeare is a great poet and much is known of his life. _____
6. Keats, Shelley and Byron brought the Romantic Movement to its height. _____
7. *Robinson Crusoe* tells the story of a shipwreck and solitary survival. _____
8. Writers of romantic literature are more concerned with imagination and feeling than with the power of reason. _____
9. *Don Juan* is an epic poem composed by John Milton. _____
10. Thomas Hardy, the author of *Tess of the D'Urbervilles*, was also a first-class poet. _____

**III. Fill in the blanks:**
1. One of the oldest of the early "Old English" literary works is a long poem from Anglo-Saxon times called _____.
2. _____ written by Geoffrey Chaucer is often studied by middle school and college

students today.

3. Shakespeare's plays fall into three categories. They are _____, _____ and history plays.
4. Name two of the tragedies written by Shakespeare: _____ and _____.
5. Charlotte Brontë and Emily Brontë are noted for their respective novels _____ and _____ which are largely the love stories of a woman for a man.
6. Charles Dickens is regarded not only as _____ but also as social critic in the 19th century. His novel _____ tells the story of an orphan child drawn into crime in the London underworld.
7. The author of *Ivanhoe* was _____.
8. Twentieth-century literature can be broadly divided into two stylistic periods: _____ and _____.
9. Virginia Woolf was one of the most famous writers of the 20th century. Her work was concerned with the individual consciousness, especially _____ consciousness. She sometimes used the technique of _____ in her writing.
10. *The Heart of Darkness* was written by _____; the author of the book *1984* was _____.

IV. **Questions:**

1. Who was Christopher Marlow? What is his most famous play?
2. Shakespeare's plays are divided into three categories: tragedies, comedies, and history plays. Can you name two plays under each category? Which of his plays do you like best? Explain your views.
3. Who was John Milton? What do you know about his epic *Paradise Lost*?
4. Who wrote *Gulliver's Travels*? What is this book about? Why is it an important work of British literature?
5. What were writers of romantic literature concerned with? Who were the two poets whose volume of poems was called romantic poetry's "Declaration of Independence"?
6. Three men brought the Romanic Movement to its height. Who were they? What poems did they write respectively?
7. Why is Jane Austen regarded as one of the greatest of all English novelists? What are some of the distinguished styles in her novels?
8. What is the novel *Jane Eyre* about? What is the main plot of the story?

# The United Kingdom of Great Britain and Northern Ireland

9. Who was the greatest British storyteller of the 19th century? Name three novels written by him.
10. Why does the author say that Joseph Conrad is one of the most famous English Modernist writers? What are his novels concerned with?
11. What is Virginia Woolf's work concerned with? Why have her novels become important to feminists?
12. In what way is George Orwell's *1984* a powerful satire?
13. Why is Salman Rushdie the most controversial of contemporary British writers? What is his writing style?

**V. Topics for discussion or research:**

1. Do you think Elizabethan Drama occupies a significant position in British literature? Who is the most important figure in Elizabethan Drama? What are some of his well-known plays?
2. What are the most important features of Romantic Literature?
3. What is Realism? Who is the most well-known Realist writer in the 19th British literature? Have you read any of his novels? Comment on them.
4. How is Modernism different from Realism? Do you think Virginia Woolf is an important Modernist writer? Discuss the themes and writing styles of her major novels.
5. As a student of English, do you think that reading works of English literature helps improve your command of the English language? Support your view with facts and examples.

# UNIT 7

# British Education System

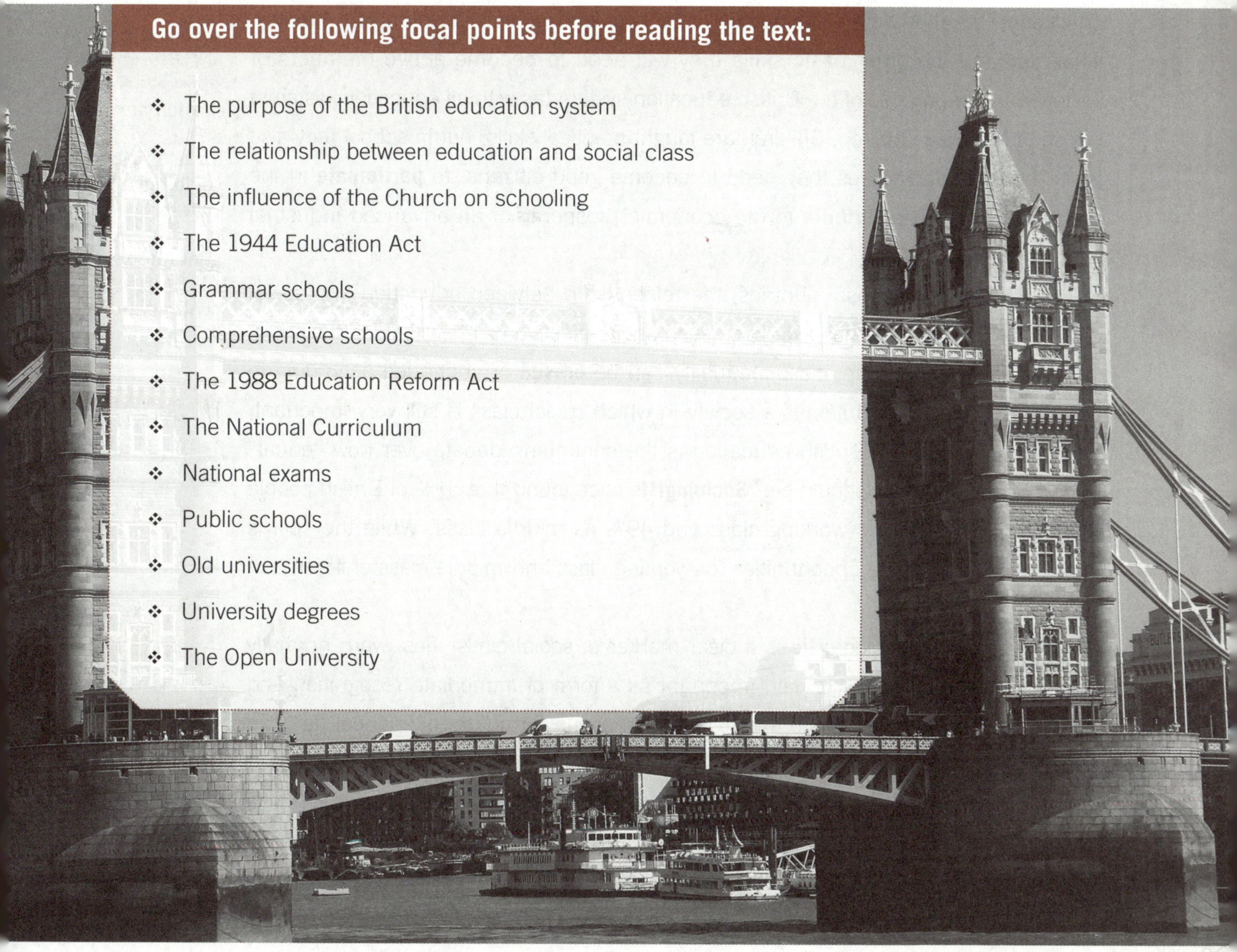

**Go over the following focal points before reading the text:**

- The purpose of the British education system
- The relationship between education and social class
- The influence of the Church on schooling
- The 1944 Education Act
- Grammar schools
- Comprehensive schools
- The 1988 Education Reform Act
- The National Curriculum
- National exams
- Public schools
- Old universities
- University degrees
- The Open University

# The United Kingdom of Great Britain and Northern Ireland

 Text

## Introduction

Many people think school is just about teaching children what are, in the UK, often called "the three R's" — "reading, 'riting and 'rithmetic" (reading, writing and **arithmetic**). In other words, the purpose of school is to provide children with **literacy**, **numeracy** and the other basic skills they will need to become active members of society. But the purpose of the British education system (as with all education systems) is also to **socialise** children. Children are taught practical skills; but in school they also learn the rules and values they need to become good citizens, to **participate** in the community, and to contribute to the economic prosperity of an advanced industrial economy.[1]

In Britain, as in most countries, the relationship between education and social class is close. Education has long been seen as an effective tool for climbing the social ladder[2]. At the same time, class inequality can be **erased** or continued according to educational policy.[3] As Britain is a society in which social class is still very important, an enduring feature of British education is the continuing debate over how "equal" educational opportunity should be.[4] **Sociologists** once found that 51% of British people identified themselves as working class and 49% as middle class. While the split is about half and half, the opportunities for working class and middle class children can be very different.

The school (or college) **tie** is a clear marker of social class. Ties, worn normally on formal occasions, may remain important as a form of immediate recognition and subsequent networking: hence the significance of the term "the old school tie".[5] To have attended the "right" schools — particularly the famous boys' public schools like Eton and Winchester[6] — and the "right" universities — Oxford and Cambridge[7] (these two rival universities have been nicknamed "Oxbridge") — are still the best means of **guaranteeing** a successful career. In 2005, 46% of Conservative Party Members of Parliament were graduates of Oxbridge. Most senior **civil servants** are also Oxbridge graduates. When people in Britain talk about "the old boys network"[8], they mean

arithmetic *n.*
算术
literacy *n.*
识字；有文化
numeracy *n.*
识数；计算能力
socialise *v.*
使合群，使适合过社会生活
participate *v.*
参加；参与
erase *v.* 消除
sociologist *n.*
社会学家
tie *n.* 领带
guarantee *v.*
保证；担保
civil servant
公务员

this **elite** group of men who went to school and university together. Not only do they dominate government, but also they are very influential in banking, the media, the arts and education. In Britain, where you are educated is still very important to your future.

## History

Nowadays, the British education system is run by the state, which provides funding, oversees standards, and tries to make sure that all British children receive a quality education. One of the largest, most important government departments is the Department for Education (DfE). In 2015–16 state expenditure on education was £83.4 billion, or about 4.4% of the UK's Gross Domestic Product (GDP)[9]. And it is worth noting here that British education system is characterised by its slightly different systems in the four regions — England, Wales, Scotland and Northern Ireland.

The state was not always involved in educating British children. Historically, education was voluntary, and many of the schools that existed were set up by churches. The influence of the Church on schooling is still strong: until very recently, religious education was the only subject which the state insisted all schools teach their pupils (other subjects were left up to schools to decide upon). Daily **prayers** and singing **hymns** are still a regular part of school life. In keeping with changes to British society, however, Christianity is no longer the only religion officially recognised. In some cities, the state funds schools which have **Islam**, **Judaism** or other religions rather than Christianity as their creed.[10]

Before 1870, only 40% of children under 10 went to school regularly. The main receivers of a more advanced education were the sons of the wealthy. One of the changes to British society brought by the Industrial Revolution was the government's decision to become increasingly involved in taking responsibility for the education of children. In 1870 the government passed a law which called for government-funded education. By 1880, attendance at school for children between 5 and 10 was **compulsory** rather than voluntary; and by the end of the First World War, the school leaving age was raised to 14 in order to **dissuade** children from leaving school in order to work to support their families. In 1938 around 80% of children left school at age 14, most having only ever attended an all-age elementary school.

Other major changes to the British education system took place **subsequent to** World War II. When the Germans began dropping bombs on British cities in 1940 and

elite *n.*
社会精英
prayer *n.*
祷告；祈祷
hymn *n.*
圣歌；赞歌
Islam *n.*
伊斯兰教
Judaism *n.*
犹太教
compulsory *adj.*
义务的；强制的
dissuade *v.*
劝阻；劝诫
subsequent to
在…之后

# The United Kingdom of Great Britain and Northern Ireland

1941, 750 000 school children were "**evacuated**" to live in the countryside where it was hoped they would be safer. Schools were closed or used for war purposes, and education continued in the countryside **on an ad hoc basis**. As a result of this **disruption** of the old system, the government, with the assistance of the Church (a conservative force) and newly powerful trade unions (a more socialist influence) began planning to reconstruct the education system. This time, the new system would emphasise equality.

The result was the 1944 Education Act which made entry to secondary schools compulsory and to universities "**meritocratic**".[11] All children were given the right to a free secondary education no matter what family background they came from and the main concern was to make sure more children had **access** to a good education. Local Educational Authorities (LEAs) were required to provide schools funded by the state. As previously, compulsion to receive full-time education began at 5, but the upper limit was extended from 14 to 15, and a provision for a later raising to 16 was made.[12] (In the event, the school-leaving age was raised to 15 in 1947 and to 16 in 1972.) Religious education was made compulsory. A "**tripartite**" system of secondary education was established after 1945, with grammar schools[13] for the most able (the top 20% of those to be prepared for university education), secondary modern schools for the majority, and technical schools for those skilled with their hands. Children were recruited into the different kinds of schools on the basis of an examination taken once at the end of primary schooling at the age of 11, known as the "11-plus". This had a huge influence over lifetime opportunity, since grammar schools were the only route to a university education for those who could not afford private education.

This first attempt to try to create a less elitist school system failed. In spite of the government's high hopes with the universal and free education, working class children still left school at a younger age and with fewer qualifications than middle class children. Because entrance to schools was based upon exam performance, the children of the middle classes performed better. They had more free time, more access to help if they were having trouble (their parents could hire **tutors**, for example) and valued education more than their working class **peers** who were often under pressure to quit school and find jobs in order to help their families.[14]

Central governments, working with teachers and local government officials, continued to experiment with policies to try to raise the quality of education of all pupils, not just the middle classes. In the late 1960s, comprehensive schools[15] were

evacuate *v.*
撤离
on an ad hoc basis
临时权宜地
disruption *n.*
中断；瓦解
meritocratic *adj.* 才智和能力出众的
access *n.* 途径
tripartite *adj.*
三方；分成三部分的
tutor *n.*
家庭教师，辅导教师
peer *n.*
同事；伙伴

introduced all over the country, which ended the division between grammar schools for the most academically capable pupils and secondary modern schools for ordinary pupils. Entrance exams were **abolished** and schools were no longer allowed to let children "compete" for places. Thus more equality of educational opportunities was achieved. In 2000, 85% of students attended comprehensive schools; the rest went to some remaining grammar schools or private schools.

In 1976 British education was the focus of a new controversy when the Labour Party started "the Great Education Debate" about national standards and styles of teaching. The Labour Government was concerned about the inadequate skill level of the labour force and a new **initiative** to prepare children for employment was launched. Just three years later, with the victory of the Conservative Government of Margaret Thatcher, education again became a big political issue. While the new government thought that job training was very important, it felt schools were not paying enough attention to teaching pupils the traditional "three Rs". Therefore, the Education Reform Act 1988 was passed, which introduced a **National Curriculum** for 5–16 year-olds that all state schools were required to follow. Thereafter children had to study the following subjects: English, mathematics, science, religious education, history, geography, technology, music, art, **physical education** (PE), and a modern foreign language. The National Curriculum occupied not less than 70% of the school timetable, the rest of the time being used for subjects of the school's choosing.[16] Students must also pass national tests (at the ages of 7, 11, 14 and 16), designed to monitor the quality of teaching and ensure what is learned is up to national standards, and schools are ranked according to the success of their pupils in reaching national targets.[17] "Key Stages" were introduced in schools. At each key stage a number of educational objectives were to be achieved. City Technology Colleges were introduced which were partially sponsored by industry and commerce, though only 15 schools were eventually set up. The Act provided for the establishment of **grant-maintained schools** independent of local authorities and under the direct funding from the central government. More power was given to schools to run their own affairs within the framework of national standards.

This is a very big change: previously, the central government only set broad education policy guidelines and provided funds. Practical decision-making was carried out by Local Education Authorities, located at regional or city levels, which based their

abolish *v.*
取消；废除
initiative *n.*
行动；倡议
national curriculum
全国教学大纲课程
physical education
体育课
grant-maintained school
中央政府拨款学校

policies on local conditions.[18] Teachers also had a lot of individual power to decide on what to do in the classroom. Now all teachers were told what to teach and their schools would be ranked according to students' performance. Thus the National Curriculum reintroduced competition between schools. Good schools attract good pupils and therefore attract more funding. More funding means they can hire better teachers, buy more books and equipment and therefore produce even better pupils. The revised second National Curriculum of 2008 continues to emphasise the importance of subjects while at the same time it places emphasis on the development of skills for life and work.

In the 21st century, specialist schools, academies and free schools[19] were promoted as part of an attempt to improve standards by "increasing diversity" in secondary schools.

In 1997 the New Labour government promoted specialist schools by encouraging secondary schools to specialise in certain areas of the curriculum to achieve school improvement. Specialist schools receive extra funding. Although they focus on one or two chosen areas (e.g. art, business & enterprise, engineering, **humanities**, languages, mathematics & computing, music, science, sports, technology), these schools must still meet the full national curriculum requirements. There were nearly 3 000 specialist schools, which was 88% of the state-funded secondary schools in England, before the new coalition government of 2010 ended the scheme.

The New Labour government in 2000 introduced academies to revive education for poor schools. Academies are publicly funded state schools independent of local authority control. They are also partially sponsored by non-governmental bodies. The first secondary academies opened in 2002 and the first primary academies opened in 2010. Academies have greater freedoms to innovate and raise standards. They do not need to follow the National Curriculum, but have to ensure that their curriculum is broad and balanced, and that it includes the core subjects of mathematics and English. The programme of creating academies was greatly expanded from 2010 by the coalition government (2010–2015) and further expanded by the Conservative government (post 2015) after 2015. In England, in November 2013, there were 3 444 such schools. The coalition government and the Conservative government have also encouraged the establishment of "free schools" — schools set up entirely outside the **aegis** of local authorities[20], set up by parents, teachers, businesses and others yet

humanity n.
人文学科
aegis n.
保护；支持

funded directly from central government. Thus, even within the state system, there are a wide range of different kinds of school — those funded directly and managed by local authorities, comprehensive schools, specialist schools, faith schools, grammar schools, academies and free schools.

## The Present Education System

Across the UK there are five stages of education: early years, primary, secondary, **further education** and higher education. Education is compulsory for all children between the ages of 5 (4 in Northern Ireland) and 16. In 2004, almost three-quarters of 16-year-olds in the UK remained in full-time education after this age, either in school or further education colleges. In 2015/16 there were 9.3 million full-time primary and secondary school students. Increasing emphasis is also placed on lifelong learning of skills to help employment in a changing labour market.

Parents can choose between sending their children to state schools or to private schools. State schools are funded by local and central government. About 93% of pupils receive free education from the public sector. The government also assists "faith schools" established by religious groups.

Since 1993, parents have had the right to express a preference for a particular state school for their children.[21] A system of "league tables" — comparative tables which rank schools according to public examination results, **truancy** rates, destinations of school leavers, and so on — are published in order to help parents make choices.[22] While children usually attend the school they live closest to, now ambitious parents sometimes move to a different neighbourhood in order to be close to a well-performing school. Needless to say, good schools tend to be in middle-class neighbourhoods and it is the wealthier middle classes who can most easily afford to move if they think it is necessary.

In the private sector there are independent schools (independent of state funding) which are commonly, but confusingly, called public schools. (They are called public schools because they were originally seen as "public" **alternatives** to having private tutors in aristocratic households.)[23] Independent schools receive their funding through the private sector and mainly through tuition fees, with some government assistance. Independent schools are not part of the national education system and are not required to follow the National Curriculum in all its details, but the quality of instruction and

---

further education
继续教育
truancy *n.*
逃学；旷课
alternative *n.*
可供选择的事物；替代物

standards are maintained through visits from Her Majesty's Inspectors of Schools[24]. Parents choose to pay fees in order to send their children to these schools because the quality of education is such that their children have a better chance of getting into good universities and/or getting better jobs when they leave school. The oldest public schools in Britain are Winchester (1394), Eton (1440), Harrow (1571), Rugby and Westminster. Independent primary schools are generally called "**prep schools**" (preparatory school). Schools for older pupils from 11,12 to 18 are often referred to as "public schools". Nowadays, most public schools are co-educational day schools. However there are still many "boarding schools" — where children live at the school throughout each term — and most of these are still single-sex. Now about 6% of British children attend independent fee-paying schools.

In state schools, each year that a pupil studies is numbered and the whole period is divided into 5 key stages[25]. Primary education starts at Year 1 and secondary education starts at Year 7. Up to age 5, children may have some pre-primary schooling in nursery schools, daycare, or play groups. The government has no obligation to provide such facilities and so many are private enterprise arrangements. However, the state realises such provision is important, especially now that many mothers work. So in England from 2010, all 3- and 4-year-olds are entitled to 15 hours (per week) of free nursery education for 38 weeks of the year.[26] Increasingly nursery education is provided by primary schools rather than specialised nurseries. Children at this stage mainly do activities and learn how to socialise with their peers. More children under 5 years old are attending school — around 20% in 1970/1971 and 64% in 1999/2000. In 2016 95% of the 3- and 4-year-old population benefitted from some funded early education.

Between the ages of 5 and 11, pupils mainly attend state sector primary schools. These schools are called **co-educational** or mixed schools because they admit both boys and girls. The primary school consists of an **infant** stage from 5 to 6 and a junior stage from 7 to 11. At the age of 7 and 11, pupils take the National Curriculum assessments called SATs (Standard Assessment Tests) for the core subjects of English, Mathematics and Science.

From the age of 11 up to around the age of 18, students attend secondary schools. More than 80% of pupils in secondary schools in England and Wales attend mixed schools; 60% in Northern Ireland; Scotland, nearly all. About 90% of secondary schools are comprehensive schools which admit children without reference to their academic

prep school
预备学校
co-educational
*adj.* 对男女学生开放的（学校）
infant *n.*
幼儿；初学者
*adj.* 幼儿的；初期的

abilities. Such schools provide a general education. Pupils can study everything from academic subjects like literature and science, to more practical subjects like cooking and **carpentry**.

Foreign languages are taught as an **integral** part of the National Curriculum, reflecting the importance of Britain's relationship with Europe.

Those children who do not attend comprehensive schools attend grammar schools instead. Grammar schools select children, usually at the age of 11, through that examination called "the 11-plus". Those who show academic potential are admitted to the grammar schools where the emphasis is on advanced academic work rather than the more general curriculum of the comprehensive schools. In Northern Ireland the grammar school/non-grammar school division is still common, but throughout the rest of Great Britain grammar schools are becoming increasingly rare.

After 5 years of secondary education, (at about age 16) English, Northern Irish and Welsh students sit their GCSE exams (General Certificate of Secondary Education[27]), usually in about eight to ten subjects, which must include English and Mathematics. GCSEs are the main means of assessing pupils' progress in their final 2 years of compulsory education. Based on these results, pupils then decide what avenue of education they would like to follow.[28] They have a number of choices. At the age of 16, they can decide to quit school and find a job; or they can prepare to sit exams for university entrance; or they can concentrate on vocational training. Every 16 and 17 year old is guaranteed a place in full-time education or training.

Pupils who hope to attend university carry on their academic study in the sixth form[29] for a further two years and then sit A-level exams (General Certificate of Education-Advanced[30]). Usually four (or five) academic subjects are studied in the first year, leading to an Advanced Subsidiary level qualification (GCE-AS Level). Then in the second year students normally specialise in three of those subjects at which they are most **proficient** for Advanced level qualification (GCE-A Level).[31] Since admittance to universities depends largely on A-level results, the two years spent in the sixth form are very important and often very **stressful** for British pupils. Among first year university students getting to know each other, the most common question after "What's your name?" and "Where are you from?" is "What A-levels did you take?"[32]

Other pupils who decide not to go to university may choose to take vocational training. The vocational equivalents of A-levels are General National Vocational

carpentry *n.*
木工手艺；木工活
integral *adj.*
完全的；缺一不可的
proficient *adj.*
熟练的；精通的
stressful *adj.*
紧张的；压力重的

Qualifications (GNVQs)[33], which provide a broadly based preparation for work or for taking further vocational.

In Britain, the academic year is divided into three terms of about twelve weeks each.

## Higher Education

British universities are public bodies which receive funds from central government. This differs from the United States which, in addition to public universities, also has privately funded universities which are often very wealthy. In the UK, the amount of funding each university receives is based on its size, the number of students it teaches, and the research it conducts.[34] So far, the UK has only one privately funded university, the University of Buckingham.

Higher education has a long history in the UK. Oxford and Cambridge date from the 12th and 13th centuries, while the Scottish universities of St Andrews, Glasgow, Edinburgh and Aberdeen from the 15th and 16th centuries. The University of London[35] was founded in 1836 and includes such famous colleges as the London School of Economics and the Imperial College of Science and Technology. Many provincial universities were set up between 1850 and 1930, for example, the "redbrick universities"[36] — Universities of Bristol, Birmingham, Liverpool, Manchester, Leeds and Sheffield, so-called because they were built of red coloured brick. In the 1960s there was a large expansion in the number of universities, with several completely new universities being built (e.g. Universities of York, Lancaster, Sussex, Kent, Warwick, Essex and East Anglia) and some colleges of advanced technology raised to university status. The Open University was established in 1969. In 1992 the number of universities grew again when polytechnics[37] and other higher education establishments were given the right to become universities. University numbers also increased from 109 in 2000/01 to 132 in 2014/15.

University campuses are full of people of different ages and nationalities studying many different things. In 2014/15 there were 1 664 000 full-time students, 438 010 of whom came from overseas. While most of the students are studying for their first degrees, about 305 400 were working on postgraduate qualifications. There are about 133 000 full time university teachers paid wholly from university funds.

First degree courses are mainly full time and last three years, except in Scotland where they take four years. Usually one receives a Bachelor of Arts (BA) or a Bachelor of Science (BSc), for a second degree Master of Arts (MA) or Science (MSc) (after a further one year full-time or two years part-time study) and Doctor of Philosophy (PhD) (after at least three years of original research).[38]

UK educational institutions are world class. The excellence of their teaching, research and scholarships is acknowledged worldwide. Such is the reputation of British education that, every year, UK institutions attract hundreds of thousands of international students. Many who come to study there pay for their courses privately and some receive financial help. UK government departments and the devolved administrations of Scotland, Wales and Northern Ireland offer a variety of scholarships and other awards to help international students study in the UK. The most well-known scholarships are the **Chevening Scholarships** and Commonwealth Scholarships. These awards are a sign of the UK's strong commitment to the rest of the world. They also show the UK's awareness of the many benefits that come from sharing the excellence of its schools, colleges and universities with visiting students and scholars from abroad. Universities and departments are also assessed once every four years by a national review body, which gives **ratings** for their research and teaching.[39] Those with good ratings get more government funding.

Universities, reflecting the trend throughout the education system, have traditionally been rather elitist. Most students were from the middle classes, attended good schools, performed well in their A-levels and received a fully-funded place in a university. In recent decades, great efforts have been made to increase the numbers and diversity of students that pursue higher education. For example, whereas in 1980, 1 in 8 pupils went on to university, by 1990 it was 1 in 5, and by 2000 it was 1 in 3. The higher education participation rates reached 48% in 2014/15, up from 42% in 2006/07, implying that, nowadays, almost half of all school students go on to study at university. Meanwhile, access for mature students and students without traditional A-level qualifications continues to widen.[40]

The Open University[41] offers a non-traditional route for people to take university level courses and receive a university degree. People can register without having any formal educational qualifications. They follow university courses through textbooks, TV and radio broadcasts, **correspondence**, videos, **residential schools** and a network of study centres. Tens of thousands of Britons, from housewives to coal miners, from teachers to ballet dancers "attend" the Open University each year.

Chevening Scholarship
志奋领奖学金
rating n.
评估；评价
correspondence n. 函授
residential school
寄宿制学校

# The United Kingdom of Great Britain and Northern Ireland

From 1998, the British government ended free higher education and started charging university students a tuition fee of £1 000 a year and student grants were replaced by loans.[42] From 2004, universities charged students up to £3 000 per year for tuition. The loan did not need to be paid back until a student earned at least £15 000 a year after graduation. The fee was further increased in 2010 to up to £9 000. A student needs to pay back when he can earn at least £21 000 a year and he pays no more than 9% of the income. There is a sharp difference in fee payment between home students[43] and international students.

In June 2016, the British public voted to leave the European Union (EU). The Brexit negotiation will take at least 2 years. While Britain is a member of the EU, EU students are treated the same as British students in tuition fees and British students are also treated as native students in other EU countries. Besides, huge numbers of staff at UK universities come from the EU countries. The UK is also part of the European Research Area and universities have received more research fund from the EU than Britain contributes. Inevitably, when Britain leaves the EU there will be a huge impact on the university sector in a variety of ways. Only time will tell as to what extent British higher education will be affected.

# Explanations

1. **Children are taught ... of an advanced industrial economy:**
   学生在学校要学习各种技能，但还要学一些成为好公民所应具备的道理规范和价值观，以便能走上社会，为一个发达的工业化国家的经济繁荣作贡献。

2. **climbing the social ladder:**
   攀爬社会阶梯，从社会较低地位向更高地位攀升。

3. **class inequality can be erased or continued according to educational policy:**
   教育政策可以铲除阶级地位的不平等，也可以使这种不平等继续存在。这说明在英国，是否受到良好教育直接影响到一个人的社会地位。

4. **an enduring feature of British education is ... how "equal" educational opportunity should be:**
   英国教育中的一个长期特点就是在教育机会"平等"的问题上争论不休。

# UNIT 7 British Education System

5. **Ties, worn normally on formal occasions ... the term "the old school tie":**

   在正式场合戴（有学校标志的）领带作为一种获得即时认可和随后的人际关系网的方式可能仍然很重要，因此这也是"母校领带"一词的重要性。

6. **Eton and Winchester:**

   伊顿公学位于伦敦以西；温切斯特公学位于英格兰南部。这两所公学是英国著名的私立贵族学校。

7. **Oxford and Cambridge:**

   牛津大学和剑桥大学是英国最古老的两所大学，分别建立于 12 世纪和 13 世纪。这两所大学有着悠久的历史，在世界上享有盛誉。英国大部分政治家和政府官员毕业于这两所大学。

8. **"the old boy network":**

   "老男孩关系网"。指毕业于私立贵族公学，之后又毕业于牛津大学或剑桥大学的老同学。因英国公学只收男孩，因此他们被称为"老男孩"。他们过去是校友，现在又占据了政府部门的要职，形成一张"关系网"。他们不仅在政府部门有地位，在银行、新闻、艺术和教育界也很有影响。

9. **Gross Domestic Product:**

   国内生产总值，略作 GDP。

10. **the state funds schools which have Islam, Judaism ... Christianity as their creed:**

    国家拨款给以伊斯兰教、犹太教或其他非基督教为宗教信仰的学校。

11. **The result was ... "meritocratic":**

    1944 年教育法案的颁布使中学教育成为义务教育，大学教育凭真才实学录取学生。Meritocratic 一词由 merit（长处、优点、成绩）加后缀 -ocratic，真才实学。

12. **As previously ... a later raising to 16 was made:**

    和过去一样，义务接受全日制教育的起始年龄还是 5 岁，但离校年龄从 14 岁延至 15 岁，并有条款建议将来进一步延至 16 岁。

13. **grammar schools:**

    文法学校，一种采取优选制的中学。儿童在 11 岁时就参加一种"小升初"的考试（11-plus exam），成绩最好者进入文法学校。这些学校的教学是为了使学生能够通过考试进入高等院校。文法学校在英国历史悠久，名称源于中世纪时学校的主要目的是教授拉丁语文法。在 20 世纪六七十年代推广综合学校的进程中，文法学校或被改造成了综合学校（不再实施优选，许多保留了"文法"的名称），或独立出来变成了付费的私立学校。那些被改造了的学校中的一部分又在 90 年代恢复优选的招生方法。文法学校如今通常指的是完全优选的国家拨款的重点公立学校，英格兰如今有 164 所。

14. **They had more free time ... to help their families:**

    他们有更多的业余时间，更能在遇到困难时获得更多帮助（如他们的家长可以雇家庭教师），比工人阶级家庭的学生更重视教育。工人阶级家庭的学生常常由于压力而辍学去找工作，以帮助他们的家庭。

15. **comprehensive schools:**

    综合学校，20 世纪 60 年代在英国广泛推行。此类学校不论学生能力如何均可入学。学生可以学习多种科目。

# The United Kingdom of Great Britain and Northern Ireland

二至三年后，可以选学自己最喜欢的专业。综合学校在英国中学中占 90% 的比例。

16. **The National Curriculum ... for subjects of the school's choosing:**
全国教学大纲课程排课量不少于学校课程表时间的 70%，其余的时间可用于学校自选的科目。

17. **Students must also pass national tests ... in reaching national targets:**
学生还必须通过全国统一的考试（在 7、11、14 和 16 岁时），旨在监测教学质量，确保所学内容符合国家标准；学校根据学生在达到国家目标方面的成绩被排名。

18. **Practical decision-making was ... on local conditions:**
地方教育局，即地区教育局或市教育局，可根据自身的条件作出切合实际的决策。

19. **specialist schools, academies and free schools:**
Specialist schools 是特色学校或特长学校。Academy 是中央政府直接拨款并负责管理的独立学院（中小学），日常运作由学院院长全权负责，具有很大的自主权。学院制的做法肇始于新工党政府将少量成绩不好的中小学改为由中央政府直接拨款并管理的做法，效果良好。但联合政府时期（2010–2015），保守党大力推进学院制。其后的保守党政府也继续发力，并计划在 2020 年以前将英格兰地区所有中小学全部改制为独立学院，不想改制的学校将会被强制执行，以最终改变自 1902 年以来中小学由地方政府管理的模式。这一改革引发了激烈的争议。Free schools 指自由学校，是联合政府的教育改革措施。2015 年英格兰地区共有 251 所自由学校。英国政府鼓励民众创办高质量的学校，同时加大对新学校办学经费的投入。自由学校的治理机制重视学校的办学自主权、市场化导向和管理机构的专业化，促进了公立学校的多样化发展。

20. **schools set up entirely outside the aegis of local authorities:**
所建学校完全不受地方教育局的管辖。

21. **parents have the right ... school for their children:**
家长有权替他们的孩子选择某一所公立学校。

22. **A system of "league tables" ... to help parents make choices:**
教育界公布一种根据各学校的公共考试成绩、逃学率、毕业去向等情况编排的学校排名表，旨在让家长基于这些信息替子女挑选好学校。

23. **They are called public schools ... private tutors in aristocratic households:**
它们被称为公学，因为它们最初被视为与贵族家庭聘请私人教师相比属"公共"教育方式。Public schools: 公学，其实是私立学校，学费昂贵。英国有名的公学有伊顿、哈罗和拉格贝等。Independent schools 也译为私立学校。

24. **Her Majesty's Inspectors of Schools:**
皇家督学。英国皇家督学制度始于 1839 年，其主要职责是：保证每所学校在规定的期限内接受监督；保证教育大臣能及时了解学校的教学质量，学生的精神、道德、社会和文化发展情况，学校财政的管理情况等。1992 年英国成立了专门督导机构——教育标准局，独立于英国教育部，统管全国教育监督和评价工作。其首脑为首席皇家督学（Her Majesty's Chief Inspector of School），由女王直接任命，其成员为皇家督学。

25. **5 key stages:**
    Key Stage 1 (Foundation year and Year 1 to 2) 对应的是 5–7 岁的学生。Key Stage 2 (Years 3 to 6) 对应的是 7–11 岁的学生。Key Stage 3 (Years 7 to 9) 对应的是 11–14 岁的学生。Key Stage 4 (Years 10 to 11) 对应的是 14–16 岁的学生。Key Stage 5 (Years 12 to 13) 对应的是 16–18 岁的学生。

26. **all 3- and 4-year-olds ... 38 weeks of the year:**
    所有三、四岁的孩子可以享受每周 15 小时、每年 38 周的免费幼儿教育。

27. **General Certificate of Secondary Education:**
    中学毕业证书。英国的义务教育制度到 16 岁结束。学生 16 岁后分流，一部分选择几门课程进一步深入学习，通过高级水平考试，从而获得进入大学的资格；另一部分则以多种方式走向职业技术教育。

28. **pupils then decide what avenue of education they would like to follow:**
    学生然后可以选择自己喜欢的教育途径。avenue of education: 教育途径。

29. **sixth form:**
    中学的最后两年，上学的第 12、13 年（Key Stage 5），相当于高中或大学预科班

30. **General Certificate of Education-Advanced:**
    普通教育高级水平证书。16 岁的学生通过中学毕业考试后，如果想进高等学府继续深造，必须通过高级水平测试。

31. **Usually four (or five) academic subjects ... for Advanced level qualification (GCE A Level):**
    在 16 岁至 18 岁的两年时间里，学生根据自己想读的大学专业选定数门有关课程学习。第一年通常选四（或五）门专业课程学习，然后考 AS（高级补充程度考试）证书。第二年学生从上述课程中选择自己学得最好的三门进行深入学习，参加高级水平测试。A-level: advanced level，即高级水平。A-level 课程成绩是大学招生的重要标准。和中国不同的是，A-level 课程中的可选科目有近 70 种。

32. **"What A-levels did you take?":**
    "你的高级水平测试选的是哪几门课程？"

33. **The vocational equivalents of A-levels are General National Vocational Qualifications (GNVQs):**
    与高级水平证书相等同的职业教育方面的证书是国家职业资格证书。国家职业资格证书是为职业技术学校毕业的学生设置的，共分 5 个级别，便于人们根据自身条件通过实际工作和专业培训由低级向高级发展。获四级证书相当于学士学位；获五级证书相当于研究生水平。英国政府十分重视职业技术教育，义务教育阶段（16 岁前），技术课是学生的必修课。

34. **In the UK, the amount of funding each university receives ... the research it conducts:**
    在英国，每所大学获得的经费是根据它的规模、学生数量和从事的研究项目而定的。

35. **University of London:**
    伦敦大学，是由 18 个学院和 10 个研究所组成的大学联邦（亦被称为"公立联邦制大学"）。它的学院有独立的大学地位和高度的自治权，有许多不同的院系，独立招生，独立排名。有 9 所学院独立颁发文凭，

# The United Kingdom of Great Britain and Northern Ireland

例如著名的伦敦政治经济学院、伦敦大学学院。帝国理工学院1907–2007年间是伦敦大学的一个加盟学院，现已脱离出来成为一所独立的大学。

36. **the "redbrick universities":**
    这包括所有1850–1930年间成立的高校，以及伦敦大学。它们很多是用当时受青睐的建筑材料红砖建造的，故而被称作"红砖大学"。

37. **polytechnics:**
    多科性技术学院，1992年后转为大学。

38. **Usually one receives ... and Doctor of Philosophy:**
    通常人们首先获得文科学士或理科学士（也称第一学位 first degree），然后获得第二学位文科硕士或理科硕士，再继续攻读可获得哲学博士。

39. **Universities and departments ... gives ratings for their research and teaching:**
    每四年还由一个国家评审机构对大学和院系进行一次评估，该机构根据其研究和教学水准给出评级。

40. **access for mature students ... continues to widen:**
    成人以及没有通过传统的高级水平测试的学生，进入高等学府的渠道继续在拓宽。

41. **the Open University:**
    开放大学。对任何人都开放，无需正式学历。完成大学的必修课程后均可拿到大学文凭。开放大学的特点就在于通过电视、广播、录像、函授等方式为学生提供就地学习的条件。开放大学不限年龄，最小的不到20岁，最大的90多岁，大多在20岁至40岁之间。

42. **student grants were replaced by loans:**
    grants 是助学金，不需要偿还；而 loan 则是助学贷款，需要毕业后偿还。英国大学生可贷款交学费以及补贴生活费，毕业后薪水达到一定数额时须将一定比例的钱用来偿还贷款。

43. **home student:**
    本土学生。这个概念包括英国本国学生以及欧盟成员国学生。其他国家生源被归为国际学生。国际学生支付的学费要远高于本土学生。

# Exercises

I. **Give the Chinese equivalents for the following:**
   1. free and compulsory
   2. Eton public school

3. National Curriculum
4. GCE-A Level
5. university rating
6. Oxbridge

## II. Decide whether the following statements are true (T) or false (F):

1. In Britain, children can legally receive free and compulsory education from the ages of 6 to 18. _____
2. More children under 5 are attending nursery education which is partly paid by the government. _____
3. Independent schools get money mainly through the private sector and tuition fees, with some government support. _____
4. The Open University charges no fees, so it does not offer degrees. _____
5. "League tables" rank schools mainly according to their public examination performance and jobs taken by school-leavers and publish the result to help parents' decisions in choosing schools. _____
6. The National Curriculum standardises teaching subjects and contents of all teaching time for all students of the country. _____
7. Some British universities are funded by central government, but some, especially the old ones like Oxford and Cambridge are private ones. _____
8. Full-time first-degree courses mainly last three years with BA or BSc degree upon graduation. _____

## III. Fill in the blanks:

1. Pupils from the ages of _____ to 11 mainly attend state-run _____ schools.
2. Students attend _____ schools from the age of 11 up to around the age of 18.
3. The _____ schools which provide a general education receive the largest number of students.
4. In the examination called "the 11-plus", students with academic potential are chosen to attend _____ schools.
5. Most parents from the wealthier middle class prefer to send their children to _____ schools and pay for better education.
6. If a student wants to receive higher education, he will carry on academic study in

# The United Kingdom of Great Britain and Northern Ireland

the _____ for a further two years after the age of 16 and then take exams called _____.

7. Two famous public schools mentioned in the text are _____ and _____.
8. Name two of the four Scottish universities dating from the 14th and 15th centuries. _____ and _____.
9. GCSE stands for _____.
10. GCE-A Level stands for _____.

## IV. Questions:

1. What role did the Church play in educating children historically?
2. How have the ages for compulsory education been changed?
3. In what ways was the Education Act 1944 very important?
4. What was the tripartite system? How do grammar schools select children?
5. Why were comprehensive schools set up in the 1960s to replace the tripartite system?
6. What are the functions of the National Curriculum?
7. What is the exam system for secondary education?
8. How do British students prepare for university entrance?
9. What are the characteristics of independent schools?
10. What are the old universities in Britain?
11. How has higher education been expanded to the present level?
12. What is the Open University in Britain? What do you think of this system?
13. When did British universities start to charge tuition fees? How much do students pay currently?
14. How should university students pay back their loans?

## V. Topics for discussion or research:

1. How does the British education system reflect social class?
2. What are the key differences or similarities in the education systems of the UK and China? Please comment on them.
3. How should Chinese students apply for post-graduate study in Britain?

# UNIT 8

# British Foreign Relations

**Go over the following focal points before reading the text:**

- The British Empire and decolonisation
- Influence on foreign policy by imperial history and geopolitical traits
- The "Three Circles" foreign policy
- A permanent member of the UN Security Council
- Britain and the Commonwealth
- Britain and the European Economic Community (the European Union)
- The Single European Act (1986) and the Single European Market
- The Schengen Agreement
- The Maastricht Treaty (1992) and the Eurozone
- Britain's entry into the EEC (EU)
- Parliamentary sovereignty vs. federalism
- The Anglo-US special relationship
- The Suez Crisis
- Military cooperation: the Falklands (Malvinas) War, the Iraq War
- Britain and the NATO

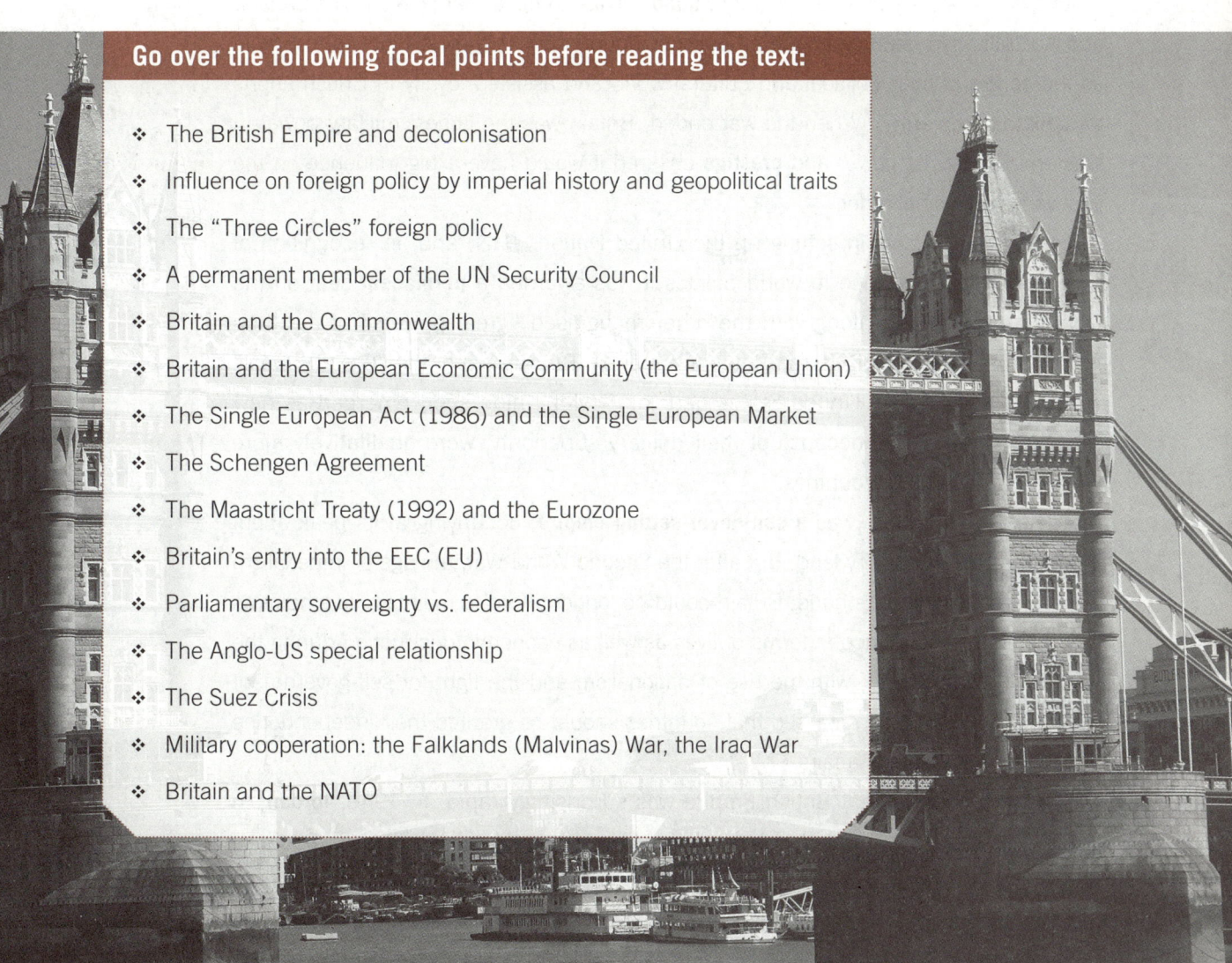

# The United Kingdom of Great Britain and Northern Ireland

 Text

### Britain Then and Now: from a World Power to a Regional Power

After a lengthy fight with the **Axis** powers[1], the United Kingdom eventually emerged victorious and with its empire still largely **intact**. While some former colonies like Canada and Australia had been **granted** their political independence, they still looked to Britain as the centre of their political and cultural world and assisted loyally in British efforts to defeat Hitler's army.[2] When the war ended, Britain was the largest military power in Western Europe. Its power and **prestige** ensured it would have a big influence on the postwar international order.

Britain was active in setting up the United Nations (UN) and, in recognition of its continuing importance to world politics it was awarded a **permanent** seat on the UN Security Council, along with the other recognised "great powers" of the then Soviet Union, the United States, China and France. But the era of the "Great Powers" was already over. The United States and the Soviet Union soon emerged as new "superpowers" which, because of their military superiority, were qualitatively more powerful than all other countries.[3]

The British Empire was **a sun-never-setting empire**, occupying at its peak about 1/5 of the world's total dry land. But after the Second World War, the age of imperialism was over too. On the one hand, Britain could no longer afford to maintain its empire as it had paid a terrible price in terms of lives as well as economic destruction during the war. On the other hand, with the rise of nationalism and the fight for self-government in many colonies, Britain realised that countries should be granted their independence and left to run their own affairs.

The end of the great British Empire was surprisingly rapid. In 1946, **Jordan**, in the Middle East, was granted independence. The following year, India and Pakistan **followed suit**. In 1948, **Burma** (now Myanmar) and **Ceylon** (now Sri Lanka) gained their independence. Throughout the next few decades, the process of **decolonisation** continued as territories and **possessions** in Africa, the Caribbean and other places received their independence or were returned to their rightful rulers. Sometimes

---

axis *n.* 轴心
intact *adj.* 未受损的
grant *v.* （尤指正式地或法律上）同意，承认
prestige *n.* 威望
permanent *adj.* 永久（性）的
a sun-never-setting empire 日不落帝国
Jordan *n.* 约旦
follow suit 仿效别人
Burma *n.* 缅甸
Ceylon *n.* 锡兰
decolonisation *n.* 非殖民（地）化，去殖民（地）化
possessions *n.* （常 *pl.*）领地，属地

the process was violent, as in Kenya and Suez.⁴ After the handover of Hong Kong to Chinese sovereignty in 1997, the most important of the 14 remaining British Overseas Territories now are the Bermuda, Gibraltar etc.⁵

So Britain has changed into a medium-sized European country. It lacks the all-powerful navy of its imperial past, but it does have an independent **nuclear deterrent** and technologically advanced armed forces. The British economy still ranks about 6th in the world in terms of size, and with London as the world's largest banking centre, it **retains** considerable influence on the international economy.

## The Foundations of Britain's Foreign Policy

The contemporary foreign policy of the UK is greatly influenced by its imperial history and also by its **geopolitical traits**.⁶ Perhaps the most important single factor which influences British policy-makers is its history. Due to its imperial past, British policy-makers frequently forget that Britain is not as influential as it used to be in world affairs. Historians argue that British foreign policy-makers retain very conservative and traditional views of Britain's role as a world power and point to many major foreign policy decisions as examples.⁷ One example was the controversial and expensive decision for Britain to build and maintain its own independent nuclear weapons to ensure it would remain superior to most other states in terms of military capability. Another sign of foreign policy conservatism lay in the debate over how much national sovereignty Britain should **relinquish** to the European Union.⁸

A second decisive influence upon the way Britain conducts its external affairs is geopolitical. Britain is an **insular** island state, and this physical isolation has influenced Britain's economic and military development. Because it is an island, Britain quite naturally developed as a nation of **seafarers** who **roamed** the globe looking for territory and economic opportunities.⁹ The settlement of Canada was based on the desire to develop the **fur** trade, and Australia proved to be a convenient place for transporting criminals¹⁰ (it was cheaper to send criminals to the undeveloped lands of Australia than to keep them in prison in Britain).

Britain's island location created a sense of **psychological** isolation in its **inhabitants**.¹¹ The physical isolation has long been reduced by the development of airlines and by the opening of the Channel Tunnel in 1994, which now links Britain to continental Europe.¹² Nevertheless, psychologically, Britons still sometimes feel cut off.

nuclear *adj.*
核的，核能的，核武器的
deterrent *n.*
威慑物
nuclear deterrent
核威慑（力量）
retain *v.*
保持，保留
geopolitical *adj.*
地缘政治的，地理政治的
trait *n.* 特点
relinquish *v.*
让给；放弃
insular *adj.*
岛屿的；孤立的；与世隔绝的
seafarer *n.*
海员；航海者
roam *v.*
漫游；游历
fur *n.* 皮货
psychological *adj.* 心理学（上）的
inhabitant *n.*
居民

# The United Kingdom of Great Britain and Northern Ireland

Britain's **schizophrenic** attitude to Europe is often attributed to its long-term physical separation from the European continent.[13]

Britain's postwar international relations were also based on Winston Churchill's[14] "**Three Circles**" **foreign policy**. In 1945, Churchill described Britain's role in the world in terms of "three circles of influence". The first circle was Britain's connection with the Commonwealth countries. The second was Britain's "special relationship" with the USA. The third was Britain's close relationship with Western Europe, where some of its armed forces were based as part of NATO's[15] defence against the Soviet Union. In the following decades, successive British governments pursued a foreign policy strategy which sought to preserve their power and influence in all three "circles".[16]

## How Foreign Policy Is Made

The Prime Minister and Cabinet decide on the general direction of Britain's foreign policy. The main government department involved is of course the Foreign and Commonwealth Office (FCO, headed by the Secretary of State for Foreign Affairs)[17], but many other government ministries also play a part in **formulating** and **executing** the government's decisions.

The Ministry of Defence is an important player. It is responsible for ensuring Britain's defence and managing Britain's involvement in its military **treaty** commitments.[18] The Department of Trade and Industry is concerned with formulating international trade policy and managing British **commercial** relations with other countries. A less obvious, but extremely influential player in Britain's foreign policy is the **Treasury**. The Treasury makes decisions on how much money other departments can have each year. If the Treasury decides to give more money to the Overseas Development Agency (the government department in charge of **distributing** foreign aid) or less money to the military, their own policies will have to be changed accordingly.[19]

## Britain and International Institutions

In the past, Britain was powerful enough to act independently in the world in order to bring about its policy objectives. Nowadays its foreign policy is largely shaped by its participation in a number of important international institutions.

Britain is one of the five permanent members of the UN Security Council[20], along

---

**schizophrenic** *adj.* 反复无常的
"**Three Circles**" **foreign policy** 三环外交政策
**formulate** *v.* 制定
**execute** *v.* 执行
**treaty** *n.* 条约；协定
**commercial** *adj.* 商业的，商务的
**the Treasury** 英国财政部
**distribute** *v.* 分配

with Russia, China, the US and France. It is the 6th largest contributor to the UN's budget (behind the US, Japan, China, Germany, France in 2016–2018). As a Security Council member, Britain retains the ability to have a large influence on world affairs.

Britain is also a member of the Commonwealth of Nations, a voluntary association of states which is made up mostly of former British colonies, established in 1949. Even though Britain granted its colonial territories independence, it continued to feel close to these new countries and wanted to continue to work with them. Many of these countries, having had similar experiences while being ruled by the British, found they shared similar histories, laws, economic concerns and cultural experiences which made them feel connected to each other. The Commonwealth was set up to provide political, economic, technical and educational cooperation and support among member countries. Two-thirds of British development aid goes to Commonwealth countries.

There are 52 members of the Commonwealth: many of these are developing countries in Africa, Asia, the Caribbean and the South Pacific; others are advanced industrial nations like Canada, Australia and New Zealand. Every two years, the heads of state meet together at the Commonwealth Heads of Government Meeting. The Queen was the head of the Commonwealth until April 2018 when Prince Charles was approved as her successor. Sixteen countries also **acknowledge** the Queen as their head of state, with a Governor-General[21] as representative of the Crown. But a majority of member countries are republics.

From 1973 up to today, more important to Britain in the day-to-day running of its affairs has been its membership of the European Union (EU). The EU has its roots in the experience of the two world wars which tore Europe apart in the first half of the 20th century.[22] In order to prevent future wars, some countries, notably France and Germany, decided that they should lock their economies closely together to make another war between them impossible. European states began to integrate their economies as a way of **fostering** cooperation and shared interests with each other.

In 1957, on the basis of the European Coal and Steel Community of 1952, France, Germany, Italy, Belgium, Luxembourg and Netherlands — the original six[23] — signed the Treaty of Rome, which led to the formation of the European Economic Community (EEC) and the European Atomic Energy Community (Euratom) in 1958. The EEC was a common market area which established a customs union with internal free trade and a common external tariff.[24] In 1973 the UK joined the EEC under the Conservative

acknowledge *v.*
承认
foster *v.*
鼓励；促进

# The United Kingdom of Great Britain and Northern Ireland

government of Edward Heath.

The pace of **integration** of the EEC was slow in the 1970s and early 1980s but **accelerated** in the latter half of the 1980s. The Single European Act of 1986[25] (SEA) was signed to complete the single internal market by December 31, 1992. The idea was to boost trade, create jobs, lower prices and reduce costs. The Single European Market opened for business on January 1st, 1993, with the free movement of goods, services, labour and capital within the EU, as if it was a single country. Routine customs clearance of commercial goods at national borders was ended. Customs barriers were removed.[26] The Schengen Agreement[27] of 1985 and the Schengen Convention of 1990, which implemented the Agreement and came into effect in March 1995, led to the creation of Europe's Schengen Area, in which internal border checks have largely been abolished and a common Schengen visa is issued. Schengen Area currently consists of 26 European countries, three of which (Switzerland, Norway and Iceland) are not EU members. The UK remains outside the Schengen Area.

The 1992 Maastricht Treaty or the Treaty on European Union (TEU)[28] marked further progress towards closer integration, particularly with a timetable towards monetary union. It established the EU based on the EEC, amending the Treaty of Rome and **incorporating** both the Single European Act and the Schengen Agreement. The single currency, the euro, was formally **inaugurated** in 1999 and notes and coins to replace national currencies of member states were introduced in 2002.[29] The current **Eurozone** includes 19 countries.[30] As with the Schengen Area, the UK remains outside the Eurozone.

By the early 1990s, the collapse of the Soviet Union had brought an end to the Cold War. The Treaty of Nice[31] (signed in 2001) reformed the institutional structure and the voting mechanisms of the EU to meet the needs of its eastward expansion with countries of Central and Eastern Europe (former allies of the old Soviet Union) joining in 2004.

The Treaty of Lisbon[32] (signed in 2007) made further revisions such as the expansion of qualified majority voting, a more powerful European Parliament, the creation of a long-term President of the European Council and a High Representative of the Union for Foreign Affairs. Its main objectives are to make the EU more democratic and more efficient and able to **tackle** today's global challenges.

Britain's membership in 1973 was an important psychological decision for the

---

integration *n.*
整合；一体化
accelerate *v.*
加速
incorporate *v.*
吸收；使合并
inaugurate *v.*
开始
Eurozone
欧元区
tackle *v.*
对付，处理

nation because traditionally Britain had looked beyond its European neighbours, feeling that really it had more in common with the United States on the one hand, and the Commonwealth on the other.[33] To many Britons, membership in the EEC meant turning its back on these "old friends". More importantly, Britain traditionally favoured free trade deals and had a natural liberal suspicion of **supranational** organisations.[34] So after the formation of the EEC, it took the lead in establishing a rival trading block — the European Free Trade Association (EFTA)[35] with six other countries. Furthermore, after the Second World War, Britain retained the illusion of great power status.

But soon, the decision to join the EEC became natural given that British economic, political and military interests were already deeply bound up with other European countries.[36] Through its involvement in NATO, Britain was committed to European defence cooperation. Although the United States was an important trade partner, so too were Western European nations, especially Germany. Trade with the Commonwealth countries had also declined greatly. Above all, Britain's economic performance was not as good as other EEC members. Recognising that Britain was now a regional rather than a global power, the country applied for membership in 1963 and 1967, but was twice vetoed by French President General de Gaulle[37], who feared that Britain's membership would bring American influence into the organisation and threaten France's leading position in it.

Britain has never been a whole-hearted member. During the negotiations on those parts of the Maastricht Treaty relating to economic and monetary union, the British government negotiated for an **opt-out**. Later, successive governments took a "wait-and-see" policy and both the Conservative Party and the Labour Party promised a referendum before taking Britain into a single currency. On the matter of the Schengen Area, Britain also believed that it should have special status. Because of the concern about national sovereignty and illegal immigration, Britain still sticks to customs check and border control while other EU countries have already got rid of them. With the refusal to join the Euro and the Schengen Area, Britain has been seen as an awkward partner in the EU.

As a matter of fact, the UK has always been very interested in encouraging free trade between countries and has therefore been very supportive of the EU as a free trade area. However, it has been less enthusiastic about giving up its national sovereignty (that is, its control over national decision-making) to a European

supranational *adj.*
超国家的；超民族的
opt-out *n.*
选择退出，不参加

# The United Kingdom of Great Britain and Northern Ireland

government. The UK likes to think of the EU as a place where economic cooperation is possible, with the free movement of goods and people. It is less certain about the possibility of the EU becoming a kind of federal "super-state" where national governments would have their powers reduced, becoming provinces **subservient** to a kind of European federal government.[38]

Here, two terms need to be explained — "**Euro-sceptics**" and "**Euro-enthusiasts**". Euro-sceptics (i.e. those people accepting Euro-scepticism) is a term commonly applied to those who are sceptical or hostile towards the UK's involvement in further European integration. Some Euro-sceptics are opposed to Britain's continuing membership of the EU. They fear that closer union threatens Britain's parliamentary sovereignty (as EU law is supreme over the law of member states in many key areas) and Britain's independence in making its own economic and monetary policies (hence its opposition to European monetary union). In the area of regulation, over 80% of rules governing the production, distribution and exchange of goods, services and capital in the British market are decided by the EU. Euro-sceptics do not want to see the EU turning into a kind of federal "United States of Europe" with the tendency towards "ever closer union". The rise of the UK Independence Party, which wants Britain to leave the EU, has been a good reflection of this **mindset**. "Euro-enthusiasts" are those who positively support the UK's involvement with the EU. They believe that EU membership is highly positive to Britain's economic development and can make Britain have its voice heard, a **state-of-affairs** which is in Britain's national interest. Without EU membership, they believe Britain would be **marginalised** as Europe continues to integrate effectively.

The controversy on the single currency seriously split the Conservative Government under John Major and partly caused the Party's loss in the 1997 general election. The Conservative-Lib-Dem Coalition Government of 2010 continued to suffer from Euro-sceptic pressure. So it passed the European Union Act 2011[39], which ensured that there would be no further transfer of sovereignty or powers to the EU without the **mandate** of referendums.

Euro-sceptics won the national referendum on June 23, 2016, which resulted in Britain's decision to leave the EU (51.9% voted Leave and 48.1% voted Remain). The term "Brexit" was coined, merging the words "Britain" and "exit". Those who wanted Britain to leave the EU held that the EU imposed too many rules on business and charged billions of pounds a year in membership fees for little in return — the UK is

**subservient** *adj.*
从属的
**Euro-sceptic** *n.*
欧洲怀疑论者
**Euro-enthusiast** *n.* 坚定的亲欧派
**mindset** *n.*
思想倾向
**state-of-affairs** *n.* 事态，情势
**marginalise** *v.*
使边缘化
**mandate** *n.*
授权，委任

one of 10 member states who pay more into the EU budget than they get out. Also, they argued that EU laws harmed parliamentary sovereignty. Immigration was also a big issue for Brexit supporters. They wanted Britain to take back full control of its borders and reduce the number of people coming to live and/or work in Britain from other parts of the EU.

The pound **slumped** the day after the referendum. Prime Minister David Cameron, who supported Remain resigned and was replaced by Theresa May. The government is now negotiating to leave the EU in the best possible way for the UK's national interest, yet this will not be easy.

## Britain and the United States

Another major factor which influences British foreign policy is the Anglo-US special relationship[40] that is claimed to exist between Britain and the United States. The term "Special Relationship" was popularised (and perhaps coined) by Winston Churchill in the mid-1940s. The special relationship was quite natural, as the two countries share common language, heritage and culture, cherish common values (e.g. the rule of law, property rights, economic liberalism, religious toleration, basic human freedoms of expression) and, more importantly, have common interests — especially common perceptions of the Soviet threat.

The UK and the USA were closely allied during World War II, and continued to work together closely in the post war years because of their shared concern about the former Soviet Union. Through the US-UK Mutual Defence Agreement signed in 1958, the United States assisted the United Kingdom in its own development of a nuclear **arsenal**. And Britain hosts a large American military presence.[41] There are currently ten US Air Force bases still operational in Britain. Because these bases are under American control and because they host the NATO nuclear deterrent, the difficulty of **dismantling** them is very complicated. The United States accounts for the UK's largest single export market. The two countries also share the world's largest foreign direct investment partnership. Even today, in many respects British and American policy-makers agree generally on, for example, how the global economy should be managed, how a warlike state should be dealt with, issues about arms control and so on. British forces participated in the US-led war in Afghanistan and unlike France, Canada, Germany, China, and Russia, the UK supported the US-led invasion of Iraq in 2003.

slump *v.*
下跌
arsenal *n.*
武器库，军火库
dismantle *v.*
废除；取消

# The United Kingdom of Great Britain and Northern Ireland

Nevertheless, the special relationship with the United States has gone through many ups and downs. Close cooperation during World War II witnessed its birth, with the **Lend-Lease Act**, the Atlantic Charter, exchange of **intelligence** and partnership in atomic weapon research. In the post-war period (1945–1963), the special relationship continued as reflected in economic aid (Marshall Plan), nuclear sharing and intelligence cooperation. Due to the common concern over the Soviet threat, Britain drew the United States into the post-war European defence commitment established in 1949 — NATO. The United States continued to contribute directly to British defence, providing Britain with the most modern nuclear defence systems in the shape of Polaris and Trident — advanced **submarine**-launched inter-continental ballistic missiles.[42] The UK took part in the Korean War (1950–1953) in support of the US-led UN forces. But Churchill resisted American pressure to dismantle the imperial preference trading system.[43]

The major test of Anglo-American relations occurred during the 1956 Suez Crisis.[44] The Egyptian president Gamal Nasser nationalised the Suez Canal, an act which harmed British and French economic interests, as the Suez Canal Company was owned by the two countries. Although Nasser offered full economic compensation for the Company, Britain and France decided to take the canal back by force. They had secret military talks with Israel, resulting in Israeli forces invading Egypt, with Britain and France landing their troops later under the pretext of protecting the Canal. To the surprise of the British, the Americans did not support this action at the UN and used America's economic power to force the Anglo-French forces to withdraw. Britain and France felt humiliated. The event demonstrated to Britain its fading imperial power and the importance of collaboration with the United States in international affairs.

The special relationship was weakened considerably between 1963 and 1979. Owing to the need for defence cuts on economic grounds, Britain was unwilling to play its traditional role of junior world policeman alongside the United States. It withdrew its troops from "East of Suez" (e.g. Singapore, Malaya and the Persian Gulf).[45] It also refused to provide troops to fight with Americans in Vietnam (Australia and New Zealand sent troops). And Atlantic ties appeared less important as Prime Ministers of the period looked increasingly towards Europe.

Margaret Thatcher came to power in 1979 as a whole-hearted **Atlanticist**. When Ronald Reagan became American President in 1981, the special relationship was

---

Lend-Lease Act
《租借法案》
intelligence *n.*
情报
submarine *n.*
潜水艇
Atlanticist *n.*
大西洋主义者

quickly revived very much on the basis of the personal friendship between Mrs Thatcher and Reagan, who were "ideological soul-mates". Both leaders shared a commitment to economic liberalism, small government, strong defence and hostility toward the Soviet Union. The nuclear relationship remained particularly special, with the US selling to the UK the more advanced Trident strategic missiles to replace Polaris at very favourable prices. In the Falklands (Malvinas) War[46] between Britain and **Argentina** (1982), the US military supported the UK by allowing it to use the American base on Ascension Island for fuel and munitions, and provided intelligence. The two leaders cooperated in being tough toward the Soviet Union, for which Mrs Thatcher was called "**Iron Lady**" by the Soviets. In the Irangate affair[47] of the mid-1980s, which concerned secret American arms sales to Iran in return for releasing American **hostages**, the UK kept silent after discovering the dealings between American national security staff and Iran arms dealers through **eavesdropping** on their hotel conversations in London. Of course there were also conflicts, e.g., American troops occupied Grenada[48] — a Commonwealth country — in October 1983 without informing Britain beforehand.

The relationship in the 1990s was less special, despite intensive cooperation in the Gulf War. The end of the Cold War removed the fundamental purpose of the alliance. Yet the special relationship survived. President Clinton contributed greatly to the Northern Ireland peace process leading to the signing of the Belfast Agreement in 1998. Prime Minister Blair and Presidents Clinton and George W. Bush enjoyed cordial personal relations despite differences. The terrorist attack of September 11th, 2001 clearly reinforced the UK-US link. Following the event, Blair's Britain emerged as Bush's most dependable ally in the "war against terror" both in Afghanistan and in Iraq.[49] However, Blair's closeness to Bush in foreign policy, particularly over Iraq, divided the UN, the NATO, the EU and the Labour Party. Acting out of step with its European partners (Germany and France), Britain was once again perceived as an awkward partner in the EU. Blair wanted British foreign policy to focus on playing a bridging role between the USA and Europe allowing greater cooperation between the political, economic and military superpower of the US and the economic "superpower" of the EU.

The relationship between Prime Minister Cameron and President Obama in the 2010s was supposed to be "solid but not **slavish**"[50]. Military and counterterrorism cooperation continued to be close. The two countries held highly similar stands on

---

Argentina *n.*
阿根廷
Iron Lady
铁娘子
hostage *n.*
人质
eavesdrop *v.*
窃听，偷听
slavish *adj.*
盲从的，奴性的

# The United Kingdom of Great Britain and Northern Ireland

Afghanistan, Syria, Iran (opposition to Iran's nuclear programme) and other issues.

But Britain was more cautious about military actions on Syria. In August 2013, Syrian opposition leaders accused forces loyal to Syrian President Bashar al-Assad of using sarin for mass killing[51] and Obama called for military strikes on Syria. But the UK parliament vetoed Cameron's calling for military reactions. *The Sun* **tabloid** ran a **mournful** front page, "Death notice: the special relationship. Died at home after a sudden illness on Thursday." After President Trump came into office, Prime Minister Theresa May was the first world leader to meet with him.

In short, in the 21st century, Britain supported the removal of the Taliban regime in Afghanistan[52] in 2001 and was the leading ally in the US-led war against Iraq in 2003. It took a leading role in alliance operations in Libya in 2011. And it is also an important US partner in efforts to pressure Iran over its nuclear activities, and to combat international terrorism.

Today, the relationship with the United States is regarded as the "most important **bilateral** partnership" in current British foreign policy while the US takes this relationship as one of its most enduring bilateral relationships, as shown in political affairs. It has perhaps always been an unequal relationship given the size and power of the US, and has always meant more to the British. The relationship has been special in personal friendships (e.g. Churchill and Roosevelt, Thatcher and Reagan, Blair and Bush), intelligence cooperation, nuclear sharing, and military and diplomatic cooperation. The special relationship has largely been a British diplomatic strategy to cope with and benefit from American power. In material terms, Britain seemed to have gained more than the US, e.g. keeping its nuclear deterrent at reasonable expenditure. Anglo-American joint operations (providing **legitimacy** to American actions in the world) to a certain degree enhanced Britain's Great Power status, giving it a sense of importance. Yet this sense of importance has affected Britain's adjustment to its post-imperial role.

## British Security and Defence Policy

Britain spends more on defence than most other advanced industrial countries and maintains larger professional forces. It is the 7th largest military spender in the world (behind the USA, China, Russia, Saudi Arabia, India and France) and is ranked 6th in terms of its military power. It is also the 2nd largest supplier of arms in the world

tabloid *n.*
通俗小报
mournful *n.*
悲伤的；哀痛的
bilateral *adj.*
双边的
legitimacy *n.*
合法（性）

behind the United States.

The **keystone** of British defence policy is its participation in the North Atlantic Treaty Organisation (NATO). The purpose of NATO is to protect member states against aggression, to provide a foundation for security in Europe, and to provide a forum for **transatlantic** defence cooperation (the USA and Canada are also members). Ninety-five percent of Britain's defence expenditure goes to meeting NATO requirements. Britain was proud to be invited to lead the Allied Rapid Reaction Corps[53] (created in 1992), which is NATO's land-based force designed to provide an early military response to a crisis.

In addition to its NATO commitments, Britain is a member of the nuclear "club", maintaining an independent nuclear capability. Since Britain is a traditional sea power, it is perhaps no surprise that its nuclear force is a naval one with nuclear-armed submarines. This nuclear force is **assigned** to NATO, but is fully under the command of the British government. Nuclear weapons are important for the prestige of a country as well as its protection. All of the permanent UN Security Council members have independent nuclear weapons capabilities.

Since September 11th, 2001, the threat of terrorist attacks has been an increasing concern. The war on terrorism may yet replace inter-state conflicts as the main means of defence policy in the 21st century: already British foreign and defence policy objectives have to prioritise homeland defence in its various forms.[54]

keystone *n.* 要旨
transatlantic *adj.* 跨大西洋的
assign *v.* 转让，派给

# Explanations

1. **the Axis powers:**
   轴心国，指第二次世界大战中的德意日轴心。

2. **While some former colonies like Canada ... to defeat Hitler's army:**
   尽管像加拿大、澳大利亚这样的前殖民地获得了政治独立，它们仍把英国视为其政治和文化的中心，并且忠诚地帮助英国打败了希特勒的军队。（它们仍然是英联邦成员，在政治上、文化上和英国保持着各种联系。）

3. **The United States and ... qualitatively more powerful than all other countries:**
   美国和苏联很快成为新的"超级大国"，因为从军事实力上讲，美苏比世界上任何国家都强大。

# The United Kingdom of Great Britain and Northern Ireland

Qualitatively: 指两个超级大国的军事优势的质量。

4. **Sometimes the process was violent, as in Kenya and Suez:**
   有时（国家独立的）过程是充满暴力的，比如肯尼亚以及苏伊士运河事件。肯尼亚 1963 年 12 月从英国的殖民统治中独立出来，为此举行过起义。埃及于 1956 年宣布将苏伊士运河收归国有，英、法、以三国因此发动战争。

5. **the most important ... Bermuda, Gibraltar etc.:**
   英国现在仍然拥有的 14 个海外领地中最重要的是百慕大和直布罗陀等。英国具有管辖权和领土主权，但海外领地不属于联合王国建制，是大英帝国的残余部分。

6. **The contemporary foreign policy of the UK ... by its geopolitical traits:**
   英国现行外交政策受其帝国史和地缘政治特点影响很大。

7. **Historians argue that ... many major foreign policy decisions as examples:**
   历史学家认为，英国外交政策的制定者对于英国作为一个世界强国应发挥的作用持有非常保守和传统的观点，并以许多外交决策为例来说明这一点。这里的"保守"和"传统"意指英国还是习惯于按照过去英国强盛时的思路出发。

8. **Another sign of foreign policy ... should relinquish to the European Union:**
   英国外交政策的保守性还表现在英国在应该向欧盟出让多少主权这一问题上的争论。

9. **as a nation of seafarers who roamed ... and economic opportunities:**
   作为一个航海国，它周游世界寻找领土和经济发展机遇。

10. **The settlement of Canada ... for transporting criminals:**
    开拓加拿大殖民地是为了发展皮货贸易（殖民者用欧洲商品与北美印第安人交换皮货），澳大利亚则证明是英国流放罪犯适宜的地方（从 1788 年起，英国就开始把罪犯流放到澳大利亚，这不仅使英国节约了开支，而且也保持了英国社会的稳定）。

11. **Britain's island location created a sense of psychological isolation in its inhabitants:**
    英国岛国的地理位置使那里的居民产生了一种心理上的孤立感。

12. **This physical isolation has ... links Britain to continental Europe:**
    航空业的发展以及 1994 年英吉利海峡海底隧道的开通早已减少了英国在地理上的孤立，英吉利海峡隧道将英国与欧洲大陆连接起来。海底隧道运营的列车名为"欧洲之星"（Eurostar）。

13. **Britain's schizophrenic attitude ... from the European continent:**
    英国对欧洲反复无常的态度也是由于它长期与欧洲大陆隔绝的缘故。

14. **Winston Churchill:**
    丘吉尔（1874–1965），英国政治家、演说家、作家。1940 年至 1945 年和 1951 年至 1955 年两次任英国首相。二战期间，丘吉尔为动员英国人民投入反法西斯战争，发表过许多精彩演说，引起轰动。

UNIT 8  British Foreign Relations

15. **NATO:**
    北大西洋公约组织，成立于 1949 年 4 月 4 日。

16. **In the following decades ... power and influence in all three "circles":**
    在后来的几十年里，英国历届政府都奉行的外交政策战略是力求在所有三个"圈子"中保持自己的权力和影响力。

17. **the Foreign and Commonwealth Office (FCO, headed by the Secretary of State for Foreign Affairs):**
    英国外交与联邦事务部，即外交部；由外交大臣领导。

18. **managing Britain's involvement in its military treaty commitments:**
    履行英国参加军事条约的义务。

19. **If the Treasury decides ... policies will have to be changed accordingly:**
    如果财政部决定给海外发展署（负责援外资金拨款的政府部门）增加拨款，或减少军费开支，那么，英国自己的外交政策也要做相应的调整。

20. **permanent members of the UN Security Council:**
    联合国安理会常任理事国。

21. **Governor-General:**
    总督。英联邦成员中有 16 个国家实行君主立宪制，承认女王为其国家元首，总督是女王的代表。总督由女王基于其中国家当选首脑（总理）的提名而象征性地任命。

22. **The EU has its roots ... which tore Europe apart in the first half of the 20th century:**
    欧盟的诞生源自 20 世纪上半叶使欧洲四分五裂的两次世界大战的惨痛经历。欧洲主要国家希望将其经济和利益捆绑在一起以避免再次发生战争。

23. **the original six:**
    欧洲经济共同体原始创始国是法国、德国、意大利、荷兰、比利时和卢森堡 6 国。1973 年英国、爱尔兰和丹麦加入；1981 年希腊加入；1986 年西班牙和葡萄牙加入；1995 年奥地利、芬兰和瑞典加入。随着苏联的解体，2004 年，东欧国家波兰、匈牙利、捷克共和国、斯洛伐克、斯洛文尼亚、拉脱维亚、爱沙尼亚、立陶宛、塞浦路斯、马耳他、保加利亚和罗马尼亚加入；2013 年克罗地亚加入，使成员国扩大到 28 个。

24. **The EEC was a common market area ... a common external tariff:**
    欧洲经济共同体是一个共同市场区域，建立了关税同盟，内部自由贸易，对外则采用共同外部关税。

25. **The Single European Act of 1986:**
    1986 年《单一欧洲法案》。主要内容为在 1992 年年底前实现商品、资本、劳工自由流动的统一内部市场。

26. **Routine customs clearance ... barriers were removed:**
    国境处的商品货物常规通关被终止，关税壁垒被取消。

# The United Kingdom of Great Britain and Northern Ireland

27. **The Schengen Agreement:**
    1985年6月，德国、法国、荷兰、比利时、卢森堡五国在卢森堡边境小镇申根签署了《关于逐步取消共同边界检查》协定，又称《申根协定》。主要内容包括：在协定签字国之间不再对公民进行边境检查；外国人一旦获准进入"申根领土"内，即可在协定签字国领土上自由通行；设立警察合作与司法互助的制度，建立有关各类非法活动分子情况的共用档案库。申根成员国现有26个。成员国对外国短期旅行者颁发统一的申根签证。

28. **The 1992 Maastricht Treaty or the Treaty on European Union (TEU):**
    《马斯特里赫特条约》或《欧盟条约》。

29. **The single currency, the euro ... were introduced in 2002:**
    单一货币欧元于1999年正式启用（发行），2002年（1月1日）正式进入流通，欧元纸币和硬币取代了成员国货币。欧盟的货币联盟（monetary union）得以实现。

30. **The current Eurozone includes 19 countries:**
    目前欧元区有19个成员国：奥地利、比利时、塞浦路斯、爱沙尼亚、芬兰、法国、德国、希腊、爱尔兰、意大利、卢森堡、马耳他、荷兰、葡萄牙、斯洛伐克、斯洛文尼亚、西班牙、拉脱维亚、立陶宛。现在，在最早的15个欧盟国家中，只有英国、丹麦和瑞典没有加入单一货币。

31. **The Treaty of Nice:**
    《尼斯条约》。该条约涉及欧洲一体化建设和东扩进程等方面的问题。在欧盟理事会内表决票数的分配上，做出了基本按成员国人口多少分配表决票数的规定，还把使用"有效多数制"表决提案的范围扩大到50多个领域，以提高欧盟的决策效率。此外，《尼斯条约》还确定了欧盟扩大到27个成员国后各国在欧洲议会中占有的席位数量，为今后接收新成员国做好了安排。

32. **The Treaty of Lisbon:**
    《里斯本条约》。该条约对欧盟机构进行了改革并简化欧盟的决策进程，以便使扩大后的欧盟更高效运转。根据条约，欧盟理事会将设常任主席，以取代之前每半年轮换一次的欧盟主席国轮替机制，任期2年半，可连任一次。设立欧盟外交和安全政策高级代表一职，全面负责欧盟对外政策，任期5年。欧洲议会的权力将增强。更多政策领域被划归到"有效多数表决制"决策的范围，以简化决策过程，成员国不再能"一票否决"。但在税收、社会保障、外交和防务等事关成员国主权的领域，仍采取一致通过原则。

33. **Britain had looked beyond ... the Commonwealth on the other:**
    过去英国的目光一向越过了欧洲邻国，他们认为自己既与美国也与英联邦国家有更多共同点。事实上，为了应对苏联的潜在威胁，英国外交部致力于将美国拉进欧洲防务中来，防止美国退守孤立主义。

34. **More importantly, Britain traditionally ... of supranational organisations:**
    更重要的是，英国传统上只青睐自由贸易协议，对超国家的组织机构有一种自然的自由主义的怀疑。

35. **the European Free Trade Association:**
    欧洲自由贸易联盟。为了与欧洲经济共同体抗衡，英国、瑞典、挪威、瑞士、奥地利、丹麦和葡萄牙七国于1960年1月在斯德哥尔摩签订了《建立欧洲自由贸易联盟公约》，组成单纯的自由贸易区。英国和

UNIT 8　British Foreign Relations

丹麦于 1972 年底退出联盟，加入欧共体。冰岛后来加入联盟。

36. **But soon, the decision to join the EEC ... with other European countries:**
    但很快，鉴于英国的经济、政治和军事利益早已与其他欧洲国家紧密连在一起，英国决定加入欧洲共同体成为很自然的事。

37. **but was twice vetoed by French President General de Gaulle:**
    （英国的申请）两次被法国总统戴高乐将军否决。英国在戴高乐将军下台后才成功被接纳为成员国。

38. **It is less certain about ... a kind of European federal government:**
    英国对欧盟成为"联邦式"超级国家的可能性持消极态度。在这种"联邦式"超级国家内，各国政府的权力将受到削弱，而成为欧洲联邦政府管辖的省份。

39. **the European Union Act 2011:**
    《2011 年欧洲联盟法》重申了英国的宪法主权和议会主权原则，规定欧盟制定新条约或做出重要条约修改在英国需由全民公决和/或议会立法形式予以认可，特别是在涉及成员国向欧盟进一步转移权力的问题上必须经过全民公决批准。

40. **the Anglo-US special relationship:**
    英美特殊关系。Anglo: 表示"英国的"。

41. **The Britain hosts a large American military presence:**
    英国有大量美国军事基地，允许大量美军驻扎在其国土上。

42. **Polaris and Trident — advanced submarine-launched inter-continental ballistic missiles:**
    "北极星"和"三叉戟"——先进的由潜艇发射的洲际弹道导弹。英国的核威慑并不是完全独立的核威慑，导弹弹头是"英国货"，但导弹发射系统长期依靠美国以极其优惠的价格提供，英国不单独研制以避免昂贵的费用。根据两国 1962 年底达成的协议，美国将向英国出售"北极星"（Polaris）海基弹道导弹，用于装备英国建造的"决心"级核潜艇。作为交换，美国获得了在英国领土上部署有关导弹、在苏格兰霍利湾建设潜艇基地以及使用英国位于世界各地（例如马耳他、巴林、新加坡、澳大利亚）的基地的权利。1979 年英美两国达成新协议，"北极星"潜射导弹将被替换成更先进的"三叉戟"（Trident）潜射洲际弹道导弹系统。英国为此建造了 4 艘"前卫"级战略核潜艇，于 20 世纪 90 年代投入海军服役，部署在苏格兰克莱德海军基地。

43. **But Churchill resisted American pressure ... imperial preference trading system:**
    但丘吉尔顶住了美国要求英国废除帝国特惠贸易制度的压力。帝国特惠制是英国和英联邦其他成员国间在贸易上实行互惠关税的制度。1932 年在渥太华帝国会议上制定，终止于 20 世纪 70 年代末。

44. **the 1956 Suez Crisis:**
    1956 年苏伊士运河危机。1956 年，埃及总统纳赛尔宣布将苏伊士运河收归国有。英国和法国为夺回运河控制权，与以色列密谋，共同发动了侵埃战争，遭到国际社会（如美国、苏联、联合国）的普遍谴责。危机以三国的失败而告终。埃及虽在军事上失利，但在美苏的干预下最终赢得了苏伊士运河的全部主权。美国因担心苏联的介入，施压英、法接受联合国停火协议，并抛售美国政府的英镑债券，导致英镑贬值。

# The United Kingdom of Great Britain and Northern Ireland

苏伊士运河危机标志着英国霸主地位的陨落，英国未来在国际事务中将不得不依赖与更强大的美国的合作。

45. **It withdrew its troops from "East of Suez" (e.g. Singapore, Malaya and the Persian Gulf):**
英国从"苏伊士（运河）以东地区"（如新加坡、马来亚和波斯湾）撤军。

46. **the Falklands (Malvinas) War:**
马岛战争。是英国和阿根廷为争夺马尔维纳斯群岛（英国殖民地，毗邻阿根廷，英国称之为福克兰群岛）主权的一场战争。美国支持了英国，让其使用大西洋中的美军海岛基地加油和加给养，否则英国舰队无法直达南美。美国这样做的代价是得罪了被它视为"后院"并一直在拉拢的南美近邻。

47. **the Irangate affair:**
伊朗门事件。1984–1985 年，西方国家驻黎巴嫩的外交人员、记者、教师等纷纷被绑架，其中有 7 名美国公民。美国希望通过伊朗斡旋，伊朗出于两伊战争的考虑（急需军火）表示愿意。于是由以色列牵线搭桥，美国卖给伊朗武器，伊朗来斡旋释放人质。美伊双方在伦敦有秘密接触，被英国情报部门窃听掌握，但英国始终没有泄密。1986 年 11 月，黎巴嫩媒体曝光了美国总统安全顾问麦克法兰 5 月份秘密访伊和运送武器的事情。美国一直宣称绝不向恐怖分子低头，绝不同他们谈判，伊朗也是武器禁运的对象，因此，以武器换人质引起世界巨大震惊。英国事前事后都保持沉默，没有对美国做出任何指责，很给面子。

48. **American troops occupied Grenada:**
美军入侵格林纳达。此举旨在推翻不亲西方的政权，以扶持亲美的反政府力量。格林纳达是英联邦国家，美国出兵理应事前告知英国，但美国没有这么做，让英国很恼火，但无法发泄。

49. **Blair's Britain emerged as Bush's most dependable alley ... in Iraq:**
在阿富汗和伊拉克的"反恐战争"中，布莱尔领导的英国成为布什最可靠的盟友。在伊拉克战争中，英美推翻了萨达姆政权。开战借口是萨达姆政权拥有大规模杀伤性武器，但美英军队始终没能找到证据。伊拉克战争没有得到联合国授权，合法性受到国际社会质疑，北约内部也有德国、法国的强烈反对，很大程度上布莱尔因此下台。

50. **"solid but not slavish":**
"牢固而不盲从"。布莱尔工党时期过分追随美国，使英国陷入伊拉克战争泥淖，引发民众强烈不满。保守党在竞选纲领中提出要同美国发展"牢固而不盲从"的关系。

51. **Syrian opposition leaders accused ... using sarin for mass killing:**
叙利亚反对派领导人指责忠于叙利亚总统巴沙尔政府的军队使用沙林毒气进行大规模屠杀（事实上到底是何方使用了沙林毒气并没有定论）。在叙利亚事件中，英国议会投票否决了首相欲追随美国出兵的建议，美国对出兵也并不坚定，后来俄罗斯从中斡旋，叙政府交出了一些化学武器，危机得到缓和。

52. **the removal of Taliban regime in Afghanistan:**
清除阿富汗塔利班政权。

53. **Rapid Reaction Corps:**
快速反应部队。它是北约快速反应军事力量中地面军事力量的关键组成部分。英国是快速反应部队的主要国家和主导力量。

54. **The war on terrorism ... prioritise homeland defence in its various forms:**
反恐战争可能在 21 世纪取代国家间的冲突作为国防政策的主要手段，英国的外交和国防政策目标已经必须优先考虑各种形式的国内防御。

# Exercises

I. **Give the Chinese equivalents for the following:**
   1. the "Three Circles" foreign policy
   2. the Commonwealth of Nations
   3. the European Union
   4. the Single European Market
   5. Brexit
   6. the Anglo-US special relationship

II. **Decide whether the following statements are true ( T ) or false ( F ):**
   1. The UK was awarded a permanent seat on the UN Security Council in recognition of its contribution in setting up the United Nations. _____
   2. The Commonwealth is made up mostly of former British colonies which feel connected to Britain after gaining independence. _____
   3. Britain was not one of the original countries in setting up the EEC because it was not invited. _____
   4. If you want to visit the UK, you can apply for a Schengen visa. _____
   5. The US backed Britain in the Falklands (Malvinas) War providing material and intelligence support. _____
   6. Britain, Germany and France supported the US in the Iraq war. _____
   7. The UK parliament vetoed the government proposal to follow the US in military strikes on Syria. _____
   8. Britain spends more money on defence than most other developed nations and is ranked 6th in terms of its military power. _____

# The United Kingdom of Great Britain and Northern Ireland

### III. Fill in the blanks:

1. The present foreign policy of Britain is greatly influenced by its _____ history as well as its _____.
2. Britain's physical isolation has long been reduced by the development of _____ and by the opening of _____, which links Britain to continental Europe.
3. Britain's postwar international relations were largely based on Winston Churchill's _____ foreign policy.
4. Britain gradually lost its empire and now it keeps contact with its former colonies through an organisation called _____.
5. In the _____, Britain and France had to withdraw their troops under American pressure.
6. The Single European Act of 1986 was signed to create a single internal market with the _____ of goods, services, labour and capital.
7. The Maastricht Treaty in 1992 established _____ for better and deeper European integration and since the beginning of 2002 the member countries have used a single currency named _____.
8. Britain is seen as an "awkward partner" because it did not join _____ or _____.
9. Euro-sceptics do not like the tendency of the EU moving towards a _____ "super-state".
10. Britain is a member of the nuclear club, yet despite its claim that it has an independent nuclear deterrent, the _____ system — Trident — is supplied by _____ at favourable prices.

### IV. Questions:

1. What are the factors that have contributed greatly to the shaping of British postwar foreign policy?
2. Which government institutions are mainly involved in British foreign policy making?
3. How did the British Empire end? What did Britain do to react to the situation?
4. Which countries set up the EEC and why?
5. What was the purpose of the Single European Act?
6. What is the Schengen Agreement and a Schengen visa?
7. What is meant by monetary union (Eurozone)?

8. Why was Britain not an original member of the EEC? Why did it want to join later?
9. Who are Euro-sceptics? What are their fears and concerns?
10. What lesson did the Suez Crisis teach Britain?
11. What are the foundations of the Anglo-US special relationship?
12. Did Britain send troops to Vietnam in support of the US in the 1960s? Why or why not?
13. In what aspects is the relationship between Britain and the US very special?
14. Explain one example of military cooperation between the UK and the US in detail, e.g. the Iraq war.

## V. Topics for discussion or research:

1. What was the purpose of establishing the NATO? What are NATO's present roles in your opinion?
2. Why does the author think that Britain has a "special relationship" with the United States? Do you think the special relationship is good for the UK or not?
3. How would you summarise Britain's present position in the world?

# UNIT 9

# The British Media

**Go over the following focal points before reading the text:**

- Popularity and functions of the media
- The quality press
- *The Observer*
- *The Times*
- *The Guardian*
- *The Telegraph*
- *The Financial Times*
- Tabloids
- Television and radio
- The British Broadcasting Corporation (BBC)
- The Independent Television Commission

# The United Kingdom of Great Britain and Northern Ireland

Text

## Introduction: Traditions and New Trends

For most British people, most days begin with a look at the morning newspaper. On an average day, 90 percent of Britons over the age of 15 read a national or local paper.[1] And in the evening, most Britons settle down to watch some television: 96 percent of the population watch TV at least once a week, making it Britain's most popular leisure activity. The third most popular pastime, after watching **telly** and reading newspapers, is listening to the radio, an activity in which 73 percent of the population engages on a weekly basis. It is obvious, then, that the media are central to British leisure culture.[2]

Not only do Britons use the media for entertainment, the media have many other functions. Newspapers and radio and TV programmes, for example, provide British people with information about political and social issues; provide weather reports; carry advertising; are used for educational purposes; and provide a **forum** for people to write letters or phone in to express their views or seek advice. The British media are considered to be vital to the British political system because they play such an important role in informing the population about problems the country may be facing and what the government is doing to solve such problems.

The media also play an important role in **engendering** a national culture. By tuning in to their favourite programme or picking up their daily paper, a worker on an oil **rig** off the coast of Scotland, a retired professor in Belfast, a London secretary and a Welsh dentist all share the same experience.[3] Even though they live in very different environments, if ever they were to meet they could discuss what they had read or seen, and this would remind them that as people living in Britain they are all part of a particular culture.[4]

In 2009 it was estimated that individuals viewed a **mean** of 3.75 hours of television per day and listened to 2.81 hours of radio. The main BBC public service broadcasting channels accounted for an estimated 28.4% of all television viewing; the three main independent channels accounted for 29.5% and the increasingly important other satellite and **digital** channels for the remaining 42.1%. Sales of newspapers have

telly *n.*
（英口语）电视
forum *n.* 论坛
engender *v.*
形成
rig *n.*
钻井架，钻井塔
mean *n.* 平均数
digital *adj.*
数码的，数字信息系统的

fallen since the 1970s, and in 2009 42% of people reported reading a daily national newspaper. In 2018, 90% adults in the UK were recent Internet users. Around 72% of adult Internet users have a social media account. **Facebook** is the leading platform.

## British Newspapers

The United Kingdom has one of the world's oldest established newspaper industries. In the late 18th and early 19th century, as the British economy began to industrialise, as the democratic **franchise** was extended to larger **segments** of the population, and as literacy levels rose through the introduction of mass education, more and more newspapers began to appear.[5] *The Observer*[6], which is still published every Sunday, first appeared in 1791, making it the world's oldest Sunday newspaper, while *The Times*[7], which began publishing in 1785, is the United Kingdom's oldest daily newspaper.

With the introduction of parliamentary democracy, candidates had to get their message to the voters. Originally this was done by giving long speeches or perhaps publishing short **pamphlets**, but increasingly newspapers took on the role of informing the electorate about politics. The very names of British newspapers — *The Times, The Observer, The Guardian*[8] — still suggest that the function of the paper is to offer the electorate objective reports about what is happening in the country. This **watchdog** function, keeping an eye on the government, is one of the reasons why a free press is considered so important to the functioning of parliamentary democracy.[9]

This role is frequently criticised, however. Many **analysts** feel that the power of the press has **usurped** the power of Parliament. Contemporary politicians prefer to speak directly to the media rather than to Parliament and of course they have their favourite, friendly reporters who will give them favourable **coverage**.[10] Journalism nowadays is not an objective recording of facts, but the writing of stories which are written to put across a particular view.[11]

Business people, even more than politicians, were quick to realise "the power of the press" to inform potential customers about their products and services, and so the **advertising** business was born.[12] While much is made of the "freedom of the press" and how important the press is to Western democratic practice, it is worth bearing in mind that newspapers are first and foremost, businesses that exist to earn money for their owners, not public services designed to inform the population.[13] In Britain, a lot

Facebook
美国一个社交网络服务网站
franchise *n.*
选举权
segment *n.*
部分
pamphlet *n.*
宣传册
watchdog *n.*
监督者
analyst *n.*
分析员
usurp *v.* 篡夺
coverage *n.*
报道
advertise *v.*
广告

# The United Kingdom of Great Britain and Northern Ireland

of advertising is carried in newspapers: in 1995, 465 million pounds were spent on advertising. Not only do companies use the press to sell products and services: people looking for a job, a house to buy, or even babysitters also turn to the classified ads and free newspapers which **consist** almost entirely of advertising.

The British media all must follow the Advertising Code which **ensures** that advertisements are legal, decent, honest and truthful; have a sense of responsibility for consumer and society; and respect the principles of fair competition.[14] Because the point of advertising is to bring your product to the attention of the public, sometimes advertisers will launch deliberately controversial ad campaigns in order to gain attention.[15] The European clothing manufacturer, Benetton, has raised much controversy by using pictures such as a man dying of AIDS and the bloody uniform of a **Bosnian** soldier to sell clothes, images which are considered in bad taste in the context of fashion marketing.[16] More often, controversies arise over the representation of women, particularly if they are not wearing many clothes. If enough people complain to the Advertising Standards Board, the company will be told to withdraw the ad.[17]

British newspaper culture is unusual in the extent to which class and educational differences are reflected in the newspapers people read.[18] In other developed countries like Japan and the United States, newspaper reading is a mainly middle-class habit, but in Britain the "lower classes" are also regular readers. Among developed countries, Britain has one of the highest levels of newspaper sales per head of population, and there are over 1 400 different newspapers which **cater for** a wide range of political views, interests and levels of education. Although most newspapers are financially independent of political parties, they often express particular political views and most people will choose to read a newspaper which **accords with** their own feelings.

Thus if you were to find yourself sitting on a London **tube** (subway) train on a Monday morning, you would be surrounded by people reading newspapers and you could tell a great deal about your fellow passengers just by the sort of newspaper he or she was reading. There are 10 different daily national papers, that is, newspapers which are available throughout the country and cover issues of national importance. About half of these are usually referred to as "the quality press" or "the broadsheets" (because they are printed on large-size paper.)[19] The quality papers carry more serious and **in-depth** articles of particular political and social importance. They also

---

consist v.
由…组成
ensure v.
保证
Bosnian adj.
波斯尼亚（人）的
cater for
迎合
accord with
与…符合，一致
tube n.
（英）地铁
in-depth adj.
深入的，彻底的

carry **reviews** and **feature articles** about high culture and will generally be read by a well-educated, middle class audience.[20] The most **left-wing** of these newspapers is *The Guardian*: you will often hear people on TV or in daily life refer to "*Guardian* readers" — this is a kind of shorthand to suggest someone who is left wing and liberal in their politics, and interested in society and social issues.[21] *Guardian* readers, for example, will be soft on crime, be quite feminist and interested in green politics. [22] The average *Telegraph* reader, on the other hand, will tend to support tough sentences for criminals, be unsympathetic to single mothers and favour free enterprise over social programmes.[23]

The other category of national newspapers is "the **tabloids**", smaller format newspapers with colour photos and **catchy** headlines. They are often called "the gutter press" because they deal in scandals and gossip, usually about famous people, whether in politics, sports or entertainment, and carry lots of crime, sports and **sensational** human interest stories.[24] The stories are short, easy to read and often rely more on opinion than fact.[25] One feature of the tabloid press which has become a national institution is the Page 3 Girl — a picture each day of a pretty, **scantily clad** young woman. Most of the scandals about the Royal Family first appeared in the tabloid press.

The tabloids, with their **lurid** and sensational stories, have been around nearly as long as the more serious newspapers. In 1843 *The News of the World* began publishing as a paper which carried mainly crime, sport and sex stories. By the 1930s it was Britain's most popular Sunday paper, selling 3.4 million copies each week. It now sells about 4.7 million papers each week, and is Britain's biggest seller.

For convenience of reading, many traditional broadsheets have switched to a more compact-sized format, traditionally used by tabloids.

Until the 1980s, almost all the national newspapers had their headquarters on or around **Fleet** Street in London, and sometimes you will hear newspaper culture referred to still as "Fleet Street", or even, sometimes, the Street of Shame, reflecting the birth of scandals which take place.[26] Now the industry, while still centred in London, is not concentrated on a single street and some newspapers are available internationally. *The Financial Times*, for example, is printed in Frankfurt, France, Hong Kong, New Jersey, Los Angeles, Tokyo and Madrid.[27]

While officially speaking the British press is "free" from government control and

---

review *n.*
评论
feature article
特写，专题报道
left-wing *adj.*
左翼的
tabloid *n.*
通俗小报
catchy *adj.*
醒目的
sensational *adj.*
耸人听闻的
scantily *adv.*
不足地，少量地
clad *adj.*
（clothe 的过去分词）穿…衣服的
lurid *adj.*
骇人听闻的
fleet *n.* 舰队

# The United Kingdom of Great Britain and Northern Ireland

**censorship** and can print what it likes, there are limits to what will appear in the daily paper. In 1990 the former chairman of the **KGB**, the Soviet Secret Service, said: "You'll never find in a British newspaper who meets who. Not like in America — their papers are big-mouthed; we used to find out a lot from their press. In England, no information could be found from the papers. I always taught my people: 'Do everything like the British.'"

While there is no particular state censorship, many British laws limit the freedom of the press. Contempt of court laws restrain newspapers from printing information about people being tried for various crimes because this can prejudice the judicial system.[28] Other laws of **libel** and **defamation** prevent papers from publishing stories about people which are not true.

The media are also affected by the Official Secrets Act, a legal act which stipulates that all government information is kept secret unless the government says it can be released. Sometimes journalists who are investigating government wrongdoing have their stories blocked,[29] are fined or are even sent to prison because they reveal information that the government does not want the public to know about. For example, in 1984 a young foreign office clerk, Sarah Tisdall, learned through her job that the government had secretly devised a plan to allow the **deployment** of American **nuclear missiles** without the public knowing because the government feared the public would protest. She felt that the government was **abusing** its power and therefore she took the information to *The Guardian*, which published it. Subsequently, Tisdall was jailed for six months for leaking information to the newspaper.

Television and the Internet have brought great changes to mass media. By the late 1990s, news was available 24 hour a day on television channels and then on the Internet. If you use the Internet, you can get most frequently updated news free of charge. This development of television and the Internet have posed a challenge to the business model of newspapers in Britain as well as in other countries. Paid **circulation** has declined, while advertising **revenue** — which makes up the bulk of most newspapers' income — has been shifting from print to the new media, resulting in a general decline in profits. Major newspapers in the UK have launched online editions in an attempt to follow or stay ahead of their audience. For instance, if you visit the website of a newspaper, such as www.thetimes.com on your computer, you can get limited free access of news articles, and if you subscribe to it, you will be able to enjoy

---

censorship *n.*
新闻检查
KGB 克格勃（苏联国家安全委员会）
libel *n.*
（法律）诽谤罪
defamation *n.*
污蔑，诽谤
deployment *n.*
部署
nuclear missile
核导弹
abuse *v.* 滥用
circulation *n.*
发行量
revenue *n.*
收入；收益

unlimited access to all the news, sport, business, comment, analysis and reviews from the *Times*. However, many people still maintain their habit of reading a newspaper at breakfast or on a tube train.

## The Broadcast Media

One famous **commentator** on British media has written that in the UK "there is almost no escape from television." The broadcast media — television and radio — are tremendously important to British national life. In a country where 97 per cent of households have a TV set and virtually everybody has a radio, the messages and information which are sent over the **airwaves** into peoples' homes, cars and workplaces reach virtually everyone.

On average, British people spend 4 hours a day watching TV and one of the most frequently read parts of the newspaper is the TV **listings**. Newspapers also carry reviews of programmes which are being broadcast. At work, or among friends and family, conversations will frequently be about shows that were watched the evening before. To not participate in British television viewing is to effectively cut oneself off from British culture and society.[30]

What do British people watch? News, entertainment, and sport are the favourites. While **comedy**, drama and **game shows** fall in and out of favour, Britain has two long-running **soap operas**.[31] The oldest and most popular soap, which began in the 1960s, is *Coronation Street*, set in the northern city of Manchester; its more recent rival is *East Enders*, which takes place in a **fictitious** east London working class neighbourhood.[32] Central to the action of both soap operas is the local pub, where the characters gather to gossip, celebrate, **commiserate**, fall in and out of love, fight, laugh and cry.

In contrast to American soap operas, which feature improbably rich, famous and exciting characters, British soaps present **gritty** and realistic accounts of the everyday life of Britons.[33] They often tackle contemporary social issues like racism, AIDs, **homosexuality**, divorce, **drug abuse**, **wife battering** and so on. They are of very high quality and are popular abroad: whether in New Zealand or Canada, you can keep up with your favourite characters. And in Manchester a popular tourist attraction is the actual set of *Coronation Street*, where fans go to have their photos taken outside of the pub, "The Rover's Return".

Daily news and weather forecasts are also popular viewing. British newscasts are

---

commentator *n.* 评论员
airwave *n.* 电波
(TV) listing *n.* （电视）节目单
comedy *n.* 喜剧
game show 智力比赛节目
soap opera 肥皂剧
fictitious *adj.* 虚构的
commiserate *v.* 同情，怜悯
gritty *adj.* 勇敢的，坚定的
homosexuality *n.* 同性恋
drug abuse 吸毒
wife battering 殴打妻子

# The United Kingdom of Great Britain and Northern Ireland

renowned for the quality of their reporting. And a fairly recent and extremely popular show is the **live broadcast** of the National **Lottery** each week, where viewers can watch the lucky numbers being drawn for weekly big cash prizes.

In North America there are literally scores of different channels to watch, from home shopping channels to 24-hour news channels, to channels that specialise in old comedy shows. Britain, in contrast, still has a fairly conservative television culture. There are still only a limited number of television channels, and satellite TV is still not as popular or as widely available as in the United States.[34] This limited number of channels and the state control of the ownership of such channels, helps to unify the entire country. The Broadcasting Act is designed to keep ownership of broadcast media widely spread so there are no concentrations of media power in the hands of a few, and foreign ownership (that is ownership outside the European Union) is mainly prohibited.[35] The same legislation also contains safeguards to maintain certain standards of decency, taste, accuracy and balance.[36]

Because of the limited number of channels, not only does nearly everyone watch TV, but nearly everyone watches the same thing. The top ten programmes of the year will attract audiences of between 16 and 23 million. In fact, during especially popular programmes, the national utility companies have to make special preparations because during commercial breaks, a surge of demand for electricity is created when millions of British viewers rush out of the living room to make a cup of tea.[37]

The British Broadcasting Corporation[38] — more familiarly known as the BBC or even "the Beeb" — is Britain's main public service broadcaster. It was founded in 1927 as a public service radio station, and later moved into TV. BBC TV was renamed BBC1 when sister channel BBC2 was launched in 1964. They are now called BBC One and BBC Two. BBC One specialises in shows with broad appeal, such as sport, entertainment, current affairs, drama, and kids' shows. It is currently the most watched television channel in the United Kingdom. BBC Two aims at a wide range of subject matter and interests, specialising in intelligent yet popular programme genres. With the new development in media technologies, BBC Three and BBC Four were both launched after the beginning of the 21st century. BBC Three is a television channel from the BBC broadcasting via digital cable, terrestrial, **IPTV** and satellite platforms. The channel is an outlet for new drama, talent shows, comedy, films, etc. BBC Four is a BBC television channel available to digital television viewers in the UK. It shows

live broadcast
直播
lottery  *n.* 彩票
IPTV
交互式网络电视

a wide variety of programmes including drama, documentaries, music, international film, comedy and current affairs, an alternative to programmes on the mainstream TV channels. In November 2008, all standard BBC television channels were made available to watch online.

The BBC is funded by **license** fees and viewers must buy a license each year for their TV set. Because the BBC is funded by license fees, there are technically no commercials, although between shows there are **trailers** for upcoming shows and **promotions** for products associated with the BBC.

The BBC is no longer just about TV shows. Nowadays it is a **multimedia** business with wide publishing and educational interests. Not only can you watch BBC shows about cars, pop music, cooking, holidays and gardening, but you can buy magazines which **complement** the shows by providing further information, recipes, and competitions.[39] Now, the BBC news can be read and its videos can be watched on the Internet.

The international **arm** of the BBC is the BBC World Service, which broadcasts in English and over 40 other languages throughout the world. Its global weekly audience is estimated to be at least 140 million people.

The other two channels are run by the Independent Television Commission (ITC)[40] and are funded by advertising.

Given the vast amounts of coverage in British homes, TV, like the press, is very important to British politics. In the past, politicians addressed public meetings and gave long speeches. The most successful politicians, like Churchill, are remembered as great **orators**. TV places different demands on politicians and so the whole style of politics has changed. With TV, politicians literally "come into our living room" and so they have to seem more relaxed and friendly, as if they are speaking to us personally.[41] Long speeches are out; contemporary politicians have just 2 to 3 minutes to get their messages across, before the attention of the viewer drifts and they change the channel. As a result, politicians speak in "sound bites" and slogans.[42] They use professional writers to help them write their speeches, "spin doctors" who manage their images and appearances, and even advertising agencies.[43] The Conservative Party in particular embraced TV and advertising as the best way to reach the hearts, minds and — more importantly — votes of the masses.[44] Spending on government advertising has risen considerably in the last few decades, and now the British government is one of the

license *n.*
（政府的）许可，特许
trailer *n.* 预告片
promotion *n.*
促销
multimedia *n.*
多媒体
complement *v.*
补充；与…相配
arm *n.* 分部
orator *n.* 演说家

# The United Kingdom of Great Britain and Northern Ireland

country's ten biggest advertisers.

After much reluctance, the House of Commons finally agreed to allow its sessions to be televised in 1990. While Commons debates are always open to the public, parliamentarians feared the power of the camera, which can easily broadcast a small detail — a government minister yawning during an important debate, for example — and therefore **detract** from the seriousness and dignity of the House. The sorts of **shots** the cameras were allowed to broadcast were strictly limited at first, but now MPs are more relaxed with their roles as TV personalities.[45]

Politicians from all parties spend a lot of time worrying about their TV images. Mrs. Thatcher took lessons from a voice **coach** who taught her to speak in a deeper voice more **befitting** a serious national leader, and changed her hair colour, make-up and clothing in order to enhance her dignified image.[46] Mr. Tony Blair changed his hairstyle in order to appear more handsome to women voters. The current Prime Minister Theresa May is known for a love of fashion and in particular distinctive shoes, wearing **leopard-print** shoes at her final Cabinet meeting as Home Secretary in 2016. However she has been critical of the media focusing on her fashion instead of her achievements as a politician.

## Conclusion

Media play an essential role in people's social, cultural, political and economic lives. They have developed and changed fast in the past decades, and are still changing. What will happen to the current media forms we have today in the next decade or even the next few years? It is hard to predict. What we know for sure is that information spreading and sharing through media will always remain important.

detract *v.* 损伤
shot *n.* 镜头
coach *n.* 教练
befitting *adj.* 适合的
leopard-print *adj.* 印有豹纹图案的

# Explanations

1. **On an average day, 90 per cent of Britons over the age of 15 read a national or local paper:**
   平均每天，15 岁以上的英国人中有 90% 的人阅读一份全国性的报纸或地方报纸。

2. **It is obvious, then, that the media are central to British leisure culture:**
   显然，新闻媒介对英国休闲文化是十分重要的。Media 是 medium 一词的复数形式。The media 这里指

# UNIT 9  The British Media

传统的媒体，包括电视、电台、报纸等为公众提供信息的各种媒介的总和。

3. **By tuning in to their favourite programme or picking up their daily paper ... same experience:**
   通过收听个人喜爱的节目，或者阅读一份日报，无论是在苏格兰海岸油井架上工作的工人，还是居住在贝尔发斯特的退休教授，还是在伦敦工作的秘书，或者威尔士牙医都可以分享同样的经历。

4. **Even though they live in very different environments ... of a particular culture:**
   尽管他们生活的环境不同，但是如果他们相遇，他们能讨论他们所共同听到或看到的事情，这使他们感到，作为生活在联合王国的人们，他们都同属于一种特殊文化。

5. **In the late eighteenth and early nineteenth century ... newspapers began to appear:**
   18世纪末、19世纪初，英国经济开始工业化，民主选举权扩大到人口中的大部分，大众教育提高了文化水平，这时，越来越多的报纸开始出现了。

6. **The Observer:**
   《观察家报》，于1791年首发出版，是世界上最早的全国发行的报纸，现在仍每周日出版。

7. **The Times:**
   《泰晤士报》，按照泰晤士河（the Thames River）的音翻译。1785年首发出版，是英国最早的日报。

8. **The Guardian:**
   《卫报》，被认为是英国的左翼报纸。

9. **This watchdog function, keeping an eye on the government ... to the functioning of parliamentary democracy:**
   新闻媒体对政府的监督作用是人们认为新闻自由对于行使议会民主极为重要的原因之一。**watchdog:** 监督者、监督机构，其作用是防止浪费、腐败以及其他非道德行为。

10. **Contemporary politicians prefer to speak directly to the media rather ... favourable coverage:**
    当代的政治家宁愿直接与新闻媒体沟通，也不愿意与议会沟通，当然了，他们有自己喜欢的、对他们友好的记者，这些记者将对他们做有利的报道。

11. **Journalism nowadays is not an objective recording of facts, but the writing ... across a particular view:**
    在今天，新闻报道已经不是客观地记录事实，而是通过编写故事来表达某种观点。

12. **Business people, even more than politicians ... so the advertising business was born:**
    商人甚至比政客更快意识到新闻的力量，新闻在向顾客提供有关产品及服务信息方面发挥巨大作用，因此，广告业产生了。

13. **While much is made of the "freedom of the press" ... designed to inform the population:**
    尽管人们大谈"新闻自由"的重要性，以及新闻对西方民主的实施如何至关重要，但是值得牢记的是，报纸首先是一种商业，是为报业老板赚钱而存在的，报纸不是为人民提供信息而设立的公共服务事业。

14. **The British media all must follow the Advertising Code which ensure ... fair competition:**
    英国所有的媒体必须遵守"广告法规"，该法规保证广告必须是合法的、得体的、诚实的、真实的，对顾客和社会有责任感，遵循公平竞争的原则。

# The United Kingdom of Great Britain and Northern Ireland

15. **Because the point of advertising is to bring your product to the attention ... in order to gain attention:**
    由于广告的目的是使公众注意到你的产品,有时广告商会故意发起有争议的广告活动,以便吸引注意力。

16. **The European clothing manufacturer, Benetton, has raised much controversy ... fashion marketing:**
    欧洲服装制造商贝纳通曾经引起很大的争论,他们用表现濒临死亡的艾滋病患者以及波斯尼亚士兵血迹斑斑的军服的图片来推销服装。这些形象在服装市场上被认为品位糟糕。

17. **If enough people complain to the Advertising Standards Board, the company will be told to withdraw the ad:**
    如果向"广告标准委员会"投诉的人超过了一定数额,该公司将被通知撤销这一广告。

18. **British newspaper culture is unusual in the extent to which class and ... the newspapers people read:**
    英国的报纸文化极不寻常,选读的报纸种类反映出读报人的阶级以及所受教育的差异。

19. **About half of these are usually referred to as "the quality press" ... printed on large-size paper.):**
    大约半数的报纸被称为"严肃的报纸"或者"大版的报纸",因为这些报纸印在大张的纸上。相对来说,通俗小报印在只有"严肃的报纸"版面一半的纸张上。但是,情况在不断变化,现在已经不能用报纸版面的大小来区分"严肃报纸"和所谓"通俗小报"了。

20. **They also carry reviews and feature articles about high culture ... middle class audience:**
    这些报纸也刊登关于高雅文化的评论文章和特别报道(也称专稿),这些文章的读者是受过良好教育的中产阶级。

21. **The most left wing of these newspapers is *The Guardian*: you will ... in society and social issues:**
    最为左翼的报纸是《卫报》。你可能在电视上或日常生活中听到有人被称为"卫报读者",这是对这些人的简称,他们属于左翼,在政治上持自由化观点,对社会和社会问题非常关注。

22. ***Guardian* readers, for example, will be soft on crime, be quite feminist and interested in green politics:**
    例如,《卫报》读者在犯罪问题上比较宽容,具有女性主义观点,对绿色政治较为关注。绿色指环境保护。欧洲和世界其他地区有致力于环保的绿党(Green Party)以及绿色和平组织(Greenpeace organisations)。

23. **The average *Telegraph* reader, on the other hand ... favour free enterprise over social programmes:**
    另一方面,一般的《电讯报》的读者则倾向于支持严惩犯罪分子,对单亲母亲缺乏同情,支持自由企业而不是社会福利项目。这一对比表明《电讯报》读者在政治问题上比较保守。

24. **They are often called "the gutter press" because they deal in scandals ... human interest stories:**
    这些小报经常被称为"低级趣味报纸",因为它们主要刊登丑闻和流言蜚语,通常是关于名人的,无论是政治、体育或娱乐方面的,而且还刊登许多犯罪、体育和耸人听闻的趣闻。Gutter 的原义是阴沟,the gutter 则指社会最贫困的底层的恶劣状况。Human interest story 也称 soft news,是新闻报道的一种类型,报道人们通常感兴趣的题材,没有时事新闻 (hard news) 的时效性,不能成为报纸的头条新闻。

# UNIT 9 The British Media

25. **The stories are short, easy to read and often rely more on opinion than fact:**
这些新闻故事一般短小、易读、通常重观点而不重事实。新闻的重要原则之一是讲求客观性，尊重事实，显然，课文作者批评这些故事为了迎合读者的口味而违反新闻报道的原则。

26. **Until the 1980s, almost all the national newspapers had their headquarters ... which take place:**
直到 20 世纪 80 年代，几乎所有的全国发行的报纸的总部都设立在伦敦的舰队街。现在有时你仍可以听到人们把报纸文化称为"舰队街"，或者"羞耻街"，反映了此地是丑闻的诞生地。

27. **The *Financial Times*, for example, is printed in Frankfurt, France, Hong Kong ... and Madrid:**
比如，《金融时报》在法兰克福、法国、香港、新泽西、洛杉矶、东京和马德里都印刷发行。

28. **While there is no particular state censorship ... because this can prejudice the judicial system:**
虽然英国不存在特殊的国家新闻检查，但许多英国的法律限制新闻自由。法庭蔑视法阻止报纸发表因种种原因而正接受审讯的人们的信息，因为此时发表报道有可能影响法律制度的公正性。**contempt of court:**
蔑视法庭；**contempt of court law:** 相关蔑视法庭行为的法律。**prejudice:** 影响某人使其对某人或某事产生不公正的意见。

29. **Sometimes journalists who are investigating government wrongdoing have their stories blocked:**
有时记者调查政府错误行为的报道遭到禁止。

30. **To not participate in British television viewing is to effectively cut oneself off ... culture and society:**
不观看英国电视等于有效地将自己从英国文化和社会中分割出去。此句说明电视是构成英国文化和社会生活的重要组成部分。

31. **While comedy, drama and game shows fall in and out of favour, Britain has two long-running soap operas:**
当喜剧、戏剧和智力比赛节目时而受欢迎，时而遭到冷落时，英国一直放映两部长篇肥皂剧。**fall in favour:** 受宠；**fall out of/from favour:** 失宠；**soap opera:** 肥皂剧，原为白天播放的情节剧，因观众多为家庭妇女，故剧间播放肥皂广告，因此这一类型的电视连续剧被称为肥皂剧。

32. **The oldest and most popular soap, which began in the 1960s ... working class neighbourhood:**
20 世纪 60 年代开始播放的《加冕典礼街》是最老的也是最受欢迎的肥皂剧，该剧以英格兰北部城市曼彻斯特为背景。后来能与《加冕典礼街》竞争的是《东区人》，该剧的故事发生在一个虚构的伦敦东区的工人阶级邻里。**East End** 是东伦敦或伦敦东区，在泰晤士河的北岸，为港口附近地区，居民多是工人。**West End** 是伦敦西区，内有大型商场、剧院和豪华酒店，与东区形成鲜明对照。

33. **In contrast to American soap operas, which feature improbably rich ... the everyday life of Britons:**
美国的肥皂剧里的人物往往是大富豪和名人，英国的肥皂剧则与此不同，呈现了英国人坚定、现实的日常生活。

34. **There are still only a limited number of television channels ... as in the United States:**
现在只有为数不多的电视频道，卫星电视还没有美国那样流行和普及。

# The United Kingdom of Great Britain and Northern Ireland

35. **The Broadcasting Act is designed to keep ownership of broadcast media ... is mainly prohibited:**
    广播法案的目的是分散广播媒介的所有权，防止媒介力量集中在少数人手中，外国所有权（即欧盟以外的所有权）一般是被禁止的。

36. **The same legislation also contains safeguards to maintain certain standards ... accuracy and balance:**
    这个法案也包含某些条款，以维护电视节目的健康、品位、准确、平衡等标准。

37. **In fact, during especially popular programmes, the national utility companies ... to make a cup of tea:**
    实际上，在特别受欢迎的节目播出时，国家公用事业公司必须为播放广告时段做好供电准备，来应付急剧猛增的用电量。因为在这一时间，数以百万的英国观众同时冲出客厅去沏茶。由于许多人家用电炉，此时的用电量大增。

38. **The British Broadcasting Corporation (the BBC):**
    英国广播公司，成立于1927年。

39. **Not only can you watch BBC shows about cars, pop music, cooking, ... and competitions:**
    你不仅能观看英国广播公司的各种节目，如有关汽车的节目、流行音乐、烹饪、假期、园艺，等等，你还可以买到配套的杂志，为你提供更多的信息、食谱和比赛。

40. **Independent Television Commission (ITC):**
    独立电视委员会，前身为独立电视局，于1954年创办。该委员会负责发放商业电视广告的许可证，就教育、宗教、慈善和广告业提出建议，但不负责安排具体的电视节目。

41. **With TV, politicians literally "come into our living room" ... as if they are speaking to us personally:**
    有了电视，政治家真正地"进入我们的客厅"，因此他们必须看上去更放松和友好。注意此处作者强调"真正地进入我们的客厅"。政治家为了争取百姓的支持，在发表演讲时常常强调他们要进入百姓的客厅里，可是在电视普及以前，人们只能通过报纸和收音机间接地接触政治家，电视使普通百姓坐在家中就可以看到演讲的政治家，犹如面对面坐在客厅里。

42. **Long speeches are out; contemporary politicians ... "sound bites" and slogans:**
    冗长的演讲过时了，现在的政治家只能用两三分钟把自己的意思表达清楚，否则观众的注意力分散，他们会转换频道。结果是，政客们演讲时必须运简短的语录和口号。 sound bite: 简短的，可引用的语录，或演讲的片段，一般指政客的演讲，暗示这样的演讲缺乏深度。

43. **They use professional writers to help them write their speeches, "spin doctors" ... advertising agencies:**
    他们聘用专业作家帮他们写讲演稿，还有"公众形象医生"负责他们的形象和容貌，他们甚至雇佣广告代理为他们服务。spin: 旋转；对向公众发布的信息给予侧重和倾斜，以便制造出所需要的效果，如为某个政客制造有利的形象。

44. **The Conservative Party in particular embraced TV and advertising ... votes of the masses:**
    保守党尤其欢迎电视和广告，因为这些媒介是赢得广大群众的感情、思想，特别是选票的最佳途径。

45. **The sorts of shots the cameras were allowed to broadcast were ... roles as TV personalities:**
    起初，播放议会开会的电视镜头是受到严格限制的，不过现在议员们对作为电视人物的角色已经比较放松自如了。

46. Mrs. Thatcher took lessons from a voice coach who taught her to speak ... enhance her dignified image:
撒切尔夫人曾专门上过声音教练的课程，学习用比较深沉的声音讲话，这样的声音更符合一个严肃的国家领导人的身份，她还改变了头发的颜色、化装以及服装，以便提高她的尊严形象。

# Exercises

## I. Give the Chinese equivalents for the Following:

1. *The Times*
2. a watchdog
3. freedom of the press
4. quality papers
5. tabloids
6. the BBC

## II. Decide whether the following statements are true (T) or false (F):

1. On an average day, an overwhelming majority of Britons over the age of 15 read a national or local paper. _____
2. The British media play an important role in shaping a national culture. _____
3. In the late 17th and early 18th century, more and more newspapers began to appear. _____
4. Free press has the function of keeping an eye on the government, and therefore it is called the watchdog of parliamentary democracy. _____
5. The Advertising Code ensures that advertisements are legal, decent, honest and truthful; have a sense of responsibility for consumer and society; and respect the principles of fair competition. _____
6. It is incorrect to say that class and educational differences are reflected in the newspapers people read. _____
7. *The Telegraph* readers, for example, will be soft on crime, be quite feminist and interested in green politics. _____

# The United Kingdom of Great Britain and Northern Ireland

8. The tabloids are smaller format newspapers with colour photos and catchy headlines. They are often called "the gutter press". _____
9. The British Broadcasting Corporation is funded by license fees, and viewers must buy a license each year for their TV set. _____
10. The BBC World Service, the international branch of the BBC, broadcasts in English and over 40 other languages throughout the world. _____

### III. Fill in the blanks:

1. Britain's three most popular activities are watching TV, listening to the radio and _____.
2. Britain has one of the world's oldest established newspaper industries. *The Observer*, which appeared in 1791, is the world's oldest _____ newspaper, while *The Times*, which began publishing in 1785, is Britain's oldest _____ newspaper.
3. The _____ newspapers carry more serious and in-depth articles of particular political and social importance.
4. _____ is regarded as the most left-wing newspaper in Britain.
5. The other category of newspapers is _____ which are often called "gutter press".
6. Officially speaking the British newspapers are free from government control and _____ and can print what they like, but many British laws limit the freedom of newspapers.
7. *The News of the World*, which began publishing in 1843, is considered as one of _____.
8. _____ carries business stories, and this paper is printed not only at home but also in many other countries of the world such as Germany, France, Spain and Japan.
9. The media are also affected by _____, a legal act which demands that all government information is kept secret unless the government agrees to release it.
10. The media have many _____. They provide people with information about political and social problems. They carry advertising and also play an important role in forming a national _____.

## IV. Questions:

1. What functions do the media have in the British life?
2. What role do the media play in forming a national culture according to the author?
3. What are some of the most popular quality papers in the UK?
4. What are the classified ads?
5. What are tabloids? Why are they often called "the gutter press"?
6. Why are television and radio tremendously important to British national life?
7. What is a soap opera? What are the most popular soap operas *Coronation Street* and *East Enders* about?
8. What does the BBC stand for? What do you know about it? Have you ever listened to or watched its programmes? What do you think of them?
9. How is the British Broadcasting Corporation funded?
10. What does the author mean when he says, "With TV, politicians literally 'come into our living room'"?
11. What examples does the author give to show how politicians from all parties spend a lot of time worrying about their TV images?
12. Can you give examples to show how media have developed, changed in the past decades, and are still changing?

## V. Topics for discussion or research:

1. Why does the author say, "The media are central to British leisure culture"? What are some of the similarities and differences in terms of functions between the British media and the Chinese media?
2. What are some of the characteristics of British newspaper culture? In what way is it different from the newspaper culture of the United States?
3. Is the British press free from the government control and censorship? What is the relationship between the British press and politics or business?
4. How does the BBC operate? How is it different from American broadcasting systems?

# UNIT 10

# Sports, Holidays and Festivals in Britain

**Go over the following focal points before reading the text:**

**Sports:**
- Football
- "Football hooligans"
- FA
- Tennis
- Wimbledon
- Cricket
- Golf
- Horse racing
- The Grand National
- Royal Ascot
- Hunting

**Holidays and Festivals:**
- Christmas
- Three traditions of Christmas
- Boxing Day
- Easter
- Bonfire Night
- The Battle of the Boyne
- Orange Marches
- St Patrick's Day
- Hogmanay
- Halloween
- The Eisteddfod

# The United Kingdom of Great Britain and Northern Ireland

 **Text**

## Sports

Having a drink at the local **pub**, going for a walk in the country, working in the garden or watching sports on the telly (television) — these are all ways in which many British people like to relax on weekends or when their daily **shifts** at work have ended. Such activities tell us about how modern **Brits** like to spend their free time; but if we look more closely, we can see these activities are not just recent inventions, but are deeply rooted in the British experience over centuries. Going to a **public house** for a glass of **ale** and working the land or going to watch a ball game were familiar activities in Shakespeare's time.[1] If today's British person were to be transported 500 years into the past, he or she would find many familiar **pursuits** and games played in rough but recognisable forms.[2] And because many of the sports we see played throughout the world today were born in Britain, the history of such activities is of interest to people everywhere.[3]

In the past, Britain was a mainly agricultural society with most people involved in farming. Britain was also a very religious society and the influence of the Christian Church on peoples' lives was very great. Such influences are still evident in today's sports and **leisure** activities. One very obvious example is how Sunday — the day of the week when everyone traditionally went to Church — is still the day that most people have off in the UK.[4] In recent years the government has changed the laws and now some shops and pubs are allowed to open on Sundays, but such changes are very recent and very controversial.

## Football

The idea of sports having seasons — like the football season — also comes from the natural rhythms of an agricultural society, where the timing of harvests and the general weather affected how people spent their time.[5] Football is a **boisterous** sport still played in winter and early spring when the weather is cool and often wet. In the winter, bad weather kept people in doors and there was not so much work to do on

---

pub *n.*
（主英）酒吧
shift *n.* 轮班
Brit *n.*
（口）英国人
public house
（正式）酒吧
ale *n.* 麦芽酒
pursuit *n.*
爱好，娱乐
leisure *n.* 休闲
boisterous *adj.*
粗鲁的；喧闹的

the farm. Men used to doing hard, physical labour found they needed to release their energies and so got together regularly to play rough, fast games like football.⁶ There are legends that suggest that games like football and **rugby** actually derived from the "sport" of ancient warriors celebrating victory by kicking around the **decapitated** head of an enemy.⁷ There is a similar grisly tale told about the origins of **bowling**: it is said that in ancient times, Scottish warriors rolled the **skulls** of their enemies along the grass for sport.

While all social classes used to join in the local football match, during the Renaissance the idea began to emerge that some sports were too rough for **aristocratic** young men. One influential writer of the era described football as "nothing but **beastly fury** and extreme violence" and not at all suitable for gentlemen. In Shakespeare's time, football was played in the cities as well as the countryside. Visitors from abroad sometimes complained about stumbling into the midst of a rough and dangerous game when walking the streets of London, while local householders and merchants were troubled by having their windows broken by stray footballs. Drinking hard went along with playing hard, and at half-time players and spectators often got very drunk, which led to even more unrefined behaviour.⁸

Today, violence is still associated with football. "Football **hooligans**", supporters of rival teams, sometimes clash before, during and after matches and occasionally run **riot** through the town, breaking windows and beating each other up.⁹ Some football fans paint their faces and sing or chant football songs and it is not too difficult to imagine their warrior-ancestors. While football violence gets a lot of attention, before big matches when trouble is expected police patrol the streets, pubs near the football grounds are closed, and shops lock their doors and shutter their windows. The selling of tickets, the seating in stadiums and security in general are more strictly controlled and every effort is made to ensure that spectators can just sit down and enjoy the game, which they do in their millions.¹⁰ Over 20 million tickets are sold to Football Association (FA) games each season. The FA is the league or association that the major teams compete in, for a **trophy** title known as the FA Cup.¹¹

## Tennis

A more gentle sport that is a sure sign that summer has arrived is the popular game of tennis. Wimbledon, actually a London suburb, is where the world's best players

rugby *n.*
英式橄榄球
decapitated *adj.*
将…斩首
bowling *n.*
保龄球
skull *n.*
头骨，颅骨
aristocratic *adj.*
贵族的
beastly *adj.*
野兽般的；野蛮的
fury *n.* 愤怒
hooligan *n.*
小流氓
riot *n.*
骚乱，大混乱
trophy *n.* 奖杯

# The United Kingdom of Great Britain and Northern Ireland

gather to compete on grass courts[12]. It is one of the major events of the British sporting calendar and probably the most famous tennis event in the world. Besides actually watching the tennis matches, other activities closely associated with the "Wimbledon **fortnight**" are eating strawberries and cream, drinking champagne and hoping that it doesn't rain[13].

Tennis was invented in Britain and it owes its origins, literally, to the Church.[14] Church records indicate that by the mid-fifteenth century, people were making a game of **bouncing** a ball off the side of their local churches or **cathedrals**, first using the hand, and later a **racquet**.

## Cricket

**Cricket** was one of the very first team sports in Britain to have organised rules and to be played according to the same rules nationally[15]. By 1787 the rules were fixed, a full century before national rules were fixed for other sports like tennis, rugby and football. (In other sports, each local village or county played by different rules.) The reason that fixed rules were applied to cricket so early on was a financial one: aristocrats loved betting on cricket matches and if people were going to risk money on a game, they wanted to ensure that the game would be played fairly.

Before the Victorian era, people from all walks of life played cricket, but in the 19th century, cricket became a sport associated with the upper classes. It was a kind of a "snob" game played by boys who attended public schools.[16] Cricket also became popular in places where the public school system was adapted, like in the colonies of Australia, New Zealand, India and Pakistan.

As generations of public school boys grew up to become the civil servants and rulers of the UK and its colonies, cricket became associated with a set of moral values, in particular the idea of "fair play" which characterised British government.[17] Sir Ian Bancroft, a high level civil servant in the 1980s, remembered that when he began his career in Whitehall, one day his government minister was so angry that he threw the telephone at him. Sir Ian said he knew exactly how to respond: "Having played cricket I was able to catch it and hand it back to him politely."[18]

British English is still full of phrases and references which those not familiar with the game will be **baffled** by.[19] To be "on a sticky **wicket**" is to face difficulties:[20] to "throw a googly" is to act unpredictably.[21] And if someone tells you that what you are doing is

---

fortnight n. 十四天，两星期
bounce v. 弹起，反弹
cathedral n. 主教座堂，教区总教堂
racquet n. 球拍
cricket n. 板球
baffle v. 使困惑
wicket n. （板球）三柱门

"not cricket" it means that you are not behaving **ethically** or honourably in a situation, whereas if you are "playing with a straight bat", you are an honest person.

The rules of cricket are as **obscure** as the language. With most sports, you can understand what is going on by simply watching for a while, but with cricket this is not the case. However, whether you understand the game or not, it is enjoyable to watch. It is a very distinctive sport: the players wear white trousers and appear quite formally dressed. Spectators gather around the "green," a large field, in chairs, enjoying the sun, sipping drinks and watching the teams play. Another unusual thing about cricket is that matches do not last just a few hours. They can go on for days.

## Golf

The game of golf was invented by the Scottish and today **avid** golfers around the world dream of playing on the famous and ancient golf course at St Andrews, not far from Edinburgh.[22] The Scots took their recreation seriously: by the sixteenth century, golf was already so popular that the **Archbishop** of St Andrews was only allowed to keep his rabbit **warrens** on the links (golf course) as long as his rabbit-raising activities didn't interfere with people who wanted to play golf.[23] And while many students of British history have heard of Mary Queen of Scots,[24] the tragic and beautiful queen who was **beheaded** in the sixteenth century during a controversy over the succession to the throne, few know that she liked to play golf. Indeed, she became the object of gossip and criticism because she was seen out on the links shortly after the death of her second husband.

## Horse Racing, Hunting and Equestrianism

The true sport of British Kings (and Queens) is not golfing, but horse racing. Organised national horse races have been held throughout Britain for hundreds of years. At the heart of medieval life was the horse, a symbol of authority and wealth and necessary to travelling, hunting and warfare.[25] The age of English **chivalry** is full of stories, songs, poems and depictions of the brave Knight on his **steed**. In fact, racing was not a good sport for knights who were clad in heavy iron **armour**. Medieval **tournaments** more commonly had activities to show off the bravery and military **prowess** of the knights, such as **jousting**. Sports which involve the riding of horses are still

ethically *adv.*
合乎道德地
obscure *adj.*
晦涩的，费解的
golf *n.*
高尔夫球
avid *adj.*
劲头十足的
archbishop *n.*
大主教
warren *n.*
养兔场
behead *v.*
斩首
horse racing
赛马
equestrianism *n.* 马术
chivalry *n.*
骑士精神；骑士制度
steed *n.*
坐骑；骏马
armour *n.* 盔甲
tournament *n.*
（中世纪骑士）马上比武
prowess *n.*
英勇；勇猛
jousting *n.*
马背长矛打斗

# The United Kingdom of Great Britain and Northern Ireland

considered rather snobbish or aristocratic sports because the average British family cannot afford to own a horse. However, there are **stables** which rent horses and offer riding lessons at affordable prices. And of course just about everyone can afford to place a bet on a horse race now and then.

There are two kinds of horse racing: flat racing, where horses and riders compete on a flat, oval track; and **steeplechase**, which is racing either across the countryside, or around a course designed to represent the obstacles you might encounter in the countryside (**hedges**, ponds, hills, and so on). The Grand National[26] is the world's most famous steeplechase. Established in 1837, in recent years the Grand National has become increasingly controversial because of the dangers involved. Every year some horses (and riders too) can be injured in trying to **negotiate** a jump for example. Badly hurt horses are usually shot, and animal lovers find it unacceptable that animals should be hurt and killed just for our enjoyment.[27] Now the Grand National course is designed to be difficult enough to be exciting, but not so difficult as to cause serious injuries.

While it is the sport of kings, kings and **commoners** alike enjoy betting on the horses. In any town centre you can go into a betting shop and place a bet on the horses. The biggest social event associated with horse racing is Royal Ascot[28], where people dress up and go to show off how fashionable they are as well to watch the races and place their bets. Women especially wear very elaborate and exotic hats, and after the races the television and newspapers will often have stories featuring the sorts of hats and outfits that were worn.

Another horsy sport associated with the aristocracy is equestrianism, sports which can involve riding skills such as show jumping and carriage driving, as well as speed.

Hunting for wild **game** was born of necessity, but it developed into a recreational pursuit in medieval England.[29] It became so popular that great lords surrounded their houses with deer parks where they could go hunting conveniently. They sometimes arranged for the servants to **herd** the deer into a corner of the park so that even the delicate aristocratic ladies could take their bows and arrows and **bag** a deer for dinner. Many of the ancient **manor** houses you can still visit in Britain have their herds of deer, although now these are more for decoration than for sport.

More common than hunting within an enclosed park was chasing an animal across the countryside on horseback, with a spear, arrows, and dogs and servants to assist.[30] In the Middle Ages, the **boar** was the favourite **quarry**, and later the wolf. Both

---

stable *n.* 马厩
steeplechase *n.* 障碍赛马；越野赛马
hedge *n.* 围栏；障碍物
negotiate *v.* （口）顺利通过
commoner *n.* 平民
game *n.* 猎物；打猎的目标
herd *n., v.* （牲口）群；赶在一起
bag *v.* 猎获；捕杀
manor *n.* （封建领主的）领地，庄园
boar *n.* 野猪；公猪
quarry *n.* 猎物

were hunted into near **extinction**. Modern hunters usually chase foxes nowadays: their medieval **forebears** would sneer at such an insignificant quarry. Hunting foxes and rabbits is also disapproved of by many British animal lovers.

A hunting **meet** is a very exciting thing to watch: huntsmen and women mounted, traditionally clad in red jackets, white **jodhpurs** and high boots. On their beautiful horses surrounded by barking, excited hunting dogs and anxious servants, they charge across the green fields and hedgerows of the countryside. But as the reason for all this activity is to chase and kill a tiny rabbit or fox, Animal Rights groups find this an unacceptable recreation for a society that is supposed to be civilised.[31] There have been recent attempts to pass laws in Parliament to ban these blood sports. These attempts have been defeated by narrow margins. Since many MPs and Lords are from wealthy families that enjoy hunting, they tend to vote against these efforts to ban one of their **pastimes**.

## Holidays and Festivals

Knowing a little bit about British holidays and customs and their origins is a good way of understanding what Britons find important in their lives and communities. Throughout the year the British celebrate many holidays which reflect the religious, historical, social and cultural diversity of their country. Some holidays are celebrated throughout the country and mark important events of the Christian calendar. Other holidays are based on local customs and traditions which reflect the variety of experience in different regions. What almost all of the holidays have in common — whether they are local, regional or national — is that they provide an opportunity for families and friends to get together to visit, eat, exchange good wishes and enjoy each other's company and hospitality.

## Religious Holidays

Although Britain remains a mainly Christian nation, most Britons do not go to church regularly or engage in Christian worship. Because of immigration and changing beliefs, most of the world's religions are practised in Britain, with sizeable **Hindu**, Jewish, Muslim and **Sikh** communities and numerous smaller groups.[32] The result is that although many Christian festivals are observed they have been adapted to fit the

extinction *n.*
消亡，灭绝
forebear *n.*
祖先
meet *n.*
（运动）会
jodhpur *n.*
马裤
pastime *n.*
消遣
Hindu *n., adj.*
印度人（的）；印度教徒（的）
Sikh *n., adj.*
锡克教信徒（的）

# The United Kingdom of Great Britain and Northern Ireland

needs of a modern, **secular** society. It is not unusual to find non-Christians as well as Christians participating in some of the activities surrounding Christmas and Easter.[33]

Christmas, December 25th, is the biggest and best loved British holiday. Schools close for the holiday period, as do shops and offices, so people can spend time at home with their families. While Christmas has a Christian meaning — it **commemorates** the birth of Jesus Christ — celebrations of the **Winter Solstice** have taken place since ancient times and some "Christian" traditions such as decorating the house with evergreen plants like **holly** and **ivy**, or kissing under a **twig** of **mistletoe**, are actually Celtic or **pagan** traditions.[34] Nowadays, Christmas is celebrated by most Britons by exchanging gifts and Christmas cards, preparing holiday foods, and decorating homes and workplaces with coloured lights, Christmas trees and ornaments.

There are three Christmas traditions which are particularly British: one is the Christmas **Pantomime**, a comical musical play. The "panto" is usually based on a version of a traditional children's story like Cinderella, written to include songs and jokes which can be enjoyed by adults and children. The main male character — the "principal boy" — is played by a young woman. In the days when women wore long skirts, it was considered rather naughty to see a woman appear in an outfit revealing the shape of her legs.[35] The main female character is a middle-aged, often ugly woman called "the **Dame**." The Dame is played by a man, often a famous actor or sportsman. When he appears in heavy make up, skirts and woman's shoes, it is considered very humorous. The audience is encouraged to cheer the hero on and **boo** when the villain appears.

Another British Christmas tradition is to hear the Queen give her Christmas message to her realm over the television and radio. The British Queen is also the Queen of other nations, like Canada and Australia, and a large number of smaller countries, and so her message is broadcast to her millions of **subjects** throughout the world. She usually talks about the year that has passed and expresses her hopes for the future.

A third British tradition, which is also celebrated in countries with British heritages, is Boxing Day[36], which falls on the day after Christmas. Traditionally, it was on Boxing Day that people gave Christmas gifts or money to their staff or servants. Now that most British people do not have servants, this custom is no longer observed and most people cannot even tell you what one is supposed to do on Boxing Day. However, a new Boxing Day custom has emerged, in the cities at least: shopping. Shops open up to sell off all their Christmas stock decorations, food, cards and gift items at low prices. But for most

---

secular *adj.*
世俗的
commemorate
*v.* 纪念
Winter Solstice
冬至
holly *n.*
冬青属植物
ivy *n.* 常春藤
twig *n.* 细枝
mistletoe *n.*
美洲寄生子属植物
pagan *n.*
异教徒的；无宗教信仰的
Pantomime *n.*
（圣诞节期间演出的）童话剧
dame *n.*
夫人；女士；（英哑剧中由男子扮演的）滑稽老太婆
boo *v.* 起哄
subject *n.*
臣民，国民

people, however, Boxing Day is a day for visiting, eating and relaxing.

For church-goers it is **Easter**, not Christmas, which is the most important Christian festival. Easter commemorates the **Crucifixion** and **Resurrection** of Jesus Christ.[37] It occurs in the spring, when schools and universities close for a break. While Christians attend many church services over the Easter period, for most people the main symbol of Easter is the Easter egg, originally a Christian symbol of new life. Nowadays people give each other chocolate or candy Easter Eggs, which are often very large, elaborate and expensive.

Christmas and Easter have been adopted and celebrated by non-Christian people who emphasise the secular rather than the religious aspects of the holidays. There are also many non-Christian festivals which are observed by people with different beliefs and many schools and workplaces will allow such people to take time off to allow them to celebrate a particular special day. For example, there were over 3.3 million Muslims in Britain in 2017, and the number is still growing. Most of them observe traditional Islamic festivals such as **Ramadan**, a **fast** which lasts 29 days during which nothing can be eaten or drunk between dawn and nightfall, and ends with a festival. There are also Jewish, Hindu, Sikh, Buddhist and even Pagan groups which observe days important to their communities. In London, the overseas Chinese community marks Chinese New Year with dragon dances, fireworks, parades and family celebrations.

## National Holidays

One of Britain's most impressive and colourful festivals happens on the second Saturday in June when the Queen's Birthday is officially celebrated by "Trooping the Colour"[38] around Buckingham Palace in London. The UK, unlike most countries, does not have a "national day", but the **pomp** and ceremony surrounding the Queen inspecting her troops draws large crowds of people. The ceremony derives from old military traditions in which regimental flags were paraded before the monarch. In the 18th century such **pageantry** used to occur daily, but early in Victoria's reign it was decided that this ceremony should only be held on the sovereign's birthday. British diplomats abroad will often have a special party or event to celebrate the Queen's birthday.

Easter *n.*
复活节
Crucifixion *n.*
（耶稣）钉在十字架上
Resurrection *n.*
（耶稣之）复活
Ramadan *n.*
斋月
fast *n.* 吃斋
pomp *n.* 盛况
pageantry *n.*
盛大的庆典

# The United Kingdom of Great Britain and Northern Ireland

## Holidays in the Four Nations

It is in the local festivals of England, Wales, Northern Ireland and Scotland that the distinctive cultural and political identities of the four nations of the United Kingdom can be seen. Many festivals and customs have been invented, adopted and used to serve political or religious functions in times of conflict. For example the historic battles between the Protestants and Catholics in the 17th century are commemorated, often with symbolic or even real violence, in England and Northern Ireland. Special days in Scotland and Wales demonstrate their national pride in their unique languages and cultures and remind us that there is much more to the UK than "the English" and "England."[39]

## England

The English do not celebrate their famous writers or battles or **patron** saints, although they have all these things. However, one truly English holiday is **Bonfire Night** — sometimes called Guy Fawkes Night — celebrated in the early autumn.

On the evening of November 5, 1605, a plan to blow up the British Parliament, kill the Protestant King and replace him with a Catholic king was discovered. One of the **conspirators**, Guy Fawkes, was found in the cellars of Westminster with gunpowder. He and the other members of his gang were arrested, tortured and killed. Protestant politicians decided that the Gunpowder Plot had failed because God wanted the Protestants to continue to rule England. Parliament passed a legal act calling for a "Public Thanksgiving to Almighty God" for revealing the plot, to be held on the anniversary of the event.[40] Nowadays, English people still celebrate this event in the traditional way. In early November, gangs of small children appear on British streets, often with a straw **effigy** called the "Guy".

The biggest Bonfire Night celebration is held in the small medieval town of Lewes, where torchlight parades wind through the narrow streets. The **paraders** wear costumes and carry models of severed heads on **pikes**, which represent Protestantism's enemies. When the paraders reach the Bonfire, fireworks are used to fight mock battles between Catholics and Protestants. At the end of these battles, giant effigies of the **Pope** and Guy Fawkes are blown up with fireworks.

**patron** *n.* （教会、城镇、个人等的）守护神
**Bonfire Night** 篝火之夜
**conspirator** *n.* 阴谋家
**effigy** *n.* 模拟像
**parader** *n.* 游行者
**pike** *n.* 长矛
**Pope** *n.* 罗马教皇，天主教教皇

## Northern Ireland

Another festival which comes from the 17th century battles between Catholics and Protestants is the Protestant celebration of their victory at the Battle of the Boyne (July 12) in 1690. The Catholic King James II was forced off the throne in 1688. William of Orange,[41] affectionately known as King Billy, was invited to take the throne and James was driven into exile. With the help of the French and the Irish — both Catholic nations — James tried to retake the throne but his forces were defeated by King Billy on the banks of the Boyne River in County Kildare, now a part of Ireland.

The Twelfth is the high point of what is known as the Marching Season,[42] when Protestant "Orangemen"[43] take to the streets wearing their traditional uniforms of **bowler hats**, black suits and orange **sashes**, marching through the streets singing, banging drums and playing in marching bands. The Orangemen often clash — verbally, legally or sometimes violently — with the Catholics as they attempt to parade through Catholic neighbourhoods, symbolically asserting their continued dominance over the Irish.[44] During Orange Marches there is a massive police and army presence surrounding the parades and the atmosphere can be very tense.

Northern Irish Catholics celebrate the birthday of the **patron saint** of Ireland, St Patrick, on March 17 each year. Patrick was a Catholic bishop who lived in the 5th century and is thought to have brought Christianity to Ireland. He lived in Great Britain, but at the age of 16 was captured by Irish raiders, taken to Ireland and made a slave. He eventually escaped and returned to Britain, where he had a dream in which the Irish begged him to return. Although his memories of years of slavery in Ireland made him hesitate, he followed this call and had a very successful missionary career.

According to popular legend, St Patrick drove snakes (the Christian symbol of evil) out of Ireland. In another legend it is said that he used the three leafed **clover**, or **shamrock**, to explain the Christian trinity (Father, Son and Holy Ghost) to the pagan Irish.[45] The shamrock is a popular symbol to wear on St Patrick's Day, and it is also considered very lucky to wear something green.

## Scotland

While most British people welcome the coming of the New Year with parties, in Scotland, New Year's Eve called **Hogmanay** — is the major winter celebration, and

---

bowler hat
圆顶高帽
sash *n.*
饰带，肩带
patron saint
主保圣人
clover *n.*
三叶草
shamrock *n.*
三叶草（爱尔兰国花）
Hogmanay *n.*
（苏格兰）除夕

# The United Kingdom of Great Britain and Northern Ireland

overshadows Christmas, which is a very quiet affair. How Hogmanay is celebrated varies throughout Scotland, but one widely practised custom is "first footing". There is a superstitious belief that the first person to cross the threshold of a household in the New Year can bring luck and prosperity: the appearance of a young, preferably dark haired and handsome man is considered particularly lucky. First footers often bring a bottle of spirits, alcohol, a lump of coal or a **peat** as a gift and are given a "**dram** of whisky" as their reward.

Each year Scottish people all over the world celebrate their most beloved national poet, Robert Burns,[46] by holding a Burns supper, commonly known as Burns Night, on or near his birthday (January 25). Burns wrote mainly in the Scots dialect and his poems drew on older traditions of Scottish folk songs and stories and so have a wide popular appeal.

Halloween is a Scottish festival that comes from the great feast of the pagan Celts which marked the arrival of the winter half of the year.[47] Halloween is notable for showing the darker, supernatural side of Celtic custom — **communion** with the dead, mischief, fortune-telling and **masquerades** are common practices. Children make "turnip lanterns". Turnips are hollowed out and holes are cut to make eyes, nose and mouth.[48] Then candles are placed inside the turnip and it is set in the windows to scare away witches and other evil spirits.

## Wales

Wales has some of the oldest and richest literary, musical and poetic traditions in Europe. Poems written in the traditional Welsh language and style are governed by ancient codes and conventions which can be traced back to the Druids, who instituted rigid rules of composition to help them to correctly memorise and pass on poems and stories.[49] In pre-14th century Wales, to become a **bard** required years of study and was considered a profession, like law or medicine.

This poetic tradition has been celebrated for centuries in eisteddfod, a Welsh word meaning a gathering where people recite verses and sing songs. In 1536 Wales was officially joined with England (it had been controlled by England for hundreds of years) and English became the national language. Speaking Welsh was seen as a bad thing. As recently as the 19th century, Welsh schoolchildren could be punished for speaking Welsh. The Welsh language began to die, but Welsh speakers fought hard to preserve

peat *n.* 泥炭块
dram *n.* 少量的（烈）酒；少量饮料
communion *n.* 契合
masquerade *n.* 假面舞会，化装舞会
bard *n.* （古代凯尔特族）吟游诗人

it. One way they accomplished this was to celebrate their culture and their language each August with a really large Eisteddfod which would remind people throughout the UK of Wales' special cultural heritage.⁵⁰ The Eisteddfod is now the largest popular festival of music making and poetry writing in Europe.

At the Eisteddfod, tents and pavilions are erected around a big open space: in the different tents competitions are held to find the best **choirs**, translators, essayists and poets. The highlight is the crowning of the two bards who have written the best poems of the festival.⁵¹

choir *n.*
唱诗班；合唱团

## Conclusion

The British calendar is full of holidays and festivals which demonstrate the different cultures and histories of the people who make up Britain. Holiday customs have changed as times have changed. Ancient pagan traditions were adapted by the church as Britain became a nation of Christians. Now that the Christian church is not as influential as it was in the past, Christian holidays and customs have changed again so they can be shared by people throughout the country whatever their backgrounds and beliefs. Thus Welsh people can celebrate Burns Night, Londoners can watch Dragon dances at Chinese New Year, Muslims can enjoy chocolate Easter eggs and Christians can go shopping on Boxing Day. Such holidays remind us of how cultures change and influence each other; they also give us an opportunity to share in the rich cultural heritage of the United Kingdom.

# Explanations

1. **Going to a public house for a glass of ale, working the land ... in Shakespeare's time:**
   去酒吧喝一杯麦芽酒，在地里干活，或去观看球赛，这些活动在莎士比亚时代就习以为常了。

2. **If today's British person were to be transported 500 years ... rough but recognisable forms:**
   假设今天的英国人倒回到 500 年前的过去，他/她会看到许多熟悉的娱乐活动和比赛，虽然这些活动的形式比较粗糙但完全可以辨认。

3. **And because many of the sports we see played throughout the world ... people everywhere:**
   而且由于我们现在看到世界上的许多体育项目发源于英国，了解这些运动的历史对其他地方的人们是有

# The United Kingdom of Great Britain and Northern Ireland

一定意义的。

4. **Such influences are still evident in today's sports ... that most people have off in the UK:**
   这些影响在体育和休闲活动中的存在仍是明显的。一个非常显而易见的例子是，英国人大多还是礼拜天休息，因为传统上星期天是去教堂做礼拜的日子。作者这里说的休息包括商店、娱乐场所大多关门，不营业。

5. **The idea of sports having seasons — like the football season ... how people spent their time:**
   体育运动也有季节，如足球赛季，这一点来自农业社会的自然节奏。在农业社会里，收获的时间以及天气影响着人们如何度过他们的时光。

6. **Men used to doing hard, physical labour found ... play rough, fast games like football:**
   习惯于干粗重体力活的男人们发现他们需要释放一下剩余的精力，于是他们经常聚在一起开展足球一类的粗野快速的运动比赛。

7. **There are legends that suggest that games like football and ... head of an enemy:**
   根据有些传说，像足球和英式橄榄球实际上来源于古代勇士的"体育"：他们将斩下的敌人的头踢来踢去，以此庆祝胜利。

8. **Drinking hard went along with playing hard and at half-time ... unrefined behaviour:**
   豪饮伴随着疯狂的比赛，赛到一半时，运动员和观众都烂醉如泥，这往往导致更加粗鲁的行为。

9. **"Football hooligans," supporters of rival teams ... and beating each other up:**
   那些"足球流氓"，也就是支持比赛队的球迷们，常常在赛前、赛中和赛后发生冲突，有时骚乱扩展到整个城镇，他们砸碎窗户，互相殴打。

10. **The selling of tickets, the seating in stadiums and security ... they do in their millions:**
    从售票、体育场座位的安排到整个保安措施都更加严格地控制，所有的措施都为了保障成千上万的观众能坐下来欣赏比赛。

11. **The FA is the league or association that the major teams compete in ... the FA Cup:**
    主要球队都在英国足球协会里比赛，争夺足协杯的冠军称号。英国足球协会成立于 1863 年，是主管英国职业和业余足球队的组织。

12. **Wimbledon, actually a London suburb, is where the world' best players ... grass courts:**
    温布尔登，实际上是伦敦的一个郊区，它是世界上最优秀的网球手聚会进行草地比赛的场所。室外网球比赛场地分为草地、红土以及硬地三种。

13. **hoping that it doesn't rain:**
    希望不要下雨。因为温布尔登是室外场地，而英国的天气又是多阵雨，比赛进行时经常下雨，这时比赛不得不中断，等待天晴才能继续。

14. **Tennis was invented in Britain and it owes its origins, literally, to the Church:**
    网球是英国发明的，它的起源的确要追溯到教会。

UNIT 10　Sports, Holidays and Festivals in Britain

15. **Cricket was one of the very first team sports in Britain to ... the same rules nationally:**
    板球比赛是英国最早有统一规则的并全国遵守同一规则进行比赛的团体运动项目之一。

16. **It was a kind of a "snob" game played by boys who attended public schools:**
    板球是种"势利"的比赛项目，玩板球的都是就读于公学的男孩。snob: 势利的，自以为优越的人

17. **As generations of public school boys grew up to ... British government:**
    当一代一代的公学男孩长大成人，当了公务员或者英国及其殖民地的统治者时，板球与一整套道德价值观产生了联系。具体地说，"公平竞赛"的思想成为英国政府的特点。"Fair play"在中国最初曾音译为"费厄泼赖"。

18. **"Having played cricket I was able to catch it and hand it back to him politely":**
    由于打过板球，我能接住他扔过来的电话机，然后礼貌地递还给他。

19. **British English is still full of references and phrases to cricket ... will be baffled by:**
    英式英语里有许多关于板球的典故和短语，那些不熟悉这一项运动的人会感到困惑。

20. **To be "on a sticky wicket" is to face difficulties:**
    "在泥泞的三柱门"的意思是面对困境。sticky wicket 原指雨后周围场地泥泞的三柱门，因这种情况使球弹不高而难于击打，因而比喻困难的处境。

21. **to "throw a googly" is to act unpredictably:**
    Googly 原指"变向曲线球"，喻指"行动无法预测，捉摸不透。"

22. **The game of golf was invented by the Scottish and today ... not far from Edinburgh:**
    高尔夫球由苏格兰人发明，今天全世界的高尔夫球迷们都梦想在离爱丁堡不远的圣安德鲁著名的古老高尔夫球场上打球。

23. **The Scots took their recreation seriously: by the sixteenth century ... wanted to play golf:**
    苏格兰人对待娱乐的态度十分严肃。比如说，到 16 世纪，高尔夫球已很风行，以至于当时的圣安德鲁大主教必须保证他养兔子不会干扰人们打高尔夫球才得到允许将养兔场留在高尔夫球场上。

24. **Mary Queen of Scots:**
    苏格兰的玛丽女王（1542–1587），出生六天即继承王位，成为苏格兰女王后嫁给法王法兰西斯二世，1561 年返苏格兰后两次再嫁，被迫逊位，逃亡英格兰，后因图谋暗杀英格兰女王伊丽莎白一世而被斩首。

25. **At the heart of medieval life was the horse, a symbol ... travelling, hunting and warfare:**
    中世纪生活的中心是马，马是权威与财富的象征，并且是旅行、打猎和战争的必需之物。

26. **The Grand National:**
    一年一度在利物浦举行的全国越野障碍赛马。

27. **Badly hurt horses are usually shot, and animal lovers ... just for our enjoyment:**
    受重伤的马通常被杀死（以免遭受痛苦）。动物爱好者认为，动物为了人们的娱乐而不得不受伤害，甚至遭到杀戮，这是不能接受的。

# The United Kingdom of Great Britain and Northern Ireland

28. **Royal Ascot:**
    皇家阿斯科特赛马会。每年6月在伯克郡的阿斯科特举行为期4天的赛马会，是英国最重要的赛马会之一，王室成员常参加。

29. **Hunting for wild game was born of necessity, but it developed ... in medieval England:**
    捕猎野兽最早是出于生存的必需，但是到中世纪打猎发展成为英国的娱乐消遣活动。

30. **More common than hunting within an enclosed park ... dogs and servants to assist:**
    比在一个圈围起来的公园里打猎更寻常的是骑在马背上在田野里追逐动物，这些猎手持着长矛和弓箭，有猎狗和仆人相助。

31. **Animal Rights groups find this an unacceptable recreation for a society that is supposed to be civilised:**
    维护动物权利组织认为这项娱乐对一个文明社会是不可接受的。

32. **Because of immigration and changing beliefs ... and numerous smaller groups:**
    由于移民和变化的信仰，世界上大多数宗教都在英国存在，较大的派别有印度教、犹太教、穆斯林教和锡克教以及众多较小的宗教派别。

33. **It is not unusual to find non-Christians as well as Christians ... Christmas and Easter:**
    非基督教徒与基督教一起参加围绕圣诞节和复活节的一些活动，这并不足为奇。

34. **... celebrations of the Winter Solstice have taken place ... Celtic or pagan traditions:**
    自古以来就有庆祝冬至的活动，一些基督教传统，如用冬青和常春藤等常青植物布置房子，或者在寄生子细枝下接吻，这实际上是凯尔特人或异教徒的传统。按照这一传统，站在寄生子细枝下的女子，男人都可与之接吻。

35. **In the days when women wore long skirts, it was considered ... the shape of her legs:**
    在那个时代妇女穿长裙，如果看到一个妇女穿着暴露腿型的衣着在大众场合露面，那是不符合习俗的。

36. **Boxing Day:**
    节礼日。在圣诞节的次日，如遇星期日则推迟一天。按英国习俗，这天向雇员、仆人、邮递员等赠匣装的礼物。

37. **Easter commemorates the crucifixion and resurrection of Jesus Christ:**
    复活节是纪念耶稣受难和复活的节日，具体日子每年可不同，一般在每年春分月圆后的第一个星期日。

38. **"Trooping the Colour":**
    每年女王生日之际在白金汉宫前举行的盛大检阅庆祝活动。the Colour: the regimental flag, 团旗，军旗。

39. **Special days in Scotland and Wales demonstrate ... "the English" and "England":**
    苏格兰和威尔士的一些特殊节日表现了这些地区的人民对自己独特的语言与文化的民族自豪感，同时也提醒我们大不列颠与北爱尔兰联合王国不仅只有"英格兰人"和"英格兰"。

40. **Parliament passed a legal act calling for a "Public Thanksgiving to Almighty God" ... on the anniversary of the event:**
    议会通过了一项法案，要求"公开感谢全能的上帝"暴露了这一阴谋，每年此日纪念这一事件。

# UNIT 10　Sports, Holidays and FESTIVALS in Britain

41. **William of Orange:**
    奥伦治王子 (Prince of Orange)，（1533–1584），后为威廉三世，新教徒，原是尼德兰（荷兰联省共和国）执政者。他的妻子玛丽是英国詹姆士二世之女，也是新教徒。1689 年，英国议会邀请他们夫妇到英国共同执政，把信奉天主教的詹姆士二世赶下王位，史称"光荣革命"或"不流血的革命"。

42. **The Twelfth is the high point of what is known as the Marching Season:**
    12 日是游行季节的高潮。1690 年 6 月 12 日，威廉三世在博因河畔击败了詹姆士二世，北爱尔兰的新教徒每年都要游行庆祝这个纪念日。1969 年，庆祝游行的新教徒与天主教徒发生了大规模的流血冲突事件。

43. **"Orangemen":**
    奥伦治会会员。奥伦治会于 1795 年创立于爱尔兰，是英国基督教新教反对天主教的政治团体，取名于英王威廉三世（William of Orange）。

44. **The Orangemen often clash — verbally, legally or sometimes ... dominance over the Irish:**
    奥伦治会会员的游行试图穿过天主教徒居住地，象征他们继续统治爱尔兰人，他们这样做时和天主教徒经常发生语言上的、法律上和暴力上的冲突。

45. **In another legend it is said that he used the three leafed ... to the pagan Irish:**
    另一则传说是，他用三叶草做比喻，为异教的爱尔兰人讲解基督教的三位一体（即圣父、圣子和圣灵）。

46. **Robert Burns:**
    罗伯特·彭斯（1759–1796），公认为苏格兰最伟大的诗人，主要用苏格兰语言写诗，歌颂自然、爱情、农民生活和对民族的热爱。代表诗歌包括《一朵红红的玫瑰》和世界各地的人民会唱的《友谊地久天长》。

47. **Halloween is a Scottish festival that comes from ... of the winter half of the year:**
    万圣节在每年的 10 月 31 日，是苏格兰的节日，源自于异教的凯尔特人庆祝一年中冬季来临而举行的盛大节日。

48. **Turnips are hollowed out and holes are cut to make eyes, nose and mouth:**
    把萝卜挖空，切出洞来，做成眼睛、鼻子和嘴。在北美，万圣节的灯是用南瓜做的。

49. **Poems written in the traditional Welsh language ... pass on poems and stories:**
    用传统的威尔士语言和文体写的诗歌必须遵循古老的法则和规律，这些法则和规律可追溯到德鲁伊特的时期。德鲁伊特为了能正确地记忆和传诵诗歌与故事而创造了这些规范。**Druids:** 德鲁伊特，古代凯尔特人中有学识的人，担任祭祀，教师和法官等。

50. **One way they accomplished this was to celebrate their culture ... cultural heritage:**
    他们做到这点的一个方法是每年的 8 月举行一次大型的诗歌音乐比赛会，以庆祝他们的文化和语言，这个诗歌音乐比赛会提醒英国各地的人们威尔士有其独特的文化遗产。

51. **The highlight is the crowning of the two bards who have written the best poems of the festival:**
    比赛会的高潮是本赛会写出最佳诗歌的两位诗人被授予桂冠。

# The United Kingdom of Great Britain and Northern Ireland

 **Exercises**

I. **Give the Chinese equivalents for the following:**
   1. Wimbledon
   2. equestrianism
   3. fair play
   4. Easter
   5. Bonfire Night
   6. Burns Night

II. **Decide whether the following statements are true (T) or false (F):**
   1. The tradition of having Sunday off derived from the Christian Church. _____
   2. The origin of bowling lies in the victory celebration ceremony by ancient warriors. _____
   3. Tennis is usually regarded as a winter and spring sport. _____
   4. The game of golf was invented by the Scottish. _____
   5. Animal-lovers' groups would like to have hunting on horseback banned. _____
   6. Easter is the biggest and best loved British holiday. _____
   7. The Christmas Pantomime is one of the three Christmas traditions that are particularly British. _____
   8. It is commonly believed that Boxing Day involves the sport of boxing. _____
   9. The biggest Bonfire Night celebration is held in London. _____
   10. In Ireland, New Year's Eve called Hogmanay (December 31st) is the major winter celebration. _____

III. **Fill in the blanks:**
   1. The FA Cup stands for _____.
   2. Phrases like "on a sticky wicket" and "playing with a straight bat" are associated with the sport of _____.
   3. There are two kinds of horse racing: flat racing and _____.

UNIT 10   Sports, Holidays and Festivals in Britain

4. People usually dress up and show off their fashionable clothes and elaborate hats for the social event called _____.
5. Compared with football, _____ is a more gentle sport which owes its origins to the Church.
6. Traditionally, people gave Christmas gifts or money to their staff or servants on _____, which is the day after Christmas.
7. Many Muslims in Britain observe a traditional Islamic festival called _____, during which nothing can be eaten or drunk between dawn and nightfall.
8. Bonfire Night, which is celebrated in November, sometimes is also called _____.
9. On March 17 each year, Northern Irish Catholics celebrate the birthday of _____, who is said to have brought Christianity to Ireland.
10. The overseas Chinese community in London often celebrates Chinese New Year with _____ dances and fireworks.

## IV. Questions:

1. Why do some sports have seasons? Where does the idea of sport seasons come from?
2. Why is football a rough and boisterous sport? What is the origin of this sport according to legends? How is violence still associated with football today?
3. What is a popular sport for summer in Britain? What activities take place during the "Wimbledon fortnight"?
4. Why is cricket one of the very first team sports in Britain to have organised rules and to be played according to the same rules nationally? How is it connected with English culture?
5. What is the idea of "fair play"? Where does it come from?
6. Where was the game of golf invented?
7. What is regarded as the true sport of British Kings or Queens? Why? How does this sport reflect British history?
8. How did hunting for wild game develop into a sport in medieval England?
9. Christmas is the biggest and best loved British holiday. Could you describe how it is celebrated in Britain?
10. What are the three Christmas traditions that are particularly British?
11. Why is Easter the most important Christian festival for church goers?

# The United Kingdom of Great Britain and Northern Ireland

12. Who was Guy Fawkes? How was he connected with the one truly English holiday — Bonfire Night?
13. What are Orange Marches? Why are policemen present during the Marching Season? What is the historical background for this festival in Northern Ireland?
14. Why do the Scottish people all over the world celebrate Robert Burns' birthday?
15. What does the word "eisteddfod" mean? How is the Eisteddfod celebrated in Wales?

**V. Topics for discussion or research:**

1. Discuss how Christian Church has influenced the sports and leisure activities of the British.
2. How do sports reveal class differences in Britain? Which team sport is regarded as very English? Why is this sport associated with a set of English values?
3. How do the British celebrate Christmas? In what way do the three Christmas traditions reflect British history and culture?
4. Christmas has been adopted and celebrated by non-Christian people, emphasising its secular aspects. It is even becoming a popular holiday among some Chinese people, especially the young. Are you worried about this? Why or why not?
5. What comparisons can you make between British and Chinese festivals, holidays and celebrations?

# The Republic of Ireland

**UNIT**

- ⑪ Land, People, and History — *211*
- ⑫ Politics and Economy — *233*
- ⑬ Irish Culture: How the Irish Live Now — *255*
- ⑭ Irish Culture: Language, Literature and Arts — *277*

# UNIT 11

# Land, People, and History

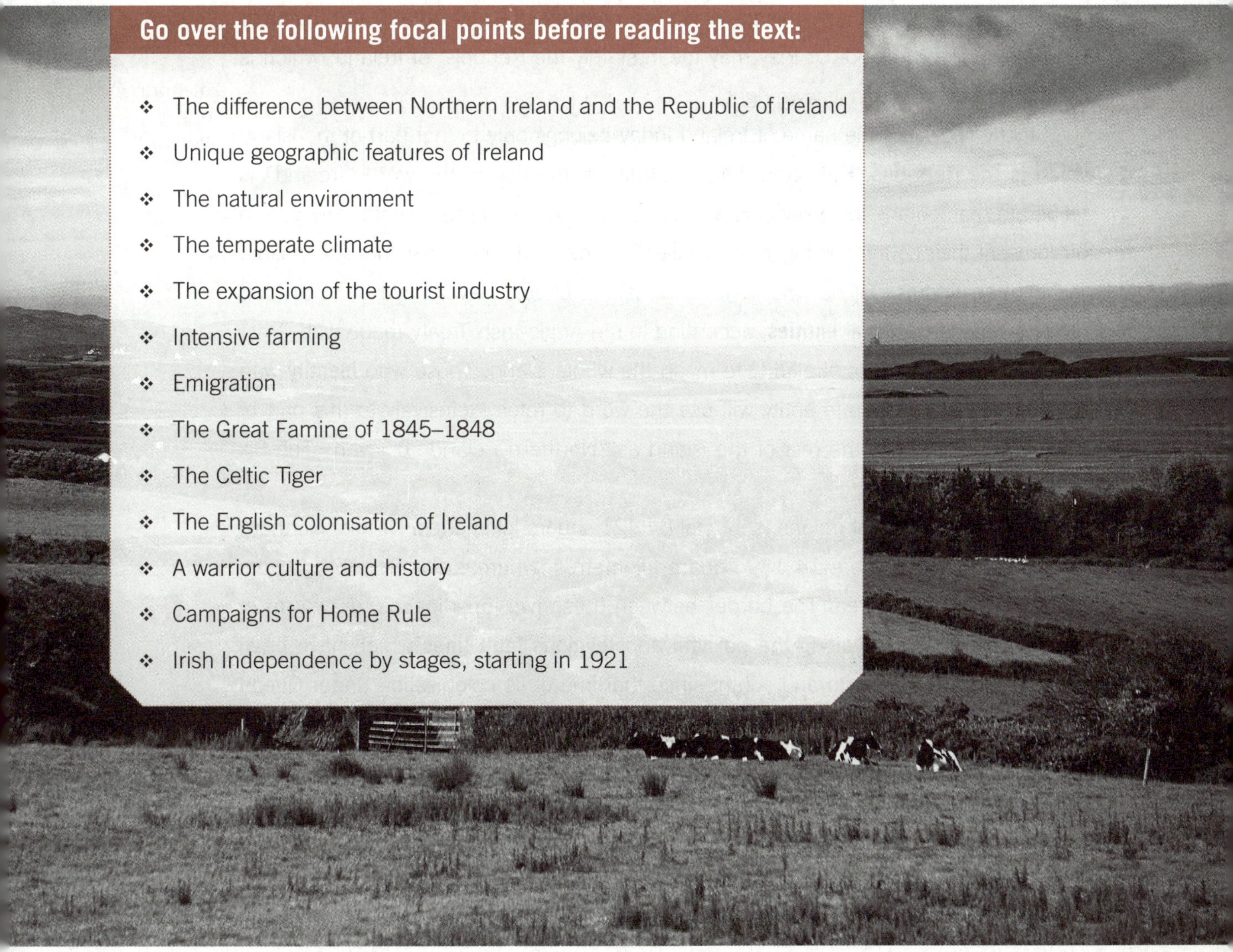

**Go over the following focal points before reading the text:**

- The difference between Northern Ireland and the Republic of Ireland
- Unique geographic features of Ireland
- The natural environment
- The temperate climate
- The expansion of the tourist industry
- Intensive farming
- Emigration
- The Great Famine of 1845–1848
- The Celtic Tiger
- The English colonisation of Ireland
- A warrior culture and history
- Campaigns for Home Rule
- Irish Independence by stages, starting in 1921

# The Republic of Ireland

 Text

## Land

Ireland is a small island off the northwest coast of Great Britain, divided from Scotland by a narrow strait of water.¹ Today, when people use the word "Ireland" they may mean the whole island, which is actually divided into two quite distinct **jurisdictions**: one is Northern Ireland, which is a province of Great Britain, and the other is the Republic of Ireland. Or they may mean simply the Republic of Ireland, which is an independent nation in its own right.

Strictly speaking, the name of Ireland today belongs only to that part of the island which is the Republic. But often this ambiguity in the use of the word "Ireland" is deliberate, particularly for politicians and diplomats, depending on whether they wish to represent their country as bigger or smaller.² Or the name used may indicate distinct political **convictions**. Those who believe the island should never have been divided into two separate political **entities**, according to the Anglo-Irish Treaty made with Great Britain in 1921, may use "Ireland" to mean the whole island. Those who **identify** with the Republic as a separate entity will use the word to refer exclusively to this part of the island, referring to the rest of the island as "Northern Ireland" or even "The Six Counties".

In size, the island of Ireland is in total 84 421 square kilometres. Of this, Northern Ireland comprises a mere 14 139 square kilometres, whereas the Republic covers about five times that area. The border between these two jurisdictions, drawn up in 1920, was constructed along the political and religious **fault lines** which have been a feature of Irish life, north and south, since the time of its colonisation under Queen Elizabeth I in the late sixteenth century.³ Essentially, the border marked off the areas inhabited by the dominantly Protestant population in the north from those inhabited mostly by Roman Catholics in the south. Following traditional county lines, the border is long and **meandering** and impossible to **police** effectively, so that, in effect, people can move easily, if illegally, between one jurisdiction and another.⁴

Geographically, Ireland is situated in the extreme northwest of Europe. Ireland is not very hot during summer, nor is it, despite its location in northern **latitudes**, very

---

jurisdiction *n.* 管辖权，司法权
conviction *n.* 信念，信仰
entity *n.* 实体
identify *v.* 认同
fault lines （宗教、政治冲突）分界线
meandering *adj.* 曲折的
police *v.* 维持治安
latitude *n.* 纬度

cold in winter. Ireland is washed by the Gulf Stream, with prevailing winds from the southwest, so that it actually has a quite temperate climate.[5]

Seen from the air, the visitor's first impression of Ireland is an intense green, or rather mixture of many different greens. Temperate climates together with frequent rain ensure that the grasslands flourish in all seasons. Snow and ice are not common. Ireland is almost always damp, although the **humidity** may vary from dramatic downpours, to showers **interspersed** with sunny periods, to misty mornings which clear to **intermittent** blue skies. While this may not be the ideal climate for human beings, it is perfect for growing grass, thus feeding Ireland's many domestic animals — in particular, cows, sheep, and horses.

In terms of geographical **elevations**, the island of Ireland resembles a tea saucer, with a large central lowland with a discontinuous border of mountains which often slope **precipitously** into the sea.[6] Whereas the middle of the island has rich agricultural land, it becomes poorer in quality as one travels to the edges, so that in the west, in particular, farmland is poor and often confined to hills which are used to **graze** sheep. For most of its history Ireland has been an agricultural country, and one in which cattle are particularly valued.

In terms of native **flora** and **fauna**, Ireland has a smaller range than is found elsewhere in Europe.[7] This probably occurred as a result of the Ireland becoming separated from the European mainland in the period following the last Ice Age. Originally, much of the island was covered with **primeval** forest. Most of these trees were **oak**, a tree worshipped in the ancient **druidic** [*i.e., pantheistic*] religions. Unfortunately oak was also a valuable timber for ship-building. Much of the primeval forest was cut down by the British in the sixteenth and seventeenth centuries as timber to build their famous navy. This exploitation of Ireland, when remembered, is still resented.[8]

Today, there are only **remnants** of the old natural forest in the Killarney area, which indicates that the oak was originally interspersed with **holly** and **birch** trees, with **ash**, **hazel**, and **yew** growing in limestone areas. Remains of far older forests are preserved in the raised **peat bogs**, for which Ireland is famous. These are found in the large central plain and also in mountainous areas of the west.

Traditionally Ireland had a quite unspoiled landscape, mostly due to the comparative poverty of the country.[9] Since the 1960s, however, both the natural landscape and such resources as clean water have come under threat from increasing

---

humidity *n.* 湿度
intersperse *v.* 散布，点缀
intermittent *adj.* 间歇的，断断续续的
elevation *n.* 海拔，高度
precipitously *adv.* 陡峭地
graze *v.* 放牧
flora *n.* 植物群
fauna *n.* 动物群
primeval *adj.* 原始的，远古的
oak *n.* 橡树
druidic *adj.* 占卜的，督伊德教的
pantheistic *adj.* 泛神论的
remnant *n.* 残余，剩余
holly *n.* 冬青树
birch *n.* 桦树
ash *n.* 白蜡树
hazel *n.* 榛树
yew *n.* 紫杉
peat *n.* 泥炭，泥煤
bog *n.* 泥塘，沼泽

# The Republic of Ireland

economic development. At that time, the Irish government began a vigorous campaign to promote modern industry and change the patterns of agriculture to ensure more intensive production. As a consequence, conflicts often arise between those who seek development and those who seek to protect the environment. Many of these conflicting claims are now **mediated** through the European Union. The EU has not only provided the Irish people with a wealth of comparative experience but has also **furnished** legislation now used to protect some of the unique features of the Irish environment, for instance, in a system of national parks and nature reserves mostly located in the west of the country.

Despite the actions of the EU and the establishment of governmental protection agencies, the quality of the Irish environment is today still very much under threat. The decline in water quality is the most noticeable, with an estimated 25% of rivers and 66% of lakes now **degraded** if not actually polluted.[10] Ireland's love-affair with the automobile has led to nitrogen oxide emissions that are well over the EU "ceiling." Greenhouse gas emissions from electricity generating plants are among the highest in the EU.[11]

Over-development of multiple tourist **resorts** has also led to a **despoliation** of many landscapes.[12] The expansion of the tourist industry is particularly dangerous for the environment, as it effectively destroys what it is selling.[13] The Burren in County Clare, for instance, once famous for its silence, now **resounds** to the roar of tour buses. Its rare flora, although protected, are being dug up by **vandals**; even its limestone rocks have sometimes been taken away for suburban gardens. Tourist facilities and holiday **bungalows** have **over-taxed sewage** systems, so that nearby rivers and lakes are increasingly polluted, although recent measures have resulted in 93% of Ireland's coastal waters reaching good ecological status.

Agriculture has also contributed to the same **paradoxical** situation, as new methods of intensive farming with fertilizers have led to pollution of springs and lakes, and sometimes even the water schemes subscribed to by the farmers themselves. Thus the environment, which is itself the very source of wealth for both the tour operator and the farmer, is being itself eroded as a resource. Fortunately, the Irish people are becoming environmentally conscious, and eager to cooperate with the Irish government to reverse this trend. Recycling among Irish households is now the norm. There is far less illegal dumping of industrial waste than previously. And the Irish are becoming increasingly

---

mediate *v.*
调停，仲裁
furnish *v.*
（使）完备
degrade *v.*
降级，退化
resort *n.*
（旅游）胜地
despoliation *n.*
掠夺
resound *v.*
回响，回荡
vandal *n.*
蓄意破坏者
bungalow *n.*
（印度）孟加拉式平房；平房，小屋
over-taxed *adj.*
使负担过重，课税过重
sewage *n.*
污水，下水道
paradoxical *adj.*
自相矛盾的；悖理的

conscious of the value of a "green economy" — especially for the tourist industry — as well as the health benefits of eating organic food.[14]

## Population

The rural landscape of Ireland is highly populated but mostly by ghosts.[15] Although the visitors may believe themselves alone in a landscape that looks positively wild, they will find that every field has a name and a history, and that often the **undergrowth** will conceal a Stone-Age **ring fort** or an old field wall or the outlines of a farmhouse or even a deserted village.

Thus the Irish landscape itself records its many layers of history.[16] The ring-fort would belong to the Bronze Age, about 3 000 years ago, but the deserted villages remind us of more recent events. Two hundred and fifty years ago, Ireland was a highly populated island. As the result of starvation, disease, and consequent mass **emigration** from the mid-1840s onwards, by 1926 that part of the island that is now the Republic of Ireland had lost about half of its people.

Emigration did take place before the Great Famine, mostly from the northern part of Ireland, known as the province of Ulster.[17] These emigrants were often the younger sons of farmers who were seeking to better their economic position by seeking land in the areas of the New World which were opening up in Canada and the United States. These people were not desperately poor; they usually had some education and a modest amount of money to start their new life. In common with many other settlers of these new territories, they were Christians of the Protestant faith. Many of these emigrants went on to become heads of families which were to become prominent in the political and economic life of the United States.[18] Seven US Presidents as well as prominent American financiers like Thomas Mellon came from an Ulster emigrant background.[19]

Later migrations to the United States and Canada were entirely different in character. These migrants left the southern, agricultural part of Ireland as the result of the Great Famine. When successive potato crops failed during the years of 1845–1848, many people of Ireland literally starved to death, or died of the diseases linked with malnutrition.[20] According to the 1841 census, the population was close to 6.5 million. By 1851, it had been reduced by at least 2 million and was still falling. Many who did not die, emigrated. They made their passage to the New World on what were called

undergrowth *n.*
低层林木，灌木
ring fort
（古代）圆形堡垒
emigration *n.*
向外国移民

# The Republic of Ireland

"coffin ships" because of the huge **mortality** among the passengers, due to crowding, **unsanitary** conditions, poor food, and their already weakened conditions.

Before the Famine, two-thirds of the Irish population depended on agriculture for a living. For the most part, the rural Irish were poor, subject to a system of **tenant** farming, which effectively meant they owned nothing except the clothes on their backs and the food they could produce from small garden patches at the back of their cottages. The tenant farmers of the early nineteenth century tended to marry young and produce large families. The potato produced enough food to nourish them, and children were always needed as a cheap source of labour. Of course, the small plots of land which the farmers worked could be sub-divided but soon were too small to support a whole family, so many of these children emigrated when they grew up, either to nearby towns or cities, or to England and America.

The new factor that triggered the Great Famine was a **blight** on the potato crop. This **devastating** plant disease occurred during a time when the British attitude was essentially that the poor were poor because they deserved to be poor. This hard capitalist attitude was compounded by the fact that the British commonly **despised** the Irish, and particularly the poor Catholic Irish. The stereotype of the Irish in the British popular press of this period is of a people who were, at best, lazy, impractical, and dreamy; at worst, dirty, untrustworthy, and close to animals.[21]

Thus the Great Famine became a **watershed** in Irish history. Not merely because there was mass starvation and mass emigration, but because the British government seemed indifferent to the fate of the poorest people in its nearest colony. The population was **decimated** and continued to decline dramatically during the second half of the century. In the Irish Republic, it remained just above 2.5 million until the late 1980s, when a rising birth rate and net immigration caused by increased prosperity brought the population up to its present level of approximately 4.6 million in the Republic (roughly comparable to that of New Zealand).[22]

In the latest census (2011), the average age of the population was 36 years. With such an average age, Ireland is no longer considered a comparatively young country within Europe. Surprisingly, during the severe economic downturn starting in 2008, the latest census recorded the highest number of births since records began in 1896.

It is also notable that today over half of all people in the Republic live in **Dublin**. Once a rural society, today Ireland sees increasing internal migration to cities as well

mortality *n.*
死亡数，死亡率
unsanitary *adj.*
不卫生的，有碍健康的
tenant *n.* 佃农
blight *n.*
（由昆虫引起的植物的）枯萎
devastating *adj.*
毁灭性的
despise *v.* 蔑视
watershed *n.*
分水岭
decimate *v.*
毁掉大部，大批屠杀
Dublin *n.*
都柏林市（爱尔兰首都）

as substantial emigration out of Ireland as a whole, leaving country villages and towns largely to the middle-aged and the old. As a result, the traditional family farm, which has been the norm in Ireland for centuries, is a dying enterprise. **Propped** up by grants from the EU Common Agricultural Policy (CAP), the small farmer sustains himself by taking other jobs.[23] Increasingly he or she is reduced to "**hobby farming**", while many smaller farms have been consolidated into larger holdings which operate them now as a business.

Ireland is still mostly a rural country. Livestock farming in particular is an important resource for the Irish economy; there are almost two million cows in the Republic of Ireland, and roughly one sheep for every one of its citizens. Although milk and beef production are still a major occupation, farming as a way of life is changing radically and the shape of its future is uncertain.

In other crucial ways, Irish life as a whole is entering a period of radical uncertainty. In 2008, the boom economy of the late 1990s to 2005, known as the "Celtic Tiger", descended suddenly and shockingly into **recession**.[24] As a result, the increasingly better-educated young people of this generation had to make hard choices. As of 2010 unemployment stood at 13.5% (not quite as bad as the 17% of the mid-1980s, but still very high). Consequently, emigration, which had slowed to a trickle in the early 1990s, became a flood as young people sought jobs elsewhere in the world.

Now, once again, the situation has turned around but not without a high price. Through a series of drastic **austerity** measures, including a universal social charge on all incomes, Ireland has slowly clawed its way back to recovery. Today, unemployment stands at 7.5%. Incomes are being slowly restored, although the rate of restoration is slow and patchy, resulting in threats of public strikes (such as that by secondary school teachers and — unbelievably — the police, or "*gardai*" as they are known). Now that the fear has diminished, there is a great deal of anger about how the downturn was officially managed and the massive debts Ireland still must pay back.

As this overview is being finalized, there are two major worries on the minds of Irish people about their future. One is Great Britain's vote to exit the European Union (Brexit), endangering Ireland's largest export market for its products, agricultural and otherwise.[25] The election of Donald Trump as American president puts a question mark over the future of American multinationals in Ireland as well as that of thousands of **undocumented** Irish immigrants now living in the United States.[26]

---

prop *v.* 支撑
hobby farming 小型的不以挣钱为目的的休闲农场
recession *n.* 经济衰退
austerity *n.* （财政）紧缩
undocumented *adj.* 无正式文件的

# The Republic of Ireland

Such turns and turnabout seems highly ironic, as Ireland during its boom years had itself, for the first time in its history, become a target for many new immigrants. Most of these came from the late-arriving EU members from Eastern bloc countries such as Poland, **Lithuania** and **Latvia**, joining incomers from the UK and Germany. As a result, the population of the Republic of Ireland is no longer **homogeneous**. According to the 2008 census, 17% of its people were born outside of Ireland. The country is now home to people from 188 different countries speaking at least as many languages. It is estimated that about 40 000 Chinese people (most of them students) are now resident in Ireland. These numbers are an indication of the growing intercultural mix in the Irish population, the result of more open immigration procedures.

But, as might be predicted from such a sudden transition from a largely homogeneous society to one of great diversity, there are tensions over the integration of these radically diverse people into Irish society. In Ireland the process of evolving a genuinely intercultural society has only just begun.

Yet none of this should seem particularly new. Throughout the ages, Ireland's history has been one of invasions of vastly different peoples — Celts, Christians, Vikings, Normans, English — each of which has made a distinctive contribution to its present population. From this history, present-day Ireland emerges as a complex society with a distinctive culture, into which many elements of the past have been **incorporated**.

## History

### Early History

The earliest settlers arrived around 7 000 BC in the **Mesolithic** or middle Stone-Age period. Evidence suggests that they arrived in the north of the island, across what is now the narrow strait from northern Britain — but then might have been an actual landbridge. These people were mainly hunters.

Rival colonialists of the **Neolithic**, or new Stone Age, period reached Ireland around 3 000 BC. These were farmers who raised animals and cultivated the soil. Within about another thousand years, around 2 000 BC, **prospectors** and metalworkers arrived. They discovered deposits of gold and manufactured bronze. As seen in the National Museum of Ireland in Dublin, Ireland had a very sophisticated Bronze Age.

It is important to emphasize that Ireland already had quite a sophisticated

---

Lithuania *n.* 立陶宛
Latvia *n.* 拉脱维亚
homogeneous *adj.* 单一的
incorporate *v.* 融合
Mesolithic *adj.* 中石器时代的
Neolithic *adj.* 新石器时代的
prospector *n.* 勘探者，采矿者

civilisation before the **incursions** which were to transform it radically: that of the Celts.[27] It is believed that the Celts, originally thought to be invaders, gradually **infiltrated** into Ireland along established trade routes, perhaps as early as the 6th century BC, with subsequent groups arriving up to the time of Christ, about two thousand years ago. The Celts had long dominated central and western Europe before the Romans.

Of all the legacies of the Celts, it is their language (now known as "Irish") that has proved the most lasting. By order of the government of the Republic of Ireland, the language of Irish must be learned by all Irish schoolchildren up to the age of sixteen. To obtain entry to all Irish universities (except Trinity College Dublin) and to the Irish civil service, candidates must show **competence** in Irish. Legally, Irish is also the first official language of the Republic of Ireland (the second being English). Making Irish official is a good example of how the past has been used, quite consciously, by those seeking to create the Republic of Ireland by this crucial marking of its difference from other nation/states, in particular, Great Britain, whose English language was seen as **imposed** on the Irish people starting from the first modern invasion of the island in the 12th century.[28]

With the language, the Celts brought an instrument of social and cultural unity to the island, which **transcended** political and social divisions. Before the arrival of Christianity in the fifth century, there were few other unifying forces. Politically, the Celts were warlords, who established their tribes on the basis of a family **lineage** or clan which **descended** purely through the male line.

Along with their language, the Celts also brought a legal system. Under Brehon Law, the primal unit was the *fine* (pronounced "FEEN e") or the family unit comprising all relations of the male descent for five generations.[29] It is this family group — loosely described as a "tribe" or "**clan**" — that was responsible for the conduct of the whole group; individuals had no rights apart from their *fine*. In Ireland today, the emphasis on the importance of family groupings over several generations may **derive** from this ancient arrangement.

Outside the family group, society was rigidly **stratified**. Rank depended on birth as well as wealth. Learning was one important marker of status: poets and lawyers were respected and even feared. All freemen were landowners, and personal property helped establish rank. The importance of land and personal property is still well-established in modern society of the Ireland of today, which has the highest rate of home-ownership

incursion *n.* 入侵
infiltrate *v.* 渗入
competence *n.* 能力，胜任
impose *v.* 强加（于）
transcend *v.* 超越
lineage *n.* 家系，家族
descend *v.* 祖传，世代相传
fine *n.* （爱尔兰语）家庭单位
clan *n.* 宗族
derive *v.* 源于
stratify *v.* 分层，阶层化

# The Republic of Ireland

in Europe. But some things have changed. Under Brehon Law, women were given a high status and a certain degree of independence. They were allowed to keep their own names after marriage; they had certain defined property rights and could easily obtain a divorce from a husband they found unsatisfactory.[30]

At some time in the 5th century (late by European standards), Christianity was introduced into Ireland. Traditionally it was said to have been brought by Saint Patrick. Although there were some Christians in Ireland before Patrick's arrival, by the time of his death in AD 461, much of the island was effectively Christian: providing a unity of culture and an administrative structure, north and south, which had not existed on the island beforehand.[31]

It was through the **monasteries** that Irish influence on Britain and Europe was exerted from the 6th century onwards. Setting out first as **pilgrims**, Irish monks **preached** the **gospel** and established new scholarly communities across the continent. The Irish monks were also great **missionaries** as well as scholars, founding important monastic centers throughout Europe.

## The Middle Ages

From around 800 onwards Viking **marauders** from Scandinavia attacked Ireland as well as England. These raids continued right through the 9th and 10th centuries. In time, when they actually settled in Ireland, the Vikings became known as great traders and did much to develop the commerce of medieval Ireland. As such, they are credited with founding most of the major towns, including Dublin, Cork, Limerick, and Waterford.

The next centuries are often regarded as a period of progress in Ireland. Cultural activity in the arts prospered. It was a great era of religious reform; a powerful effort was made to bring the church more fully into line with Roman Catholic **orthodoxy**. In politics, others sought to follow Brian Boru's (c. 941–1014) example in seeking (unsuccessfully, as it turned out) to establish themselves as kings of all Ireland.[32]

This trend was interrupted by the arrival of the Normans as of 1167. In 1171 the Norman monarch, Henry II, King of England, invaded Ireland, establishing himself as an **overlord** of the country. With his **ascendancy** began the political involvement of England in Ireland which was to dominate the country's history for the next seven hundred and fifty years. During the course of the 13th century, the Normans were the first to attempt to impose on Ireland a centralised administration which **mimicked** the

---

monastery n.
隐修院，修道院
pilgrim n.
朝圣者
preach v. 传道
gospel n.
教义，福音
missionary n.
传教士
marauder n.
劫掠者
orthodoxy n.
正统观念，正统信仰
overlord n.
最高统治者
ascendancy n.
优势，支配地位
mimic v. 模仿

parliament and legal systems and administrative practices of their native England.

The success of the Norman Conquest was, however, compromised as time went on. Although the last serious effort to overthrow Norman rule in Ireland failed in 1315, the native Irish won by other means. Through intermarriage and **Gaelicisation** of leading Norman families, the area of effective English rule in Ireland had, by the end of the 15th century, shrunk to a small **enclave** around Dublin known as "**The Pale**."[33] Ireland had managed to **assimilate** their Norman invaders, making them "more Irish than the Irish themselves".

**Early Modern Period**

By the 16th century it became clear to the Tudor monarchy that a re-conquest of Ireland had now become a political necessity if Ireland were to remain English.[34] In 1541, Henry VIII declared himself King of Ireland — the first English monarch to do so. In order to secure their political hold, the Tudor monarchs introduced new English settlers into Ireland. They also **embarked** on a series of military campaigns against the Gaelic Irish and the Anglo-Norman lords who had fallen away in their **allegiance** to the crown. Queen Elizabeth I continued and **amplified** her father's Irish campaigns. When her army defeated the Irish at the Battle of Kinsale in 1601, the native political system was overthrown and, for the first time, the entire island was controlled by a strong English central government.

Also from the 16th century onwards, the English sought to impose their own brand of Christianity, a branch of Protestantism called the Church of Ireland.[35] Partly because of its close association with the **repressive** policies of the English administration, this version of Christianity was resisted fiercely in Ireland.

Thus issues of religious allegiance added even more complexity to an already complicated political situation. Divisions soon appeared as the Irish **factions** became **enmeshed** in the 17th century civil war carried out in England between King and Parliament.[36] When the new (and so far, only) English Republic was established in 1649 under Oliver Cromwell, he took such drastic measures to crush the rebellion on Irish soil that the **massacres** of his parliamentary army are still recalled in the folk memory of Ireland today.

---

Gaelicisation *n.*
盖尔语化；盖尔化
enclave *n.*
飞地（指在本国境内的隶属另一国的一块领土）
the Pale
都柏林地区的古称
assimilate *v.*
同化
embark *v.*
着手，从事
allegiance *n.*
效忠，忠诚
amplify *v.*
扩大，增强
repressive *adj.*
镇压的，压制的
faction *n.*
派别，帮派
enmesh *v.*
使…陷入
massacre *n.*
大屠杀，残杀

# The Republic of Ireland

## The 18th Century

Throughout this century, Roman Catholics were seen as a threatening faction which might **rally** in support of James II's Catholic followers in an attempt to regain what he regarded as his rightful place on the English throne.[37] Thus the British government enforced a severe code of penal legislation against Catholics, preventing them from owning land, attending university, or entering the professions (among other restrictions). Those Protestants (Presbyterians known as "Dissenters") who did not accept the King of England as the head of their church, also suffered religious disabilities but on a much lesser scale. As a result, power over the Irish people was increasingly concentrated in the hands of the small minority, loyal to England, known as the Protestant Ascendancy.

In implementing such repressive measures, the island of Ireland appeared to have been rendered among the most **compliant** of the British colonies.[38] But it was the revolt of another British colony — in the American War of Independence (1776–1783) — that initiated radical changes in Irish politics. Encouraged by the American example, the Protestant Ascendancy began to press for a measure of colonial self-government. As a result, in 1782 the Irish parliament, hitherto **subservient** to London, was granted independence. Ireland was now effectively a separate kingdom sharing a monarch with England, although the Dublin administration was still appointed by the King.

The French Revolution of 1789, with its new ideas, had an equally profound impact on Ireland. Following its slogans of "Liberty, Equality, Fraternity," the Society of the United Irishmen was founded in 1791 to press for radical reform. A famous revolt was initiated in 1798 by the United Irishmen under Theobald Wolfe Tone. This was a group aiming, for the first time, to unite Catholics and Protestants in a **coalition** that would forever break Ireland's link with England. Yet, in spite of French help, the rebellion was badly organised and easily **suppressed**.

After the defeat of the 1798 rebellion, the London government took drastic action to **curtail** any notions of Irish independence. They decided to **institute** a formal political **fusion** between the British and Irish parliaments in what was called The Act of Union. Thus the Irish parliament, newly dismissed as an unrepresentative assembly, was induced to vote itself out of existence in 1800.[39] With its **demise** ended the hopes of the Irish for a nation of their own separate from that of Great Britain.

---

rally *v.*
团结，集合
compliant *adj.*
遵从的，顺从的
subservient *adj.*
屈从的，恭顺的
coalition *n.*
联合，联盟
suppress *v.*
抑制，镇压
curtail *v.*
抑制，剥夺
institute *v.*
制定，创立
fusion *n.*
融合
demise *n.*
死亡，终止

## Modern Ireland

From 1801 onwards Ireland had no parliament of its own; Irish Members of Parliament, drawn from the Protestant Ascendancy, sat in the Westminster parliament in London where they constituted a small minority. The Westminster government was unwilling to grant major **concessions** to Roman Catholics.

Meanwhile, the end of the Napoleonic wars in Europe in 1815 had a drastic impact on the economy. The war had led to a huge growth in **tillage** farming to supply the armies, and, in Ireland, a dependence on the potato as a staple food. When the war ended there was a change from tillage to **pasture**, causing agrarian unemployment. At the same time, the Irish population was increasing rapidly, reaching 8 million by 1841, two-thirds of whom depended solely upon agriculture. In this **precarious** agrarian economy the failure of the potato crop in 1845, due to blight, proved disastrous. The crop failed again in 1846, 1847, and 1848 and, coupled with severe weather, resulted in a disastrous **famine**, known in Ireland as "The Great Hunger." By 1851 the population had been reduced by at least 2 million due to starvation, disease and emigration to Britain and North America.

The shadow of the famine, and what was seen as English indifference if not downright cruelty to the Irish, hung over the entire latter half of the nineteenth century. Not surprisingly, this period is characterized by campaigns for national independence and land reform. The Irish Republican Brotherhood (the IRB, later known as the Irish Republican Army or IRA) was founded in 1858 to promote, by violence if necessary, Irish independence from Great Britain.[40] Although this secret society staged an armed uprising in 1867, it proved no more than a token gesture.

To counter just such bloody and **futile** rebellions, a constitutional movement seeking Home Rule was instituted by an Irishman elected to the Westminster Parliament, Isaac Butt.[41] The Home Rulers, who sought a separate Irish parliament subordinate to London, won half of the Irish seats in the 1874 election.

The constant friction between English colonial masters and the Irish colonists was, during this period, made worse by those between English landlords and their Irish tenant farmers. Although Catholics were allowed once again to own property under the acts of Catholic Emancipation (1823–1829), benefits from property extended only to the well-off. In 1879 Michael Davitt founded the National Land League, which aimed to secure the most basic rights for tenant-farmers — fair rent, free sale of land and fixity

concession *n.* 让步
tillage *n.* 耕作，耕种
pasture *n.* 牧场，草场
precarious *adj.* 危险的，不稳的
famine *n.* 饥荒
futile *n.* 无用的

# The Republic of Ireland

of tenure. Charles Stuart Parnell — ironically, both an Irish Protestant and a landlord — became president of the movement. The result was a great national campaign of mass **agitation** which forced the British government to pass a series of reforming land acts. These eventually abolished the old landlord system and transferred ownership of the land to the people who worked it.

Using the agrarian movement as the basis for agitation, Charles Stuart Parnell stood for the Home Rule party in the 1885 election. The Home Rule party swept the whole island outside eastern Ulster. In effect, the **impetus** of the Home Rule campaign had been effectively lost with the scandal that attended a divorce action against Parnell — followed by his tragically early death in 1891.

Subsequently, as of 1905, Arthur Griffith developed a new political party known as *Sinn Féin* (pronounced "SHIN-fane"), meaning "we ourselves" in the Irish language.[42] The *Sinn Féin* policy was that Irish MPs should withdraw from the Westminster government entirely to establish an independent parliament. *Sinn Féin* had close links with the Irish Republican Brotherhood and later with its successor, the Irish Republican Army (or IRA).

The Home Rule bill was finally passed in 1914 but was **shelved** upon the outbreak of World War I with a promise of implementation afterwards. Not trusting that commitment, in 1916 the Irish Volunteers, led by Patrick Pearse and the Irish Citizen Army, led by James Connolly, staged another, and final, rebellion against British rule. The Easter Rising of 1916 was put down in a matter of days. But the decision of the British to **execute** several of the imprisoned leaders one by one, over a period of nine days, violently **alienated** Irish public opinion, which had hitherto **wavered** between condemnation and **detachment**.[43] As a consequence, in the 1918 general election, *Sinn Féin* totally defeated the Irish parliamentary party.

Once again, the Irish won a symbolic victory, although the actual revolt of Easter 1916 resulted in a military defeat. How did this come about? By choosing Easter Monday as the day of the rebellion, the rebels consciously **invoked** the symbolic sacrifice of Jesus Christ, an act which seemed at the time to be a defeat but which was believed to end in triumph when, on the third day after his death (Easter Sunday), Jesus was said to have been **resurrected** from the dead.[44] Thus, even though the Irish rebels were defeated and then executed, they were seen as **martyrs** to the cause of Irish freedom, which itself took on a symbolic life of its own as a result of their sacrificial

---

agitation *n.*
鼓动，骚动
impetus *n.*
动力
shelf *v.* 搁置
execute *v.* 处死
alienate *v.*
（使）疏远，异化
waver *v.* 动摇，犹豫不决
detachment *n.*
超然，漠不关心
invoke *v.* 唤起
resurrect *v.*
（使）复活
martyr *n.*
烈士，殉道者

deaths.

Once elected, the *Sinn Féin* representatives constituted themselves as the first Dáil (pronounced "DOYLE"), or independent Parliament, in Dublin. A **belated** British attempt to smash *Sinn Féin* led to the War of Independence of 1919-21. After more than two years of guerrilla struggle, a **truce** was agreed. In December, 1921 the Anglo-Irish Treaty was signed, with the result that 26 counties gained independence as the new Irish Free State. Six counties in Ulster, however, refused to become part of the new nation. These were largely Protestant and their people identified more strongly with the British than with the southern Irish. As a consequence of the new Treaty, these counties were granted their own parliament at Stormont in Belfast in 1920 and, with it, the right to remain as part of the United Kingdom. Today these six counties, still a part of the United Kingdom, are known as Northern Ireland. As we shall see, **aspirations** to unite the island as a whole may be put into effect (according to the Belfast Agreement of 1998) under certain given conditions.

belated *adj.*
延误的，迟来的
truce *n.*
休战，停战（协定）
aspiration *n.*
抱负

# Explanations

1. **Ireland is a small island ... by a narrow strait of water:**
   爱尔兰是一个靠近英国西北海岸、与苏格兰一水之隔的小岛。strait: 海峡。

2. **But often this ambiguity ... as bigger or smaller:**
   但"爱尔兰"这一词汇的模糊用法是有用意的，尤其是对于政治家和外交家，这取决于他们希望代表的国家是较大或较小的概念。

3. **The border between these two jurisdictions, ... in the late sixteenth century:**
   这两个管辖范围之间的界限于 1920 年划分，沿其政治和宗教冲突分界线建立，形成南北局面。其实，早从 16 世纪末伊丽莎白一世殖民统治时期开始，这一直是爱尔兰生活的特征。

4. **Following traditional county lines, ... between one jurisdiction and another:**
   沿传统各县界线划分的边界漫长曲折，无法有效地加以警戒，所以两边人员很容易越界流动。

5. **Ireland is washed by the Gulf Stream, ... so that it actually has a quite temperate climate:**
   爱尔兰受到墨西哥湾流和常年西南风的影响，所以实际上气候相当温和。

6. **In terms of geographical elevations ... which often slope precipitously into the sea:**
   从地形上来看，爱尔兰像一个茶碟，中间是大片低地，间或有些起伏的山丘，这些山丘的周边则是断续

# The Republic of Ireland

的山脉，经常在入海时形成悬崖峭壁。

7. **In terms of native flora and fauna, ... elsewhere in Europe:**
   与欧洲其他地区相比，爱尔兰当地的动植物种类较少。

8. **Much of the primeval forest was cut down ... is still resented:**
   16–17 世纪，大多数原始森林被英格兰人砍伐，建造他们著名的海军舰队。人们一想起英国掠夺爱尔兰的这段历史仍然愤愤不平。

9. **Traditionally, ..., mostly due to the comparative poverty of the country.:**
   爱尔兰历来自然风景优美，没有被破坏，这主要是因为该地区相对贫困落后。

10. **The decline in water quality ... if not actually polluted:**
    水质的下降最为明显。即使还未到被污染的程度，估计有 25% 的河流和 66% 的湖泊水质下降。

11. **Ireland's love-affair with the car ... among the highest in the EU:**
    爱尔兰对汽车的喜爱使其氮氧化物的排放量大大超过了欧盟规定的"上限"标准。发电厂所产生的温室气体排放量在欧盟国家中也是最高的之一。

12. **Over-development of multiple tourist resorts has also led to a despoliation of many landscapes:**
    多种旅游胜地的过度开发也使许多风景遭到破坏。

13. **The expansion of the tourist industry ... destroys what it is selling:**
    旅游业的发展对环境的破坏尤为危险，对其本身的卖点有着极大的破坏性。旅游业的最大卖点是优美的环境，但过度开发却在不同程度上破坏了环境。

14. **And the Irish are ... the health benefits of eating organic food:**
    爱尔兰人越来越意识到在旅游业领域"绿色经济"的价值，以及吃有机（绿色）食品对健康的益处。

15. **The rural landscape of Ireland is highly populated, but mostly by ghosts:**
    爱尔兰乡村住着许多人，但其中大多是鬼魂。意思是指爱尔兰有着悠久的历史。

16. **Thus the Irish landscape itself records many layers of its varied history:**
    所以，爱尔兰的山山水水本身记录着它丰富历史的许多层面。

17. **Emigration did take place ... the province of Ulster:**
    大饥荒之前就有爱尔兰人移居海外，这些移民主要来自爱尔兰北部被人们称作阿尔斯特的省份。The Great Famine：大饥荒。1845–1848 年，爱尔兰重要农作物马铃薯因受灾大面积减产，造成人口锐减以及大批爱尔兰人移民至美国，寻找生计。

18. **Many of these emigrants ... the United States:**
    这些移民中许多人自立门户，而这些家族后来成为美国政治经济生活中的名门望族。

19. **Seven US Presidents ... came from an Ulster emigrant background:**
    七位美国总统以及如托马斯·梅隆这样的著名金融家具有阿尔斯特移民家庭背景。Thomas Mellon：

UNIT 11 Land, People, and History

托马斯·梅隆（1813–1908）为爱尔兰裔美国企业家、律师和法官，梅隆银行的创建者。

20. **When successive potato crops failed ... linked with malnutrition:**
1845–1848 年，马铃薯连年受灾减产，许多人被饿死，或死于营养不良造成的疾病。

21. **The stereotype of the Irish ... dirty, untrustworthy, and close to animals:**
这一时期英国流行报刊上的爱尔兰人的典型形象从最好方面讲是懒惰、不切实际、好梦想，从最坏方面讲则是肮脏、靠不住以及近乎牲畜。

22. **In the Irish Republic, ... (roughly comparable to that of New Zealand):**
爱尔兰共和国的人口在 20 世纪 80 年代末之前一直停留在 250 万多一点；80 年代末以来，由于出生率增高以及经济繁荣造成的净流入移民，爱尔兰共和国的人口才达到现在约 460 万的水平（相当于新西兰的人口）。

23. **Propped up by grants ... by taking other jobs:**
得益于欧盟共同农业政策的补贴，小农场主们通过兼职做其他工作来维持其生计。肇始于 1962 年的欧盟共同农业政策通过对成员国农民的补贴来维持农业生产及其在国际市场的竞争力。

24. **In 2008 the boom economy ... into recession:**
2008 年，1990 年代末期到 2005 年"虎虎有生气"的爱尔兰经济出人意料、令人震惊地突然陷入了衰退。"Celtic Tiger"："虎虎有生气的爱尔兰（经济）"。由于爱尔兰的经济在加入欧盟之后持续高速增长，又由于爱尔兰人的祖先为凯尔特人，故被称为"凯尔特之虎"，正如新加坡、中国香港、中国台湾与韩国等国家和地区在经济持续高速增长时期被称为"亚洲四小龙"。

25. **One is Great Britain's vote to exit the European Union ... its products, agricultural and otherwise:**
其中的一项关切是英国的脱欧公投会危及爱尔兰最大的工业品、农产品和其他产品出口市场。2016 年 6 月 23 日，英国就脱离还是留在欧盟举行全民公决，造成脱欧的结果。这自然会影响作为欧盟成员国的爱尔兰未来与英国的经贸关系（英国是爱尔兰最大的出口市场）。

26. **The election of Donald Trump as American president ... now living in the United States:**
唐纳德·特朗普当选美国总统给爱尔兰的美国跨国公司以及现居美国的数以千计的非法爱尔兰移民的未来打上了一个问号。Donald Trump：唐纳德·特朗普，美国第 45 任总统（2017– ）。特朗普上任之后宣布奉行"美国第一"和"重振美国"的政策，曾下达总统令，限制一些伊斯兰国家的移民入境。

27. **It is important to emphasize ... that of the Celts:**
应当重点强调的是爱尔兰在被后来的入侵彻底改变之前，已有了很精致的文明，即凯尔特文明。The Celts：凯尔特人，铁器时代到中世纪时期欧洲的一个民族，讲凯尔特语并有着相似的文化，主要活跃在欧洲的中部和西部。爱尔兰的语言和文化即属于延续下来的凯尔特文化。

28. **Making Irish official is a good example of how the past ... the island in the 12th century:**
将爱尔兰语规定为官方语言是谋求创立爱尔兰共和国的人们古为今用、使爱尔兰区别于其他国家，尤其是区别于英国的经典好例证，后者的英语被爱尔兰人视作英国自 12 世纪第一次开始入侵爱尔兰以来强加给爱尔兰人民的。

# The Republic of Ireland

29. **Under Brehon Law ... the male descent for five generations:**
    布莱恩法规定，基本的社会单位为"家族"，由五代以内的男性血亲关系网构成。布莱恩法为爱尔兰早期的法律，其条文规范着中世纪早期爱尔兰人的日常生活。诺曼人 1167–1169 年的到来对其造成了部分侵蚀和破坏，但从 13 到 17 世纪该法规在爱尔兰的主要地区出现过复兴，并幸存到近代早期，与英国法规并行使用。

30. **They were allowed to ... obtain a divorce from a husband they found unsatisfactory:**
    （布莱恩法规定）妇女有权在婚后保留自己的姓氏；她们拥有一定的财产权，而且与自己不满意的丈夫离婚也并非难事。

31. **Although there were some Christians in Ireland ... on the island beforehand:**
    尽管在帕特里克之前爱尔兰就有一些基督徒，只是到帕特里克于公元 461 年去世时，该岛大部分地区才真正皈依了基督教；基督教从北到南提供了文化和行政上的统一，这在该岛的历史上尚属第一次。圣帕特里克为公元五世纪罗马–不列颠基督教使团驻爱尔兰的传教士和主教，在该岛传播基督教，后来被尊为爱尔兰的保护神。圣帕特里克节（St. Patrick's Day）每年的 3 月 17 日（据信是帕特里克去世的日子）举行，五世纪末期起源于爱尔兰，如今已成为爱尔兰的国庆节。随着爱尔兰后裔遍布世界各地，圣帕特里克节逐渐在一些国家成为节日。圣帕特里克节的传统颜色为绿色。

32. **In politics, others sought to ... to establish themselves as kings of all Ireland:**
    在政治上，一些爱尔兰人则以布莱恩·博茹为榜样，寻求（但结果并不成功）建立统一的爱尔兰，成为该岛的国王。布莱恩·博茹（941–1014）是爱尔兰历史上力图统一该岛的国王。

33. **Through intermarriage ... a small enclave around Dublin known as "The Pale.":**
    通过通婚和诺曼望族的凯尔特（盖尔）化，到 15 世纪末的时候英国人对爱尔兰的实际控制已经缩小到仅为都柏林周围的一小片飞地。

34. **By the 16th century ... if Ireland were to remain English:**
    到 16 世纪，都铎王朝清楚地意识到，如果英国人想要控制爱尔兰就必须对其进行再征服，这在当时已属必然的政治需要。Tudor Monarchy: 都铎王朝（1485–1603），统治英国和爱尔兰的英国王室，历经五任君主，其中包括亨利八世和伊丽莎白一世。

35. **Also from the 16th century onwards, ... the Church of Ireland:**
    而且自 16 世纪以后，英国人试图在爱尔兰推行自己的基督教教派形式，被称作"爱尔兰圣公会"的一种新教。Protestantism: 新教，亦称基督新教，是基督教的一派，与天主教、东正教并称为基督教三大派别。因对罗马公教（即天主教）持抗议态度，不承认罗马主教的教皇地位，故西方一般称基督新教为"抗罗宗"或"抗议宗"。词源出自德文"Protestanten"（抗议者），最初指 1529 年在德意志帝国会议中对恢复天主教特权之决议案提出抗议的新教诸侯和城市代表，后演变为新教各教派的共同称谓。主要分布在英、美、德、瑞士、北欧各国及新西兰、澳大利亚等国。

36. **Divisions soon appeared ... between King and Parliament:**
    随着爱尔兰各派卷入英国国王与议会之间爆发的内战，爱尔兰也出现了拥护国王与拥护议会派别之间的纷争。

UNIT 11　Land, People, and History

37. **Throughout this century, Roman Catholics ... his rightful place on the English throne:**
整个 18 世纪，罗马天主教徒被视作詹姆士二世追随者的危险支持派别，试图重新夺回国王对英国王位的继承权。James II：詹姆士二世（1633–1701），英格兰国王（1685–1688），詹姆士一世之子和继承人，天主教徒，因与议会发生宗教和权力之争而被罢黜，史称"光荣革命"。

38. **In implementing such repressive measures ... of the British colonies:**
由于实施了这些高压政策，爱尔兰似乎变成了英国殖民地中最驯服的地区。

39. **Thus the Irish parliament ... was induced to vote itself out of existence in 1800:**
这样，刚刚被以不具代表性为由而解散的（爱尔兰）议会于 1800 年被诱导投票终止了自己本身的存在。

40. **The Irish Republican Brotherhood ... Irish independence from Great Britain:**
爱尔兰共和兄弟会（后来以爱尔兰共和军的名号著称）成立于 1858 年，旨在促进爱尔兰脱离英国的独立进程，必要时诉诸暴力手段。

41. **To counter just such bloody and futile rebellions ... the Westminster Parliament, Isaac Butt:**
为了逆转这样徒劳流血的反抗，被选入英国议会的爱尔兰人艾萨克·巴特发动了寻求地方自治的宪政运动。Home Rule：地方自治，1870 年，由艾萨克·巴特提出并广为传播，成为 1870–1914 年爱尔兰国民运动的口号，号召建立英帝国制度内的独立爱尔兰议会。

42. **Subsequently, as of 1905 ... "we ourselves" in the Irish language:**
随后，亚瑟·格里菲斯于 1905 年建立了一个新政党，称作"新芬党"，爱尔兰语的意思是"我们自己"。

43. **But the decision ... wavered between condemnation and detachment:**
然而，英国人在九天的时间里逐一处决（复活节起义）被俘领袖的决定强烈地异化了爱尔兰的民意，而在此之前爱尔兰人对复活节起义（以及英国人镇压）的态度是谴责和漠然之间的摇摆。The Easter Rising of 1916：爱尔兰人民争取独立的复活节起义，于 1916 年 4 月爆发于都柏林，随后很快被镇压，但其影响深远。

44. **By choosing Easter Monday ... Jesus was said to have been resurrected from the dead:**
选择复活节星期一作为起义日，反叛者们有意将起义与耶稣基督的象征性牺牲联系起来，这一行动在当时看似失败了但却注入了最终胜利的信念，因为耶稣死后第三天（复活节星期日）据说又被上帝复活了。Easter：复活节，纪念耶稣基督复活的节日。在西方教会传统里，春分之后第一次满月之后的第一个星期日即为复活节，节期大致在 3 月 22 日至 4 月 25 日之间。《圣经·新约全书》记载，耶稣被钉死在十字架上，第三天身体复活，复活节因此得名。复活节是基督教最重大的节日，其重要性甚至超过圣诞节。

# The Republic of Ireland

## Exercises

**I. Give the Chinese equivalents for the following:**
1. The Great Famine
2. The Celts
3. St. Patrick
4. *Sinn Féin*
5. The Easter Rising

**II. Decide whether the following statements are true (T) or false (F):**
1. When referring to Ireland, people mean either the Republic of Ireland or Northern Ireland, a province of Great Britain. _____
2. The area covering the Republic of Ireland is five times of that of Northern Ireland. _____
3. Most of the people in Northern Ireland are Catholics while the majority of the people in the Republic are Protestants. _____
4. Ireland has an extreme climate and four distinct seasons. _____
5. The present population of Irish Republic is less than 4 million. _____
6. After the Great Famine, there was a rapid decline of population, and many Irish people emigrated to other countries. _____
7. The average age of the population in the Republic of Ireland in the latest census is 36. _____
8. Although the language of the Celts survived through history, their language is not the official language of the Republic of Ireland. _____

**III. Fill in the blanks:**
1. Ireland is situated off the northwest coast of _____.
2. The whole island has two jurisdictions, one is _____ and the other _____.
3. "The Six Counties" are referred to as _____.
4. Ireland has a _____ climate, in other words, it does not change much from one season to another.

5. Because of the Great Famine, many people in Ireland emigrated to _____.
6. Ireland has a population equivalent to that of _____.
7. The booming economy of Ireland between the late 1990s and 2005 earned it the name as "the _____ Tiger".
8. In 1171 the Norman monarch, _____, King of England, invaded Ireland, establishing himself as an overlord of the country.
9. In 1541, _____ declared himself King of Ireland — the first English monarch to do so.
10. The population of the Republic of Ireland is no longer homogeneous as _____ of its people were born outside of Ireland according to the 2008 census.

## IV. Questions:

1. What is Ireland's geographical location in Europe?
2. What are the major geographical features of Ireland?
3. What are the differences in the meanings of "Ireland", "Northern Ireland", and "the Republic of Ireland"?
4. What was the landscape of Ireland like traditionally? What changes and conflicts have taken place since the 1960s? What role has the EU played in this respect?
5. What is the climate like in Ireland? What factors cause such a climate?
6. Why does Ireland have a smaller range, in terms of native flora and fauna, than is found elsewhere in Europe?
7. What impact did the Great Famine have on Ireland?
8. Where did many Irish emigrate to during the Great Famine? What happened to them after their emigration to the New World? Give examples to prove your point.
9. What was the stereotype of the Irish in the British popular press in the 19th century? Why?
10. What legacies have the Celts left for Ireland?
11. Who was Saint Patrick? How did he influence the history and culture of Ireland?
12. What was the impact of the English colonisation on Ireland?
13. How did the conflict between Catholics and Protestants come about?
14. What were the major divisions of opinions among the Irish concerning their independence movement in the early 20th century?
15. What was the significance of the Easter Rising of 1916?

# The Republic of Ireland

V. **Topics for discussion or research:**
1. What are some of the distinctive features of Ireland's geography? Find out similarities and differences in terms of climate, landscape, plants and animals between Ireland and Britain.
2. What are the causes and effects of the Great Famine in the history of Ireland?
3. Do research on the history of English colonisation of Ireland and the consequences it brought to the two countries.
4. Discuss the causes of the conflict between the Protestants and Catholics in Irish history. Explore possible solutions to the conflict.
5. If you have a chance to visit Ireland, what would you like to see most? Explain your reasons.

# UNIT 12

# Politics and Economy

**Go over the following focal points before reading the text:**

- Representative democracy
- The structure of Irish government
- Checks and balances
- The civil service
- The Irish legal system
- A small, open, trade-dependent economy
- Economic transformation
- Ireland's accession to the EU
- Social changes
- Multinational culture
- New prosperity
- New inequalities

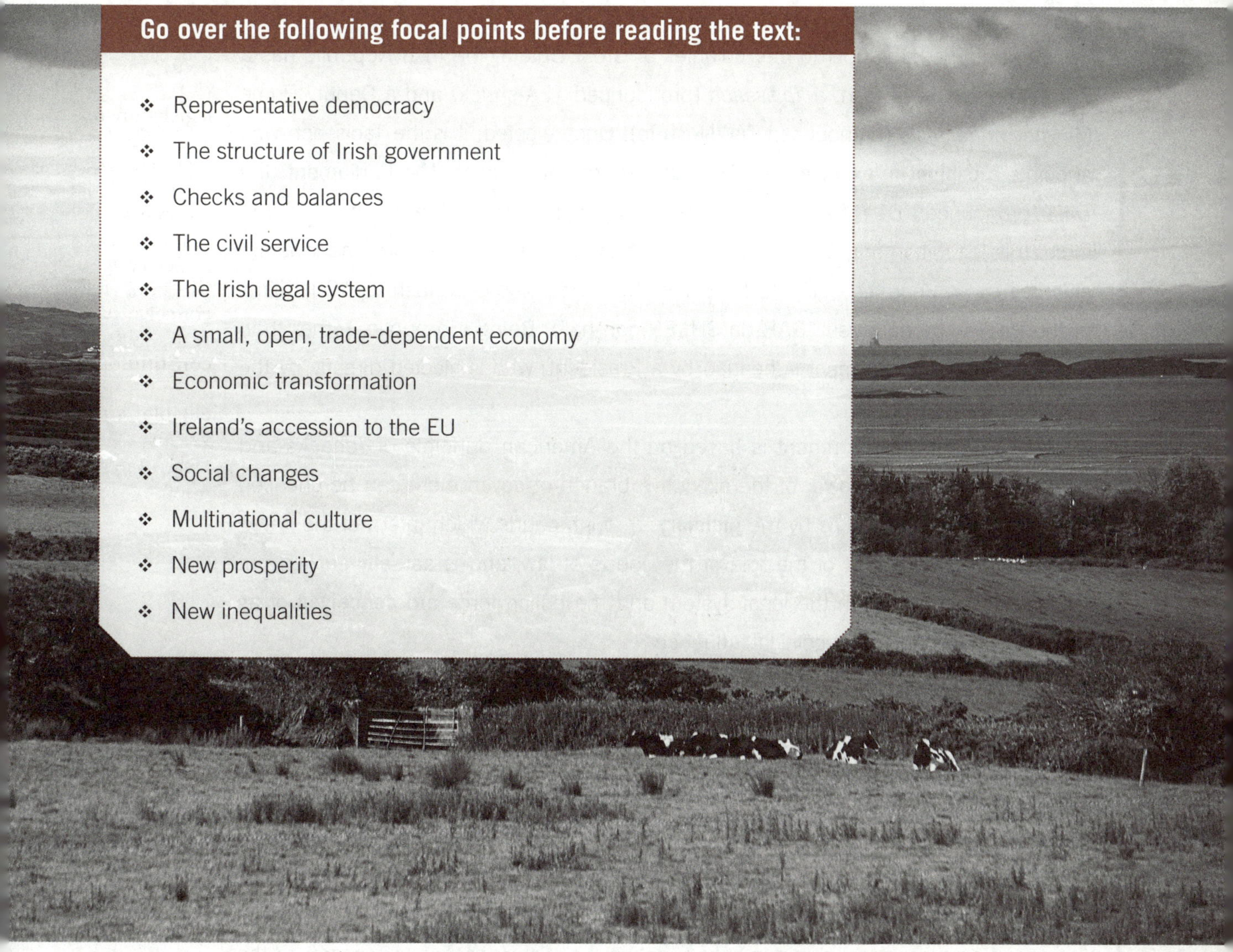

# The Republic of Ireland

## Politics

In common with most countries in Western Europe, Ireland is a **representative** democracy: that is to say, most of its offices are filled through election, either direct or indirect, by the Irish people.[1]

In structure, like most former colonies of Great Britain, the Irish Republic has a Prime Minister or, in Irish, a *Taoiseach* (pronounced TEA-shuck) and a Deputy Prime Minister or *Tánaiste* (pronounced TAWN-ish-ta). Once elected, it is the Taoiseach who appoints a **cabinet** to **execute** the daily business of government. The Parliament (the *Dáil*) (pronounced DOYLE) frames and **enacts** all **legislation** for the country. Once in force, this legislation may be interpreted by a **hierarchy** of courts. Finally, the laws are **enforced** by an unarmed police force, called the *Garda Siochana* (Irish for "Guardians of the Peace" pronounced "GAR-da SHEER-con-ha"). Being a republic, rather than a monarchy, the government is headed by a President, who is elected directly by the people.

The system of government is based on the American principle of "checks and balances": that is, the power of the executive branch of government can be checked by the legislature as well as by the **judiciary**, through courts which interpret the laws.[2] Enforcement is also part of the role of the courts of law, and is actually carried out by the police force. Both the legal system and the police force are **conceived** of as completely independent of political influence.

### The President

Under the **Constitution**, the President (*Uachtarán*, pronounced "UCH-ter-an") is usually elected by the direct vote of the people. Every citizen of 35 years of age or over is **eligible** to run for President. Every citizen has a right to vote as of age 18.

The President's term of office is seven years. A President can be reelected once only. The President acts as a symbolic Head of State and only has executive functions in case of emergencies. In its symbolic function the Irish Presidency is nearer to the

---

representative *adj.* 代议制的
cabinet *n.* 内阁
execute *v.* 实施,执行
enact *v.* 颁布,制定(法律)
legislation *n.* 立法,法律
hierarchy *n.* 层级,等级制度
enforce *v.* 实施,执行
judiciary *n.* 司法系统
conceive *v.* 设想,想象
constitution *n.* 宪法
eligible *adj.* 合格的,符合条件的

status of the present Queen in the United Kingdom than to that of the President of the United States.

The President has one power which may require exercising his or her **discretion**. This allows the President to refuse to dissolve the *Dáil* on the advice of a *Taoiseach* who has ceased to **retain** the support of a majority in the *Dáil*.[3] Such an action would then force the *Taoiseach* to form a new government rather than calling a general election.

## The Government

The executive powers of the State are exercised by, or on the authority of, the Government. The Government consists of the *Taoiseach* and the ministers that he or she appoints to the cabinet. All must be elected members of the Irish parliament. It is the cabinet which determines, and then enacts, government policy. As such, the Government acts collectively and is responsible to the *Dáil* or Irish Parliament.

The Prime Minister or *Taoiseach* is appointed by the President on the **nomination** of the Parliament. *Taoiseach* literally means "**chieftain**". Thus the *Taoiseach* must emerge as an agreed candidate of the largest political party of the Parliament, or one that is agreed by a **coalition** of Parliament parties. In turn the *Taoiseach* nominates one member of the government to be *Tánaiste*, or the Deputy Prime Minister.

The *Taoiseach* also assigns different areas of responsibility or Departments of State to members of the Government. Government ministers are assisted in their work by **Ministers of State**, who are not members of the cabinet.

The *Taoiseach* also appoints an Attorney General. Although not a member of the Government, the Attorney General acts as legal adviser to the Government and may attend Cabinet meetings.[4]

## Parliament

The sole power of making laws for the state is **vested** in the Irish Parliament. The Parliament of Ireland is comprised of two houses: the *Dáil* and the *Seanad* (pronounced "SHAN-uth") or the Senate. Government policy and administration may be examined and criticized in both Houses; but under the Constitution the Government is responsible to the *Dáil* alone.

In the passage of legislation the **primacy** of the *Dáil* is clearly shown in relation to legislation regarding money (allocation and spending).[5] On this central issue, the

---

discretion *n.*
自由裁量权
retain *v.*
保持，持有
nomination *n.*
提名
chieftain *n.*
酋长，首领
coalition *n.*
联合（政府），联盟
Minister of State
国务部长
vest *v.*
授予，归属
primacy *n.* 首位

# The Republic of Ireland

Senate is empowered only to make recommendations (not amendments). In fact, the primary function of both Houses is to operate as forums for public discussion, with the *Dáil* clearly the more visible and powerful. But in actuality, the power of the Parliament is secondary to that of the Government cabinet and to the work of the various *Dáil* committees.[6]

At present the Irish Parliament has 158 members called *Teachtai Dála* ("Deputies to the *Dáil*" or TDs; pronounced "TOCH-ta DAW-la"). TDs have two jobs. First of all, they must represent the region which elected them, making themselves available there to hear personal comments and requests from their **constituents**. Secondly, they must serve in the national *Dáil* to pass laws, particularly those dealing with funding.

The *Seanad* or Senate was designed by the Constitution as a second House of Parliament. There specific issues are considered and debated in conjunction with the *Dáil*. Although its **efficacy** is under question today, the *Seanad* was originally conceived as a second house which could serve to balance and check the powers of the *Dáil*.[7]

At present the *Seanad* has 60 members. Unlike TDs Senators are not directly elected. Eleven members are nominated directly by the Prime Minister. Forty-three members are elected from five **panels** of candidates under different headings. Each panel consists of persons with knowledge and practical experience of the interests represented by the panel (such as that in agriculture, for instance). The remaining six members are elected by two universities — three by the National University of Ireland and three by the University of Dublin (Trinity College, Dublin)

### Voting in Elections and Referenda

As a democracy, Ireland entrusts a great deal of power in the ordinary people to decide on their own government through the election of representatives of their choice. Popular voting is also crucial in deciding important changes to Ireland's written Constitution. The general public may vote in five separate decision-making procedures:

1. the election of the President (every seven years);
2. *Dáil* (or parliamentary) elections (at least every five years);
3. **referenda** on proposed Constitutional **amendments** (as they are called);
4. the election of representatives to the European Parliament (every five years);
5. elections to local authorities (usually every five years).

---

constituent *n.*
选民
efficacy *n.*
功效，效力
panel *n.*
小组，委员会
referendum（复数为 referenda）
*n.* 全民公决，公投
amendment *n.*
修正案

The electoral system used in Ireland is called "**proportional representation**". As opposed to the "first-past-the-post" or "winner-take-all" system in the UK or the USA, proportional representation is a **calibrated system** of voting which is very sensitive to electoral preferences.[8] It is therefore of great value in a small country with a history of political divisions in which the voters may have a large **spectrum** of different political **persuasions**.[9]

In practical terms, the system of proportional representation has had several notable outcomes. First of all, it means that even a small political party may still have a **credible** level of representation at government level. Secondly, it may also mean that small parties **have access to** power beyond their actual numbers. Increasingly, the larger parties can only stay in power by building coalitions with one or two smaller parties.

## The Civil Service

The **civil service** is divided into sixteen Government Departments, each headed by a Minister appointed by the *Taoiseach*. Ministers have final responsibility for these areas. Recruitment to the civil service is by public competitive exams administered by the independent Civil Service Commission and is open to every citizen of the Republic. It is generally regarded as steady, life-long employment with a secure **pension** after **mandatory** retirement at age 65.

## The Irish Legal System

Essentially, the Irish Constitution (composed in 1937, later somewhat revised) sets forth the principles by which Irish law is made. The *Dáil* **frames** specific laws in accordance with these principles. And, finally, these laws are interpreted through the courts as the occasion arises.

Justice is **administered** in courts of law administered by a judge. What happens in an Irish court is usually public and open to being reported in the media.

The way the system works is as follows. When a person is **wronged**, he **files** a formal complaint through a lawyer. A person with a **grievance** would first consult a **solicitor** and ask him to prepare a **case** to bring to court. If the case does go to court, that person or client will be represented there by a **barrister**. Some lower courts have only a judge while others have both judge and **jury**.

---

proportional representation 比例代表（代议）制
calibrated system 标准制度
spectrum *n.* 频谱，范围
persuasion *n.* 信念，派别
credible *adj.* 可靠的，可信的
have access to 可以获得或使用
civil service 行政部门，公务员系统
pension *n.* 退休金，养老金
mandatory *adj.* 强制的
frame *v.* 规定，制定
administer *v.* 管理，执行
wrong *v.* 冤枉
file *v.* 提起（诉讼）
grievance *n.* 冤情，委屈
solicitor *n.* （文案）律师
case *n.* 官司，案件
barrister *n.* （出庭）律师
jury *n.* 陪审团

# The Republic of Ireland

Judges are appointed by the President on the advice of the Government. They are guaranteed independence in every exercise of their functions — that is, by law, they cannot be influenced in their work by political or personal pressures.[10]

A jury is composed of 12 ordinary citizens, chosen to hear the arguments in the case. In criminal trials, it will be up to the jury to decide, in private, whether **the accused** is guilty or innocent. According to the jury's judgment, the judge will then release the accused or sentence him according to the seriousness of the crime. In Ireland a judge has considerable discretion as to what the punishment will be. But Ireland has abolished the death sentence.

The legal courts in Ireland are arranged in a hierarchy, in such a way that the judgment of one may be **appealed** to a higher court.[11] Sometimes a case will work its way up the entire hierarchy of courts. At the bottom of this ladder is **the District Court**. The District Court is presided over by a judge sitting without a jury. It tries minor criminal and civil offenses.

The next **rung** is represented by **the Circuit Court**, which tries more serious cases. The Circuit Court can try all criminal cases except murder, **treason**, **piracy** and allied offenses. It also acts as an appeal court from the District Court. In criminal cases the Circuit Court is constituted by a judge and a jury.

If the accused is not satisfied that justice has been done at a lower court or if there has been a flaw in procedures, he may appeal to **the High Court**. The High Court has full **jurisdiction** and determining power in all matters of law or fact, civil or criminal. It can decide the **validity** of any law, having regard to the provisions of the Constitution.

Further review of the judgments of any or all of the lower courts may be carried out by **the Court of Criminal Appeal**: a court consisting of three judges drawn from the High Court and **the Supreme Court**.

The court of final appeal is, however, the Supreme Court. It consists of the **Chief Justice**, four other judges and, **in an ex-officio capacity**, the President of the High Court. The Court hears appeals from the High Court and the Court of Criminal Appeal. Whatever the Supreme Court's decision, it will not be subject to any further appeals.

## The Economy

Ireland is a small, open, trade-dependent economy. That it is small is self-evident. That it must be open follows from its size and Ireland's geographical position as an

---

the accused
被告
appeal *v.* 上诉
the District Court
地方法院，初级法院
rung *n.*
梯级，层次
the Circuit Court
巡回法院
treason *n.*
叛国（罪）
piracy *n.*
剽窃，盗版
the High Court
高等法院
jurisdiction *n.*
司法权，管辖权
validity *n.*
有效性
the Court of Criminal Appeal
刑事上诉法院
the Supreme Court
最高法院
Chief Justice
首席法官，审判长
in an ex-officio capacity
依据职位的权限（高低）

island on the western edge of Europe.[12] Its openness is reflected in the international mobility of its labour and capital. In recent decades, the Irish economy has been transformed from combining agriculture with a traditional manufacturing base into an economy increasingly based on internationally traded services as well as on high-tech medical and **pharmaceutical** industries.[13] In 2011 estimates, the services sector accounted for 78% of employment, industry for 19%, and agriculture for only 5%. Thus, by a large margin, services continue to account for the most significant percentage of Ireland's present trade.

From its founding in 1922 until the 1970s, Ireland as an economy tended to be inward-looking, and concentrated on goals now seen to be futile, such as becoming economically self-sufficient. By the end of the 1950s, this goal of self-sufficiency had distorted the economy through a series of measures designed to protect Irish products from cheaper imports. Predictably, the result of this protectionism was high prices at home and a virtual **stagnation** of trade.

From approximately 1995 to 2005, unprecedented economic growth almost doubled the level of Irish real GNP. What changed this stagnant economy into one of the fastest-growing in Europe? There are many answers — and they all have to do with radical change and growth. First of all, there was a **population boom**, so that the number of young people increased dramatically. Secondly, the reform of education meant that these young people were better educated and more aware of their **options** in life and better able to take them up. During this period, instead of emigrating, Irish people were returning to Ireland to take up employment. As a result of a radical change of attitudes (and EU legislation enforcing equal rights) more women were also entering the workforce.

Finally, the government had a **conversion** to market economics, instituted under the **aegis** of a visionary economist, Ken Whitaker. Its subsequent institution of a low corporation tax rate for trading profits (of 12.5%) has led to a significant **multinational** presence, especially for those in the technology sector. Ireland is now a European base for Amazon, Apple, Dell, Facebook, Google, Microsoft and Yahoo, among others. What made it possible for Ireland to sell itself as a gateway to the European market? The answer is its accession into the European Union in 1973. While transforming labour practice, this momentous event gave Ireland, at one move, immediate access to the Single Market: an extended trade area with relatively free movement of capital and of

pharmaceutical *adj.* 制药的
stagnation *n.* 滞胀，停滞
population boom 人口激增，人口繁荣
option *n.* 选项，选择权
conversion *n.* 转换，转化
aegis *n.* 庇护，支持
multinational *adj.* 跨国的；涉及多国的

services.[14]

## The European Union: Economic Policies

Over the last forty years, strenuous efforts have been made by the Irish government to transform Ireland from a traditional agricultural economy into a post-industrial economy. Unlike Great Britain, Ireland never had an industrial revolution. So its economic transformation had to be achieved politically, rather than by the more ruthless practices of **untrammeled** capitalism.[15] The new government programmes for economic expansion, initiated in the late 1950s, moved Ireland away from its insular and protective economic policies into a new era of industrialisation and urbanisation.

As a result of an elaboration of these policies, by the 1990s Ireland became a rich country for the first time in its history. Mimicking the boom in Asia, the media called Ireland's sudden success "the Celtic Tiger" economy.[16] Indeed, Ireland became wealthy with all the swiftness and **ferocity** of that beast. From about 60% of the European average, Irish incomes went to 110%. House prices in Dublin **quadrupled**. Many people went out and bought expensive cars and vacation houses **availing** themselves of historically low interest-rate loans mandated by EU policy. On the other hand, not all the Irish people benefited from the economic boom. The inequalities of Irish society also increased dramatically.

Where did this sudden wealth come from? It came from Ireland's entry into the Common Market (now known as the European Union) as of 1973. In fact, much of the actual money initially came from the European Union itself in the form of structural funds — used to improve the infrastructure and to aid education and training. Other large grants were for implementing the Common Agricultural Policy (CAP), used for assisting traditional farmers to make the transition to more market-oriented methods of agriculture. During its early years of membership, Ireland benefited disproportionately from EU funding, as it was deemed on its accession to be among the most impoverished regions of the EU.

Apart from the massive **infusion** of structural funds, the EU's most important benefit for Ireland has been in granting it access to Europe. With its accession to the EU, all of Ireland's citizens now hold EU citizenship and travel on EU passports. They are now entitled to work, to be educated in, and to claim the social benefits of any other European member state. With this access, Ireland's dependence on its traditional

---

untrammeled *adj.* 自由放任的
ferocity *n.* 凶猛
quadruple *v.* 翻两番
availing *adj.* 有益于
infusion *n.* 灌输，输入

trading partner, Great Britain, has been dramatically **modified**.¹⁷ Moreover, the EU forced the removal of many of the barriers which had previously restricted trade as well as protecting Ireland's surplus labour.

When "the Celtic Tiger" died in late 2008, Ireland's membership of the EU proved crucial in keeping it from **going under**. Although there were fears that the grave economic crisis involving Greece's **credit rating** would spread, on the whole EU policy has guaranteed stability for the Euro currency used in Ireland.¹⁸ During the economic crisis of 2010 and onwards, the EU also provided actual monetary **back-up** as well as policy advice. But as these policies involved severe **austerity** measures for Ireland, it was resented. The result for the general population has been a significant cut in income, social welfare benefits and services, and a funding crisis for healthcare and **third-level education**.

While it is not unusual in the West for an economic boom to be followed by an economic **bust**, in Ireland's case, the bust of 2008 was particularly dramatic. There are several reasons for this. First of all, as a small, open economy, Ireland is more vulnerable than most countries to economic **downturns** elsewhere. Secondly, Ireland's government was **complicit** in a large property "bubble", that is, an unsustainable growth in goods which were not worth as much as was paid for them.¹⁹

What is a property bubble? Over the centuries, the majority of Irish people lived as **tenants** on other people's property. To own one's own place was therefore a long-held ambition over many centuries. Thus, when Ireland became richer, many people borrowed to buy their own house — and sometimes a holiday home or an apartment to rent out as well. Banks in Ireland were only too willing to loan them the money at very low or even no interest at all, and the government simply did not exercise sufficient regulation over these transactions because real estate "**stamp duty**" added much to its income.²⁰ The result was what is known as "**over-heating**" of the property market. So that when the crisis came, too many people owed too much money on property they could sell only at a loss or perhaps not at all. Not only could these people not repay their loans, the banks themselves (given the general economic downturn) could not sustain the sheer volume of their loans.

The result has been a full-blown economic crisis, affecting not only Ireland but many other European countries: Greece, Spain, Portugal, and Italy, in particular. One result of Ireland's sudden economic downturn has been that the future for the

modify *v.*
调整；弱化
going under
沉没，破产
credit rating
信用评级
back-up *n.*
支援，后援
austerity *n.*
紧缩
third-level education
高等教育
bust *n.*
破产，萧条
downturn *n.*
经济衰退
complicit *adj.*
串通一气的
tenant *n.*
承租人，佃户
stamp duty
印花税
over-heating *n.*
（经济）过热

# The Republic of Ireland

upcoming generation of Ireland's young people appears very uncertain. Unlike previous generations, a far greater **proportion** of Irish people now have a third-level education. Yet, since 2008, almost every family has seen one or more of its grown children emigrate — and not only to Europe but to Australia, the United States, Canada, and even Asia.

Now that the economic tide is starting to turn once again (unemployment which once stood at 13.5% is now at 7.5%: down to the levels of the time of the crash in 2008), young people are beginning to trickle back to Ireland to take up employment here.[21] But often these jobs are not the same kind of jobs they left. The government, for instance, has lowered **pay scales** for newly employed public servants such as teachers, nurses, and the police.

In other words, the recent recovery of the Irish economy is still a large gamble. The Irish economy today remains dominated by many multinationals, particularly in the technological and financial services as well as the electronic and pharmaceutical industries. However, this kind of industry is already proving a **mixed blessing**. Multinationals do provide jobs, which are important if Ireland is to keep its young people in Ireland and to prevent more mass emigrations. But the large multinationals have, in the end, no loyalty except to their own **cash flows**. They may provide jobs, but their substantial profits are normally **repatriated** to their home countries. Once they have reaped the immediate benefits of the **tax concessions**, or once the price of labour in Ireland exceeds that of another country (such as those in Eastern Europe or India), these **multinationals** have little difficulty in simply deciding to pack up and to **relocate** elsewhere.

Other large uncertainties concern the European Union itself. Having survived a financial and banking crisis since 2008, the EU now faces its biggest crisis in the Great Britain's referendum vote in June 2016 to exit the EU (known as "Brexit"). What the outcomes for the EU or for Ireland are hard to predict but are widely seen as negative. Yet, given all these uncertainties, what is clear is that the Irish are a very **resilient** and creative people, used to hardship and determined to make a success of their relatively new independence. Known as the poor man of north-west Europe for most of the 20th century, Ireland, residing on the **periphery** of Europe, long faced issues of **isolationism**, and policy mistakes which **mired** the country in relative poverty and stagnation.[22] Then everything changed as, in the 1990s, the Irish economy exploded into life.

proportion *n.*
部分，比例
pay scale
工资标准
mixed blessing
好坏参半之事
cash flows
现金流量
repatriate *v.*
遣返，返还
tax concession
税收减让
multinational *n.*
跨国公司
relocate *v.*
迁移新址
resilient *adj.*
有弹性的，有复原能力的
periphery *n.*
边缘
isolationism *n.*
孤立主义
mire *v.*
（使）陷入困境

After a decades-long stagnation, employment almost doubled in just a dozen years, encouraging more workers to immigrate. In terms of income per person, as **gauged** by GDP measures, Ireland finally caught up with its European peers by the year 2000.

Furthermore, the centrality of European market access to Irish prosperity is reflected in public and elite opinion.[23] There are very few voices challenging the overwhelming **consensus** that EU membership has been good for Ireland. The latest EU-wide **Eurobarometer opinion poll** showed that the Irish had the third most positive view of the union among its 28 members. Only 14% viewed the EU negatively. In a world in which electorates are angry and often willing to blame first and ask questions later, this **turnaround** is remarkable. It is due not merely to the EU's economic workings but also to its distinctive social policies.

### The European Union: Social Policies

Over the last forty years, Ireland's membership in the European Union has brought about social changes which can only be described as revolutionary. If one were to identify one of the most obvious markers of the way that EU membership has changed Ireland, it would be in the status of women. In Irish law, up to 1973 Irish women were forbidden to take up state or semi-state jobs after marriage, largely in order to preserve professional jobs for men. Legally, women during this period were of the status of "**chattel**" — that is, they (and their children, if any) belonged to their husbands as if they were a kind of property.

All of this changed with accession to the EU when the women of Ireland were granted legal status as persons in their own right. No one could advertise any longer for jobs along with the phrase "Men only need apply." In 1974 the "**marriage bar**" (as it was called) was removed from state and semi-state jobs. **Paid maternity leave** of 20 weeks (and later, parental leave, which is unpaid, up to 14 weeks) eventually became a matter of legal right. It was no longer possible to dismiss a woman from her job because she was pregnant or refuse to take her back to her current position once she had had a child. Equality legislation guaranteed that women also had (at least in theory) equal access to jobs, as well as equal opportunities for **subsequent** promotions and pay awards.

It would be unfair to the Irish people or to their government to imply that all these changes came about as the result merely of Ireland's joining the EU. What happened

---

gauge *v.*
测量，估计
consensus *n.*
一致，共识
Eurobarometer
欧洲晴雨表（一个民意测验机构）
opinion poll
民意测验
turnaround *n.*
变化，转变
chattel *n.*
动产，奴隶
marriage bar
妇女婚后不得工作的障碍
paid maternity leave
带薪产假
subsequent *adj.*
随后的

# The Republic of Ireland

was that a vigorous women's liberation movement, originating in the early 1970s, brought pressure to bear on public opinion, and thus on the Irish government, to change the status of women.[24] When these women encountered resistance on the home front, they found that **appealing to** the more liberal legislation of the EU placed the Irish government in a position in which they either had to reform legislation by its own **legal mechanisms** or be subject to the more lengthy procedures involving a legal appeal to the EU.[25] More often than not, under such conditions the Irish government would **frame** home-grown legislation in an effort to be responsive to prevailing political conditions.

Sometimes the attempt at compromise between traditional Irish attitudes and the more liberal ones of the EU resulted in legislation that was odd, if not downright bizarre: a situation that gave rise to the saying that such compromise was "An Irish solution to an Irish problem."[26] This is still the case, for instance, in Irish legislation which virtually bans **abortion** in the country (even for cases of rape and fatal **foetal abnormality**) except for those in which the mother's life is clearly **at stake**. Hence some 3,500 Irish women now travel abroad (usually to the UK) for this procedure. Finally this has become a live issue for the Irish people, who are demanding a formal parliamentary debate followed by amending legislation.

The other striking change brought about by Ireland's accession to the EU has been a change of attitude towards the environment. Before 1973, widespread and illegal **dumping** was common in the Irish countryside. Sea-coasts and rivers and lakes were becoming polluted, both through industrial pollution and the chemicals used by farmers to increase production. Now, thanks to the **enlightened** policies of the EU, such dumping has been virtually halted. Industrial pollution and agricultural chemicals are more regulated, although they still remain a significant problem. Recycling is now standard practice for most Irish households. And conscious concern for the environment is growing, along with demands for more ecologically produced, or "organic", foods.

But in terms of everyday experience, the most obvious outcome of the accession to the EU today is a change in Ireland's labour market. Now all Irish citizens are **entitled to** an EU passport, which allows them to work legally in any member country. In turn, any other citizen of an EU country may work legally in Ireland. Thus, in common with the rest of Europe, Ireland is benefitting from these labour exchanges, in particular from the

appeal to
呼吁，诉诸
legal mechanisms
法律机制
frame  v.
设计，制定
abortion  n.
堕胎
foetal abnormality
胎儿畸形
be at stake
处于险境
dumping  n.
倾倒（垃圾等）
enlightened  adj.
开明的，进步的
be entitled to
有…的资格，有权享有

countries of Eastern Europe. But especially during the economic boom years **preceding** the crash of 2008, Ireland also suffered a significant **influx** of illegal immigrants, particularly from troubled Middle Eastern and African countries.

Predictably, such a sudden opening up of Ireland to foreign nationals has meant a dramatic shift of attitudes. Previously an almost oppressively **homogeneous** population (ten or twenty years ago it would have been rare to see anyone other than **Caucasians** on the street), the Irish people have been slow to welcome what is now a steady influx of people who are visibly foreign. When one considers that Ireland now is a host to legal immigrants from 188 countries, speaking as many languages, one can understand the shock to this generation of Irish people. This has led to a subdued **backlash** against foreigners in general, but nothing so stridently expressed as the current hostility in the UK.

Thus, in general, despite general public approval, the Irish regard the actual outcomes of European Union membership as something of a mixed blessing. For a new nation, such as Ireland, there are always issues relating to those of shared sovereignty — issues which surfaced loudly during the period in which the EU imposed harsh austerity measures to stabilize the sinking Irish economy. For these, among other reasons, the EU often proves controversial in its official policies. But regarding its liberal policy initiatives in many areas, particularly in labour law and women's rights as well as protection of the environment, most Irish people welcome Ireland's accession to the EU as a watershed in its history.[27]

### Ireland Today

Those born in the Republic of Ireland sixty years ago barely recognise the Ireland of today. In the first decade of the twenty-first century, Ireland has experienced radical changes financially, socially, and morally. Once a society based largely on land-ownership and rural values, the young Irish person of today is **in flight from** the land and the traditional culture tied to it. Rather than leaving school at fifteen, he or she will now likely be university-educated and headed for a professional or semi-professional career. Since 2008, the high rate of unemployment led many young people to seek work outside Ireland. But, rather than searching for employment only in the United States or Great Britain, they now look towards the new member states of the European Union and even further afield (in places such as China) for job opportunities. Thus,

---

preceding *adj.* 在…之前的
influx *n.* 涌入
homogeneous *adj.* 同类的，同质的
Caucasian *n.* 白种人
backlash *n.* 抵制，反对
in flight from 逃离

# The Republic of Ireland

while many Irish families are now learning through their sons and daughters about life in **far-flung** places, these same grown children are more likely to think of their future more in global rather than local terms.

And, in fact, even if they remain at home in Ireland, the Irish are now far more likely than a generation ago to meet many more non-Irish people at university or at work. EU policies mean that many more people from other European countries live and work in Ireland; particularly during the boom years before 2008 immigration into Ireland was widespread, especially from such countries as Poland. Now, with the current migrant crisis (accelerated by wars in the Middle East), increased pressure to open its citizenship to economic **refugees** from Eastern Europe as well as from other non-EU countries means that Ireland is swiftly becoming a more multinational culture.[28] In their turn, universities have fostered this new **ethos** by actively seeking to recruit talented students, particularly from China, to fill out the places left after the decline of the Irish population from the mid-1980s onwards.

Most Irish people now have at some time in their lives also lived and/or worked abroad. But they prefer to live in Ireland and will now often return to raise their families there if possible. On return, however, they would seek to live in a city or a large town rather than on an isolated farm or rural village.

Because of a lack of houses, most young people often have to go back to living with their parents or find a place to live in far-flung suburbs. Because property ownership was historically a mark of status, the Irish are very determined to own their own houses — and, in fact, Ireland has historically one of the highest rates of **home-ownership** in Europe (more than 80%). However, many young married couples found themselves in financial trouble because they bought a house during the boom that is now worth less than they paid for it. Today, the stress of meeting the **mortgage** to finance that house is causing serious pressure, especially during a time when more people are in low-paid jobs.

Even if one has a job, commuting into the city centre has become something of a nightmare, with gridlocked traffic now costing the economy an estimated billion Euro **per annum**. Public transport is still relatively poorly financed, and perhaps as a result of their history of being poor, the Irish love their cars. The traditional **layout** of many Irish towns, essentially medieval in character, is being destroyed to accommodate wider roads and more car parks. And the Irish do not consider seriously the costs of the

---

far-flung *adj.*
遥远的
refugee *n.*
难民
ethos *n.* 精神
home-ownership *n.*
自有住房权
mortgage *n.*
按揭（贷款）
per annum
每年，年度
layout *n.*
布局

car in terms of public health — such as the risks of increased air pollution or lack of physical exercise — that accompany intensive car use.[29]

In sum, over the last two decades, Ireland's living standards have first increased dramatically and then taken a sudden and shocking downturn before starting on a modest recovery. During the economic boom, the new wealth had not been shared equally; the wealthy had become almost indecently rich. The poor survived but, because of the high visibility of the new wealth, became more aware of their **deprivation**. During the prosperous times, the Irish government did little to tackle these inequalities or see their danger for the **coherence** of a society that now **resembles** more closely that of North America than, say, of Denmark.[30]

Ireland's boom years have led to other costs. In the last few years, **tribunals** have been set up by the Irish government to examine a wide variety of corruption, some of it involving trusted figures in leading institutions: bankers, accountants, business executives, as well as corrupt politicians.[31] While in the 1980s the ordinary citizen was **exhorted** to be financially prudent, and was subject to high levels of personal tax, some in the higher **echelons** of society were practicing tax avoidance and evasion on a grand scale. The exposure of these practices has shocked the ordinary Irish citizens and made them (in common with the rest of the Western world) increasingly cynical about politicians in particular. It might say something about Ireland as a society that few of those exposed for corruption have been sent to jail: the shame of their exposure has been itself considered sufficient punishment.[32]

What is really striking in Ireland, however, has been the government's lack of initiative during the boom years to finance adequate public programmes to tackle these emerging problems. In terms of social welfare, the rising housing prices have led to a rapid increase in homelessness, which has now reached crisis levels in some cities such as Dublin. Despite this, there are not sufficient hostels for the homeless. In 2008, at the end of the biggest economic boom in its history, Ireland still had not funded adequate drug or drink **rehabilitation** programmes. The facilities for the disabled and mentally handicapped are a disgrace to a once-wealthy and still moderately well-off country. Rather than dealing with these problems according to best European practice, there is a perception that Ireland is trying to cope with the social problems of rapid urbanisation more by producing repressive legislation rather than by setting up programmes for housing or for those with special needs or acute problems.[33]

---

deprivation *n.*
贫困
coherence *n.*
连贯；统一
resembles *v.*
看起来像
tribunals *n.*
特别法庭
exhort *v.*
告诫
echelon *n.*
阶层
rehabilitation *n.*
康复，戒除（酒瘾等）

# The Republic of Ireland

As a result, at a time when Ireland is just recovering from the shock of severe economic downturn, the Irish public have mixed feelings about their government. Although they know that, as a small, open economy, Ireland is particularly vulnerable to forces outside it, they consider that the government (historically ruled by the Fianna Fáil party: the same one which presided over the economic downturn) is largely responsible. In part, the Irish public sees, for example, **slack** regulation of the banks. In Ireland, often links at the top of society are controlled by *guanxi* connections. In Ireland's case, people are not pleased to see that members of this "golden circle" — both in financial and construction services — are being rescued by those in power, while the ordinary citizen is left to pick up the bill.[34] Ireland still owes vast amounts of money, borrowed to **stay afloat** during the crisis years. Everyone, through taxes, will be called upon to manage this debt.

Today, the political parties that once enjoyed a popular majority (Fianna Fáil and Fine Gael) have had to share their government seats with a **ragtag** collection of independents who have few common policies but considerable popular support. And now that the economic recovery seems to be official, there have been numerous, successive threats from public service unions to strike for a **restoration** of the wages **docked** during the recession.

What seems still to be missing in this debate is a general sense of civic responsibility. While the Irish now think of their future as bound up with that of Europe as well as that of Great Britain and the United States, they are still reluctant to acknowledge that it is also bound up with the most deprived of their own society. Often the newly wealthy seem blind to the abuses and deprivation on their own doorstep. Government cannot do everything. But until these new inequalities are addressed, the ideals of equality and **fraternity** which for generations drove the Irish people to seek their own Republic, will remain empty words for many of Ireland's people.

**slack** *adj.*
松弛的，疏忽的
**stay afloat**
坚持，维持
**ragtag** *adj.*
松散的，杂乱的
**restoration** *n.*
恢复
**dock** *v.*
扣除（部分工资）
**fraternity** *n.*
友爱，博爱

# Explanations

1. **In common with ... by the Irish people:**
   和大多数西欧国家一样，爱尔兰是个代议制民主国家，也就是说，政府部门的大多数官员都是爱尔兰人民通过直接或间接选举产生的。

2. **The system of government ... through courts which interpret the laws:**
   爱尔兰的政体是依据美国的"三权分立"原则建立起来的，也就是说政府的行政权力受到立法部门以及司法部门各级法院释法权的制约。

3. **This allows the President to ... retain the support of a majority in the *Dáil*:**
   这种自由裁量权允许总统在首相失去议会多数议员支持时依照首相的建议可以拒绝解散议会（重新举行大选）。

4. **Although not a member of the Government ... Cabinet meetings:**
   虽然司法部长不是政府的阁员，但他却是政府的法律顾问并且可以出席内阁会议。Attorney General: 司法部长，是政府的主要法律顾问，并负责全国的司法、检察等方面的工作。

5. **In the passage of legislation the primacy of the *Dáil* ... (allocation and spending):**
   在通过法案方面，下议院的首要地位在涉及预算案（财政拨款及开支）时表露无遗。

6. **But in actuality, the power of the Parliament is really secondary ... *Dáil* committees:**
   但实际上，议会的权力在政府内阁和各种议会委员会之下。

7. **Although its efficacy is under question today, ... balance and check the powers of the *Dáil*:**
   尽管其效率在当今遭到质疑，建立参议院（第二院）的最初设想是为了平衡和制约下院的权力。

8. **As opposed to the "first-past-the-post" ... very sensitive to electoral preferences:**
   与英国或美国实行的"简单多数制"或"赢者通吃"的选举制度不同，比例代表制度是一种对选民喜好极为敏感的标准选举制度。

9. **It is therefore of great value in a small country ... different political persuasions:**
   所以，比例代表制度在一个历史上存在政治纷争、选民可能具有广泛而不同政治信仰的小国具有极大价值。

10. **They are guaranteed independence ... by political or personal pressures:**
    法官们被赋予每次行使其权力时的独立性，也就是说，依据法律规定，法官们的审理工作不受政治或人情压力的影响。

11. **The legal courts in Ireland are arranged in a hierarchy ... appealed to a higher court:**
    爱尔兰的法院系统实行层级制，这样任何一级法院的判决均可向更高一级法院上诉。

12. **That it must be open ... on the western edge of Europe:**
    爱尔兰必须实行开放的政策，这是由其国土面积和位于欧洲西部边缘的地理位置所决定的。

13. **In recent decades ... as well as on high-tech medical and pharmaceutical industries:**
    在近几十年时间里，爱尔兰的经济已经实现了从农业与传统制造业基地向日益倚重国际服务贸易以及高科技和制药业的转变。

14. **While transforming labour practice ... free movement of capital and of services:**
    在改变劳工法的同时，这一重大事件（指加入欧盟）使爱尔兰一举进入欧盟统一市场——一个具有资本

# The Republic of Ireland

和服务相对自由流动的广泛的贸易区。

15. **So its economic transformation had to be achieved politically ... untrammeled capitalism:**
    所以，它的经济变革必须通过政治途径，而不是通过无情的（并且是破坏性的）自由资本主义法则。

16. **Mimicking the boom in Asia ... "the Celtic Tiger" economy:**
    效仿亚洲（四小龙）的经济繁荣，媒体将爱尔兰在经济上取得的快速成功称作"凯尔特之虎"。

17. **With this access, Ireland's dependence ... severely modified:**
    由于加入了欧盟，爱尔兰对其传统贸易伙伴英国的依赖大大减弱了。

18. **Although there were fears ... for the Euro currency used in Ireland:**
    尽管人们担心希腊的经济危机和信用评级（降低）会扩散（到爱尔兰），总体来说欧盟的政策确保了爱尔兰使用的欧元货币的稳定性。

19. **Ireland's government was complicit ... which were not worth as much as was paid for them:**
    爱尔兰政府对房地产"泡沫"起了推波助澜的作用，泡沫的产生是由于商品（住房）价格的不可持续的增长远远超过了它们的实际价值。

20. **Banks in Ireland were only too willing to ... added much to its income:**
    爱尔兰的银行很乐意给购房人提供低息甚至无息贷款，而政府则根本没有对这些贷款交易进行充分的监管，因为房地产"印花税"给政府带来了丰厚的财政收入。

21. **Now that the economic tide ... take up employment here:**
    由于经济形势又开始好转（曾经高达13.5%的失业率现在已下降到2008年金融危机发生前的7.5%水平），年轻人又开始逐渐回到爱尔兰工作。

22. **Known as the poor man of north-west Europe ... in relative poverty and stagnation:**
    在20世纪的大部分时间里，位于欧洲边缘的爱尔兰向来以西北欧的穷国著称，长期面临孤立主义以及使国家陷入相对贫困和停滞的决策失误等问题。

23. **the centrality of European market access ... in public and elite opinion:**
    获准进入欧洲市场对于爱尔兰繁荣的关键作用反映在公众和精英的意见和主张上。

24. **What happened was ... to change the status of women:**
    事实上，起始于20世纪70年代初期的蓬勃的妇女解放运动极大地影响了公众以及爱尔兰政府的态度，从而改变了妇女地位。

25. **When these women encountered resistance ... involving a legal appeal to the EU:**
    当这些妇女在国内遇到阻力时，她们发现向具有更大限度自由法律的欧盟上诉会把爱尔兰政府置于不得不对自身法律制度进行改革的情形下，否则爱尔兰政府将不得不应对更加漫长的欧盟法律上诉程序。

26. **Sometimes the attempt at compromise ... "An Irish solution to an Irish problem.":**
    有时，传统爱尔兰态度与欧盟更加自由的态度之间的妥协努力会产生奇怪甚至荒唐的立法：由此产生了人们对这种妥协的称呼——"爱尔兰问题的爱尔兰式解决方案"。

27. **But regarding its liberal policy initiatives in many areas ... as a watershed in its history:**
    但是涉及欧盟在许多领域进步的政策举措，尤其在劳工法、妇女权益以及环境保护领域方面，大多数爱尔兰人则欢迎爱尔兰加入欧盟并将此举视作爱尔兰历史上的一个转折点（分水岭）。

28. **Now, with the current migrant crisis ... a more multinational culture:**
    现今的移民流动危机（中东的战争使之更加恶化）以及向东欧和非欧盟国家经济移民开放公民资格的压力意味着爱尔兰正快速变成一个更具多元文化的国家。

29. **And the Irish do not consider seriously the costs ... that accompany intensive car use:**
    爱尔兰人没有认真考虑伴随汽车的大规模使用给公众健康带来的沉重代价——例如恶化的空气污染和缺乏体育锻炼的风险。

30. **During the prosperous times ... that of North America than, say, of Denmark:**
    在经济繁荣期，爱尔兰政府几乎没有采取措施来解决这些不平等的问题，也没有预见到原本和谐统一的爱尔兰社会现今变得更像北美（贫富差距较大）而不是丹麦（贫富差距较小）。

31. **In the last few years ... as well as corrupt politicians:**
    过去几年，爱尔兰政府成立了专门的法庭来审查各种各样的腐败，其中有的腐败涉及重要机构受到公众信赖的人物：银行家、会计师、公司高管以及腐败政客。

32. **It might say something about Ireland as a society that ... sufficient punishment:**
    那些被曝光的腐败分子很少被判刑入狱：曝光给他们造成的羞耻感本身被认为已经是足够的惩罚了。这或许能够说明爱尔兰是一个什么样的社会了。

33. **Rather than dealing with these problems ... those with special needs or acute problems:**
    人们有一种感觉，爱尔兰政府没有根据欧洲的最高标准处理这些问题，而是试图通过建立压制性的法律来应对快速城市化所产生的社会问题，没能为那些有特殊需要或严重缺房的人们解决住房问题。

34. **In Ireland's case ... while the ordinary citizen is left to pick up the bill:**
    爱尔兰的情况是：人们很不愿意看到这个"黄金圈子"的成员（金融与建筑行业）被那些大权在握的人拯救，而他们所造成的问题却由普通老百姓来买单。

# Exercises

## I. Give the Chinese equivalents for the following:

1. representative democracy
2. checks and balances
3. civil service

## The Republic of Ireland

4. European Union
5. multinationals

II. **Decide whether the following statements are true (T) or false (F):**
1. Ireland is a representative democracy, which means most of its government offices are filled through election by the Irish people. _____
2. Ireland is a republic with a government headed by a Prime Minister, elected directly by the people. _____
3. In Ireland, the President is only a symbolic Head of State and does not have executive power. _____
4. The Irish Parliament is responsible for making laws. _____
5. The Senate, designed by the Constitution as a second House of Parliament, is directly elected by the Irish people. _____
6. All lower courts have both a judge and a jury to try a case. _____
7. In the Irish economy, the manufacturing industry is the most important sector. _____
8. Ireland's accession to the European Union in the 1970s has helped to transform its economy and brought an economic boom. _____

III. **Fill in the blanks:**
1. The power of the executive branch of government can be checked by the _____ as well as by the judiciary, through courts which interpret the laws.
2. Every citizen of 35 years of age or over is eligible to run for _____.
3. The _____ is appointed by the President on the nomination of the Parliament.
4. The Irish legal system is arranged in a hierarchy with the District Court at the bottom and _____ at the top.
5. The electoral system used in Ireland is called "_____", a calibrated system of voting which is very sensitive to electoral preferences.
6. One of the main reasons for the present economic boom in Ireland is its accession to the _____.
7. Ireland has received massive _____ from the EU to improve its present infrastructure and aid its education and training.

8. Over the last forty years, strenuous efforts have been made by the Irish government to transform Ireland from a traditional agricultural economy into a _____ economy.
9. One of the most notable markers of the way the EU membership has changed Ireland is the status of _____ in the society.
10. Because of a lack of _____, most young people often have to go back to living with their parents or find a place to live in far-flung suburbs.

## IV. Questions:

1. What American principle is the system of the Irish government based on? Explain how this system works.
2. How is the President elected in Ireland? What is the function of the President?
3. What is the Cabinet composed of? What part does it play in the government?
4. What is the role of the Attorney General in the government?
5. What are the two houses that the Parliament is comprised of? Which house is more important? Why?
6. What are the five separate decision-making procedures that the general public may participate in through voting?
7. What are the benefits a civil servant can get by serving in the government?
8. Distinguish the functions of various courts in the judiciary hierarchy (District Courts, Circuit Court, High Court, Court of Criminal Appeal, and the Supreme Court).
9. What is the order of importance of agriculture, industry, and the services sector in the Irish economy?
10. What happened to the Irish economy during the period from 1995 to 2005? Why was Ireland called "the Celtic Tiger" during this period?
11. In what way did the Common Market help the Irish economy?
12. What was the property bubble like before the financial crisis in 2008? Why did it go bust?
13. Why does the author say that the multinationals in Ireland are a mixed blessing?
14. How has Ireland's accession to the EU changed the Irish people's attitude towards the environment?
15. Why did the Irish government lack initiative to finance adequate public programmes concerning urbanisation and poverty during the economic boom years?

# The Republic of Ireland

V. **Topics for discussion or research:**
1. What is the "first-past-the-post" or "winner-take-all" election system in the UK or the USA? What is the "proportional representation" election system in Ireland? Compare these two systems in terms of their respective advantages and disadvantages.
2. Discuss the economic and social changes, both positive and negative, brought by Ireland's accession to the European Union.
3. Compare Ireland's judicial system with China's in terms of court hierarchy, the role of the judge, lawyers (solicitor and barrister) and jury.

# UNIT 13

# Irish Culture: How the Irish Live Now

**Go over the following focal points before reading the text:**

- Rapid social change
- Irish attitudes to England and the English
- Irish identity
- Roman Catholic values
- The conflict between Catholics and Protestants
- Catholic and Protestant stereotypes
- An extended family
- The women's movement
- Pub culture
- Flexibility in work places
- Trade unions
- First-level, second-level, and third-level education
- Investment in education

# The Republic of Ireland

## Text

### What Culture Means

Culture may have many definitions; but the most useful is to use the term to identify the way people live: the patterns and normal expectations of their lives as passed within a certain place. After these patterns are understood, it is then easier to understand the role that "high culture" — such as art or music — plays within that particular tradition, as a cultivated expression of a particular people's perspective on the world. Accordingly, Unit 13 offers observations on how Irish people live, and Unit 14 will then turn to an examination of the kinds of artistic expression they value.

### How the Irish Live Now

The average young person in Ireland today would have grown up with rapid social change, as Ireland made a transition from a largely rural and traditional to a newly urban and modern **cosmopolitan** society. These changes register largely in terms of new and changed expectations

The son of a farmer, for instance, would come to understand that his generation is very different from any that have gone before. His father would probably have been the first son of a first son. Land in Ireland is inherited according to the law of "**primogeniture**", favouring the first-born male. His father's family may have lived on this farm for a hundred, two hundred years, maybe longer. For generations the members of his family have been born, raised, and died in this place, perhaps in this very same house. But this young man would have been urged by his father to get a university education — and never to come back to the family farm except to visit. Having seen his father struggle year in and year out to keep the farm going, the son would understand that his father wanted to be the last to farm the land in this way. In coming times, the farmland would go to a younger brother or to a sister, who would seek training in other work and run the farm as a second income, perhaps commuting into a nearby town to earn money.[1]

The daughter of a middle-class family in Dublin today might even be a little weary

*cosmopolitan adj.* 世界主义的, 国际化的
*primogeniture n.* 长子继承权

of her mother's tales of "how it used to be when I was growing up". Girls in the 1950s and 1960s and even the early 1970s were not urged to get a university education; so her mother would have left school at 17, having taken the **Leaving Certificate exams**, and then found a suitable job as a secretary, perhaps in a department of the civil service. There she met the man who was to be her husband. They dated for five years before they became engaged, and then postponed the marriage for another three years until they had saved enough for a house. Once they married, in the "bad old days" she was compelled under the state's "marriage bar" to leave her job working for the State.[2] As there was no legal access to **contraception** (and her mother, who was a devout Roman Catholic, would have **frowned on** such precautions in any case), she immediately became pregnant, and subsequently had five children in eight years.[3]

Her daughter considers that her mother belonged to the Stone Age. The daughter herself went to a leading university, and decided to enter what in the 1990s was still considered a man's field, chemical engineering. She has recently bought her own apartment, has a fancy car, and an enviable life-style. She survived the economic **downturn** with financial help from her parents and by living a more modest lifestyle (expensive holidays a thing of the past). Now that there is a modest economic recovery she worries that she might lose her job, which is with a large American multinational company, specializing in **biotechnology**. If that happens, she does not know how she would be able to pay the **mortgage** for her apartment.

The child whose life differs least from that of his parents is one born into Ireland's **underclass**, those of the **chronically** unemployed.[4] Jason's parents considered emigrating, but found England a hostile and difficult country for someone without education beyond the age of 15. His parents did not even do the Leaving Certificate — they just left school, considering that it had little to teach them. His father worked for the building trade, seeking casual labour but never learning a specific skill. As he is now no longer as young as he was, he regrets not signing up for an **apprenticeship** that would have qualified him as a **plasterer** or carpenter. He sees no way that the so-called economic "recovery" has helped him or his prospects. He still cannot find work and lives on the government's welfare benefit. This is very damaging to his **self-esteem**, which he tries to recover by meeting regularly with his mates for outings to football matches and to the pub.[5]

Rapid social change does not benefit everyone. For the first time in its history,

---

Leaving Certificate exam 中学毕业考试
contraception *n.* 避孕
frown on 皱眉，不同意
downturn *n.* （经济）衰退
biotechnology *n.* 生物技术
mortgage *n.* 抵押，分期贷款
underclass *n.* 下层阶级
chronically *adv.* 长期地
apprenticeship *n.* 学徒期
plasterer *n.* 泥水匠
self-esteem *n.* 自尊（心）

# The Republic of Ireland

Ireland is a wealthy country. This has changed everyone's expectations, while at the same time, with the recent recession, disappointing them. Now there is a modest economic recovery. For the first time, a majority of Irish people could **aspire** to attend university, find a good job, and lead a secure middle-class existence. With the UK decision to leave the EU ("Brexit") — involving Ireland's closest trading partner, Great Britain — all of these expectations are now at risk. What remains, out of what was once a society united in a kind of **genteel** poverty, are now glaring inequalities between rich and poor.[6]

Apart from the **dislocations** of a boom-and-bust economy, there are also the confusions that attend a young nation, which is in a sense, still seeking to define its identity.[7] Traditionally, the Irish people differentiated themselves from their colonial masters by several important cultural markers. While the English are largely Protestant, the Irish of the Republic largely belong to the Roman Catholic faith. While the English speak English, the first official language of the Irish Republic is the Irish language. Nonetheless Irish is spoken at home by only a small minority and those few who speak it routinely also speak English. While England is an industrialised country, Ireland is only now leaving behind its reliance on a traditional agricultural economy. While the English seem to have become even more **self-absorbed** in being English, the Irish have consciously become more European.[8]

### Attitudes toward the English

In common with many post-colonial nations, Ireland has contradictory and sometimes even downright **paradoxical** attitudes to their former masters, the English.

On the one hand, the English political domination of Ireland has left the Republic with a secure and workable administrative, educational, and judicial system. It has also ensured that most Irish people now speak English, although that is a **sore point** among those nationalists who believe the Irish should speak their own ancient language, not one forced on them by colonial masters. Finally, it should be said that there has been so much movement back and forth between the British Isles and Ireland that almost every Irish family has some relations in England or Scotland or Wales, or most probably has had members who worked in these places for some portion of their lives.[9]

On the other hand, the Irish are proud they do not have a monarchy: they think of themselves as citizens, not as subjects. But, in line with the general confusion that

---

aspire *v.*
渴望，追求
genteel *adj.*
文雅的；装体面的
dislocation *n.*
错位，混乱
self-absorbed *adj.* 自私的，固执己见的
paradoxical *adj.* 自相矛盾的，似非而是的
sore point
痛点，心病

attends their attitudes to the English, an occasion such as a royal wedding will have most of the Irish nation glued to their TV sets to watch the ceremonies.[10] It should not be surprising, then, that on the occasion of Queen Elizabeth II's state visit to Ireland in May 2011 (the very first such visit since Ireland became a nation), she was greeted warmly. When this visit was **reciprocated** by the Irish President, Michael D. Higgins, three years later, it was regarded as a sign that relations between the two nations had at last been "normalised."

Despite these gestures, "Brexit" has again reminded the Irish — particularly the Irish in Britain — of the kind of racism which has, over centuries, **dogged** relations between the two countries.[11] And in Ireland itself, there are still **vestiges** of such enduring **ambivalence** towards England in the way most Irish people regard members of the Irish **aristocracy**, who describe themselves as Anglo-Irish and are often descended from colonisers of the 16th and 17th centuries.[12] Despite their long involvement with Ireland, these may still be rejected as "not Irish".

In its public expression, such ambivalence often takes the form of a full-blown love/hate relationship, one in which admiration and condemnation of the English tend to go hand-in-hand.[13] In cultural terms, perhaps it might be considered a sign that Ireland as a nation is still growing up — in terms of defining its relationship to the colonial heritage of its past.

Just as the Irish have sought to define their culture in opposition to that of Great Britain, the British have for their part been responsible for many of the stereotypes that are still in force about the Irish. For centuries, the British **caricatured** the Irish as, at best, dreamy and impractical; at worst, lazy and given to drinking in excess. It is clear, from Ireland's once-dazzling economic success, that the Irish are neither lazy nor incompetent. Quite the opposite: the Irish workforce is now young, highly educated, **entrepreneurial**, and disciplined.

But, perhaps of all these changes, the most startling is the decline of the authority of the Roman Catholic Church; this alone would serve as a marker to the emergence of new **parameters** as what now constitutes a modern Irish identity.[14]

## The Roman Catholic Church

In the past fifty years, Ireland has passed from being a traditional culture to a post-industrial one, without many of the **intervening** phases.[15] In other words, Ireland

reciprocate *v.* 回应，回访
dog *v.* （长期）困扰；尾随
vestige *n.* 痕迹
ambivalence *n.* 矛盾心理
aristocracy *n.* 贵族（阶层）
caricature *v.* 画成漫画讽刺
entrepreneurial *adj.* 具有企业家精神的
parameter *n.* 规范；范围
intervening *adj.* 介于中间的

# The Republic of Ireland

since the mid-1970s has been subject to very rapid social change, which has led to an apparent rejection of many of the traditional values associated with being Irish.

It is during this period that the Roman Catholic Church has lost its dominance as an **arbiter** of moral values in Irish culture. Although many Irish people (85% of the population in 2011) still **profess** to being practicing Roman Catholics, and many still seek to be married in and buried from the Church, there is serious disillusion with the institution itself and the way it has sought to shape the lives, both private and public, of Irish people.[16]

Much of this reaction has to do with the unthinking **piety** of the Irish people in previous generations, in which the authority of the Roman Church was obeyed as a matter of course. This was particularly true in matters **pertaining to** sexual conduct. For historical reasons, the kind of Roman Catholicism which shaped the Irish **priesthood** was very **puritanical**, with the result that one of the distinguishing characteristics of Irish Roman Catholicism (as distinct from that in Italy, for instance, or even France) was that Irish Catholicism concentrated on what it saw as matters of sexual purity. Contraception was traditionally banned by the Catholic Church because it went against the will of God, and so many Irish women had many more children than they wished to have or even could afford. Sometimes the health, and even the lives of the women themselves, might be put at risk for the sake of this principle. How far this principle has been **eroded** may be judged from the fact that today it is considered normal for even unmarried people to use contraceptives. Again, although the Irish Catholic Church vigorously opposed divorce, the Irish people voted divorce into legislation as of 1996. Now the Church's authority is once again to be tested in a renewed debate about the availability of abortion in Ireland: currently banned, for instance, even in cases of **incest** or rape or fatal foetal abnormality.[17]

Apart from **dictating** sexual morality, in traditional Ireland, the Catholic Church also exercised a firm hold over educational structures, hospitals, and the media, affecting the way people thought about themselves and their lives. How did this come about? Historically, the Irish people believed they had found a political ally against England in the Roman Catholic Church — to such an extent that, when Ireland achieved its independence, the 1937 Constitution of the new Free State, while instituting freedom of religious practice, granted the Roman Catholic Church a "special status".[18] This meant that the Irish government, who were making the laws, consulted the Roman

arbiter *n.* 仲裁者
profess *v.* 声称
piety *n.* 虔诚
pertaining to 与…有关，关于
priesthood *n.* 神职人员
puritanical *adj.* 清教徒的，禁欲的
erode *v.* 侵蚀
incest *n.* 乱伦
dictate *v.* 强行规定，指示

Catholic authorities about any aspect of Irish law in which the Catholic Church might have a **doctrinal** interest. Consequently, by law, birth control was effectively forbidden even to married couples until 1979; neither divorce nor abortion were legally available; books and movies were **censored**; schools and hospitals were set up with administrative boards that would dictate the "**ethos**" or religious ideology of the institution.

What weakened the grip of the Catholic Church was a combination of events. From the 1970s onwards, mass education, particularly at the tertiary level, served to broaden people's views. And as Irish people became wealthier, they travelled more; they saw that other European countries could still be "Roman Catholic" in ethos without being subject to the dictates of the clergy. Also, when Ireland joined the European Community (now the EU) many of the Irish laws drawn up under the influence of the Catholic Church were challenged in the European Union court and found to be overly restrictive.[19] Finally, the conflict within the North of Ireland, which is effectively a **sectarian** conflict between Roman Catholic and Protestant traditions, made people in the Republic more conscious of how sectarian (Catholic) their own laws were. If that conflict were to be resolved, and the island of Ireland reunited (as some hope it eventually will be), then it was important that the bias of the Irish state towards Roman Catholicism be modified.

Certainly the final blow to the Catholic Church's authority was the publication in 2009 of what is known as the Ryan Report, which detailed fifty years of abuse, sexual and otherwise, of vulnerable young people by members of the Roman Catholic **clergy**. After centuries of preaching sexual purity to the Irish people, in the end it was discovered that it was some of the priests themselves who were impure in the most dangerous sense. With that report, the trust of the Irish people in the Catholic Church was so severely damaged that some now describe Ireland as a "post-Catholic" country.

### The Republic of Ireland: Catholic and Protestant

Over the last forty-five years, the conflict in the North has also changed attitudes in the Republic of Ireland about the sectarian divisions within their own society.

The Republic of Ireland is still overwhelmingly Roman Catholic in ethos. Despite the unofficial **disillusionment** with the Church, most of Ireland's population will, if asked in public, say they are members of the Roman Catholic faith. Catholics believe they are members of the "one true" Christian Church. They also believe that the Pope speaks with the authority of Jesus Christ himself, as his own representative on earth. It is this

doctrinal *adj.*
教义的
censor *v.*
审查（和删节）
ethos *n.*
道德观，道德思想
sectarian *adj.*
宗派的，狭隘的
clergy *n.*
神职人员，牧师
disillusionment *n.* 幻灭

# The Republic of Ireland

claim of supreme authority for the Pope speaking from Rome for a world-wide Church that is the distinguishing characteristic of Roman Catholicism and which once gave rise to the Protestant complaint that, for Ireland, "Home Rule means Rome rule".[20]

Protestants are those who "protest" against these claims. Protestants challenge the right of the Pope to tell them what to believe. Essentially, Protestants believe that they themselves can have direct access to God through prayer and study of God's word in the Christian sacred book, the Bible.

For historical reasons, the Irish tend to identify the Roman Catholic Church as an ally of their nationalist ideals. In Ireland, Protestantism is, historically, identified with the English. In the case of Roman Catholicism, under the English, Irish Catholics endured centuries of persecution and legal discrimination (both at home and abroad), exile, and even death. Yet at no earlier time in the history of post-Reformation Ireland has it mattered less than now whether a person is identified as Protestant or Catholic.[21] Ironically, the bitter sectarian violence of the Northern Ireland conflict has led people in the Republic to become disillusioned with religion, particularly with the sectarian divisions of historical Christianity.

Having said that, it is also important to note that there are still many markers in the Republic as to what has become **acculturated** as "Protestant" or "Catholic". Protestants, for instance, are still associated with old, big houses, such as those they lived in during **the Ascendancy** (the 18th and 19th centuries). They are still associated with horse-riding (historically, only a Protestant was wealthy enough to own a good horse) and gardening (part of owning a big house) and also with English sports such as **cricket**. Protestants are also thought to be more plain-spoken and open about their motives than Catholics.

Catholics, on the other hand, are usually associated with being somewhat indirect and manipulative in speech, for instance, praising people before asking for something. Because of the traditional ban on contraceptives, Catholics of an older generation come from large families. They would be more likely to speak the Irish language or practise native "Gaelic" sports such as **hurling**. They also value owning their own house, however modest, a clear reaction to the times when most Catholics were tenant farmers and owed everything to their land owner. Catholics from the Republic also send their children to Catholic schools and universities, such as University College, Dublin (founded initially as The Catholic University in 1851). Before that time, Catholics and those

---

**acculturate** *v.* 文化适应，文化移入
**the (Protestant) Ascendancy** 18、19世纪英国新教徒统治爱尔兰时期
**cricket** *n.* 板球
**hurling** *n.* 爱尔兰式曲棍球

Protestants who did not agree with the teachings of the Anglican state church (called "Dissenters") were forbidden access in Ireland to university education.

Although these stereotypes are now fading in the Republic, the art of "telling" or guessing whether a person is Protestant or Catholic is still a preoccupation, as underneath a modern cosmopolitan **veneer**, the force of these cultural divisions may still at times be registered.

In both North and the Republic, however, joining the European Union has provided a larger, federal context which gives a more generous perspective on Ireland's particular sectarian difficulties. In the Republic, especially, a growing secular society as well as an expanding non-Christian population (marked by the recent construction of several **mosques** in different parts of Dublin), makes the old conflicts between two sects of Christianity seem to belong more to Ireland's history than to its present-day concerns.

**The Family**

In common with most European cultures, the family is central to Irish life. Traditionally, Irish families were large, with up to sixteen or more children, families of eight or nine children not being uncommon in the last generation. Farm families in particular often regarded many children as a guarantee of an adequate labour supply for the farm — and security in their old age. But it should be said that children are also valued very much for their own sake in Irish society and are generally given a warm welcome.

Although the number of children per family fell dramatically, from 3.76 in 1960 to 1.98 in 2001 (around the European average), 2008 saw the highest number of births recorded in over a century. Although this has now settled back to an average of 1.4 children per family, the Irish still value highly their extended family or "tribe". Consequently, of Irish families that have children, about a quarter, have three or more. But however many children there are, Irish people tend to maintain close relations with other members of an extended family, such as grandparents, cousins, aunts, and uncles.

What has changed dramatically in the last forty years has been the structure of Irish family life. Before 1970, children born outside of marriage were regarded as a matter of shame, often given up for adoption. Since the early 1980s, however, the situation has changed dramatically. Now about a quarter of all children are born to

veneer *n.*
外表
mosque *n.*
清真寺

# The Republic of Ireland

single mothers. Although such mothers tend to be poorer than those in marriages, having a child outside marriage is no longer considered a matter of shame; most single mothers would choose to keep their children and raise them themselves. In fact, it is now not unusual for the mother of the child (or even children) to marry their **biological father** some years after the birth of their children. In some ways this goes back to the ancient Brehon Law in Ireland, where it was considered good for a woman to have a child or two before marriage, in order to "prove" her **fertility**.

The primary agent in effecting change in traditional family life has been the movement for women's liberation. **Inaugurated** in the early 1970s, the women's movement concentrated first on gaining control of women's own fertility, demanding contraceptives, divorce, and the right to have an abortion if necessary. The first two goals have been achieved over a span of about twenty years, and a referendum held in May 2018 finally legalised abortion in the Republic of Ireland.

The second objective of the women's liberation movement was to secure the right of women, and that particularly of married women, to work. Until 1973, married women were forbidden by law to hold down any state or semi-state job, which effectively barred them from permanent and **incremental** positions in the civil service or the many other institutions funded by the government, such as health boards and public universities. Once the "marriage bar" was lifted thanks to the EU, however, the structures that remained were still designed for men with a supporting spouse at home. There was, for instance, no **maternity leave**; no provisions for childcare; no equal **pension** arrangements for married women; and, once the law preventing them being hired was removed, a determined resistance to the promotion of women within the career structure of these jobs still remains. Consequently, many married women had to take sick leave to have their babies, or were simply driven out of the jobs by poor pay and poor promotion prospects.

Today, about 60% of the women of Ireland of working age hold down jobs. Their way has been paved over the last generation by the hard work of women's groups, trade unions — and, most significantly — of the European Union, which has passed legislation on hiring practice, paid maternity (and now, parental) leave, and **legislation** for job protection that makes it very difficult to dismiss a woman on grounds of pregnancy.[22]

Just as the status of women has changed radically over the last generation, so has

---

biological father 生父
fertility *n.* 生育能力
inaugurate *v.* 开始，开创
incremental *adj.* 递增的；渐进的
maternity leave 产假
pension *n.* 养老金，退休金
legislation *n.* 立法

that of men. Traditionally, Irish men were very secure in their status. They were usually the only breadwinners. Their role in family life was usually limited to that of authority figure, wage earner, and sometimes, of role model. They had wives who provided the services needed to raise children and keep a home. A generation ago, a young Irishman might be proud he did not know how to cook or to iron a shirt or look after a baby.

Today that is all changed. It is now quite usual to see a man carrying a young baby or wheeling it in a **pushchair**. Now that their wives increasingly work outside the home, young husbands make an effort to share in domestic duties, although often theirs is only a symbolic contribution, leaving the bulk of the work at home to the working wife.

Thus it is safe to say family life — and with it, shifts of gender expectations — have changed almost beyond recognition in the space of a generation or so. While a "family" in Ireland still implies a man and a woman (who may be married or simply co-habiting) with children, there is an increase in couples without offspring as well as a notable number of single, separated, or divorced parents heading families. For better or worse, the model for work practice in Ireland is still the "male model": based on the assumption that whoever works will have some full-time support at home, usually unpaid and thus undervalued.

**Community**

Traditionally, Ireland has been a rural and agricultural culture. The centres of the big cities (such as Dublin, Limerick and Cork) belonged historically to the ruling elite and the agents of the English government, and were settled mostly by Anglo-Irish Protestants. The Catholics tended to live in towns and villages or isolated farms. When Ireland was under English rule, the Irish who did live in cities such as Dublin were usually confined to **ghettos** marked by such names as "Irishtown".

Today about a third of all Irish people live in or near Dublin. Many of the present city dwellers who are Irish are only one or at most two generations away from the village, and still maintain close ties to the relatives who still live there. The new ghettos are settled by the immigrants who arrived during the Celtic Tiger years of the late 1990s. From both EU and non-EU countries (like Nigeria, where the schools were often run by Irish missionaries), these recent immigrants have now been **marooned** in Ireland. Having found jobs, bought houses, and had children, they found, when the economic

pushchair *n.*
折叠式婴儿车
ghetto *n.*
贫民区
maroon *v.*
陷入困境

# The Republic of Ireland

bust came, that they could not move back to their countries of origin as their houses were unsalable or in negative equity — and their children had already, in a real sense, become Irish.

Thus "community," like "family" has also become a **fragmented** concept in Ireland. Most shocking is the housing crisis. As people lost their jobs and with them, the ability to pay the mortgages on their houses, they became homeless. Homelessness is no longer the fate of those with mental health or addiction problems; it has spread to the working and even the middle class and is now the largest, most visible social crisis in the Irish state.

The predictable result of such rapid social change is that the Irish still have a poorly developed urban culture — as well as an underdeveloped sense of civic responsibility. Thus, although Irish households may be **meticulous** about maintaining their own property, they may not pay much attention to the state of public property.[23] It is also often difficult to get Irish people to volunteer for public projects. But one is still talking about a society increasingly divided: by wealth, housing status, and origin. Racism, although not yet violent, has risen along with the number of immigrants, now totaling about 17% of the population. Indifference to, and (perhaps even more dangerous) anger at the sacrifices necessitated to turn the economy around, have taken a political turn, most recently in opposition to charges for water — a commodity increasingly under threat due to Ireland's rapid urbanisation.[24]

If one were to look for a place where the Irish community is most reliably represented, that would most probably be the public house or "pub". In common with British society, the Irish recognise the pub as a place to gather to meet friends and neighbours on an informal basis. Every neighbourhood will have a pub, and often many more than one, to which a customer shows a kind of loyalty, and which offers a kind of social base, particularly for men. In rural areas especially the pub functions as a kind of informal community center. It has many valuable aspects: for instance, it is often the place where the people of a particular **locality** go to meet others, as well as a place where, traditionally, music and story-telling are often heard. Unfortunately, because of its association with alcohol, "pub culture" as it is called, is also held responsible for Ireland's considerable (and notorious) drink problem.

fragment v.
使…碎片化
meticulous adj.
一丝不苟的
locality n.
地方，地点

## Work Culture

The Irish have long been stereotyped by outsiders as lazy, but actual experience contradicts this: the Irish are as hard-working as any of their European counterparts, but often have a different style in regard to work practice.

In general, that style can be described as informal. The Irish pay less attention to schedules than to completing a task. One of the reasons why these informal work practices are **congenial** is that there is little division in an Irish person's life between his work and his social life. An Irish worker will know a great deal about the personal life of his or her fellow workers, and thus be more sympathetic to appeals for flexibility if he or she knows there is a personal situation that needs support. As a result, Irish workers generally cooperate well as a team in completing the task at hand. That team spirit extends beyond the office: it is not uncommon for office colleagues to have lunches together to mark important social occasions, or to **adjourn** to a pub at the close of work on Friday to enjoy each other's company. In Ireland, trade unions play a significant part in maintaining job security. Many trades and professions have access to their own union, which is a legally constituted **interest group** designed to negotiate for its members' appropriate pay and **protocols** of work practice, and, if necessary, institute legal procedures against an employer if it considers an injustice has been done. Legal cases are usually brought before the Labour Court, which attempts to **mediate** between workers and managers to settle work disputes. Failing resolution, trade unions may initiate strikes. Many workers pay to become members of unions, knowing that membership provides them with some degree of protection in an uncertain marketplace.

All this having been said, it is important to note that there is a big difference between the work-practices of the traditional Irish job and those available in the new multi-national companies which increasingly now employ Irish workers. In an international financial corporation such as **Citibank**, the work practices would be very similar to that in its parent institution in America: that is, strict adherence to schedules, with a tendency to come in early and demonstrate that one is working hard during the entire work-day; rigid adherence to company procedures and protocols; teamwork that includes marked **deference** to those further up in the hierarchy. There is also a certain amount of job insecurity, as multinationals have no reason to be loyal to the country in which they are sited, and the home office may well decide in adverse circumstances

---

congenial *adj.*
相宜的，合适的
adjourn *v.*
休会，休息
interest group
利益集团
protocol *n.*
协议，条款
mediate *v.*
调停，斡旋
Citibank
（美国）花旗银行
deference *n.*
顺从，尊重

# The Republic of Ireland

to close the Irish offices at short notice, offering workers only the **statutory** redundancy payments.[25]

**statutory** *adj.* 法定的
**denominational** *adj.* 教派的，宗派的

### Education and Training

In the last fifty or so years, the Irish government has come to recognise that if they are to modernise the economy, significant resources would need to be diverted into the educational system.

Traditionally, Irish education was undertaken by various religious orders, mostly Roman Catholic, with the result that forty years ago, almost three-quarters of existing schools were "**denominational**" — that is, associated with one religious denomination or another. In Ireland today, there are still many schools of Catholic orientation, far fewer of Protestant; one Jewish and one Muslim school. But there are also a growing number of "neighbourhood" or "interdenominational" schools, as families demand a more secular basis for education. Historically, by offering education to the Irish people, the religious orders provided a cheap and largely inclusive service. However, often the price to the Irish state was an education system that was rigorously sectarian and sometimes poorly administered.

From about 1960 onwards, the Irish government made educating its young people a priority. Right up to 1960, about half of each generation of young people emigrated, often to low-level jobs in the United Kingdom or America. But very rapidly the Irish government turned this around, by instituting a system of teacher payments and per capita grants for sectarian or "denominational" schools, thus rendering them virtually free for students while maintaining the former sectarian structure of education. As a result, after 1960, the participation in second-level education rose from about 45% to up to 90%.

In 1996–1997 the Irish government extended free education to cover all public universities, as is common in most of the countries of Europe. As a result, today the Irish educational system is among the cheapest and best in Europe, but the universities themselves complain they are chronically starved of funding. It should be noted that "tuition-free" education at Irish universities is open only to established EU and Irish residents.

In Ireland, education is compulsory for children aged six to fifteen years. In terms of curriculum, the Irish system resembles that of the United Kingdom with the significant difference that, from entry, all children in the Republic must learn the Irish language. Furthermore, to gain entry into every Irish university (except that of Trinity College Dublin, which is exempt for historical reasons) every student must pass a compulsory exam in the Irish language.

The education system is administered centrally by the Department of Education which provides the bulk of current and capital funding. Education at first and second level schools, as well as university level, remains free in terms of tuition costs, although there are still substantial attendant expenses at all levels in terms of administrative fees, books, and accommodation.

orientation n.
方向，定位
craft n.
手工（课）
sizeable adj.
相当大的
the Junior Certificate
初中毕业证书

### First-level Schools

The vast majority of children receive their primary education in "national schools"; i.e., state-aided primary schools. Each school is run by its own board of management, comprising representatives of parents, teachers and local clergy, but receives most of its funding, including teachers' salaries, from the State. They remain for the most part denominational in **orientation** (that is, under the management of a specific religious group) with the exception of some new "multi-denominational" or community schools which are set up by groups of involved parents with the help of the Irish state.[26] The present curriculum includes Mathematics, English, Irish, French, History, Geography, Art, Music, **Crafts**, Social and Environmental Studies and Physical Education.

### Second-level Schools

Second-level schools are designed for students from twelve years of age upwards. There are various types of second-level schools. There are a comparatively small number of comprehensive and community schools which are state-owned second-level schools. But most secondary schools are privately owned, many by Catholic religious communities — and are hence sectarian or denominational in orientation. Although their expenditure is largely funded by the State, many of the "private" secondary schools also require **sizeable** annual fees.

Second-level education in Ireland has two cycles. The junior cycle is a three-year course leading to a series of exams that result in the awarding of **the Junior Certificate**.

At one time, many pupils left school after the Junior Cert, as it is called. But now most students stay on for the senior cycle. This consists of a two-year course leading to the awarding of the Leaving Certificate, the basic qualification for admission to third-

# The Republic of Ireland

level education. Between the junior and senior cycle, there is an optional Transition Year. Available at an increasing number of schools, this is a time during which students may pursue non-examination subjects and gain some work or volunteer experience.

At the end of the senior cycle, all students take the Leaving Certificate exams. Like the Chinese *gaokao*, these are state exams set by the Department of Education which are uniform for all Irish students. They take place over two weeks and offer a menu of exams, of which English and Mathematics are compulsory (and Irish for all universities other than Trinity). These Leaving Certificate exams are designed to measure the students' level of academic achievement, and also generate scores that are the only **criterion** used for entrance to a certain university or even a certain programme within a university. Thus these exams are both highly competitive and very stressful; if a student fails any or all of these exams, they may be repeated (but only a year later, in the following June).

Vocational schools are owned and operated by the State through local Vocational Education Committees. Vocational Schools were, originally, mainly concerned with technical education and thus, if a student wishes to enter a specific trade, are considered a sound **alternative** to university.

### Third-level Education

There are five public universities in the State. The University of Dublin comprises one college, Trinity College. This is the oldest and most **prestigious** university in the State, founded in 1592 by Queen Elizabeth I for the education of Protestants. Until forty or so years ago, this University was banned to Roman Catholics, who had to have special permission from their Church to attend classes there.

The National University of Ireland (NUI) has colleges in Dublin, Cork, Galway and Maynooth. The largest of these, University College, Dublin (UCD), was founded after Catholic Emancipation as The Catholic University in 1851. The National University of Ireland, Maynooth, once the primary training school or **seminary** for Roman Catholic priests, is now established as an independent university in its own right. Both these institutions, UCD and Maynooth, are attended largely by Catholic students, in line with their historical evolution. Others such as the University of Limerick and Dublin City University are comparatively new universities (established as such only in 1989) and so have escaped much of this sectarian history.

---

**criterion** *n.*
标准
**alternative** *n.*
供替代的选择
**prestigious** *adj.*
久负盛名的
**seminary** *n.*
神学院

The Regional Technical Colleges and the Dublin Institute of Technology place a heavy emphasis on applied science and on technological education, particularly in the area of the new technologies such as computer science.

Many of these third-level institutions expanded rapidly in the 1970s to meet the government's demand for more inclusive university education for the Irish people. Since the mid-1980s, however, the Irish population has begun to decline, with the result that the Irish university sector is expanding rapidly into the foreign market. Irish third-level institutions are now actively **recruiting** Asian, as well as American, students in order to boost their **enrollments**. Chinese students, in particular, are valued for their disciplined and committed attitude to their studies.

Other third-level institutions specialise in particular areas such as law, medicine, art, music, and teacher training.

The Irish government has now determined that university education is an important factor in Ireland's struggle to regain its former economic status. Hence new funding is being directed in particular to post-graduate training, and to those university centres concentrating on public/private enterprises; that is, **cooperative ventures** between business and university research projects. Given its investment in the medical and pharmaceutical industries, bio-technology has emerged as one of the leading fields for both investment and research. But the most employable are the graduates from the many computer studies programmes, who, if they prove competent, are almost guaranteed immediate employment in the many tech- and financial-service multinationals that have **gravitated** to Ireland, citing the high quality of its university graduates.[27]

recruit *v.*
招收
enrollment *n.*
入学（人数）
cooperative ventures
合作机构（企业等）
gravitate *v.*
被吸引到

# Explanations

1. **In coming times ... perhaps commuting into a nearby town to earn money:**
   在不久的将来，农田将传给较年轻的兄弟或姐妹；他（她）们有着其他职业或工作，例如坐车到附近的城镇打工，而经营农田只是其收入的次要来源。

# The Republic of Ireland

2. **Once they married ... to leave her job working for the State:**
   一旦结婚，在那"糟糕的过去岁月里"她将被迫遵从国家的"婚姻禁令"，放弃国家公务员的工作。marriage bar 指爱尔兰禁止已婚妇女工作的传统法律。

3. **As there was no legal access to contraception ... five children in eight years:**
   由于没有合法的避孕措施（再说，她那虔诚的天主教徒母亲对这个措施也会皱眉头的），她马上就怀孕，并且在八年的时间里连续生育五个孩子。

4. **The child whose life differs least ... those of the chronically unemployed:**
   与父母的生活方式差别最小的子女来自爱尔兰的下层社会，即那些长期失业的阶层。

5. **This is very damaging to his self-esteem ... football matches and to the pub:**
   这（领救济）很伤他的自尊；他试图通过定期与工友会面去看足球赛或到酒吧聊天来恢复自尊。

6. **What remains ... are now glaring inequalities between rich and poor:**
   曾一度贫困却不失优雅的和谐社会现在只剩下尖锐而明显的不平等和贫富分化。

7. **Apart from the dislocations of a boom-and-bust economy ... define its identity:**
   除了经济兴衰所带来的错位，还有这个年轻国家在努力建立其民族认同感时伴随而来的迷惘。

8. **While the English seem ... become more European:**
   英国人似乎变得愈加顾影自怜、孤芳自赏，而爱尔兰人却已经自觉自愿地越来越欧洲化了。

9. **Finally, it should be said that ... for some portion of their lives:**
   最后，应该说，不列颠群岛与爱尔兰之间的来往如此之多以至于几乎每个爱尔兰家庭在英格兰、苏格兰或威尔士都有或近或远的亲戚，或者说多数爱尔兰家庭都有家庭成员曾在这些地方工作过。

10. **But, in line with the general confusion ... to watch the ceremonies:**
    但是，由于对英国人爱恨交加的复杂感情，英国王室婚礼这样的节目也会将爱尔兰全国大部分人紧紧吸引到电视屏幕前。

11. **Despite these gesture ... dogged relations between the two countries:**
    尽管有这些（友好）往来，"英国脱欧"再次提醒爱尔兰人——尤其是在英国的爱尔兰人——伴随两个国家几个世纪交往史的是英国的种族主义。

12. **And in Ireland itself ... colonisers of the 16th and 17th centuries:**
    而且在爱尔兰本土，对英国人长期的矛盾心态仍然存在，这反映在多数爱尔兰人对待爱尔兰贵族阶层爱恨交加的态度上；这些贵族将自己描绘成 16 和 17 世纪英国殖民者的英裔爱尔兰人的后代。

13. **In its public expression, such ambivalence ... to go hand-in-hand:**
    在爱尔兰的公众表达上，这种矛盾心理常常以充分发展的既爱又恨的方式出现，对英国人的钦佩与谴责并行。

UNIT 13  Irish Culture: How the Irish Live Now

14. **Perhaps of all these change ... a modern Irish identity:**
    也许在所有这些变化中，最令人吃惊的是罗马天主教会权威的衰落；仅此一项变化即可成为正在形成的当代爱尔兰身份新标准的一个标志。

15. **In the past fifty year ... without many of the intervening phases:**
    在过去的五十年中，爱尔兰已从传统文化转变为成后工业文化，跳过了许多中间阶段。后工业时代指以服务业（第三产业）为主的时代。

16. **Although many Irish people ... both private and public, of Irish people:**
    虽然许多爱尔兰人（2011年人口普查时为85%）声称尊奉罗马天主教，而且许多人的婚礼在教堂举行，死后由教堂安葬，但人们对教会本身以及它寻求左右爱尔兰人民个人与公共生活的方式产生了巨大的幻灭。

17. **Now the Church's authority ... incest or rape or fatal foetal abnormality:**
    现在，教会的权威在新一轮关于堕胎合法化的辩论中再次经受考验：爱尔兰现行法律禁止堕胎，即使是因乱伦或遭到强奸而怀孕或者胎儿有致命缺陷的情况下也如此。

18. **Historically ... granted the Roman Catholic Church a "special status":**
    在历史上，爱尔兰人民认为罗马天主教会是他们反对英格兰统治的政治同盟，以至于爱尔兰取得独立后1937年的爱尔兰自由邦宪法在规定宗教信仰自由的同时，赋予罗马天主教"特殊的地位"。

19. **Also, when Ireland joined ... to be overly restrictive:**
    而且，爱尔兰加入欧共体（现为欧盟）后，很多深受天主教教会影响而制定的爱尔兰法律受到欧盟法庭的挑战，并暴露出其过于限制自由的性质。

20. **It is this claim ... "Home Rule means Rome rule":**
    罗马教皇被视作代表上帝统领全世界教会的最高权威正是罗马天主教会的明显特征，也导致了新教徒对此的抱怨："所谓（爱尔兰）地方自治，不如说是罗马统治"。

21. **Yet at no earlier time in the history ... as Protestant or Catholic:**
    在宗教改革以来的爱尔兰历史上，人们从未像现在这样对一个人是新教徒还是天主教徒持无所谓的态度。

22. **Their way has been paved ... on grounds of pregnancy:**
    上一代的妇女组织、工会，尤其重要的是欧盟，它们的艰苦努力为当今的妇女扫除了障碍；欧盟在雇用政策、带薪产假（父母都享有）以及工作保护等方面的立法使得以怀孕为理由解雇妇女变得非常困难。

23. **Thus, although Irish households may be meticulous ... the state of public property:**
    因此，虽然爱尔兰家庭对维护自己的财产很精心，但并不会特别关注公共财产的状况。

24. **Indifference to ... due to Ireland's rapid urbanisation:**
    随着政治气候的变化，对于振兴经济所做出必要牺牲的要求往往招致公众的漠不关心，甚至（更危险的是）愤怒，这体现在最近政府决定收取水费（由于爱尔兰的快速城市化，水资源作为一种商品正日益受到威胁）时所遭到的反对。

## The Republic of Ireland

25. **There is also a certain amount of job insecurity ... redundancy payments:**
    还有一定程度的工作不稳定，因为跨国公司没有理由忠于其投资设址的国家，其总部可以在经营条件不好的时候随时关闭其爱尔兰分支，而仅给予被裁人员以法律规定的失业补偿。

26. **They remain for the most part ... with the help of the Irish state:**
    国立学校在性质上大都有派别之分（也就是说，分属某个具体宗教团体管理），而一些新的"多教派"或社区学校则属例外，它们是在爱尔兰政府的帮助下由相关家长团体成立的。

27. **But the most employable ... citing the high quality of its university graduates:**
    但是最有可能被雇用的员工是许多计算机专业的毕业生，他们如果证明自己的能力，可以说就可以立即被许多科技或金融服务领域的跨国公司雇用，足以证明爱尔兰大学毕业生的高素质。

# Exercises

**I. Give the Chinese equivalents for the following:**

1. Catholics
2. Protestants
3. abortion
4. maternity leave
5. Leaving Certificate exam

**II. Decide whether the following statements are true (T) or false (F):**

1. The average young person in Ireland today would have grown up in an environment of less social change than the previous generation. _____
2. Girls in the 1950s and 1960s were urged to get a university education because they had to find a good job. _____
3. The attitude of the Irish toward the English is contradictory or even paradoxical because of the colonial past. _____
4. With the support from the Catholic Church, the Irish people voted divorce into legislation. _____
5. The majority of the Irish population is Protestant. _____
6. The Catholic Church is opposed to contraception and abortion. _____
7. When Ireland was under English rule, the Irish who did live in cities such as Dublin were

usually confined to ghettos marked by such names as "Irishtown". _____
8. Today free education provided by the Irish government covers all public universities, as is common in most of the countries of Europe. _____

III. **Fill in the blanks:**
1. Culture in this text refers to the _____ people live: the patterns and normal expectations of their lives as passed within a certain place.
2. The child whose life differs least from that of his parents is one born into Ireland's _____, those of the chronically unemployed.
3. Ireland since the 1970s has been subject to very rapid social change, which has led to an apparent rejection of many of the _____ associated with being Irish.
4. Apart from dictating sexual morality, in traditional Ireland, the _____ also exercised a firm hold over educational structures, hospitals, and the media.
5. In common with British society, the Irish recognise the _____ as a place to gather to meet friends and neighbours on an informal basis.
6. _____ are widely recognised in Ireland and many workers pay to become members, knowing this provides them with some protection in an uncertain marketplace.
7. One of the reasons why these informal work practices are congenial is that there is little _____ in an Irish person's life between his work and his social life.
8. Today the Irish educational system is among the cheapest and best in _____.
9. Currently there are _____ public universities in the Republic of Ireland.
10. _____ were, originally, mainly concerned with technical education.

IV. **Questions:**
1. How is culture defined in the text? What is "high culture"?
2. How different is the life of a farmer's son from that of his father?
3. What is the content of the law of "primogeniture"? How has it affected the life of the Irish?
4. How do the Irish look at the English? Why?
5. In what aspects has the Catholic Church lost its grip in Irish society? In what aspects is it still influencing people's life?
6. What are the major differences between the Catholics and the Protestants in terms of doctrinal faith and life style?

## The Republic of Ireland

7. In what way has joining the European Union given a more generous perspective on Ireland's particular sectarian difficulties?
8. Why did the Irish families tend to have more children traditionally? Why has this practice changed over time?
9. What were the two objectives of the women's liberation movement inaugurated in the early 1970s?
10. How has men's status changed in the last generation?
11. What role does the "pub" play in the Irish community?
12. What is the general work culture in Ireland in terms of teamwork and interpersonal relationships?
13. What role does the Trade Union play in maintaining workers' job security?
14. How has religious division affected Ireland's education system?
15. What is the difference between the Junior Certificate and the Leaving Certificate in the Irish education system?

V. **Topics for discussion or research:**
1. Do research on the Women's Liberation Movement, particularly pay attention to the specific social changes it has brought to the Irish women.
2. Sum up the major differences between the Catholics and the Protestants in the Irish society, and explore the root causes.
3. Compare the general work culture of the Irish with that in China.
4. Describe the education system in Ireland and compare it with that in China.

# UNIT 14

# Irish Culture: Language, Literature and Arts

**Go over the following focal points before reading the text:**

- The Irish language and colonial policy
- Hiberno-English
- The Irish oral tradition
- Folk heritage
- *Riverdance*
- Irish literature
- Nobel Prize winners for Literature
- James Joyce
- Irish music and dance
- Popular sports
- Science and technology
- Irish identity in the world

# The Republic of Ireland

 Text

## Language

The issue of language, like much else in Ireland, is heavily politicized. Traditionally, the Irish people spoke their own language, called Irish or **Gaelic**. It is a very ancient (and difficult) language with a rich oral culture. However, under English colonial policy, much pressure was brought to bear to stop the Irish people speaking their own language and to learn standard English instead. Since the Irish people felt, **instinctively**, that to lose their language was to lose their native culture, they resisted this policy strongly. Until the mid-nineteenth century Irish was still spoken widely by the peasant classes — although those who had to deal with the British administration (particularly middle-class and professional people) — chose to use English. Many of these lost their Irish and never regained it.

The **death blow** to the Irish language was the Great Famine of 1845-48, in which almost two million Irish people emigrated or died. As most of these were peasants, and thus Irish-speakers, much of the native culture, including the language and its music, songs and poems and stories, would have emigrated or died with them.

As part of the **move** for Irish independence in the late nineteenth century, a conscious attempt was made to revive the use of the Irish language among the middle and professional classes. After the first Irish national state was set up (the Free State of 1922), a **concerted** official attempt was made to make Irish once again the national language. Under Eamon de Valera's government (1932–1959)[1], the school system was **reconfigured** so that it taught the Irish language to all Irish children from the age of four until they left school at fifteen. This was **reinforced** by making it mandatory to have a **competent** level of Irish in order to enter the universities of Ireland, with the exception of Trinity College in Dublin which was, until recently, a Protestant university with its own laws and which drew many of its students from Great Britain.[2] These requirements still stand for university entrance, as does de Valera's provision that no one may enter the Irish civil service or the **diplomatic corps** or the teaching profession in first- and second-level schools without having a certain level of competence in the Irish language.

---

Gaelic *n.* 盖尔语
instinctively *adv.* 本能地
death blow 致命的打击
move *n.* 提议，要求
concerted *adj.* 齐心协力的
reconfigure *v.* 重新调整，重新设定
reinforce *v.* 加强，强化
competent *adj.* 胜任的
diplomatic corps 外交使团

# UNIT 14 Irish Culture: Language, Literature and Arts

Despite such official pressures, today Irish is spoken at home by a diminishing number of people. The language that is spoken universally in the Republic of Ireland is a version of standard English known as **Hiberno-English**. This idiom is distinguished from the kind of English spoken in the British Isles by a certain vocabulary (in which many of the words are either **provincial**, **archaic**, or derived from the Irish language) and by certain **semantic idiosyncrasies**.[3] Some of these have been mocked by Irish playwrights, who have their Irish characters speaking with a heavy **brogue** (Irish accent) and systematically using the wrong word (a "**malapropism**") or committing illogical speech acts ("an **Irish bull**").

The other notable aspect of Hiberno-Irish to the foreign ear is the variety and difficulty of the regional accents, from Cork to Donegal. Although these accents are largely **intelligible** to most Irish people, many English people have difficulty in understanding what is being said. These **mannerisms** mark the English spoken by the Irish, although increasingly urban Irish people speak in an accent and manner completely intelligible to their peers in the USA.

**Oral Culture**

Although only a small minority in the Republic of Ireland now speak fluent Irish, they do **retain** one element of their native culture: they talk. Ireland is a culture which operates most obviously on an oral level. The Irish value good talk, and they love a good story. An Irish person will very likely take an opportunity to talk even if pressed for time, and a business transaction is often conducted with a great deal of **banter**, even when — to an outsider — the **discourse** seems **superfluous**, beside the point.

The basis for this is, of course, the original peasant culture, which made the transfer from an oral to a written culture only slowly in the late 19th century. But even among the most literate classes, great value is extended to the ability to talk **spontaneously** and with grace and force.[4] What this means in practical terms is that doing even ordinary business in Ireland may take a great deal more time than a more **reticent** culture would allow.[5] But although this habit may look like a sheer waste of time to a visiting German or American businessman, in practical terms it also means that the routine business of getting through a day will be **enlivened** by a whole **array** of verbal exchanges, from personal stories to **lame jokes**, and will be accompanied by a good deal of personal interaction, teasing (called "**slagging**") and laughter.[6] This is part of the

---

Hiberno-English n. 爱尔兰（式）英语
provincial adj. 地方性的
archaic adj. 陈旧的，古体的
semantic idiosyncrasy 语义特点
brogue n. 土腔，方言
malapropism n. 文字（词语）误用
Irish bull 自相矛盾的说法
intelligible adj. 可理解的
mannerism n. 言谈举止；（写作中）过分的独特风格
retain v. 保留，保有
banter n. 无恶意的玩笑
discourse n. 讲话，论述
superfluous adj. 多余的，不必要的
spontaneously adv. 即兴地，自发地
reticent adj. 寡言少语的
enliven v. 使活跃
array n. 系列，大量
lame joke 蹩脚的笑话
slagging n. 戏弄，调侃

# The Republic of Ireland

legendary charm of the Irish, and in a world in which the time to talk or to get to know other people is constantly under pressure from other concerns, this quality adds great pleasure to the day-to-day routine. Perhaps it is also one key to Ireland's very effective business and diplomatic efforts. It is **indisputably** the very basis for Ireland's reputation as a culture of great writers.

## Art Culture

Ireland is a traditional culture and it is true to say virtually every art form in Ireland derives from its rich **folk heritage**.

In Ireland, writers may publish in either the Irish or the English language. The number of new writers, particularly poets, who choose to write in Irish is striking, given the fact that it is reputed to be a dying language.

Similarly, although Ireland is renowned for its fine traditional music culture, it now can boast of classical composers of considerable merit. Many of them use Irish folk tunes or modes as the basis for their new compositions.

Again, in dance, Ireland is known throughout the world for the **intricacy** and **fervour** of its folk dances, modernised in the current stage productions of *Riverdance*.[7]

Thus it is useful to see contemporary Ireland as consciously rooted in the traditions, as well as the language, of its past, rather than as the art of a **self-consciously** "new" nation.[8]

## Literature

As all writers know, good talk is the basis of good literature. Thus, as a talk culture, Ireland rightly has a reputation for being a culture in which writers flourish.

Originally most stories began in the oral culture and many still remain there. The first stories told in Ireland were not only oral, but were recited in the Irish language. The first poem identified as "Irish" is the **saga** of the *Tain* (pronounced "TOIN"), which was transmitted orally for centuries before it was written down.[9] Other forms of oral recitation, such as **genealogies**, local myths and legends, folk poetry, anecdotes and jokes are still current in the present oral culture. Other traditional material, such as folk songs and folk tales, have been collected intensively over the last seventy years; some of the most **avid** collectors have been those poets and writers who have sought to assert the importance of Ireland's traditional culture as a basis for its claim to be a distinct and

indisputably *adv.* 无可争议地
folk heritage 民间传统
intricacy *n.* 繁复
fervour *n.* 热情
self-consciously *adv.* 刻意地，自己意识到地
saga *n.* 英雄事迹，传说
genealogy *n.* 家谱（学），血统
avid *adj.* 渴望的，热切的

independent nation.[10]

Now that Ireland is an independent Republic in its own right, it has developed the habit of laying claim to all writers who have been born or have worked/written within its national boundaries over many centuries.[11] Of course most of these, in historical terms, were, like Jonathan Swift or Oscar Wilde, in fact English — as they lived or wrote in Ireland during the time it was officially a British colony. But the Irish see no reason why history should prevent them from **appropriating** these writers as "Irish" (or Anglo-Irish) in order to **boost** national pride in Ireland as a land of literary giants.[12]

And giants they have been. In modern times alone, the territory that has become the Republic of Ireland has been the origin of four winners of the Nobel Prize for Literature: the poets, W.B. Yeats (1865–1929) and Seamus Heaney (1939–2013); the **playwrights**, George Bernard Shaw (1856–1950) and Samuel Beckett (1906–1989).[13] Apart from these well-known writers, there have been many writers over the centuries who have demonstrated themselves to be Irish in sympathy or in technique. Of these, it is important to name Jonathan Swift[14] (1667–1745), who **satirized** English attitudes towards the Irish in such works as *Gulliver's Travels* or *A Modest Proposal*. Another notable writer is Laurence Sterne[15] (1713–1768), who **ridiculed** the conventions of the English novel in *Tristram Shandy*, employing a typically Irish tactic, that of **digression**, and carrying it to its logical extreme.

Satire was also the mode for the Irish playwrights Richard Sheridan[16] (1751–1816) and Oscar Wilde[17] (1856–1900), whose plays made them famous in London. Wilde is known also for his **trenchant** essays, particularly "The Soul of Man under Socialism" and his **controversial** novel, *The Picture of Dorian Gray*. After the turn of the century, the novelist James Joyce[18] (1882–1941) is famous as the writer who changed the nature of the traditional English novel forever. Two important qualities enabled Joyce to do this. In common with many of the writers before him, Joyce was extraordinarily self-conscious about the language in which he was writing. As he has his hero say in *The Portrait of the Artist as a Young Man*, he did not feel that English was his native tongue: it was a foreign language, even though it resembled Hiberno-English. This sense of language as **alien**, and having a life of its own, made it easier for Joyce to experiment with it and to play with its expression.[19]

Perhaps for this reason, the work of James Joyce, as well as that of Samuel Beckett, was self-consciously **avant-garde**: playing with different **dialects** and styles of

---

appropriate *v.* 占用，挪用
boost *v.* 促进
playwright *n.* 剧作家
satirize *v.* 讽刺
ridicule *v.* 讥讽
digression *n.* 离题，题外话
trenchant *adj.* 犀利的
controversial *adj.* 引起争议的
alien *adj.* 外国的，异域的
avant-garde *adj.* 前卫的，先锋派的
dialect *n.* 方言

# The Republic of Ireland

English as if they were part of a game.[20] Beckett, in particular, was fascinated by the different shapes and patterns one can make out of language.

Following the path of the great writers before him, Joyce's work often took a satirical look at the society around him, particularly the values of "proper" **genteel** society identified with the British. Beckett's great play, *Waiting for Godot*, carries this satire to its logical extreme, asking his middle-class audience seriously to **contemplate** the lives of two **tramps**, who have no purpose except to wait for someone who may never come and who do nothing for the entire performance but play trivial word-games. As a critique of bourgeois **obsessions** with hard work and accomplishment, purpose and meaning, the play could scarcely be more **savage**.[21]

Like the experimental attitude towards language, the impulse to satirize undoubtedly also arises from the Irish experience of **colonialism**. English ways are not Irish ways, and Irish adaptations of them often led to ridicule from those who perceive the coloniser's manners as foreign and often offensive.[22] A poet such as Seamus Heaney, originally from the North of Ireland but a long-time resident of the Republic, is regarded as someone who sought to speak with **conscience** about what had been happening there: not as someone who takes one side or the other, but who records, in the **authentic** accents of those who suffer, the history of his people.[23] He is honoured because what he says is true, but also because it recalls, in the midst of cruel divisions, the original unity of a **pastoral** culture which is the common inheritance of all Irish people, North and South.[24]

In Ireland, the poet and the writer are honoured above all other artists because what is said in Ireland still has the ancient force of the binding word. Like Joyce's artist, the writer in Ireland is bound over to a sacred mission, to "forge the **uncreated** conscience of his race". It is no mean vocation.[25]

## Music and Dance

Like literature, music has its roots in ancient Irish culture. Perhaps the oldest form of music is that embodied by the *sean nos* or "old style" of singing. Traditionally, *sean nos* is sung by the **unaccompanied** voice. The singer will often close his or her eyes and hold one hand behind the ear, the better to hear himself or herself. The words are always in Irish. Usually the song is about unrequited (*unreturned*) love and is a **lament** for lost love. The last line is spoken, not sung.

---

genteel *adj.* 上流社会的，文雅的
contemplate *v.* 沉思，反思
tramp *n.* 流浪汉
obsession *n.* 迷恋
savage *adj.* 野蛮的，残酷的
colonialism *n.* 殖民主义
conscience *n.* 良心
authentic *adj.* 真正的，可信的
pastoral *adj.* 乡村的，田园生活的
uncreated *adj.* 永生的，永存的
unaccompanied *adj.* 无伴奏的
lament *n.* 挽歌

# UNIT 14 Irish Culture: Language, Literature and Arts

The **modalities** of *sean nos* often sound strange to European ears, and, indeed, in form and style they may seem closer to the music of North Africa than to Europe. The same is true of the **pipe** music. In tone, the Irish pipes are sweeter and less noisy than those of the Scots, which are employed as war-pipes. The Irish pipes are usually played indoors, for private entertainment and for dancing.

Dancing is traditionally part of Irish culture; in former centuries every village would have a dancing-master and some villages still boast figures of dance that are named after them. If a piper were not available, then a **fiddler** might be found. Fiddles (violins played with an informal technique) became common in the early 19th century in Ireland. Irish fiddlers today are well-known for their **repertoire** of jigs and reels, hornpipes and slides.[26] The music usually sounds fast and furious — and so is the dancing. Whether done by individuals or in "sets", Irish dancing involves fancy **footwork** in intricate patterns. Most of the action is from the waist down, with the arms held rigidly at the sides. Shows like the recent *Riverdance* demonstrate that this type of dancing can be very expressive indeed.

In common with most of the old culture, words are central to music in Ireland. The oldest poems or sagas were probably recited to the Irish **harp**, still regarded as Ireland's most ancient instrument (and now adopted as its national symbol). In such a recitation, the words would have equal status to the music. Historically, long narrative songs or **ballads** often acted as a political **commentary** on actual events. This is particularly true of songs that criticized the **recruiting** methods of the British Army (in which young men were forced into military service) or those that gave accounts of the heroes of the latest popular rebellion against England.[27] Some of these songs, such as those associated with the Irish Republican Army, are still regarded as politically sensitive. Among the saddest songs, however, associated with emigration, particularly of emigration to Australia and America, which the Irish who stayed home regarded as a kind of living death for those who were leaving.

Things are changing. In architecture, for instance, Irish innovators are now asserting a strong presence (such as the award-winning buildings in Milan, Italy and in Lima, Peru, by the firm of Grafton Architects). **Visual** creativity in Ireland is also thriving across a host of areas, from fashion and **graphics** to **animation** and video games. As Ireland has become more modern, the image is catching up with the written word, because modernity is itself bound up with **spectacle**. Thus rock concerts and theatrical

---

modality *n.* 形式，方式
pipe *n.* 管，笛
fiddler *n.* 小提琴手
repertoire *n.* （演出的）全部节目
footwork *n.* 步法
harp *n.* 竖琴
ballad *n.* 民谣
commentary *n.* 评论
recruit *v.* 征募
visual *adj.* 视觉的
graphic *n.* 图形
animation *n.* 动画
spectacle *n.* 壮观的景象，壮观的场面

# The Republic of Ireland

gigs such as *Riverdance* are increasingly bound up with both image and spectacle.

## Sports Culture

Again, in terms of spectacle, the performance culture which **elicits** the most passionate response in the Irish people is sports. Soccer or "football", introduced to Ireland in 1878, has a large social importance. The Irish team made its first appearance in the World Cup finals in Italy in 1990. Since then, soccer has become the fastest growing sport in the country.

**Rugby football**, originally from England, is also very popular with the Irish. Every year the Irish rugby team competes in the Six Nations' Cup (the nations represented are England, France, Ireland, Italy, Scotland, and Wales). But usually the high point of the rugby season (in winter) is the Triple Crown match, in which Ireland plays against the other three original "home" countries — England, Scotland, and Wales.

Note that in speaking about "football" to an Irish person, it is important to distinguish between rugby and soccer (both British) and the ancient Irish sport known as Gaelic football. A kind of **hybrid** of the two other games in the way it is played, Gaelic football has recently become (in terms of attendance) the most popular sport in Ireland while, outside Ireland, Gaelic football is mainly played among members of the Irish **diaspora** (including teams fielded in Beijing and Chengdu).

The game that is most natively Irish is called **hurling**. It has a reputation of being one of the oldest field sports in the world, as well as one of the fastest. The oldest date, which is **mythological**, given for its origin is 1272 BCE, when, according to ancient tradition, two teams of twenty-seven were locked in a mighty heroic contest. It is taken as a mark of its Irish **authenticity** that the English banned the playing of this game not once but twice during their 800-year rule over Ireland.[28]

The newest and most fashionable ball game in Ireland is, of course, golf. Such is the **upsurge** of interest in the game worldwide, that Ireland's golf courses have now become major tourist attractions, especially given the long daylight hours Ireland enjoys in summer, thanks to its northerly latitude.[29] Other widely popular sports are sailing, tennis, and running. The annual Dublin marathon is now the 4th largest in Europe.

But the sport nearest the Irish heart must be horse-racing. The Irish have a high regard for horses and for centuries the country has been established as an important center for horse-breeding. Watching horse racing is a spectacle that combines several

---

elicit *v.* 引起
rugby football 英式橄榄球
hybrid *n.* 混合（体）
diaspora *n.* 流散在海外的人
hurling *n.* 爱尔兰式曲棍球
mythological *adj.* 神话的，虚构的
authenticity *n.* 真实性，正宗
upsurge *n.* 高涨

elements that the Irish particularly enjoy: it is very sociable, involves valuable and elegant animals, and is an occasion for having a drink while placing a bet. It is said that the Irish love to gamble, and horse-racing is still regarded as an almost respectable **outlet** for this pastime.

## Science and Technology

It is in the name of such stereotypes that Irish culture is often thought of as having an "**arty**" tradition, not a scientific or technological one. This stereotype, interestingly enough, has been traced back to the English, who regarded the Irish character as vague and **unworldly** — utterly unsuited to the hard and practical expertise involved in observing and modifying the natural world.

For a time after declaring their own independence as a nation, the Irish even played up to this stereotype, marketing themselves to incoming tourists as charming but essentially **ineffectual** people who could offer the harassed tourist a **respite** from the pressures of the modern world.

Nothing could be further from the truth.[30] As the historical record shows, Ireland has a rich tradition of scientific enquiry and technological invention.

In science and technology Ireland has been represented by such distinguished names as Robert Boyle (1627–1691), often called the "father of chemistry"; John Tyndall (1820–1893) whose many inventions include the **fireman's respirator**, the **fiber optic** and the **infra-red analyser**. The explanation for the color of the sky that comes from the scattering of light is known as the "Tyndall effect".[31] Also memorable is William Thompson, Lord Kelvin (1824–1907), renowned for his work on transatlantic cables as well as the scale for measuring temperatures.

While all these worked in international circles, others maintained a strong tradition at home. Among these were William Rowan Hamilton (1805–1865), who made important contributions to classical mechanics, optics, and algebra; William Parsons (1800–1867), builder of the world's first great telescope; his son, Charles Parsons (1854–1931) who invented the **steam turbine engine**; John Philip Holland (1841–1914), who invented the first modern **submarines**; Harry Ferguson (1884–1960), who developed the tractor; and Nicholas Callan (1799–1864), the father of battery technology and **magnetism**. It should also be noted that Ernest T. Walton of Trinity College, Dublin, who won the Nobel Prize for Physics in 1951, helped to split the atom.

---

outlet *n.*
发泄的方法
arty *adj.*
艺术气息的，附庸风雅的
unworldly *adj.*
不谙世事的，精神上的
ineffectual *adj.*
效率不高的
respite *adj.*
暂时的休息，缓解
fireman's respirator
消防面具
fiber optic
光纤（技术）
infra-red analyser
红外线分析仪
steam turbine engine
蒸汽涡轮发动机
submarine *n.*
潜水艇
magnetism *n.*
磁力，磁学

# The Republic of Ireland

He helped proved Einstein's theories to be correct.

Irish institutions have also been **innovators**. The Dublin Society (later the Royal Dublin Society), established in 1731, was among the early schools of science in Europe and became a model for other such societies. The establishment of the Royal Irish Academy in 1785 gave Irish science and technology an independent focus. The work of these bodies, together with that of the universities, made Dublin an important center for mathematics and **astronomy** in the nineteenth century. Today, Trinity College, Dublin, in particular, is known for its outstanding international work in the fields of **biotechnology** and **genetics**.

## What is Irish about Irish Culture?

As the above history demonstrates, the stereotypes many have of the Irish are at least partly true. Ireland is a culture where art flourishes, although the arts that flourish most vigorously are those associated with the ear, not the eye. The stereotypes are also partly false: Ireland has always had distinguished scientists and mathematicians and inventors — though many were identified as English during Ireland's eight centuries of colonial subordination.

What tourists most note, however, is that Ireland is also an intensely **people-oriented** society. Family is central to its values. It is very congenial: a society which loves talk and outings and drinking. Unfortunately, the drinking habits of the Irish at times sometimes get out of control and now are a matter for some public concern. The work culture is also very sociable, with little distinction being made between people's public and private lives.

But, as we have seen in looking at its work culture, the Irish have a way of escaping stereotypes. Although they may seem sociable and relaxed at work, they actually work as hard, and as many hours, as their European **counterparts**. In other ways, the Irish have been **hindered** by the stereotypes **foisted** upon them. The Irish have always been proud of their writers, and perhaps Ireland is one of the last countries in the world where being a poet is regarded as a serious and honorable profession. But the Irish are also now rediscovering their heritage in terms of scientific and technological innovation. Certainly in the last two decades they have made their name in the international community in the development and production of electronic technology as well as in such fields as **biogenetics** and biotechnology.

---

innovator n. 创新者，革新家
astronomy n. 天文学
biotechnology n. 生物技术
genetics n. 遗传学
people-oriented adj. 以人为本的，重视人际关系的
counterpart n. 对方，对应的人
hinder v. 阻碍
foist v. 把…强加于
biogenetics n. 生物遗传学

# UNIT 14  Irish Culture: Language, Literature and Arts

What is clear today is that Ireland is still a nation that is in the process of making itself — and the first place a nation makes itself is in its own imagination.[32] During the early years when Irish independence became a national ideal, writers such as W. B. Yeats and his contemporaries were very important in helping the Irish to imagine themselves as a people with a special **destiny**, separate from that of their British colonial masters. They gave **nobility** and purpose to the idea of Ireland as an independent nation. Later, the figure of Eamon de Valera (1882–1975), who began as a freedom fighter, served as the head of government (1932–1959) first for the Free State and then for the Republic of Ireland. He imagined an Ireland that was independent of Britain, culturally and economically. De Valera understood that such independence would have a price: Ireland would not become rich this way. But he did not **aspire** to wealth; his **vision** for Ireland was of a rural economy that had a modest and simple existence.

Inevitably, de Valera's economic policies, particularly those that resulted in the economic tensions of the 1930s, **engendered** an inward-looking and **stagnant** nation, preoccupied with making its own way alone in the world.[33]

All of that changed with Ireland's **accession** to the European Market. From the early 1970s onward, Ireland has now been able to take its place among the nations of Europe, and with it, of the world.[34] In doing so, Ireland has also been forced to modernise its laws and along with its legal framework, the very structure of Irish society. Finally, Ireland has now made its entry into a global economy, to which its fate is now **inextricably** bound.

In fact, today Ireland is now considered to be one of the most **globally-oriented** societies in the Western world. After all, they are inheritors of the **legacies** of two great empires: first of all, that of the British Empire; secondly, that of the world-wide Roman Catholic Church. They also have had a long history of emigration. The Irish diaspora, as it has been called, is a scattering of Irish people across the world, sometimes as the result of better job opportunities abroad — but more often as the result of **dire** conditions at home — famine, foreign domination, low employment, and poverty. As a result, Irish people can today be found in significant concentrations in countries such as Australia, America, Canada, Great Britain and New Zealand, as well as in smaller but significant numbers in Argentina, the Caribbean, and in all parts of the world which were once former British colonies, such as India.[35] In fact, it is hard to go anywhere and *not* find Irish people — and an Irish pub.

---

destiny *n.* 命运
nobility *n.* 高贵的品质
aspire *v.* 渴望，立志
vision *n.* 想象力，眼力
engender *v.* 产生，造成
stagnant *adj.* 停滞的
accession *n.* 加入
inextricably *adv.* 逃不掉地，难解难分
globally-oriented *adj.* 面向全球的
legacy *n.* 遗产
dire *adj.* 悲惨的

# The Republic of Ireland

This global outlook extends to more than merely physical ties across the world. Because of its past as a developing country, Ireland recognises the claims of poorer nations on the wealth of more developed countries, and, for the same reason, is often regarded as an ally of the developing nations.[36] Further, as a politically **neutral** country, Ireland has given **disproportionately** of its services to such international organisations as the United Nations.

From the perspective of North America, Ireland's geographical position also allows itself to be represented as a gateway to the nations of Europe. Because it is English-speaking, as well as having a significant **proportion** of **descendants** living in America, Ireland is often chosen as a site for American business operations in Europe.

But all these perspectives can explain only in part the complex fate of being Irish. To be Irish is to be different — although the Irish themselves would differ about the ways in which they are different. But they feel different, and centuries of colonialism have confirmed them in their conviction that to be Irish is to be like no one else. Racially, the Irish feel more allied to the Celtic peoples of Scotland and Wales and **Brittany** (in western France) who also consider themselves as a race distinct from that of their rulers.[37]

Historically, the Irish have defined themselves by centuries of resistance, political and cultural. Even today, the Irish still have a **residual resentment** against the British, and against any large nation (including the United States) which they feel might try to **bully** them. The Irish tend to identify with the **under-dogs**, with oppressed nations or aspiring nations — with those they see as being denied their rights as a people.

Perhaps because of such a complex heritage, the Irish appear to have a permanent identity crisis. What does it mean to be Irish? The ways the Irish have of being Irish differs from person to person. Some Irish people identify their difference by speaking the Irish language or recovering the traditional arts of Ireland. Others do so by working as volunteers with non-governmental organisations in the Third World, knowing they will be welcome there as politically neutral workers who understand what it means to live in a former colony — or even what it might mean to starve. Other Irish people travel widely, secure in the knowledge that they will be welcome almost everywhere that the British and the Americans are not — as they say, everyone loves the Irish.[38] But even if they have forgotten their lessons in the Irish language, or don't know any traditional dance steps or a **bar** of the old music, the Irish live secure in the conviction

---

neutral *adj.*
中立的
disproport-
ionately *adv.*
不成比例地
proportion *n.*
比例
descendant *n.*
后裔
Brittany *n.*
不列塔尼（群岛）
residual *adj.*
残存的
resentment *n.*
不满，气愤
bully *v.* 欺负
under-dog *n.*
弱者，处于劣势的人
bar *n.*
（音乐）小节

that they have a special destiny, and one that will be gradually revealed to them in the newly evolving global context in which they now make their lives.

# Explanations

1. **Eamon de Valera:**
   埃蒙·德·瓦勒拉（1882–1975），爱尔兰政治家、总理（1932–1948，1951–1954，1957–1959）。早年积极参加爱尔兰独立运动并在 1916 年复活节起义后当选新芬党主席（当时在英国的监狱中）。瓦勒拉于 1959 年成为爱尔兰共和国总统，1973 年退休。

2. **This was reinforced by making it mandatory ... its students from Great Britain:**
   这一政策得到了强化，规定进入爱尔兰的大学必须具有足够的爱尔兰语水平。唯一的例外是设在都柏林的三一学院。本来该校就是具有自己法规并从英国招收许多学生的新教学校。

3. **This idiom is distinguished from ... by certain semantic idiosyncrasies:**
   这种语言以某些词汇（其中的许多词来自于地方、古语或者爱尔兰语）和某些句子结构特点区别于英国人讲的英语。

4. **Even among the most literate classes ... with grace and force:**
   即使在受过最好教育的阶层，人们还是非常重视自然、优雅和有力的谈话能力。

5. **what this means in practical terms is ... than a more reticent culture would allow:**
   这在实际生活中意味着即使是在爱尔兰做普通生意也可能比在重行轻言的社会要花更多的时间。

6. **But although ... by a good deal of personal interaction, teasing (called "sagging") and laughter:**
   尽管对来访的德国或美国商人来说这种习惯看上去纯粹是浪费时间，但实际上这意味着一天的日常活动会由于诸如亲历故事、蹩脚笑话等口头交流而变得活跃起来，整天都是由很多的人际交往、打趣（被称为"乱开玩笑"）以及笑声陪伴度过的。

7. **Again, in dance ... in the current stage production of *Riverdance*:**
   还有，在舞蹈方面，爱尔兰以其繁复而热烈的民间舞蹈闻名于世，体现在现代化的当代歌舞"大河舞"上。

8. **Thus it is useful ... art of a self-consciously "new" nation:**
   因此，应该将当代爱尔兰看作是一个意识根植于其过去传统、语言和艺术的民族而不是自觉的"新"国家。

9. **The first poem identified as "Irish" ... before it was written down:**
   被认定为第一首"爱尔兰语"诗歌的《泰恩》传奇已经在口头上流传了几个世纪之后才被用文字记录下来。

10. **some of the most avid collectors ... as a basis for its claim ... independent nation:**
    其中一些最积极的收集者是诗人与作家，他们努力宣扬爱尔兰传统文化的重要性，以其作为爱尔兰具有

# The Republic of Ireland

鲜明特色独立国家的基础。

11. **Now that Ireland is an independent republic ... over many centuries:**
既然爱尔兰已经成为独立的主权国家,该国养成了一种习惯,即宣布几百年来所有在爱尔兰境内出生或写作过的作家均属于爱尔兰。

12. **But the Irish see no reason ... as a land of literary giants:**
但是,爱尔兰人认为历史没有理由阻止他们将这些作家视为"爱尔兰人"(或英裔爱尔兰人)用来增加爱尔兰作为文豪之国的民族自豪感。

13. **In modern times alone, ... Bernard Shaw (1856–1950) and Samuel Beckett (1906–1989):**
仅仅在现代,爱尔兰共和国的这片土地成为四位诺贝尔文学奖得主的祖国:诗人叶芝(1865–1929)与谢默斯·希尼(1939–2013),以及剧作家萧伯纳(1856–1950)和塞缪·贝克特(1906–1989)。

14. **Jonathan Swift (1667–1745):**
乔纳森·斯威夫特,爱尔兰作家,代表作品为《格列佛游记》(*Gulliver's Travels*)。

15. **Laurence Sterne (1713–1768):**
劳伦斯·斯特恩,出生于爱尔兰的英国作家,代表作为《项狄传》(*Tristram Shandy*)。

16. **Richard Sheridan (1751–1816):**
理查德·谢力丹,爱尔兰剧作家,代表作有《丑闻学校》(*The School for Scandal*)。

17. **Oscar Wilde (1856–1900):**
奥斯卡·王尔德,爱尔兰剧作家、诗人,代表作有《道林·格雷的画像》(*The Picture of Dorian Gray*)、《温德密尔夫人的扇子》(*Lady Windermere's Fan*)、《理想丈夫》(*An Ideal Husband*),等。

18. **James Joyce (1882–1941):**
詹姆斯·乔伊斯,爱尔兰小说家,其作品风格为现代主义的意识流,作品有《都柏林人》《一个青年艺术家的画像》《尤利西斯》和《芬尼根的守灵夜》。

19. **This sense of language as alien ... to play with its forms:**
这种视英语为具有自身活力外来语的感受使得乔伊斯对其进行实验并在形式上做游戏(比英国人)容易得多。乔伊斯在小说语言上做了大胆的实验,他时常自造词汇,或者不用规范的句法和标点符号,让语言自由流动,就像人物潜意识的复杂活动。

20. **Perhaps for this reason, ... as if they were part of a game:**
也许正是由于这个原因,乔伊斯以及贝克特的作品具有自我意识的先锋派风格,把玩不同的方言和英语文体,就像在玩游戏。

21. **As a critique of bourgeois obsessions ... more savage:**
作为对资产阶级迷恋努力工作、建功立业以及追求目的和意义的批判,该剧可算是最为辛辣猛烈的。

UNIT 14  Irish Culture: Language, Literature and Arts

22. **English ways are not Irish ways, ... as foreign and often offensive:**
    英国人的生活方式并非爱尔兰人的生活方式，如果爱尔兰人采用了英国方式，那他们会引起那些认为殖民者生活方式为外来而且可恶的人们的讽刺和挖苦。

23. **A poet such as Seamus Heaney, ... the history of his people:**
    像谢默斯·希尼这样的诗人，出生在北爱尔兰但后来长期居住在爱尔兰共和国，被尊奉为敢于对发生在那里的冲突凭良心讲话的人。他超脱于两派纷争之外，以受到纷争之苦的人们真正代言人的身份记录下自己人民的历史。

24. **He is honoured ... which is the common inheritance of all Irish people, North and South:**
    他被人们尊崇不仅仅因为他说真话，还因为这些话在严酷的分裂之中，使人们回想起原本统一的田园文化，即所有爱尔兰人，不管北方还是南方，拥有的共同传统。

25. **Like Joyce's artist, ... It is no mean vocation:**
    和乔伊斯笔下的艺术家一样，爱尔兰的作家天生具有一种神圣的使命感，来"塑造本民族永存的良心意识"。这可不是一般的职业。

26. **Fiddles became common in the early 19th century ... hornpipes and slides:**
    在爱尔兰，19世纪初期小提琴手已很常见，而现在的爱尔兰小提琴手更是以演奏吉格舞曲、瑞尔（回旋）舞曲、号笛舞曲和滑动舞曲等一系列保留曲目闻名于世。

27. **This is particularly true of songs ... rebellion (of which, over the centuries, there were many):**
    这尤其体现在抨击英国征兵制度（在这一制度下年轻人被强征服役）或讲述最近一次率领民众反抗英国的英雄的歌曲上。

28. **It is taken as a mark ... during their 800-year rule over Ireland:**
    由于被视为纯正的爱尔兰体育运动标志，英国在对爱尔兰长达800年统治期间曾两度禁止该项运动。

29. **Such is the upsurge of interest ... thanks to its northerly latitude:**
    全世界对高尔夫球运动的兴趣如此高涨，以至于爱尔兰的高尔夫球场现在成为主要的旅游胜地，尤其吸引游客的是其高纬度给夏季的爱尔兰带来的漫长日光。

30. **Nothing could be further from the truth:**
    没有比这离事实更远的了。意思是，这根本不是事实。

31. **In science and technology Ireland ... and the infra-red analyzer:**
    在科学与技术方面，爱尔兰产生了如雷贯耳的杰出科学家：经常被称为"化学之父"的罗伯特·波伊尔（1627–1691）；发明了包括消防面具、光纤以及红外线分析仪（对天空颜色来自散射光线的解释被称为廷道尔效应）的约翰·廷道尔（1820–1893）。

32. **What is clear today is that ... in its imagination:**
    现在很清楚的一点是，爱尔兰仍是一个自我塑造中的国家，而一个国家自我塑造的首要条件就是自己的想象力。

# The Republic of Ireland

33. **Inevitably, de Valera's economic policies ... making its own way alone in the world:**
    不可避免，他的政策，尤其是导致20世纪30年代经济紧张的那些政策，造就了一个内向和停滞的国家，致力于以自己的方式在世界上独自发展。

34. **From the early 1970s onward, ... of the world:**
    自20世纪70年代初以来，爱尔兰已经能够自立于欧洲民族国家之林，随之而来的是确立了在世界上的地位。

35. **As a result, ... such as India:**
    结果，在澳大利亚、美国、加拿大、新西兰和英国都能找到集中并可观的爱尔兰人群，数量少一些的国家有阿根廷、加勒比海地区以及曾为英国殖民地的所有国家，如印度。

36. **Because of its past as a developing country, ... as an ally of the developing nations:**
    由于过去曾为发展中国家，爱尔兰认可较穷国家对富裕国家财富的诉求，而且出于同一原因，经常被看作是发展中国家的盟友。

37. **Racially, the Irish feel more allied to the Celtic peoples ... distinct from that of their rulers:**
    在种族认同方面，爱尔兰人感到更贴近苏格兰、威尔士和不列塔尼（在法国北部）的凯尔特人种。他们都认为自己与其统治者是截然不同的民族。

38. **Other Irish people travel widely, ... everyone loves the Irish:**
    另外一些爱尔兰人经常在世界各地旅行，他们对在英国人和美国人不受欢迎的地方他们都受到欢迎这一点深信不疑——正如他们所说，人人都喜欢爱尔兰人。

# Exercises

**I. Give the Chinese equivalents for the following:**

1. Hiberno-English
2. *Riverdance*
3. James Joyce
4. Robert Boyle
5. the Irish diaspora

**II. Decide whether the following statements are true (T) or false (F):**

1. Traditionally, the Irish people spoke their own language, called Irish or Gaelic. _____

UNIT 14  Irish Culture: Language, Literature and Arts

2. The language spoken universally in the Republic of Ireland is known as Hiberno-English, a version of standard English. _____
3. The Irish people have a weak oral culture, that is to say, they don't like talking to people. _____
4. *Riverdance* is not a form of Irish dance. _____
5. The Republic of Ireland has produced four Nobel Prize winners among its writers. _____
6. The work of James Joyce and that of Samuel Becket are not self-consciously avant-garde. _____
7. The *sean nos* or "old style" of singing is sung by the unaccompanied voice. _____
8. The most natively Irish game is hurling, enjoying a reputation of being one of the oldest field sports in the world. _____

III. **Fill in the blanks:**

1. Irish or Gaelic is a very ancient (and difficult) language with a rich _____ culture.
2. Until the mid-nineteenth century Irish was still spoken widely by the _____ classes.
3. The first poem identified as "Irish" is the _____ of the *Tain*, which was transmitted orally for centuries before it was written down.
4. As an independent Republic in its own right, Ireland has developed the habit of laying claim to all _____ who have been born or have worked/written in Ireland.
5. Among the Irish Nobel Prize winners for literature, W. B. Yeats and Seamus Heaney were _____; George Bernard Shaw and Samuel Beckett were _____.
6. Samuel Becket's most famous play is _____.
7. _____ is a very popular sport among the Irish because they can have a drink and place a bet for the occasion.
8. The explanation for the color of the sky that comes from the scattering of light is known as the "_____".
9. The _____, established in 1731, was among the early schools of science in Europe and became a model for other such societies.
10. Today Ireland is considered to be both _____-oriented and _____-oriented.

# The Republic of Ireland

IV. **Questions:**

1. What are the two languages used by the Irish people? What accounts for the phenomenon?
2. Why is the number of people speaking Irish diminishing despite official advocating?
3. What is the basis of the Irish oral cultural tradition? How does the Irish oral culture influence the life and work of the Irish people?
4. What role does satire play in the works by some major Irish writers such as Jonathan Swift and Oscar Wilde?
5. Why did James Joyce like to experiment with the English Language and play with its expression?
6. Which writers' works were self-consciously avant-garde? What are the reasons?
7. Why are the poet and the writer honoured above all other artists in Ireland ?
8. What is the usual style and theme of the traditional Irish singing *sean nos*?
9. What are the characteristics of Irish dancing as represented by *Riverdance*?
10. What is the newest and most fashionable ball game in Ireland? What advantageous conditions can Ireland offer regarding the game?
11. Why is Irish culture often thought to have an "arty" tradition, rather than a scientific or technological one?
12. What are the three most important inventions by John Tyndall?
13. What contributions did Eamon de Velera make to the formation of the Irish national identity? Are there any limitations in his vision and policies?
14. Why does Ireland often regard itself as an ally of the developing nations?

V. **Topics for discussion or research:**

1. Research one of the four Nobel Prize winners for Literature mentioned in the text: W. B. Yeats, Seamus Heaney, George Bernard Shaw or Samuel Beckett.
2. What is Irish about Irish culture according to the author? What are your observations and comments?
3. Discuss the phenomenon of the Irish diaspora and how it provided benefits to Ireland.

# Australia

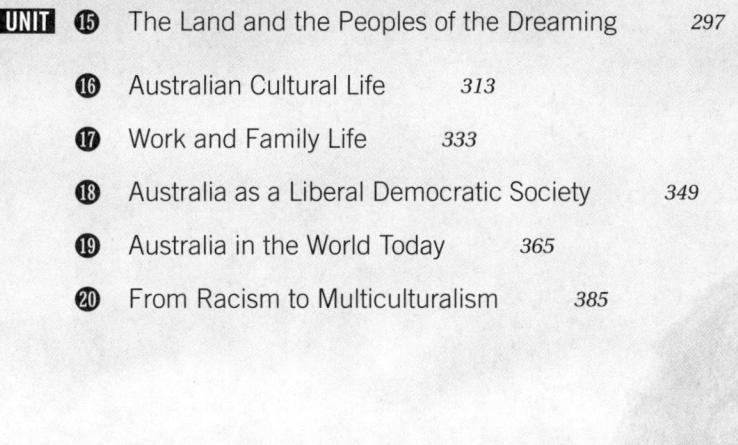

**UNIT 15** The Land and the Peoples of the Dreaming — 297

16 Australian Cultural Life — 313

17 Work and Family Life — 333

18 Australia as a Liberal Democratic Society — 349

19 Australia in the World Today — 365

20 From Racism to Multiculturalism — 385

# UNIT 15

# The Land and the Peoples of the Dreaming

> **Go over the following focal points before reading the text:**
>
> ❖ The natural environment of Australia
> ❖ Distinctive features of the land
> ❖ Distinctive animals of the land
> ❖ The indigenous peoples
> ❖ Dreaming and Dreamtime
> ❖ *Terra Nullius*
> ❖ The impact of colonisation on the indigenous peoples
> ❖ Policies of segregation and assimilation
> ❖ The assimilation policy

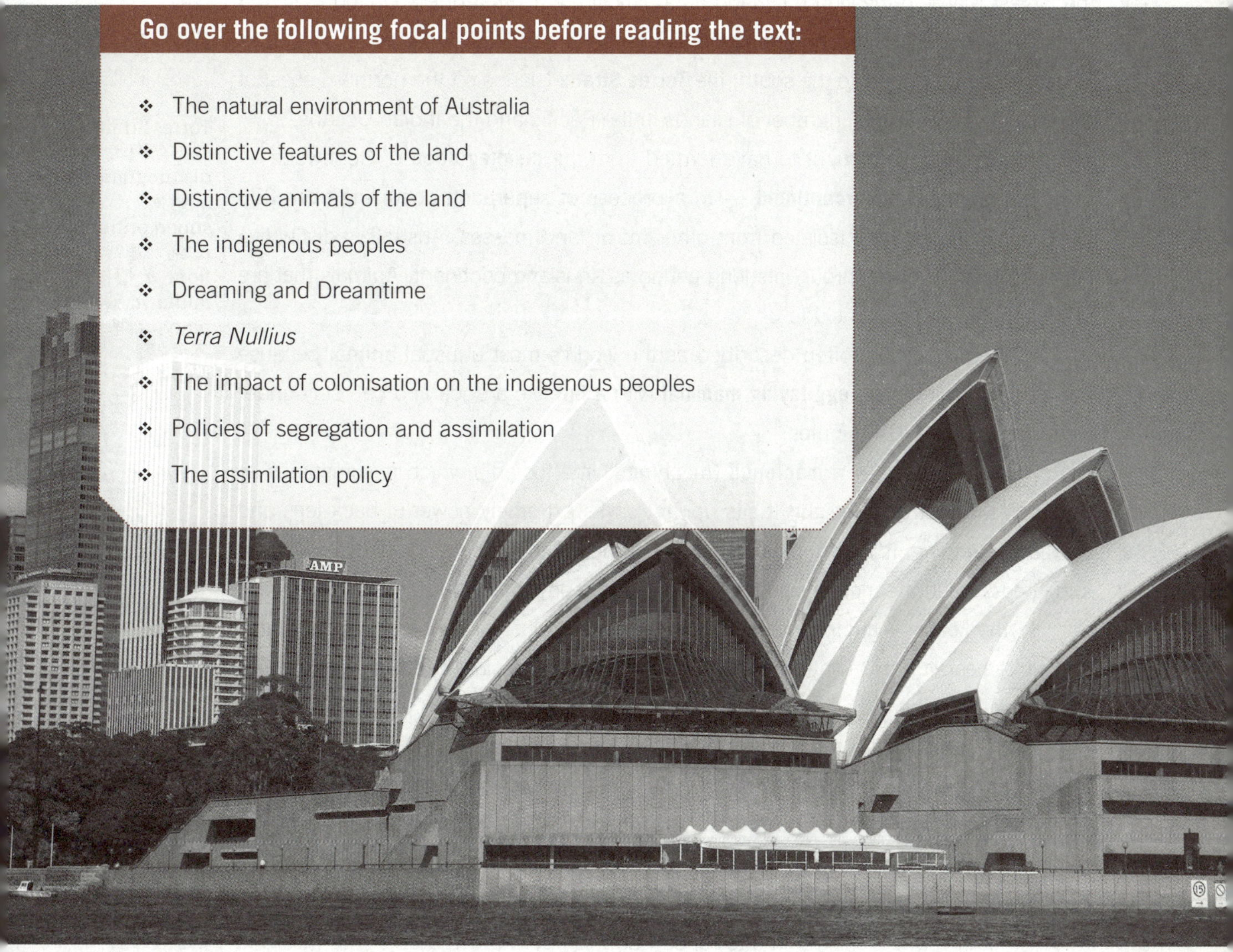

# Australia

 Text

## The Land

The continent of Australia lies between **equatorial** South East Asia and the **Antarctic**. With a coastline of 30 000 kilometres and a land area of 7 692 000 km$^2$, it is the largest island in the world. Its land area almost equals that of the United States. It is also the smallest, flattest and driest continent in the world. The country also includes **Tasmania**, an island just to the south, the **Torres Straits** Islands off the northern coast of the mainland and a small number of islands in the Pacific and the Indian Oceans.[1]

The continent is thought to have formed from the **disintegration** of Gondwana — the great southern **supercontinent** — in a process of separation occurring from 250 to 90 million years ago.[2] Isolated from other major land masses, Australia's distinctive **flora** and **fauna** evolved through its long period as an island continent. Animals that are unique to the continent include:

- the **platypus** — often described as the world's most unusual animal because it is a small, **web-footed**, **egg-laying mammal** with a **bill** like a duck and can stay under water for as long as 14 minutes;

- the **kangaroo** — a **macropod** (meaning "large footed") which is sometimes as much as two metres in height. It sits upright on its extremely powerful back legs and moves by jumping. It is also a **marsupial** which means that the young "joeys", or baby kangaroos, live in the mother's **pouch** until they are ready to **fend** for themselves;[3]

- the **koala** — another marsupial but one which looks like a small, woolly, grey and white bear. It lives mainly in the branches of trees, especially the **eucalyptus** whose leaves comprise the koala's main diet[4];

- the **wombat** — a **squat**, round, bear-like, **burrowing** marsupial, about one metre in length, with short legs, small ears and eyes and a thick, coarse fur of brown or grey.

The landscape of the country is extremely variable. In the north are tropical rainforests; snowfields occupy the plateau landscapes of the southeast whilst, in the centre and the western areas of the continent, two thirds of the land is desert or semi desert.[5] However, it is in the Mediterranean and temperate climates of the hills and fertile plains bordering the east, south and the south west of the continent that eighty

---

equatorial *adj.*
（在）赤道的；赤道附近的
Antarctic *adj.*
南极的，南极附近的
Tasmania *n.*
塔斯马尼亚岛（澳大利亚东南部）
Torres Straits
托雷斯海峡
disintegration *n.* 解体
supercontinent *n.* 超大陆
flora *n.* 植物群
fauna *n.* 动物群
platypus *n.*
鸭嘴兽
web-footed *adj.*
长蹼足的（动物）
egg-laying *adj.*
产卵的
mammal *n.*
哺乳动物
bill *n.* 鸟嘴
kangaroo *n.*
袋鼠
macropod *adj.*
大足的
marsupial *n.*
有袋动物
pouch *n.*（袋鼠等的）育儿袋
fend (for oneself)
能独立照顾自己
koala *n.* 树袋熊
eucalyptus *n.*
桉树
wombat *n.*
毛鼻袋熊
squat *adj.*
低矮的，矮胖的
burrow *v.*
挖地洞，住地洞

per cent of Australians live today.[6]

Two of the country's most distinctive physical features are the Great Dividing Range[7] and the Great Barrier Reef[8]. The Great Dividing Range extends as an almost unbroken series of plateaus down the East Coast of Australia, from northern Queensland, through New South Wales and into Victoria, whilst, off shore, The Great Barrier Reef, the largest **coral** structure in the world, extends for over 2 000 kilometres along the coast of Queensland.

coral *n.* 珊瑚

## The Peoples

We do not know exactly how long the country has been occupied but the earliest discovered site of occupation is about forty-seven thousand years old. To put this in perspective, since the First Fleet arrived in 1788 there have been only eight generations of settlers. On the other hand, there have been at least 18 500 generations of the Peoples of the Dreaming.[9]

The Peoples of the Dreaming belonged to over 500 different groups or nations with different languages and cultures but they were bound together by their belief in the Dreaming. "The Dreaming" or "The Dreamtime"[10] is the most enduring religion in Australia today. It is based on the central principle that the people who live on the continent have special responsibilities to the land — that the land owns them and that they hold it in trust as the home of their creator.[11] However, in the immensely variable landscape of the country, different cultures and different languages developed within this broad framework of the Dreamtime.

There were somewhere between 200 to 250 different languages spoken on the continent. Some of these languages still exist today: about 20 of them are still strong, but over 150 are now lost. We do not now know the names of all the languages that were spoken throughout the continent but these are some of the language groups who lived in the country's wide variety of landscapes and climates.

- The Arrernte people lived in the desert regions of Central Australia[12].
- The Thurrawai, the Dhurga and the Dyirringa peoples, lived on the fertile plains of the Illawarra[13] in the South East.
- The Gundungurra and the Ngarigu are the People of the tablelands and the snowfields to the west of these plains, in the land on which Canberra[14], the Australian capital now stands.

# Australia

- Pitjanjara is the language of a number of different family groups whose country is in the central and southern desert region. Uluru[15], a huge rock (called a **monolith**) that sticks out in the middle of the flat desert, and the Devils Marbles[16], massive **boulders** which are scattered along the highway near Alice Springs, belong to the Dreaming of the Pitjanjara peoples.
- The Jawoyn people belong to the tropical north of the country. Their people are responsible for the rich artwork, the rock paintings in the **gorge** country of what is now the Nitmiluk National Park.

Membership in a particular language group was of great social and cultural significance. Traditionally, languages belong to **tracts** of country which, in the belief system of the Dreamings, have been put in their places by Dreamtime creator figures.[17]

### "Dreamtime" or "Dreaming"

The expression "Dreamtime" is most often used to refer to the "time before time", or "the time of the creation of all things", while "Dreaming" refers to an individual's or group's set of beliefs or spirituality. For instance, an **indigenous** Australian might say that they have Kangaroo Dreaming, or Wombat Dreaming. These are the many separate stories that explain the creation of whichever features of the land that form the country of any one group.[18]

In most of the languages there is no distinction between the words for "belief", "law" and "knowledge".[19] The sacred creation stories are not only explanations about how the country came to be formed, they also provide principles of how people should live and interact with others, especially with whom they may or may not intermarry. These stories and the rules of how to live are very intricate: the Peoples of the Dreaming lived in a complex spiritual and social world. The several stories of creation also provide a memorable map of the landscape[20]. For people outside of this culture the desert seems to be empty and life threatening. However, the intricate and specific detail of the stories of the Dreaming transform the desert into a familiar and life sustaining landscape: the Peoples of the Dreamtime know how to find water, even in the desert areas, because the special stories within the Dreaming provide a detailed knowledge of their land.[21]

Within the **clan** grouping, all speaking the same language or the same dialect, small bands of families carried out their daily living as a group. They moved around their clan country, from place to place, depending on the season and the availability of

---

monolith *n.* 独块巨石
boulder *n.* 巨砾，漂砾
gorge *n.* 峡谷
tract *n.* 广阔的土地，地域
indigenous *adj.* 本地的，本土的
clan *n.* 家族

## UNIT 15  The Land and the Peoples of the Dreaming

food. In coastal areas and the more fertile parts of the continent, groups were relatively **static**, because food was readily obtainable, but in the desert areas vast tracts of land could support only a few people who had to travel long distances in their **quest** for food.[22]

Because the Peoples of the Dreaming developed an intricate understanding of the land their intellectual skills became important to the colonists and developers who took over the country after 1788. The first industries that were developed after the settlements were the **sealing** industries. White **sealers**, in Tasmania, and on Kangaroo Island in South Australia, were quick to understand the value of the knowledge of the local peoples whose land they had invaded. On both islands the sealers **abducted** young indigenous women and used their manual and intellectual labour to catch and prepare the seal skins and the meat and **blubber** from which the sealers extracted their profit[23]. Later, the **pastoralists** exploited the Peoples' understanding of the land in the development of the great cattle and sheep stations that created massive wealth for the new white "owners".[24]

In both of these examples the indigenous people were paid no wages and were treated as though they were part of the fauna of the country rather than as people with human rights. Their intellectual skills were used but devalued by the colonists who, from 1788, invaded, took over the land and, eventually, reconstructed the continent into the nation of Australia.[25]

From 1788 until today the relationship between the Peoples of the Dreaming and the colonisers has passed through several different stages. In the next section of this unit we look at the impact of contact and colonisation. After we have examined the construction of modern Australia in Units 16 to 19 we return, in the final unit, to this central relationship to examine the Peoples' 20th century struggles to reclaim their culture and their rights to the land.

## Contact and the Concept of *Terra Nullius*

The British were not the first foreigners to make contact with the Peoples of the Dreaming. In 1405, Zhu Di the Ming emperor commissioned his **admiral** Zheng He to take 317 of his ships to the Middle East and Eastern Africa. Between 1405 and 1433 Zheng He made seven trips routinely passing through what we now call Southeast and South Asia and there is evidence that several ships from that **armada** landed on the

static *adj.* 静态的
quest *n.* 寻求
sealing *adj.* 捕猎海豹的
sealer *n.* 捕猎海豹者
abduct *v.* 诱拐，劫持，绑架
blubber *n.* 海兽脂
pastoralist *n.* （澳）牧场主
admiral *n.* 海军将军；商船队长
armada *n.* 舰队

# Australia

Aru Islands to the north of Arnhem Land[26]. Some Northern Territory stories incorporate concepts, for example of **reincarnation**, that are more often associated with Buddhism than with the Dreaming[27] and there are rock paintings in the Northern Territory which could be interpreted as portraying **Chinese junks** weighing **anchor** or images of the Buddha. Moreover, the kangaroo, an animal indigenous only to Australia was known in 15th century China.

Although Chinese, Malaysian, Indonesian, and Arab **seafarers** may have landed in northern Australia well before 1500 AD, Australia was essentially unknown in the West until the 17th century. However it did exist in late medieval European logic and mythology as a great Southland, or Terra Australis, which was thought necessary to balance the weight of the northern landmasses of Europe and Asia.[28] Terra Australis often appeared on early European maps as a large, globe-shaped mass in about the location they expected it to be.[29]

There are records in the art of the Peoples of the Dreaming of the arrival of various European travellers, Portuguese, Spanish and Dutch explorers. However, it was the British who took over the country in the late 18th century, declaring it to be "*terra nullius*"[30] — an un-owned wasteland which could, legitimately, be colonised.

By declaring Australia "*terra nullius*" the British were not only claiming that they could take possession of the land but that they could dismiss those who had lived there for 18 000 or so generations as a people who were not fully human and who were certainly not "civilised".[31] The 500 Peoples of the Dreaming were not recognised. These one million or so people who lived on the land were instead grouped together under the one name: "the **Aborigines**", the **generic** term meaning "the original natives of the land."[32]

## The Impact of Colonisation

Approximately a large number of Aborigines were killed in violent **skirmishes** and **massacres** in the first decades of colonisation. The ratio of white to black deaths in these battles and skirmishes was about 1:10. Chilla Bulbeck makes the point that more White Australians were killed in these "frontier wars" than in the conflicts in Vietnam and Korea. In some areas **martial law** was declared against those Aborigines who attempted to prevent the settlers from taking over their hunting and collecting grounds[33]. This was especially the case in Tasmania where the indigenous people were hunted down systematically. However, even Lachlan Macquarie, the Governor of NSW[34]

---

reincarnation *n.* 转世化身
Chinese junk 中国式帆船
anchor *n.* 锚
seafarer *n.* 水手，航海者
Aborigine *n.* 土著居民
generic *adj.* 一般的，通用的
skirmish *n.* 小规模战斗，小冲突
massacre *n.* 大屠杀，残杀
martial law 军事管制，戒严令

who is usually regarded as the most humane and liberal Governor of the early period of the settlement of NSW, wrote in 1816 that he approved of the way his soldiers attacked the indigenous peoples even though innocent men, women and children had been killed, because this attack would strike terror in the heart of "the natives"[35].

Even more disastrous to the Peoples of the Dreaming were the diseases that the colonists brought with them. Many were killed by the imported diseases, and as a result the Peoples were soon no longer seen as a threat to settlement[36].

## The Policies of Segregation and Exclusion

By the mid 1800s the government practices of violence changed to policies of segregation and exclusion. The aboriginal people were forcibly taken from their own land and put on **reserves** where they were placed under the absolute control of white officials, often Christian missionaries, who were given the title of Protectors[37].

Throughout the 19th century, Europeans — **bolstered** by the image of themselves as the superior, civilised peoples — colonised several countries around the world. In Australia, the 19th and early 20th century social scientists legitimated this view. Social scientists of the time adapted the general **Darwinian** theory of evolution to develop a theory of a hierarchy of races, with the white colonising peoples located at the top and the black **nomadic** peoples, whom they colonised and exploited, at the bottom of the scale.[38] Herbert Spencer the most prominent social **evolutionist** of this period, introduced the term "the survival of the fittest" to **validate** the military, political and cultural superiority of the colonial Europeans.[39] In Australia these racist theories legitimated even further forms of exploitation and **appropriation** of land as the white settlers took over more of the country. Meanwhile, on the reserves, the Peoples of the Dreaming were denied basic rights and freedoms.

## The Policy of Assimilation

By the beginning of the 20th century the policy of protection had been replaced by the policy of assimilation. "Assimilation" was founded on the belief that the white culture was the progressive and superior whereas the Dreamtime was only a form of **superstition**[40]. Children were taken away from their parents to be placed in church-run institutions and the missionaries on the "protected reserves" set out to destroy

---

segregation n.
隔离
exclusion n.
排斥
reserve n.
保留地
bolster v.
支撑，支持
Darwinian adj.
达尔文的
nomadic adj.
游牧的
evolutionist n.
进化论者
validate v.
使有法律效力；证实
appropriation n. 占用，盗用
assimilation n.
同化
superstition n.
迷信

the culture of the Dreamings and to replace it with Christianity. As the children grew to adulthood, many of them had lost both their families and their culture. They were known as the Stolen Generations. They were employed as domestic servants or on cattle stations but were paid only with food and clothes or with wages that were only a fraction of those paid to white workers. Young Aboriginal women were continually at risk of rape on the reserves, institutions, and in their places of employment[41].

There was a major contradiction underlying the official relationship of "Assimilation". Whilst it officially meant that both peoples would become as one, with the Aboriginal people merging into the larger Australian society, in practice, assimilation was accompanied by segregation.[42] Aboriginal people were excluded from the social, the political and the working life of mainstream Australians. They had unequal conditions of entry into public houses, swimming pools and cinemas and were excluded from mainstream education and health services. They were also excluded from many forms of employment and from citizenship: Aboriginal people could not vote.

The double loss, of traditional culture and exclusion from mainstream Australian society and culture, led to Aboriginal people being labelled as lazy, stupid and drunken and dirty. This combination of exclusionary practices and cultural prejudices paralleled the systems of **apartheid** practised in the United States and South Africa.[43] **Racism** was an **entrenched** part of Australian culture until the 1960s and operated at the personal and the institutional level.

## Conclusion

The history of contact has been a history of loss for the Peoples of the Dreaming, a history of:
- stolen land
- stolen wages
- stolen culture and
- stolen children

In the final unit we investigate the continuing tragedy of social inequality but, as well, we record the successes of the Peoples' struggles for Land Rights and for social and cultural equality. However, before we examine these current relationships, we need to outline the development of mainstream Australia society and culture by investigating

apartheid *n.*
种族隔离
racism *n.*
种族主义
entrench *v.*
确立，使处于牢固地位

the alternative belief systems and the construction of the political, economic and family systems that comprise mainstream Australian society and culture today.

## Explanations

1. **The country ... in the Pacific and the Indian Oceans:**
   澳大利亚还包括位于其大陆南方的一个岛，即塔斯马尼亚岛（Tasmania），和距其大陆北部海岸不远的托雷斯海峡群岛，以及太平洋和印度洋中的一些岛屿。塔斯马尼亚岛与澳大利亚大陆隔巴斯海峡（Bass Strait）相望，是澳大利亚最大的岛和最小的省。

2. **The continent is thought ... from 250 to 90 million years ago:**
   人们认为，澳大利亚大陆形成于两亿五千万到九千万年前发生的一系列板块分离运动中的冈瓦纳板块的解体。地质学研究认为，两亿年前，地球由两个大陆地板块组成，即冈瓦纳大陆（Gondwana）和劳亚古大陆（Laurasia）。冈瓦纳古大陆解体后形成了南极洲、澳洲、非洲、南美洲和印度次大陆，而劳亚古大陆解体后形成了北美洲、欧洲、亚洲和格陵兰岛。

3. **It sits upright ... to fend for themselves:**
   袋鼠站立时是坐在自己强有力的后腿（和尾巴）上，行走时进行跳跃式的运动。它是有袋动物，小袋鼠在能独立照顾自己之前，一直生活在妈妈的袋子里。joey 源自澳大利亚原住民的语言，指幼袋鼠。

4. **... especially the eucalyptus whose leaves comprise the koala's main diet:**
   特别是栖息在桉树上，因为桉树叶是它们的主要食物。

5. **In the north are ... is desert or semi desert:**
   北部有热带雨林；东南部的高原区被雪地覆盖，而澳大利亚大陆的中部和西部的三分之二地区是沙漠或半沙漠。

6. **However, it is in ... that eighty per cent of Australians live today:**
   然而，今天80%的澳大利亚人都住在澳大利亚大陆的东部、南部和西南部边缘地区的山丘和肥沃的平原上，处于地中海式气候或温带气候区内。

7. **The Great Dividing Range:**
   大分水岭。如下文所说，澳大利亚大分水岭沿着大陆的东部边缘，从昆士兰省的北部开始绵延不断，形成一系列几乎不间断的高地，一直穿过新南威尔士省和维多利亚省，延伸到塔斯马尼业南部海边。

8. **The Great Barrier Reef:**
   大堡礁，位于昆士兰省东北部海洋中，沿着昆士兰省的海岸绵延 2 000 多公里，由 3 000 个不同阶段的珊瑚礁、珊瑚岛沙洲和泻湖组成，总面积 20.7 万平方公里，是世界七大自然景观之一。大堡礁是一个重要

# Australia

的海洋生态系统，其中的岛屿和珊瑚礁中生存着许多稀有的海洋动植物。大堡礁被列为世界自然遗产。

9. **To put this in perspective ... the Peoples of the Dreaming:**
   为了对此有正确的理解，（我们知道）自从 1788 年（英国载着罪犯的）第一批舰队到达澳大利亚以来，一共才只经过了八代人，而梦创时代的后人（即原住民）从四万七千年前开始已有 18 500 代人在这片土地上生活。

10. **"The Dreaming" or "The Dreamtime":**
    梦创时代，是原住民文化的重要组成部分。它是指原住民的神话中所指的远古时期，那时地球得到了其目前的形态，生命和自然的形式和周期也在那时开始。关于梦创时代的传说构成了今天原住民的价值观和社会关系。澳大利亚原住民认为只有在梦境之中，人才可以得到对远古创始期的认知，故称其为 Dreaming。

11. **It is based on ... as the home of their creator:**
    梦创时代的信仰基于一条最重要的原则，即生活在澳大利亚大陆上的人们对土地有着特殊责任——即他们属于土地，他们只是受托保管他们先人创造者的家园。

12. **The Arrente people:**
    这里和后文中所列的八个名字是在澳大利亚不同地区土著部落的名称。

13. **Illawarra:**
    伊拉瓦拉地区，位于澳大利亚新南威尔士省的东南沿海地区。

14. **Canberra:**
    堪培拉，澳大利亚首都，位于澳大利亚东南部澳大利亚首都特区内（ACT）。

15. **Uluru:**
    乌鲁如岩，曾被白人定居者称为艾尔斯岩（Ayres Rock），位于澳大利亚中部，是一块在平坦的沙漠中天然形成的巨大岩石。它也是当地原住民部落的圣地，被列为世界自然和文化遗产。

16. **Devils Marbles:**
    原住民称其为 Karwekarlwe，位于澳大利亚中部、北方领土内，巨大的花岗岩巨石叠摞在一起，颇为壮观。同时，这里也是当地原住民的圣地，他们认为这些巨石是他们的祖先彩虹蛇的卵。

17. **Traditionally, languages belong ... by Dreamtime creator figures:**
    从传统意义上讲，梦创时代的信仰体系中认为，语言都是属于某一特定地区的，而这是由远古梦创时代的造物者安排的。澳大利亚原住民分为 500 多个部落，每个部落都有自己的语言和活动区域。原住民认为这都是在梦创时代就划分好的。

18. **The expression "Dreamtime" is ... of any one group:**
    "Dreamtime"（梦创时代）这一说法经常用来指"远古时期"或"创世纪的时候"，而"Dreaming（梦创）"则是用来指个人或群体的信仰或精神崇拜。如一位澳大利亚原住民会说他们有 Kangaroo Dreaming（袋鼠信仰）或 Wombat Dreaming（毛鼻袋熊信仰）。 这是因为原住民部落有许多不同的故事来演绎他们土地上的地貌特征是如何形成的。

## UNIT 15  The Land and the Peoples of the Dreaming

19. **In most of the languages ... "law" and "knowledge":**
    大部分语言中"信仰""法律"和"知识"词意没有差别。意指这三者都有约束和指导人们思想与活动的作用。

20. **The several stories of creation also provide a memorable map of the landscape:**
    原住民的几个有关创造天地的故事也为他们了解土地提供了难忘的地图。

21. **However, the intricate and specific detail ... knowledge of their land:**
    然而,梦创故事中复杂而具体的细节帮助原住民把沙漠变成了他们熟知的、帮助他们维持生命延续的地方:梦创时代的传人们即使在沙漠中,也知道如何找到水,因为一些特殊的梦创故事中为他们提供了土地的详细信息。

22. **In coastal areas ... in their quest for food:**
    在沿海地区和土地较肥沃的地方,原住民群体相对运动较少,因为他们能较容易地得到食物;但是在沙漠地区,一大片土地的食物只够些许人生存之用,原住民就会为寻找食物而长途跋涉。

23. **On both islands ... extracted their profit:**
    在这两个岛上,海豹捕猎者绑架年轻的原住民妇女,利用她们的体力劳动和知识抓捕海豹,加工海豹皮、肉和油脂,以从中获利。

24. **Later, the pastoralists exploited ... the new white "owners":**
    后来,在发展大型牛羊牧场的过程中,牧场主又利用原住民对土地的理解,为这些澳大利亚土地的新白人"拥有者"赚取了巨额财富。

25. **Their intellectual skills ... into the nation of Australia:**
    他们的知识技能被殖民者利用,但同时又遭到他们的贬损。从 1788 年开始,殖民者侵略并抢走了他们的土地,并最终把这片土地重新构建为澳大利亚。

26. **Arnhem Land:**
    阿纳姆地,是澳大利亚北部一个地区。

27. **Some Northern Territory stories ... with the Dreaming:**
    一些北方领土的原住民故事中融入了一些与佛教相关的观念,而非原住民的梦创信仰,例如转世投生等观念。

28. **However, it did exist ... of Europe and Asia:**
    但是,在中世纪后期欧洲的逻辑和神话中确实存在着一片南方大陆。那时人们认为南方大陆一定存在,以便能平衡北半球欧亚板块的重量。"Terra Australis",西班牙语,意为"南方大陆"。

29. **Terra Australis often appeared ... they expected it to be:**
    在欧洲绘制的早期地图上,南方大陆经常显示为一个巨大的球形大陆,并标在欧洲人认为的位置上。

30. ***terra nullius*:**
    (拉丁语)无主地,无人拥有的土地,指荒地,在法律上不属于任何国家的土地。无主地概念在 18 世纪国际法中流行,被欧洲各国用来辩护帝国主义行为。

# Australia

**31. By declaring Australia ... who were certainly not "civilised":**
英国殖民者把澳大利亚称为"无主地",这不仅使他们能合法地占有土地,还使他们能把已在这片土地上生活了 18 000 代的原住民看成半人类,当然也就是没有文明进化的人。

**32. "the Aborigines", the generic term meaning "the original natives of the land":**
原住民在白人定居者到来之前有五百多个部落,各有自己的名称和语言。但白人定居者抹杀了他们的文化差异,统称其为"土著人"。

**33. to prevent the settlers from taking over their hunting and collecting grounds:**
以阻止白人定居者侵占他们狩猎和采食的土地。

**34. Lachlan Macquarie:**
拉克伦·麦夸利,1810 至 1821 年间任新南威尔士总督。在任期间致力于提高殖民地的道德水平,发展教育,以其对罪犯的人道关怀著称。

**35. he approved of the way ... in the heart of "the natives":**
他赞同他的士兵攻击原住民,因为尽管在攻击中会杀害无辜的男人、女人和孩子,但是这样的攻击可以让这些"土著人"心里产生恐惧。

**36. Many were killed ... as a threat to settlement:**
大量的原住民被白人带来的疾病夺取了生命,(他们的人数迅速减少)很快他们就对英国定居者构不成任何威胁。白人定居者的到来给当地的原住民带来了天花等传染病。原住民对这些传染病没有任何免疫力,从而导致他们人口锐减。

**37. The aboriginal people were ... given the title of Protectors:**
原住民被从他们自己的土地上强行带走,关进土著人保护区。在保护区内,他们处于白人官员的绝对控制中。这些白人官员通常都是基督教传教士,却被冠以土著人"保护者"的头衔。

**38. Social scientists of the time ... at the bottom of the scale:**
那时的社会科学学者将普通的达尔文进化论发展为种族优劣等级论,并据此将白人殖民者置于种族等级制最上层,而把被他们殖民、剥削的黑人游牧民族置于等级制的最下层。

**39. Herbert Spencer ... of the colonial Europeans:**
当时最著名的社会进化论者赫伯特·斯宾赛,提出了"适者生存"的观念,使欧洲殖民者在军事、政治和文化上的优越感有了理论依据。Herbert Spencer(1820–1903),英国哲学家、社会学家,将进化论引入社会学,提出"适者生存"说。

**40. "Assimilation" was founded ... only a form of superstition:**
"同化"政策是基于这样一种认识上的,即白人文化是进步的、高级的,而梦创文化只是一种迷信。

**41. Young Aboriginal women ... in their places of employment:**
年轻的土著女性在保护区、宗教慈善机构和工作的场所常常有被强奸的危险。**Institutions:** 指为收容土著人使他们忘记自己的文化而设置的宗教慈善机构。

## UNIT 15 The Land and the Peoples of the Dreaming

42. **There was a major contradiction ... was accompanied by segregation:**
    在官方的所谓同化政策中存在着根本性的矛盾。它表面上是要两个民族融合成为一个民族，使原住民融入澳大利亚社会，但实际上，融合政策永远是与种族隔离政策相伴而行的。

43. **The double loss ... in the United States and South Africa:**
    这种失去传统文化并被拒之于澳大利亚主流社会之外的双重损失，导致原住民被认为是懒惰、愚钝、酗酒成性和肮脏不堪的。这种隔离和文化偏见相结合的做法与当时美国和南非的种族隔离制度是相类似的。

# Exercises

**I. Give the Chinese equivalents for the following:**

1. koala
2. the Dreaming
3. *Terra Nullius*
4. the Great Barrier Reef
5. the Darwinian theory
6. the policy of assimilation

**II. Decide whether the following statements are true (T) or false (F):**

1. The continent of Australia is the largest island in the world. _____
2. Most of Australia's unique plants and animals are imported from other continents. _____
3. The Great Barrier Reef goes along the eastern coast of Australia, from Queensland to Tasmania. _____
4. Dreaming is shared by the members of an indigenous group about how the features of their land were created. _____
5. Dreaming helps the indigenous people to survive in the harsh environment of the desert of Australia. _____
6. White sealers and pastoralists exploited the indigenous people's knowledge of the land and created wealth for the colonisers. _____
7. European travellers like Portuguese and Spanish explorers declared the continent of Australia *terra nullius* before the British did. _____

## Australia

8. The diseases brought by the white settlers to Australia did not contribute to the drastic decline of the indigenous population. _____

### III. Fill in the blanks:

1. In terms of its size, Australia is the largest _____ and the smallest _____ in the world.
2. _____ is Australia's largest island.
3. _____ and _____ are animals that are unique to the continent of Australia.
4. Most of Australia's population lives in the _____ and _____ climates of the hills and fertile plains.
5. The two most striking geological features of the Australian continent are _____ and _____.
6. _____, bringing the first convicts to Australia, arrived in 1788.
7. _____ refers to belief systems of the indigenous people of Australia.
8. Young indigenous women were forced to help the white settlers in _____, which was one of the first industries of Australia.
9. The concept of _____ legitimised British colonisation of the Australian continent in the late 18th century.
10. Under the assimilation policy, _____ were taken away from their parents to be placed on the "protected reserves".

### IV. Questions:

1. Where is Australia located? How is the continent thought to be formed?
2. What are the two most distinctive physical features of Australia? In what way are they distinctive?
3. Who were the Peoples of the Dreaming? How were these people with different languages and cultures bound together?
4. What is the central principle on which "the Dreaming" is based? How does this belief view the relationship between land and people?
5. What does "Dreamtime" mean? What does "Dreaming" refer to?
6. What does the author think of the sacred creation stories in different cultures?
7. What does the author mean when she says: "The several stories of creation also provide a memorable map of the landscape"? How does she explain her point?

8. How did the white colonists and settlers such as sealers and pastoralists take advantage of the intellectual skills of the peoples of the Dreaming?
9. Who were the first foreigners to make contact with the Peoples of the Dreaming? What evidence shows that Zheng He's fleet reached Australia?
10. What does *terra nullius* mean? Why did the British declare the country *terra nullius*?
11. What happened to the Aborigines in the first decades of colonisation?
12. What happened to the aboriginal people under the policies of segregation and exclusion in the 1800s?
13. What belief underlay the new policy of assimilation at the beginning of the 20th century?
14. Who were the stolen children or the stolen generations?
15. The aboriginal people were truly assimilated into the mainstream of Australian society. Do you agree or disagree?

V.  **Topics for discussion or research:**
    1. What are the unique natural features of the Australian continent?
    2. Do research on the Peoples of the Dreaming.
    3. Discuss the understanding of the land of the Peoples of the Dreaming and their other social and cultural values.
    4. Discuss the changes brought by colonisation, and their impacts on the aboriginal people.

# UNIT 16

# Australian Cultural Life

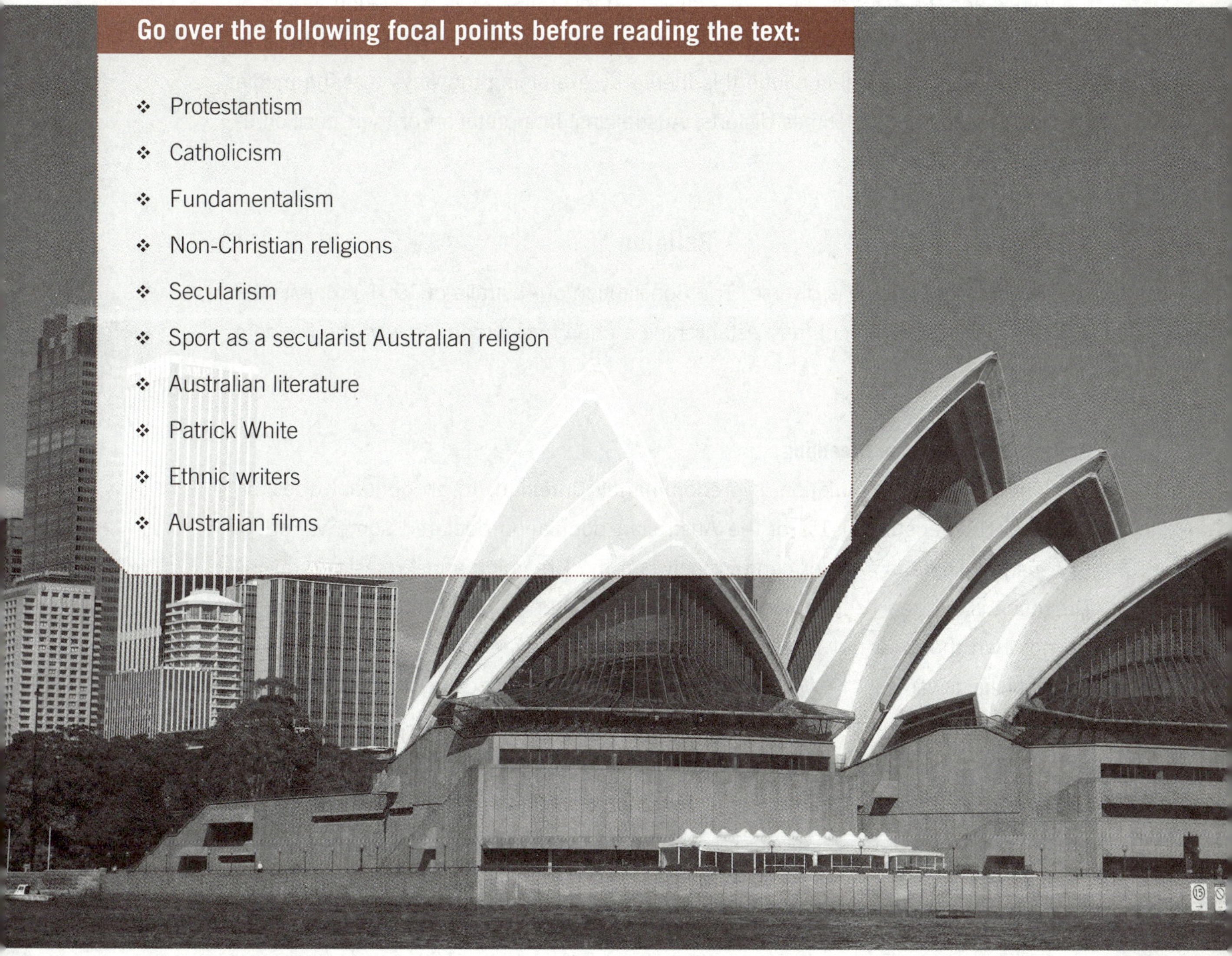

**Go over the following focal points before reading the text:**

- Protestantism
- Catholicism
- Fundamentalism
- Non-Christian religions
- Secularism
- Sport as a secularist Australian religion
- Australian literature
- Patrick White
- Ethnic writers
- Australian films

# Australia

 **Text**

In Unit 15, we saw that the Dreaming was the basis of the culture of the Peoples of Australia until 1788. Over the past two centuries Australian culture has changed in many ways. There is now a much wider range of cultural sites generating the ideas, the values and the ways of "being Australian". In this unit we will be looking at four of these cultural sites: religion, sport, literature, and film. Then in Unit 19 "Australia in the World Today", we will continue this theme by examining the ways that the media communicates, and sometimes distorts, Australians' interpretation of their position in the world.

## Religion

Religion in Australia is diverse. The Constitution of Australia of 1901 prohibits the Commonwealth government from establishing a church or interfering with the freedom of religion.

### Protestantism[1] and the Dreaming

The Australian population is predominantly Christian. In an optional question on the 2011 Census, 61.1% of the Australian population declared some variety of Christianity. There is a major contrast between the Dreaming and Protestantism: the Dreaming is about a people being at one with the country, which means that people do not own the land but the land owns the people, who have responsibilities of **guardianship** towards it.[2] However, after 1788 Protestantism became the dominant form of religion, and a central concept of Protestantism is that individual people own, and are obliged to use and exploit the land for the greater glory of their God.[3] This difference in the key values of the two religions is basic to understanding how Australian society and Australian culture have developed over the past two centuries.

When Australia was colonised by the British, Protestantism was already the religion of the Western governing colonial class. It was the form of Christianity that came to dominate Northern Europe (and eventually the USA) from the 16th century to today.

---

Protestantism *n.* 新教，新教教义

guardianship *n.* 守卫，保护，监护

Its development **coincided with** the development of the new form of political economy of the West — liberal, democratic, colonialist, capitalist. So, when the British brought their particular form of Protestantism, **Anglicanism**, to their new colony, they brought a religious culture that supported the values of the new Australian ruling class, the military and government leaders, the business owners and large scale agriculturalists of the 19th century. Protestantism spread the idea that the people at the top of society, the wealthy and the powerful, were successful because they were the ones doing God's will by dominating the land and by dominating those who worked for them on the land.[4] Thus, the majority of people in this new colony — the **convicts** and the poorer free men and women — were seen as being not only lower in the social scale, but lower in the eyes of God. So, religion helped to create not only a new political economic system, but a set of clearly separated social positions based on class, a system and a culture very different from those of the communities of people who had lived here over the previous 40 thousand years.[5]

### The Variations of Christianity and the Introduction of Non-Christian Religions

By the 1850s these social class differences had led to different versions of Protestantism, with the upper and middle classes remaining with Anglicanism, whilst **Congregationalism**, **Methodism** and the **Salvation Army** gave greater emphasis to the view that "we are all equal before God" which appealed more to working class communities or to those in the middle classes who preferred this more **egalitarian** approach to society.[6] In addition, as more migrants came from countries other than England, other forms of Christianity, and other non-Christian religions, were established.

### Catholicism

In the latter half of the 19th century, it was the **Catholics**, most notably the Irish political convicts and refugees from famine, who played a significant part in the establishment of the alternative working class culture. Catholics, working class Protestants and **Secularists** combined to establish unionism and to create the political party that represented labour — the Australian Labor Party (the ALP).

A separate system of Catholic schools was established in this period and today Catholic education still plays an important part in the Australian education system, partly because the move to multiculturalism in the 1970s led to much higher rates of

# Australia

migration from Catholic countries.

### The Non-Christian Religions: Buddhism, Islam, Hinduism and Judaism

The histories of Buddhism, Islam and Hinduism in Australia have similar patterns: a modest mid-19th century growth; a cut back at the beginning of the 20th century due to the racist White Australian.Policy, and a significant proportional increase when Australia became a **multicultural** society in the 1970s.[7] Buddhism is now the fastest growing belief system in Australia. According to the 2011 census, 2.5 percent of the total population of Australia identified as Buddhist. This includes both new immigrants and many non-Asian converts. Buddhism is the second largest religion in the country after Christianity. However, as yet, only just 6.5 % of Australians are committed to these various non-Christian religions. The other modern changes in religious commitment have been the rise of two very different movements: **Fundamentalism** and **Secularism**.

### Fundamentalism and Evangelicalism

Fundamentalism is often a feature of a society in a rapid state of change. When cultural values seem to be shifting too quickly a form of cultural anxiety or "**anomie**" can occur.[8] For some people there is a need to reaffirm the values of one's earlier life. These earlier values are those in which one's sense of self and society was developed. Rapid social shifts in values and behaviours can be associated with such a strong social and psychological **disquiet** that there is a need to take active steps to resist the changes.[9] Fundamentalism is not confined to any one religious belief. In Australia, there are fundamentalist forms of Protestantism, Catholicism, Islam, and Judaism. Fundamentalists want to maintain or to recreate what was (or what was thought to have been) the fundamental values of an earlier culture.

Laura Tiernan (2005) connects this shift in the religious culture with the return of the right-wing political values of the early 19th century, where the religion was tied to clearly **segregated** and unequal classes in society.[10]

### Secularism

Secularism is the rejection of any religious belief. Secularists use a set of non-religious values to guide their lives. As only 13% of the population attends church each week, Australia could be described as a secular society. However, there is not a

---

Buddhism *n.* 佛教
Islam *n.* 伊斯兰教
Hinduism *n.* 印度教
Judaism *n.* 犹太教
multicultural *adj.* 多元文化的
Fundamentalism *n.* 原教旨主义，基要主义
Secularism *n.* 现世主义
Evangelicalism *n.* 福音主义
anomie (anomy) *n.* 社会道德沦丧
disquiet *n.* 不安，忧虑，担心
segregated *adj.* 隔离的

clear distinction between "believers" and "non-believers". Many non-churchgoers stay committed to a form of belief. Moreover, at key points of change in peoples' lives — at death, birth, marriage or when going to war — the church becomes an important institution, the site at which many Australians want to **commemorate** the significance of the event.[11] So, although only a minority of Australians attends church regularly, Australia could be called a "**lukewarm**" religious society. In 2011, 22.3% of Australians stated "no religion." However, if these "lukewarm believers" are not closely tied to their religions, from where is the majority of Australians deriving their cultural values? What other sources of cultural and social influences are there today? Consider sport.

## Is Sport a Secularist Australian Religion?

Many features of sport in Australia seem to reflect the patterns of religion. Ritually, every Saturday hundreds of thousands of Australians gather at sports fields and **arenas** in every city. They are dressed in their sports team's special colours. Many carry **emblems** representing the team's symbolic creatures — the **Magpies**, the **Bulls**, the **Roosters** and many others. The fans enter the great "coming-together" place — the arena — and chant their team's special songs.[12] They watch a performance that is **ritualistic** in its weekly repetition of the moves of the game.[13] The skills, **virtues** and **vices** of the players on either side are keenly followed and discussed endlessly for the rest of the week.[14] Pictures of the heroes/players adorn bedroom walls across the country like the pictures of **saints**. At the end of the day, the same games are watched on TV whilst sports experts, the "priests" of sport, commentate on the week's games and the actions of the individual players, interpreting it all in terms of the more abstract idea of "the Game" and the way it should be played.[15]

Although the principal games are usually a form of football — Rugby League (ARL), Australian Football League (AFL), Rugby Union (RU)[16], or Soccer[17] — the above scene is common to a range of spectator sports. Sport is like Christianity: it has many **variants**. Other games and sports, **cricket**, **hockey**, basketball, beach volleyball, and swimming have their fervent followers. **Netball** is the most popular game in terms of the numbers who play the game, although it doesn't attract as many spectators as football, perhaps because it is usually played by women.[18] The second most popular participation sport is fishing.

In Australia today sport plays a dominant role. How does this contemporary major

commemorate v. 纪念
lukewarm adj. 不冷不热的，不热情的
arena n. 竞技场
emblem n. 象征，标志；徽章
magpie n. 喜鹊
bull n. 公牛
rooster n. 雄禽；公鸡
ritualistic adj. 仪式的
virtue n. 德行，高尚的道德；正直的品质
vice n. 邪恶（行为）；道德败坏（行为）
saint n. 圣贤，圣人
variant n. 变体
cricket n. （体）板球
hockey n. 冰球，曲棍球
netball n. 无挡板篮球

# Australia

institution affect the broader culture? The sociologist Hugh Mackay points out that Australians spend far more, per capita, on the training of **elite athletes** than they do on the training of doctors, scientists, musicians and philosophers.[19] He then warns that, as Australia so glorifies competitive sport, it is as if sport is now the basis of the country's values and **priorities**.[20] Thus, he argues, Australians should take care not to glorify sporting **rituals** above other kinds of social **interactions**, nor centre their culture on the principle that success should always be achieved at someone else's expense.[21] Similarly, Elizabeth Broderick, the Federal Sex Discrimination Commissioner, is concerned about the excessive **masculinism** of Australian sport, exemplified by the 98:2 ratio of male: female sport **coverage** on television, the excess of **allegations** of sexual **harassment** and violence by **high-profile** sportsmen and, most importantly, the parallels between the issues of pay **equity**, the lack of women in leadership positions, discrimination on the basis of sex, and the celebration of an extremely masculinist form of male ideal in which women are constructed as the weaker sex.[22]

However, sport also has positive characteristics. It creates a sense of community, potentially balances the spirit of competition within the broader culture of fair play, and encourages exercise and physical fitness. Moreover, there are forms of sport which are neither overly competitive, nor gender biased, and the beach is one of the most popular places for these activities.[23] Every week thousands of girls and boys who are the young trainee **recruits** to life saving clubs practice life saving skills, **rowing**, and swimming. They share with the millions of Australians who love **body surfing**, sea swimming, practicing **board surfing**, **picnicking**, playing beach cricket, or building sand **castles**, all just for the fun of it. Australians are lucky in that their summers are long and, because they have so many beautiful beaches surrounding the major cities, the sands are rarely overcrowded.[24]

## Australian Literature

The history of Australian literature covers an immense field, from the Dreamtime stories, **myths** and **legends** that have been passed on orally or visually by artistic representations on rocks and on bark over 40 000 years, through to the various forms of Australian literature in the English language which covers the period 1788 to the present day and includes not only fiction, verse, drama, history, biography and autobiography, but also journals, diaries, letters and **memoirs**.[25] So this section must

---

elite *adj.*
杰出的，精锐的，卓越的
athlete *n.*
运动员
priority *n.*
优先，重点
ritual *n.* 仪式
interaction *n.*
互动
masculinism *n.*
男权主义
coverage *n.*
报道
allegation *n.*
宣称；指控
harassment *n.*
骚扰
high-profile *adj.*
引人注目的
equity *n.*
公平，公正
recruit *n.*
新手，新成员
rowing *n.*
划船；赛艇运动
body surfing
人体冲浪（指不用冲浪板而以胸腹冲浪）
board surfing
冲浪板冲浪
picnic *n.* 野餐
castle *n.* 城堡
myth *n.* 神话
legend *n.*
传奇故事
memoir *n.*
回忆录

comprise only a very small glimpse of the range that should be covered. It's narrowed here to some of the major works and authors but remember this means that many interesting texts and aspects of the topic will have to be omitted. For a broader coverage have a look at some of the web sites listed at the end of this section.

The **journals** of Captain Cook[26] and Sir Joseph Banks[27] give detailed insights into how these English explorers and settlers interpreted the Peoples, the country and their own experiences of the Australian continent. However, these and other writings from Australia over the first few decades were written in the English style for an English audience. During the next few decades Australian writers began to write from a more Australian perspective focusing on constructing this new Australian identity as convicts, **bushrangers**, and pioneering bush families. The classic novel of convict life was Marcus Clarke's *For the Term of His Natural Life* (1874). The life of "the **Bush**"[28], the Australian countryside, was described in the works of Henry Lawson (1867–1922) and A. B. (nicknamed "Banjo" ) Paterson (1864–1941). Paterson, although a city lawyer, wrote **yearningly** in *The Man from Snowy River and Other Verses* (1895) of the "**romance** of the Bush", creating stereotypes that appealed to Australians' wish to see themselves as a tough, hardy, egalitarian set of characters, different from "people back Home"[29]. In contrasts, in *While the Billy Boils* (1896) Lawson uses a more **laconic**, **sparse** and harshly realist style of verse, in which egalitarianism has to be fought for, not taken for granted.

It was this "realism" that defined the early 20th century: writings including Miles Franklin's *My Brilliant Career* (1901) and Barbara Baynton's *Bush Studies* (1907) which powerfully describes the problems that women in particular faced and conveys such a sense of an alive, threatening and **alienating** landscape that "the Bush" becomes almost a character in her novels.[30]

The increasing industrialisation of the early 20th century meant a move away from the rural bases of the earlier Australian literature. Urban Australian life was represented by both the Romantics and the Realists: C.J. Dennis' (1876–1938) patriotic novels and poetry celebrated the simple pleasures of life of an "ideal" set of ordinary Australians. His most celebrated character, the urban **larrikin** in "The Songs of a Sentimental Bloke", together with his mates and girl friend, all lived in an idealistic time of innocence. In contrast, one of the most important Australian writers of the early 20th century, Ethel Richardson (1880–1946), is a realist writer whose works include

journal *n.* 日志
bushranger *n.* 灌木丛护林员
bush *n.* 灌木丛
yearningly *adv.* 怀念地；渴望地
romance *n.* 浪漫故事，浪漫作品
laconic *adj.* 简洁的
sparse *adj.* 稀少的
alienating *adj.* 疏远的；荒无人烟的
larrikin *n.* 无赖

# Australia

*The Getting of Wisdom* (1910) and her **trilogy**, *The Fortunes of Richard Mahoney* (1930). Similarly, Christina Stead (1902–1983), author of *The Man Who Loved Children* (1940)[31], realistically portrays the power struggles of Australian family life. Yet, an interesting **paradox** occurs here as both of these realist authors had to hide their status as female Australian authors. Ethel Richardson worked under the male **pseudonym**, Henry Handel Richardson, and Christina Stead increased her readership by setting her novel, not in Australia, but in the USA.

Similarly, in the 1950s and 1960s many Australian writers echoed Christina Stead's earlier awareness that to gain a name they had to leave Australia. Most went overseas to Europe: Charmaine Clift (1923–1969) and George Johnston (1912–1970), at that time the most celebrated literary couple in Australian literature, who wrote *High Valley* (1948), *My Brother Jack* (1963) and *Clean Straw for Nothing* (1969), went to Greece. Germaine Greer (1939–), author of *The Female Eunuch* (1970)[32], and Clive James (1939–), author of *Unreliable Memoirs* (1979) left for Britain and have lived and worked in the UK since 1962. The Australian book industry was described in this era as a colonial **depot** for excess stock from British publishers who decided the reading habits of Australian readers[33]. In this, the publishing industry reflected the broader **obeisance** to British culture. However, this period was also notable for the 1955 production of Ray Lawler's (1921–) drama *Summer of the Seventeenth Doll*, which was later produced on both the London and New York stage. Lawler's criticism of Australian cultural stereotypes, combined with a natural style and a language free of **cliché**, represented a major break with tradition and inspired a new phase of dramatic realism in Australia[34]. Then, in the late 1960s and 1970s, Australians developed a different, broader sense of self identity, less **deferential** to the British culture and greater self confidence in being Australian, especially in being Australian in the Asia Pacific region[35]. Both the Whitlam and Fraser governments invested in the arts to further encourage this more independent Australian voice as it was given expression in films, art, music and books.[36]

In 1973, the dominating figure in Australian literature Patrick White (1912–1990)[37], the author of *The Aunt's Story* (1948), *The Tree of Man* (1955), *Voss* (1957), *The Solid Mandela* (1966) etc., was awarded the Nobel Prize for Literature, and earned world status as a novelist. White's fiction employs humor, shifting narrative perspectives and a stream of consciousness technique. He is praised "for an epic and psychological narrative art" in the Swedish Academy's **citation**. Ruth Park (1917–2010), a New

---

trilogy *n.* 三部曲
paradox *n.* 悖论
pseudonym *n.* 笔名
depot *n.* 库房
obeisance *n.* 景仰
cliché *n.* 陈腐的套话
deferential *adj.* 尊重的
citation *n.* 颁奖词

Zealander who spent most of her life in Australia, also won many literary awards for works including the trilogy of *The Harp in the South* (1948), *Poor Man's Orange and Missus* (1949) and the children's book the *Muddle-Headed Wombats* series. Her work was translated into 37 languages. This greater self confidence was being expressed in different ways. Australian publishing flourished, with new firms specialising in indigenous and feminist writing, producing the wide range of novels, textbooks and journals that characterised the 1960s concerns with **inequalities** of **gender** and racism. Self confidence was expressed in a more critical examination of life in Australia. On the stage David Williamson's (1942– ) work as a playwright focuses on themes of politics, loyalty and family in contemporary urban Australia, particularly in two of its major cities, **Melbourne** and **Sydney**. His work covers the four decades from the early 1970s to the present, with *Don's Party* (1971), *The **Removalists*** (1971), *The Department* (1975), *The Club* (1977), *Travelling North* (1979), *The **Perfectionist*** (1982), ***Emerald** City* (1987), *Money and Friends* (1991), *Brilliant Lies* (1993), *Dead White Males* (1995) and his most recent work *Influence* (2005).

Thomas Keneally (1935– ) similarly has a long career as an Australian author. His work spans six decades and ranges over a wide **spectrum**: Irish immigration, American political biography, Nazi Germany, civil strife in **Ethiopia**, racism in the Australian Bush, Joan of Arc, **priesthood** in the Catholic Church and motherhood in the Australian **outback**.[38] The common theme of this **eclectic** list of topics is the **authenticity** and the humanity of his subjects. Several of his books have been made into films. His novels and non-fiction works include *Three Cheers for the **Paraclete*** (1968), *The Chant of Jimmy Blacksmith* (1972), *The Playmaker* (1987), *The Great Shame* (1998), and *A Commonwealth of Thieves* (2006), the story of Australia's late 18th-century beginnings as a colony for transported prisoners. Peter Carey (1943– ) has made a parallel contribution. His novels include *The Tax Inspector* (1991), *The Unusual Life of Tristan Smith* (1994), *Jack Maggs* (1997), *True History of the Kelly Gang* (2001), and *Parrot and Olivier in America* (2009).

In the 1990s, this variety of ways of "being Australian" was further broadened when the voices of second generation migrants were published in novels, journals, essays, and poetry.[39] This **genre** includes the young adults' novel, *Looking for Alibrandi* (2000), in which Melina Marchetta's (1965– ) own experiences informs her story of the relationships between three generations of Italian Australian women from the

inequality *n.*
不平等
gender *n.*
性别
Melbourne
墨尔本
Sydney
悉尼
removalist *n.*
迁移者
perfectionist *n.*
完美主义者
emerald *n.*
绿宝石
spectrum *n.*
范围
Ethiopia *n.*
埃塞俄比亚
priesthood *n.*
牧师的职位
outback *n.*
内地
eclectic *adj.*
包罗万象的
authenticity *n.*
真实性
paraclete *n.*
圣灵；调解人；辩护人
genre *n.*
体裁；类型

# Australia

perspective of the youngest, the twelve year old schoolgirl. This theme, not simply of the issues and complexities of multiculturalism, but of the insights this brings to our humanity in general, similarly **underpins** Christos Tsiolkas' (1965– ) novels.[40] In 2006, Tsiolkas won the Age Fiction Prize and the Melbourne Best Writing Award for his novel *Dead Europe* (2005). In 2009, his novel *The Slap* (2008) won the Australian Literary Society Gold Medal.

In the same year, Alice Pung's book, *Unpolished Gem* (2006), based on her family's migration from China to Australia, became a national bestseller, winning the Australian Book Industry Newcomer Award, 2009, for her portrayal of what it is like to be caught between two cultures.[41] Again in 2009, Nam Le's[42] set of short stories, *The Boat*, was the winner of the 2009 NSW Premiers Literary Awards Book of the Year. Nam Le (born 1978) is a Vietnamese-born Australian writer. What caught the attention of the jury was Nam Le's ability to engage the reader in a range of experiences across the world, from **Tehran**, the slums of **Columbia**; to the USA and Australia. Nam Le conveys the language and the mind sets of aging American painters, Japanese schoolgirls, Australian **Ockers** and Vietnamese migrants.

Australian literature here is positioning Australians in the world in a new way, as global citizens oriented not only to Europe but to the Pacific, to Asia and South America. This is in notable contrast to the 1950s writers, who felt they had to go abroad to write about Australia.

Also included in this wider range of genres is Tim Winton (1960– ), who is a contemporary writer who echoes the skills of Patrick White in connecting the inner **consciousness** of his characters with the outer landscapes of Australia. In his novels, which include *Cloud Street* (1991), *Dirt Music* (2001) and *Breath* (2008), he uses simple Australian prose and basic everyday issues to write with extraordinary effect of ordinary people. Similarly, David Malouf's (1934– ) novels are often firmly grounded in the physical spaces of the Australian landscape, using a heightened sense of spatial relations to focus on the complexity and **tenuousness** of identity. His work, *Remembering Babylon* (1993) was described by the international IMPAC Dublin Literary Award judges as "the best novel written by anyone, anywhere, in any language, in the last three years". In 2016, he received the Australian Council Award for Lifetime Achievement in Literature.

In other genres: Sonya Hartnett (1968– ) is one of several novelists working in

---

**underpin** *v.*
构成
**Tehran**
德黑兰（伊朗首都）
**Columbia**
哥伦比亚
**ocker** *n.*
无教养的澳大利亚人
**consciousness** *n.* 意识
**tenuousness** *n.* 脆弱

the new field of "young adult novels". *Butterfly* (2009), her latest novel is about the terrifying **vulnerability** of early **adolescence**, the costs of interfering in the lives of others, and of how we must all eventually leave childhood behind. Peter Temple (1946– ) is noted for his crime novels, *Bad Debts* (1996), *Black Tide* (1998), *The Broken Shore* (2005), and *Truth* (2009), which are accepted as mainstream literary gems. In the late 1990s, Dorothy Porter (1954– ) re-visited one of the oldest forms of literature — the verse novel. It's essential too to recommend the works of Helen Garner, Peter Carey, Kate Grenville, Geraldine Brooks, J.M. Coetzee, Robert Dessaix and Cate Kennedy to readers wanting to know the **multiplicity** of ways that Australian literature today is reflecting and **reshaping** the culture.

vulnerability *n.*
易伤性，脆弱性
adolescence *n.*
青春期
multiplicity *n.*
多样性
reshape *v.*
重塑
obsession *n.*
困扰
miniseries *n.*
短篇电视连续剧
going to the pictures
看电影

## Books that Have Been Made into Films

There is a strong link in Australia between literature and film. *For the Term of His Natural Life, The Man from Snowy River, My Brilliant Career, Picnic at Hanging Rock* and *The Sentimental Bloke* are just five films based on the earlier Australian novels. There are too many recent novels that have been translated into films to list here, but some of the most notable include this variety of genres.

From popular drama, there are Neville Shute's *A Town like Alice* and *On the Beach* (which has been filmed twice) and Colleen McCulloch's *Tim and an Indecent* **Obsession**. Her most popular novel *The Thorn Birds* was made into a major TV **miniseries**.

From young adult literature, Colin Thieles *Storm Boy*, John Marsdens's *Tomorrow When the War Began* series and Melina Marchett's *Looking for Alibrandi* were made into films.

From texts based on the treatment of indigenous peoples, there are *The Chant of Jimmy Blacksmith* and *The Rabbit Proof Fence*.

From award winning novels are Peter Cary's *Bliss*, and *Oscar and Lucinda*, Helen Garner's *Monkey Grip*, and Patrick White's novel *The Eye of the Storm*. However, probably the most influential film based on a novel by an Australian author has been Spielberg's film of Thomas Keneally's *Schindler's Ark*, renamed as *Schindler's List*.[43]

## Films

Although many other forms of entertainment today compete with films, "**going to the pictures**" is still one of the most popular forms of entertainment in Australia.

# Australia

However, with the introduction of "**talking pictures**", then **technicolour films**, in the 1920s and 1930s, it became much cheaper for Australian film and TV **distributors** to buy ready made overseas films and TV programmes from the UK and from **Hollywood**. This led to a concern that Australian culture was being swamped by these two film producing **giants**. So the Australian government intervened in the 1970 and 1980s by providing funding bodies both for the production of films and in the training of film makers.[44] This led to a **revival** of the film industry creating "the New Wave" lasting from 1970 to 1985 when Australia produced nearly 400 films — more than had been made in the previous 70 years. In this era, Australian film directors flourished, producing films with strong Australian themes: *Sunday Too Far Away, Caddie, The Devil's Playground, Don's Party, My Brilliant Career, Mad Max: the Road Warrior, Gallipoli,* and *Breaker Morant*. Since then, further government policies have helped to finance the industry and over the next decades. Australian films generated another new wave of Australian directors producing internationally successful films like the Academy Award winning *Shine*, and films reflecting contemporary Australian values about comedy, romance and sexuality: **Crocodile** *Dundee, Strictly Ballroom, Muriel's Wedding,* and *Priscilla, Queen of the Desert*. This period saw the rise of actors Nicole Kidman, Cate Blanchett, Toni Collette, Russell Crowe, and Heath Ledger, all eventually becoming either Oscar or Tony Award winners. More recently, films have begun to explore the experiences of identity and cultural conflicts between old and younger generations in Italian, Greek and Chinese immigrant families in Australia. Notable amongst these are *Looking for Alibrandi*, the comedies *Wog Boy* and *Wog Boy 2* and *Home Sung Story*. This latter film is written and directed by the Chinese-Australian script-writer Tony Ayers and stars Joan Cheng.

Although these have all been notable Australian films, the next three, all made in the 21st century, have particular cultural significance. They have been created and driven by the experiences of the Peoples of the Dreaming and their descendants: *The Rabbit Proof Fence*, *The Ten* **Canoes** and *Samson and Delilah*. *The Rabbit Proof Fence* is based on the book by Doris Pilkington Garimar and tells of her mother's experience as part of the "Stolen Generation". *The Ten Canoes* is the first Australian film made in an Australian language other than English — the Yolngu[45] language and is a comedy of the parallel experiences of two young Yolngu men, centuries apart, having trouble in making the journey to becoming a man and in getting a wife. The actors representing

---

talking pictures 有声电影
technicolour films 彩色电影
distributor *n.* 发行人
Hollywood 好莱坞
giant *n.* 巨商
revival *n.* 复苏
crocodile *n.* 鳄鱼
canoe *n.* 独木舟

the Yolngu people are all indigenous artists, although the director, Rolf de Heer, is a **Netherlander** born Australian. Both the actors and the director of the most recent of these three films, *Samson and Delilah*, are indigenous Australians. This film tells the story of two young lovers, belonging to the Warlpiri[46] community in the Central Australian desert, who attempt to move to Alice Springs only to experience extreme forms of racism there.

So these three movies are giving Australians new **narratives**. Although these stories have always underpinned Australian history, they have rarely before been a significant part of the way the majority of Australians see and define themselves through film. This is an important stage in Australian culture because for the first time it is the indigenous peoples of Australia who are in charge of constructing the stories and the values underpinning those stories of the films that we watch.

Netherlander *n.*
荷兰人
narrative *n.*
描述

# Explanations

1. **Protestantism:**
   新教（教义）。新教是指公元 16 世纪从罗马天主教中分离出来的基督教教派，与天主教、东正教并称为基督教三大教派。16 世纪初，欧洲新兴城市市民阶级反对封建主义，掀起宗教改革，在西欧、中欧一些国家出现许多脱离天主教的基督教派，总称为新教。后文中提到的 Anglicanism 也属新教。

2. **the Dreaming is about a people being at one with the country ... guardianship towards it:**
   梦创信仰认为人与土地应该合而为一，这意味着人不拥有土地，而是土地拥有人，人有守护它的责任。

3. **However, after 1788, Protestantism became the dominant form ... for the greater glory of their God:**
   然而，1788 年之后新教成为宗教的主导形式，它的中心理念是个人拥有土地，并有义务利用开发土地来为他们信仰的上帝赢得更大的荣耀。

4. **Protestantism spread the idea that the people at the top of society ... them on the land:**
   新教宣传的理念是，在社会上层的人们，即有钱有势的人们之所以成功是因为他们通过主宰土地和在土地上耕耘的人来实践上帝的意旨。

5. **So religion helped to create not only a new political ... over the previous 40 thousand years:**
   所以，宗教不仅协助制造了一个新的政治经济体系，还协助制造了一套界线分明的社会地位，其基础是阶级，以及一种有别于当地群体在过去的 4 万年生活的体系和文化。

# Australia

6. **By the 1850s these social class differences had led to different versions ... approach to society:**
   到 19 世纪 50 年代，这些社会阶级的差异导致了不同的新教派别，中上层阶级坚持信仰圣公会教义，而公理教义、循道教义和救世军更强调"在上帝面前我们人人平等"的观点，这一观点对工人阶级或者中产阶级里那些更赞成社会平等主义的人们更有号召力。

7. **The histories of Buddhism, Islam and Hinduism in Australia ... a multi–cultural society in the 1970s:**
   在澳大利亚的佛教，伊斯兰教和印度教有着相似的发展模式：19 世纪中期这些宗教有小幅度的发展，20 世纪初由于白人澳大利亚的种族歧视政策而有所减少，当 20 世纪 70 年代澳大利亚成为多元文化社会后，信仰这些宗教的人数比例有了显著的增长。

8. **When cultural values seem to be shifting too quickly a form ... can occur:**
   当文化价值观似乎变化太快时，就会产生文化焦虑感和"社会道德沦丧"。

9. **Rapid social shifts in values and behaviours can be associated ... take active steps to resist the changes:**
   社会上价值观和行为的快速变迁可能与需要采取积极行动来抵制这些变化的强烈的社会与心理不安联系起来。

10. **Laura Tiernan (2005) connects this shift in the religious culture ... and unequal classes in society:**
    2005 年 Laura Tiernan 发表的著作将宗教文化的这一变迁与 19 世纪初右翼政治价值观的回归联系起来，那时，宗教和明显隔离的、不平等的阶级密切关联。

11. **Moreover, at key points of change in peoples' lives — at death ... the significance of the event:**
    况且，在人生变化的关键时刻，比如，死亡、诞生、婚姻或者上前线打仗，教堂就成为重要的机构和场所。在那里，澳大利亚人想要纪念这一事件的意义。

12. **The fans enter the great "coming–together" place — the arena, and ... special songs:**
    球迷们走进神圣的"聚集场所"——运动场，唱着他们所支持的球队的队歌。

13. **They watch a performance that is ritualistic ... the moves of the game:**
    他们观看的表演相当仪式化，因为每个星期比赛的动作都是重复的。

14. **The skills, virtues and vices of the players on either side ... for the rest of the week:**
    接下来的一周内，人们津津乐道地、没完没了地谈论比赛双方球员的技巧、道德品质和恶劣行径。

15. **At the end of the day, the same games ... the way it should be played:**
    晚上，电视上播放同样的比赛，由体育专家们也就是体育"牧师"评论一周的赛事以及球员的个人表现，用比较抽象的"比赛"来解释一切，以及"比赛"应该怎样进行才对。

16. **Rugby League (ARL), Australian Football League (AFL), Rugby Union (RU):**
    都是最吸引观众的橄榄球和足球赛事。Rugby: 英式橄榄球，是一种接触性的团队竞赛运动，采用椭圆形橄榄球，在一片矩形草场上比赛，每队各 13 名球员。

UNIT 16　Australian Cultural Life

17. **Soccer:**
    足球，不同于美式足球（橄榄球）或英式橄榄球。

18. **Netball is the most popular game in terms ... because it is usually played by women:**
    无挡板篮球就参加的人数来说是最流行的比赛，虽然这项比赛不如足球更吸引观众，因为打这种球的一般是女性。

19. **The sociologist, Hugh Mackay, points out ... musicians and philosophers:**
    社会学家休·麦凯指出，澳大利亚在训练优秀运动员上的人均费用远远超过了培养医生、科学家、音乐家和哲学家的费用。

20. **He then warns that, as Australia so glorifies competitive sport ... and priorities:**
    他警告说，澳大利亚如此崇尚竞技体育，好似体育现在成了国家价值观和优先性的基础。

21. **Thus, he argues, Australians should take care ... achieved at someone else's expense:**
    因此，他认为澳大利亚应该注意不要过于颂扬体育仪式，将其置于其他社会互动形式之上，也不要把国家的文化中心建立在胜利必须以他人的失败为代价的原则上。

22. **Similarly, Elizabeth Broderick, the Federal Sex Discrimination ... the weaker sex:**
    同样，联邦性别歧视委员伊丽莎白·布罗德里克对澳大利亚体育中的过度男权主义也表示关注。这种男权主义的一个典型例子是电视上的男女赛事的报道比率是 98 比 2，即电视体育报道的 98% 是关于男运动员的。同时，关于性骚扰的指控也非常多，还有，引人注目的运动员打人的事件也不少。更重要的是存在和社会上一样的报酬公平问题、妇女缺乏领导地位、性别歧视、推崇男性思想的男权主义的极端形式、把妇女塑造成弱势性别等一系列问题。

23. **Moreover, there are forms of sport which are neither ... for these activities:**
    而且，有些运动形式既不过度竞争，也没有性别偏见，海滩就是这样的体育活动最受欢迎的地方。

24. **Australians are lucky in that their summers are long ... sands are rarely overcrowded:**
    澳大利亚人很幸运，因为他们的大城市周围都有美丽的海滩，所以海滩地区很少出现拥挤的情况。Sands:（英式英语）海滩地区。

25. **The history of Australian literature covers an immense field ... letters and memoirs:**
    澳大利亚文学史涵盖面很广，从梦创时代的故事、神话和传说开始，这些文学形式由口头流传下来，或者由具有 4 万年历史的呈现在石头和树皮上的艺术视觉形象流传下来，直到 1788 年到今天的用英语写成的澳大利亚文学的各种形式，不仅包括小说、诗歌、戏剧、历史、自传和传记，还包括日志、日记、信件和回忆录。

26. **Captain Cook:**
    库克船长。詹姆斯·库克（James Cook，1728–1779），英国著名探险家、航海家和制图学家。他进行了三次探险航行，给人们关于大洋——特别是太平洋的地理学知识增添了新的内容。

27. **Sir Joseph Banks:**
    约瑟夫·班克斯爵士 (1743–1820)，英国植物学家，于 1768–1771 年随同詹姆斯·库克航海探险。

28. **"the Bush":**
    澳大利亚的"灌木丛地带"。灌木丛生长在灌木和森林之间，是和城市相对立的广阔乡村地带，土地干旱贫瘠，上面长着灌木丛，几乎没有草，只有几棵桉树。这一风景是澳大利亚独特的，与欧洲移民所习惯的景象截然不同。"灌木丛地带"在澳大利亚文化中具有代表性。本文提到的作家将其浪漫化，塑造独特的澳大利亚自我身份。

29. **different from "people back Home":**
    大写的"家"指英国。早期来到澳大利亚定居的罪犯来自英国。

30. **It was this "realism" that defined the early 20th century ... a character in her novels:**
    这一"现实主义"成为20世纪初期文学的特点，其间的作品包括迈尔斯·富兰克林所著的《我的光辉事业》(1901)以及巴巴拉·贝恩顿所著的《灌木丛研究》(1907)，该作品强烈地描写了妇女面临的问题，生动地描述了活生生的、带有威胁性的和使人异化的风景，以至于灌木丛变成了小说的人物之一。

31. ***The Man Who Loved Children* (1940):**
    《爱孩子的男人》虽然于1940年出版，但在1965年再版后才得到文学评论的重视和获得大批读者，被《时代》杂志列入1923–2005年英语最佳100本小说。

32. **Germaine Greer (1939–), author of *The Female Eunuch* (1970):**
    吉梅茵·格丽尔是《女阉人》的作者。该作品于1970年出版后立即在澳大利亚、英国、美国、加拿大等国引起轰动，成为国际畅销书。吉梅茵·格里尔是作家、学者和记者，被认为是20世纪末期最重要的女性作家之一。她还著有许多其他著作，如《性与命运》(1984)以及《莎士比亚的妻子》(2007)。

33. **The Australian book industry was described in this era ... of Australian readers:**
    这个时期的澳大利亚出版业被称为英国出版商剩余库存的殖民地仓库，英国出版商决定澳大利亚读者的阅读习惯。

34. **Lawler's criticism of Australian cultural stereotypes ... dramatic realism in Australia:**
    劳勒对澳大利亚刻板形象的批评结合了自然的风格以及没有陈词滥调的清新语言，其作品代表了对传统的重要突破，并激发了澳大利亚戏剧现代主义的新阶段。

35. **Then, in the late 1960s and 1970s ... in the Asia Pacific region:**
    之后，在20世纪60年代后期和70年代，澳大利亚人发展了一个不同的、更为广泛的自我身份意识，对英国文化少了些恭敬，而对作为澳大利亚人则增加了自信心，特别是作为亚太地区的澳大利亚人。

36. **Both the Whitlam and Fraser governments ... in films, art, music and books:**
    惠特拉姆和弗雷泽（自由党，1975–1783任总理）政府都投资文化，进一步鼓励更为独立的澳大利亚声音通过电影、艺术、音乐和书籍表现出来。

37. **Patrick White (1912–1990):**
    帕特里克·怀特，是20世纪重要的英语作家，1973年获诺贝尔文学奖，是澳大利亚第一位获此殊荣的作家。从1935年到他逝世，共发表了12部小说、2个短篇故事集、8部戏剧。代表作为《人树》和《探险家沃斯》。写作风格多运用变化的叙述视角和意识流。

UNIT 16　Australian Cultural Life

38. **Thomas Keneally (1935– ) similarly has a long career ... in Australian outback:**
托马斯·基尼利（1935–）同样也有着很长的作家生涯。他的作品跨度六十年，题材内容丰富多彩，其中包括爱尔兰移民、美国政治性传记、纳粹德国、埃塞俄比亚的内战、澳大利亚乡村的种族歧视、法国民族英雄圣女贞德、天主教牧师以及澳大利亚内地的母亲生活。

39. **In the 1990s, this variety of ways of "being Australian" ... and poetry:**
在20世纪90年代作为澳大利亚人的不同经历又得到了进一步丰富和拓展，因为第二代移民通过小说、日志、散文和诗歌发出了他们的声音。

40. **This theme, not simply of the issues and complexities ... Christos Tsiolkas'(1965– ) novels:**
这个主题，不仅仅是其多元文化的问题及其复杂性，而是其带给我们人类的洞察力给Christos Tsiolkas的小说赋予了力量。

41. **In the same year, Alice Pung's book, *Unpolished Gem* ... between two cultures:**
同年，艾丽斯·彭根据她家庭从中国到澳大利亚的移民经历创作的小说《没有抛光的宝石》成为全国畅销书，2009年获得澳大利亚出版业新人奖，她的小说刻画了夹在两种文化之间的感受。艾丽斯·彭（1981–）是青年作家，中文名字方佳。她的父母是来自柬埔寨的华人，移民到澳大利亚。艾丽斯·彭出生在澳大利亚。她是作家和律师，任《在澳大利亚成长的亚裔人》杂志的主编。她的其他作品有 *Her Father's Daughter* (2011) 和 *Laurinda* (2014)。

42. **Nam Le:**
南勒，澳大利亚青年作家，1978年他出生于越南，还不到一岁时和父母作为难民坐船来到澳大利亚，他毕业于墨尔本大学和美国的爱荷华大学。

43. ***Schindler's List*:**
电影《辛德勒的名单》（1993），是犹太导演斯皮尔伯格对二战期间德国纳粹屠杀600万犹太人惨剧的回顾。影片以悲观阴郁的基调和富于强烈戏剧张力的惊悚元素，透过主人公辛德勒的眼睛，重回二战时波兰的科拉科，带领人们经历这个城市从繁荣到废墟的一切，同时在那个没有人性的年代中努力寻找人性的微芒，最终揭示了一个主题——人类的良知在任何恶劣的境况中都不会完全地泯灭。该片获当年奥斯卡最佳影片奖。

44. **So the Australian government intervened ... of film makers:**
所以澳大利亚政府在20世纪70、80年代进行了干预，为制作电影和培训电影制作者设立基金组织。

45. **Yolngu:**
居住在澳大利亚北部地区的一个土著民族。

46. **Warlpiri:**
澳大利亚一个土著民族，人口约5 000–6 000。

# Australia

## Exercises

I. **Give the Chinese equivalents for the following:**
1. Protestantism
2. Secularism
3. masculinism
4. convicts
5. genre

II. **Decide whether the following statements are true (T) or false (F):**
1. Dreaming is about a people being at one with the country, which means that people do not own the land but the land owns the people, who have responsibilities of guardianship towards it. _____
2. Anglicanism is the British particular form of Protestantism. _____
3. Fundamentalism is only confined to Christianity. _____
4. Hugh Mackay points out that Australians spend far more, per capita, on the training of elite athletes than they do on the training of doctors, scientists, musicians and philosophers. _____
5. Female sport coverage on television is far below that of male sports. _____
6. The history of Australian literature dates back to the Dreamtime stories, myths and legends that have been passed on orally or visually by artistic representations on rocks and on bark over 40 000 years. _____
7. The main feature of Australian literature in the early 20th century is realism. _____
8. Ethel Richardson is a realist writer. Her works include *The Getting of Wisdom* and her trilogy, *The Fortunes of Richard Mahoney*. _____
9. In the 1950s and 1960s many Australian writers thought that to gain a name they had to leave Australia, and most went overseas to the US. _____
10. The Whitlam and Fraser governments invested in the arts to further encourage a more independent Australian voice as it was given expression in films, art, music and books. _____

UNIT 16  Australian Cultural Life

## III. Fill in the blanks:

1. After 1788, _____ became the dominant form of religion.
2. Congregationalism, Methodism and the Salvation Army gave greater emphasis to the view that "we are all equal before God" which appealed more to _____ communities.
3. At key points of change in peoples' lives — at death, birth, _____ or when going to war, the church becomes an important institution, the site at which many Australians commemorate the event.
4. Many Australian sport fans carry _____ representing the team's symbolic creatures — the Magpies, the Bulls, the Roosters and many others.
5. The _____ of Captain Cook and Sir Joseph Banks give detailed insights into how these English explorers and settlers interpreted the Peoples, the country and their own experiences of the Australian continent.
6. Then, in the late 1960s and 1970s, Australians developed a different, broader sense of self identity and greater self confidence in being Australian, especially in being Australian in _____ region.
7. The second generation migrants published novels, journals, essays, and poetry in the _____.
8. As an Australian author, _____ has a long career, and several of his books have been made into films including the Oscar-winning *Schindler's List*.
9. Neville Shute's most popular novel _____ was made into a major TV mini series.
10. Critics show that _____ is still one of the most popular forms of entertainment in Australia.

## IV. Questions:

1. What was the basis of the culture of the Peoples of Australia until 1788?
2. What is a major contrast between the Dreaming and Protestantism concerning the land?
3. What idea did Protestantism spread in the colonisation of Australia? How did it influence Australia socially, politically and culturally?
4. How did the variations of Christianity reflect class differences?
5. What is the title of the section about sport? What does the title reveal about the author's view of sport in Australia? Why does she use a question mark here?
6. When the author says that in Australia today sport plays a dominant role, does she mean it as a compliment or a criticism?

# Australia

7. What positive characteristics does sport have? What is fair play?
8. How did the works of the 19th and early 20th century Australian writers differ from the journals of Captain Cook and Sir Joseph Banks? How did the 20th century writers identify themselves in their works?
9. Why was Patrick White awarded the Nobel Prize for Literature in 1973?
10. Who was Ruth Park? What are her major works?
11. Can you name some films based on Australian novels?
12. Why did the Australian government provide funding bodies both for the production of films and in the training of film makers in the 1970 and 1980s?
13. Can you name any Australian actors who have won Oscar or Tony Awards?
14. What is common among the three films *The Rabbit Proof Fence, The Ten Canoes* and *Samson and Delilah*? What particular cultural significance do they share?

**V. Topics for discussion or research:**

1. Compare Protestantism and the Dreaming in their different relationships with land. In the past, people were led to think that the European settlers were more civilised than the indigenous people. Do you still think so after this comparative study?
2. What is Fundamentalism? How is it related with social change?
3. The author is critical of the dominant role that sport plays in Australia. Do you agree with her? What role does sport play in China? What do you think should be the role of sport?
4. How has Australian literature evolved over the past decades? Illustrate your point with examples. How is Australian self-identity expressed through literature?
5. How are literature and films related in Australia?

# UNIT 17

# Work and Family Life

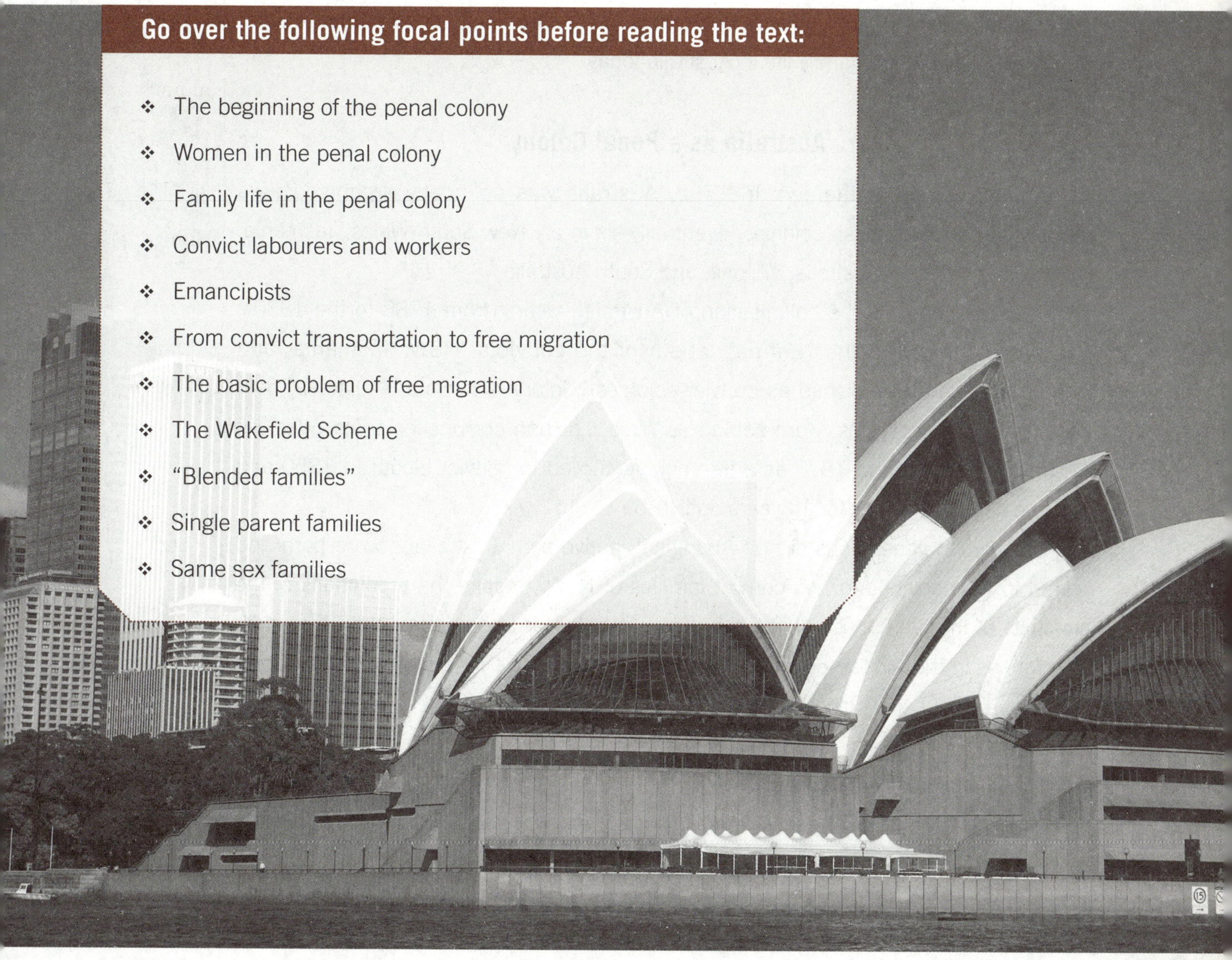

**Go over the following focal points before reading the text:**

- The beginning of the penal colony
- Women in the penal colony
- Family life in the penal colony
- Convict labourers and workers
- Emancipists
- From convict transportation to free migration
- The basic problem of free migration
- The Wakefield Scheme
- "Blended families"
- Single parent families
- Same sex families

# Australia

## Introduction

Work and family life have been constructed in very different ways in Australia. This section covers three major stages in this development: Australian work and family life in the **penal colony**, Australian work and family life in a free migration and free market economy, and work and family life in Australia today.

## Australia as a Penal Colony

After European settlement in 1788, Australia was politically organised as a number of separate British colonies, eventually six in all: New South Wales, Tasmania, Queensland, Western Australia, Victoria, and South Australia.[1]

The first period of the colonisation of Australia, lasting from 1788 to the 1830s, was based largely on the "unfree" labour of the convicts: NSW, Tasmania, and Queensland were established as convict colonies; Victoria and South Australia, both established in the 1830s, were settled as "free", or non-convict, colonies. Western Australia, established in 1828 as a free colony, turned to convict labour in 1850 and became a convict colony for 19 years until 1869.

So the first generations of non-Aboriginal, native-born Australians were born and reared in the convict and non-convict families of NSW. Despite the **predictions** of the **moralists** of the time, these children turned out to be far less criminal than their **peer** generations in the Mother country.[2] What was family life like in this extraordinary form of society — the penal colony of NSW?

### Family Life in the Convict Colony

At the end of the 18th century families in Europe, especially those in Britain, were in a state of transition, moving from the families of rural life to the new urban families of the manufacturing towns and **slums** of the early industrial revolution.[3] So life in the penal colony was based on a culture that was itself subject to changing values. Moreover, for the first few decades after 1788, the colonial workforce was based largely

penal *adj.*
有关刑罚的，作为刑罚的
penal colony
罪犯流放殖民地
prediction *n.*
预言，预料，预计
moralist *n.*
道德主义者，道德说教者
peer *n.*
同等地位的人，同辈
slum *n.* 贫民区

on convict labour. Men vastly outnumbered women. However, family life was being established in the colony although with some significant variations from life in the "Mother country".[4]

Portia Robinson's description of the lives of working families in the convict era from 1788 to the 1830s reveals that many wives of convicts made desperate efforts to be brought out to live with their husbands. The majority of requests were denied[5]. For these wives, being left behind in the UK, often meant **deprivation**, even death, for them and their children. However, a few wives were allowed to sail with their convict husbands. In 1791, for example, the human **cargo** on the convict ship *Albemarle* comprised one thousand convicts and six wives of convicts[6]. In 1802, thirty free wives sailed with their convict husbands on the convict ship *HMS Calcutta*. By the 1820s this practice had increased, although the rules often seem to have been applied **arbitrarily**.[7]

In the first decades new families were often formed in the colony in a brutal way. When a ship with women convicts or "free" women migrants **docked**, first the government officials and senior officers, then the sailors and "free" working men were allowed to go on board to claim a woman as a servant and/or a **concubine**[8]. Convicts could claim the remaining women. The women who were not claimed either slept on the streets or were sent to the "Female Factory"[9] — a prison in Paramatta. Single women were at risk of being **viciously** treated and this abuse was so much part of the institutional culture of the colony that Governor Macquarie was **censured** for punishing one group of his officers for their **abominable** treatment of women.[10] For women this vicious system meant that they were obliged to work and sleep with one man or bear the considerable risks of being shared between men.[11] Women in the colony had little choice between an informal family relationship and **prostitution**.

So families were formed in various ways: some arrived together, or arrived separately and were reunited, whilst others were newly formed in NSW. The convict husbands of free wives could be **allotted** to them as "ticket-of-leave" servants[12]. In these cases, the husband was expected to provide for the family[13] through his labour on land that had been formally allocated to the wife.

The **partnerships** between convict men and convict women were less secure[14]: Margaret McDonald, a convict from Edinburgh, applied to have her convict husband assigned to her but the authorities deliberately separated the couple by assigning them to masters in different areas of the colony. Moreover, whether the wife was "free"

deprivation *n.*
贫困，缺乏生活来源
cargo *n.*
（装载的）货物
arbitrarily *adv.*
武断地
dock *v.*
使（船）靠码头
concubine *n.*
妾
viciously *adv.*
恶性地，恶劣地
censure *v.*
指责，公开谴责
abominable *adj.* 令人憎恶的
prostitution *n.*
卖淫
allot *v.*
分配，分给
partnership *n.*
伙伴关系

# Australia

or "convict", if the convict husband had a special skill required by the government, he was less likely to be assigned to her. For example, Ann Evans, a free wife with two children, came to the colony two years after her husband, a carpenter, had been transported for life[15]. Portia Robinson records the response of the authorities to Ann's petition. The government would not free him from his convict **servitude** because "The husband of the **Petitioner** is a **Cabinet Maker** and in the present state of the Public Works he cannot be spared"[16].

Many of the women and men who had been transported as convicts, lived together and had children without having been officially married in church. In Australian terms, these were "*de facto*" families. Samuel Marsden, a Protestant **clergyman** and an influential moralist in the colony, was critical of these "unofficial" families. Portia Robinson, the historian of family life in the colony, strongly disputes Marsden's account of the **immorality** of these early Australian families[17]. Her research details the care and responsibility that parents displayed towards their children. "Currency children" was the name given to these first generations born in NSW, and several visitors to the colony favourably compared the physical **stature** and easy **demeanour** of the "Currency children" with those of the children reared in the industrial towns and slums of England[18].

Convict partnerships were not the only form of family of this era. There were also "free" families of people who came over with the transported convicts, families of soldiers or administrators of the colony or people who arrived as "free settlers". However, the majority of men in the early years of the colony did not have wives. The majority of men, of course, were also convicts.

## Work Life in the Penal Colony

Most convicts lived as servants and labourers, but there were also convict tradesmen and **clerical** and administrative workers. Francis Greenaway, a convict architect who had been convicted of **forgery**, was responsible for some fine buildings that still stand in Sydney today.[19] Initially the convict work force rarely received wages, and for some years imported **rum** was the currency of the colony. Lachlan Macquarie, who took over as governor of NSW in 1810, used this massive force of convict labour to expand the colony by building up to fifty townships around Sydney. At this time some convicts, especially those who were "**mechanics**" or tradesmen, were able to

---

**servitude** n. 奴役（状态），束缚
**petitioner** n. 请愿人，请求人
**cabinet maker** （熟练的）细木工人，家具木工
*de facto* （拉丁）实际的，事实上的
**clergyman** n. 牧师
**immorality** n. 不道德
**stature** n. 身材，身高
**demeanour** n. 行为，举动
**clerical** adj. 职员的，办事员的，文书工作的
**forgery** n. 伪造
**rum** n. 朗姆酒，糖蜜酒
**mechanic** n. 机械工，机修工

earn wages in their spare time — that is, after three o'clock in the afternoon. They could earn between six and eight **shillings** a day, higher wages than those earned by free workers back in Britain. Other convicts, especially those who worked for the **pastoralists**, were not so lucky.

The pastoralists, the major landowners, built their wealth on the unpaid labour of the convicts. Pastoralists' obligations were only to **house**, feed and clothe their convict servants and agricultural labourers. Moreover, as pastoralists were also often **magistrates** they could use their legal powers to enforce hard labour from their workers. Approximately 40 per cent of convicts received the **lash** at some time during their period of penal labour. However, once the convicts gained their 'ticket of leave' and became "free" workers or "**emancipists**", these early generations of colonists created family businesses, in shops or inns, building **works**, small factories and farms that spread with the rapid growth of the colony. Some of the businesses of these emancipist families became immensely successful. For example, the convicts Elizabeth and James Ruse made history in the colony by being the first successful farming family. In 1788, they were allocated land at Paramatta, the most fertile land in the new colony. Married in 1790 and, still technically convicts, they enjoyed considerable freedom and later had other convicts **assigned** to work for them. After Ruse's **sentence expired** in 1792, he was allotted the first land **grant** to any convict in the colony. At times it was Elizabeth who had to maintain the farm, single-handedly. Today a suburb and a major roadway are named after him, and the James Ruse Agricultural High School is one of the most respected schools in NSW.

Emancipists also became lawyers, architects, editors, successful business people, and even government administrators. By the 1820s, a third of the richest men in the colony were emancipists.

By 1821 the population of NSW had increased to 40 000, and the majority of women in the colony were "free" colonists: by 1820 only 17% of women were convicts. Women ran the new businesses of the colony with their husbands. Those who had been **widowed** were operating as independent **publicans**, dealers, traders, and shopkeepers able to request in their own names assigned extra servants and grants of extra land.[20] Mary Reiby[21] became the most famous of these successful, and wealthy, ex-convict businesswomen. In the next stage of the history of the colonial family economy, however, we trace the decline of this female independence.

shilling n.
先令（1971年前英国货币单位，20先令为1镑）
pastoralist n.
（澳）牧场主
house v.
提供住宿
magistrate n.
地方行政官；执法官
lash n.
笞刑
emancipist n.
（澳史）刑满释放者
works n. 工厂
assign v.
分配（工作）
sentence n.
刑期
expire v. 到期
grant n.
授予物（如土地、权利等）
widow v.
使丧偶
publican n.
（英）酒馆老板，小旅馆老板

# Australia

## From Convict Transportation to "Free" Migration

By the early 1820s there was pressure from the majority of the "free" settlers in NSW to replace convict transportation with "free migration" and to establish a "free market" economy. This move was opposed by some, especially the pastoralists and the merchant class who wanted to maintain transportation as a source of cheap labour[22]. Nevertheless, convict transportation was **suspended** in New South Wales in 1840. Attempts by the British Colonial Office to reinstate the practice in the colony brought about mass anti-transportation demonstrations in Sydney and Melbourne. The British Government then lost its political nerve for reintroducing convicts to eastern Australia[23]. Transportation to Van Diemen's Land[24] was suspended in 1852 and to Western Australia in 1868.

The **agitation** against transportation paralleled civil agitation for representative government, which was introduced in NSW in 1842.[25] By the middle of the 19th century, all six States had achieved virtually complete internal self-government under their own colonial parliaments. So the 1830s and 1840s formed the early years of the modern (non-convict) system of the Australian political economy.

By the mid 1830s, the free migrants considerably outnumbered the convict population of Australia.

During the period of the **gold strikes**[26] in Australia in the 1850s so many people made their own way to Australia that the population nearly doubled without the help of government-assisted migration.

## Work and Family Life in the Expanding "Free Market" Society: Mid-19th to Mid-20th Century

Work life in this period was reconstructed around the "free market" model: the economy would be largely based on the class system of individual entrepreneurs investing in agricultural and industrial business. So the convict colony gave way to a class economy. The three major class groups in this period were the "free labourers" who sold their labour on the "free labour market", their employers, who had invested capital to develop agricultural, mining and industrial businesses and needed to employ the workers' labour to produce their commodities and, thirdly, the in-between group. This middle class group were the owners of the small farming, mining, manufacturing and commercial businesses who employed only themselves and their families.

---

suspend *v.*
暂停，中止
agitation *n.*
躁动不安，骚乱
gold strike
金矿的发现

In some situations especially in Western Australia and South Australia, this system did not work too well at first because too many migrants wanted to become self-employed workers rather than the employees. This meant that migrants had to be channelled into selling their labour in the labour market. Thus, the "free market" system became less "free" and more controlled by the government. In South Australia, for example, the government used the Wakefield[27] scheme to develop the colony.

**The Wakefield Scheme**

- The government would make grants of land to investors at a "Sufficient Price".
- The "Sufficient Price" would be set high enough to finance an ongoing migration programme.
- Labourers of both sexes would be brought out to the colony thus ensuring that the cost of one generation's migration would result in several future generations of labourers.[28]
- The "Sufficient Price" would also provide a "sufficient" balance: it would be low enough to encourage the relatively wealthy to invest, yet sufficiently high to prevent labourers from immediately becoming landowners themselves.[29]
- The emigrant labour would be "bonded". That is to say, the workers had to provide their paid labour to the government, or to the land holder, for a specified number of years before being free to choose whether to continue working as labourers under the scheme, to work elsewhere, or even, if they had saved "sufficient" money, to apply for land themselves.

The government was also concerned to ensure that family life would take a particular shape. Their preferred model of the family was the one in which the wife and mother would be economically dependent on her husband. This was articulated in Catherine Helen Spence's recommendations to the NSW government. She argued that there were two dangers if women migrants had equal pay. Firstly, women would delay getting married and delay producing children, i.e. the next generation of labourers. Secondly, some men would become lazy, they would come to depend on their wives' income and thus withdraw their own masculine labour from the "free market". As the political economy grew, and more areas of employment and education developed, the government enacted legislation to ensure that women would be excluded from these new improved labour markets. In the jobs that women were allowed to enter, their pay would be less than the male rate, even if they were widowed and had dependent children. This meant that women and women-headed families were always at risk of having to live below the poverty line.

One further change affected family life. From the late 19th century women began to control the numbers of children they had. Increasingly families became smaller. By the mid-20th century family life was constructed as a classic nuclear family. This means: a family with only two or three children, with the husband as the major bread winner and the wife being responsible for all the unpaid domestic labour. In addition, the classic nuclear family had fewer ties with the husband's and the wife's family of birth. This family form fitted the increasingly changing economy, in which new forms of industry and employment were constantly being generated. The classic nuclear family is a more mobile family, enabling the husband to move around the country as the economy and the employment market change shape.

## Work and Family Life in Australia Today

Over the past 60 years, work and family life have changed in several ways. By the 21st century, the fights for equal pay and equal rights to education and employment have given both men and women much greater choice about the ways they want to live. Today in Australia, people get married and have children much later in life. Often, the parents of families remain unmarried. There are more "blended families" as people separate and remarry, bringing their two sets of children into their new partnerships.[30] Single parent families now comprise a higher proportion of all families. The extension of longer periods of education and training means that children are dependent on their families for much longer periods, in some cases staying at home with their parents until they are in their late twenties or thirties. The fight for gay rights means that same sex families are not unusual. However, families still include a few people living in the classic nuclear family form. Nevertheless, more commonly, Australian children live in families where both their mothers and fathers share their paid work and family responsibilities.

So there is much greater freedom about what kind of families Australians create, much greater equality between men and women, and greater equality between gay and **straight** families. However, these new freedoms operate in a work economy that has not yet fully adapted to meet their needs. The "nine to five" work day, or sometimes the "nine to seven o'clock work day", puts strains on families with babies or dependent children

straight *adj*.
非同性恋的

whose school day ends at four o'clock. So one of the major problems that Australian fathers and mothers experience today is just how to balance work and family life. The total numbers of hours that parents spend on paid and unpaid work is increasing and this can place strains on both partners. In addition, as health care improves, enabling disabled and ageing family members to live longer, the unpaid work of caring for the family increases. Moreover, although 20% of **lesbians** and up to 10% of gay men are parents, these single sex families not only face the same "work/family balance" problems, but face a range of other issues in work and in the community.[31]

Complete gender equality has still not been achieved as it is mainly women who have the major responsibility for the unpaid caring work for children and other dependents. This often means that it is women who have breaks in their careers just when promotions to the next levels of their occupations are opening up.[32] These are problems that are on the agenda today. It is no longer taken for granted that family and work life are separate issues. The government funds two major research institutes: HILDA, (the Household and Labour Dynamics Institute) and the AIFS (the Australian Institute of Family Studies). Both constantly research the problems of the **intersection** of family and work life today and make recommendations about the ways in which these problems could be addressed. Similarly there are several political **lobby** groups who raise issues about the problems that people in same sex families face in adopting and raising children.

lesbian *n.*
女同性恋者
intersection *n.*
交叉
lobby *n.*
议会院外活动集团

# Explanations

1. **After European settlement ... and South Australia:**
   1788年欧洲定居点开始在澳大利亚建立后，澳大利亚被分为多个相互独立的英国殖民地。最终它们合并成六个殖民地，即新南威尔士、塔斯马尼亚、昆士兰、西澳大利亚、维多利亚和南澳大利亚。其中新南威尔士建立得最早，是1788年第一只舰队的登陆地。南澳大利亚成立最晚，1836年才建立。如下文所说，新南威尔士、塔斯马尼亚和昆士兰被作为罪犯流放地，维多利亚和南澳大利亚是自由定居殖民地。西澳大利亚初建时是自由定居殖民地，后又接受了流放罪犯。本文中 the colony 代指1901年成立联邦之前的澳大利亚。

## Australia

2. **Despite predictions ... in the Mother country:**
尽管一些当时的道德说教者这样预言（即这些出生在澳大利亚的罪犯和自由定居者的孩子长大后会成为罪犯），这些孩子的犯罪率实际上远远低于在英国与之同龄的孩子的犯罪率。

3. **At the end ... the early industrial revolution:**
在 18 世纪末，欧洲的家庭，特别是英国家庭，正处于变化时期，从农村生活方式的家庭转变为工业革命早期以制造业为主的城市和城市贫民窟中的新型城市家庭。

4. **Men vastly outnumbered ... life in the "Mother country":**
男人的人数远远超过了女人，但是在澳大利亚正在逐步形成家庭生活，只是澳大利亚的家庭生活与英国的家庭生活有着一些重要的差异。意指在罪犯流放地的罪犯妻子或罪犯丈夫不能过正常的家庭生活，有的还无法在一起。家庭的组成方式也和在英国的不同。

5. **The majority of requests were denied:**
（罪犯的妻子不顾一切地要求同丈夫一起流放到澳大利亚，）但这样的要求通常都被拒绝了。

6. **the human cargo ... six wives of convicts:**
运载罪犯的 Albemarle 号船上装了 1 000 名罪犯和 6 名罪犯的妻子。human cargo: 人体货物。指运罪犯的船上条件极差，把人当成货物运输。

7. **By the 1820s ... applied arbitrarily:**
到 19 世纪 20 年代，这种做法更为普遍了，但对相关规定的执行却显得无章可循。即尽管越来越多的罪犯妻子随着丈夫一起流放，但对此并没有明确的条文规定。

8. **When a ship ... and/or a concubine:**
当载有女犯或女性自由移民的船靠岸时，首先是政府官员和高级军官，然后是水手和自由民工人到船上去领一个女人回家做仆人兼 / 或情妇。

9. **The Female Factory:**
女子工厂，位于新南威尔士的 Paramatta，在 1804 到 1848 年间关押女罪犯。罪犯在里面从事纺线、织布等工作。

10. **Single women were at risk ... their abominable treatment of women:**
单身女子很可能会受到粗暴虐待，而这已成为殖民地长期形成的文化中的一部分。因此，当麦夸里总督惩罚了自己手下一群虐待妇女的军官时，他却因此受到了公开批评。Governor Macquarie: 1809–1821 任新南威尔士总督。任内主张提高殖民地的道德水平，建立教育机构，鼓励开发蓝山以西地区，对罪犯给予人性关怀，被后人誉为"澳大利亚之父"。

11. **For women ... or prostitution:**
对妇女来说，这种残酷的体制迫使她们要么为一个男人做仆人和情妇，要么就会变成多个男人摧残的对象。在澳大利亚的妇女除了选择非正式的家庭关系（即做情妇）或卖淫以外，没有其他的选择。

# UNIT 17　Work and Family Life

12. **The convict husbands ... "ticket-of-leave" servant:**
    自由人妻子的犯罪丈夫可以获得假释以分配给他们的妻子做"仆人"。Ticket-of-leave：是 18 世纪末和 19 世纪前半叶实行的一种让获得减刑或免刑的罪犯做工以换取酬劳的做法。

13. **provide for the family:**
    供养家人。

14. **The partnerships ... less secure:**
    罪犯丈夫和罪犯妻子的婚姻关系就不那么有保障了。

15. **had been transported for life:**
    被终生流放（永远不得回英国）。

16. **The husband of ... cannot be spared:**
    申请人的丈夫是一名熟练的家具木工，目前不能离开正在进行的公共工程。

17. **Portia Robinson, ... early Australian families:**
    Portia Robinson 是研究殖民地时期澳大利亚家庭生活的历史学者，她对 Marsden 有关早期澳大利亚家庭的不道德性的观点表示坚决反对。

18. **several visitors to ... slums of England:**
    一些到过澳大利亚的人认为，在澳大利亚出生长大的儿童，在体格和行为做事上，都要优于在英格兰的工业城镇和贫民窟中长大的儿童。Currency children：又叫 currency lads and lasses，用于指在早期新南威尔士殖民地出生长大的孩子。与 sterling 相对，即自由移民到澳大利亚的出生在英国的孩子。

19. **Francis Greenaway ... in Sydney today:**
    弗朗西斯·格林纳威（1777–1837），罪犯、建筑师，因伪造罪被判刑。他负责设计的一些杰出的建筑仍然矗立在今天的悉尼。弗朗西斯·格林纳威因伪造建筑合同被流放到新南威尔士。麦夸里总督赦免了他，并任命他为悉尼的建筑师。他先后共设计了 40 多座建筑，其中包括现在的新南威尔士音乐厅等。

20. **Those who had been widowed ... grants of extra land:**
    失去丈夫的妇女可以做独立的酒吧老板、做买卖、经商或做店主，她们可以用自己的名字获得额外的仆人并得到政府额外特批的土地。

21. **Mary Reiby:**
    玛丽·莱蓓（1777–1855），商人，13 岁时因盗窃马匹被流放到澳大利亚。后嫁给托马斯·莱蓓，帮助他在悉尼获得地产，并帮他经营生意。1811 年托马斯·莱蓓去世后，玛丽·莱蓓继续扩大他的生意规模，积累了巨额财富。

22. **This move was ... of cheap labour:**
    这一动议遭到一些人的反对，特别遭到了大牧场主和商人阶层的反对。他们希望能继续接收流放罪犯以便得到廉价劳动力。

# Australia

23. **The British Government ... to eastern Australia:**
    英国政府失去了向澳大利亚东部重新遣送罪犯的政治勇气。

24. **Van Diemen's Land:**
    范迪门的土地,即如今的塔斯马尼亚岛。荷兰航海家 Abel Tasman 于 1642 年到达塔斯马尼亚岛的西部,便以派他进行航海探险的荷兰东印度公司总督 Anthony Van Diemen 的名字对其命名。1855 年该岛正式更名为塔斯马尼亚。

25. **The agitation ... in NSW in 1842:**
    反对罪犯流放制的运动与要求建立代议制的运动同时发生,1842 年,新南威尔士成立了代议制政府。

26. **The gold strikes:**
    发现金矿,淘金热。1851 年在新南威尔士州巴瑟斯特市(Bathurst)发现金矿后,澳大利亚开始了淘金热,大量人口涌入澳大利亚,对澳大利亚的经济、社会和政治造成深远影响。

27. **Wakefield:**
    威克菲尔德(1796–1862),英国殖民地开发理论家,他的思想影响了澳大利亚,特别是南澳大利亚的发展。1829 年,在服刑期间,他写了《悉尼来信》,阐述了一个简单易行而又非常巧妙的殖民体制。他认为土地不能无偿分配或廉价出售,而应以"足够高的价格"出售,确保只有资本的人才能买得起;出售土地的收入用于资助经过筛选的自由移民到澳大利亚,成为当地的劳动力。

28. **Labourers of both sexes ... generations of labourers:**
    到殖民地的劳动力移民应男女都有,以使一代移民的成本可以带来将来几代移民。

29. **The "Sufficient Price" ... landowners themselves:**
    "足够高的价格"也应能建立起"恰好的"平衡:价格不应很高以促使相对富裕的人进行投资,但同时也不应很低,以阻止劳动力能很快成为土地拥有者。

30. **There are more "blended families" as people separate ... into their new partnerships:**
    现在有许多"混合家庭",因为人们分居并再婚,把他们各自的孩子带到新的家庭中。partnership: 伙伴关系。

31. **Moreover, although 20% of lesbians and up to 10% of gay men ... in the community:**
    虽然 20% 的女同性恋和 10% 的男同性恋有孩子,这些同性家庭不仅面临上述的工作与家庭的平衡问题,而且还在工作和社区中还面临一系列其他问题。

32. **This often means that it is women who have breaks ... occupations are opening up:**
    这经常意味着妇女当有机会被提升到更高一级水平时却不得不(因为家庭问题而)中断她们的事业。

**UNIT 17  Work and Family Life**

# Exercises

I. **Give the Chinese equivalents for the following:**
   1. a penal colony
   2. New South Wales
   3. emancipists
   4. publicans
   5. the "blended family"

II. **Decide whether the following statements are true (T) or false (F):**
   1. The European settlement in Australia started in 1788. _____
   2. Victoria and South Australia were established as convict colonies. _____
   3. At the beginning of the settlement, there were roughly equal numbers of men and women. _____
   4. Convicts' wives in England were discouraged from following their husbands to Australia. _____
   5. The convict husbands of free wives could be assigned to work for their own families as ticket-of-leave servants. _____
   6. Mary Reiby was a successful farmer who received the first land grant in NSW. _____
   7. Convict transportation to the Australian continent was stopped in 1852. _____
   8. From the late 19th century women began to control the number of children they had. _____
   9. Today, the parents of families often remain unmarried. _____
   10. Complete gender equality has been achieved in Australia today. _____

III. **Fill in the blanks:**
   1. Elizabeth and James Ruse became the first successful _____ family in Australia.
   2. _____ was established as a free colony, but turned to convict labour in 1850.
   3. Female convicts who were not claimed by any man upon arriving in Australia were sent to the _____.

## Australia

4. The first generation of children who were born in NSW were called _____.
5. In 1810, Lachlan Macquarie became the _____ of NSW.
6. Pastoralists often used their legal power as _____ to force labourers to work hard.
7. One important factor of the Wakefield Scheme was that the land should not be available _____ and _____.
8. One of the major problems that Australian fathers and mothers experience today is just how to balance work and _____ life.

IV. **Questions:**
1. What was a penal or convict colony during the first period of colonisation of Australia?
2. Why did men vastly outnumber women in the early colonial period?
3. Why does the author say, "In the first decades new families were often formed in the colony in a brutal way"?
4. What was the "Female Factory"? How were women convicts treated there?
5. What were "*de facto*" families? Who were the "Currency children"? Did Portia Robinson agree with Samuel Marsden's criticism of the "unofficial" "*de facto*" families?
6. Who was Francis Greenway? What is he remembered for?
7. How did Governor Macquarie use the massive force of convict labour to expand New South Wales?
8. Who were the emancipists? What role did they play in the economic growth of the colony?
9. Who was Mary Reiby? What does her story show?
10. Why was convict transportation suspended in NSW in 1840 and later in other parts of Australia?
11. What was a class economy? What were the three major class groups in the period when the convict economy gave way to a class economy?
12. What were the main points of the Wakefield Scheme? Did the scheme solve the problem in the early development of Australian economy? Why or why not?
13. What family model was preferred by the government? Why?
14. What were the two dangers described by Catherine Helen Spence if women had equal pay?
15. Why has "how to balance work and family life" become one of the major problems that Australian fathers and mothers experience today?

V. **Topics for discussion or research:**
1. What was convict transportation in colonial Australia? How did it affect family life in the colonies?
2. Describe the situation of women in colonial Australia.
3. Do you think the two issues of family and work life are separate or related? How would you describe the relationship between family and work life in today's China?
4. What changes have taken place in family life over the recent decades in Australia? Has complete gender equality been achieved in Australia today? Support your view with facts.

UNIT 18  Australia as a Liberal Democratic Society

# UNIT 18

# Australia as a Liberal Democratic Society

**Go over the following focal points before reading the text:**

- Commitment to difference as the central value of Australian society
- The Washminster form of polity
- The three-tier system of government
- The two houses of parliament
- The Governor-General
- Political parties
- Advantages of the pluralist form of government
- The Australian government's role in the national economy
- Interventionist government
- Economic rationalism

# Australia

## Text

### Introduction: Different Perspectives

Australians understand and conduct life upon a basic commitment to difference[1]. This central value has implications for all areas of life. There are many different religions. Politics is based upon conflicts — and their resolution — between major political parties[2]. Newspapers are identified with different political **biases**. So too, are various television and radio programmes. Students are expected to interpret their subjects from different perspectives and are encouraged to use considered arguments to contest other students' and even their lecturers' interpretation of the subject[3].

The emphasis is upon the principle that there are different ways of thinking and knowing about the world: there is neither absolute truth nor one single way to run the country. Instead, there has to be debate about how we know the world and how we should behave in the world. Even core values — which tend to be long lasting — can be changed over time, not by a violent overthrow of the cultural system but through discussion, education and gradual cultural change.[4]

The **corollary** of this approach is that **objectivity** can only be obtained by being aware of, and honest about, the particular perspective or interpretation we are using.[5] The major differences in the perspectives of Australians are, to some extent, represented by the major political parties. Over the past 100 years, government in Australia, in the main, has been represented by either the Labour Party or the Liberal/National **Coalition**.

### The Formation of the Australian Political System

Australia has what has been called a "Washminster" form of **polity**[6]. In other words it is a mixture of the US, Washington system of government and the British Westminster system: the political structure is based on a Federation of States and has a three-tier system of government but the chief executive is a Prime Minister not a President.

Although Australia has a three-tier system of government — the Australian Parliament at Federal level, six State governments and about 900 Local government

---

bias *n.* 偏见
corollary *n.* 必然结果
objectivity *n.* 客观性
coalition *n.* 联合政府；结合体，同盟
polity *n.* 政治机构

bodies — the Prime Minister and his **Cabinet** at federal level is the acknowledged centre of Australian parliamentary power.[7] For example, there are some parliamentary powers which are shared by Federal and State governments but, when there is any **inconsistency** between the decisions of the two levels of government, the Commonwealth or Federal laws **overrule** the laws of the State.

At the Federal level there are two houses of parliament — the House of Representatives, or the Lower House, and the Senate. The Senate, even though it is called the Upper House, does not have the power to enact legislation. Its role is to consider and propose amendments to the Bills, that is, the proposed pieces of legislation, which the Lower House **initiates**. If there is sufficient disagreement between the House of Representatives and the Senate, then the Governor General can call a "double **dissolution**": both Houses of Parliament are stood down and there is an early general election.[8] However, this power of the Senate is employed rarely.

Within the pluralist **paradigm**, it is citizens who ultimately control the government through the electoral system. Citizens vote for members of parliament. The members of parliament generally belong to one of the two major political parties, the Australian Labor Party (ALP)[9] or the Coalition. As its name implies, the Coalition comprises a combination of two parties — the Liberals[10] and the Nationals[11]. Each party sets out a party programme[12] — a set of basic principles and policies that align with those principles.

This system has the following advantages:

• The difference between the two party programmes means that citizens can choose, at each election, which set of policies they would prefer to be enacted over the following three years of government[13]. It is this ability to help to elect one's own government from parties with reasonably clearly defined political programmes that underpins the political citizenship of the Australian people.[14]

• This system secures **transparency** and thus **accountability**[15]. Even when the major party is in power their policies should be subject to the continuous **scrutiny** of the opposing party, both on the floor of the house[16], in the Senate committee system and through political debates in the media.

• **Pluralism** provides for a ready made alternative government as the major Opposition party comprises not only **back-benchers**, but also "shadow ministers" and a "shadow cabinet", who are sufficiently informed about current aspects of their shadow

# Australia

**portfolios** for the opposition to be competent to take over should any government collapse.[17]

- Citizens can exert their power between elections through their membership of major interest groups. These include not only the political parties, but also other associations such as unions, employers' groups and environmental groups. Citizens, according to the pluralist interpretation, can have a continuing input into party policies through their membership of such groups. Nevertheless, it is the voting system which is the **keystone** of the pluralist and liberal theory of citizen power.

In contrast with many other liberal democratic societies, Australia has a system of compulsory voting[18]. At each election all citizens of voting age (over 18 years) must attend their local electoral station. However, there is no law saying that citizens cannot spoil their vote, so casting a vote *per se* is not compulsory[19].

Formally, the executive branch of government is headed by the Governor-General who is the representative of the Queen. However, the British monarch has no real power in Australia. The Governor-General acts only on the advice of the Executive Council that comprises himself and the Cabinet[20].

The only recent exception to this rule was the 1975 dismissal of Gough Whitlam[21] who was then the Labor Prime Minister of Australia. The leader of the opposition, Malcolm Fraser[22] had persuaded Sir John Kerr, the Governor-General, that as the Upper House had refused to pass the Supply Bill granting money to the government, Whitlam should be dismissed, and that he, Fraser, should be appointed as a caretaker Prime Minister[23]. This dismissal was generally interpreted as a major constitutional crisis created by the **flouting** of the **uncodified** or unwritten conventions of government[24]. The Governor-General attracted such political and popular **animosity** that it is unlikely that any future Governor-General would attempt to exert this power again[25].

## The Relationship between the Political and Economic Spheres

According to the principles of liberal theory, governments should play only a minor part in the nation's economy[26]. The major principle is that the economy should be run as a "free market" system with as little interference from the government as possible. However, the actual history of the Australian political economy demonstrates a very uneven application of this principle[27]. We saw in Unit 16 how, even at the establishment of the Australian "free market" system, there was a need for major political intervention

---

portfolio *n.*
部长职，大臣职
keystone *n.*
基础，主旨；基本原则
*per se*（拉丁）
（不涉及其他因素的）自身，本身
flout *v.*
蔑视，藐视
uncodify *v.*
没有编成法典
animosity *n.*
憎恶，仇恨

to help provide a supply of cheap labour through the assisted migration scheme[28].

The long wool boom[29] of the 1820s and 1830s, and later the gold rush, sucked in British investment. This investment raised the Australian standard of living up to, or beyond, many first-world levels.

The 1850s gold rushes attracted a flood of self-funded immigrants. The population of Australia doubled in that decade. It also opened up the land as not only a source of agricultural but also of mineral wealth[30]: gold, silver, **iron ore**, **nickel** and **alumina** became major export industries by the end of the 20th century. However, it was agriculture, especially the wool trade, that formed the basis of the Australian economy for over 130 years when Australia was described as "riding on the sheep's back". From the 1840s to the 1970s agriculture regularly accounted for over 75% of Australia's export trade. The period from the 1840s to the end of the 19th century was an era of expanding agricultural settlement. This economic and population expansion in turn both depended upon and supported the growth of towns and railways.

By the last few decades of the 19th century the government was playing a very large part in the economy. It was a major employer. It invested in massive capital works programmes in provision of railways and communications, and urban infrastructures of water and sewage[31]. In the education "industry" the introduction of universal primary education was based upon state funding. By the time of Federation in 1901, the colonial governments had developed a large bureaucracy of government workers to administer and run these several aspects of economic life[32].

In further moves away from the **purist** form of a "free" market, the Federal Government chose in 1901 a programme of **tariff** protection[33], rather than a free trade policy, to develop manufacturing industries in the secondary sector of the Australian economy; pursued a White Australia Policy of labour immigration in the Immigration Restriction Act of 1901[34] and initiated, through the 1907 Harvester Judgement[35], a central **arbitration** system which, amongst other responsibilities, would set a basic minimum wage for all workers.

The Government continued to play a large part in the economy in the post-WWII period. By the 1970s the Government was responsible for 30% of the GDP (Gross Domestic Product). It was involved in:
- labour migration programmes,
- wage setting through the arbitration system,

iron ore 铁矿石
nickel *n.* 镍
alumina *n.* 氧化铝，矾土
purist *n.* 纯粹主义者
tariff *n.* 关税
arbitration *n.* 仲裁，裁决

# Australia

- controls of industry through occupational safety legislation[36],
- control of foreign exchange dealings and
- tariff protection, especially in the manufacturing industries.

By this period the secondary or manufacturing sector had reached its highest level. However, major changes occurred in the 1970s/1980s. Increased overseas competition together with the lowering of the tariff system wiped out some major manufacturing industries[37]. Unemployment levels rose considerably.

This led to a significant **dismantling** of the government's involvement in and regulation of the Australian economy:

- Tariff rates were lowered.
- The centralised wage system was replaced by a focus on individual work place bargaining with the Coalition's "Work Choices Act".
- The foreign exchange markets were **deregulated**.

Economic **rationalism** has been the major policy **orientation**. There have been significant shifts away from government involvement in communication, banking, and in the provision of water and sewerage services. Even in those spheres which are more usually associated with the government, the provision of social welfare and social security services and the administration of the punishment system, the government has **contracted out** some of its responsibilities to the private sector, sometimes even to overseas corporations[38]. In addition, the government has been introducing greater private sector involvement in its provision of both education and health services. The Australian Broadcasting Corporation (the ABC)[39], a central and **iconic** source and reflection of Australian culture, is being encouraged to focus on producing programmes as marketable commodities to reduce its dependence upon government funding.

## The Australian Political Economy in the 21st Century

As citizens, Australians today are debating whether the loss of "social capital" — the cut-backs of public spending on education, health and the public broadcaster — is a necessary cost in maintaining Australia's position as one of the "strong" economies in global **league tables**[40]. Both the Labor and the Coalition parties have been **instrumental** in deregulating the economy. However, the Coalition is associated with the most **stringent** forms of economic rationalism especially with making a balanced budget the keystone of its policies whilst the Labor Party is aligned with a political programme

---

**dismantle** *v.* 废除，取消
**deregulate** *v.* 解除管制，使自由化
**rationalism** *n.* 理性主义
**orientation** *n.* 方向
**contract out** 外包，立合同把工作包出
**iconic** *adj.* 标志性的
**league table** 名次表，排名表
**instrumental** *adj.* 起重要的作用
**stringent** *adj.* 严格的

focusing more on the balance between social and economic aspects of Australian life.

By 2007, after twelve years of Coalition Government, the Labour Party was returned to power. Then, the following major factors affected Australian politics:
- The government was returned on its promises to revoke some of the transfers of power away from the workers.
- Economies around the world experienced the G.F.C. (the global financial crisis).
- Governments around the world had to consider the consequences of climate change.
- There was a continued military and diplomatic commitment to the USA but also an extension of commitments to other political economies, especially those in the Asian Pacific Region.

So some key changes were introduced after 2007. The government withdrew its troops from Iraq, although it maintained military support for the USA involvement in Afghanistan. On the industrial front, it re-established some of the rights, and negotiating power, of workers, by abolishing the "Work Choices Act" and replacing it with the "Fair Work Act" (2009). This was accompanied by a major change in the language that the Labour Party now uses. It tends no longer to talk of "workers" but of "working families": a change that indicated its acknowledgement of the key cultural shift outlined in Unit 17 Work and Family Life. Today, both men and women share the responsibilities of paid and unpaid work in the market and in the home.

The Labour Government also abandoned the Liberal Party's commitment to a balanced budget by making major government investments in education, health, communications and the environment. This set of policies was aimed at counteracting the effects of both the global financial crisis, and of Australia's relatively high levels of environmental pollution. Thus the government increased its role as a regulator of and player in the market especially in the labour market. So, the government was once again in debt. One policy, to reduce the government debt incurred by these programmes, was an attempt to make the mining corporations pay higher taxes on their profits. This policy was very controversial. Thus, it **pinpointed** the key aspect of the Australian political system that we noted in the introduction to this section: Australian politics is based on managing conflict by recognising the value of difference and debate.

At the federal election on Sept. 7, 2013, Tony Abbott led the Liberal/National

pinpoint *v.*
准确描述，确定

Coalition to victory over the incumbent Labour government, led by Kevin Rudd. Abbott had a conservative reputation. Soon his government was criticized for his decision to only include one woman, Julie Bishop, in his cabinet. The Prime Minister was the subject of criticism also because of his opposition to same-sex marriage and the reintroduction of the British Honours system of Dames and Knights among other reasons. However, it is generally acknowledged that the government led by Abbott did achieve some major accomplishments. His policy and attitude concerning the Indigenous people won some support and acclaim. As Prime Minister, Abbott oversaw free trade agreements signed with Japan, South Korea and China. But Malcolm Turnbull criticized Abbott for failing to exercise the economic leadership Australia needed. Turnbull became Prime Minister after defeating Abbott in the Liberal Party. The former is considered to be a part of the moderate wing of the Liberal Party. His views on issues such as climate change, republicanism, same-sex marriage and abortion differ from those held by the conservative wing, and are more progressive. At the beginning, his performance was quite satisfactory, but he lacked internal support from his own party. In fact, both the Labor and Liberal parties were faced with serious internal conflicts. The leaders of both parties were successfully challenged by their colleagues, and therefore, were unable to complete their term as Prime Minister. This in turn reveals the defects and problems existing in the political system in Australia.

*interventionist adj.* 干涉主义的

## Conclusion: Current Differences of Perspectives

For most of its history the Australian political economy has been characterised by a relatively **interventionist** government. The majority of Western democracies, including Australia, have attempted to balance three contradictory political economic programmes:

(a) to ensure that the country runs a profitable economy with little interference by the State in the market economy

(b) to invest in the kind of human capital necessary for each era of the political economy[41]

(c) to prevent the accompanying inequalities of a "free market" economy becoming too socially divisive[42].

All Western democracies vary in the way they deal with the contradictions inherent in the attempt to balance these three programmes whilst responding to the demands of

**UNIT 18  Australia as a Liberal Democratic Society**

their electorates.⁴³

    Until the 1970s, the balance chosen by the Australian polity had been to place greater emphasis on the second and third of these programmes. It had always had relatively interventionist governments. This placed it in the category of a welfare state. In contrast, the USA has followed the more purist liberal line by paying much greater attention to the first programme. However, with Australia's greater participation in the global economy it increasingly has moved towards the USA **neo-liberal** pattern.

    Although both political parties in Australia have pursued this more liberal form of a deregulated political economy, the Liberal Party has been its keenest **proponent**. Nevertheless, from the perspective of a pluralist theorist both parties still have to respond to their citizens who are likely to place limits on the extent to which any government can move away from a commitment to welfare programmes.⁴⁴

> neo-liberal *adj.*
> 新自由经济主义的（强调自由放任理论与政策的经济学）
> proponent *n.*
> 倡导者，支持者

# Explanations

1. **Australians understand and conduct life upon a basic commitment to difference:**
   澳大利亚人对生活的理解和行事是基于对于差异的一种基本承认与承诺。

2. **Politics is based ... major political parties:**
   政治的主要活动就是主要政党间的冲突和冲突的解决。

3. **... to use considered arguments ... of the subject:**
   鼓励学生用经过深思熟虑的观点来反驳其他学生——或者甚至是老师——对某一课题的解读。

4. **Even core value ... gradual cultural change:**
   即便是核心价值观——核心价值观一般会长期保持不变——也会随时间推移而改变。这种变化不是靠猛烈地推翻文化体制来实现的，而是通过讨论、教育以及渐进的文化变革实现的。

5. **The corollary of this approach ... we are using:**
   这种看问题的方法就必然意味着，我们只有意识到并承认我们看问题时采用的视角或解读方式，才能真正具有客观性。即绝对客观是不可能的，每个人都受不同因素的影响，以不同视角看问题。只有意识到这一点才能更客观地看问题。

6. **a "Washminster" form of polity:**
   英美政治体制相结合的政治制度。Washminster 是 Washington 和 Westminster 的缩写，分别是美国议会和英国议会所在地。如后文所说，澳大利亚的政治体制是英美政治体制的混合体，即其结构采用的是

# Australia

各州联邦制，并设有三级政府，但政府的首席执行官是总理，而不是总统。

7. **Although Australia has ... Australian parliamentary power:**

   尽管澳大利亚设有三级政府——联邦议会、六个州政府和 900 个地方政府机构——联邦政府的总理和他的内阁是公认的澳大利亚议会权力的中心。即如果联邦政府和州政府的政策之间出现分歧，联邦法律可以否决州法律。

8. **If there is ... an early general election:**

   如果众议院和参议院发生严重意见分歧，总督可以下令解散众议院和参议院（双解散）：议会两院结束任期，提前举行大选。

9. **the Australian Labour Party:**

   澳大利亚工党，简称 ALP，是澳大利亚最早成立的政党。它起源于 19 世纪末的工会运动。成立之初，致力于改善工人的工作条件，主张政府应对教育和农业给予支持，主张"白澳"政策。随着澳大利亚国内和国际形势的变化，工党摒弃了"白澳"政策，提倡多元文化主义；尽管仍和工会保持着传统关系，在经济上也逐渐实行了经济理性主义的一些政策。

10. **the Liberals:**

    The Liberal Party，自由党。自由党最初成立于 1909 年，遵循当时英国自由党的一些理念和政策。后经过分裂、重组，目前的澳大利亚自由党成立于 1945 年。澳大利亚自由党是澳大利亚主要保守派政党。

11. **the Nationals:**

    The National Party，澳大利亚国家党，是澳大利亚第三大党，代表农场主的利益。

12. **a party programme:**

    政党政纲，即政党的基本方针及如何贯彻实行这些方针的政策。

13. **which set of policies ... the following three years of government:**

    他们希望在以后的三年中政府执行哪套政策。澳政府的任期为三年。

14. **It is the ability ... of the Australian people:**

    公民有能力帮助从施政纲领明确合理的政党中挑选出自己想要的政府，这种能力对巩固澳大利亚人的公民政治权具有重要意义。

15. **This system secures transparency and thus accountability:**

    这一体制保证了政府的透明度，因此也就保证了政府官员问责制。

16. **the floor of the house:**

    议会中议员的座席，议员席。

17. **Pluralsim provides for ... any government collapse:**

    主要在野党不仅包括普通议员，还包括"影子大臣"和"影子内阁"，他们对目前政府相应部门的工作有相当的了解，如果出现政府不能运作的情况，他们有能力接替政府继续工作。因此，多元主义体制还保证了可替补政府随时可投入工作。

UNIT 18  Australia as a Liberal Democratic Society

18. **compulsory voting:**
    强制选举。澳大利亚规定，所有年满 18 岁的公民都必须到投票站参加投票选举。

19. **there is no law ... is not compulsory:**
    没有法律规定公民不能在选票上不按规定涂抹选票，因此就投票本身而言，并不是强制性的。即公民必须到投票站登记，领取选票，但可投空票、废票，法律对此未予禁止。Spoil their vote: 使投票作废。

20. **The Governor–General acts ... and the Cabinet:**
    总督只能依照执行委员会的建议行事。执行委员会由总督和政府内阁组成。尽管对此并无明文规定，但这已成公认的准则。

21. **Gough Whitlam（1916–2014）**
    高夫·惠特拉姆，澳大利亚工党政治家，1972 年在工党连续失利 23 年后，率澳大利亚工党取得联邦大选胜利，组成工党政府。在其任内，工党政府从越南撤回军事顾问，取消兵役制，与中国建立了外交关系并访问了中国。同时他也在国内推行改革，增加对教育和艺术、医疗卫生和土著事务的投入。1975 年 11 月，惠特拉姆政府被总督解散，引起了宪政危机。

22. **Malcolm Fraser（1930–2015）**
    马尔科姆·弗雷泽，澳大利亚自由党政治家。从 1975 年惠特拉姆政府被解散后，至 1983 年任澳大利亚政府总理。

23. **a caretaker Prime Minister:**
    看守政府总理。

24. **This dismissal was ... unwritten conventions of government:**
    普遍认为，解散政府这一举动是对不成文的政府行为准则的嘲弄，导致宪政危机。Constitutional Crisis 1975：惠特拉姆政府尽管对国内社会改革有一系列设想，但由于其财政计划出现问题，工党占少数派的参议院拒绝批准其拨款草案，使得政府没有基本运作资金，形成对峙局面。当时的总督 John Kerr 爵士解散了惠特拉姆政府，因此引起轩然大波。

25. **The Governor-General attracted ... this power again:**
    总督解散政府招致了政治和社会上的强烈不满，恐怕以后的总督不会再行使这一权力。

26. **According to the principles ... the nation's economy:**
    自由主义理论主要是关于个人和政府关系的理论。自由主义认为个人是自由的，有理性的，对自己的劳动和财产享有权力。政府在国民经济中的作用是次要的，不应过多干涉经济运作和发展。

27. **a very uneven application of this principle:**
    对此项原则的应用是不一致的。

28. **even at the establishment ... the assisted migration scheme:**
    即便是在澳大利亚自由市场体系形成的时候，也必须采取政策上的干涉，以通过资助移民计划为经济发展提供廉价劳动力。

## Australia

29. **wool boom:**
 因羊毛产业而带来的经济繁荣。从 19 世纪上半叶开始，羊毛产业就成为澳大利亚经济发展的领头羊，产量居世界第一，曾为澳大利亚带来经济繁荣，因此人们也称澳大利亚为"骑在羊背上的国家"。

30. **It also opened up ... of mineral wealth:**
 淘金热使人们认识到，土地不仅可用于农业生产，而且还有矿产资源宝藏。

31. **It invested in ... and water and sewage:**
 政府对大型基本建设工程进行投资，建设铁路和通讯、城市基础设施，如供水系统、排水系统。Capital works：基本建设工程。

32. **By the time of Federation ... of economic life:**
 到 1901 年成立澳大利亚联邦时，殖民地政府都已建立了庞大的政府官僚机构，雇佣许多人员管理经济生活中这些工作。

33. **a programme of tariff protection:**
 在澳大利亚联邦成立前，各殖民地间就关税和自由贸易问题进行了长期的争论和协商。1901 年，澳大利亚联邦成立，为保护澳大利亚制造业不受海外竞争的威胁，采用了关税制。

34. **the Immigration Restriction Act:**
 1901 年的《移民限制法案》以法律的形式确立了白澳政策，限制非欧洲移民进入澳大利亚。此法案的出台在当时有三个原因：一是种族歧视；二是经济原因，防止廉价劳动力进入澳大利亚，导致澳大利亚人生活水平的下降；再就是社会原因，即防止种族冲突。此法案于 1973 年被废除。

35. **Harvester Judgement:**
 1907 年，联邦和解与仲裁法庭对 Sunshine Harvester Works 一案所进行的裁决。1907 年，Sunshine Harvester Works 以其付给工人的工资是"公平合理"为由申请免税。Higgins 法官认为，一名每周工作六天的普通雇员，如已婚并有三个孩子的话，其生活在一个文明社区中所需的最低工资为每天 7 个先令。这一裁决在澳大利亚建立了最低工资的概念。

36. **controls of industry through occupational safety legislation:**
 通过职业安全立法对工业加以控制。

37. **increased overseas competition ... major manufacturing industries:**
 越来越激烈的海外竞争和关税降低，导致一些主要的制造业产业倒闭。

38. **Even in those spheres ... to overseas corporations:**
 甚至在一些人们通常认为应由政府管理的领域内，如社会福利和社会保障服务、惩罚体制的运作等，政府都把它的一部分责任转包给私人经济，有时甚至转包给外国公司。

39. **The Australian Broadcasting Corporation:**
 澳大利亚广播公司，简称 ABC。成立于 1932 年，资金主要来源是政府拨款，但节目制作等政策上是独立运作的，不受政府影响。其节目水平高，质量精良，成为澳大利亚文化的标志性产业。

40. **Australians today are debating ... in global league tables:**
    为保住澳大利亚在全球经济中排名前列的地位，是否必须丧失"社会资本"，即削减在教育、卫生医疗和公共广播方面的公共支出，这是今天的澳大利亚人正在争论的话题。

41. **to invest in ... the political economy:**
    对不同的政治经济时期所需的人力资本进行投资（使其能再生）。

42. **to prevent ... too socially divisive:**
    避免与自由市场经济相伴而生的不平等导致社会分裂。

43. **All Western democracies ... of their electorates:**
    平衡这三方面的发展不可避免地有其内在矛盾，而所有的西方民主国家都以不同的方法处理这些矛盾，同时还要照顾到选民的要求。

44. **Nevertheless, from the perspective ... to welfare programme:**
    尽管如此，从一个多元主义者的角度来看，两党都必须要顺应公民的要求，而公民会对政府可以在多大程度上放弃福利制度提出限制。

# Exercises

## I. Give the Chinese equivalents for the Following:

1. Washminster
2. a party programme
3. pluralism
4. compulsory voting
5. coalition
6. a welfare state

## II. Decide whether the following statements are true (T) or false (F):

1. The Australian political system follows the Western democratic tradition, reflecting British and USA expericncc. _____
2. It is general acknowledged that the Prime Minister and the Cabinet at the federal level is the center of the Australian parliamentary power. _____
3. Laws of the State should be changed if they don't agree with the Federal laws. _____

## Australia

4. The Senate of the parliament is responsible for initiating the bills and enacting legislation. _____
5. The Coalition party is made up of the Australian Labour Party and the National Party. _____
6. It is generally expected that the Governor-General should follow the advice of the Cabinet. _____
7. The "shadow cabinet" of the opposition can take over the government when there is a constitutional crisis. _____
8. Many migrants poured into Australia during the 1850s. As a result, the Australian population increased by 50% in that decade. _____
9. The Labour Party is more conservative than the Liberal Party. _____
10. Over the past 100 years, government in Australia has been mainly represented by either the Labour Party or the Liberal/National Coalition. _____

### III. Fill in the blanks:

1. The Immigration Restriction Act was passed in _____.
2. From the 1840s to the 1970s, the agricultural exports made up _____ of Australia's total.
3. In the massive post-WWII immigration programme, Australia favoured the migrants from _____ than those from _____ and Eastern Europe.
4. The Australian Broadcasting Corporation is encouraged to rely less on _____.
5. The two houses of the federal parliament are _____ and _____.
6. The Governor-General is the representative of _____.
7. _____ and _____ are at the center of the Australian parliamentary power.
8. Shadow Cabinet is made up of the members of the major party _____.

### IV. Questions:

1. What does the author mean when she says, "Australians understand and conduct life upon a basic commitment to difference"? What examples does she give to support her point?
2. What are the major political parties representing government over the past 100 years in Australia? How are they different in their party programmes?
3. What is the "Washminster" form of polity?

# UNIT 18 Australia as a Liberal Democratic Society

4. What is the three-tier system of government?
5. Who is the centre of Australian parliament power?
6. What are some of the advantages political pluralism has in the author's opinion?
7. What role do governments play in the national economy according to the principles of liberal theory?
8. Did the government play a large role in the economy by the last decades of the 19th century? Why?
9. In what way did the government continue to play a large part in the economy in the post WWII period? Give examples to illustrate your point.
10. After the Labour Party returned to power in 2007, what factors affected Australian politics?
11. What key changes took place after 2007?
12. Who is Tony Abbott? What was his performance as the Prime Minister? Who is Malcolm Turbull? How are they different in their policies?

## V. Topics for discussion or research:

1. What is the central value of the Australian people? How is it reflected in the political life in Australia?
2. Do you agree with the author's view on the advantages of political pluralism? Why or why not?
3. Do research on the Labour Party and the Liberal/National Coalition. If you had the right to vote in Australia, which party would you vote for? Why?
4. In what way has the Australian government been an interventionist government?
5. What three contradictory political economic programmes have the majority of Western democracies attempted to balance? How has Australia tried to balance them?

# UNIT 19

# Australia in the World Today

**Go over the following focal points before reading the text:**

- The three stages in Australian foreign relations
- Australia and APEC
- Australia's economic relations
- Education in Australia
- The tourist industry in Australia
- The Australian media
- Environmental risks and efforts to address them
- The impact of climate change on Australia

# Australia

## Introduction

Australia today is a wealthy, middle power nation with a small population, occupying a large continent located a great distance from its historical sources of security and prosperity. In this unit we are examining six major aspects of Australia's role in the globalised world.

**Globalisation** is a complex concept. It has been defined as comprising four **flows**: of **capital**, of technology, of people, of culture.[1] In the later sections of this unit we will be looking at how Australia engages with the rest of the world through these flows in the fields of foreign relations, economic relations, education, tourism, media and the environment. We begin by a brief **overview** of Australian foreign relations.

## Australia: Foreign Relations

To understand Australia's role in the world today we need a brief review of the historical background, the three major historical stages in Australia's relationship with the rest of the world. Each of these stages has a common **theme**: Australia's need as a small to middle power to find both security, and its own active role in the Asia Pacific region.[2] This concern has taken different directions in these three stages.

### Stage One: 1788–1940s

Until 1900 Australia **comprised** a group of six British **colonies** whose relationship to the rest of the world was dictated by the British government. On Federation in 1901 Australia became an independent colony, but until the 1940's it had little control in the field of foreign affairs.[3] In 1907 it was decided that the "great colonies" including Australia should no longer be called colonies but should be styled "the self-governing dominions beyond the seas".[4] However, this made little difference to Australia's control over its foreign relations. The British government declared that Britain's "**authority** cannot be shared" even on the decisions on the formation of the Australian military and naval services. During WWII, the Japanese bombed Darwin in February 1942, and the Australian government was horrified at the British neglect of the dangers that Japanese

---

globalisation *n.* 全球化
flow *n.* 流动
capital *n.* 资本，资金
overview *n.* 概述
theme *n.* 主题
comprise *v.* 包括
colony *n.* 殖民地
authority *n.* 管辖权

**militarism posed** to Australia. The government turned from the UK to the USA to cooperate in defending Australia. The Statute of Westminster Adoption Act, passed by the Curtin Government in 1942, provided that in future the British Government could only legislate for Australia at Australia's specific request.[5] It was a major step forward in Australia's preparedness to **forge** its own legal **identity** in the world.

### Stage Two: 1940s–1970s

The danger now was that Australia had simply exchanged **domination** by the UK for domination by the USA. The post-war successes of communism in Russia and China bred **paranoia** in the West. In this **scenario**, Australia was positioned as the "West's outpost" in the Asia Pacific region within the ANZUS treaty, signed by Australia, New Zealand and the United States in 1951.[6] From the 1950s to the 1970s Australia became involved in the American "**crusade** against communism" in the Korean War and the Vietnam War. During this time, the deeply unpopular policy of **conscription-by-ballot** became one of the major factors leading to a negative reaction to Australia's relationship with the USA.[7]

### Stage Three: 1970s to date, Australia in the world today

The Whitlam Government (1972–1974) was voted in on the wave of this opposition to Australia's commitment as a minor ally in an unpopular USA war.[8] The government made a conscious decision that Australia would take a more independent position. It abolished conscription, **withdrew** troops from Vietnam in 1972, and in the longer term, moved to increase trade relations with Asia, most notably in order to have a more open political and trading relationship with China. It officially recognised the People's Republic of China. Since Whitlam, relations with China and with the whole Asia Pacific region have continued to evolve.

Today, Australia is a member of the APEC[9], G20[10], OECD[11] and WTO[12] organisations. APEC was established from an Australian **initiative** in 1989, when **Canberra** hosted the first informal dialogue with 12 members. Since then the **forum** has grown to include 21 member **economies** and has become one of the most significant world economic bodies: the 21 APEC Member Economies represent over 40 per cent of the world's population, 56 per cent of global GDP, and around 48 per cent of world trade. Australia takes its turn, along with other member nations, to host **assemblies** with leaders from the United States, the People's Republic of China, Indonesia, the Russian Federation and Japan and other Asia-Pacific partners to promote regional **stability**

---

militarism *n.*
军国主义
pose *v.*
构成，造成
forge *v.* 打造
identity *n.*
身份
domination *n.*
统治
paranoia *n.*
恐惧，多疑
scenario *n.*
事态，局面
crusade *n.*
运动
conscription-by-ballot
（以抽签方式的）征兵制
withdraw *v.*
撤军
initiative *n.*
提议
Canberra
堪培拉
forum *n.*
论坛
economy *n.*
（某个国家的）经济制度；经济体
assembly *n.*
会议
stability *n.*
稳定

# Australia

and to **address** global issues including **counter-terrorism**, nuclear **non-proliferation** and health. APEC member economies account for approximately 70 per cent of Australia's trade and include eight of its top 10 export markets. So APEC provides an important base for Australia's current economic and political role in an increasingly globalised world.

## Economic Relations

### Globalisation: Flows of Capital

Australia's capital investment in its own manufacturing industries declined significantly in the late 20th century. Capital investment in these industries shifted globally to cheaper labour markets in Asia. So the Australian economy now depends primarily upon its other two major sectors, the resources and services industries. The Australian service sector now represents 68% of Australian GDP, however, the agricultural and mining sectors combined (representing only 10% of GDP) account for 57% of the nation's exports.

In various ways then, these flows of capital are affecting the flows of people and technologies in both the services and the resources sectors. The two way flow of capital, of people and of culture is most marked in its resources, education and tourism industries.

### The Resources Industry: Flows of Capital, Culture and People

According to the CIA World Factbook[13], in 2007 Australia imported AU $228 billion of goods and services and exported AU $216 billion. Australia is a major exporter of natural gas, coal, iron, **bauxite**, copper, **tin**, gold, silver, **uranium**, **tungsten**, **mineral sands**, **lead**, **zinc**, **opals**, **diamonds**, grains, wool, meat and food products. The agricultural and mining sectors comprise approximately 57% of the country's exports. Australia's main export partners are China, Japan, Korea, the USA and India, and the main import partners are the USA, China, Japan, Singapore, and Germany. In 1972, Japan became Australia's largest trading partner. Then, in 2007 China overtook Japan.

The China-Australia Free Trade Agreement (ChAFTA) was signed between the two countries on June 17, 2015, and entered into force on Dec. 20, 2016. It lays an historic foundation for the next phase of Australia's economic relationship with China. The agreement opened significant opportunities for Australia in China which is Australia's largest export market for both goods and services, accounting for nearly a third of total

---

address *v.* 处理
counter-terrorism 反恐（反恐怖主义）
non-proliferation 不扩散；防止（核）扩散
bauxite *n.* 铝土矿
tin *n.* 锡
uranium *n.* 铀
tungsten *n.* 钨
mineral sands 矿砂
lead *n.* 铅
zinc *n.* 锌
opal *n.* 猫眼石，蛋白石
diamond *n.* 钻石

exports, and a growing source of foreign investment. However, the strength of the new trading relationship with China is viewed with a mixture of feelings within Australia.[14] It is seen both as a major benefit because China is Australia's biggest trading partner thanks mainly to its strong demand for iron ore, coal and **liquefied** natural gas. These exports to China helped Australia escape the worst effects of the global economic **meltdown** in the years following the 2007 global financial crisis. However, there is also some **trepidation**. After shaking off the domination of first, the British, then the USA, there is a concern that Australia has to be careful not to overbalance its current strong relationship with China.[15] In her "Submission to the Senate Inquiry into Australia's Relationship with China", Professor Ann Kent argued that the Australian government is at risk of becoming simply a "market society" where all human interactions with China are based only on market connections. Professor Kent argued not that China is trying to put pressure on Australia, but rather that Australia will sink back into its old "junior partner" position, of being over eager to submit to the demands of its major economic partner.[16] She argues that, in doing this, Australian politicians, bureaucrats and media also show a lack of understanding of China's own **sophistication** and ability to **compartmentalise** issues in its foreign policy.

This contradictory set of attitudes about Australia's role in the world today is reflected, although in different ways, in education, tourism, the media and in Australia's environmental policies.

## Education: Global Flows of Capital and People

Australia attracts students from around the world wishing to gain a top-quality education. In 2015, over 645 000 international students were enrolled in education programmes in Australia. Of these over 272 000 international students were enrolled in the higher education sector. The largest numbers of enrollments in this sector were from China, India and Malaysia. In 2015, 170 212 Chinese students studied in Australian schools and universities.

Education has become Australia's third-biggest export industry. According to AEI, (Australian Education International, the government organisation responsible for overseeing and promoting the overseas students) education services attract annual **earnings** of $15.5 billion and remains Australia's third largest export, behind coal and iron ore ($46 billion and $30.2 billion respectively) and the largest services export

liquefied *adj.* 液化的
meltdown *n.* 衰退
trepidation *n.* 惊恐
sophistication *n.* 老于世故
compartmentalise *v.* 划分
earning *n.* 收入

# Australia

industry, ahead of tourism services ($11.7 billion). It's a "**mushrooming** industry": foreign-student numbers in Australia increased almost three times from 2002 to 2015. This increase was driven largely by the rapid growth of **vocational** colleges. However, by 2010, this rapid expansion had created problems, necessitating a government review: "Stronger, Simpler, Smarter ESOS: Supporting International Students"[17]. Bruce Baird, author of the report, said the education industry had been harmed by institutions that cashed in on foreigners who used education as a pathway to immigration.[18]

"We have **permanent-residency** factories," Mr. Baird said in his critique of this situation. To convert the colleges from this "factory status", Baird recommended greater government control of the educational standards of the colleges and better information flows to the prospective students to enable them to make informed choices about the standards of the education they are buying.[19]

## Tourism in Australia: Global Flows of Capital, People and Culture

Tourism is the second major service industry in the Australian export economy. In 2007, it brought approximately 12 billion dollars into Australia. Visitors from China alone, contributed over $2 billion to this total. **Prior to** the 2007 global financial **downturn**, over 10 million overseas tourists visited Australia every year, a figure equal to nearly half of the population of Australia. This means that Tourism Australia has to work in cooperation with a range of other government bodies with specific concerns about **sustainability** and security. However, its major goal is to increase international and domestic travelers' intention to visit Australia. The most successful tourist marketing campaign, the "Put another Shrimp on the Barbie" campaign, focused on the friendly casualness of an Australian barbecue against the backdrop of Uluru, the magnificent **megalith** set in the vast and beautiful desert centre of Australia.[20]

Australia's climate and its unique environment attracted over 11 million visitors during the two year period ending on January 31, 2010. Of these, 187 696 were tourists on Working Holiday **visas**. These jobs, usually taken up by younger tourists, especially those from Ireland and Korea, include fruit picking, working in an Australian country pub, and a range of other, relatively unskilled and temporary forms of labour. However, for the majority of overseas visitors, the most popular tourist features include the Great Barrier Reef, Uluru, Kakadu and the key city attractions and beaches of Sydney, the Gold Coast, and the other metropolitan centres.[21]

---

mushrooming *adj.* 快速增长的
vocational *adj.* 职业的
permanent-residency 永久居留
prior to *prep.* 在…之前
downturn *n.* 衰退，下降
sustainability *n.* 可持续
megalith *n.* 巨石
visa *n.* 签证

Of these, let's look in more detail at Kakadu National Park which is managed by the traditional Aboriginal **clans**. Kakudu covers 19 000 square kilometres comprising rainforest, wetlands with **paperbark** trees, **pandanus**, **cycads** and **lotus lilies**. The wildlife includes **crocodiles, barramundi**, and a variety of birds: **magpie geese, brolgas, jabirus** and **white-bellied sea eagles**. The area contains 1 000 different plant **species**, and a quarter of all Australian freshwater fish species. A number of Aboriginal clans still live within the Park as their people have done for over 40 000 years, and tourists can visit, with their guidance, some of the largest concentrations of Aboriginal rock art in the world.

Tourism is a major factor in the Australia economy. It is a major source of employment and wealth. However, this means that the country continually must "sell itself". The dangers here are that town planning and land management decisions can be over influenced by the interests of the tourist industry. This bias has sometimes led to the **degradation** of the very resources on which tourism is built. Clean water, beautiful beaches, plentiful wild life, and the basic culture of the people have all been threatened by a narrow focus on building large-scale tourist developments.[22] In response to this problem, the concept of "sustainable tourism" now **underpins** the debate about how to "Sell Australia".

## The Australian Media: Flows of Capital, Culture and Technology

In any one year, just under a million Australian live overseas and approximately 3 million have overseas holidays. However, Australians' major source of information about foreign countries is the media. Similarly, the image that other people have of Australia is accessed through this same set of media **filters**. Most of us now live in an "information society" in which media technologies have "shrunk the world", compressing time and space, as the print and the electronic media bring the news of the wider world instantly into our own lives. So what are the effects of these media filters on the way we know the world and the way the world knows us? Let's look at the impact of the major forms of media: newspapers, radio and TV.

### Newspapers or "The Press"

Fifty-four English language newspapers, and several non-English publications in 20–25 other languages, are published in Australia. The major non-English speaking

---

clan *n.* 宗族
paperbark *n.* 白千层属植物
pandanus *n.* 露兜树
cycad *n.* 苏铁植物
lotus lilies 荷花睡莲
crocodile *n.* 鳄鱼
barramundi *n.* 澳洲肺鱼
magpie geese 鹊鹅
brolga *n.* 澳洲鹤
jabiru *n.* 美洲大白鹳
white-bellied sea eagles 白肚皮海鹰
species *n.* （生物）种，类
degradation *n.* 削弱
underpin *v.* 加强
filter *n.* 滤器

# Australia

papers include *Il Globo* and *La Fiamma*, *The Greek Herald*, *The Independence Daily*, which is a Chinese paper, and *El Telegraph*, the Arabic paper. This group provides information from "home" for non-Anglo-Australians: news which is often lacking in the mainstream Australian media. The mainstream press comprises one national newspaper, *The Australian*, and State-based newspapers, including *The Sydney Morning Herald* and *The Age*. These major newspapers are owned by media corporations.

**TV and Radio**

Unlike the press, the TV and radio programmes are provided by a mixture of government networks, private business companies and by small community groups. The publicly owned channels include SBS which runs news, information and entertainment programmes from a wide range of other countries. However, the programmes with the highest ratings are those owned by the private, **profit-oriented** media corporations.

**Ratings and the Content of Media Messages**

Most of the information about foreign countries that the majority of Australians access in both the TV and radio programmes and in the press is provided by profit-based media organisations. Media businesses are like other businesses: they have something to sell at the best possible profit. What they have to sell is "audiences to advertisers". So "audiences" become "ratings". Thus, media corporations must be constantly asking "which media items attract the biggest audiences". The answer is "those with the highest news values". There is then, an important downside to this process: the goal of producing the most "attractive" news stories limits the range of information about other countries to the most dramatic and entertaining items.[23] Information about other countries, especially about non-English speaking countries, tends to be covered only if it includes negative images, for example, of massive disasters: wars, massacres, **tsunamis** or earthquakes. In addition, the non-news programmes, dramas, **comedies** or **quiz shows** nearly always come from the English-speaking countries, the USA and the UK. This is because TV series are expensive to make, so it is cheaper for the commercial TV channels to buy ready-made programmes from overseas. Thus the only positive images of the world that most Australians choose

profit-oriented *adj.* 以赢利为导向的
tsunami *n.* 海啸
comedy *n.* 喜剧
quiz show 知识竞赛

to consume are of Americans and Britons or of Australians themselves. Otherwise the images tend to reflect back an image of the world in which "foreigners" are dangerous, dehumanised, or undemocratic "Others".[24]

The public controlled programmes on radio and TV have fewer commercial pressures and can provide a wider, more informed, picture of the outside world. In addition, the major newspapers, *The Australian*, *The Sydney Morning Herald*, *The Age* and *The Financial Times*, are able to sell more expensive advertisements although their ratings are lower, because their readers are from higher income **brackets**. This means that they can provide wider, less distorted images of the world. Thus, although these images are usually accessed only by a minority of the Australian audience, it is possible to choose between the narrow and the wider images of "what is going on in the world out there". This leads us to address the key issue that concerns Australians about their role in the world today: the issue of Australia's use of environmental resources.

## Globalisation and Environmental Risks: Flows of Pollution

Over the past few decades globalisation has altered the kinds of **hazards** that nations face. A major example is the current threat of climate change. Global flows of pollution are created by the overproduction of **greenhouse gases**. These pollution flows are produced mainly by the high and medium power nations but affect all nations. The next section examines three aspects of climate change as it relates to Australia: the role that Australia has played in contributing to climate change, the impact of climate change on Australia, and the country's political and technological attempts to **redress** the problem.

### Australia's Greenhouse Gas Emissions

Australia only accounts for around 1.5% of global greenhouse gas **emissions**, but its **per capita** emissions are more than four times the world average. Australia's relatively high per capita emissions can be **attributed to** factors such as the high usage of coal in electricity generation, the agricultural emissions from large numbers of sheep and cattle, and **land clearing**. This means that Australia needs to reduce each person's **intake** by 75% to reach the world per capita average. Thus Australia is one of the major contributors to this global problem. Moreover, it takes on an even bigger responsibility for creating climate change as the Australian economy is heavily dependent on its coal

---

bracket *n.*
等级
hazard *n.*
危害
greenhouse gas
温室气体
redress *v.*
纠正
emission *n.*
排放
per capita
人均
attribute to *v.*
把⋯归因于
land clearing
开垦土地
intake *n.* 吸入

## Australia

export trade.

One of the ways in which Australia contributes to the worlds greenhouse gas emissions is through the destruction of its forests. Australia has the sixth largest area of forest in the world with 4% of the worlds forests, with only Russia (20%), Brazil (12%), Canada (8%), the US (8%) and China (5%) having more. There are 164 million **hectares** of forest in Australia, covering 21% of the continent. The Australian Conservation Foundation's Michael Krockenberger has argued that native vegetation clearance represents one of the largest contributors to greenhouse emissions in Australia.[25] In 1990, **carbon dioxide** emissions from forest clearing for agriculture totaled 156 million tonnes, which is some 27.35% of Australia's **net** emissions in carbon dioxide equivalent.[26] The rate of clearing then doubled. Land cleared in Australia in 1994 was equal to that which was cleared in the previous five years. This included 640 000 hectares of **virgin bush** land.

It is the clear felling form of land clearing, when the logging procedure fells every tree that has the most devastating effect on both the production of carbon emissions and on species loss.[27] About 20% of Australia's known species of flowering plants are endangered, vulnerable, or threatened with extinction, with these logging operations, especially in the southwest of the country and Tasmania.[28]

**Impact of Climate Change on Australia: Droughts, Fires, Cyclones and Floods and Species Loss**

There are a range of risks that Australians face from climate change. Australia is the driest continent in the world with a long history of **cycles** of **droughts**, fires, **cyclones** and floods. So it is particularly vulnerable to the possibility that, with the current rate of climate change, the intensity of these cycles will increase by up to 20% by 2030.

Today, Australia faces reduced water supplies to households, reduced river flows affecting the health and breeding patterns of its bird, animal and fish species, and threats to the production of domestic food resources and to the country's agricultural and manufacturing industries. In addition, global warming increases the risk of fiercer and more widespread bushfires, threatening both households and farming regions. **Paradoxically**, climate change also increases the hazards of increased flooding, especially in the **tropical** northern regions. These northern floods eventually trickle south to increase the flows of the Murray-Darling[29], Australia's major river-system.

---

hectare *n.*
公顷
carbon dioxide
二氧化碳
net *adj.*
净的，纯的
virgin bush
未开垦的灌木
cycle *n.* 周期
drought *n.*
干旱
cyclone *n.*
旋风
paradoxically
*adv.* 自相矛盾地
tropical *adj.*
热带的

However, **evaporation** reduces this benefit, whilst the problems of flood include loss of lives, increased dangers of infection, the death of livestock, damage to homes, businesses, roads, equipment and **ecosystems**. Overall, flooding has been Australia's costliest form of natural disaster, with even the pre-climate-change losses estimated at over $400 million a year. Nevertheless, it is the cycle of droughts, fires, cyclones and floods, rather than any one feature of the cycle, that makes Australia especially vulnerable to climate change.

However, these are not Australia's only environmental hazards. Rising sea levels are already creating problems for people living close to the ocean. The Great Barrier Reef, the world's largest natural reef system, is under threat of pollution from urban and agricultural **run-off**. Almost 40 % of all mammal **extinctions** that have occurred around the world in the last 200 years have occurred in Australia. The World Wildlife Fund for Nature (WWF)[30] argues that as most Australian species aren't found anywhere else, the loss of Australian species is a loss for the whole world. The clear felling of forests is one of the major causes of species loss, and climate change is **exacerbating** this process. The Australian Museum has listed over 40 species currently under threat, including species of frogs, snakes, **turtles**, **lizards**, **possums**, tree kangaroos, **wallabies**, and birds. This list even includes Victoria's State **emblem** — the **helmeted honey eater**.

**Technological and Political Responses**

Efforts are being made to address species loss and carbon emissions. There are several community-based programmes focused on saving specific species, but the Australian Academy of Science is concerned that whilst Australians will spend energy in safeguarding our "emblematic species" like koalas, and the helmeted honey eater, problems arise when we consider other species that have no public appeal. For example, how do you think Australians might feel about saving rats, snakes and **spiders**?

Species loss and carbon emissions are associated with the clear felling of forests. This method is being addressed in two ways. The Australian and Tasmanian Governments have introduced **alternatives** to the use of clear felling in **old growth forests**. Clear felling, the logging procedure which fells every tree, still continues, but it has been reduced from more than 50 % in 2004/05 to less than 20% by 2010. In addition, forests which are being clear felled are being replaced by logging **plantations**.

---

evaporation *n.* 蒸发
ecosystem *n.* 生态系统
run-off 排放
extinction *n.* 灭绝
exacerbate *v.* 加剧
turtle *n.* 海龟
lizard *n.* 蜥蜴
possum *n.* （澳、新）袋貂
wallaby *n.* 沙袋鼠
emblem *n.* 象征，标志
helmeted honey eater 头盔吸蜜鸟，黄披肩吸蜜鸟
spider *n.* 蜘蛛
alternative *n.* 替代品
old growth forest 天然林
plantation *n.* 人造林

# Australia

So to some extent, the problem of increased carbon emissions from clear felling is being addressed. However, replacing old growth forests by logging plantations does little to reduce species loss.

By the 21st century six of Australia's seven states and **territories**, and all of Australia's major cities, were officially "in drought" and had been for years. The most recent assessment by the Intergovernmental Panel on Climate Change (IPCC) was that climate change would make the southern regions of Australia, where most people live, even warmer and drier and even more **susceptible** to extreme **variations** in weather.[31]

As the agricultural industry uses two thirds of the country's water supply, the political control of the industry's use of the river systems is the key issue in addressing drought. For most of their history, the Australian State governments have been generous in granting irrigation rights to both small and large scale agriculturalists until the state of the river systems has **deteriorated** to a dangerous level.[32] Although there have been major storms and floods, the surge of water has often been sucked up by lands that have become too dry. This problem is being addressed by major political changes in water management, including governments' "water buyback" of major sections of its river systems; by water-recycling and **desalination** schemes and by government support for household rainwater tanks.[33]

Alternative forms of **renewable** energy — **wind farms**, **solar panels**, **biofuels**, **geothermal**, ocean power and **biomass** — are replacing some of the unsustainable and carbon polluting forms of energy resources. However, **fossil fuel** products still dominate Australian energy consumption. In 2015, approximately 73% of the electricity used by Australian homes and by industry came from coal. Coal is both non-renewable and the major source of pollution. So the key political question is how to exchange these polluting, fossil fuel forms of energy for the non-polluting, renewable forms.

In 2015, Australia's annual electricity production based on renewable power was less than 5.9% of electricity consumption for that year, an increase of 1.2 % compared with 2011. The current Australian Government has a Mandatory Renewable Energy Target to increase that level to 20% by 2020.

## Political Issues

The public concern about the environment has seen the rise of a new political party, the Australian Greens[34]. The party's first Federal Senator, Bob Brown, was

---

territory *n.*
领地
susceptible (to) *adj.* 易受影响的
variation *n.*
变化
deteriorate *v.*
恶化
desalination *n.*
（化学）脱盐
renewable *adj.*
可再生的
wind farm
风能发电厂
solar panel
太阳能电池板
biofuel *n.*
生物燃料
geothermal *n.*
地热
biomass *n.*
（在一个单位面积或体积内的）生物量
fossil fuel
矿物燃料

elected in 1996. Since then the party has grown. Following the 2016 Australian federal election, the Australian Greens had eight senators and one member in the lower house in the Parliament of Australia, 23 elected representatives in State and Territory Parliaments, and more than 100 local **councilors**. Moreover, both of the two major parties — the Labor Party and the Liberal Party — now accept that climate change is an issue that needs to be addressed. However, there are major differences about which policies should be followed.

In 2007 the government commissioned the Garnaut Review[35] to address the issue of climate change. In 2008, The Garnaut Review's key recommendation was that the government should introduce an emissions trading[36] scheme. The Labour government implemented this proposal with a "Carbon Pollution Reduction Scheme (CPRS) Bill" to cap industry's use of coal and to encourage their use of renewable energies. This proposal was opposed by the major opposition party, the Liberal/National Coalition, for imposing too many costs on industry. Finding bipartisan agreement on the most appropriate policies to achieve reductions has been challenging. The former ALP Government established a carbon pricing **mechanism** in 2012. However, the "**carbon tax**" was **repealed** by the Abbott government in 2014. The current government led by Turnbull pledges to consider carefully Australia's progress in reducing emissions, and ensure the Government's policies remain effective in achieving Australia's 2010 target and Paris Agreement commitments.

councilor *n.*
议员
mechanism *n.*
机制
carbon tax
碳税（对二氧化碳排放所征收的税）
repeal *v.*
废除，撤销

# Explanations

1. **It has been defined as comprising four flows ... of people, of culture:**
   全球化的定义包括四方面的流动：资本、技术、人和文化的流动。

2. **Each of these stages has a common theme ... its own active role, in the Asia Pacific region:**
   每一个阶段都有一个共同的主题，即澳大利亚作为中小国力的国家需要寻求在亚太地区的安全及其积极作用。

3. **On Federation in 1901, Australia became an independent ... in the field of foreign affairs:**
   1901年联邦成立，澳大利亚成为独立的殖民地，但直到20世纪40年代之前澳大利亚在外交领域几乎没

# Australia

有控制权。

4. **In 1907 it was decided that the "great colonies" ... "the self-governing dominions beyond the seas":**
1907年决定包括澳大利亚在内的"大殖民地",不应该还成为殖民地,而应改称为"海外自治领"。

5. **The Statute of Westminster Adoption Act ... at Australia's specific request:**
1942年澳大利亚科廷政府通过"威斯敏斯特接受法案"。该法案规定,在未来,英国政府只能在澳大利亚的特殊要求下才能为澳大利亚立法。威斯敏斯特法案(The Statute of Westminster Act)是英国政府于1931年通过的,该法案规定,英国的自治领——加拿大、澳大利亚、新西兰、南非和爱尔兰——均为英联邦内自由和平等的国家,它们与联合王国一起组成英联邦,共奉英王为国家元首;各自治领议会与帝国议会平等,英国议会的任何一项法律,未经自治领承认对自治领均不适用。加拿大和南非批准并确认了该法案,但当时澳大利亚并没有。1942年科廷政府才批准确认该法案,向塑造在国际舞台上的独立立法身份迈出了关键的一步。

6. **In this scenario, Australia was positioned as the "West's outpost" ... in 1951:**
在这种局面下,澳大利亚被定位为亚太地区《澳新美安全条约》内部的"西部前哨基地"。该条约于1951年由澳大利亚、新西兰和美国共同签署。ANZUS treaty 全称为 Australia, New-Zealand and the United States Mutual Security Pact。

7. **During this time, the deeply unpopular policy ... relationship with the USA:**
在此期间,人们极力反对的"征兵制度"(义务兵役制,即由抽签决定服兵役的制度)成为导致人们对澳美关系负面反应的主要因素之一。

8. **The Whitlam Labour government (1972–1974) was voted in ... unpopular USA war:**
在这股反对澳大利亚作为一个小同盟卷入美国在越南的不得人心的战争浪潮下,惠特拉姆政府(1972-1974)当选执政。

9. **APEC:**
全称为 Asia-Pacific Economic Cooperation。亚太经济合作组织,是亚太地区的一个主要经济合作组织,1989年11月5日至7日,澳大利亚、美国、加拿大、日本、韩国、新西兰和东盟等在澳大利亚首都堪培拉举行亚太经济合作会议首届部长级会议,这标志着亚太经济合作会议的成立。该组织的宗旨是保持经济的增长和发展,促进成员间经济的相互依存,加强开放的多边贸易体制,减少区域贸易和投资壁垒,维护本地区人民的共同利益。

10. **G20:**
全称为 The Group of Twenty Finance Ministers and Central Bank Governors (known as the G-20 and also the G20 or Group of Twenty)。20国集团,由19个成员国和欧盟共同组成,是一个国际经济合作论坛。

11. **OECD:**
Organisation for Economic Co-operation and Development 的缩写,即经济合作与发展组织,OECD成立于1961年,其前身是欧洲经济合作组织(OEEC),目前共有36个成员国。还包括国际能源代理机构、核能代理机构、欧洲交通部长会议、发展中心、教育研究和创新、Sahel and West Africa Club 等6个半

# UNIT 19 Australia in the World Today

自治的代理机构。包括了几乎所有发达国家，国民生产总值占全世界三分之二。OECD 的职能主要是研究分析和预测世界经济的发展走向，协调成员国关系，促进成员国合作，经常为成员国制定国内政策和确定在区域性、国际性组织中的立场提供帮助。

12. **WTO:**

    是世贸组织的英文简称（World Trade Organisation）。是一个独立于联合国的永久性国际组织。1995年 1 月 1 日正式开始运作，负责管理世界经济和贸易秩序，总部设在瑞士日内瓦。世贸组织是具有法人地位的国际组织，在调解成员争端方面具有更高的权威性。世贸组织与世界银行、国际货币基金组织一起，并称为当今世界经济体制的"三大支柱"。

13. **CIA World Factbook:**

    《CIA 世界各国概况》，由美国中央情报局每年出版，书中提供世界各国的一些资料信息，包括国旗、地图、地理情况、人文风俗以及当地风土人情。

14. **The strength of the new trading relationship with China ... within Australia:**

    在澳大利亚，人们对加强与中国的新贸易关系的看法是不相同的。

15. **After shaking off the domination of first, the British ... strong relationship with China:**

    在先后摆脱了英国和美国的主宰之后，人们认为澳大利亚必须小心谨慎，不要在目前与中国的紧密关系上失去平衡。

16. **Professor Kent argued not that China is trying ... major economic partner:**

    肯特教授说，其实不是中国给澳大利亚压力，而是澳大利亚可能会重新退回到以前的"小伙伴"地位，过于热切服从其主要经济伙伴的要求。

17. **However, by 2010, this rapid expansion ... Supporting International Students":**

    但是，到 2010 年这种快速的增加产生了新问题，使得政府所有必要做出题为"更强、更简单、更精明的海外学生教育服务：支持国际学生"的评论报告。ESOS 是 Education Services for Overseas Students 的简称。

18. **Bruce Baird, author of the report, said the education ... pathway to immigration:**

    评论报告的作者布鲁斯·贝尔德说，教育行业受到一些机构的损害，这些机构利用外国人想通过教育移民的心理从中牟利。布鲁斯·贝尔德曾担任交通部长（1988–1995），悉尼申奥会的主席（1990–1993），澳大利亚众议院议员（1998–2007）。2009 年澳大利亚教育部长请他领导评议留学生工作。2010 年 3 月此评论报告发布。

19. **To convert the colleges from this "factory status" ... education they are buying:**

    为了扭转大学成为"工厂身份"的局面，贝尔德建议政府加大对大学生教育标准的控制，同时对潜在学生提供更好的信息，以便他们能根据掌握的信息选择他们将要付费接受的教育。

20. **The most successful tourist marketing campaign ... centre of Australia:**

    最成功的旅游市场销售活动是"在烧烤上再放上一只虾"，中心是体现澳大利亚烧烤的友好和休闲，背景是艾尔斯岩，这是澳大利亚中部宽广又美丽的沙漠上的一块壮观的巨石。艾尔斯岩高 348 米，周遍长 9.4

# Australia

公里，是澳大利亚国家的象征之一，对当地土著人有着宝贵的文化价值。"A Shrimp on the Barbie"原是八九十年代澳大利亚旅游局的一句家喻户晓的电视广告词。现在变为"Put another Shrimp on the Barbie"，表示澳大利亚人更加热情地欢迎世界各地的游客。Barbie 是 barbecue 的澳大利亚俚语。

21. **However, for the majority of overseas visitors, the most popular ... metropolitan centres:**
不过，对大多数海外旅客来说，最著名的景点包括大堡礁、乌卢鲁/艾尔斯岩、卡卡都国家公园以及主要城市旅游点和悉尼海滩，黄金海岸和其他大城市中心。大堡礁是世界上最大最长的珊瑚礁群，被列入世界遗产，这里孕育了各式各样的动植物，种类堪称世界之冠，同时也是最为著名的潜水乐园。乌卢鲁是全世界上最大的单体巨石，也是八大自然奇迹之一，1984 年被列入联合国世界自然文化遗产名录。卡卡都公园地处澳大利亚北方热带地区，总面积 19 000 平方公里，由一系列冲积平原构成，其互动生态系统自然衍化，几乎未受人类干扰。卡卡都国家公园有 1 600 种植物、64 种哺乳类动物、290 种雀鸟和 120 种爬虫类、25 种青蛙和 55 种鱼类。悉尼海滩上的歌剧院是悉尼的标志，世界最豪华的文化建筑之一，全部建筑群长 183 米，宽 118 米，由一道海堤与陆地相连。黄金海岸是澳大利亚昆士兰州东南的一处海滨休养地，也是澳大利亚著名的旅游点，因为有一段绵延长达 32 公里的金黄色海滩而得名，全年平均气温 25 度，保证了 300 多个晴天可供游客来度假游玩。

22. **Clean water, beautiful beaches, plentiful wild life ... large–scale tourist developments:**
清澈的水，美丽的海滩，丰富的野生动植物以及澳大利亚人的基本文化都受到大规模发展旅游的狭隘目的之威胁。

23. **There is then, an important downside to this process ... dramatic and entertaining items:**
这个过程有一个重要的负面作用，即制作最"吸引人"的新闻节目限制了关于其他国家的信息，使节目只能是最戏剧化和最有娱乐性的内容。

24. **Otherwise the images tend to reflect back an image ... undemocratic "Others":**
否则，电视图像趋向于反应世界的这样形象，其中"外国人"是危险的，非人性化的，或者是非民主的"他者"。本句中的第一个"images"的意思是指电视上的图像、画面。第二个"image"的意思是形象。

25. **The Australian Conservation Foundation's Michael Krockenberger ... in Australia:**
澳大利亚保护基金会的 Michael Krockenberger 指出，当地植被的毁灭性砍伐是造成澳大利亚温室气体排放的最重要的因素。澳大利亚保护基金会（ACF）是一个非营利的、以社区为基础的环保组织，其中心任务是倡导、政策研究和社区协助。

26. **In 1990, carbon dioxide emissions from forest clearing ... carbon dioxide equivalent:**
1990 年为开垦农田而砍伐森林所造成的二氧化碳排放量总计 1.56 亿吨，占澳大利亚二氧化碳当量的总排放量的 27.3 5%。Carbon dioxide equivalent (CDE)：二氧化碳当量，是描述某种或某量的温室气体可能造成的全球变暖程度的测量方法。

27. **It is the clear felling form of land clearing ... carbon emissions and on species loss:**
砍伐全部树的这种土地清除形式对制造碳排放和物种灭绝有着破坏性的作用。

28. **About 20% of Australia's known species of flowering ... the country and Tasmania:**
这些滥砍滥伐的行径使得澳大利亚大约 20% 的开花植物种类受到危险，变得脆弱，甚至濒临灭绝，特别

UNIT 19  Australia in the World Today

是在澳大利亚的西南部和塔斯马尼亚州。塔斯马尼亚州位于澳大利亚南面，是澳大利亚最小的州，也是澳大利亚唯一的岛州，面积只有 67 800 平方公里，地处巴尔斯海峡以南，与澳洲本土的南部海岸隔海相望。

29. **The Murray–Darling:**

墨累–达令河流域。由墨累河和达令河形成的流域，河流全长 3 375 公里，流经澳大利亚国土的七分之一，是澳大利亚最重要的农业区。

30. **The World Wildlife Fund for Nature (WWF):**

世界自然基金会（WWF）是在全球享有盛誉的、最大的独立性非政府环境保护组织之一，自 1961 年成立以来，WWF 一直致力于环保事业，在全世界拥有将近 520 万支持者和一个在 100 多个国家活跃着的网络。

31. **The most recent assessment by the Intergovernmental Panel ... variations in weather:**

联合国政府间气候变化委员会的最近评估显示，气候变化将使澳大利亚南部地区，即人口集中的地区，更加干旱炎热，发生极端天气变化的可能性更大。联合国政府间气候变化委员会 (IPCC) 是世界气象组织 World Meteorological Organisation (WMO) 及联合国环境规划署（United Nations Environment Programme）(UNEP) 于 1988 年联合建立的政府间机构。其主要任务是对气候变化科学知识的现状，气候变化对社会、经济的潜在影响以及如何适应和减缓气候变化的可能对策进行评估。

32. **For most of their history, the Australian State governments ... a dangerous level:**

历史上，澳大利亚州政府长期以来，不论对经营规模大或小的农民，在给予灌溉权方面一向是很慷慨的，直到河流系统的状况恶化到危险的水平为止。

33. **This problem is being addressed ... support for household rainwater tanks:**

水管理的重要政治变化正在解决这一问题，其措施包括"政府赎回"河流系统的主要部分，水的再循环、水的脱盐计划及政府支持发展推广家庭雨水收集储蓄池。

34. **the Australian Greens:**

澳大利亚绿党。由澳大利亚东部的水利环保运动和澳大利亚西部的解除核武器运动发展而来。1991 年成立，1996 年首次获得参议院席位，澳大利亚绿党的政治理念是"社会公正""可持续发展""草根民主"和"非暴力"四项。其政治立场多在争议性问题中引起关注：反对 1991 年海湾战争、反对 2003 年伊拉克战争、反对铀开采与核动力、倡导可再生能源、倡导水资源管理的可持续方法等。

35. **Garnaut Review:**

全称为 Garnaut Climate Change Review，于 2007 年由澳大利亚政府授权 Ross Garnaut 教授独立研究气候变化对澳大利亚经济的影响。该报告于 2008 年 9 月 30 日公布，为改善可持续繁荣的前景推荐中长期政策和政策框架。2010 年 11 月政府授权更新 2008 年的报告，为多党气候变化委员会以及澳大利亚公众提供最新的研究成果。

36. **emissions trading:**

碳排放交易。碳排放交易是一种交易成本最小化的制度安排，是市场化的减污手段。简单地说，就是一个政府机构规定一个地区碳排放的总限额，并将其分别卖给排放碳的企业，使企业在排放权的限制下排放，

# Australia

不得超过自己的排放限额。如果某一企业需要超出自己的排放量，它必须向限额有富裕的企业购买排放权。这种排放权的交易就是碳排放交易。这样，排放量大的企业将为自己的排放付款，而排放量小于自己额度的将有经济收益。碳排放交易的最终目的是控制碳排放，从而减少污染。

## Exercises

I. **Give the Chinese equivalents for the following:**
1. global flow of capital
2. APEC
3. counter-terrorism
4. World Wildlife Fund for Nature (WWF)
5. renewable energy
6. ChAFTA

II. **Decide whether the following statements are true (T) or false (F):**
1. Australia today is a big power nation in the world. _____
2. In this text, globalisation has been defined as comprising four flows: of capital, of technology, of people, of culture. _____
3. Today, Australia is a member of the APEC, G20, OECD and WTO organisations. _____
4. The strength of the new trading relationship with China is viewed with completely negative feelings and views within Australia. _____
5. Uluru, the magnificent megalith set in the vast and beautiful desert centre of Australia, is one of the most striking symbols of Australia. _____
6. A number of Aboriginal clans still live within the Kakadu National Park. _____
7. Information about other countries, especially about non-English speaking countries, tends to be covered only if it includes negative images, for example, of massive disasters, wars, earthquakes etc. _____
8. It is the clear felling form of land clearing (when the logging procedure fells every tree) that has the most devastating effect on both the production of carbon emissions and on

species loss. _____
9. The Abbott Government adopted the "carbon tax" in 2014. _____

III. **Fill in the blanks:**
 1. There are _____ major historical stages in Australia's relationship with the rest of the world.
 2. On Federation in 1901, Australia became an independent colony but until the 1940's it had little control in the field of _____.
 3. During WWII the Australian government turned from the UK to _____ to cooperate in defending Australia.
 4. The _____ Labour government (1972–1974) was voted in on the wave of this opposition to Australia's commitment as a minor ally in an unpopular USA war.
 5. APEC's mission is to promote regional stability and to address global issues including _____, nuclear non-proliferation and health.
 6. At present, the Australian economy now depends primarily upon its other two major sectors: the resources and _____ industries.
 7. According to Australian Education International education services attract annual earnings of $15.5 billion and remains Australia's _____ largest export.
 8. The concept of _____ now gives strength to debates about how to "Sell Australia".
 9. Global flows of pollution are created by the overproduction of _____.
 10. The risk of fiercer and more widespread bushfires, threatening both households and farming regions is increased by _____.

IV. **Questions:**
 1. How does the author define globalisation? What four flows does it comprise?
 2. What are the three stages in Australia's relationship with the rest of the world?
 3. Why did Australia turn from the UK to the USA for cooperation in defending itself during WWII?
 4. In what way was the Statute of Westminster Adoption Act a major step forward in Australian foreign relations?
 5. What decision did the Whitman Government make in Australia's foreign policy?
 6. What role did Australia play in APEC?
 7. What two sectors does the Australian economy depend on?

# Australia

8. Why is Australia's new trading relationship with China viewed with a mixture of feelings within Australia?
9. Why is education viewed as a "mushrooming industry" in Australia?
10. Why does Australia attract large numbers of tourists every year? What are some of the most popular tourist features in this country? What is the concept of "sustainable tourism"?
11. Are Australian media objective in presenting the image of the world? Explain your point of view.
12. Is Australia a major carbon emitter per capita? How does the destruction of its forests increase greenhouse gas emission?
13. What impact does climate change have on Australia?
14. What are the attitudes of the major political parties — the ALP, the Liberal/National, and the Green Party — towards climate change and their respective policies to address this issue?

**V. Topics for discussion or research:**

1. What are the three major stages in Australia's foreign relations? How have Australian foreign relations changed through the three stages?
2. Discuss Australia's relationship with China.
3. Do research on the most popular tourist attractions in Australia. If you have a chance to visit Australia, which of them would you like to see most? Why?
4. What impacts does climate change have on Australia?

# From Racism to Multiculturalism

**Go over the following focal points before reading the text:**

- Ethnicity and immigration
- The White Australia Policy
- Multiculturalism
- Pauline Hanson and the One Nation Party
- Immigration to Australia today
- The four stages of settler-Aboriginal relations
- The struggle for Land Rights for the Indigenous people
- The Mabo decision
- The Wik decision

# Australia

## Ethnicity and Inequality

Ethnic divisions have been a part of Australia's history since the 18th century. There have been several stages in this history, from periods of **outright** racism to the current era of multiculturalism. In this final unit, we examine the 20th century history of the two aspects of racism and ethnicity that have underpinned the development of Australian society and culture:

- ethnicity and immigration
- the relationship between Aboriginal and non-Aboriginal Australians.

### Ethnicity and Immigration

Since the earliest days of European settlement, immigration has accounted for up to 50 % of Australia's population increase. During the middle of the 19th century immigrants were predominantly British, and those who benefited from assisted migration were almost all from Britain. However, the population also included migrants from Italy, Greece, the **Lebanon**, **Afghanistan** and the Pacific Islands. The large numbers of non-assisted migrants attracted to the country in the **gold rushes** from the 1850s came from many other countries especially from Germany and China[1]. By the 1870s, the Chinese **constituted** the third largest group in Australia, after the British (including the Irish) and Germans.

Racism was an accepted part of the culture of 19th century Australia, but it was the Chinese and the Pacific Islanders (or **Kanakas**) who were subject to the fiercest forms of discrimination[2].

Chinese migrants suffered from racism at many levels. They were the target of physical attacks, especially in the anti-Chinese **riots** at Lambing Flat in NSW[3] and Crocodile Creek in Queensland[4].

Pacific Islanders experienced a different history of racism in Australia. They were **kidnapped** by the infamous "**Blackbirders**" from their own islands and brought to North Queensland to be sold as **indentured** labourers to work in the sugar industry[5]. However

outright *adj.*
完全的，彻底的
Lebanon *n.*
黎巴嫩
Afghanistan *n.*
阿富汗
gold rush
淘金热
constitute *v.*
构成
Kanaka *n.*
夏威夷及南太平洋群岛土著人
riot *n.* 暴乱
kidnap *v.* 绑架
Blackbirder
黑奴船
indenture *v.*
以契约约束

these workers were also subjected to the "Whites only" fever that resulted in the 1901 The Pacific Island Labourers Act[6]. Of the 10 000 Pacific Islanders who were living in Queensland and northern New South Wales when this Bill became law, only 700 were **exempt from deportation**. This Act, directed specifically at the Pacific Islanders, was part of the broader form of institutional discrimination — the White Australia Policy.

## The White Australia Policy

The White Australia Policy was manifested in the Immigration Restriction Act (1901)[7]. It remained a guiding principle of Australian migration until its gradual abolition between 1966 and 1973. The **framers** of the policy made it clear that Chinese and other 'non-whites' had to be stopped from permanently settling here. They did this chiefly through the biased "**dictation test**", whereby anyone seeking admission could be tested in a European language. Failure of the test automatically imposed "**prohibited** immigrant" status on the individual[8]. The test was applied selectively to Chinese and other "non-whites". Even those who spoke perfect English could be excluded as the examiners could choose to use Welsh or Gaelic as the test of admission.

## From White Australia to Multiculturalism

In 1947, almost 90% of the population were of British backgrounds. However, after the Second World War, the Labour Government introduced a massive programme of assisted migration. The policy was aimed at supporting a large scale expansion of the economy which, in turn, was expected to boost what was seen as a relatively defenceless **outpost** of Western culture against the threat of Eastern Communism[9]. The aim was to keep Australia "white and free". It took another thirty or so years before Australia became less racist and more ethnically **egalitarian**.

Racism was still central to the culture and remained the normal way of life of Australia. The preferred migrant groups were British, followed by other northern, then southern and central Europeans, and it was expected that the new settlers would assimilate and be easily absorbed into the culture of their host country[10].

People were recruited essentially because they were a convenient source of labour. The non-British migrants, especially those from non-English speaking backgrounds,[11] entered the bottom of the labour market. This period of "assimilation" was not completely successful. Many migrants responded to the difficulties that they

---

exempt from
被免除，被豁免
deportation *n.*
驱逐出境，遣返
framer *n.*
制定者，创作者
dictation test
听写测验
prohibit *v.*
禁止
outpost *n.*
前哨
egalitarian *adj.*
平等主义的，平等的

# Australia

experienced by returning to Europe. In the 1960s the Government began to address the disadvantages by providing a series of supportive programmes that led in 1973 to the policy of Multiculturalism.

**Multiculturalism: from 1973**

With the adoption of Multiculturalism, a series of non-discriminatory programmes was introduced to enable Australians from non-English speaking backgrounds (NESB) to have greater equality of access to education, health and social services, and pensions. In addition, "ethnic groups" were positioned to have greater access to government channels and to be accorded the rights to speak for their "minority groups"[12].

Australian culture became much richer. Ethnic schools and ethnic newspapers flourished. The Special Broadcasting Service (SBS)[13] television channel began broadcasting in 1980. It currently broadcasts in 68 languages and provides a variety of programmes in English that cover a much wider field of overseas stories than other channels. It also provides news services in 15 different languages including Chinese, Indonesian, French, Italian, Spanish and German.

In 1989 Multiculturalism was identified as comprising three areas of policy:
- Cultural Identity: the right to express and share one's cultural heritage.
- Social Justice: the right to equal treatment and opportunity.
- Economic efficiency: the need to maintain and develop the skills of all Australians regardless of their backgrounds[14].

**Critical Reactions to Multiculturalism**

There are two major sets of critical responses to Multiculturalism: those from the Right and those from the Left of Australian politics.

Pauline Hanson and the One Nation Party[15] most notoriously represented the right wing response. Hanson was elected to Parliament as an independent. Her **platform** was based on her claim that there was an increasing division in Australian society caused by government policies favouring migrants, Multiculturalism and Indigenous Australians.

The critique from the left is that Multiculturalism has not gone far enough. The emphasis upon cultural aspects of ethnic relationships has not altered the **dominance** of Anglo-Australians in the Australian political economy. Non-English Speaking migrants,

platform *n.*
政纲
dominance *n.*
优势，支配地位

especially **refugees**, are still discriminated against in the work force. Multiculturalism has permitted a few specially targeted people from non-Anglo communities to become an elite but, as De Lepervanche wrote in 1990, "Most ethnic leaders and **spokespeople** are men and bourgeoisie (who do not) represent the interests of women and the working class."[16]

Look at the list of evidence in the next section of the chapter to judge whether you think that Multiculturalism is working alright, or whether you agree with the right wing or the left wing criticisms of Multiculturalism.

refugee n.
难民
spokespeople n.
发言人

## Immigration Today

Since 1945, almost 6.9 million have arrived in Australia as new settlers. During the same time, Australia's population has risen from around 7 million to over 24 million (2016). A 2014 sociologist study concluded that: "Australia and Canada are the most receptive to immigration among Western nations."

In 2008–2009, more than 171 000 migrants were granted visas under the Skill and Family Streams of Australia's Migration Programme, and by 2010 migration was more significant than the birth rate in contributing to Australia's annual increase in population.

In this same period nearly 670 000 people received temporary entry visas to Australia to undertake specific work or business, or to entertain, play sport, have a working holiday or study.

There is now a much higher proportion of settlers arriving from Asia although white migrants still predominate. In 2010, 39% of migrants came from Asia, and in terms of specific countries most migrants were born in New Zealand (17.6 %), the United Kingdom (9.8%), China (7.5%), South Africa (6.4 %), India (5.7%) and Indonesia (4.7%).

### The evidence for social inequality and ethnicity in the 21st century
- Northern European and Asian Australians share much the same occupational characteristics as Australian born workers while Southern and Eastern Europeans and Middle Eastern immigrants occupy the lower range of occupations[17].
- Those who do not speak English at all are far more likely to be women. It is

this group of Australians who are most at risk of becoming the workers earning below poverty-level wages in Australia. NESB women workers are much more likely to be employed as home based workers in the clothing industry, where they earn sometimes less than a dollar an hour although the legal minimum weekly wage is almost AU $570.

- 61% of immigrants from Europe had their trade qualifications recognised but only 30% of people from South East Asia gained such recognition[18]. In 1999, only a fifth of migrant workers with trade qualifications were working in the trades for which they are qualified. (A 2004 study of professional migrants from China found that women whose professional skills were not recognised had to work as home based clothing machinists.)

## Aboriginality Today

We saw in Unit 15 that the history of Australian society and culture has a very dark side: the massacres, exploitation and cultural **dispossession** of the 500 or so Peoples who have lived on the continent for over 18 000 generations.

The relationship between the colonisers and the Peoples of the Dreaming has gone through various stages:

- **expropriation** of land and the killing of the Peoples;
- segregation and "protection";
- assimilation, segregation and the attempted destruction of the cultures of the Dreaming; and
- from the mid-20th century, citizenship and the fight against racism.

We examine here this last stage: the ways in which the Aboriginal peoples have resisted the cultural imperialism of "white Australia". Before we do this, however, it is important to consider the names by which the Indigenous peoples of Australia are known today.

### Naming and Aboriginal English

Although the European term "Aborigine" simply means "the original people of the region" it has become so associated with the history of exploitation and degradation **inflicted** on the Peoples of the Dreaming by the white invaders that, today, Aboriginal people in Australia prefer to use their word for "the people"[19]. There are several

dispossession n. 剥夺，夺取
expropriation n. 征用，没收，据为己有
inflict v. 使遭受（损害、痛苦等），强加

variations of this term depending upon the region. The Aboriginal English words for "the people" meaning the original peoples of the continent are:
- Kooris and Yuin in NSW and Victoria
- Nungas in South Australia
- Murris and Bama in Queensland
- Noongars, Wongais and Yamajis in Western Australia
- Palawa in Tasmania and
- Yolngu in parts of the Northern Territory of Australia

It is not always **feasible** to use these names, for example when speaking generally or historically, but you will see these alternative names being used at times throughout the following account. In addition you will also see the word "gubba", another Koori English word which means non-Aboriginal or "white" people.

feasible *adj.*
可行的
validation *n.*
批准，确定
tenure *n.*
（对土地、财产的）保有权，保有期
mourn *v.*
哀悼，忧伤
pass *n.* 通行证
whereabouts *n.*
行踪，下落，所在

### From Segregation to Citizenship: Cultural and Social Struggles in the 20th Century

The Aboriginal Protection Act of 1909 introduced powers to move people away from towns and reserves[20]. By 1910 there were 116 reserves totalling 10 500 hectares, 65 per cent of which were created as **validation** of Aboriginal occupation or in response to requests for land. However, in 1911 the Aboriginal Protection Board ceased to defend **tenure** on reserves, and by 1915, it was seizing reserve land to lease to whites[21]. By 1927, of the 27 000 acres of reserve land, 13 000 were lost.

### The Struggle for Land Rights: from the 1920s–1960s

On January 26[22], 1938, one hundred Koori men and women gathered in Sydney's Australia Hall to **mourn** the loss of their lands and to demand the same basic rights as the rest of the population. It was the first national Aboriginal civil rights gathering. They called it the "Day of Mourning and Protest"[23].

From the 1920s on, Aboriginal groups had been protesting against the denial of their citizenship. In this period of segregation, they had no rights of citizenship. They were forced to carry a **pass** to control their **whereabouts**[24]. Free movement was restricted. For those one hundred people in Sydney in 1938, simply to advertise and hold the meeting was a declaration of social revolution.[25]

During World War II, Aborigines became soldiers, defended the northern and western coastlines, worked on wartime construction projects and in some cases earned

# Australia

the same wages as non-Aboriginal workers. Nevertheless, when the war was over they were expected to return to the limited and exploitative working conditions of pre-war times, some receiving food and clothing but no pay while others were paid only up to twelve shillings a week, when the average Australian's weekly pay was between 4 and 5 pounds.

### The 1946 Stockmen's Strike of Western Australia

On May 1st, 1946, Aboriginal **stockmen** throughout the north of Western Australia refused to work until they had been guaranteed a minimum wage of thirty shillings a week[26].

This strike played a major part in Australian history. It challenged the "white" control of Aboriginal labour and provided an alternative perspective of freedom from that control. Further strikes took place in the late 1940s and in 1949 wages were introduced for Aboriginal workers though their pay was still below the award rates for white workers.

### From the 1960s

The next notable fight to secure these rights was the strike by the Gurindji people against their pastoral employers in the Northern Territories[27]. Vincent Lingiari[28] was one of the Gurindji people. He worked on the traditional lands of his people on which the Vestey family, British aristocrats, ran the Wave Hill **cattle station**. He believed that his ancestral lands were wrongly occupied and that his people were oppressed and exploited by what he referred to as the "Vestey **mob**". The strike lasted nine years, through the 1960s to the 1970s.

Throughout the strike, white support, financial, material and political, was critical in protecting the Gurindji from isolation and physical intimidation. Frank Hardy, the novelist, Nugget Coombs, the respected political administrator, and broad union support were able to **mobilise**, preventing some of the more ruthless efforts to break the strike[29].

There were contradictions in this alliance between white labour unions and the Gurrindji strikers. The Australian Workers Union (AWU), which was the union most relevant to the work of Aboriginal people in the Northern Territory, was a racist organisation which believed that Aboriginal labour was inferior to, and a threat to, white

---

stockmen *n.*
（主澳）畜牧工，饲养员
cattle station
放牛场
mob *n.*
暴民，乱民
mobilise *v.*
动员

labour[30]. Nevertheless, even this union was eventually **won around** to the cause of the Gurindji.

The success of the Gurindji struggle for equal wages was a **pyrrhic victory**[31]: when they achieved this goal the landowners replaced them. However, it had a greater significance. The Gurindji strike was not the first, nor the only demand, by Aborigines for the return of their lands — but it was the first one to attract wide public support within Australia for Land Rights.

win around
说服，争取过来
pyrrhic victory
代价过高的胜利，得不偿失的胜利
outback *adj.*
（尤指澳大利亚的）内地，内陆
assault *v.* 攻击
repossess *v.*
重新拥有

### The Freedom Rides and Cultural Change

The support for the Gurindji's rights became a part of the general movements for civil rights for exploited groups that characterised the late 1960s. In the mid-1960s Charles Perkins, an Arrernte man who became the second Aboriginal person to graduate from university in Australia, led a group of white university students on "Freedom Rides" to **outback** Australia.[32] They demonstrated outside public swimming pools demanding that black children be allowed entry. The demonstrators were spat at and **assaulted**, but the publicity that surrounded the "Freedom Rides" played a major part in raising the consciousness of Australians about the level of segregation and racism that existed in the country, and demonstrated the need for social change[33].

From 1966 to 1993, the State and Federal levels of government enacted legislation or established Royal Commissions to begin to restore land rights to different groups of Aboriginal people. For example, Ayres Rock[34], a megalith in the Central Desert and one of the most important features of the Australian landscape, was **repossessed** by its traditional owners and renamed Uluru. However, it was in 1993 that the most significant legal fight for land rights took place when Eddie Mabo challenged the legal concept of "*Terra Nullius*" (i.e. "Empty Country").

### The Mabo Decision: the Death of Australia as *Terra Nullius*

In North Queensland, Torres Strait Islanders wear T-shirts bearing a picture of Eddie Koiki Mabo and the slogan CAPTAIN COOK STOLE OUR LAND — KOIKI MABO GOT IT BACK[35].

Eddie Koiki Mabo was a Torres Strait Islander. He lived on Murray Island, which lies off the North Queensland coast and is administered by the Queensland government. Here he had traditional rights to land that had been in his family for generations.

# Australia

However, the courts had never recognised customary land title[36]. Their views rested on the general belief of "*terra nullius*" and the particular claim that on **annexation** of the Islands in 1879, all the land had become the property of the Crown.[37] Eddie Mabo took the case to court. He, and his two fellow traditional landowners, James Rice and David Passey, were opposed by the Queensland government.

By a six to one majority, the High Court found in favour of Mabo and his **co-plaintiffs**. Eddie Mabo was now entitled to claim ownership of his land, but the Mabo decision had a much wider significance. This finding was a major cultural reconstruction of the very concept of "Australia". The High Court had rejected the principle of "*terra nullius*". The recognition of native title is now **enshrined** in The Commonwealth Native Title Act (1993). However, a major assumption upon which The Commonwealth Native Title Act had first been drafted was that existing pastoralist leases automatically gave exclusive possession to the pastoralist.[38] This assumption was challenged in 1996.

## The Wik Decision

In 1996 the Wik Peoples of Cape York Peninsula took the State of Queensland to the High Court of Australia. The Wik People were claiming rights over two pastoral **leases** in Northern Queensland. The pastoralists did not own the land; they only **leased** it from the Crown.

The findings of the court in 2006 had both positive and negative consequences for the rights of the Aboriginal owners of the land.

The court held that native title rights could exist side-by-side with the rights of pastoralists on cattle and sheep stations. This is called coexistence. But it said that when pastoralists and Aboriginal rights were in conflict, the pastoralists' rights would prevail, giving pastoralists certainty to continue with grazing and related activities.

Despite this, the Wik decision led to a **hysterical** attack from pastoralists and conservative leaders, who demanded that native title be extinguished, or wiped out, on pastoral leases. The Howard Government used the decision as an excuse to severely attack native title rights with its Native Title Amendment Bill, based on the so-called Ten Point Plan for native title.

The Wik decision was significant not only because it recognised native title rights on pastoral leases, but also because these leases covered a vast area — some 42% of

annexation *n.*
合并
co-plaintiff *n.*
共同起诉人，共同原告
enshrine *v.*
铭记
lease *n., v.*
租借，出租
hysterical *adj.*
歇斯底里的

the Australian land mass. The coexistence of native title provides the means whereby thousands of Aboriginal people, previously the backbone of the grazing industry, who were locked off cattle and sheep stations in the late 1960s and early 1970s, may gain some rights to their traditional lands.

The Mabo and the Wik decisions have made major material and cultural differences to the relationship between the Aboriginal and non-Aboriginal people in Australia. However, this does not mean that there is now an end to the social inequality between them. The urban Kooris and Murris, Nungas and Yalawi who were dispossessed from the land, and even dispossessed from their families and their culture, do not have these rights. There are still many social issues of equity that need to be addressed.

## Social Inequality Today

In her book *Aboriginal Child Poverty* (1990), Christine Choo found that in measures of income, employment, housing, and health, the Aboriginal people are the most disadvantaged people in Australia today. The 2003 Senate Commission in Poverty in Australia also found that although the majority of those in poverty in Australia were in the category of "relative poverty", Indigenous people in remote communities were at risk of being in the much severer category of "absolute poverty" in which their lack of access to basic resources deprived them of necessities for life.[39]

The rates of policing and imprisonment in NSW are much higher for Kooris than for non-Koori people[40]. Police are likely to label an action of Koori adolescents, for example, the act of swearing at policemen, as criminal while the same act performed by "white" adolescents is likely to simply be ignored. This form of institutional racism exists across all other States in Australia[41].

Aboriginal people today, however, see themselves as survivors rather than as victims. From the urban Kooris and Murris in **metropolitan** Sydney or Brisbane, to the Jawoyn people who still live on their land, and speak their own language, in the Nitmilik area of northern Australia, there is a great pride in belonging to a culture that has been part of the "country" for 18 000 or more generations. The Kooris, Murris and Nungas of NSW, Victoria, Queensland, and South Australia and the several other Peoples of Western Australia, Tasmania, the Northern Territory are, today, major contributors to Australian life and culture.

metropolitan
*adj.* 大都市的

# Australia

### Aboriginal Culture Today: "Double Consciousness" and "the Deadly"

W.E.B. Du Bois, the African-American sociologist, talked of the "**double consciousness**". This "double consciousness" is the basis of much creativity in all fields of art.

The "**two-way identity**" of being both Australian and Aboriginal resounds
- in the music of the singer Archie Roach[42], and the bands "Yothu Yindi"[43], "No Fixed Address", and the Djarridjarri Saltwater Band[44];
- in the writing of David Unaipon[45], Sally Morgan[46], Jack Davis[47], and Oodgeroo Noonuccal[48];
- in Tracey Moffat's[49] photography and films and
- in the stage and film work of the Bangarra Dance Company and the major films directed by and starring indigenous actors.

In each of these fields, these are only a few of the most prominent names. There are also over 5 000 Aboriginal artists and crafts people who combine traditional and contemporary **motifs** in works that have achieved international recognition, most notably the "dot paintings"[50] of the Western desert peoples and the "X-ray" paintings of Arnhem Land[51].

This extraordinary level of creativity is also associated with several successful business ventures, especially in the field of tourism and culture. Across Australia, Indigenous communities are introducing visitors to their country and their culture in the tropical **savannahs** in the north, the red deserts of the centre, the rainforests of Northern Queensland, or along the beaches and harbours of Sydney.

In Koori or Murri or Nunga terms, all these successes, and the people who have achieved them, are "Deadly" — the highest level of praise in contemporary Koori English.

The work of Aboriginal women and men who are administrators, teachers, political activists and academics provide a much fuller understanding of the complexities of the social and political economic relationships which comprise Australian society and culture. There has been, since the mid 1960s, what amounts to a revolution in the way in which Australians now interpret their history — an acknowledgement that there is another tragic dark side after the suffering the convicts endured.

---

double consciousness
双重意识
two-way identity
双向身份
motif *n.*
主题，中心思想，中心情景
savannah *n.*
（热带或亚热带）稀树草原

## History Wars, Sorry Speech and Close the Gap Programmes

From the mid-1990s there was a strong re-action against this approach. This fierce debate was between those historians and politicians who want to "**disremember**", and those who want to reveal, the racism that has been part of the construction of modern Australian society. These "History Wars" are not only an important feature of Australian society and culture, but they are also a feature of other Western societies — Canada, the United States, and South Africa. Dirk Moses points out that this revisionism also parallels the Japanese denial of history in Tanaka Masaaki's *The Fabrication of the Nanking Massacre*[52].

By 2007, a strong popular demand had developed that the government should apologise to the indigenous peoples for the injustices and pain of the past. In the 2007 election debates, the Labor Party made a strong commitment to do this. This promise was one of the policies which helped it to win the election that year. The first major political action of the new Labour government, on February 3, 2008, was the Parliamentary Apology or "The Sorry Speech". It included an **acknowledgement** that the injustices of the past must never happen again. More specifically, the government promised to close the gap between the indigenous and non-indigenous Australians in **life expectancy**, educational achievement and economic opportunity.

This parliamentary Apology was not only a response to the popular demand that the government should "Say Sorry". The speech also reinforced that commitment, as **polling** before the speech showed that 55% of Australians supported the Government's decision to say "sorry" and to work towards greater equality. After the Apology, that level of support rose to 78%. The government began work on fulfilling the promises by declaring a Close the Gap Statement of **Intent**. It invested several billions of dollars into Close the Gap programmes. Nevertheless by 2010, Indigenous peoples continued to experience major forms of inequality in education, housing, employment, **imprisonment**, health and life expectancy rates. Tom Calma, Aboriginal and Torres Strait Islander Social Justice **Commissioner**, has argued that the goals of equality would be better achieved by strengthening Aboriginal community controls over the programmes and by providing greater security for Aboriginal land rights.

In "Closing the Gap: Prime Minister's Report 2016" Mr Turnbull pointed out: "We pride ourselves on having built an equalitarian society where everyone has the same chance to realise their dreams and to fulfil their potential. But it is not until Aboriginal

disremember *v.* 忘记
acknowledgment *n.* 承认
life expectancy 预期寿命
poll *v.* 民意测验
intent *n.* 意图
imprisonment *n.* 关押，监禁
commissioner *n.* （委员会的）委员

and Torres Strait Islander people have the same opportunities for health, education and employment that we can truly say we are a country of equal opportunity."

documentation
n. 文献证据，文献资料

## Conclusion

Social inequalities based around ethnic differences are still a feature of Australian society. However, the institutional support for racism is no longer uncontested. Both of the major parties have enacted legislation to support Multiculturalism and to legislate against racism in the broader culture.

The extensive **documentation** of the wrongs done to non-British immigrants and to the Peoples of the Dreaming and their descendants is now a recognised part of the history of Australia. It forms part of the curriculum in schools. It is a central feature of the National Museum and, even more significantly, it has been used in the courts and in parliament to validate claims for Land Rights and proposals for various forms of positive discrimination.[53] However, as the indigenous social policy researcher, Dr. Maggie Waters, says "There is still a long way to go."

# Explanations

1. **The large numbers of ... from Germany and China:**
   在19世纪50年代的淘金热中，大量没有得到政府资助的移民来到澳大利亚，许多是从德国和中国来的。

2. **it was the Chinese ... the fiercest forms of discrimination:**
   华人和南太平洋岛国人受到了最强烈的种族歧视。Kanaka：南太平洋岛屿的土著人，也指这些地区种植园中的苦工。

3. **The anti-Chinese riots at Lambing Flat in NSW:**
   1861年，在淘金热末期，在种族主义情绪的煽动下，为争夺金矿资源，白人金矿工在新南威尔士的Lambing Flat金矿区发动了大规模暴乱，对华人淘金矿工的营地进行攻击，焚烧掠夺了他们的物品，把他们赶出了金矿。

4. **anti-Chinese riot at Crocodile Creek in Queensland:**
   1867年1月7日，在昆士兰的Crocodile Creek附近的金矿区，为争夺金矿资源，200名白人矿工烧毁了华人矿工的营地，抢掠了他们的商店，将他们赶出了金矿区。四名白人暴乱者因此被判入狱九个月。

# UNIT 20  From Racism to Multiculturalism

5. **They were kidnapped ... in the sugar industry:**
   臭名昭著的贩卖黑奴船到他们的岛上，将他们绑架到昆士兰北部，卖给蔗糖业做包身工。

6. **The Pacific Island Labourers Act:**
   《太平洋岛国劳工法案》，1901年成立澳大利亚联邦后通过的第一批法案中的一个，与《移民限制法案》一起确立了白澳政策的合法性。该法案规定所有太平洋岛国劳工都应被遣返回太平洋岛屿。1907年，所有劳工均被遣返。

7. **The White Australia Policy ... the Immigration Restriction Act 1901:**
   1901年的《移民限制法案》充分体现了白澳政策。在澳大利亚联邦成立之前，各殖民地都执行了白澳政策，限制非欧洲裔移民进入澳大利亚。1901年的《移民限制法案》将白澳政策合法化，是澳大利亚联邦议会通过的第一个法案。

8. **They did this ... on the individual:**
   （为避免明显地表现出法案对亚洲移民的针对性）他们主要通过进行不公平的"听写测验"排斥亚裔。任何申请进入澳大利亚的人必须进行一门欧洲语言测试，考试不合格者会被归入"禁止移民"的类别。

9. **The policy was ... of Eastern Communism:**
   该政策的目的是为大规模经济扩建提供劳动力支持，使没有什么防御能力的澳大利亚得到发展，能作为西方文化前哨阵地去对抗所谓"东方共产主义"的威胁。

10. **it was expected ... their host country:**
    新来的定居者应该能毫不费力地融入移居国的文化中。

11. **non-English speaking backgrounds:**
    非英语国家背景。指南欧、东欧及亚洲等地的移民。

12. **"ethnic groups" were ... their "minority groups":**
    "少数民族群体"能够得到更多与政府沟通的机会，并得到代表"弱势群体"讲话的权利。

13. **Special Broadcasting Service:**
    特殊广播节目。SBS广播电台成立于1977年，电视台成立于1980年，播放英语和非英语的新闻和其他节目，为少数民族群体提供服务。

14. **Economic efficiency ... of their backgrounds:**
    经济效益：所有澳大利亚人，无论他们来自何处，他们的技能都应得到保持和发扬。

15. **Pauline Hanson and the One Nation Party:**
    Pauline Hanson，昆士兰省一个快餐店店主。1996年代表自由党参加大选，因其"种族性福利"和"土著人享有过多特权"的言辞受到自由党开除。但她以独立候选人的身份赢得选举，成为联邦议会议员。1997年成立One Nation Party（单一民族党），认为政府给土著人的拨款过多，土著人已成为特权阶层；认为澳大利亚亚洲移民过多，有被亚洲人吞没的危险；认为政府的政策倾向移民；多元文化主义和原住民使社会产生分裂。尽管她和单一民族党的言论遭到主流舆论的批评，但还是在澳大利亚工人阶层中引起较强反响。

## Australia

16. **Multiculturalism has permitted ... the working class"**:
    多元文化主义允许非英语背景的社团中的个别人成为社会精英，但是，"大多数的少数民族领袖和代言人都是男人和资产阶级，（不能）代表妇女和工人阶级的利益。" De Lepervanche：女权主义学者。

17. **Northern European and ... lower range of occupations:**
    在澳大利亚的北欧和亚洲移民与在澳大利亚出生的人的职业特点相同，而南欧、东欧和中东的移民从事着较为低层次的职业。

18. **61% of migrants ... such recognition:**
    61％的欧洲移民的行业资质得到认可，而只有30％的东南亚移民的行业资质得到认可。一些移民在本国的行业资质，如医生、会计师等，在澳大利亚得不到认可，因此不能从事相关职业。

19. **Although the European ... for "the people":**
    尽管Aborigine在欧洲语中只有"本地区最早的居民"的意思，但由于它与白人入侵者剥削和欺辱梦创后人的历史有着密切联系，今天的澳大利亚原住民更愿意用他们自己的语言来表示"the people"。"The people"是指1788年前作为澳大利亚大陆上唯一的人群的原住民。下文中的Koori、Yuin、Nungas等大多是土著部落的名称，现用来代指原住民。

20. **The Aboriginal Protection Act ... towns and reserves:**
    1909年的《原住民保护法》允许将原住民从城镇和保护地带走。此法案的出台，意味着对原住民的所谓"保护性"的隔离政策的改变，即将土著和白人混血的土著人从保护地带走，对他们进行培训，使他们逐步忘记自己的文化，成为免费劳动力，达到消灭土著文化的目的。

21. **By 1910 there were ... to lease to whites:**
    到1910年，总共有116个原住民保护地，占地10 500公顷，其中65％是在原住民已占有土地上成立的，或因原住民对土地的要求而成立。但1911年，原住民保护委员会不再保护原住民保护地对土地的占有权，转而抢夺保护地出租给白人。

22. **January 26:**
    每年的1月26日，又称为Australian Day，即澳大利亚国庆日，纪念1788年1月26日欧洲第一只舰队在悉尼植物湾（Botany Bay）登陆，开始建立殖民地。

23. **The Day of Mourning and Protest:**
    哀悼与抗议日。对澳大利亚原住民来说，1788年1月26日是白人对他们的土地的占领的开始。从那以后，他们失去土地，在自己的土地上丧失了基本的生存权利。因此，这一天成为他们的哀悼与抗议日。

24. **They were forced to carry to a pass to control their whereabouts:**
    他们被迫要随身携带通行证，以便当局能控制他们的行踪。

25. **For those one hundred people ... of social revolution:**
    对这些1938年在悉尼集会的100多名Koori土著人来说，能发布消息、举行集会就是一种社会革命的宣言。

UNIT ⓴ From Racism to Multiculturalism

26. **On May 1st, ... thirty shillings a week:**
1946年5月1日，北方领土土著畜牧工人要求得到每周30先令的最低工资保障，否则，拒绝继续工作。

27. **The next notable fight ... in the Northern Territories:**
另一场为争取权利而进行的斗争是北方领土的Gurindji原住民反对他们的农场主的罢工。1966年8月，Vicent Lingiari要求Wave Hill牧场将土著工人的工资提高到每周25镑，尽管这一数目低于当时非土著工人的平均工资标准，还是遭到了牧场经理的拒绝。8月22日，200名土著畜牧工和家政服务人员开始罢工。随着罢工的进行，它不仅是一场要求提供工资的斗争，而变成了原住民要求独立和平等权利的象征。Lingiari要求政府归还租借给Wave Hill农牧公司的500平方英里土地。经过九年的斗争后，澳大利亚联邦政府总理惠特拉姆于1975年，象征性地将Wave Hill的土壤倒入Lingiari的手中，表示将土地归还给了当地的原住民。

28. **Vicent Lingiari:**
他领导了Wave Hill的土著人罢工，以其出众的领导才能取得了九年罢工的胜利，成为澳大利亚原住民争取土地权利斗争的里程碑。Vicent Lingiari被公认为是最伟大的原住民领袖。

29. **Frank Hardy and ... to break the strike:**
小说家弗兰克·哈迪和受人尊敬的政府公务员Nugget Coombs都支持Gurindji原住民的罢工，同时它还赢得广泛的工会支持，阻止了许多不择手段地破坏罢工的企图。弗兰克·哈迪，小说家，著有 *Power without Glory*（《没有荣耀的权力》）和 *The Unlucky Aborigines*（《不幸的原住民》）等。Nugget Coombs（1906–1977）是澳大利亚最杰出、最有影响力的国家公职人员，曾前后共三十年担任7任政府总理工作，曾担任澳大利亚联邦储备银行行长、澳大利亚原住民事务委员会主席、澳大利亚战后重建委员会主任、澳大利亚国立大学（ANU）校长等职。他为改善澳大利亚原住民的社会经济和政治地位做了很大贡献。

30. **There was contradictions ... white labour:**
在白人工会和Gurindji罢工者的联盟中是有矛盾的。澳大利亚工人联合会是与北方领土的原住民工作有直接利害关系的工会，有很强的种族主义思想，认为原住民劳工比白人劳工卑微，而且对白人构成威胁。

31. **Pyrrhic victory:**
皮洛士式的胜利，代价过高的胜利。指参加罢工的土著工人后来都失去了工作。Pyrrhus (319–272BC)，皮洛士，是古希腊伊庇鲁斯国王，曾率兵至意大利与罗马交战，以惨重的代价打败罗马军队。Pyrrhic victory一词由此得来。

32. **In the mid-1960s ... to outback Australia:**
20世纪60年代中期，Arrente部落的Charles Perkins成为澳大利亚第二个从大学毕业的土著人。他带领白人大学生深入澳大利亚内陆进行了"自由行"。1965年2月12日，受美国民权运动的影响，Charles Perkins带领29名白人大学生乘公共汽车到新南威尔士的乡镇发动运动，反对种族隔离制度，争取土著人使用咖啡馆、游泳池等公共设施的权力。借助媒体的影响，他们的活动使澳大利亚人意识到了种族思想对澳大利亚社会的影响，为结束白澳政策做出了重要贡献。Charles Perkins：1963年进入悉尼大学学习，成为悉尼大学的第一批原住民学生之一。之前他曾作为足球运动员到国外踢球，接触到了

# Australia

不同的思想，相信澳大利亚原住民应该有权利享有土地、平等和公民权。

33. **The demonstrators were ... for social change:**
"自由行"的示威者被人吐唾沫，遭到人身攻击，但有关"自由行"的报道为提高澳大利亚人对在澳大利亚存在的种族隔离和种族主义的认识做出了重要贡献，说明了进行社会变革的需要。

34. **Ayres Rock:**
艾尔斯岩，位于澳大利亚北方领土，土著人将其奉为圣地。白人殖民者将其命名为艾尔斯岩，现已回归给当地的土著人，重新命名为"Uluru"。

35. **In North Queensland ... GOT IT BACK:**
在昆士兰北部，托雷斯海峡岛民穿的 T 恤衫上印有 Eddie Koiki Mabo 的画像以及这些字："库克船长偷走了我们的土地，Koiki Mabo 重新赢回了土地"。Torres Strait Islanders：托雷斯海峡岛民，和土著人一样，是澳大利亚最早的居民。Eddi Koiki Mabo（1937–1992），出生于托雷斯海峡北部的 Murray 群岛中的 Mer 岛。他是土著艺术家，曾在澳大利亚理事会下设的原住民艺术委员会任职。他发起成立了当地的原住民医疗卫生机构和原住民社区学校。1982 年，他和另外四名托雷斯海峡岛民提出法律诉讼，要求承认他们对自己土地的所有权，这就是著名的 Mabo Case（马博案）。1992 年，在 Mabo 去世四个月后，昆士兰省最高法院裁定，Mer 人拥有对他们的土地的所有权，此权利先于白人对土地的占领，并不因白人的占领而终止。此裁决的历史意义在于，它承认了土著人对土地的所有权，也就从法律上否认了在白人到达澳大利亚时，澳大利亚是"无人占有的土地"（terra nullius）的理念。

36. **customary land title:**
对土地的传统所有权。

37. **Their views rested ... of the Crown:**
这种观点基于一种普遍接受的观点，即澳大利亚在殖民者到来时，是无人占有之地，而且，在 1879 年托雷斯海峡岛屿被并入昆士兰后，所有的土地都属于国王及其政府。The Crown：指英国国王，或英国政府和殖民地政府。

38. **The recognition of ... to the pastoralist:**
对原住民对土地所有权的承认已经写入了 1993 年的《联邦原住民土地所有权法案》。但是，该法案最初起草时是建立在一种推断上，即目前的牧场主对土地的租用权中包括牧场主对土地的全部占有。

39. **The 2003 Senate Commission ... necessities for life:**
2003 年参议院澳大利亚贫困调查委员会发现，大多数生活在贫困中的澳大利亚人都属于"相对贫困"，而偏远土著社区中的原住民很可能会变成非常严重的"绝对贫困"，即没有基本生活来源,没有生活必需品。

40. **The rates of ... non–Koori people:**
在新南威尔士省，警察对土著社区的巡查和土著人被关进监狱的可能性要远远高于非土著人。

41. **This form of institutional racism exists across all other states in Australia:**
这种存在于体制中的种族主义在澳大利亚其他各省都存在。

42. **Archie Roach:**
    歌手，歌曲创作者，杰出的艺术家。生于维多利亚省南部的一个土著保护地内，很小的时候就被从父母身边带走送进了政府为逐步消灭土著文化而设立的"保护性"机构中，成为"被偷走的一代"中的一员。后被墨尔本一个白人家庭领养。他的歌曲既有梦创的传统故事，也有他生活的真实故事，在原住民中引起共鸣。歌曲 *Took the Children Away* 讲述了融合政策下的澳大利亚政府是如何将土著孩子从他们的父母身边带走。

43. **Yothu Yindi:**
    澳大利亚著名的土著乐队，由来自北方领土东北部沿海地区的 Yolngu 土著人组成，他们的歌曲讲述原住民与土地的关系及这种关系如何在今天继续发展。他们的表演本身就包括土著人的舞蹈和仪式。

44. **The Djarridjarri Saltwater Band:**
    一支来自北方领土 Arnhem 地区的土著乐队。他们的表演既有现代的土著音乐，也有传统的土著艺术形式。他们希望通过表演，将土著的传统传给下一代人，使他们不要在西方的物质主义中失去自己的传统文化。

45. **David Unaipon（1872–1967）：**
    作家、公共演说家和发明家。他由于有多项发明，被誉为"澳大利亚的达·芬奇"。1914 年，他利用飞去来兮的原理预见了直升机的发明。他是第一个作品被公开发表的土著人，作品包括《土著人：他们的传统与习俗》和《土著人的神话与传说》等。为纪念他为澳大利亚所做的贡献，他的头像被印在澳大利亚 50 元的纸币上。

46. **Sally Morgan（1951– ）：**
    出生于珀斯。14 岁以前，家人为躲避种族歧视，一直对其谎称她们是印度人，因此肤色与白人不同。十四岁时，Sally Morgan 知道了自己是土著人的真实身份。其后，通过了解家史和写作，她逐渐找到了自己的真正自我。

47. **Jack Davis:**
    剧作家、诗人、演说家和政治家。他在土著文化中占有象征性的中心地位：他是最后的传统口述故事者，也是繁荣的土著写作传统的开启者。主要作品有 *The Dreamers* 和 *No Sugar*。

48. **Oodgeroo Noonuccal（1920–1993）：**
    原名 Kathleen Walker，诗人、政治活动家、艺术家和教育家。Oodgeroo Noonuccal 上过小学，13 岁在布里斯班开始做女仆，1942–1944 年，参加了澳大利亚女子兵团，1964 年出版了第一本诗集。她一生致力于保护土著文化，为土著人赢得平等权利和保护环境，1970 年，获得大英帝国勋章。1984 年，为抗议澳大利亚政府无视土著人的感情和白人对土著人的伤害，在 1988 年庆祝建国两百周年时，她将勋章退回给澳大利亚政府。

49. **Tracey Moffat:**
    Tracey Moffat 是澳大利亚当代最成功的艺术家之一。她创作的主要艺术形式有摄影、电影短篇、纪录片和音乐电视。创作内容来自她的生活，主题包括种族、性别与身份。

# Australia

50. **dot painting:**
点画，澳大利亚原住民的一种绘画方式。将不同颜色的点组成不同的图案，代表不同的意思。主要出现在澳大利亚中部的沙漠中。

51. **X–ray painting:**
十字晕画，澳大利亚原住民的一种绘画方式，将不同颜色的线条交叉排列组成图案，一般画在树皮上。主要出现在昆士兰北部。

52. **Tanaka Masaaki's *The Fabrication of the Nanking Massacre*:**
田中正明，日本作家，其著作《南京屠杀的虚构》(1985) 否认日军在南京的暴行。

53. **It is a central ... of positive discrimination:**
它成为澳大利亚国家博物馆的重要内容。更重要的是，这些文献被法庭和议会采用，用于支持土著人对土地的权利，支持各种形式的对弱势群体的优惠政策。

# Exercises

**I. Give the Chinese equivalents for the following:**

1. The White Australia Policy
2. a gold rush
3. a Blackbirder
4. Queensland
5. "The Sorry Speech"

**II. Decide whether the following statements are true (T) or false (F):**

1. Few non-British migrants benefited from assisted migration. _____
2. The third largest ethnic group in Australia by the 1870s was the Japanese. _____
3. The Pacific Islanders were abducted to work in the sugar industry of Northern Queensland. _____
4. The Immigration Restriction Act, which was passed in 1901, reaffirmed the White Australia Policy practiced in the colonies. _____
5. The original intention of the massive post-war immigration programme was to keep Australia "white and free". _____

## UNIT 20 From Racism to Multiculturalism

6. The SBS was set up in 1977 to broadcast news programmes in English and other different languages. _____
7. The One Nation Party complained that the government had paid too much attention to the welfare of the Indigenous people and the development of Multiculturalism. _____
8. The first national Aboriginal civil rights gathering was on Jan. 26, 1938, when the Aboriginal people celebrated together with the white people the arrival of the First Fleet. _____
9. The Gurindji people's strike at the Wave Hill cattle station won support not only from the black community, but also the white workers' union as well. _____
10. The Freedom Riders confined their activities mostly to the urban areas of Australia. _____

### III. Fill in the blanks:

1. The gold rushes attracted large numbers of _____ from Germany and China.
2. Pacific Islanders were kidnapped and brought to _____ to be sold as _____ to work in the sugar industry.
3. Under the White Australia Policy, immigrants to Australia had to take a test in _____; the individual who failed would be given the status of _____.
4. The aim of the massive immigration programme after WWII was to support a large scale expansion of the _____, and to defend Australia against the threat of _____.
5. _____, which was formed by Pauline Hanson in 1997, believed Multiculturalism was a divisive policy to the Australian society.
6. Australia's population now is just around _____.
7. The Day of Mourning and Protest for the Aboriginal people is _____.
8. The _____ of being both Australian and Aboriginal is the basis of much creativity in all fields of art by the Indigenous people.
9. _____ were organised by an Aboriginal university graduate to go to the outback of Australia to raise people's consciousness about the level of racism.
10. The _____ and _____ decisions both recognised the native titles on the traditional lands of the Aboriginal people.

# Australia

IV. **Questions:**
   1. Why did many Chinese immigrate to Australia from the 1850s? How were they treated in this country?
   2. What racism did the Pacific Islanders experience in Australia?
   3. What was the White Australia Policy? What was a "dictation test"? Why was it biased?
   4. What non-discriminatory programmes were introduced to assist Australians from non-English speaking backgrounds from 1973? Why were these programmes introduced?
   5. What various stages has the relationship between the colonisers and the Peoples of the Dreaming gone through?
   6. What is the dark side of the history of Australian society and culture in the author's opinion?
   7. What did one hundred Koori men and women gathering in Sydney's Australia Hall in 1938 demand? Why was the event regarded as a "declaration of social revolution"?
   8. Why did Aboriginal stockmen go on strike throughout the north of Western Australia in 1946? How did the struggle challenge the white control of the Aboriginal people?
   9. Which fight was the first one put up by the Aborigines to attract wide public support within Australia for Land Rights?
   10. Who was Eddie Koiki Mabo? How did the High Court rule in his case?
   11. What was the Wik Decision? What was its significance for the Aboriginal people?
   12. What were the three areas of policy that Multiculturalism was identified as comprising in 1989?
   13. What is "double consciousness"? How does it serve as the basis of creativity in the fields of art created by the Aboriginal people?
   14. Who made "The Sorry Speech"? What was it about?
   15. What is the Close the Gap Statement of Intent? What did Prime Minister Turnbull say in his 2016 Closing the Gap Report about the current status of the Aboriginal and Torres Strait Islands peoples?

V. **Topics for discussion or research:**
   1. Compare the different ways in which white and non-white immigrants were treated in Australia under the White Policy.
   2. Does racism exit in Australia today ? Illustrate your view with examples and facts.
   3. What is multiculturalism? How is it reflected in Australia today?
   4. How does the two-way identity of being both Australian and Aboriginal resound in Aboriginal art?

## 郑重声明

高等教育出版社依法对本书享有专有出版权。任何未经许可的复制、销售行为均违反《中华人民共和国著作权法》，其行为人将承担相应的民事责任和行政责任；构成犯罪的，将被依法追究刑事责任。为了维护市场秩序，保护读者的合法权益，避免读者误用盗版书造成不良后果，我社将配合行政执法部门和司法机关对违法犯罪的单位和个人进行严厉打击。社会各界人士如发现上述侵权行为，希望及时举报，本社将奖励举报有功人员。

反盗版举报电话　（010）58581999　58582371　58582488
反盗版举报传真　（010）82086060
反盗版举报邮箱　dd@hep.com.cn
通信地址　北京市西城区德外大街4号　高等教育出版社法律事务与版权管理部
邮政编码　100120

## 防伪查询说明

用户购书后刮开封底防伪涂层，利用手机微信等软件扫描二维码，会跳转至防伪查询网页，获得所购图书详细信息。用户也可将防伪二维码下的20位密码按从左到右、从上到下的顺序发送短信至106695881280，免费查询所购图书真伪。

反盗版短信举报
编辑短信"JB,图书名称,出版社,购买地点"发送至10669588128

防伪客服电话
（010）58582300

## 网络增值服务使用说明

一、注册/登录

访问http://abook.hep.com.cn/，点击"注册"，在注册页面输入用户名、密码及常用的邮箱进行注册。已注册的用户直接输入用户名和密码登录即可进入"我的课程"页面。

二、课程绑定

点击"我的课程"页面右上方"绑定课程"，正确输入教材封底防伪标签上的20位密码，点击"确定"完成课程绑定。

三、访问课程

在"正在学习"列表中选择已绑定的课程，点击"进入课程"即可浏览或下载与本书配套的课程资源。刚绑定的课程请在"申请学习"列表中选择相应课程并点击"进入课程"。

如有账号问题，请发邮件至：abook@hep.com.cn。